DEMOCRACY IN AMERICA

Alexis de Tocqueville

Alexis de Tocqueville

DEMOCRACY
IN AMERICA

Edited by Eduardo Nolla

Translated from the French by James T. Schleifer

VOLUME 2

LIBERTY FUND

This book is published by Liberty Fund, Inc., a foundation established to encourage study of the ideal of a society of free and responsible individuals.

𒂼𒄄

The cuneiform inscription that serves as our logo and as the design motif for our endpapers is the earliest-known written appearance of the word "freedom" (*amagi*), or "liberty." It is taken from a clay document written about 2300 B.C. in the Sumerian city-state of Lagash.

The French text on which this translation is based is *De la démocratie en Amérique*, première édition historico-critique revue et augmentée. Edited by Eduardo Nolla. Librairie Philosophique J. Vrin; 6, Place de la Sorbonne; Paris, 1990.

Frontispiece: Portrait of Alexis de Tocqueville by Léon Noël, reproduced with kind permission of the Beinecke Library, Yale University.

Map of the United States appearing in the first edition of *Democracy in America* (1835), reproduced with kind permission of the Special Collections Research Center, University of Chicago Library.

18 19 20 21 22 P 7 6 5 4 3

Library of Congress Cataloging-in-Publication Data
Tocqueville, Alexis de, 1805–1859
[De la démocratie en Amérique. English]
Democracy in America/Alexis de Tocqueville;
edited by Eduardo Nolla;
translated from the French by James T. Schleifer.—[Student ed.]
p. cm.
Includes bibliographical references and index.
ISBN 978-0-86597-840-9 (set: pbk.: alk. paper)
ISBN 978-0-86597-838-6 (v. 1: pbk.: alk. paper)
ISBN 978-0-86597-839-3 (v. 2: pbk.: alk. paper)
1. United States—Politics and government. 2. United States—Social conditions—To 1865. 3. Democracy—United States. I. Nolla, Eduardo. II. Schleifer, James T., 1942– III. Title.
JK216.T713 2012
320.973—dc23   2011041363

LIBERTY FUND, INC.
11301 North Meridian Street
Carmel, Indiana 46032

DEMOCRACY IN AMERICA

Contents

DEMOCRACY IN AMERICA
(1835)

VOLUME I

Part I

Part II

DEMOCRACY IN AMERICA
(1840)

VOLUME II

Foreword   690

Part I: Influence of Democracy on the
Intellectual Movement in the United States

Part II: Influence of Democracy on the Sentiments of the Americans

Part III: Influence of Democracy on Mores Properly So Called

Part IV: Of the Influence That Democratic Ideas and Sentiments Exercise on Political Society

VOLUME 2

DEMOCRACY
IN AMERICA[a]

a. Introduction to the third volume./
Ideas about the plan of this volume./
Perhaps most of the things contained in this bundle will be useful for the large final chapter in which I intend to summarize the subject./
Influence of democracy. *Ter* [three (ed.)]:

I. Ideas
II. Sentiments. This relates only to man in isolation.
III. Customs. They include the relationships of men with one another.

What is American or English without being democratic.
Great difficulty in disentangling what is *democratic, commercial, English* and *Puritan.*
To explain in the foreword.
My principal subject is not *America,* but the *influence of democracy on America.* As a result, the only one of the four causes set forth above that I must dwell upon seriously and at length is the *democratic.* Perhaps not because it is the principal one (what I believe, moreover), but because it is the one that is most important for me to show. I must speak about the others only: 1. To interest the class of readers who want above all to know America, 2. To make myself clearly understood, 3. To show that I am not exclusive and entirely given to a single idea.
[In the margin: I see all the other causes, but I am only looking at the democratic.]
If, among these various causes, I always choose by preference to deal with the democratic cause, let me not therefore be accused of an exclusive mind.
I do not believe it necessary to treat the *commercial, English* and *Puritan* causes separately. I only think that I must show in the course of the book that I know and appreciate them.
To speak about the four causes only in the preface and only there give them their respective places.
Important idea.
After finishing, look carefully at the places where I could point out how the things produced by democracy help democracy in turn and indirectly.
[On the following page] Perhaps in the large final chapter.
Idea of democratic liberty and idea of religion.

Foreword[b]

The Americans have a democratic social state that has naturally suggested to them certain laws and certain political mores.[c]

In civil society as in political society, these two points of departure explain nearly everything. And I must come back to that in a general way, either at the beginning or at the end of the third volume (YTC, CVk, 1, pp. 39–41).

b. Several notes and fragments indicate that Tocqueville had considered writing a long preface that contained a good number of ideas present in the fourth and last part of the book (it constituted a single chapter in the first drafts). Did the sheer size of the last chapter lead him to sacrifice the preface? This preface was reduced to a foreword, and certain ideas of the introduction (including the admission of his error concerning the weakening of the federal bond) did not finally find their place in the first pages of this volume.

Some notes of rough drafts that present a version of the foreword very similar to the final version bear the date 5 February 1838. In the following months, however, Tocqueville did not stop coming back to the idea of writing a long introduction to the second volume and hesitated about whether to place certain fragments at the beginning or at the end of the book.

"One of the principal ideas of the preface must be, it seems to me, to show in brief all the dissimilarities that exist between the American democracy and ours. Democracy pushing men further in certain directions in America than it does among us (sciences, arts), in certain others pushing them not as far (religion, good morals)" (YTC, CVk, 1, p. 48).

Note relative to the preface of my great work.
It must be shown how recent events justify most of the things that I said.
Indians.
Texas.
Negroes.
The necessity of having troops in the cities.
Ultra-democratic tendencies.
Admit my error. The weakening of the federal bond (YTC, CVk, 1, p. 39).

c. First paragraphs of the book in a rough draft:

The work which appears at this moment (illegible word) the public is not an entirely new work. It is the second and last part of a book that I published five years ago on democracy in the United States.

This same social state has, moreover, given birth among them to a multitude of sentiments and opinions that were unknown in the old aristocratic societies of Europe. It has destroyed or modified relationships that formerly existed and established new ones. The appearance of civil society has been no less changed than the physiognomy of the political world.

I dealt with the first subject in the work that I published five years ago on American democracy. The second is the subject of the present book. These two parts complement one another and form only a single work.[d]

I must immediately warn the reader against an error that would be very prejudicial to me.

Seeing me attribute so many diverse effects to equality, he could conclude

---

When there are no more castes, distinct features, particular and exclusive rights, permanent riches, entailed estates, citizens differ little from each other by their conditions, and they constantly change conditions; they naturally adopt certain laws, and contract certain habits of government that are appropriate to them.

This same equality and these same causes influence not only their political ideas and habits, but also all their habits and all their ideas. The men who live in this democratic social state conceive new opinions; they adopt new mores; they establish relationships among themselves that did not exist or modify those that already existed. The appearance of civil society is not less changed than the physiognomy of the political world.

[To the side, with a bracket that includes the two previous paragraphs: Louis would say that only about the Americans.]

≠The object of the book that I published five years ago was to show the first effects of equality; this one wants to depict the second. The two parts united form a single whole.≠

It is this second portion of the subject that I wanted to treat in the present book.

I am assuredly very far from claiming to have seen everything on so vast a ground. I am even certain that I have discovered only a small part of what it includes.

The Revolution that reduced to dust the aristocratic society in which our fathers lived is the great event of the time. It has changed everything, modified everything, altered everything. [v: hit everything].

[In the margin, with a bracket that includes the two previous paragraphs] To delete, I think (YTC, CVk, 1, pp. 35–36).

d. "The first book more American than democratic. This one more democratic than American" (YTC, CVk, 1, p. 53).

that I consider equality as the unique cause of all that happens today.[e] This would assume a very narrow view on my part.

There is, in our time, a host of opinions, sentiments, instincts that owe their birth to facts foreign or even contrary to equality. Thus, if I took the United States as an example, I would easily prove that the nature of the country, the origin of the inhabitants, the religion of the first founders, their acquired enlightenment, their previous habits, exercised and still exercise, independently of democracy, an immense influence on their way of thinking and feeling. Different causes, also distinct from the fact of equality, would be found in Europe and would explain a great part of what is happening there.

I recognize the existence of all these different causes and their power, but talking about them is not my subject. I have not undertaken to show

e. In Preface, I believe.

Explain somewhere what I understand by centuries of equality [v: democratic centuries]. It is not that chimerical time when all men will be perfectly similar and equal, but those:

1. When a great number among them will be in (two illegible words) and when a greater number will fall either above or below, but not far from the common measure.

2. Those when there will be no more permanent classification, caste, class, any insurmountable barrier or even one very difficult to surmount, so that if all men are not equal, they can all aspire to the same point; some being able (illegible word) to fear falling, others to hope to rise, so that a common measure makes itself (illegible word) against which all men measure themselves in advance, which spreads the sentiment of equality even within unequal conditions.

—22 June 1838 (YTC, CVk, 1, pp. 45–46).

In another place, he explains:

Two close but distinct propositions:

1. I cannot show all that equality does and will do.

2. I do not claim to link everything to equality, but only to show where equality acts (YTC, CVk, 1, p. 53).

"Idea of the preface or of the last chapter./

"That democracy is not the cause of everything, but that it mixes with everything, and has a part in all the causes" (YTC, CVk, 1, p. 42).

the reason for all our inclinations and all our ideas; I have only wanted to show to what extent equality had modified both.[f]

You will perhaps be surprised that, since I am firmly of the opinion that the democratic revolution we are witnessing is an irresistible fact against which it would be neither desirable nor wise to struggle, I have often ended up addressing such harsh words in this book to the democratic societies created by this revolution.

I will simply reply that it is because I was not an adversary of democracy that I have wanted to be candid about it.[g]

Men do not receive the truth from their enemies, and their friends hardly ever offer the truth to them; that is why I have spoken it.

I have thought that many would take it upon themselves to announce the new good things that equality promises to men, but that few would dare to point out from a distance the perils with which it threatens them. So it

---

f. Principal object. Somewhere.

I want to make *everyone* understand that a democratic social state is an invincible necessity in our time.

Dividing then my readers into enemies and friends of democracy, I want to make the first understand that for a democratic social state to be tolerable, for it to be able to produce order, progress, in a word, to avoid all the evils that they anticipate, at least the greatest ones, they must at all costs hasten to give *enlightenment* and *liberty* to the people who already have such a social state.

To the second, I want to make them understand that democracy cannot give the happy fruits that they expect from it except by combining it with morality, spiritualism, beliefs . . .

I thus try to unite all honest and generous minds within a small number of common ideas.

As for the question of knowing if such a social state is or is not the best that humanity can have, may God himself say so. Only God can say (YTC, CVk, 2, pp. 55–56).

g. "I am profoundly persuaded that you can succeed in making democratic peoples into prosperous, free, powerful, moral and happy nations. So I do not despair of the future, but I think that peoples, like men, in order to make the most of their destiny, need to know themselves, and that to master events, it is above all necessary to master yourself" (YTC, CVk, 1, p. 33).

"Idea of bringing democracy to moderate itself. Idea of the book" (YTC, CVk, 1, p. 39).

is principally toward these perils that I have directed my attention, and, believing that I have clearly discerned them, I have not had the cowardice to say nothing about them.[h]

I hope that you will find again in this second work the impartiality[j] that seemed to be noted in the first. Placed in the middle of the contradictory opinions that divide us, I have tried to eradicate temporarily in my heart the favorable sympathies or contrary instincts that each one of them inspires in me. [I have wanted to live alone in order to keep my mind free.] If those who read my book find a single sentence that aims to flatter one of the great parties that have agitated our country, or one of the small factions that bother and enervate it today, may those readers raise their voices and accuse me.

The subject that I have wanted to embrace is immense; for it includes most of the sentiments and ideas that the new state of the world brings forth. Such a subject assuredly exceeds my powers;[k] while treating it, I have not succeeded in satisfying myself.

But, if I have not been able to achieve the goal that I set, readers will at least do me the justice of granting that I have conceived and followed my enterprise in the spirit that could make me worthy to succeed in it.[m]

---

h. In a first version of this paragraph, Tocqueville added: "<Far from wanting to stop the development of the new society, I am trying to produce it>" (YTC, CVk, 1, p. 44).

j. "This in the preface.

"I am often obliged to repeat myself because I want to divide what is indivisible, the soul. The same soul constantly produces an idea and a sentiment. Place there the already completed piece in which I compare the soul to a milieu whose ideas and sentiments are like beams . . ." (YTC, CVk, 1, p. 30).

k. "Not only do I not claim to have seen everything in my subject, but I am certain I have seen only a very small part. The democratic revolution is the great event of our days, it spreads to everything, it modifies or changes everything. There is nothing that cannot or perhaps should not be dealt with while speaking about it. I have said all that I have seen clearly, leaving to those more skillful or to men enlightened by a longer experience to portray the rest" (YTC, CVk, 1, p. 47).

m. Ideas of the preface or of the last chapter:

In order to make myself well understood I have constantly been obliged to depict extreme states, an aristocracy without a mixture of democracy, a democracy without a mixture of aristocracy, a perfect equality which is an imaginary state. Then I come to attribute to one or the other of the two principles more complete effects than those that they generally produce because, in general, they are not alone. In my words, the

---

reader must distinguish what my true opinion is, from what is said in order to make it well understood (YTC, CVk, 1, p. 51).

To say in the preface, if not in the book.
Idea of races.
I do not believe that there are races destined for liberty and others for servitude, some for happiness and enlightenment, others for misfortunes and ignorance. These are cowardly doctrines.

Doctrines, however. Why? That is due to the natural vice of the human mind in democratic times [and of the heart that makes these peoples tend toward materialism. This idea of the invisible influence of race is an essentially materialistic idea], apart from the weakening of beliefs.

That the generative idea of this book is directly the opposite, since I begin invincibly at this point that whatever the tendencies of the social state, men can always modify them and ward off the bad tendencies while appropriating the good (YTC, CVk, 1, p. 37).

FIRST PART[a]

Influence of Democracy on the Intellectual Movement in the United States

a. The rough drafts indicate that in the beginning the first chapter included a large portion of the ideas that now constitute the following chapters: the taste for general ideas, general ideas in politics and certain considerations from chapter V on religion. Chapters VI and VII are not in the summary of chapters copied in notebook CVf, which suggests that they were included when the work of writing was already well advanced.

Concerning the other chapters of the first part, a note mentions:

A chapter IV was found here in which I explained at length the influence that the philosophical method of the Americans exercised on the relationships of father and children, of master and servant, on women, the customs of societies.

This spoiled the subject and treated it incompletely, for all these things have a particular character under democracy not only because of the philosophical doctrine given birth by equality, but also for a thousand other causes that cannot, consequently, be treated here.

I believe however that for the mind of the reader, tired by the long theory that precedes, to rest in applications, I would do [well (ed.)] in a very short chapter to point out how in fact the philosophical method of the Americans can *influence* (not cause) all these things (YTC, CVj, I, pp. 91–92).

In a letter to Beaumont of 14 June 1836 (*Correspondance avec Beaumont, OC*, VIII, 1, p. 160), Tocqueville announced his intention to finish the first part before his departure for Switzerland in mid-July, which allows us reasonably to date the first version of this part to the summer of 1836. It is in November 1838, when he begins the revision of his manuscript, that Tocqueville, in another letter to Beaumont (*ibid.,* pp. 325–26) alludes to the confusion of the first two chapters and the necessity to review them. In the following letter (*ibid.,* p. 328), he says he has thrown the first one hundred pages of the manuscript into the fire and entirely rewritten them. Another letter of the same month to Francisque de Corcelle confirms these statements (*Correspondance avec Corcelle, OC,* XV, 1, p. 105).

CHAPTER I^a

In the beginning, the organization of the first chapters probably must have appeared as follows: (1) A long chapter on philosophical method, including a certain number of ideas that were later moved or that formed independent chapters, like the one on pantheism, which now bears number 7. (2) The origin of beliefs among democratic peoples. (3) A chapter on religion. (4) The influence of philosophical method on the relations of the father with his children, of the master with his servants, on woman and on habits. (5) The taste for general ideas. (6) Science and the arts.

a. "While rereading and recasting my manuscript, do, after each chapter, a small outline of what it contains; a kind of *assets* and *liabilities* of democracy; that will marvelously facilitate for me the final tableau, which it is immensely important to do well" (YTC, CVk, 1, pp. 11–12).

Notebook F of the manuscript collection of Yale reproduces short summaries of each chapter. The first page bears the date April 1840. Here is the summary of this chapter:

1. That the Americans show by their actions that they have a philosophical method, even though they have neither philosophical school nor philosophical doctrine strictly speaking.

2. That this method consists principally of drawing your opinions only from within yourself, as Descartes indicates.

3. That it is principally from their social state that they have drawn this method and that it is the same cause that has made it adopted in Europe.

4. That the Americans have not made so great a use of this method as the French: 1. Because they got from their origin a more fixed religion. 2. Because they are not and have never been in revolution. 3. As a result of a still more general and powerful cause that I am going to develop in the following chapter and that in the long run must limit, among all democratic peoples, the intellectual independence given birth by equality (YTC, CVf, pp. 1–2).

The first draft of this chapter (YTC, CVj, 1, pp. 42–82) contains some ideas that afterward will acquire sufficient importance to constitute independent chapters (chapters 2 to 8). Tocqueville clearly hesitated a great deal about the content of the first chapter, finding himself inclined to speak about individualism before everything else.

"Perhaps," Tocqueville noted again in a rough draft, "begin the whole book with the chapters on individualism and the taste for material enjoyments. Nearly everything flows from there in ideas as well as in sentiments" (YTC, CVk, 1, p. 12).

It is probably on the advice of Kergorlay, who spent the autumn of 1838 at the Tocqueville château at the very time when the author worked on the revision of the first version

Of the Philosophical Method of the Americans[b]

I think that in no country in the civilized world is there less interest in philosophy than in the United States.

The Americans have no philosophical school of their own, and they worry very little about all those that divide Europe; they hardly know their names.

---

of his manuscript, and who found the first two chapters remarkably well written, that Tocqueville changed his mind.

In another place:

> Of all the chapters that precede the IXth where I am now (December 1838), there is not a single one in which I have not felt the need to assume that the reader knew either what leads democratic peoples to *individualism,* or what leads them to the *taste for material enjoyments.* The experience of these eight chapters tends to prove that the two chapters on *individualism* and material enjoyments should precede the others.
>
> L[ouis (ed.)]. thinks that whatever logical interest there might be in beginning with the two chapters above, I must persevere in placing the chapter on method at the beginning. That, he says, opens the subject very grandly and makes it immediately seen from a very elevated perspective (YTC, CVk, 1, p. 11).

Chapter 9 in the manuscript is now number 11, entitled: IN WHAT SPIRIT THE AMER-ICANS CULTIVATE THE ARTS.

Another note, probably prior, suggested: "Perhaps do a chapter on the influence of democracy on the moral sciences. I do not believe that the first chapter of the book corresponds to that" (YTC, CVa, p. 45).

b. Chap. 1.

This first chapter treats a very abstract matter. Extreme efforts must be made to make it clear and perceptible, otherwise the reader would be discouraged.

In this chapter there are two ideas that I take up and leave alternately in a way that is fatiguing for the mind, it is that of an *independent method* and of the *inclination and aptitude for general ideas.*

Either these two ideas must be intimately linked with each other, or they must be separated entirely and treated individually.

Perhaps explain in a few words the meaning of the expressions: general ideas, generalization, method (YTC, CVj, 1, p. 42).

The jacket that contains the manuscript of the chapter bears this note: "≠There is no society without common ideas and no common ideas if on each point each person is abandoned to the solitary and individual effort of his reason.≠"

It is easy to see, however, that nearly all the inhabitants of the United States direct their minds in the same way, and conduct them according to the same rules; that is to say, they possess, without ever having taken the trouble to define its rules, a certain philosophical method that is common to all of them.

To escape from the spirit of system, from the yoke of habits, from the maxims of family,[c] from the opinions of class, and, to a certain point, from the prejudices of nation; to take tradition only as information, and present facts only as a useful study for doing otherwise and better; to seek by yourself and in yourself alone the reason for things, to strive toward the result without allowing yourself to be caught up in the means, and to aim for substance beyond form: such are the principal features that characterize what I will call the philosophical method of the Americans.[d]

If I go still further and, among these various features, look for the principal one and the one that can sum up nearly all the others, I discover that, in most operations of the mind, each American appeals only to the individual effort of his reason.

So America is one of the countries of the world where the precepts of Descartes are least studied and best followed.[e] That should not be a surprise.

c. In the rough drafts and first versions: ". . . from the maxims of State" (YTC, CVj, I, p. 21; another version, p. 43).

d. In the margin, in pencil: "{And religion, Ampère?}"

Jean-Jacques Ampère, writer and historian with eclectic tastes, son of the famous physicist. Tocqueville met him in 1835 in the salon of Madame Récamier, with whom Ampère was in love for fifteen years. We know little about the beginning of the friendship between Tocqueville and Ampère, but we know that the author of the *Democracy* read several chapters of this volume to him and asked for his advice on several occasions. From 1841, the Tocqueville château sheltered in one of its towers a *room of Ampère,* always ready to receive him. Indefatigable traveler, Ampère ended several of his long journeys by a visit to the Tocquevilles.

Upon the death of the author, Ampère published a touching article on "his best friend": "Alexis de Tocqueville," *Correspondant,* 47, 1859, pp. 312–35. The correspondence of Tocqueville with Ampère has been published in volume XI of *Œuvres complètes.*

e. "Although Descartes professes a great scorn for the crowd, his method is based on the idea of the equality of minds, for if I must rely on myself why would you not do the same?

"Protestantism itself already announced that society had become very democratic" (YTC, CVj, 1, p. 13).

Americans do not read the works of Descartes, because their social state diverts them from speculative studies, and they follow his maxims because the same social state naturally disposes their mind to adopt them.[f]

Amid the constant movement that reigns within a democratic society,[g] the bond that links generations together weakens or breaks; each man easily loses track of the ideas of his ancestors, or is hardly concerned about them.

Nor can the men who live in such a society draw their beliefs from the opinions of the class to which they belong, for there are so to speak no longer any classes, and those that still exist are composed of elements so fluid, that the corps can never exercise a true power over its members.[h]

As for the action that the intelligence of one man can have on that of another, it is necessarily very limited in a country where citizens, having become more or less similar, all see each other at very close range; and, not noticing in any one of them the signs of incontestable greatness and superiority, they are constantly brought back to their own reason[j] as the most

----

"Descartes, the greatest democrat" (YTC, CVj, 1, p. 53).

A letter from Kergorlay dated 27 June 1834 (*Correspondance avec Kergorlay, OC,* XIII, 1, pp. 384–89) suggests that the two friends had had the project of reading together the *Discours de la méthode.* It contains the first impressions of Kergorlay on reading this work.

f. In the margin: "<Perhaps transfer here several of the things that I say in the chapter on *revolutions.* Here the foundations are found, they must be well secured before building.>"

g. "A democratic people, society, time does not mean a people, society, time in which all men are equal, but a people, society, time in which there are no more castes, fixed classes, privileges, particular and exclusive rights, permanent riches, properties fixed in the hands of families, in which all men can constantly rise or descend and mingle together in all ways.

"When I mean it in the political sense, I say *democracy.*

"When I want to speak about the effects of equality, I say *equality*" (YTC, CVk, 1, pp. 50–51).

h. In the margin: "<They escape the rule of their own habits, for they change them constantly.>"

j. "Imagine men entirely equal in knowledge, in enlightenment, in reason; rationalism[1] comes into the world.

visible and nearest source of truth. Then it is not only confidence in a particular man that is destroyed, but the taste to believe any man whatsoever on his word.

So each person withdraws narrowly into himself and claims to judge the world from there.

The custom that the Americans have of only taking themselves as guide for their judgment leads their mind to other habits.

Since they see that they manage without help to solve all the small difficulties that their practical life presents, they easily conclude that everything in the world is explicable, and that nothing goes beyond the limits of intelligence.

Thus, they readily deny what they cannot understand; that gives them little faith in the extraordinary and an almost invincible distaste for the supernatural.

Since they are accustomed to relying on their own witness, they love to see the matter that they are dealing with very clearly; so in order to see it more closely and in full light, they rid it as fully as they can of its wrapping; they push aside all that separates them from it, and clear away everything that hides it from their view. This disposition of their mind soon leads them to scorn forms, which they consider as useless and inconvenient veils placed between them and the truth.

So the Americans did not need to draw their philosophical method from books, they found it within themselves. I will say the same about what happened in Europe.

This same method became established and popularized in Europe only as conditions there became more equal and men more similar.

Let us consider for a moment the train of events:

"Rationalism, general ideas: two things produced by equality, but distinct.

"Necessity that religions have in democratic centuries of winning over common opinion.

"1. I use this modern word without understanding it well. The most natural meaning to give it is the *independence of individual reason*" (YTC, CVj, 1, pp. 10–11).

In the XVIth century, the men of the Reformation[k] subject some of the dogmas of the ancient faith to individual reason; but they continue to exclude all the others from discussion.[m] In the XVIIth, Bacon, in the natural sciences, and Descartes, in philosophy strictly speaking, abolish accepted formulas, destroy the rule of traditions and overthrow the authority of the master.[n]

k. In the margin of a first version belonging to the rough drafts: "The Protestant religion (perhaps religions should only be touched as little as possible for fear of burning my fingers)" (YTC, CVj, 1, p. 45).

m. I suppose that knowing the language that our fathers spoke, I do not know their history. I open the books of the (three illegible words) of the XVIth century. I understand that there one preaches to men that each one of them has the right and the ability to choose the particular road that should lead to heaven. I am assured that half of the nations of Europe have adopted this new doctrine. That is enough. I do not need to be taught that a great political revolution has preceded and accompanied the religious revolution whose history is provided for me.

[v: That is enough. I already know without anyone telling me that in a nation in which intellectual equality is thus professed and accepted, a very great inequality in conditions cannot exist and that whatever the external appearances of political society may still be, men have already come very close to a common level]" (YTC, CVj, 1, pp. 13–14).

n. Fragment on a separate sheet of the manuscript:

Read the preliminary portion of the *Novum Organum* entitled *subject and plan,* p. 263 and following, and compare the manner in which Bacon explains his method concerning the physical senses to the manner in which Descartes, more or less at the same time, conceived and explained his method concerning the moral sciences, and you will be astonished to see to what degree the two methods are identical and how these new truths occur in the same way to these two minds.

This is obviously not the result of chance, but indicates a general direction of the human mind in this period. Bacon and Descartes, like all great revolutionaries, made ideas that were already spread in all minds *clear and systematic./*

They gave the general formula applicable to all the particular truths that each person began to find at hand everywhere./

Bacon, 1561–1626.

The *Novum Organum* (instrument) was published in 1620./

"Our method," says Bacon (p. 264), "submits to examination what ordinary logic adopts on the faith of others and by deferring blindly to authority. [. . . (ed.) . . .] Instead of rushing, so to speak, as is commonly done, toward the most elevated principles and the most general propositions in order then to deduce middle propositions, it begins on the contrary with natural history and particular facts and

The philosophers of the XVIIIth century, finally generalizing the same principle, undertake to submit to the individual examination of each man the object of all his beliefs.°

---

climbs only imperceptibly and with an extreme slowness up the ascending ladder, to entirely general propositions and to principles of the first order./

"The seat of human understanding," he says below, "must be rid of all received opinions and methods, then the mind must be turned in an appropriate way toward the facts that must enlighten it; finally, when it is sufficiently prepared, these facts must be presented to it."/

Obviously not only is a new scientific method introduced there, but also a great revolution of the human mind is begun or rather *legalized, theorized.*

From the moment when observation, the detailed and analytical observation of facts, is the condition of all scientific progress, there is no longer a means to have anything other than individual and formed beliefs in scientific matters. Received or dogmatic beliefs are chased from that entire portion of the human mind.

Tocqueville takes this quotation from the preface of Bacon's work which is entitled: "Spirit, Subject, Purpose, and Plan of the Work."

o. The manuscript says:

If I put aside the opinions of the French philosophers of the XVIIIth century and their actions, which must be considered as fortuitous accidents caused by the particular state of their country, in order to envisage only the fundamental principles that constituted their method, I discover that the same rules that directed their minds lead that of the Americans today. I see that in the period when they wrote the old aristocratic society among us was finally dissolving; this makes me see clearly that the philosophical method of the XVIIIth century is not only French but democratic, and that is why it was so easily adopted in all of Europe and why it contributed so powerfully to changing the face of Europe. I do not claim that this method could only arise in democratic centuries, but I am saying that men who live during these centuries are particularly disposed by their social state to find and to accept this method, and that it is only during that time that it can become usual and popular.

If someone asks me why, today . . .

In a rough draft, the author specified:

The first use that the French philosophers made of their liberty was to attack all religions with a kind of fury and particularly the Christian religion. I believe that this must be considered as a pure accident, a fact particular to France, the result of extraordinary circumstances that might never have been found and that already to a great extent no longer exist.

Who does not see that Luther, Descartesᴾ and Voltaire used the same method, and that they differ only in the greater or lesser use that they claimed to make of it?

Why did the men of the Reformation enclose themselves so narrowly in the circle of religious ideas? Why did Descartes want to use it only in certain matters, although he made his method applicable to everything, and declare that only philosophical and not political things must be judged by oneself? How did it happen that in the XVIIIth century general applications that Descartes and his predecessors had not noticed or had refused to see were all at once drawn from that same method? Finally, why in that period did the method we are speaking about suddenly emerge from the schools to penetrate society and become the common rule of intelligence, and why, after becoming popular among the French, was it openly adopted or secretly followed by all the peoples of Europe?

The philosophical method in question was able to arise in the XVIth century, to take shape and become general in the XVIIth; but it could not be commonly adopted in either one of the two. Political laws, the social state, the habits of the mind that flow from these first causes, were opposed to it.

It was discovered in a period when men began to become equal and similar to each other. It could only be generally followed in centuries

---

I am persuaded that the revolutionary influence (two illegible words) France is due much less [to (ed.)] its very ideas than to the philosophical method that provided them. It is not because they shook Christianity in their country, changed their laws, modified their mores that they turned Europe upside down. It is because they were the first to point out to the human mind a new method by the aid of which you could easily attack all things old and open the way to all things new.

And if someone asks me why foreign peoples so readily conformed to the new method that the French brought to light, I will answer that like the French, although to a lesser degree, they were naturally disposed by their social state to adopt it (YTC, CVj, 1, pp. 54–56).

The same idea appears at the beginning of his "Social and Political State of France Before and Since 1789" (*OC,* II, 1, p. 34).

p. "Descartes was Catholic by his beliefs and Protestant by his method" (YTC, CVj, 1, p. 32).

when conditions had finally become nearly similar and men almost the same.

So the philosophical method of the XVIIIth century is not only French, but democratic,q which explains why it was so easily accepted everywhere in Europe, whose face it so much contributed to changing. It is not because the French changed their ancient beliefs and modified their ancient mores that they turned the world upside down; it is because they were the first to generalize and bring to light a philosophical method by the aid of which you could easily attack all things old and open the way to all things new.

If someone now asks me why, today, this same method is followed more rigorously and applied more often among the French than among the Americans, among whom equality is nonetheless as complete and older, I will answer that it is due in part to two circumstances that must first be made clear.

It is religion that gave birth to the Anglo-American societies: that must never be forgotten; so in the United States religion merges with all national habits and all sentiments that the country brings forth; that gives it a particular strength.r

q. "It is not Luther, Bacon, Descartes, Voltaire that must be blamed. They only gave form or application; the substance emerged from the state of the world in their time" (*Rubish*, 1).

r. All the peoples of Europe were born in centuries when the ardor of religious passions reigned, but American society was established especially in order to satisfy these very passions. It was created in order to obey rules prescribed by a positive belief and it is a direct product of faith. The influence of this premier fact grows weaker each day; it is still powerful; and if the Americans are dogmatic in the matter of religion that is not because their social state is democratic, but because their origin is Puritan.

Although philosophy and religion are two distinct things, there nevertheless exists between them a very close link that makes them in some way depend on each other. When the human mind has indeed stopped within the fixed limits of a religious belief, philosophy merges so to speak with religion or at least it becomes as exclusive and nearly as stable as religion itself. When on the contrary religious beliefs are shaken, philosophical systems proliferate.

The Americans do not concern themselves with proving by metaphysical reasons the existence of God and the immortality of the soul, they do not try to mark out the rules of human morality, and do not claim to discover the common principle that should govern the actions of man. They believe in the authenticity of a book in which God himself, addressing immortal creatures, took care to set down with his powerful hand the limit of good and evil.

[In the margin: This is very good and merits being kept; perhaps it should be placed where I show how aristocracy immobilizes the mind.]

(three illegible words) the greatest of the philosophical questions that have divided the world for six thousand years seem hardly to preoccupy the mind of the Americans.

This results from yet another cause than the one indicated above.

Although philosophical systems can in the long run exercise a powerful influence on the destinies of the human species, they seem to have only a very indirect connection with the fate of each man in particular; it follows that it can excite only a secondary interest in the latter. So men never feel carried toward philosophical studies by an actual and pressing need, they devote themselves to them for pleasure or in order to fill the leisure that the principal affairs of life leave to them. Now in {small} democratic countries generally and in particular in the United States, where so many various raw materials are offered to human activity, few men are found who can be concerned with philosophy, and the latter, should they be found, would lack a public that would be interested in their work and would encourage their efforts.

When a man incessantly pursues well-being or wealth, leads ships to the antipodes of the earth, cuts down forests each day, fills in swamps, transforms the wilderness, he willingly leaves to another the trouble of discovering the limits of free will and of trying to find out the origin of evil.

Of all the branches of human study, philosophy will be, if I am not mistaken, the one that will suffer most from the establishment of democracy. If men, whose social state and habits are democratic, wanted to occupy themselves with philosophy, I do not doubt that they would bring to this matter the boldness and freedom of mind that they display elsewhere. But it can be believed that rarely will they want to be concerned with it.

It is right moreover to distinguish two things with care.

A nation can have a philosophy of its own and have no philosophical system *strictly* speaking. When each of the men who compose a people proves individually by his actions that they all have a certain uniform way of envisaging human affairs, you can say that the people in general have a philosophy even though no one has yet taken on the task of reducing these common notions to a body of knowledge, of specifying these general ideas spread throughout the crowd and of linking them methodically together in a logical order.

When you study the life of the Americans you discover without difficulty that the greater part of all their principal actions are naturally linked to a certain small number of theoretical philosophical opinions to which each man indistinctly conforms his conduct.

Do you know why the inhabitant of the United States (illegible word) does not undertake to control the private conduct of his servants and scarcely reserves the right to counsel his children?

To this powerful reason add this other one, which is no less so: in America, religion has so to speak set its own limits; the religious order there has remained entirely distinct from the political order, so that they were able to change ancient laws easily without shaking ancient beliefs.

So Christianity retained a great dominion over the mind of the Americans, and, what I want to note above all, it reigns not only as a philosophy that you adopt after examination, but also as a religion that you believe without discussion.

In the United States, Christian sects vary infinitely and are constantly changing, but Christianity itself is an established and irresistible fact that no one attempts to attack or defend.

The Americans, having admitted the principal dogmas of the Christian religion without examination, are obliged to receive in the same way a great number of moral truths that arise from it and are due to it. That confines the work of individual analysis within narrow limits, and excludes from it several of the most important human opinions.[s]

Do you understand why he (illegible word) lavishly (two illegible words) of himself . . .

[In the margin: *Examples* drawn from the American theory of the *equality of men,* of the *doctrine of interest.* Each one for himself.

I know that there is a multitude of American actions that have their driving power in these two doctrines, but they do not come back to me at this moment.

End in this way:

So the Americans have a [v: their] philosophy even though they do not have philosophers, and if they do not preach their doctrines in writings, they at least teach them by their actions.

Perfectibility. Nothing draws visible limits to man.

Another very fruitful principle for the Americans.

All philosophical doctrines that can have a close connection to human actions are very fixed in America. Purely theoretical opinions are intermingled with religious doctrines strictly speaking.]

The fact is that the Americans have allowed the Christian religion to direct the small actions of life, and they have adopted [v: have created for themselves] a democratic philosophy for most of the large ones (YTC, CVj, 1, pp. 63–69).

s. I am firmly persuaded that if you sincerely applied to the search for the true religion the philosophical method of the XVIIIth century, you would without difficulty discover the truth of the dogmas taught by Jesus Christ, and I think that you would arrive at Christianity by reason as well as by faith. So I am not astonished to see in

The other circumstance that I spoke about is this:

The Americans have a democratic social state and a democratic constitution, but they have not had a democratic revolution. They arrived on the soil that they occupy more or less as we see them. That is very important.

There are no revolutions that do not turn ancient beliefs upside down, enervate authority and cloud common ideas. So every revolution has more or less the effect of leaving men to themselves and of opening before the mind of each one of them an empty and almost limitless space.

When conditions become equal following a prolonged struggle between the different classes that formed the old society, envy, hatred and contempt for neighbor, pride and exaggerated confidence in self, invade, so to speak, the human heart and for some time make it their domain. This, apart from equality, contributes powerfully to divide men, to make them mistrust each other's judgment and seek enlightenment only within themselves alone.^{t}

Each person then tries to be self-sufficient and glories in having beliefs that are his own. Men are no longer tied together except by interests and

---

the Americans sincere Christians, but at first glance, I am surprised by the manner in which they become so. Within Christianity the American mind is deployed with an entirely democratic independence, but it is very rare for it to dare to go beyond these limits that it does not seem to have imposed on itself (YTC, CVj, 1, pp. 59–60).

t. General revolt against all authority. Attempt to appeal to individual reason in all things. General and salient character of the philosophy of the XVIIIth century, character essentially democratic.

But much more so when conditions are becoming equal than when conditions are equal. An intellectual anarchy that is revolutionary and not democratic. We see on this point more disorder than we will ever see.

The XVIIIth century exalted the individual (illegible word). It was revolution, not democracy.

Skepticism is found at the beginning of democratic centuries rather than in these centuries.

The philosophy of the XVIIIth century was revolutionary rather than democratic. Try to find out what was revolutionary in it and what was democratic (YTC, CVj, 1, pp. 11–12).

not by ideas, and you would say that human opinions no longer form anything other than a kind of intellectual dust that swirls on all sides, powerless to come together and settle.

Thus, the independence of mind that equality suggests is never so great and never appears so excessive as at the moment when equality begins to become established and during the painful work that establishes it. So you must carefully distinguish the type of intellectual liberty that equality can provide, from the anarchy that revolution brings. These two things must be considered separately, in order not to conceive exaggerated hopes and fears about the future.

I believe that the men who will live in the new societies will often make use of their individual reason; but I am far from believing that they will often abuse it.

This is due to a cause more generally applicable to all democratic countries and that, in the long run, must keep individual independence of thought within fixed and sometimes narrow limits.

I am going to speak about it in the chapter that follows.[u]

u. In the manuscript, you find here these two fragments:

TWO GOOD FRAGMENTS THAT WILL PERHAPS BE NECESSARY TO PUT TO USE.
  [In the margin: To join to the chapter on method./
  This piece would have been excellent in the chapter on *method* if before showing why democratic peoples have an independent individual reason, I had shown why aristocratic peoples do not have it. *To see.*]
  In the Middle Ages it was believed that all opinions had to follow from authority. Philosophy, this natural antagonist of authority, had itself, in those times, taken the form of authority; it had taken on the characteristics of a religion. After creating certain opinions by the free and individual force of some minds, it imposed these opinions without discussion and by repressing the force that had given birth to it (see what Aristotle was in the Middle Ages and until the beginning of the XVIIth century when the *Parlement* of Paris forbid under penalty of death either to uphold or to teach any maxim against ancient and approved authors.)
  In the XVIIIth century the extreme of the opposite state was reached, that is to say that people claimed to appeal for all things only to individual reason and to chase dogmatic beliefs away entirely, and just as in the Middle Ages the form and the appearance of a religion was given to philosophies, in the XVIIIth century the form and the appearance of philosophy was given to religions.
  Today the movement still continues in minds of a second order, but the others understand and accept that received beliefs and discovered beliefs, authority and lib-

erty, individualism and social force are needed at the very same time. The whole question is to decide the limits of these two things.

My whole mind must be bent to that.

24 April 1837.

The other fragment says:

There is no society possible without social conventions, that is to say without a simultaneous agreement of the majority of citizens on certain beliefs, ideas or certain customs that you accept once in order to follow them forever.

There are conventions of this type in democracies as elsewhere, but at the same time that the social state and mores become more democratic, the number of these conventions becomes less. Agreement is reached on very general ideas that place wider and wider limits on the independence of each person and allow variety in a multitude of particular cases and secondary facts to be introduced progressively. It is like a circle that is constantly growing larger and in which individual liberty expands in proportion and becomes agitated.

I will take as an example what is happening in the United States in the matter of religion. It is clear that the Americans to [*sic*] accept the truth of the Christian religion without discussing it.

They have in a way moved the limits of discussion back to the extreme limits of Christianity, but there the spirit of innovation must stop and it stops in fact as if by itself, by a type of tacit and general agreement; while within the interior of Christianity the individual independence given birth by democracy is exercised without constraint and there is no interpretation of the Gospel so strange that does not find . . . [interrupted text (ed.)]

[To the side: Good sentence to introduce in the chapter on philosophical method, in the place where I speak about the religion of the Americans.]

On a strip of paper: "D[emocratic (ed.)] method.

"The democratic tendency that consists of getting to the substance of things without paying attention to the form; in fact, through the formality, [this] is clearly seen in the civil code. Marriage is perfected by consent and only in consent; sale by the desire to sell. . . ."

CHAPTER 2[a]

Of the Principal Source of Beliefs among Democratic Peoples[b]

a. 1. That man cannot do without dogmatic beliefs:

1. Without dogmatic beliefs there are no common ideas and consequently no common action; so they are necessary to society.

2. The individual can have neither the time nor the strength of mind necessary to develop opinions that are his own on all matters. If he undertook it, he would never have anything except vague and incomplete notions. So dogmatic beliefs are necessary to the individual.

2. Therefore, there will always be beliefs of this type. It is only a matter of finding their sources.

3. It is in humanity and not above or beyond that democratic men will place the arbiter of their beliefs.

4. Within the interior of humanity, it is to the mass alone that each individual hands over the care of forming for him opinions that he cannot form for himself on a great number of matters.

5. So intellectual authority will be different, but it will perhaps not be less.

6. Far from fearing that it is disappearing, it must instead be feared that it is becoming too great (YTC, CVf, pp. 2–3).

b. New sources of beliefs. Authority. Sources of beliefs among democratic peoples.

To put in, before or after the chapters in which I treat the influence of equality on philosophy and religion.

Religion—authority.

Philosophy—liberty.

What is happening in the United States in the matter of religion is proof of this.

(Illegible word) difficulty for men to stop at common ideas. Remedy for that in the future. This difficulty is something more *revolutionary* than *democratic.*

The same ideas from this chapter recur two or three times in the course of the work, among others in *associations* and above all in *revolutions;* I must try to treat them completely here, with verve and without being concerned about what I said elsewhere; because that is their natural and principal place. But afterward it would

Dogmatic beliefs are more or less numerous, depending on the times. They are born in different ways and can change form and object; but you cannot make it so that there are no dogmatic beliefs, that is to say, opinions that men receive on trust and without discussion. If each person undertook to form all his opinions himself and to pursue truth in isolation, along paths opened up by himself alone, it is improbable that a great number of men would ever unite together in any common belief.[c]

---

be necessary to compare this chapter to those I named above, so as to avoid monotony as much as possible, particularly with the chapter on revolutions. There is the danger. I believe however that it can be avoided by painting with moderation in this chapter the natural and true state of democratic peoples relative to beliefs and in the chapter on revolutions by showing (illegible word) and more (illegible word) the exaggeration and the danger of the same tendencies (YTC, CVj, 1, pp. 1–2).

The first title of the second chapter had been: OF PARTICULAR CAUSES THAT IN AMERICA CAN HARM THE FREE DEVELOPMENT AND THE GENERALIZATION OF THOUGHT (YTC, CVj, 1, pp. 33–42, 82–88). The principal cause, Tocqueville wrote, is the rule of the majority. This idea reappears at the end of the chapter, but without the development and the attention it had received in the rough drafts.

c. Note to reread before reworking this chapter. Capital.

The weakening of beliefs is much more general and more complete during the democratic revolution than when democracy is settled.

Since a multitude of beliefs is then renounced, general confidence in beliefs is shaken.

By belief I mean an opinion that you have not had the time to examine yourself and that you accept on trust because it has been transmitted to you, and because those more clever profess it or because the crowd follows it.

Dogmatic beliefs are supports necessary for the weakness [of (ed.)] men. There is no human mind that is able to find [prove? (ed.)] by itself all the truths that it needs to live. A belief is an instrument that you have not fabricated yourself, but that you use because you lack the time to look for something better.

You cannot hide the fact that equality of conditions, democracy . . . is essentially contrary to *dogmatic beliefs,* that is a capital idea, which I must face throughout this chapter, clarify, explain and carefully delimit in my mind (YTC, CVj, 1, p. 2).

Wilhelm Hennis ("La 'nueva ciencia politica' de Tocqueville," *Revista de estudios politicos* 22, 1981, pp. 7–38) notes that Tocqueville is more like Rousseau than he is a Cartesian because he accepts the necessity of dogmatic beliefs and because he places the grandeur of man in the coincidence of the sentiment of liberty with religious sensibility.

Now, it is easy to see that no society is able to prosper without similar beliefs, or rather none can continue to exist in such a way; for, without common ideas, there is no common action, and, without common action, there are still men, but not a social body. So for society to exist, and, with even more reason, for this society to prosper, all the minds of the citizens must always be brought and held together by some principal ideas; and that cannot happen without each one of them coming at times to draw his opinions from the same source and consenting to receive a certain number of ready-made beliefs.[d]

If I now consider man separately, I find that dogmatic beliefs are no less indispensable for him to live alone than to act in common with his fellows.[e]

But to us this anti-cartesianism seems instead to be a sign of Pascal's influence. Like the author of the *Pensées,* Tocqueville believes that, at the time of his fleeting passage in the world, man must accept certain general ideas that he is incapable of proving or of discovering by himself and that all free human action finds itself within the circle limited by these truths. As Tocqueville wrote to Kergorlay in 1841: "Experience teaches me more and more that the success and the grandeur of this world reside much more in the good choice of these general and generative ideas than in the skillfulness that allows you each day to get yourself out of the small difficulties of the moment" (*Correspondance avec Kergorlay, OC,* XIII, 2, p. 100).

Luiz Díez del Corral has more than once demonstrated the influence of Pascal on Tocqueville (as in "El liberalismo de Tocqueville. (La influencia de Pascal.)," *Revista de Occidente* 3, no. 26 (1965): 133–53). See also Luis Díez del Corral, *El pensamiento político de Tocqueville* (Madrid: Alianza, 1989); and Aurelian Craiutu, *Liberalism Under Siege* (Lanham, Md.: Lexington Books, 2003).

d. "I know only two states bearable for peoples as for men: dogmatic beliefs [v: ignorance] or advanced knowledge, between these two extremes are found doubt and all miseries" (YTC, CVa, p. 41).

e. [In the margin: Beccaria said that authority, society, was the portion of liberty that individuals left to the mass in order to retain a more complete and more assured enjoyment of (illegible word).]

By philosophy I mean all that the individual discovers by the individual effort of his reason.

By religion I mean all that he accepts without discussing it. So philosophy and religion are two natural antagonists. Depending on whether the one or the other predominates in humanity, men tend toward an intellectual individualism without limits, or tend toward having only common opinions and ending at intellectual slavery. These two results are impractical and bad. Philosophy is needed and religions are needed.[1]

If man was forced to prove to himself all the truths that he uses every day, he would never finish doing so; he would wear himself out with preliminary demonstrations without advancing; as he has neither the time, because of the short span of his life, nor the ability, because of the limitations of his mind, to act in this way, he is reduced to holding as certain a host of facts and opinions that he has had neither the leisure nor the power to examine and to verify by himself, but that those more clever have found or that the crowd adopts. On this foundation he builds himself the structure of his own thoughts. It is not his will that leads him to proceed in this manner; the inflexible law of his condition compels him to do so.

There is in this world no philosopher so great that he does not believe

---

It is clear that the democratic social state must make philosophy as I (illegible word) it predominate.

You must not hide from the fact that when you dogmatically teach a child or a man a doctrine, you are taking away from him the part of liberty that he could have applied to discovering this doctrine himself. From this perspective you put him into slavery. But it is a slavery often necessary for the preservation of the liberty that you leave to him. Thus the beautiful definition of Beccaria is found again.

[In the margin: When a philosophical opinion, after being discovered by the individual reason of one man, spreads by the authority of the name of this man, such a philosophy is temporarily in the state of religion.

I would say as much about all political, scientific, economic doctrines that reign in the same manner.]

When men associate for whatever object, each one gives up a certain portion of his freedom to act and to think that the association can use. Outside of the association, each one regains his individual independence and occupied [*sic*] his mind or his body with what pleases him. Men make associations of all types.

They make some very durable ones that they call societies; they make some very temporary ones by the aid of which they gain a certain precise object that they had in view. A religion (the word is taken here in the common sense) is an association in which you give up your liberty in a permanent way. Associations of this type are necessary.

If man was forced to prove by himself . . .

1. These two principles are arranged in each century and among each people in various proportions; that is nearly the entire history of humanity (YTC, CVj, 1, pp. 3–5).

The library of the Tocqueville château had a copy of Beccaria, *Traité des délits et des peines* (Philadelphia [Paris], 1766), translated by Morellet. The contractualist principle that Tocqueville refers to above appears in the second chapter of the edition cited (pp. 6–9).

a million things on the faith of others, and who does not assume many more truths than he establishes.[f]

This is not only necessary but desirable. A man who would undertake to examine everything by himself would only be able to give a little time and attention to each thing; this work would keep his mind in a perpetual agitation that would prevent him from penetrating any truth deeply and from settling reliably on any certitude. His intelligence would be independent and weak at the very same time. So, among the various subjects of human opinions, he must make a choice and adopt many beliefs without discussing them, in order to go more deeply into a small number that he has reserved to examine for himself.[g]

[<In this manner he is misled more, but he deceives himself less.>]

It is true that every man who receives an opinion on the word of others

---

f. "The great Newton himself resembles an imbecile more by the things that he does not know than he differs from one by the things that he knows" (YTC, CVk, 1, p. 36).
In a note destined for the introduction, Tocqueville had written:

Preface.
There is no man in the world who has ever found, and it is nearly certain that none will ever be met who will find the central ending point for, I am not saying all the beams of general truth, which are united only in God alone, but even for all the beams of a particular truth. Men grasp fragments of truth, but never truth itself. This admitted, the result would be that every man who presents a complete and absolute system, by the sole fact that his system is complete and absolute, is almost certainly in a state of error or falsehood, and that every man who wants to impose such a system on his fellows by force must *ipso facto* and without preliminary examination of his ideas be considered as a tyrant and an enemy of the human species.
[To the side: They intercept some beams from time to time, but they never hold the light in their hand.]
The idea is not mine, but I believe it good. 8 March 1836.
Not to accept or to disregard a fact because the cause escapes you is a great weakness and a great foolishness in the moral and political sciences, as in all the others (YTC, CVk, 1, pp. 46–47).

g. In the margin, in pencil: "To reexamine. Ampère."

puts his mind into slavery; but it is a salutary servitude that allows making a good use of liberty.[h]

[That is noticeable above all in dogmatic beliefs whose subject is religion.

Religion, by providing the mind with a clear and precise solution to a great number of metaphysical and moral questions as important as they are difficult to resolve, leaves the mind the strength and the leisure to proceed with calmness and with energy in the whole area that religion abandons to it; and it is not precisely because of religion, but with the help of the liberty and the peace that religion gained for it, that the human mind has often done such great things in the centuries of faith.][j]

So, no matter what happens, authority must always be found somewhere in the intellectual and moral world. Its place is variable, but it necessarily

---

h. Uncertainty of human judgments./
    The one who receives an idea is almost always more convinced of its correctness and absolute truth than the one who conceived and produced it. This appears at first view contrary to good sense and even to experience, but it is so.
    The work to which the one who conceived the idea devoted himself in order to make it ready to appear before the public, almost always made him discover certain weak, obscure or even incomplete sides that escape others. The reader or the listener who sees the result of the operation without seeing the operation itself, notices at first the plausible and likely side that is presented to him and, without being concerned about the other side, he seizes the former and holds on to it firmly. I am persuaded that everything considered skepticism is more common among those who teach where certitude is to be found than among those who go to the latter to find certitude.
    27 December 1835 (YTC, CVa, pp. 54–55).

And in another place:

A doctrine must never be judged by the one who professes it, but by those who accept it.
    [In the margin: That a doctrine must not be judged by the teacher, but by the disciples.]
    The most harmful doctrines can lead the man who invented them to very beautiful practical consequences; because, apart from his doctrine, he has the strength of mind, the imagination, the ambition and the energy that made him discover the doctrine and bring it to light. His disciples have nothing more than the doctrine and in them it bears its natural fruits.
    29 December 1836 (YTC, CVa, p. 34).

j. "I would readily compare dogmatic beliefs to algebraic quantities by the aid of which you simplify the operations of life" (YTC, CVj, I, pp. 5–6).

has a place. Individual independence can be greater or lesser; it cannot be limitless. Thus, the question is not to know if an intellectual authority[k] exists in democratic centuries, but only to know where its repository is and what its extent will be.

I showed in the preceding chapter how equality of conditions made men conceive a kind of instinctive unbelief in the supernatural, and a very high and often exaggerated idea of human reason.

So men who live during these times of equality are not easily led to place the intellectual authority to which they submit outside and above humanity. It is in themselves or their fellows that they ordinarily look for the sources of truth. That would be enough to prove that a new religion cannot be established during these centuries, and that all attempts to bring it to life would be not only impious, but also ridiculous and unreasonable. You can predict that democratic peoples will not easily believe in divine missions, that they will readily scoff at new prophets and that they will want to find the principal arbiter of their beliefs within the limits of humanity and not beyond.

When conditions are unequal and men dissimilar, there are some individuals very enlightened, very learned, very powerful because of their intelligence, and a multitude very ignorant and very limited. So men who live in times of aristocracy are naturally led to take as guide for their opinions the superior reason of one man or of one class, while they are little disposed to recognize the infallibility of the mass.

k. Two effects of authority:

1. More *time* and *freedom of mind* to examine and go deeper into the questions that you reserve for yourself.

2. More assurance in holding your own in the portion that you reserved for yourself and in defending yourself there against external attacks than if you did not have one certain and firmly established point.

Not only are you strong on beliefs that you have *received*, but you are also more confident about beliefs that you formed yourself. The soul acquired the habit of firmly believing and energetically defending all its beliefs, the dogmatic ones as much as the philosophical ones (*Rubish,* 1).

The contrary happens in centuries of equality.[m]

As citizens become more equal and more similar, the tendency of each blindly to believe a certain man or a certain class decreases. The disposition to believe the mass increases, and more and more it is opinion that leads the world.

Not only is common opinion the sole guide that remains for individual reason among democratic peoples; but also it has among these peoples an infinitely greater power than among any other. In times of equality, men,

m. Influence that equality of conditions exercises on philosophy.

The further I go the more I am persuaded that equality of conditions pushes man with an unequaled energy to lose sight of the individual, his dignity, his strength, his value . . . , in order to think no longer of anything except the mass. This single given fact influences nearly all the points of view that men have about humanity in that time. The trace [of it (ed.)] has been found everywhere.

In democracy you see only *yourself* and *all*.

After the influence that equality exercises on philosophical method, say what it exercises on philosophy itself.

[To the side: Question of realists and nominalists, to examine when I treat the influence of equality on philosophy. You tend more and more today to lose sight of the individual in order to see only humanity, that is to say, to become, I believe, *realist*.

See *Revue des deux mondes* of May 1837, literary review of the year]" (YTC, CVj, I, p. 7).

It concerns A.C.T., "Mouvement de la presse française en 1836," *Revue des deux mondes,* 4th series, X, 1837, pp. 453–98. On page 456, an account is given of the edition done by Victor Cousin of the works of Abelard and of his definition of the words *realist* and *nominalist.*

In 1840, Tocqueville writes, on the same question, to his English translator:

I believe that the realists are wrong. But above all I am sure that the political tendency of their philosophy, dangerous in all times, is very pernicious in the time in which we live. The great danger of democratic ages, be sure of it, is the destruction or the excessive weakening *of the parts* of the social body in the presence of *the whole.* Everything today that raises up the idea of the individual is healthy. Everything that gives a separate existence to the species and enlarges the notion of the type is dangerous. The mind of our contemporaries runs in this direction by itself. The doctrine of the realists introduced into the political world pushes toward all the abuses of democracy; it is what facilitates despotism, centralization, scorn for particular rights, the doctrine of necessity, all the institutions and all the doctrines that allow the social body to trample men underfoot and that make the nation all and the citizens nothing (Letter to Henry Reeve of 3 February 1840, *Correspondance anglaise, OC,* VI, I, pp. 52–53).

because of their similarity, have no faith in each other; but this very similarity gives them an almost unlimited confidence in the judgment of the public; for it does not seem likely to them that, since all have similar enlightenment, truth is not found on the side of the greatest number.[n]

When the man who lives in democratic countries compares himself individually to all those who surround him, he feels with pride that he is equal to each of them; but, when he comes to envisage the ensemble of his fellows and to place himself alongside this great body, he is immediately overwhelmed by his own insignificance and weakness.

This same equality that makes him independent of each one of his fellow citizens in particular, delivers him isolated and defenseless to the action of the greatest number.[o]

So the public among democratic peoples has a singular power the idea of which aristocratic nations would not even be able to imagine. It does not persuade, it imposes its beliefs and makes them penetrate souls by a kind of immense pressure of the mind of all on the intelligence of each.

In the United States, the majority takes charge of providing individuals with a host of ready-made opinions, and thus relieves them of the obligation to form for themselves opinions that are their own. A great number of theories in matters of philosophy, morality and politics are adopted in this way by each person without examination on faith in the public; and,

n. In the margin: "Before having this entire part of my discussion printed, I must reread the analogous things that I say in the chapter on *revolutions* and consider for myself what I should leave there or transfer here."

o. 1. Absence of those intermediate authorities between his own reason and the collective reason of his fellows leaves nothing else as guide except the mass.

2. Each individual, finding himself isolated and weak, finds himself overwhelmed in the presence of the mass.

3. It is only during democratic centuries that you clearly conceive the idea of the mass [{human species}], when you follow it without hesitating, you believe it without discussion and beliefs penetrate souls by a kind [of (ed.)] immense pressure of the mind of the greatest number [v: of all] on the intelligence of each (*Rubish,* 1).

if you look very closely, you will see that religion itself reigns there much less as revealed doctrine than as common opinion.p

p. When you look very closely, you see that equality of conditions produces three things:

1. It isolates men from one another, prevents the reciprocal action of their intelligence and allows their minds to diverge in all directions.

2. It gives to nearly all men the same needs, the same interests, the same sights, so that in the long run, without knowing it or wanting it, they find themselves having on a host of points the same ideas and the same tastes.

3. It creates the *moral* power of the majority (I saw in another place its political power). Man, feeling very weak, seeing around him only beings equally weak and similar to him, the idea of the collective intelligence of his fellows easily overwhelms him. That gives to common opinion a power over minds that it never attains to the same degree among aristocratic peoples. Among the latter, where there are individuals very enlightened, very learned, very powerful due to their intelligence and a crowd of others very ignorant, very limited, you readily trust the superior reason of a man, but you believe little in the infallibility of the mass. It is the time of prophets.

Faith in common opinion is the faith of democratic nations. The majority is the prophet; you believe it without reasoning. You follow it confidently without discussion. It exerts an immense pressure on individual intelligence. The moral dominion of the majority is perhaps called to replace religions to a certain point or to perpetuate certain ones of them, if it protects them. But then religion would live more like common opinion than like religion. Its strength would be more borrowed than its own. All this can be supported by the example of the Americans.

Men will never be able to deepen all their ideas by themselves. That is contrary to their limited nature. The most (illegible word) and the most free genius believes a million things on the faith of others. So *moral authority* no matter what you do must be found somewhere in the moral world. Its place is variable, but a place is necessary for it. Man needs to believe dogmatically a host of things, were it only to have the time to discuss a few others of them. This authority is principally called *religion* in aristocratic centuries. It will perhaps be named *majority* in democratic centuries, or rather *common opinion.*

[In the margin: Somewhere make the state of transition felt in which each person is pulling in his direction and forms purely individual opinions, beliefs, ideas.]

As men become more equal, the disposition to believe in one man decreases, the disposition to believe in the mass increases, and is more and more the opinion that leads the world.

Religion is an authority (illegible word) [prior? (ed.)] to humanity, but manifested by one man or one class of men to all the others, who submit to it. Common opinion is an authority that is not prior to humanity and that is exercised by the generality of men on the individual.

The source of these two authorities is different, but their effects come together.

I know that, among Americans, political laws are such that the majority governs society as a sovereign;q that greatly increases the dominion that it naturally exercises over intelligence. For there is nothing more familiar to man than recognizing a superior wisdom in the one who oppresses him.r

---

Common opinion like religion gives ready made beliefs and relieves man from the unbearable and impossible obligation to decide everything each day by himself. These beliefs were originally discussed, but they are no longer discussed and they penetrate minds by a kind of pressure of all on each.

[In the margin: I spoke elsewhere about the political and violent dominion of the majority. Here, I am speaking about its moral and peaceful dominion. To say that.]

It is very difficult to believe that equality does not weaken the first of these authorities, but you can think that it will make up for it in part by the second, and that the moral power of common opinion will be called upon to limit much more than is supposed the errors of individual reason. This will be a change of power rather than a destruction of power (YTC, CVj, 1, pp. 8–10).

q. The manuscript says "governs despotically."

r. Of particular causes that can harm the free development and generalization of thought in America./

I showed in the preceding chapter that dogmatic and traditional opinions maintained in the matter of religion limited the innovative mind of the Americans in several directions so to speak. There is another cause perhaps less powerful, but more general that threatens to stop and already hinders the free development of thought in the United States. This cause, which I already pointed out in another part of this work, is nothing other than the (illegible word) power that the majority exercises in America.

A religion is a power whose movements are regulated in advance and that moves within a known sphere, and many people believe that within this sphere its effects are beneficial, and that a dogmatic religion better manages to obtain the desirable effects of a religion than one that is rational. The majority is a (illegible word) power that moves in a way haphazardly and can spread successively to everything. Religion is law, the omnipotence of the majority is arbitrariness.

Religion leads the human mind to stop by itself and makes obedience the free choice of a moral and independent being.

The majority forces the human mind to stop, despite what they have [sic] and by forcing it constantly to obey ends by taking away from it even the desire to be free to act for itself.

In the United States, the pernicious influence that omnipotence of the majority exercises over thought makes itself noticeable above all in politics. It is principally on political questions that public opinion has formed until now; but the laws of the Americans are such that the majority, in whatever direction it decided to head, would make its omnipotence equally felt. Its own will and not the constitution of the country limits it.

You cannot hide from the fact that the Americans have, in that, allowed themselves to be carried away by the usual tendency of democratic peoples. In democracies, whatever you think, the majority and the power that represents it are always provided with a rough power and no matter how little the laws favor instead of combat this tendency, it is nearly impossible to say where the limits of tyranny will be. Now, despotism, whoever imposes it, always produces a kind of dullness of the human mind. Freed from the opinions of family and of class, the human mind bends itself to the will of the greatest number. I say that among purely aristocratic peoples the interest of class, the habits of family, the customs of profession, the maxims of the State . . . form as so many barriers that enclose within them the imagination of man.

If in place of these (two illegible words) that hinder and slow the progress of the human mind, democratic peoples substituted the uncontrolled power of the majority, it is easy to see that the evil would only have changed character. You could say that the human mind is oppressed in another way, but you could not maintain that it is free. Men would not have found the means to live independently; they would only have discovered, a difficult thing, a new mode of servitude.

In aristocracies the power that curbs the imagination of man is one and the prejudices of all types that are born and maintained within an aristocracy take certain paths and prevent the imagination from proceeding in that direction, but they do [not (ed.)] attack intellectual liberty in its principle and in an absolute way; in democracies constituted in the manner that I spoke about above, the majority hangs in a way over the human mind, it curbs in a permanent and general way all its springs of action and by means of bending men to its will ends by taking away from each one of them the habit and the taste *to think* for themselves. So it could happen, if you were not careful, that democracy, under the dominion of certain laws, would harm the liberty of *thought* that the democratic social state favors, and after escaping from the interests of class and the traditions of family the human mind would chain itself to the will of the greatest number.

I think that is something that should make all those who see in human liberty a holy thing and who do not hate the despot, but despotism, reflect deeply. For me, when I feel the hand of power pressing on my head, knowing who is oppressing me matters little to me [and I (ed.)] do not feel more inclined to (illegible word) [put (ed.)] my head in the yoke because a million hands present it to me.

[two illegible lines]

I say that among democratic peoples I clearly notice two contrary tendencies. One leads men toward new and general thoughts, the other could reduce them, so to speak, to not thinking.

So if I found myself suddenly charged with giving laws to a democratic people, I would try to distinguish these two tendencies clearly and make them not cancel each other out or at least make it so that the second does not become preponderant. With

This political omnipotence of the majority in the United States increases, in fact, the influence that the opinions of the public would have without it on the mind of each citizen there; but it does not establish it. The sources of this influence must be sought in equality itself, and not in

---

this purpose, I would attempt not to destroy the dominion of the majority, but to moderate its use and I would work hard to get it to limit itself after overturning all rival powers. In this way, in order to provide not a complete picture but an example, if I lived among a democratic people, I would prefer to see it adopt the monarchical constitution rather than the republican form, I would prefer that you instituted two legislative assemblies rather than one, an irremovable judiciary rather than elected magistrates, provincial powers rather than a centralized administration. For all of these institutions can be combined with democracy, without altering its essence. As the social state becomes more democratic I would attach more value to gaining all or a few of these things, and by acting in this way I would have in view not only, as I said in another part of this work, to save political liberty, but also to protect the general progress of the human mind. If you say that such maxims will not be popular, I will attempt to console myself with the hope that they are true.

I understand that you serve the cause of democracy, but I want you to do so as a moral and independent being who retains the use of his liberty even as he lends his support. That you see in the majority the most bearable of all powers, I understand, but I would like you to be its counselor and not its courtier, and I would want you to say to it just as Massillon said to the young king, Louis XV, Sire [interrupted text (ed.)]" (YTC, CVj, 1, pp. 33–42).

The library of the Tocqueville château contained a 1740 edition, in five volumes, of the sermons of Massillon. Tocqueville is perhaps referring to the following passage from the second part of the sermon on the Incarnation:

The liberty, Sire, that princes owe to their peoples is the liberty of laws. You are the master of the life and the fortune of your subjects; but you can dispose of them only according to the laws. You know only God alone above you, it is true; but the laws must have more authority than yourself. You do not command slaves, you command a free and quarrelsome nation, as jealous of liberty as of its liberty.

Another note mentions:
"Chap. II. Of the particular causes that can harm the free development and the generalization of thought in America.
The pieces of Massillon, on which you can draw, are found:
Petit carême. 1. Sermon of Palm Sunday, first and third part. 2. Sermon of the Incarnation, second part.
You could still look for and, in any case, knit together separate sentences. There would be nothing improper about that" (YTC, CVj, 1, p. 33).

the more or less popular institutions that equal men can give themselves. It is to be believed that the intellectual dominion of the greatest number would be less absolute among a democratic people subject to a king, than within a pure democracy; but it will always be very absolute, and, whatever the political laws may be that govern men in centuries of equality, you can predict that faith in common opinion will become a sort of religion whose prophet will be the majority.

Thus intellectual authority will be different, but it will not be less; and, far from believing that it must disappear, I foresee that it would easily become too great and that it might well be that it would finally enclose the action of individual reason within more narrow limits than are suitable for the grandeur and happiness of the human species. I see very clearly in equality two tendencies: one that leads the mind of each man toward new thoughts and the other that readily reduces him to thinking no more. And I notice how, under the dominion of certain laws, democracy would extinguish the intellectual liberty that the democratic social state favors, so that after breaking all the obstacles that were formerly imposed on it by classes or men, the human mind would bind itself narrowly to the general wills of the greatest number [*volontés générales du plus grand nombre*— Trans.].[s]

If, in place of all the diverse powers that hindered or slowed beyond measure the rapid development of individual reason, democratic peoples substituted the absolute power of a majority, the evil would only have changed character. Men would not have found the means to live independently; they would only have discovered, a difficult thing, a new face of servitude. I cannot say it enough: for those who see liberty of the mind as

---

s. Liberty and authority will always divide the intellectual world into two parts. These two parts will be more or less unequal depending on the centuries./

Authority can be exercised in the name of one certain power or in the name of another; but authority itself will continue to exist.

[In the margin: If men had only dogmatic beliefs, they would remain immobile. If they had only non-dogmatic beliefs, they would live in an ineffectual agitation. On the one hand, despotism; on the other, anarchy.] (*Rubish,* 1).

a holy thing, and who hate not only the despot but also despotism, there is in that something to make them reflect deeply. For me, when I feel the hand of power pressing on my head, knowing who is oppressing me matters little to me, and I am no more inclined to put my head in the yoke, because a million arms present it to me.

CHAPTER 3ª

Why the Americans Show More Aptitude and Taste for General Ideas Than Their Fathers the English

God does not consider the human species in general. He sees at a single glance and separately all the beings who make up humanity, and he notices

a. 1. What is the strength and the weakness of general ideas. Result greater, less exact.

2. That general ideas arise principally from enlightenment.

3. This is not sufficient to explain why the Americans and above all the French, who are not more enlightened than the English, show much more aptitude and taste for general ideas than the latter.

Apart from the common cause of enlightenment, these other causes must therefore be recognized:

1. When men are (illegible word) [similar? (ed.)] their similarity leads them to conceive ideas about themselves applicable to the entire species, which gives them the habit and the taste for general ideas in all things.

2. Men being equal and weak, you do not see individuals who force them to march along the same path. So a great cause must be imagined that acts separately but in the same way on each one of them. That also leads to general ideas.

3. When men have escaped from the spirit of class, profession, (illegible word) in order to search for truth by themselves, they are led to study the very nature of man. New form of general idea.

4. All men of democracies are very busy practically. That gives them a great taste for general ideas, which produce great results in little time.

5. Writers of democratic centuries, like all the other men of those centuries, want quick successes and present enjoyments. That leads them vigorously toward general ideas.

4. Also, aristocratic peoples do not esteem general ideas enough and do not make enough use of them; democratic peoples are always ready to abuse them and to become excessively impassioned about them (YTC, CVf, pp. 3–5).

each of them with the similarities that bring each closer to the others and the differences that isolate each.

So God does not need general ideas; that is to say he never feels the necessity to encompass a very great number of analogous objects within the same form in order to think about them more comfortably.

It is not so with man. If the human mind undertook to examine and to judge individually all the particular cases that strike it, it would soon be lost amid the immensity of details and would no longer see anything; in this extremity, it resorts to an imperfect, but necessary procedure that helps its weakness and proves it.[b]

b. The human mind naturally has the taste for general ideas because its soul is an emanation of God, the most generalizing being in the universe. So it is only by a kind of constraint that you keep the human mind contemplating particular cases. And if it sees a way to escape by some path, it rushes in that direction; and, the more restrained it is in all the other directions, the more violently it does so.

That is why when aristocratic societies become enlightened without yet ceasing to be aristocratic, you find minds who force their bonds and, in a way losing sight of earth, go far away from the real world in order to create the most general principles in matters of politics, morality, and philosophy.

During this time real society continues to follow its routine existence; and while castes, professions, religions, fortunes divide and classify men, interests, ideas, an entirely imaginary society is in a way built in the air outside of real society; it is an entirely imaginary society in which the human (illegible word) [v: mind], no longer limited by the desire for application, subjects everything to general principles and common rules.

So you must not judge the state of a people by a few adventurous minds that appear within it. For it could happen that they might be all the more given to generalizing the less the people itself is given to doing so, and that the impossibility of establishing anything that pleases them in the real world might be what pushes them so energetically into entirely imaginary regions. I doubt that More would have written his *Utopia* if he had been able to realize a few of his dreams in the government of England, and I think that the Germans of today would not abandon themselves with so much passion to the search for general truth in philosophy if they were allowed to generalize a few of their ideas in politics.

When some men put forward very general ideas, it is not proof therefore that the social state is already democratic; it is only an indication that it is beginning to become so.

But if you find among an entire people a visible tendency to apply the same rules to everything, if you see it, while still remaining in the practical and the real, try hard to extend the same moral, intellectual, political condition to all men at once, do not

After considering a certain number of matters superficially and noticing that they are alike, the human mind gives them all the same name, puts them aside and goes on its way.

General ideas do not attest to the strength of human intelligence, but rather to its insufficiency, for there are no beings exactly the same in nature: no identical facts; no rules applicable indiscriminately and in the same way to several matters at once.[c]

---

hesitate any longer and say without fear that here the revolution is accomplished, and it is from now on no longer a matter of destroying democracy, but only of regulating it.

The state of slavery in which the woman lives among savage tribes, her complete separation from men and her imprisonment among Orientals, her inferiority and more or less great subjugation among the civilized peoples of Europe can provide arguments about what I have said concerning the intellectual effects of aristocracy.

The aristocracy of sex is the most natural, the most complete and the most universal that is known. And the greater and more exclusive it is, the more it tends to specialize and to (illegible word) the circle of human ideas.

In the Orient there are the thoughts of men and the thoughts of women. In Europe you imagine ideas that apply at the same time to the two types that compose the human species.

By mixing the sexes in activities and in pleasures you thus give to the intelligence of men and of women something more daring and more general.

That also suffices to explain well the differences that are noticeable in the march of intelligence in the west and in the east (YTC, CVj, 1, pp. 27–29).

Cf. conversation with Clark of 9 August 1833 (*Voyage en Angleterre, OC,* V, 2, p. 25).

c. Earlier version in a rough draft:

. . . at once. When man says that something is, he assumes a fact that he knows does not exist but that he uses, lacking anything better; he leaves better clarification for later when he has the time, just as the algebrist expresses by "a" or by "b" certain quantities whose value he will examine later (three illegible words).

So general ideas are only means by the aid of which men advance toward truth, but without ever finding it. You can even say that, to a certain extent, by following this path they are moving away from it.

For if they limited themselves to examining certain matters individually they (two illegible words) the former, while by considering them together he cannot have anything except a confused and inexact idea of everything.

General ideas are not any less the most powerful instruments of thought, but you must know how to use them.

That men often form general ideas out of laziness as much as out of weakness and need (YTC, CVj, 1, p. 15).

General ideas are admirable in that they allow the human mind to make rapid judgements about a great number of matters at the same time; but, on the other hand, they never provide it with anything other than incomplete notions, and they always make it lose in exactitude what it gains in breadth.

As societies grow older, they acquire knowledge of new facts and each day, almost without knowing it, they take hold of a few particular truths.

As man grasps more truths of this nature, he is naturally led to conceive a greater number of general ideas. You cannot see a multitude of particular facts separately, without finally discovering the common bond that holds them together. Several individuals make the notion of the species emerge; several species lead necessarily to that of the genus. So the older and more extensive the enlightenment of a people, the greater will always be their habit of and taste for general ideas.

But there are still other reasons that push men to generalize their ideas or move them away from doing so.

The Americans make much more frequent use than the English of general ideas and delight much more in doing so; that seems very strange at first, if you consider that these two peoples have the same origin, that they lived for centuries under the same laws and that they still constantly communicate their opinions and their mores to one another. The contrast seems even much more striking when you concentrate your attention on our Europe and compare the two most enlightened peoples that live there.[d]

---

d. It is possible that certain .-.-.- a natural genius that leads them to generalize their ideas. Great writers have said so and yet I still doubt it. I see nothing in the physical constitution of man that disposes him to one order of ideas rather than to another, and nothing in historical facts leads me to believe that this particular disposition of the mind is inherent in one of the human races rather than in the others. I see that the peoples most avid for general ideas and the best disposed to discern them have not always shown the same taste for seeking them and the same facility for discerning them. So I reject a reason that analysis cannot grasp and that, supposedly applicable to all times, explains only what is happening today (*Rubish*, 1).

You would say that among the English the human mind tears itself away from the contemplation of particular facts only with regret and pain in order to return from there to causes, and that the human mind generalizes only in spite of itself.

It seems, on the contrary, that among us the taste for general ideas has become a passion so unrestrained that it must be satisfied in the slightest thing. I learn each morning upon waking that a certain general and eternal law has just been discovered that I had never heard of until then [and <I am assured> that I obey with all the rest of my fellows some primary causes of which I was unaware]. There is no writer so mediocre for whom it is enough in his essay to discover truths applicable to a great kingdom and who does not remain discontent with himself if he has not been able to contain humanity within the subject of his discourse.ᵉ

---

e. There are several causes that make men form general ideas.

A man by dint of research discovers numerous and new connections among diverse matters, beings, facts, . . . and he draws a general idea from it.

Another discovers a certain number of connections among other matters. He knows that the general idea that these connections (illegible word) bring forth is inexact, but he wants to go further and he uses it as an imperfect means that nonetheless helps him reach the truth.

These are the learned, considered, philosophical ways to create general ideas. General ideas created in this way attest to the vigor of the human mind.

But most men do not set about doing it in this way. After an inattentive and short examination, they believe they have discovered a common connection among certain matters. To continue research is long and tiresome. To examine in detail if the matters that you are comparing are truly alike and to what degree would be difficult. So you hasten to pronounce. If you considered most of the general ideas that are current among men you would see that most do not attest to the vigor of the human mind, but to its laziness.

[In the margin] Men do in the matter of government what they do in the fact of language. They notice at first only particular cases, then when they begin to know general ideas, they want to generalize too much; as they become more learned, they complicate their sciences and establish classifications, distinctions that they had not at first noticed. Thus with government. The idea of centralization belongs to the middle age of human intelligence (YTC, CVj, 1, pp. 16–17).

And in the *rubish* of the end of volume II:

The man who puts forth general ideas is exposed to two great dangers from the perspective of criticism.

Such a dissimilarity between two very enlightened peoples astonishes me. If finally I turn my mind toward England and notice what has been happening for half a century within that country, I believe I am able to assert that the taste for general ideas is developing there as the ancient constitution of the country is becoming weaker.

So the more or less advanced state of enlightenment alone is not sufficient to explain what suggests love of general ideas to the human mind or turns it away from them.

When conditions are very unequal, and inequalities are permanent, individuals become little by little so dissimilar that you would say that there are as many distinct humanities as there are classes; you see only one of them at a time, and, losing sight of the general bond that gathers all within the vast bosom of the human species, you envisage only certain men and not man.

So those who live in these aristocratic societies never conceive very general ideas relative to themselves, and that suffices to give them a habitual distrust of these ideas, and an instinctive disgust for them.

The man who inhabits democratic countries, on the contrary, sees near

---

He is exposed to the danger common to all those who put forth ideas which is that they are false and it is noticed. He is also exposed to another danger which is particular to the subject.

The more general an idea (and I suppose it true as well as general), the more it allows particular cases to escape. A very great number of particular cases opposed to a general idea would prove that the idea is false, but a few particular cases do not prove it. The one who raises against the maker of a general idea a certain number of particular cases does not therefore prove absolutely that this idea is false, but he advances the beginning of embarrassing [doubtful reading (ed.)] evidence.

Now, since this beginning of evidence exists against all general ideas true or false, it is like a weapon at the disposal of all narrow or ill-intentioned minds. General ideas can be appreciated in a competent manner only by very enlightened and very impartial minds. There is the evil.

Special ideas leave less room for partiality and require much less enlightenment in those who judge them" (*Rubish*, 2, in a jacket belonging to the bundle of the last part that is entitled SOME RUBISH THAT DO NOT FALL INTO ONE SECTION OF THIS CHAPTER RATHER THAN INTO ANOTHER).

him only more or less similar beings; so he cannot consider whatever part of the human species, without having his thought widen and expand to embrace the whole. All the truths that are applicable to himself seem to him to apply equally or in the same way to each one of his fellow citizens and of his fellow men.[f] Having contracted the habit of general ideas in the one area of his studies that concerns him most and that interests him more, he transfers this same habit to all the others, and this is how the need to find common rules in everything, to encompass a great number of matters within the same form, and to explain an ensemble of facts by a sole cause, becomes an ardent and often blind passion of the human mind.[g]

Nothing shows the truth of what precedes better than the opinions of antiquity relative to slaves.

The most profound and far-reaching geniuses of Rome and of Greece were never able to reach this idea so general, but at the same time so simple,

f. In democracies, since men are all more or less equal and similar to each other, subject to sensations little different, and provided with analogous ideas, it is nearly always found that what is applicable to one is applicable at the same time and in the same way to all the others.

So democratic nations are led naturally and so to speak without wanting to be toward conceiving general ideas in what interests them the most, which is themselves. They thus contract the general taste for generalization of ideas and carry it into all the inquiries of the mind.

In this way the smallest democratic people will be closer to searching for and finding the general rights that belong to the human species than the greatest nation whose social state is aristocratic.

There is only a step for the human mind between believing that all the citizens of a small republic must be free and considering that each man has an equal right to liberty (YTC, CVj, 1, pp. 22–23).

g. The Americans are a democratic people who since its birth was able to act in all ways; the French form a democratic people who for a long time was able only to think. Now I know nothing that leads men more vigorously toward general theories than a social state that disposes them naturally to discover new ideas and a political constitution that forbids them from rectifying these ideas by practice and from testing them by experience.

In this sense, I think that the institutions of democracy prudently introduced are, everything considered, the best remedy that you can set against the errors of the democratic mind (YTC, CVj, 1, p. 71).

of the similarity of men and of the equal right to liberty that each one of them bears by birth; and they struggled hard to prove that slavery was in nature and that it would always exist. Even more, everything indicates that those of the ancients who had been slaves before becoming free, several of whom have left us beautiful writings, themselves envisaged servitude in the same way.

All the great writers of antiquity were part of the aristocracy of masters, or at least they saw this aristocracy established without dispute before their eyes; so their minds, after expanding in several directions, were limited in that one, and Jesus Christ had to come to earth in order to make it understood that all members of the human species were naturally similar and equal.[h]

In centuries of equality, all men are independent of each other, isolated and weak; you see none whose will directs the movements of the crowd in

---

h. Proofs of the limits that the classification of ranks puts on the free development of thought.

Plato and Aristotle were born in the middle of democratic republics. Cicero saw the greatest part of the human species gathered under the same laws. These are ample reasons that should have made general thoughts come to the mind of these great men. Neither those men, however, nor any other of antiquity was able to discover the so simple idea of the equal right to liberty that each man [has (ed.)] by birth.

The slavery that has not existed for so many centuries appeared to them in the nature of things, and they seemed to consider it as a necessary and eternal condition of humanity.

Even more, nothing indicates that the men of that time who had been slaves before becoming free and several of whom were great writers, had considered from a different perspective the servitude from which they had suffered so much. How to explain this?

All the ancients who have left us writings were part of the aristocracy of masters, or at least they saw this aristocracy established without dispute among the men of their time. Their minds, so expansive in so many directions, were limited on that one and J[esus (ed.)]. C[hrist (ed.)]. had to come to earth in order to consider the general value of man and to make it understood that similar beings could and must be equal.

When I see Aristotle make the power of Alexander serve the progress of the natural sciences, ransack all of Asia weapons in hand in order to find unknown animals and plants, and when I notice that after studying nature at such great cost he ended up finally by discovering slavery there, I feel myself led to think that man would do better to remain at home, not to study books and to look for truth only in his own heart (YTC, CVj, 1, pp. 30–31).

a permanent fashion; in these times, humanity always seems to march by itself. So in order to explain what is happening in the world, you are reduced to searching for some general causes that, acting in the same way on each one of our fellows, therefore lead them all voluntarily to follow the same route. That also naturally leads the human mind to conceive general ideas and causes it to contract the taste for them.

I showed previously how equality of conditions brought each man to search for truth by himself. It is easy to see that such a method must imperceptibly make the human mind tend toward general ideas.

When I repudiate the traditions of class, of profession and of family, when I escape from the rule of example in order, by the sole effort of my reason, to search for the path to follow, I am inclined to draw the grounds of my opinions from the very nature of man, which brings me necessarily and almost without my knowing, toward a great number of very general notions.j

Everything that precedes finally explains why the English show much less aptitude and taste for the generalization of ideas than their sons, the Americans, and above all than their neighbors, the French, and why the English today show more of such aptitude and taste than their fathers did.k

The English have for a long time been a very enlightened and at the same time very aristocratic people; their enlightenment made them tend constantly toward very general ideas, and their aristocratic habits held them in very particular ideas. From that this philosophy, at the very same time bold

j. In the margin: "≠All this portion seems to me of contestable truth and to delete≠."
k. "The (illegible word) reason for the difference.

"1. In practical life.

"2. The second . . . in physical nature; although I am in general little in favor of arguments based on the physical nature of peoples, I believe nonetheless that I am able to make use of them here" (YTC, CVj, 1, pp. 69–70).

and timid, broad and narrow, that dominated in England until now, and that still keeps so many minds there restricted and immobile.[m]

Apart from the causes that I showed above, you find still others, less apparent, but no less effective, that produce among nearly all democratic peoples the taste and often the passion for general ideas.

These sorts of ideas must be clearly distinguished. There are some that are the product of a slow, detailed, conscientious work of intelligence, and those enlarge the sphere of human knowledge.

m. First version in a rough draft:

The English have for a long time been one of the most enlightened and most aristocratic people of the globe. I think that the singularities that you notice in their opinions must be attributed to the combination of these two causes. Their enlightenment made them tend toward general ideas, while their aristocratic habits held them within the circle of particular ideas. From that this philosophy at the very same time bold and timid, broad and narrow, liberated and addicted to routine that characterizes the march of the human mind in England. Certainly, the country that produced the two Bacons, the great Newton {Adam Smith and Jeremy Bentham}, that country is not naturally sterile in men who can conceive general ideas and put them within reach of the common people, but these extraordinary men lacked a public. They opened wide roads where they marched alone; mores and laws formed like intellectual barriers that separated their minds from that of the crowd, and if they were able to open their country to new and general ideas in the particular matters that they treated, they did not succeed in giving it the taste for new and general ideas in all matters. The various causes that I have just enumerated can exist without the social state and institutions having yet become democratic, and I do not claim that lacking the auxiliary causes they cannot develop more or less power. I am only saying that democracy places men in a situation favorable to the conception of new and general ideas and that uniting with other causes, it pushes them vigorously toward them. If the Americans were neither enlightened nor free, I doubt that they would have very general and very bold ideas, but I am sure that their social state coming to be combined with their enlightenment and their liberty has singularly helped them to conceive these sorts of ideas.

[In the margin] There is only one aristocracy in America, that of skin. See the consequences: more *narrow* ideas . . ." (YTC, CVj, 1, pp. 80–81).

You find a variant of this fragment in YTC, CVj, 1, pp. 31–32, where Tocqueville adds (p. 32): "In America there is less freedom of mind in the slave countries. Among equal men, there cannot be lasting classification."

There are others that arise easily from a first rapid effort of the mind, and that lead only to very superficial and very uncertain notions.

Men who live in centuries of equality have a great deal of curiosity and little leisure; their life is so practical, so complicated, so agitated, so active, that little time remains for them to think. The men of democratic centuries love general ideas, because they exempt them from studying particular cases; they contain, if I can express myself in this way, many things within a small volume and in little time produce a great result. So when, after an inattentive and short examination, they believe they notice among certain matters a common relationship, they push their research no further, and, without examining in detail how these diverse matters are similar or different, they hasten to arrange them according to the same formula, in order to move on.

One of the distinctive characteristics of democratic centuries is the taste that all men there feel for easy success and present enjoyments. This is found in intellectual careers as in all others. Most of those who live in times of equality are full of an ambition intense and soft at the same time; they want to gain great successes immediately, but they would like to excuse themselves from great efforts. These opposing instincts lead them directly to the search for general ideas, by the aid of which they flatter themselves to portray very vast matters at little cost, and to attract the attention of the public without difficulty.

And I do not know if they are wrong to think this way; for their readers are as much afraid to go deeper as they themselves are and ordinarily seek in the works of the mind only easy pleasures and instruction without work.

If aristocratic nations do not make enough use of general ideas and often show them an ill-considered scorn, it happens, on the contrary, that democratic peoples are always ready to abuse these sorts of ideas and to become impassioned excessively for them.[n]

n. In the margin: "I believe that in this matter what can be said most generally true is this."

CHAPTER 4[a]

Why the Americans Have Never Been as Passionate as the French about General Ideas in Political Matters

[<I showed in the preceding chapter that equality of conditions suggested to the human mind the taste for general ideas. I do not want to abandon this subject without pointing out here in passing how the great liberty that the Americans enjoy prevents them from giving themselves blindly to this very taste in politics.>]

I said before that the Americans showed a less intense taste than the

---

a. Chapter 4 (a).[1]

Why the Americans have never been as passionate as the French about political theories.

The Americans have never shown the same passion as the French for political theories.

That comes from the fact that they have always done politics in a practical way. On this point their liberty combatted the excessive taste for general ideas to which their equality, all by itself, would have given birth. This seems contrary to what I said in the preceding chapter, that it was the practical life of democratic peoples that suggested the love of theory to them. These two things are reconciled, however, by means of a distinction.

The busy life of democratic peoples gives them in fact the taste for theories, but not in the thing with which they are occupied.

It is even enough to make them occupy themselves with something in order to make them accept general ideas relative to this thing only after examination (YTC, CVf, pp. 5–6).

1. ≠The chapters marked (a) are those that still leave me most unsatisfied and that must principally attract my attention at a *last* reading≠ (YTC, CVf, p. 1).

In the jacket that contains the manuscript of the chapter: "This chapter leaves me with something to be desired, I do not know what."

737

French for general ideas. That is above all true for general ideas relative to politics.

Although the Americans introduce infinitely more general ideas into legislation than the English, and although they concern themselves much more than the latter with adjusting the practice of human affairs to the theory, you have never seen in the United States political bodies as in love with general ideas as were our own Constituent Assembly and Convention; never has the entire American nation had a passion for these sorts of ideas in the same way that the French people of the XVIIIth century did, and never has it shown so blind a faith in the goodness and in the absolute truth of any theory.

This difference between the Americans and us arises out of several causes, but principally this one:

The Americans form a democratic people that has always run public affairs by themselves, and we are a democratic people that, for a long time, has only been able to think about the best way to conduct them.

Our social state already led us to conceive very general ideas in matters of government, while our political constitution still prevented us from rectifying these ideas by experience and from discovering little by little their inadequacy; while among the Americans these two things constantly balanced and mutually corrected each other.

It seems, at first view, that this is strongly opposed to what I said previously, that democratic nations drew from the very agitation of their practical life the love that they show for theories. A closer examination reveals that there is nothing contradictory there.[b]

Men who live in democratic countries are very avid for general ideas, because they have little leisure and because these ideas excuse them from wasting their time in examining particular cases; that is true, but it must be extended only to the matters that are not the habitual and necessary

---

b. "This in not a contradiction, but it is due to the fact that the Americans are not only equal but are republican" (*Rubish*, 1).

object of their thoughts.[c] Tradesmen will grasp eagerly and without looking very closely all the general ideas that are presented to them relative to philosophy, politics, the sciences and the arts; but they will accept only after examination those that have to do with commerce and accept them only with reservation.

The same thing happens to statesmen, when it is a matter of general ideas relative to politics.

So when there is a subject on which it is particularly dangerous for democratic peoples to give themselves to general ideas blindly and beyond measure, the best corrective that you can employ is to make them concern themselves with it every day and in a practical way; then it will be very necessary for them to enter into details, and the details will make them see the weak aspects of the theory.

c. Let us consider Germany.

The human mind there shows itself excessively (illegible word) and generalizing as regards philosophy and above all metaphysics, regular and specialized, enslaved, in nearly all the rest. What causes that?

In America, on the contrary, where the human mind is regular as regards philosophy, it is bold and generalizing in all the rest.

Wouldn't the result be that equality of conditions leads to bold and general ideas only in matters of civil and political society and exercises only an imperceptible influence on all the rest?

Or rather isn't there a hidden reason that makes it so that bold and general ideas in philosophy can occur to a mind that does not conceive the others?

Or rather finally must you search for the explanation for all of that in the facts and say:

First of all, that it is not correct that in the United States the common mind is routine as regards philosophy. If you give the name philosophy to the principles that direct human actions, even if the principles were not reduced to theory and science, the Americans certainly have a philosophy and even a very new and very bold philosophy.

Secondly, equality of conditions is already very great; that the philosophical movement that you are speaking about has above all been noticeable since a half-century ago when equality of conditions really came about. That its consequences come about only in philosophy because it is suppressed by force everywhere else and that it brings them about all the more vigorously there because it can bring them about only there. Philosophy is in fact only the complete exercise of thought, separate from the practice of action (YTC, CVa, pp. 36–37).

See the first chapter of book III of the *Old Regime* (*OC,* II, 1, pp. 193–201), where, using the same reasoning, Tocqueville explains the appearance of the French pre-revolutionary intellectuals and their passion for general ideas in politics.

The remedy is often painful, but its effect is certain.

In this way democratic institutions, which force each citizen to be oc-cupied in a practical way with government, moderate the excessive taste for general theories in political matters that equality suggests.[d]

d. Usefulness of varying the means of government. Ideas too general as regards gov-ernment are a sign of weakness in the human mind, like ideas too particular. Be-longing to the middle age of intelligence. Danger of allowing a single social principle to take without objection the absolute direction of society.

General idea that I wanted to make emerge from this work.

[In the margin: Perhaps use here the piece on general ideas.]

.-.-.-.-.-.-.- men ordinarily {judge} ideas much more perfect, more effective and more beautiful in proportion to their being more simple, and that it [sic] can be reduced much more easily to a single fact.

This judgment arises in part from our weakness. Complications tire the human mind, and it willingly rests [v: with a kind of pride] in the idea of a single cause producing by itself alone an infinity of great effects. If however we cast our eyes on the work of the being par excellence, of the creator of man, of his eternal model, of God, we are surprised by the strange complications that present themselves to our sight. We are obliged to renounce our (illegible word) of beauty and to place perfec-tion in the grandeur of the result and not in the simplicity of the means.

God ties together a multitude of bones, muscles, nerves, each of which has a sepa-rate and distinct function. The first elements are themselves the products of a mul-titude of primary causes. In the middle of this machine so complicated, he places an intelligence that resides there without being part of it. An invisible bond unites all these things and makes them all work toward a unique end. This assemblage feels, thinks, acts, it is man, it is the king of the world after the one who created it.

The same diversity is found in all the works of the Creator. . . .

Man himself is only a means, among the millions of means that God uses to reach the great end that he proposes, the government of the universe. God indicates as much to us. .-.-.-.- great results can be obtained only with the help of a great diversity of efforts, with variety of chosen means. If your machine can function as well with one wheel as with two, only make one; but make ten if that is useful for the object that you have in view. If the machine thus composed produces what you must expect from it, it is no less beautiful than if it were simpler.

The error of men comes from believing that you can produce very great things with very simple means. If you could do it, they would be right to put the idea of beauty partially in the simplicity of means.

[v: So God, if I can express myself in this way, puts the idea of grandeur and perfection not in executing a great number of things with the help of a single means, but in making a multitude of diverse means contribute to the perfect execution of a single thing.]

Theoretical .-.-.-.-.- have more connection to practice than you think. This opinion that you can achieve a very great result with the help of a single means and that you should aim for that, this opinion applied to the matter of government has exercised a strange and fatal influence on the fate of humanity. It has singularly facilitated and still facilitates every day the establishment of despotism on the earth. What is more simple than (illegible word) organized government of a (illegible word)? What is more complicated than liberty?

If men had enough strength of mind to combine easily a great number of means, they would succeed better in this way.

It is their weakness and not their strength that leads them to the idea of (illegible word).

Not able to do something very well with a great number of means, they hope to do it more or less well with the help of one single means.

The human mind, not being able to coordinate a great number of means, got the idea that it was glorious to employ only a single one of them (YTC, CVk, 2, pp. 37–41).

CHAPTER 5[a]

How, in the United States, Religion Knows How to Make Use of Democratic Instincts[b]

a. 1. I showed that dogmatic beliefs were necessary; the most necessary and the most desirable are dogmatic beliefs in the matter of religion. Reasons to believe.

[In the margin: To change the title. Put one that places it more clearly under the rubric of ideas and operations of the mind.]

1. Fixed ideas on God and human nature are necessary to *all* men and *every* day to *each* man, and it is found that there are only a few, if any, men who are capable by themselves of fixing their ideas on these matters. It is a science necessary to all at each moment and inaccessible to the greatest number. That is unique. So it is in these matters that there is the most to gain and the least to lose by having dogmatic beliefs.

2. These beliefs particularly necessary to free peoples.

3. Id. to democratic peoples.

2. So I am led to seek *humanly* how religions could most easily assert themselves during the centuries of equality that we are entering.

Development of this:

1. Necessity that religions be based on the idea of a *unique* being imposing at the *same* time the *same* rules on *each* man.

2. Necessity of extricating religion from forms, practices, figures, as men become more democratic.

3. Necessity of not insisting on remaining immobile in secondary things.

4. Necessity of trying to purify and regulate the love of well-being, without attempting to destroy it.

5. Necessity of gaining the favor of the majority.

3. All this proved by the example of America (YTC, CVf, pp. 6–7).

b. Twice there must be the question of religion in this book.

1. The first *principally* in a separate chapter placed I think after the first in which I would examine *philosophically* the influence of democracy on religions.

742

I established in one of the preceding chapters that men cannot do without dogmatic beliefs, and that it was even much to be desired that they had such beliefs. I add here that, among all dogmatic beliefs, the most desirable seem to me to be dogmatic beliefs in the matter of religion; that very clearly follows, even if you want to pay attention only to the interests of this world alone.

[≠Religions have the advantage that they provide the human mind with the clear and precise answer to a very great number of questions.≠]

There is hardly any human action, no matter how particular you assume it to be, that is not born out of a very general idea that men have conceived of God, of God's relationships with humanity, of the nature of their soul and of their duties toward their fellows. You cannot keep these ideas from being the common source from which all the rest flows.^c

[Experience has proved that they were necessary to all men and that each man needed them daily in order to solve the smallest problems of his existence.]

So men have an immense interest in forming very fixed ideas about God, their soul, their general duties toward their creator and toward their fellows; for doubt about these first points would leave all their actions to chance and would condemn them in a way to disorder and impotence.

So this matter is the one about which it is most important for each one of us to have fixed ideas, and unfortunately it is also the one on which it is most difficult for each person, left to himself and by the sole effort of his reason, to come to fix his ideas.

Only minds very emancipated from the ordinary preoccupations of life,

---

2. The second *incidentally* somewhere in the second volume where I would say more oratorically how it is indispensable in democracies in order to immaterialize man (*Rubish,* 1).

See Agnès Antoine, "Politique et religion chez Tocqueville," in Laurence Guellec, *Tocqueville et l'esprit de la démocratie* ([Paris:] Presses de Sciences Po, 2005), pp. 305–17; and also by the same author, *L'impensé de la démocratie* (Paris: Fayard, 2003).

c. In the margin: "<What is most important is not so much that they are correct, it is that they are clear and fixed.>"

very perceptive, very subtle, very practiced are able with the help of a great deal of time and care to break through to such necessary truths.

Yet we see that these philosophers themselves are almost always surrounded by uncertainties; at each step the natural light that illumines them grows dark and threatens to go out, and despite all their efforts they still have been able to discover only a small number of contradictory notions, in the middle of which the human mind has drifted constantly for thousands of years, unable to grasp the truth firmly or even to find new errors. Such studies are far beyond the average capacity of men, and, even if most men were capable of devoting themselves to such studies, it is clear that they would not have the leisure to do so.

Fixed ideas about God and human nature are indispensable for the daily practice of their life, and this practice prevents them from being able to acquire those ideas.

That seems unique to me. Among the sciences, there are some, useful to the crowd, that are within its grasp; others are only accessible to a few persons and are not cultivated by the majority, which needs only the most remote of their applications. But the daily practice of this science is indispensable to all, even though its study is inaccessible to the greatest number.

General ideas relative to God and to human nature are, therefore, among all ideas, those most suitable to remove from the habitual action of individual reason, and for which there is the most to gain and the least to lose by recognizing an authority.

The first object, and one of the principal advantages of religions, is to provide for each of these primordial questions a clear, precise answer, intelligible to the crowd and very enduring.

There are very false and very absurd religions. You can say however that every religion that remains within the circle that I have just pointed out and that does not claim to go outside of it, as several have tried to do in order to stop the free development of the human mind in all directions, imposes a salutary yoke on the intellect; and it must be recognized that, if religion does not save men in the other world, it is at least very useful to their happiness and to their grandeur in this one.

This is above all true of men who live in free countries.

When religion is destroyed among a people, doubt takes hold of the highest portions of the intellect and half paralyzes all the others. Each person gets accustomed to having only confused and changing notions about the matters that most interest his fellows and himself. You defend your opinions badly or you abandon them, and, since you despair of being able, by yourself, to solve the greatest problems that human destiny presents, you are reduced like a coward to not thinking about them.

Such a state cannot fail to enervate souls; it slackens the motivating forces of will and prepares citizens for servitude.

Then not only does it happen that the latter allow their liberty to be taken, but they often give it up.

When authority no longer exists in religious matters, any more than in political matters, men are soon frightened by the sight of this limitless independence. This perpetual agitation [<and this continual mutation>] of all things disturbs and exhausts them. Since everything shifts in the intellectual world, they at least want everything to be firm and stable in the material order, and, no longer able to recapture their ancient beliefs, they give themselves a master.

For me, I doubt that man can ever bear complete religious independence and full political liberty at the same time; and I am led to think that, if he does not have faith, he must serve, and, if he is free, he must believe.

I do not know, however, if this great utility of religions is not still more visible among peoples where conditions are equal, than among all others.

It must be recognized that equality, which introduces great advantages into the world, nevertheless suggests, as will be shown below, very dangerous instincts to men; it tends to isolate them from one another and to lead each one of them to be interested only in himself alone.

It opens their souls excessively to love of material enjoyments.

The greatest advantage of religions is to inspire entirely opposite instincts. There is no religion that does not place the object of the desires of men above and beyond the good things of the earth, and that does not naturally elevate his soul toward realms very superior to those of the senses. Nor is there any religion that does not impose on each man some duties toward the human species or in common with it, and that does not in this way drag him, from time to time, out of contemplation of himself. This is found in the most false and most dangerous religions.

So religious peoples are naturally strong precisely in the places where democratic peoples are weak; this makes very clear how important it is for men to keep their religion while becoming equal.

I have neither the right nor the will to examine the supernatural means that God uses to make a religious belief reach the heart of man. At this moment I am envisaging religions only from a purely human viewpoint. I am trying to find out how they can most easily retain their dominion in the democratic centuries that we are entering.[d]

I have shown how, in times of enlightenment and equality, the human mind agreed to receive dogmatic beliefs only with difficulty and strongly felt the need to do so only as regards religion [<and dogmatic beliefs are readily adopted in the form of common opinions>]. This indicates first of all that, in those centuries, religions must be more discreet than in all other centuries in staying within the limits that are appropriate to them and must not try to go beyond them; for, by wanting to extend their power beyond religious matters, they risk no longer being believed in any matter. So they must carefully draw the circle within which they claim to stop the human mind, and beyond that circle they must leave the mind entirely free to be abandoned to itself.

Mohammed made not only religious doctrines, but also political maxims, civil and criminal laws, and scientific theories descend from heaven and placed them in the Koran. The Gospel, in contrast, speaks only of the general relationships of men with God and with each other. Beyond that, it teaches nothing and requires no belief in anything. That alone, among

d. "If God allowed me to lift the veil of the future, I would refuse to do so; I would be afraid to see the human race in the hands of clerks and soldiers" (*Rubish*, 1). The same idea appears in another draft: "I would be afraid to see the entire society in the hands of soldiers. A *bureaucratic, military* organization. The soldier and the clerk. Symbol of future society" (YTC, CVa, p. 50). Cf. note a of p. 1245.

a thousand other reasons, is enough to show that the first of these two religions cannot long dominate during times of enlightenment and democracy, whereas the second is destined to reign during these centuries as in all others.[e]

If I continue this same inquiry further, I find that for religions to be able, humanly speaking, to persist in democratic centuries, they must not only carefully stay within the circle of religious matters; their power also depends a great deal on the nature of the beliefs that they profess, on the external forms that they adopt, and on the obligations that they impose.

What I said previously, that equality brings men to very general and very vast ideas, must principally be understood in the matter of religion. Men similar and equal easily understand the notion of a single God, imposing on each one of them the same rules and granting them future happiness at the same cost. The idea of the unity of the human race leads them constantly to the idea of the unity of the Creator, while in contrast men very separate from each other and strongly dissimilar readily come to make as many divinities as there are peoples, castes, classes and families, and to mark out a thousand particular roads for going to heaven.

You cannot deny that Christianity itself has not in some way been sub-

e. Tocqueville explained in a letter to Richard Milnes (Lord Houghton), dated 29 May 1844:

> You seem to me only like Lamartine to have come back from the Orient a bit more Moslem than is suitable. I do not know why some distinguished minds show this tendency today. For my part, I have experienced from my contact with Islam (you know that through Algeria we touch each day on the institutions of Mohammed) entirely opposite effects. As I got to know this religion better, I better understood that from it above all comes the decadence that before our eyes more and more affects the Moslem world. Had Mohammed committed only the mistake of intimately joining a body of civil and political institutions to a religious belief, in a way to impose on the first the immobility that is in the nature of the second, that would have been enough to doom his followers in a given time at first to inferiority and then to inevitable ruin. The grandeur and holiness of Christianity is in contrast to have tried to reign only in the natural sphere of religions, abandoning all the rest to the free movements of the human mind.

With the kind permission of Trinity College, Cambridge (Houghton papers, 25/200).

jected to the influence exercised by the social and political state on religious beliefs.

At the moment when the Christian religion appeared on earth, Providence, which without doubt prepared the world for its coming, had gathered together a great part of the human species, like an immense flock under the scepter of the Caesars. The men who made up this multitude differed a great deal from one another, but they nevertheless had this point in common, they all obeyed the same laws; and each of them was so weak and so small in relation to the greatness of the prince, that they all seemed equal when compared to him.

It must be recognized that this new and particular state of humanity had to dispose men to receive the general truths that Christianity teaches, and it serves to explain the easy and rapid way in which it then penetrated the human mind.[f]

f. The history of religions clearly shows the truth of what I said above that general ideas come easily to the human mind only when a great number of men are placed in an analogous situation.

Since the object of religion is to regulate the relationships that should exist between man and the Creator, there is nothing that seems more natural than general ideas .-.-.-.- until the Roman Empire, however, you saw almost as many religions and gods as peoples. The idea of a religious doctrine applicable to all men came only when nearly all men had been subjected in the same manner to the same power.

I would say something more as well. You can conceive that all men should adore the same God, without accepting that all men are equal in the eyes of God. Christianity says these two things. So it is not only based on a general idea but on a very democratic idea, which is an additional nuance. I believe that Christianity comes from God and that it is not a particular state of humanity that gave birth to it; but it is obvious that it had to find great opportunities for spreading at a period when nearly all the human species, like an immense flock, was mixed and mingled under the scepter of the Caesars, and when subjects, whoever they were, were so small in relation to the greatness of the prince, that when you came to compare them to him, the differences that could exist among them seemed nearly imperceptible.

≠You wonder why nearly all the peoples of modern Europe present a physiognomy so similar? It is because the same revolution that occurs within each State among citizens, takes place within the interior of Europe among peoples. Europe forms more and more a democracy of nations; each [nation (ed.)] being nearly equal to the others by its enlightenment, its social state, its laws, it is not surprising that all envisage the

The counter-proof came about after the destruction of the Empire.

The Roman world was then broken so to speak into a thousand pieces; each nation reverted to its original individuality. Soon, within the interior of these nations, ranks became infinitely graduated; races became marked; castes divided each nation into several [enemy] peoples. In the middle of this common effort that seemed to lead human societies to subdivide themselves into as many fragments as it was possible to imagine, Christianity did not lose sight of the principal general ideas that it had brought to light. But it seemed nonetheless to lend itself, as much as it could, to the new tendencies given birth by the splitting up of the human species. Men continued to adore only a single God, creator and sustainer of all things; but each people, each city, and so to speak each man believed in the ability to gain some separate privilege and to create particular protectors next to the sovereign master. Not able to divide Divinity, his agents at least were multiplied and enlarged beyond measure; the homage due to angels and saints became for most Christians a nearly idolatrous worship, and it could be feared at one time that the Christian religion was regressing toward the religions that it had vanquished.

It seems clear to me that the more the barriers that separated nations within humanity and citizens within the interior of each people tend to disappear, the more the human mind heads as if by itself toward the idea of a single and omnipotent being, dispensing equally and in the same way the same laws to each man. So particularly in these centuries of democracy, it is important not to allow the homage given to secondary agents to be confused with the worship due only to the Creator.

[So you can foresee in advance that every religion in a democratic century that comes to establish intermediary powers between God and men and indicates certain standards of conduct to certain men will come to clash

---

same matters in the same way.≠ (*Rubish*, 1. Another version of the same passage exists in YTC, CVj, 1, pp. 85–87).

In the copy from CVj, 1 (p. 86), next to the third paragraph, in the margin, you read: "Is the social state the result of ideas or are the ideas the result of the social state?"

with the irresistible tendencies of intelligence; it will not acquire authority or will lose the authority that it had acquired at a time when the social state suggested opposite notions.]

Another truth seems very clear to me; religions must attend less to external practices in democratic times than in all others.

I have shown, in relation to the philosophical method of the Americans, that nothing revolts the human mind more in times of equality than the idea of submitting to forms. Men who live during these times endure representations impatiently; symbols seem to them puerile artifices that you use to veil or keep from their eyes truths that it would be more natural to show them entirely naked and in full light of day; the trappings of ceremonies leave them cold, and they are naturally led to attach only a secondary importance to the details of worship.

Those who are charged with regulating the external form of religions in democratic centuries must pay close attention to these natural instincts of human intelligence, in order not to struggle needlessly against them.

I firmly believe in the necessity of forms;[g] I know that they fix the human mind in the contemplation of abstract truths, and forms, by helping the mind to grasp those truths firmly, make it embrace them with fervor. I do not imagine that it is possible to maintain a religion without external practices, but on the other hand I think that, during the centuries we are entering, it would be particularly dangerous to multiply them inordinately; that instead they must be restricted and that you should retain only those that are absolutely necessary for the perpetuation of the dogma itself, which is the substance of religions,[1] of which worship is only the form. A religion that would become more minutely detailed, more inflexible and more burdened by small observances at the same time that men are becoming more equal, would soon see itself reduced to a troop of passionate zealots in the middle of an unbelieving multitude.

g. The manuscript says: "I do not deny the utility of forms." See note r for p. 1270.

1. *In all religions, there are ceremonies that are inherent in the very substance of belief and that must be carefully kept from changing in any way. That is seen particularly in Catholicism, where form and foundation are often so closely united that they are one.*

I know that some will not fail to object that religions, all having general and eternal truths as their object, cannot bend in this way to the changing instincts of each century, without losing the character of certitude in the eyes of men. I will answer here again that you must distinguish very carefully between the principal opinions that constitute a belief and that form what theologians call the articles of faith, and the incidental notions that are linked to them. Religions are obliged always to hold firm in the first, whatever the particular spirit of the times; but they must very carefully keep from binding themselves in the same way to the second, during centuries when everything changes position constantly and when the mind, accustomed to the moving spectacle of human affairs, reluctantly allows itself to be fixed. Immobility in external and secondary things does not seem to me a possibility for enduring except when civil society itself is immobile; everywhere else, I am led to believe that it is a danger.

We will see that, among all the passions to which equality gives birth or favors, there is one that it makes particularly intense and that it deposits at the same time in the heart of all men; it is the love of well-being. The taste for well-being forms like the salient and indelible feature of democratic ages.

It can be believed that a religion that undertook to destroy this fundamental passion would in the end be destroyed by it; if a religion wanted to drag men away entirely from the contemplation of the good things of this world in order to deliver them solely to the thought of those of the other, you can predict that souls would finally escape from its hands and go far from it to plunge into material and present pleasures alone.

The principal business of religions is to purify, to regulate and to limit the overly ardent and overly exclusive taste for well-being that men feel in times of equality; but I believe that religions would be wrong to try to overcome it entirely and to destroy it. Religions will not succeed in turning men away from love of riches; but they can still persuade them to enrich themselves only by honest means.[h]

h. "I believe religious beliefs necessary for all democratic peoples, but I believe them necessary for the Americans more than for all others. In a society constituted like the American republics, the only non-material conceptions [v: the only non-material tastes] come from religion" (YTC, CVa, p. 5).

This leads me to a final consideration that, in a way, includes all the others. As men become more similar and more equal, it is more important for religions, while still keeping carefully out of the daily movement of affairs, not unnecessarily to go against generally accepted ideas and the permanent interests that rule the mass; for common opinion appears more and more as the first and most irresistible of powers; outside of it there is no support strong enough to allow resistance to its blows for long.ʲ That is no less true among a democratic people, subjected to a despot, than in a republic. In centuries of equality, kings often bring about obedience, but it is always the majority that brings about belief; so it is the majority that must be pleased in everything not contrary to faith.

[It would be wrong to attribute only to the Puritan origin of Americans the power that religion retains among them; there are many other causes as well. The object of what precedes was to make the reader better understand the principal ones.]ᵏ I showed, in my first work, how American priests stand aside from public affairs. This is the most striking example, but not the only example, of self-restraint. In America, religion is a world apart where the priest reigns but which he is careful never to leave; within its limits, he leadsᵐ minds; outside he leaves men to themselves and abandons them to the independence and to the instability that are appropriate to their nature and to the time. I have not seen a country where Christianity was less enveloped by forms, practices and images than in the United States, and where it presented more clear, more simple and more general ideas to the human mind. Although the Christians of America are divided into a

---

j. "In democratic centuries religion needs the majority, and to gain this majority its genius must not be contrary to the democratic genius" (*Rubish,* 1).

k. I have already pointed out two great causes for the power of religious beliefs in America:

    1. The Puritan origin.

    2. The separation of church and State.

These two causes are very powerful, but they are not *democratic;* the ones that remain for me are *democratic* (*Rubish,* 1).

m. The manuscript says: "he subjugates."

multitude of sects, they all see their religion from this same perspective. This applies to Catholicism as well as to the other beliefs. There are no Catholic priests who show less taste for small individual observances, extraordinary and particular methods of gaining your salvation [indulgences, pilgrimages and relics], or who are attached more to the spirit of the law and less to its letter than the Catholic priests of the United States; nowhere is the doctrine of the Church that forbids giving the saints the worship that is reserved only for God taught more clearly and followed more. Still, the Catholics of America are very dutiful and very sincere.

Another remark is applicable to the clergy of all communions. American priests do not try to attract and fix the entire attention of man on the future life; they willingly abandon a part of his heart to the cares of the present; they seem to consider the good things of this world as important, though secondary matters. If they themselves do not participate in industry, they are at least interested in its progress and applaud it, and, while constantly pointing out the other world to the faithful man as the great object of his fears and of his hopes, they do not forbid him to seek well-being honestly in this one. Far from showing him how the two things are separate and opposite, they pay particular attention instead to finding in what place they touch and are connected.

All American priests know the intellectual dominion exercised by the majority and respect it. They support only necessary struggles against the majority. They do not get involved in party quarrels, but they willingly adopt the general opinions of their country and their time, and they go along without resistance with the current of sentiments and ideas that carries everything along around them. They try hard to correct their contemporaries, but do not separate from them. So public opinion is never their enemy; instead it sustains and protects them, and their beliefs reign simultaneously with the strengths that are their own and those that they borrow from the majority.

In this way, by respecting all the democratic instincts that are not contrary to it and by using several of those instincts to help itself, religion succeeds in struggling with advantage against the spirit of individual independence that is the most dangerous of all to religion.

CHAPTER 6[a]

Of the Progress of Catholicism in the United States

America is the most democratic country on earth, and at the same time the country where, according to trustworthy reports,[b] the Catholic religion is making the most progress. This is surprising at first view.

Two things must be clearly distinguished. Equality disposes men to want to judge by themselves; but, from another side, it gives them the taste and the idea of a single social power, simple and the same for all. So men who live in democratic centuries are very inclined to avoid all religious authority. But, if they consent to submit to such an authority, they at least want it to be unitary and uniform; religious powers that do not all lead to the same center [or in other words national churches] are naturally shocking to their

---

a. This chapter, which bears the number Vbis in the manuscript, as well as the one that follows, are not included in the list of notebook CVf. In the manuscript the first title is: HOW THE PROGRESS OF EQUALITY HAS FAVORED THE PROGRESS OF CATHOLICISM.

On the jacket of the manuscript you find this note: "Ask for some figures from Mr. Wash perhaps." Probably this concerns Robert Walsh, American journalist, founder of the *National Gazette.* Tocqueville and Beaumont met him in Philadelphia (George W. Pierson, *Tocqueville and Beaumont in America,* pp. 475–76, 537).

b. Several conversations with Americans had persuaded Tocqueville of the rapid increase of Catholicism in the United States. This fact has been contested by certain American critics. On this subject, it can be recalled that, in his first letters from America, Tocqueville noted that if the lower classes tended toward Catholicism, the upper classes converted instead to Unitarianism (cf. alphabetic notebook A, YTC, BIIa, and *Voyage, OC,* V, 1, pp. 230–32. YTC, BIIa contains a note on conversions in India copied from the *Asiatic Journal and Monthly Register,* 4, April 1831, p. 316. It is not reproduced in *Voyage*).

intelligence, and they imagine almost as easily that there is no religion as that there are several.[c]

You see today, more than in earlier periods, Catholics who become unbelievers and Protestants who turn into Catholics. If you consider Catholicism internally, it seems to lose; if you look at it from the outside, it gains. That can be explained.

Men today are naturally little disposed to believe; but as soon as they have a religion, they find a hidden instinct within themselves that pushes them without their knowing toward Catholicism. Several of the doctrines and practices of the Roman Church astonish them;[d] but they experience a secret admiration for its government, and its great unity attracts them.

If Catholicism succeeded finally in escaping from the political hatreds to which it gave birth, I hardly doubt that this very spirit of the century, which seems so contrary to it, would become very favorable to it,[e] and that it would suddenly make great conquests.

It is one of the most familiar weaknesses of human intelligence to want to reconcile contrary principles and to buy peace at the expense of logic.

c. "Two very curious conversations could be done, one with a Protestant minister, the other with a Catholic priest. They would be made to uphold on all points opposed [sic] to what they are in the custom of upholding elsewhere.

"These conversations would have to be preceded by a portrait of these two men and of their institutions. Very piquant details would result from all of that for the French public above all" (YTC, CVa, p. 55. See the appendix bearing the title SECTS IN AMERICA).

d. The manuscript says: "repulse them."

e. The chapter finishes in this way in the manuscript:

"and that it would end by being the only religion of all those who would have a religion.

"I think that it is possible that all men who make up the Christian nations will in the long run come to be no longer divided except into two parts. Some will leave Christianity entirely and others will go into the Roman Church."

In 1843, Tocqueville had a very different secret opinion about the relation between Catholicism and democracy.

"Catholicism," he wrote to Francisque de Corcelle, "which produces such admirable effects in certain cases, which must be upheld with all one's power because in France religious spirit can exist only with it, Catholicism, I am very afraid, will never adopt the new society. It will never forget the position that it had in the old one and every time that [it] is given some powers, it will hasten to abuse them. I will say that only to you. But I say it to you, because I want to have you enter into my most secret thought" *Correspondance avec Corcelle, OC,* XV, 1, p. 174.

So there have always been and will always be men who, after submitting a few of their religious beliefs to an authority, will want some other religious beliefs to elude it, and will allow their minds to float haphazardly between obedience and liberty. But I am led to believe that the number of the latter will be fewer in democratic centuries than in other centuries, and that our descendants will tend more and more to divide into only two parts, some leaving Christianity entirely, others going into the Roman Church.

CHAPTER 7

What Makes the Minds of Democratic Peoples Incline toward Pantheism[a]

I will show later how the predominant taste of democratic peoples for very general ideas is found again in politics; but now I want to point out its principal effect in philosophy.

It cannot be denied that pantheism has made great progress in our time. The writings of a portion of Europe clearly carry its mark. The Germans introduce it into philosophy, and the French into literature. Among the works of the imagination that are published in France, most contain some opinions or some portrayals borrowed from pantheistic doctrines, or allow a sort of tendency toward those doctrines to be seen in their authors. This does not appear to me to happen only by accident, but is due to a lasting cause.[b]

As conditions become more equal and each man in particular becomes more similar to all the others, weaker and smaller, you get used to no longer envisaging citizens in order to consider only the people; you forget individuals in order to think only about the species.

In these times, the human mind loves to embrace all at once [and to mix up in the same view] a host of diverse matters; it constantly aspires to be able to connect a multitude of consequences to a single cause.

a. In the first page of the manuscript: "≠Very small chapter done afterward and that I think should be placed after *general ideas*. Think more whether it must be included and where to place it. Perhaps it is too unique to be separate.≠"

It carries the number 3bis in the manuscript, and the first paragraph clearly indicates that at the moment of drafting it followed the current chapter 4, consecrated to general ideas in politics. The jacket of the chapter in the manuscript also contains a rough draft of the chapter.

b. In the margin, in pencil: "[illegible word]. Ampère."

The mind is obsessed by the idea of unity, looking for it in all directions, and, when it believes unity has been found, it embraces it and rests there. Not only does the human mind come to discover in the world only one creation and one creator, this first division of things still bothers it, and it readily tries to enlarge and to simplify its thought by containing God and the universe in a single whole. If I find a philosophical system according to which the things material and immaterial, visible and invisible that the world contains are no longer considered except as the various parts of an immense being that alone remains eternal amid the continual change and incessant transformation of everything that composes it, I will have no difficulty concluding that such a system, although it destroys human individuality, or rather because it destroys it, will have secret charms for men who live in democracy; all their intellectual habits prepare them for conceiving it and set them on the path to adopt it. It naturally attracts their imagination and fixes it; it feeds the pride of their mind and flatters its laziness.[c]

Among the different systems by the aid of which philosophy seeks to explain the world, pantheism seems to me the one most likely to seduce the human mind in democratic centuries.[d] All those who remain enamored of the true grandeur of man must join forces and struggle against it.

c. Religious .-.-.-.-.- of a unique being regulating all men by the same laws is an essentially democratic idea. It can arise in other centuries, but it can have its complete development only in these centuries. Example of that in the Christianity of the Middle Ages when populations, without losing the general idea of a unique god, split up the divinity in the form of saints. So in democratic centuries a religion that wants to strike minds naturally must therefore get as close as possible to the idea of unity, of generality, of equality" (With the notes of chapter 5. *Rubish,* 1).

d. "Democracy, which brings about the idea of the unity of human nature, brings men back constantly to the idea of the unity of the creator./

"Household gods, particular saints of a family, patrons of cities and of kingdoms, all that is aristocratic.

"To accept all these different celestial powers, you must not believe all to be of the same species.

[With a bracket that includes the last two paragraphs: *Hic.*]" (In the *rubish* of chapter 5. *Rubish,* 1).

CHAPTER 8[a]

How Equality Suggests to the Americans the Idea of the Indefinite Perfectibility of Man[b] [TN 7]

Equality suggests several ideas to the human mind that would not have occurred to it otherwise, and it modifies nearly all those that the mind already had. I take for example the idea of human perfectibility, because it is one of the principal ones that intelligence can conceive and because it

a. A note from the *rubish* of the foreword indicates that Tocqueville had thought of having this chapter followed by the one on interest well understood:

> After showing how a democratic social state could give birth in the human mind to the idea of indefinite perfectibility, my intention was to show how this same social state brings men to adopt the doctrine of interest well understood as principal rule of life.
>
> I would have thus pointed out to the reader the two principal ideas that in America [added: it seems to me] guide most of the actions of the Americans.
>
> But I am finding unforeseen difficulties that force me to divide my work (With notes of the foreword. *Rubish*, 1).

b. 1. The idea of human perfectibility is as old as man. But equality gives it a new character.

2. Among aristocratic peoples where everything is immobile and appears eternal, where men are fixed in castes, classes or professions that they cannot leave, the idea of perfectibility appears to the human mind only in a confused form and with very narrow limits.

3. In democratic societies where each man can try on his behalf to ameliorate his lot, where everything changes constantly and gives rise to infinite attempts, where each individual comparing himself to the mass has a prodigious idea of the form [strength? (ed.)] of the latter, the idea of perfectibility besets the human mind and assumes immense proportions.

4. This shown by America (YTC, CVf, pp. 7–8).

Translator's Note 7: For this title and chapter, I have used the cognate *indefinite,* a more literary term still carrying the sense of *without limit* or *not limited,* rather than using either *unlimited* or *infinite.*

759

constitutes by itself alone a great philosophical theory whose consequences are revealed each moment in the conduct of affairs.

Although man resembles animals in several ways, one feature is particular only to him alone; he perfects himself, and they do not perfect themselves. The human species could not fail to discover this difference from the beginning. So the idea of perfectibility is as old as the world; equality did not give birth to it, but equality gave it a new character.

When citizens are classed according to rank, profession, birth, and when all are compelled to follow the path on which chance placed them, each man believes that near him he sees the furthest limits of human power, and no one tries any more to struggle against an inevitable destiny. It is not that aristocratic peoples absolutely deny man the ability to perfect himself. They do not judge it to be indefinite; they conceive of amelioration, not change; they imagine the condition of society becoming better, but not different; and, while admitting that humanity has made great progress and that it can still make more progress, they enclose humanity in advance within impassable limits.

So they do not believe they have reached the supreme good and absolute truth (what man or what people has been so foolish ever to imagine that?), but they like to persuade themselves that they have almost attained the degree of grandeur and knowledge that our imperfect nature entails; and since nothing stirs around them, they readily imagine that everything is in its place.ᶜ That is when the lawmaker claims to promulgate eternal laws, when peoples and kings want to erect only enduring monuments and when the present generation assumes the task of sparing future generations the trouble of regulating their own destiny.

---

c. Certitude:

I imagine that after long debating a point with others and with yourself, you reach the *will* to act, but not *certitude*. Discussion can show clearly what must be done, but almost never with utter certainty what must be believed. It always raises more new objections than the old ones it destroys. Only it draws the mind from the fog in which it rested and, allowing it to see different *probabilities* distinctly, forces it to come to a decision.

[On the side: June 1838.] (YTC, CVa, p. 47).

As castes disappear, as classes come closer together, as common practices, customs, and laws vary because men are mixed tumultuously together, as new facts arise, as new truths come to light, as old opinions disappear and as others take their place, the image of an ideal and always fleeting perfection presents itself to the human mind.

Continual changes then pass before the eyes of each man at every moment. Some changes worsen his position, and he understands only too well that a people or an individual, however enlightened, is not infallible. Other changes improve his lot, and he concludes that man, in general, is endowed with the indefinite ability to improve. His failures make him see that no one can claim to have discovered absolute good; his successes inflame him in pursuing the absolute good without respite. Therefore, always searching, falling, getting up again, often disappointed, never discouraged, he tends constantly toward this immense grandeur that he half sees vaguely at the end of the long course that humanity must still cover.

[When conditions are equal each man finds himself so small next to the mass that he imagines nothing equivalent to the efforts of the latter. The sentiment of his own weakness leads him each day to exaggerate the power of the human species.]

You cannot believe how many facts flow naturally from this philosophical theory that man is indefinitely perfectible,[d] and the prodigious influ-

---

d. I am so sure that everything in this world has its limit that not to see the limit of something seems to me to be the most certain sign of the weakness of the human mind.

A man is endowed with an intelligence superior to that of the common man. He has beautiful thoughts, great sentiments; he takes extraordinary actions. How would I take hold of him in order to bring him back to the common level?

He deems that a certain truth that strikes his view is applicable in all times and to all men, or he judges that one of his fellows whom he admires is worthy to be admired and merits being imitated in everything.

That is enough to make me see his limits and to indicate to me where he comes back into the ordinary conditions of humanity.

He would place the limit of the true and the good elsewhere than where I place it myself; from that I would not conclude that he *fails at everything at this point;* I would instead feel disposed to believe that I am wrong myself.

ence that it exercises on even those who, occupied only with acting and not with thinking, seem to conform their actions to it without knowing it.

I meet an American sailor, and I ask him why the vessels of his country are constituted so as not to last for long, and he answers me without hesitation that the art of navigation makes such rapid progress each day, that the most beautiful ship would soon become nearly useless if it lasted beyond a few years.[e]

In these chance words said by a coarse man and in regard to a particular fact, I see the general and systematic idea by which a great people conducts all things.

Aristocratic nations are naturally led to compress the limits of human perfectibility too much, and democratic nations to extend them sometimes beyond measure.

But if he puts the limit nowhere, I have no further need to discuss it and I regard it as established that he is wrong.

5 April 1836. (YTC, CVa, pp. 35–36).

e. Note of Tocqueville in the manuscript: "This answer was given to me, but it concerned only steamboats."

CHAPTER 9[a]

How the Example of the Americans Does Not Prove That a Democratic People Cannot Have Aptitude and Taste for the Sciences, Literature, and the Arts[b]

a. On the jacket containing the chapter: "The first part of the chapter seems good to me. The second does not satisfy me. The evidence does not grab my mind. Something, I do not know what, is missing./

"Perhaps it will be necessary to have the courage to delete this section entirely in order to arrive immediately at the chapter on details." See note a of pp. 696–97.

The cover of the *rubish* of this chapter bears this note: "Very considerable and sufficiently finished fragments of the chapter as it was before the revision of September 1838" (*Rubish,* 1). Tocqueville already had worked on the chapters on art, science and literature in June 1836.

Bonnel (YTC, CVf, p. 1) remarks that a copy of the *Journal des débats* of 2 April 1838 exists inside a jacket on which Tocqueville wrote: "Journal to reread when I treat the direction that equality gives to the fine arts." The number of the *Journal des débats* cited contains the second part of the review, by Philarète Chasles, of the work of E. J. Delécluze, *Notice sur la vie et les ouvrages de Léopold Robert* (Paris: Rittner and Goupil, 1838); the first had been published March 18. This book contains a commentary on the industrialization of art that could have interested Tocqueville.

b. 1. The Americans have made little progress in the sciences, letters and arts.

2. This is due to causes that are more American than democratic.

1. Puritan origin.
2. Nature of the country that leads too vigorously to the sole search for riches.
3. Proximity of scientific and literary Europe and of England in particular.

3. Why other democratic peoples would be different.

1. A people who would be ignorant and (illegible word) at the same time as democratic, not only would not cultivate the sciences, letters and the arts, but also would never come to cultivate them. The law would constantly undo fortunes without creating new ones. Since ignorance and (illegible word) benumb souls, the poor man would not even have the idea of bettering his lot and the rich man of defending himself against the approach of poverty. Equality would become complete and invincible and no one would ever have either the time or the taste for devoting them-

763

It must be recognized that, among the civilized people of today, there are few among whom the advanced sciences have made less progress than in the United States, and who have provided fewer great artists, illustrious poets and celebrated writers.[c]

Some Europeans, struck by this spectacle, have considered it as a natural and inevitable result of equality, and they have thought that, if the democratic social state and institutions came at some time to prevail over all the

---

selves to the works and pleasures of the mind. But it isn't the same with a people who become democratic while remaining enlightened and free. Why:

1. Since each man conceives the idea of the better and has the liberty to strive toward it, a general effort is made toward wealth. Since each man is reduced to his own strength, he attains wealth depending on whether he has greater or lesser natural abilities. And since natural inequality is very great, fortunes become very unequal and the law of inheritance has no effect other than preventing the perpetuation of wealth in families. From the moment when inequality of fortunes exists, there are men of leisure, and from the moment when men have leisure, they tend by themselves toward the works and pleasures of the mind.

In an enlightened and free democratic society, men of leisure will have neither the usual wealth, nor the perfect tranquillity, nor the interests that the members of an aristocracy have, but they are much more numerous.

2. Not only is the number of those who can occupy their intelligence greater, but also the pleasures and the works of the mind are followed by a crowd of men who would in no way be involved in them in aristocratic societies.

[In the margin:

1. Utility of knowledge which appears to all and which arouses all to attempt to acquire some knowledge.

2. Perpetual mixture of all classes, all men continually growing closer together, emulation, ambition, envy that make even the worker claim to give his mind some culture.

3. From the moment when the crowd is led to the works of the mind, a multitude devotes itself to them with ardor in order to gain glory, power, wealth. Democratic activity shows itself there as elsewhere. Production is immense.

Conclusion. Enlightened and free democratic societies do not neglect the sciences, the arts, letters; they only cultivate them in their own way] (YTC, CVf, pp. 8–10).

c. "To begin the chapter by: It must be recognized . . . something moderate, *supple*, and not too intensely satirical. I must not put the Americans *too low*, if afterward I want to raise up other democratic peoples" (*Rubish*, 1).

earth,[d] the human mind would see the enlightenment that illuminates it darken little by little, and man would fall back into the shadows.

d. Passage that began the chapter, in a jacket of the *rubish* that carries this explanation:

≠Portion of the chapter relating to the particular reasons that turn Americans away from the sciences, literature and the arts.≠/

Portions of the old chapter./

.-.-.-.-.- the frontiers of the United States toward the Northwest still meet here and there in nearly inaccessible places and on the banks of raging torrents against whose course European boats or canoes are unable to go, small groups of beavers half destroyed, remnants of a great amphibious population that formerly extended over the major part of the continent. Although reduced to a very small number, these industrious animals have kept their habits, I could almost say their civilization and their laws.

You see them as in the past devote themselves to different types of industry with surprising dexterity and marvelous harmony. They make bridges, raise large dams that make the rivers meander and, after establishing the walls of the dwelling according to a methodical and uniform plan, they take care to isolate it in the middle of a lake created by their efforts.

That is where, in a secure and tranquil refuge, the generations succeed each other obscurely, amid a profound peace and an unbroken well-being.

Although the most perfect harmony seems to reign within this small society, you cannot find there, if the accounts of the *voyageurs* do not mislead us, the trace of a hierarchical order; each one there is busy without letup with his affairs, but is always ready to lend his aid.

One day civilized man, this destroyer or this ruler of all beings, comes to pass by and the amphibious republic [v: nation] disappears forever without leaving a trace.

[In the margin: See the description of Buffon. Order, property, comfort, work in common and the division of property, public granaries, internal peace, union of all to repulse external violence.]

Ill-humored observers have been found who wanted to see in this republic of beavers a fairly faithful symbol of the republic of the United States.

Americans have concentrated, it is true, in a surprising way on material concerns .-.-.-.- to man only to have him more easily discover the means to satisfy the needs of the body.

It is not that the inhabitant of the United States is a coarse [v: unpolished] being, but among the products of civilization, he has chosen what was most defined, most material, most positive in order to appropriate it for himself. He has devoted himself to the study of the sciences only to look immediately for the useful applications; in letters, he saw only a powerful means to create individual affluence and social well-being; and he cultivated the arts much less to produce objects of value than to decorate and beautify the existence of the rich. You could say that he wanted to develop the

Those who reason in this way confuse, I think, several ideas that it would be important to separate and to examine apart. Without wanting to, they mix what is democratic with what is only American.[e]

The religion that the first emigrants professed and that they handed down to their descendants, simple in its worship, austere and nearly primitive in its principles, enemy of external signs and of the pomp of ceremonies, is naturally little favorable to the fine arts and permits literary pleasures only reluctantly.

[≠At their arrival on the shores of the New World, these men were at first assailed by such great needs and threatened by such great dangers, that they had to dedicate all the resources of their intelligence to satisfying the first and overcoming the second.≠]

The Americans are a very ancient and very enlightened people, who encountered a new and immense country in which they can expand at will, and that they make fruitful without difficulty. That is without example in

---

intellectual power of man only to make it serve the pleasures of his physical nature and that he has employed all the resources of the angel only to perfect the animal [variant in the margin: ≠beast≠].

Among the Europeans who from their arrival in the United States have been struck by this spectacle, there are several who have seen in this tendency of the American mind a necessary and inevitable result of democracy and who have thought that if democratic institutions succeeded in prevailing over all the earth the human mind . . ." (*rubish*, 1).

In the *rubish* INFLUENCE OF DEMOCRACY ON LITERATURE, Tocqueville comments: "To make fun of those who believe that democracy will lead us to live like the *beavers*. Perhaps true if it had started with societies.

"[To the side: Democracy without liberty would perhaps extinguish the enlightenment of the human mind. You would then have only the vices of the system.]"

Cf. *Pensée* 257 of Pascal (Lafuma edition). Also see *Correspondance avec Kergorlay, OC,* XIII, 1, p. 389.

The library of the Tocqueville château contained at least two works of Buffon: *Histoire naturelle générale et particulière,* 1769, 13 vols.; and *Histoire naturelle des oiseaux,* 1770, 4 vols. (YTC, AIe).

e. In the margin: "<The Americans have appeared to concentrate on the material cares of life and they have seemed to believe that intelligence was given to man only to allow him more easily to discover the means to satisfy the needs of the body.>" On this subject, see Teddy Brunius, *Alexis de Tocqueville, the Sociological Aesthetician* (Uppsala: Almqvist and Wicksell, 1960).

the world. So in America, each man finds opportunities unknown elsewhere to make or to increase his fortune. Greed is always in good condition there, and the human mind, distracted at every moment from the pleasures of the imagination and the works of intelligence, is drawn only into the pursuit of wealth. Not only do you see in the United States, as in all other countries, industrial and commercial classes; but, what has never been seen, all men there are busy at the same time with industry and with commerce.

I am persuaded however that, if the Americans had been alone in the universe, with the liberties and enlightenment acquired by their fathers and the passions that were their own, they would not have taken long to discover that you cannot make progress for long in the application of the sciences without cultivating the theory; that all the arts improve by their interaction, and however absorbed they might have been in the pursuit of the principal object of their desires, they would soon have recognized that to reach it better, they had to turn away from it from time to time.

The taste for pleasures of the mind is, moreover, so natural to the heart of civilized man that, among the cultured nations that are least disposed to devote themselves to it, there is always a certain number of citizens who develop it. This intellectual need, once felt, would have soon been satisfied.

But, at the same time that the Americans were led naturally to ask of science only its particular applications, of the arts only the means to make life easy, learned and literary Europe took care of going back to the general sources of truth, and perfected at the same time all that can work toward the pleasures of man as well as all that must serve his needs.[f]

f. To the side: "≠America forms like one part of the middle classes of England.≠"
In the *rubish,* inside the jacket that is entitled PORTIONS OF THE OLD CHAPTER:

Among all the classes which made up the English nation there was particularly one that, placed above the people by its comfort and below the nobles by the mediocrity of its fortune, possessed the tranquil tastes [v: the love of well-being], the simple habits, the incomplete enlightenment, the good practical and [blank (ed.)] sense that in nearly all countries. .-.-.-.-.- middle classes. It was the middle classes that provided to the population of the United States its principal and so to speak its only elements.

At the head of the enlightened nations of the Old World, the inhabitants of the United States particularly singled out one with whom a common origin and analogous habits closely united them. They found among this people famous scientists, skilled artists, great writers, and they could reap the rewards of intelligence without needing to work to accumulate them.

I cannot agree to separate America from Europe, despite the Ocean that divides them. I consider the people of the United States as the portion of the English people charged with exploiting the forests of the New World, while the rest of the nation, provided with more leisure and less preoccupied by the material cares of life, is able to devote itself to thought and to develop the human mind in all aspects.

[<≠So I think that democracy must no more be judged by America than the different nations of Europe by one of the commercial and manufacturing classes that are found within them.≠>]

So the situation of the Americans is entirely exceptional, and it may be believed that no democratic people will ever be put in the same situation. Their entirely Puritan origin, their uniquely commercial habits, even the country that they inhabit and that seems to divert their intelligence from the study of the sciences, letters and the arts; the proximity of Europe, that allows them not to study them without falling back into barbarism; a thousand particular causes, of which I have been able to show only the principal ones, had to concentrate the American mind in a singular way in the concern for purely material things. The passions, needs, education, circumstances, everything seems in fact to combine to bend the inhabitant of the

---

Scarcely transported to the shores of the New World, these men were at first assailed by great needs and threatened by great dangers against which they had at first to direct their entire attention in order to satisfy the first and to ward off the second.

After these first obstacles had been conquered, it was found that the country they inhabited offered such incredible possibilities to human industry that there was no one there who could not aspire to comfort and many to wealth, so that the human mind, diverted from the pursuit of the sciences, distracted from the pleasures of the mind, insensitive to the attractions of the arts, found itself as if carried away despite itself by a rapid torrent toward only the acquisition of wealth [v: well-being]" (*Rubish,* 1).

United States toward the earth. Religion alone makes him, from time to time, turn a fleeting and distracted gaze toward heaven.

So let us stop seeing all democratic nations with the face of the American people, and let us try finally to consider them with their own features.g

g. Fragment in the manuscript:

"≠If those who think that the sciences, letters and the arts cannot prosper among democratic peoples assumed the existence of the three principal circumstances that I am going to talk about, I would perhaps share their sentiment.

I imagine a people newly emerged from the uncivilized state, among whom conditions remained equal and political power is concentrated in the hands of one man. That among a democratic nation of this type the human mind would be stopped in its development, curbed and as if struck by a sort of intellectual paralysis, I accept without difficulty.≠

[In the margin: Here take if possible a confident, simple, short, broken, didactic style. Free myself from the oratorical form.

Read Beaumont's piece.

Under democracies that come after an aristocratic order, that are enlightened and free, the sciences, literature and the arts develop, but they develop in a certain way./

America itself can provide us with illuminating details on this point.

(Note) The underlined sentence must not be lost from view and try to bind myself to it.

This chapter on general ideas must be short and followed by separate small chapters on the sciences, letters and the arts. Mix America as much as possible with all of that.]

≠But why imagine an imaginary democracy when we can easily conceive of a real one? What good is it to go back to the origin of the world≠ when what is happening before our eyes is enough to enlighten us?

I take the European peoples such as they appear before my eyes, with their aristocratic traditions, their acquired enlightenment, their liberties, and I wonder if by becoming democratic they risk, as some would like to persuade us, falling back into a kind of barbarism.

There exists at the bottom of the human heart a natural taste for things of the mind and the enjoyments of the imagination, as well as an instinctive tendency toward the pleasures of the senses. The mind of man left to itself leans from one side toward the limited, the material and the commercial, the useful, from the other it tends without effort toward the infinite, the non-material, the great and the beautiful.

So when men have once tasted, as among us, the intellectual and delicate pleasures that civilization provides, I cannot believe that he [*sic*] will ever get sick of them. Legislation, social state can direct in a certain way the natural tendency that leads men there, but not destroy it.

[To the side, with a bracket that includes the last two paragraphs: ≠All of that is perhaps too metaphysical, too long . . .≠]

You can imagine a people among whom there would be neither caste, nor hierarchy, nor class; where the law, recognizing no privileges, would divide inheritances equally; and who, at the same time, would be deprived of enlightenment and liberty. This is not an empty hypothesis: a despot can find it in his interest to make his subjects equal and to leave them ignorant, in order to keep them slaves more easily.

Not only would a democratic people of this type show neither aptitude nor taste for the sciences, literature and the arts, but also you may believe that it will never show them.

The law of inheritance would itself undertake in each generation to destroy fortunes, and no one would create new ones. The poor man, deprived of enlightenment and liberty, would not even conceive the idea of rising toward wealth, and the rich man would allow himself to be carried along toward poverty without knowing how to defend himself. A complete and

---

Give a democratic people enlightenment and liberty and you will see them, you can be sure, bring to the study of the sciences, letters and the arts the same feverish activity that they show in all the rest.

[In the margin: The first idea is this one:

A people who has acquired the habit of literary pleasures cannot get out of the habit completely. There will always remain at least a large number of men who will keep it and there will be utility and profit in satisfying the latter.

The second:

Among an enlightened and free people equality cannot fail to have limits. Many rich men, men of leisure who perhaps would not by themselves conceive the pleasures of the imagination but who take to those that they see being enjoyed.]"

Beaumont commented on the study of the sciences in America in *Marie,* I, pp. 247–48.

Some years later, Tocqueville had partially changed his opinion. In a letter dating probably from 1856 and perhaps addressed to Mignet, he asserted:

Under the spell that your reading cast on me yesterday, I forgot to make a small observation to you that has recurred to me since and [that (ed.)] I do not want to leave absolutely in silence. It concerns the very amusing portrait that you do of the Americans, above all of their scorn for letters. I know that you do not speak there in your name; nonetheless, I believe that a small correction from you would do well in that place. I am talking above all of the accusation of being indifferent to letters. You know that since then they have made, even in this direction, very notable progress. They begin to count among civilized nations, even in the sciences that relate to pure theory, like metaphysics. A single parenthesis by you on this subject will reestablish equity without reducing any of the charm of the tableau (Private archives).

invincible equality would soon be established between these two citizens. No one would then have either the time or the taste for devoting himself to the works and pleasures of the mind. But everyone would live benumbed in the same ignorance and in an equal servitude.

When I come to imagine a democratic society of this type, I immediately think I feel myself in one of these low, dark and suffocating places, where lights, brought in from outside, soon grow dim and are extinguished. It seems to me that a sudden weight overwhelms me, and that I am dragging myself along among the shadows around me in order to find the exit that should lead me back to the air and daylight. But all of this cannot apply to men already enlightened who remain free after destroying the particular and hereditary rights that perpetuated property in the hands of certain individuals or certain bodies.

[<In democratic societies of this type equality encounters necessary limits that it cannot go beyond.>]

When the men who live within a democratic society are enlightened, they discover without difficulty that nothing either limits them or fixes their situation or forces them to be content with their present fortune.

So they all conceive the idea of increasing it, and, if they are free, they all try to do so, but all do not succeed in the same way. The legislature, it is true, no longer grants privileges, but nature gives them. Since natural inequality is very great, fortunes become unequal from the moment when each man makes use of all his abilities in order to grow rich.

The law of inheritance is still opposed to the establishment of rich families, but it no longer prevents the existence of the rich. It constantly leads citizens back toward a common level from which they constantly escape; they become more unequal in property the more their enlightenment increases and the greater their liberty is.

In our time a sect celebrated for its genius and its extravagances arose; it claimed to concentrate all property in the hands of a central power and to charge the latter with distributing it afterward, according to merit, to all individuals. You were shielded in this way from the complete and eternal equality that seems to threaten democratic societies.

There is another simpler and less dangerous remedy; it is to grant privilege to no one, to give everyone equal enlightenment and an equal independence, and to leave to each man the care of making his place for himself. Natural inequality will soon appear and wealth will pass by itself toward the most able.[h]

So [enlightened] and free democratic societies will always contain within them a multitude of wealthy or well-to-do men. These rich men will not be bound as closely together as members of the old aristocratic class; they will have different instincts and will hardly ever possess a leisure as secure and as complete; but they will be infinitely more numerous than those who composed this class could have been. These men will not be narrowly confined within the preoccupations of material life and they will be able, although to varying degrees, to devote themselves to the works and pleasures of the mind. So they will devote themselves to them; for, if it is true that the human mind leans from one side toward the limited, the material and the useful, from the other, it rises naturally toward the infinite, the non-material and the beautiful. Physical needs attach the mind to the earth, but, as soon as you no longer hold it down, it stands up by itself.

Not only will the number of those who can interest themselves in the works of the mind be greater, but also the taste for intellectual enjoyments will descend, from one person to the next, even to those who, in aristocratic societies, seem to have neither the time nor the capacity to devote themselves to those enjoyments.

When there are no more hereditary riches, privileges of class and prerogatives of birth, and when each man no longer draws his strength except from himself, it becomes clear that what makes the principal difference among the fortunes of men is intelligence. All that serves to fortify, to expand and to embellish intelligence immediately acquires a great value.

---

h. ≠Give all citizens equal means [v: instruction and liberty] to achieve wealth and prevent wealth acquired by the individual efforts of one of them from then going to accumulate by itself and being transmitted without difficulty to all of his descendants, and you will very naturally approach the goal toward which the Saint-Simonians claim to go, without using the dangerous and impractical means that they indicate. Leave men alone. They will class themselves according to their capacity, just watch that nothing prevents them from doing so.≠

[In the margin] These ideas are capital. They clarify my mind and clearly show me the place where it is necessary to build (*Rubish*, 1. A nearly identical passage exists on the page that carries the number 8).

The utility of knowledge reveals itself with an extremely particular clarity to the very eyes of the crowd. Those who do not appreciate its charms value its effects and make some efforts to achieve it.

In enlightened and free democratic centuries, men have nothing that separates them or anything that keeps them in their place; they go up or go down with a singular rapidity. All classes see each other constantly, because they are very close. They communicate and mingle every day, imitate and envy each other; that suggests to the people a host of ideas, notions, desires that they would not have had if ranks had been fixed and society immobile. In these nations, the servant never considers himself as a complete stranger to the pleasures and works of the master, the poor to those of the rich; the man of the country tries hard to resemble the man of the city, and the provinces, the metropolis.

Thus, no one allows himself easily to be reduced to the material cares of life alone, and the most humble artisan casts, from time to time, a few eager and furtive glances into the superior world of intelligence. People do not read in the same spirit and in the same way as among aristocratic peoples; but the circle of readers expands constantly and ends by including all citizens.[j]

From the moment when the crowd begins to be interested in the works of the mind, it discovers that a great means to acquire glory, power or wealth is to excel in a few of them. The restless ambition given birth by equality [v: democracy] immediately turns in this direction as in all the others. The number of those who cultivate the sciences, letters and the arts becomes immense. A prodigious activity reveals itself in the world of the mind; each man seeks to open a path for himself there and tries hard to attract the eye of the public. Something occurs there analogous to what happens in the United States in political society; works are often imperfect, but they are

---

j. So I am persuaded that conditions, by becoming more equal among us, will only extend the circle of those who know and value literary pleasures. The whole question is knowing whether or not they will lose on the side of purity of taste what they gain on the side of numbers.

But I am far from believing that among democratic peoples who have enlightenment and liberty, the number of men of leisure will be as small as is supposed (*Rubish*, 1).

innumerable; and, although the results of individual efforts are ordinarily very small, the general result is always very great.

So it is not true to say that men who live in democratic centuries are naturally indifferent to the sciences, letters and the arts; only it must be recognized that they cultivate them in their own way, and that they bring, from this direction, qualities and defects that are their own.

CHAPTER 10[a]

Why the Americans Are More Attached to the Application of the Sciences Than to the Theory[b]

a. 1. Among democratic peoples, each man wants to judge by himself; no one likes to believe anyone on his word; no one talks a lot of fine words. All these instincts are found again in the scientific world, and give to the sciences among the latter peoples a free, sure, experimental, but less lofty course.

2. Three distinct parts of the sciences, one purely theoretical, another (illegible word) theoretical but close to application, a last absolutely applied.

The Americans excel in the last two and neglect the first one, why:

1. Meditation is needed to make progress in the most theoretical portion of the sciences. The perpetual movement that reigns in democratic societies does not allow devoting oneself to it. It takes away the time and also the desire. In societies where nearly everyone is constantly in action, there is little esteem for meditation.

2. It is the lofty and disinterested love of truth that pushes the human mind toward the abstract portion of the sciences. These great scientific passions show themselves more rarely in democratic centuries than in others, why:

1. Because the social state does not lead to great passions in general, and does not keep souls on so lofty a tone.

2. Because men who live in democratic societies are constantly in a hurry to enjoy, are discontent with their position and, aspiring to change it, are not led to value the sciences except as means to go by the easiest and shortest roads to wealth. So they reward scientists in this spirit and push them constantly in this direction.

[In the margin: I know something more striking, clearer, better finally than this deduction, but my mind refuses to grasp it.]

3. In democratic centuries, the government must exercise all its efforts to sustain the theoretical study of the sciences. Practical study develops by itself.

4. If men turned entirely away from theory to occupy themselves only with the practical, they could again become by themselves nearly barbarous. Example of China (YTC, CVf, pp. 11–12).

b. Order of ideas./

If the democratic social state and democratic institutions do not stop the development of the human mind, it is at least incontestable that they lead it in one direction rather than another. Their efforts, limited in this way, are still very great, and you will pardon me, I hope, for stopping a moment to contemplate them.

When it was a matter of the philosophical method of the Americans, I made several remarks that we should benefit from here.

Equality develops in every man the desire to judge everything by himself; it gives him, in everything, the taste for the tangible and the real, scorn for traditions and forms. These general instincts make themselves seen principally in the particular subject of this chapter.

Those who cultivate the sciences among democratic peoples are always afraid of being lost in utopias. They distrust systems; they love to stay very close to the facts and to study them by themselves; since they do not allow themselves to be easily impressed by the name of any one of their fellows, they are never inclined to swear on the word of the master; but, on the contrary, you see them constantly occupied with searching for the weak part of his doctrine. Scientific traditions have little sway over them; they never stop for long in the subtleties of a school, and they spin out a lot of fancy words with difficulty; they enter as much as they can into the principal parts of the subject that occupies them, and they love to explain them in

---

1. Three parts in each science: high, middle, low.

This proved by the science of laws.

These three parts hold together but can be cultivated separately.

2. Equality leads men to neglect the first, in order to occupy themselves only with the other two. Why:

1. No meditation possible in the middle of democratic movement.

2. Great political liberty that deprives science of great geniuses and great passions. This is not necessarily democratic.

First a distinction must be made between nations that possess great political liberty and those that do not have it. This is a great question: *political* genius and *scientific* genius are so different that you can say that one only inflames the other without diverting it.

3. Two types of scientific passions, one *disinterested* and lofty, the other *mercantile* and low (*Rubish*, 1).

common language. The sciences then have a freer and more certain, but less lofty allure.[c]

The mind can, it seems to me, divide science into three parts.

The first contains the most theoretical principles, the most abstract notions, the ones whose application is unknown or very distant.

The second is made up of general truths that, though still pure theory, lead nevertheless by a direct and short path to application.

The processes of application and the means of execution fulfill[d] the third.[e]

c. "Under democracy the sciences get rid of useless words, of empty formulas. Efforts of the Americans to get out of the judicial routine of the English. Code of Ohio.

See Beaumont, G. B. Q." (*Rubish*, 1). Cf. *Marie*, I, pp. 247–48.

d. Note in the margin: "Louis thinks that this piece should be modified a bit and do three classes of scientists instead of three classes of sciences. For, in fact, he says, there are only two of them."

e. At the end of the chapter, you find a jacket with the title: "Development that seemed too long to me, but which is good in itself.":

An example would make my thought easier to grasp: I would choose the science that I know best which is that of the laws. The distinctions that I have just indicated are found in the science of laws and I believe, without being able to assert it in so positive a way, that you should see at least the trace of those distinctions in all of the laws and principally in those that are called exact, because of the rigorous manner in which they proceed.

There is a science of laws whose object is lofty, speculative, general. The former works hard to find the rules by which human societies exist and to determine the laws that various peoples must impose on themselves in order to reach the goal that they propose for themselves.

There is a science of laws that, taking hold of a particular body of laws, or even of the higher portion of a body of laws, demonstrates what general principles dominate there and shows the economy that reigns and the overall view that is revealed.

There is a last one that enters into the administrative or judicial detail of the processes by which the legislator wanted to have his plans carried out, learns how political assemblies or the courts interpreted their will, and that teaches the art of making good the rights of each citizen with the aid of the laws.

A class of scholars is attached to each of these portions of the science to whom you give the name writers on law, legal experts, jurists (examine these definitions in the best authors).

If you now come to examine how these different men are related to each other, you discover that in the long run the legal expert and the jurist cannot do without

Each one of these different portions of science can be cultivated separately, even though reason and experience make it known that none of them can prosper for long when it is separated absolutely from the other two.

In America, the purely applied part of the sciences is admirably cultivated, and the theoretical portion immediately necessary to application is carefully attended to; in this regard the Americans reveal a mind always clear, free, original and fruitful; but there is hardly anyone in the United States who devotes himself to the essentially theoretical and abstract portion of human knowledge. In this the Americans show the excess of a tendency that will be found, I think, although to a lesser degree, among all democratic peoples.[f]

---

the writer on law, but that at a given moment they can easily act and prosper independently of him.

If men limited themselves to studying the whole and the detail of existing laws without ever going as far as the general theory of laws, it is clear that by degrees they would reach the point of seeing in the legislation of their country only a collection of formulas that they would end up using without exactly understanding their sense, and that they would not take long to become miserably lost in the maze of the subtleties of the school. That is how you can truthfully say that there is a necessary relation between Montesquieu and the least bailiff of the kingdom, in such a way that the enlightenment of the first gives light by a far and distant reflection to the works of the second.

But men do not need to return every day to the philosophy of law in order to know the laws in force; without having sought what the legislator must have wanted, they are able to understand what he wanted. They are able to apply the general wills [*volontés générales*—Trans.] to the particular case and draw from legal science its most useful consequences. Therefore each one of these different portions of the science of laws can be cultivated separately, although each cannot prosper in the long run when it is separated absolutely from the others. Coming back now to my subject, I want to know if democracy tends to develop the various parts of science in the same way.

In America, where the practical portion of human knowledge and the theoretical portion immediately necessary for application are admirably cultivated, there is so to speak no example of anyone interested in the essentially theoretical and general part.

I think that you would not do justice by attributing this to democracy alone. The Americans are pushed exclusively toward application by powerful causes that are due neither to the social state nor to the political constitution. I have carefully enumerated them above.

[In the margin] *Quid.*

f. Now in all free governments, a great number of men are involved in politics, and

Nothing is more necessary to the cultivation of the advanced sciences, or of the higher portion of the sciences, than meditation; and nothing is less appropriate to meditation than the interior of a democratic society. There you do not find, as among aristocratic peoples, a numerous class that remains at rest because it finds itself well-off, and another that does not stir because it despairs of being better-off. Each man is in motion; some want to attain power, others to take hold of wealth. Amid this universal tumult, this repeated clash of contrary interests, this continual march of men toward fortune, where to find the calm necessary for profound intellectual syntheses? How to fix your thoughts on some point, when around you everything moves, and you yourself are dragged along and tossed about each day by the impetuous current that drives everything?g

---

in free governments whose social state is democratic, there is hardly anyone who is not occupied by it. So among nations subject to these governments it must be expected that a kind of public scorn for the higher speculations of science and a kind of instinctive repulsion for those who devote themselves to them will be established.

I imagine that a people constituted like the Germans of today, among whom great civil liberty would be found, where enlightenment would be very widespread, where communal independence would not be unknown, but where great political liberty would not exist, would be in a more fortunate position than another to cultivate and to perfect the theoretical portion of the sciences; and I would not be surprised if, of all the countries of Europe, Germany soon became for this reason the principal center of higher human knowledge.

Despotism is hardly able to maintain what it finds existing, and by itself alone it has never produced anything great. So I am not talking about an enslaved nation, but about a people who would not be entirely master of itself.

Great political liberty seems to me so precious a thing in itself and so necessary to the guarantee of all other liberties that, as long as it does not disappear at the same time from all the countries of the earth, I am more or less sure of never inhabiting a country where it will not exist; but I cannot believe that, following the ordinary course of societies, great political liberty must favor the development of the general and theoretical part of the sciences. I recognize in it a thousand other advantages, but not that one (*Rubish*, 1).

g. "Of all branches of human studies, philosophy will be, if I am not mistaken, the one that will suffer most from the establishment of democracy. If the men whose social state and habits are democratic wanted to concern themselves with philosophy, I do not doubt that they would bring to this matter the boldness and the freedom of mind that

The type of permanent agitation that reigns within a tranquil and already constituted democracy must be clearly distinguished from the tumultuous and revolutionary movements that almost always accompany the birth and development of a democratic society.

When a violent revolution takes place among a very civilized people, it cannot fail to give a sudden impulse to sentiments and to ideas.

This is true above all of democratic revolutions, that, by moving at once all of the classes that make up a people, give birth at the same time to immense ambitions in the heart of each citizen.

If the French suddenly made such admirable progress in the exact sciences, at the very moment when they finally destroyed the remnants of the old feudal society, this sudden fertility must be attributed, not to democracy, but to the unparalleled revolution that accompanied its development. What occurred then was a particular fact; it would be imprudent to see in it the indication of a general law.

Great revolutions are not more common among democratic peoples than among other peoples; I am even led to believe that they are less so. But within these nations there reigns a small uncomfortable movement, a sort of incessant rotation of men that troubles and distracts the mind without enlivening or elevating it.

Not only do men who live in democratic societies devote themselves with difficulty to meditation, but also they naturally have little regard for it. The democratic social state and democratic institutions lead most men to act constantly; now, the habits of mind that are appropriate to action are not always appropriate to thought. The man who acts is often reduced to being content with approximation, because he would never reach the end of his plan if he wanted to perfect each detail. He must rely constantly on ideas that he has not had the leisure to study in depth, for he is helped much more by the expediency of the idea that he is using than by its rigorous correctness; and everything considered, there is less risk for him in making use of a few false principles, than in taking up his time establishing the

---

they display elsewhere. But you can believe that they will rarely want to concern themselves with it" (YTC, CVj, 1, p. 66).

truth of all his principles. The world is not controlled by long, learned proofs. The rapid view of a particular fact, the daily study of the changing passions of the crowd, the chance of the moment and the skill to grab hold of it, decide all matters there.

So in centuries when nearly everyone acts, you are generally led to attach an excessive value to the rapid flights and to the superficial conceptions of the mind, and, on the contrary, to depreciate excessively its profound and slow work.

This public opinion influences the judgment of the men who cultivate the sciences; it persuades them that they can succeed in the sciences without meditation, or turns them away from those sciences that require it.[h]

There are several ways to study the sciences. You find among a host of men a selfish, mercenary and industrial taste for the discoveries of the mind that must not be confused with the disinterested passion that is aroused in the heart of a small number; there is a desire to utilize knowledge and a pure desire to know. I do not doubt that occasionally, among a few, an ardent and inexhaustible love of truth is born that feeds on itself and gives constant delight without ever being able to satisfy itself. It is this ardent, proud and disinterested love of the true that leads men to the abstract sources of truth in order to draw generative ideas from there.

If Pascal[j] had envisaged only some great profit, or even if he had been

---

h. The taste for well-being makes a multitude ask the sciences loudly for *applications* and recompenses with money and with glory those who find them.

And acting on the soul of scientists the multitude leads them to take their research in this direction and even makes them incapable of directing it elsewhere by taking from them the taste for non-material things that is the principal motivating force of the soul (*Rubish*, 1).

j. Different motives that can push men toward science.

Material interest.

Desire for glory.

Passion to discover the truth. Personal satisfaction that is impossible to define or to deny its effects.

Perhaps the greatest scientists are due uniquely to this last passion. For will is not enough to bring action; the mind must rush forward by itself toward the object; it must aspire.

moved only by the sole desire for glory, I cannot believe that he would ever have been able to summon up, as he did, all the powers of his intelligence to reveal more clearly the most hidden secrets of the Creator. When I see him, in a way, tear his soul away from the midst of the cares of life, in order to give it entirely to this inquiry, and, prematurely breaking the ties that hold the soul to the body, die of old age before reaching forty years of age, I stop dumbfounded; and I understand that it is not an ordinary cause that can produce such extraordinary efforts.

The future will prove if these passions, so rare and so fruitful, arise and develop as easily amid democratic societies as within aristocratic ones. As for me, I admit that I find it difficult to believe.

In aristocratic societies, the class that leads opinion and runs public affairs, being placed above the crowd in a permanent and hereditary way, naturally conceives a superb idea of itself and of man. It readily imagines glorious enjoyments for man and sets magnificent ends for his desires. Aristocracies often undertake very tyrannical and very inhuman actions, but they rarely conceive low thoughts; and they show a certain proud disdain for small pleasures, even when they give themselves over to them; that gives all souls there a very lofty tone. In aristocratic times, you generally get very vast ideas about the dignity, power and grandeur of man. These opinions influence those who cultivate the sciences, like all the others; it facilitates the natural impulse of the mind toward the highest regions of thought and naturally disposes the mind to conceive the sublime and nearly divine love of truth.

So the scientists of these times are carried toward theory, and it even often happens that they conceive an ill-considered scorn for application. "Archimedes," says Plutarch,[k] "had a heart so noble that he never deigned

---

Imagine Newton or Pascal in the middle of a democracy.

The soul is given a less lofty tone in democracies. It envisages the things of life from a lower perspective (in the *rubish* THE INFLUENCE OF DEMOCRACY ON LITERATURE, *Rubish*, 1).

k. This fragment appears in the *rubish* with this bibliographic reference: "Plutarch, *Vie de Marcellus*, p. 269, vol. III, translation of Augustus." The quotation, longer in the

to leave any written work on how to erect all of these war machines [<for which he gained glory and fame, not for human knowledge but rather for divine wisdom>]; and considering all of this science of inventing and making machines and generally any art that brings some utility when put into practice, as vile, low and mercenary, he used his mind and his study to write only things whose beauty and subtlety were in no way mixed with necessity." Such is the aristocratic aim of the sciences.

It cannot be the same among democratic nations.

[Among these peoples, the opinions of the class that governs and the general mores of the nation hardly ever raise the human mind toward theory; on the contrary they draw it every day toward application.]

Most of the men who compose these nations are very greedy for material and present enjoyments; since they are always discontent with the position that they occupy, and always free to leave it, they think only about the means to change their fortune or to increase it. [Men naturally have the desire to take pleasure quickly and easily, but that is particularly true of those who live in democracies.

This sentiment to which scientists themselves are not strangers leads them to look for the consequences of a principle already known rather than to find a new principle; their work is at the very same time easier and better understood.

The same sentiment makes the public attach much more value to applications than to abstract truths.]ᵐ For minds so disposed, every new method that leads to wealth by a shorter road, every machine that shortens work, every instrument that reduces the costs of production, every discovery that facilitates and increases pleasures, seems the most magnificent effort of human intelligence. It is principally from this side that democratic peoples are attached to the sciences, understand them and honor

---

draft, contains a phrase that is missing from the book: ". . . so noble <and an understanding so profound in which there was a hidden treasure of so many geometric inventions>" (*Rubish*, 1).

m. This fragment is found on a separate sheet of the manuscript.

them.[n] In aristocratic centuries [v.: societies], people particularly demand enjoyments of the mind from the sciences; in democratic ones, those of the body.

Depend on the fact that the more a nation is democratic, enlightened and free, the larger the number of these self-seeking men who appreciate scientific genius will grow, and the more discoveries immediately applicable to industry will yield profit, glory and even power to their authors; for, in democracies, the class that works takes part in public affairs, and those who serve it have to look to it for honors as well as for money.

You can easily imagine that, in a society organized in this manner, the human mind is led imperceptibly to neglect theory and that it must, on the contrary, feel pushed with an unparalleled energy toward application, or at least toward the portion of theory necessary to those who do applications.

An instinctive tendency raises the human mind in vain toward the highest spheres of intelligence; interest leads it back toward the middle ones. That is where it puts forth its strength and restless activity, and brings forth miracles. These very Americans, who have not discovered a single one of the general laws of mechanics, have introduced to navigation a new machine that is changing the face of the world.

Certainly, I am far from claiming that the democratic peoples of today are destined to see the transcendent light of the human mind extinguished, or even that they must not kindle new light within their midst. At the age of the world in which we find ourselves and among so many lettered nations that are tormented incessantly by the ardor of industry, the ties that bind the different parts of science together cannot fail to be striking; and the very taste for application, if it is enlightened, must lead men not to neglect theory. In the middle of so many attempts at application, so many experiments repeated each day, it is often nearly impossible for very general laws

n. "So if it happens in the United States that there is no innovation in philosophy, in literature, in science, in the fine arts, that does not come from the fact that the social state of the Americans is democratic, but rather from the fact that their passions are exclusively commercial" (YTC, CVj, 1, p. 91).

not to happen to appear; so that great discoveries would be frequent, even though great inventors were rare.

I believe moreover in high scientific vocations. If democracy does not lead men to cultivate the sciences for their own sake, on the other hand it immensely increases the number of those who cultivate the sciences. It cannot be believed that, among so great a multitude, there is not born from time to time some speculative genius inflamed by the sole love of truth. You can be sure that the latter will work hard to penetrate the most profound mysteries of nature, whatever the spirit of his country and of his time. There is no need to aid his development; it is enough not to stop it. All that I want to say is this: permanent inequality of conditions leads men to withdraw into proud and sterile research for abstract truths; while the democratic social state and democratic institutions dispose them to ask of the sciences only their immediate and useful applications.

This tendency is natural and inevitable. It is interesting to know it, and it can be necessary to point it out.

If those who are called to lead the nations of today saw clearly and from a distance these new instincts that will soon be irresistible, they would understand that with enlightenment and liberty, the men who live in democratic centuries cannot fail to improve the industrial portion of the sciences, and that henceforth all the effort of the social power must go to sustain the theoretical sciences and to create great scientific passions.

Today, the human mind must be kept to theory, it runs by itself toward application, and instead of leading it back constantly toward the detailed examination of secondary effects, it is good to distract it sometimes in order to raise it to the contemplation of first causes.

Because Roman civilization died following the invasion of the barbarians, we are perhaps too inclined to believe that civilization cannot die otherwise.

If the light that enlightens us ever happened to go out, it would grow dark little by little and as if by itself. By dint of limiting yourself to application, you would lose sight of principles, and when you had entirely forgotten the principles, you would badly follow the methods that derive from them; no longer able to invent new methods, you would employ without intelligence and without art the learned processes that you no longer understood.

When the Europeans reached China three hundred years ago, they found all the arts at a certain degree of perfection, and they were astonished that, having arrived at this point, the Chinese had not advanced more. Later they discovered the vestiges of some advanced knowledge that had been lost. The nation was industrial; most of the scientific methods were preserved within it; but science itself no longer existed. That explained to the Europeans the singular type of immobility in which they found the mind of the people. The Chinese, while following the path of their fathers, had forgotten the reasons that had guided the latter. They still used the formula without looking for the meaning; they kept the instrument and no longer possessed the art of modifying and of reproducing it. So the Chinese could not change anything. They had to give up improvement. They were forced to imitate their fathers always and in all things, in order not to throw themselves into impenetrable shadows, if they diverged for an instant from the road that the latter had marked. The source of human knowledge had nearly dried up; and although the river still flowed, it could no longer swell its waves or change its course.

China had subsisted peacefully for centuries however; its conquerors had taken its mores; order reigned there. A sort of material well-being was seen on all sides. Revolutions there were very rare, and war was so to speak unknown.º

So you must not feel reassured by thinking that the barbarians are still far from us; for if there are some peoples who allow light to be wrested from their hands, there are others who trample it underfoot themselves.P

o. With a note, in the manuscript: "<Louis says that he is afraid that this last piece, although good, appears a bit exaggerated given the current state of our notions on China. It now seems certain, he says, that if the Chinese have declined, they have at least never been as advanced as I suppose and as was supposed in Europe sixty years ago.>"

p. In the *rubish:*

Louis said to me today (1 June 1838) that what had struck him as more obvious and more clear in the question of the sciences was that the applied sciences or the theoretical part of the sciences most necessary to application had, in all times, been cultivated among men as the taste for material enjoyments, for individual improvements increased, while the cultivation of the advanced sciences had always been joined with a certain taste for intellectual pleasures which found pleasure in encountering great truths, even if they were useless.

This seemed to him applicable to aristocratic peoples like the English or the men of the Middle Ages, in the period of the Renaissance, although some were occupied in this period with the things of heaven; it is clear however that there was a reaction toward the things of the earth. But he admitted that democracy drove this taste and that it could thus be considered as the mediate cause of this scientific impulse whose immediate cause would be the taste for material enjoyments./

It seems clear to me that I do not make the *taste for material well-being* suggested by this social and political state play a large enough role among the causes that lead democracies toward the applied sciences. It is however the greatest, the most incontestable, the truest reason. I have not precisely omitted it, but under-played it. This gap must be repaired. See note (a, b, c).

To cite England. The taste for well-being taking hold of the democratic classes would give these classes, thanks to liberty and commercial possibilities, a great preponderance, allowing them in a way to give their spirit to the nation, while letting the aristocratic classes subsist in its midst. What follows for [the (ed.)] sciences.

Still more intense taste; class that feels it still more preponderant in America. Practical impulse of the sciences still more exclusive.

[In the margin: Another point of view that is not sufficiently appreciated.

Peoples who have strongly devoted themselves to the application of something, very practically occupied with something, find neither the *time* nor the *taste* to be occupied with theory. I said something similar while talking about the sciences among free peoples. But I was talking only about taste.

It is clear that an aristocracy, like a democracy, can be constantly occupied in a practical way with something and neglect all the rest. It is the case of the Romans who were so devoted to the conquest of the world that they were not able to think about the sciences. They have left nothing on that. While the Greeks more *divided* made great scientific progress./

How many things are explained by the taste for material well-being!!] (*Rubish*, 1).

CHAPTER 11[a]

In What Spirit the Americans Cultivate the Arts[b]

I believe it would be wasting my time and that of my readers, if I applied myself to showing how the general mediocrity of fortune, the lack of superfluity, the universal desire for well-being and the constant efforts made by each person to gain well-being for himself, make the taste for the useful

a. 1. Democratic institutions and the democratic social state make the human mind tend toward the useful rather than toward the beautiful as regards art. I set forth this idea without proving it. The rest of the chapter comments on it or adds to it.

2. 1. In aristocracies, artisans, apart from the desire to earn money, have their individual reputation and the reputation of their corps to maintain. The aim of the arts is to make a small number of masterpieces, rather than a large number of imperfect works. It is no longer so when each profession no longer forms one corps and constantly changes members.

2. In aristocracies, consumers are few, very rich and very demanding. In democracies, they are very many, in straitened circumstances and nearly always with more needs than means. Thus the nature of the producer and of the consumer combine to increase the production of the arts and to decrease their merit.

3. An analogous tendency of the arts in democratic times is to simulate in their products a richness that is not there.

4. In the fine arts in particular, the democratic social state and democratic institutions make the aim the elegant and the pretty rather than the great; the representation of the body rather than that of the soul; they turn away from the ideal and concentrate on the real (YTC, CVf, pp. 12–13).

b. "Among the fine arts I clearly see something to say only about architecture, sculpture, painting. As for music, dance . . . , I see nothing" (in the *rubish* of chapter 5. *Rubish,* 1).

Tocqueville seems not to have appreciated the musical evenings that he attended in the United States. In his correspondence, he speaks of "caterwauling music" and "unbearable squealings." Beaumont thought it good to delete these commentaries from his edition of Tocqueville's complete works.

predominate over the love of the beautiful in the heart of man. Democratic nations, where all these things are found, will therefore cultivate the arts that serve to make life comfortable in preference to those whose object is to embellish it; they will by habit prefer the useful to the beautiful, and they will want the beautiful to be useful.[c]

But I intend to go further, and, after pointing out the first feature, to outline several others.

It happens ordinarily, in centuries of privilege, that the exercise of nearly all the arts becomes a privilege and that each profession is a world apart where no one is at liberty to enter. And, even when industry is free, the immobility natural to aristocratic nations makes all those who are occupied by the same art end up nevertheless forming a distinct class, always composed of the same families, all of whose members know each other and a class in which public opinion and corporate pride soon arise. In an industrial class of this type, each artisan has not only his fortune to make, but also his reputation to keep. It is not only his interest that regulates his behavior, or even that of the buyer, but that of the corps, and the interest of the corps is that each artisan produces masterpieces. So in aristocratic centuries, the aim of the arts is to make the best possible, and not the most rapid or the cheapest.[d]

c. What makes the taste for the *useful* predominate among democratic peoples./

[In the margin: Perhaps to philosophy. What makes the doctrine of the useful predominate.

Utilitarians.]

This idea is necessary, but perhaps it has already been treated either under this title or under another. *It must be treated separately.* It is too important to be found only accidentally in my book. The preeminence granted in all things to the useful is in fact one of the principal and fertile characteristics of democratic centuries.

There are many things that make the taste for the useful predominate in these centuries: the middling level of fortunes, the lack of superfluity, the lack of imagination or rather the perpetual straining for the production of well-being. There is imagination in the ordinary sense of the word only in the upper and lower classes; the middle ones do not have it.

There are still many other causes. Look for them.

12 April 1838 (YTC, CVk, 1, p. 10).

d. You find in aristocratic societies as well as in democracies men who cultivate the useful arts, and who even excel if not in all at least in several of them. It suffices to

When on the contrary each profession is open to all, when the crowd enters and leaves each constantly, and when its different members, because of their great number, become unknown, indifferent and nearly invisible to each other, the social bond is destroyed, and each worker, led back to himself, seeks only to earn the greatest amount of money possible at the least cost. There is nothing more than the will of the consumer to limit him. Now it happens that, at the same time, a corresponding revolution makes itself felt among the last.

In countries where wealth, like power, is concentrated in a few hands and remains there, the use of most of the wealth of this world belongs to always the same small number of individuals; necessity, opinion, the moderation of desires exclude all others.

Since this aristocratic class keeps itself immobile at the point of grandeur where it is placed, without narrowing or expanding, it always experiences the same needs and feels them in the same way. The men who compose it draw naturally from the superior and hereditary position that they occupy the taste for what is very well made and very lasting.

That gives a general turn to the ideas of the nation as regards the arts.

It often happens, among these peoples, that the peasant himself prefers to do entirely without the objects that he covets than to acquire them imperfect.

So in aristocracies, workers labor only for a limited number of buyers, who are very difficult to satisfy. The gain that they expect depends principally on the perfection of their works.

This is no longer so when, all privileges being destroyed, ranks mingle and all men constantly go down and rise up the social scale.

You always find, within a democratic people [≠and particularly in the period when they finally come to be so≠], a host of citizens whose patrimony divides and decreases. They have contracted, in better times, certain

---

see a few of the engraved breast-plates that the warriors of the Middle Ages left for us, and the gothic churches that still seem to thrust into the sky from the heart of our cities, in order to understand that the armorers and the masons of those times were often skilled men.

But they did not bring to their works the same spirit as the artisans of today (*Rubish*, 1).

needs that they continue to have after the ability to satisfy them no longer exists, and they try restlessly to find if there is not some indirect means to provide for them.

On the other hand, you always see in democracies a very large number of men whose fortune grows, but whose desires grow very much faster than their fortune and who greedily eye the goods that their fortune promises them, before it delivers them. These men try to open in all directions shorter paths to these nearby enjoyments. The result of the combination of these two causes is that in democracies you always meet a multitude of citizens whose needs are beyond their resources and who would readily agree to being satisfied incompletely rather than renouncing entirely the object of their covetous desire.

The worker easily understands these passions because he shares them himself. In aristocracies, he tried to sell his products very expensively to a few; now he understands that there would be a more expedient means to become rich, it would be to sell his products inexpensively to all [<for he begins to discover that a small profit that is repeated every day would be preferable to a considerable gain that you can expect only rarely.>

That sets his mind on a new path. He no longer tries to make the best possible but at the lowest price.].

Now, there are only two ways to arrive at lowering the price of merchandise.

The first is to find better, shorter and more skillful means of producing it.[e] The second is to fabricate in greater quantity objects more or less similar, but of less value. Among democratic peoples, all the intellectual abilities of the worker are directed toward these two ends.

He tries hard to invent procedures that allow him to work, not only better, but faster and at less cost, and if he cannot manage to do so, to reduce the intrinsic qualities of the thing that he is making without making it entirely inappropriate to its intended use. When only the rich had watches,

---

e. "Democracy leads toward the useful arts not so much because it decreases the number of those who could have demands to make on the fine arts as because it takes away from the latter even the taste to seek the beautiful in the arts" (in RUBISH OF THE CHAPTERS ON THE ARTS, *Rubish,* 1).

nearly all were excellent. Now hardly any are made that are not mediocre, but everyone has them. Thus, democracy not only tends to direct the human mind toward the useful arts, it leads artisans to make many imperfect things very rapidly, and leads the consumer to content himself with these things.

It isn't that in democracies art is not capable, as needed, of producing marvels. That is revealed sometimes, when buyers arise who agree to pay for time and effort. In this struggle of all the industries, amid this immense competition and these innumerable trials, excellent workers are formed who get to the furthest limits of their profession. But the latter rarely have the opportunity to show what they know how to do; they carefully moderate their efforts. They stay within a skillful mediocrity that is self-assessing and that, able to go beyond the goal that it sets for itself, aims only for the goal that it attains. In aristocracies, in contrast, workers always do all that they know how to do, and, when they stop, it is because they are at the limit of their knowledge.

When I arrive in a country and I see the arts provide some admirable products, that teaches me nothing about the social state and political constitution of the country.[f] But if I notice that the products of the arts there

---

f. That the perfection of certain products of the arts is not a proof of civilization./

The Mexicans that Cortés conquered so easily had reached a high degree of perfection in the manufacture of cotton. Their fabrics and the colors with which they covered them were admirable, p. 64.

In India cotton fabrics and particularly muslins have always been made and are still made whose softness, brilliance, and toughness, Europeans, with all the perfection of their arts, are still not able to imitate, p. 61.

India, however, is still in a state of semi-barbarism.

The fact is that the perfection of an isolated art proves nothing, only that the people who cultivate it have emerged from the state of a hunting or pastoral people. In this state nothing can be perfected.

Another curious fact that Baines' book provides me with is that the beautiful muslins of Dana were in all their splendor only while India had kings and an aristocracy. They have been in decline since, because of a lack of orders, p. 61 (*Rubish,* 1).

Edward Baines, *History of the Cotton Manufacture in Great Britain* (London: H. Fisher, R. Fisher and P. Jackson, 1835). Reprinted in New York by Augustus M. Kelly, 1966 (Reprints of Economics Classics).

are generally imperfect, in very great number and at a low price, I am
sure that, among the people where this is occurring, privileges are becoming weak, and the classes are beginning to mingle and are soon going to
blend.g

Artisans who live in democratic centuries not only seek to put their useful
products in the reach of all citizens, they also try hard to give all their products shining qualities that the latter do not have.

In the confusion of all classes, each man hopes to be able to appear to
be what he isn't and devotes great efforts to succeeding in doing so. Democracy does not give birth to this sentiment, which is only too natural to
the heart of man; but it applies it to material things. The hypocrisy of virtue
exists in all times; that of luxury belongs more particularly to democratic
centuries.

In order to satisfy these new needs of human vanity, there is no impos-
ture to which the arts do not resort; industry sometimes goes so far in this
direction that it ends by harming itself. The diamond has already been so
perfectly imitated that it is easy to make a mistake. Once the art of producing false diamonds has been invented so that you can no longer distinguish false from true ones, both will probably be abandoned, and they will
again become stones.

This leads me to talk about those arts that are called, par excellence, the
fine arts.

I do not believe that the necessary effect of the democratic social state
and democratic institutions is to decrease the number of men who cultivate
the fine arts. [<I even think that their number increases with democracy>];
but these causes powerfully influence the manner in which they are cultivated. Since most of those who had already contracted the taste for the fine
arts have become poor, and, on the other hand, many of those who are
not yet rich have begun, by imitation, to conceive the taste for the fine
arts, the quantity of consumers in general increases, and very rich and

g. "So democracy draws a multitude of mediocre products from the arts, but these
products are sufficient for the well-being of a multitude of our fellows, while more perfect works would serve only a small number" (in RUBISH OF THE CHAPTERS ON THE
ARTS, *Rubish*, 1).

very refined consumers become more rare. Something analogous to what I already demonstrated when I talked about the useful arts then occurs in the fine arts. They multiply their works and reduce the merit of each one of them.

No longer able to aim at the great, you seek the elegant and the pretty; you tend less to reality than to appearance.

In aristocracies you do a few great paintings, and, in democratic countries, a multitude of small pictures. In the first, you raise bronze statues, and, in the second, you cast plaster statues.

When I arrived for the first time in New York by the part of the Atlantic Ocean called the East River, I was surprised to notice, along the river bank, at some distance from the city, a certain number of small palaces of white marble,[h] several of which were of a classical architecture; the next day, able to consider more closely the one that had particularly attracted my attention, I found that its walls were of white-washed brick and its columns of painted wood. It was the same for all the buildings that I had admired the day before.

The democratic social state and democratic institutions give as well, to all the imitative arts, certain particular tendencies that are easy to point out. [<I know that here I am going back to ideas that I have already had the occasion to explain in relation to poetry, but the fault is due less to me than to the subject that I am treating. I am talking about man and man is a simple being, whatever effort is made to split him up in order to know him better. It is always the same individual that you envisage in various lights. All that I can do is only to point out the result here, leaving to the memory of the reader the trouble of going back to the causes.>][j] They often divert them from portraying the soul in order to attach them only to portraying the

h. ". . . an incredible multitude of country houses, as large as little boxes but as carefully worked . . . I was so struck by how comfortable these small houses had to be and by the good effect that they produced on the landscape, that I will try to obtain the design or the plan of one or two of the prettiest ones. Perhaps Émilie would make use of it for Nacqueville. I already know that they are not expensive." (Extract of the letter from Tocqueville to his mother, of 26 April–19 May 1831, YTC, BIa2.) Pocket notebook 1 in fact contains the plan of one of these houses (YTC, BIIa, pp. 2–3).

j. In the margin: "To delete if I put this piece before poetry."

body; and they substitute the representation of movements and sensations for that of sentiments and ideas; in the place of the ideal, finally, they put the real.

I doubt that Raphael made as profound a study of the slightest mechanisms of the human body as the artists of today. He did not attribute the same importance as they to rigorous exactitude on this point, for he claimed to surpass nature. He wanted to make man something that was superior to man; he undertook to embellish beauty itself.

David and his students were, on the contrary, as good anatomists as painters. They represented marvelously well the models that they had before their eyes, but rarely did they imagine anything beyond; they followed nature exactly, while Raphael sought something better than nature. They left us an exact portrait of man, but the first gave us a glimpse of divinity in his works.

You can apply to the very choice of subject what I said about the manner of treating it.

The painters of the Renaissance usually looked above themselves, or far from their time, for great subjects that left a vast scope to their imagination. Our painters often lend their talent to reproducing exactly the details of the private life that they have constantly before their eyes, and on all sides they copy small objects that have only too many originals in nature.[k]

k. They hasten [to (ed.)] depict battles before the dead are buried and they enjoy exposing to our view scenes that we witness every day.

I do not know when people will tire of comparing the democracy of our time with what bore the same name in antiquity. The differences between these two things reveal themselves at every turn. For me, I do not need to think about slavery or other reasons that lead me to regard the Greeks as very aristocratic nations despite some democratic institutions that are found in their midst. I agree not to open Aristotle to finish persuading me. It is enough for me to contemplate the statues that these peoples have left. I cannot believe that the man who made the Belvedere Apollo emerge from marble worked in a democracy.

[In the margin. Next to the last paragraph.] To delete. That I think raises useless objections (in the *rubish* of the chapter that follows, *Rubish*, 1).

For his part, Beaumont had written: "There exists, in the United States, a type of painting that prospers: these are portraits; it is not the love of art, it is self-love" (*Marie*, I, p. 254).

CHAPTER 12[a]

Why the Americans Erect Such Small and Such Large Monuments at the Same Time

I have just said that, in democratic centuries, the monuments of art tended to become more numerous and smaller. I hasten to point out the exception to this rule.

Among democratic peoples, individuals are very weak; but the State, which represents them all and holds them all in its hand, is very strong.[b] Nowhere do citizens appear smaller than in a democratic nation. Nowhere does the nation itself seem greater and nowhere does the mind more easily form a vast picture of it. In democratic societies, the imagination of men narrows when they consider themselves; it expands indefinitely when they think about the State. The result is that the same men who live meanly in cramped dwellings often aim at the gigantic as soon as it is a matter of public monuments.[c]

---

a. 1. In democratic societies, individuals are very weak, but the State is very great. The imagination narrows when you think about yourself; it expands immeasurably when you turn your attention to the State.

In those societies, you see a small number of very small monuments and a multitude of very large ones.

Example of the Americans proves it.

2. Nor do large monuments prove anything about the prosperity, the enlightenment and the real greatness of the nation.

Example of the Mexicans and the Romans shows it (YTC, CVf, pp. 13–14).

b. In a note: "It is their very weakness that makes its strength . . .

"A piece from *ambition* could go well there."

c. "In democracies the State must take charge of large and costly works not only because these large works are beautiful, but also in order to sustain the taste for what is great and for perfection" (in RUBISH OF THE CHAPTERS ON THE ARTS, *Rubish*, 1).

The Americans have laid out on the site that they wanted to make into the capital the limits of an immense city that, still today, is hardly more populated than Pontoise, but that, according to them, should one day contain a million inhabitants; already they have uprooted trees for ten leagues around, for fear that they might happen to inconvenience the future citizens of this imaginary metropolis. They have erected, in the center of the city, a magnificent palace to serve as the seat of Congress, and they have given it the pompous name of the Capitol.

Every day, the particular states themselves conceive and execute prodigious undertakings that would astonish the genius of the great nations of Europe.

Thus, democracy does not lead men only to make a multitude of petty works; it also leads them to erect a small number of very large monuments. But between these two extremes there is nothing. So a few scattered remnants of very vast structures tell nothing about the social state and institutions of the people who erected them.

I add, although it goes beyond my subject, that they do not reveal their greatness, their enlightenment and their real prosperity any better.

Whenever a power of whatever kind is capable of making an entire people work toward a sole undertaking, it will succeed with little knowledge and a great deal of time in drawing something immense from the combi-

---

In Beaumont's papers you find this note drafted during the journey that they made together to England in 1835:

Aristocracy. Democracy.
   Public institutions./
   One thing strikes me when I examine the public institutions in England: it is the extreme luxury of their construction and maintenance. In the United States I saw the government of democracy do most of its institutions with an extreme economy. Example: prisons, hospitals. It seems to me that these institutions cannot be done more cheaply. In England it is entirely the opposite: the government or the administration appears to try to construct everything at the greatest possible expense. What magnificence in the construction of Milbank! What luxury in the slightest details!! 20 million francs spent to hold 2,000 prisoners! And Beldlan [Bedlam (ed.)]! for 250 of the insane, 2 million 500 thousand francs (cost of construction), 200,000 pounds sterling. Isn't it the spirit of aristocracies to do everything with grandeur, with luxury, with splendor, and with great expenditures! And Greenwich! And Chelsea!
   (14 May [1835], London) (YTC, Beaumont, CX).

nation of such great efforts; you do not have to conclude from that that the people is very happy, very enlightened or even very strong.[d] The Spanish found the city of Mexico full of magnificent temples and vast palaces; this did not prevent Cortez from conquering the Mexican Empire with six hundred foot soldiers and sixteen horses.

If the Romans had known the laws of hydraulics better, they would not have erected all these aqueducts that surround the ruins of their cities; they would have made better use of their power and their wealth. If they had discovered the steam engine, perhaps they would not have extended to the extreme limits of their empire those long artificial stone lines that are called roman roads.

These things are magnificent witnesses to their ignorance at the same time as to their grandeur.

d. Many men judge the state of the civilization of a people by its monuments, that is a very uncertain measure.

I will admit that it proves that these peoples were more aristocratic, but not that they were more civilized and greater.

Ruins of Palenque in Mexico. Mexicans who still knew only hieroglyphic writing and vanquished so easily by the Spanish (*Rubish* of the previous chapter, *Rubish,* 1).

In 1845, concerning French monuments, Tocqueville made the following reflection to his friend Milnes:

France has the appearance of noticing since only ten years ago, that it is still covered with masterpieces of the Middle Ages. The idea of repairing them, of completing them, of preserving them above all from complete ruin preoccupies a great number of cities, several of which have already made great sacrifices. Do not conclude from it that society is returning to old ideas and institutions. It is the sign of precisely the opposite. Nothing indicates better that the Revolution is finished and that the old society is dead. As long as the war between the old France and the new France presented for the first the least chance of success, the nation treated the monuments of the Middle Ages like adversaries; it destroyed them or left them to perish; it saw in them only the physical representation of the doctrines, beliefs, mores and laws that were hostile to it. In the middle of this preoccupation, it did not even notice their beauty. It is because it no longer fears anything from what they represent that it is attached to them as if to great works of art and to curious remnants of a time that no longer exists. The archeologist has replaced the party man (Paris, letter of 14 April 1845. With the kind permission of Trinity College, Cambridge. Houghton papers, 25/201).

People who would leave no other traces of their passage than a few lead pipes in the earth and a few iron rods on its surface could have been more masters of nature than the Romans.[e]

e. The *rubish* continues:

Large monuments belong to the middle state of civilization rather than to a very advanced civilization. Man ordinarily erects them when his thoughts are already great and his knowledge is still limited and when he does not yet know how to satisfy it except at great expense.

On the other hand, the ruins of a few large monuments cannot teach us if the social state of the people who erected them was aristocratic or democratic since we have just seen that democracy happens to build similar ones.

In the rough drafts of the previous chapter: "They [large monuments (ed.)] are the product of centralization. Here introduce the thought that centralization is not at all the sign of high civilization. It is found neither at the beginning nor at the end of civilization, but in general at the middle" (RUBISH OF CHAPTERS ON THE ARTS, *Rubish,* 1).

And in another place in the same jacket: "Large monuments prove nothing but the destruction of large monuments proves. Warwick castle, *aristocratic.* Cherbourg sea wall, *democratic"* (*rubish* of the previous chapter. *Rubish,* 1). It was during his stay in England in 1833 that Tocqueville visited the ruins of Warwick castle, setting for *Kenilworth* of Walter Scott. To his future wife, Mary Mottley, he sent a short account of his visit entitled *Visit to Kenilworth* (YTC, CXIb, 12, reproduced in *OCB,* VII, pp. 116–19).

CHAPTER 13[a]

Literary Physiognomy of Democratic Centuries

When you enter the shop of a bookstore in the United States, and when you go over the American books that fill their shelves, the number of works appears very large, while that of known authors seems in contrast very small.[b]

a. 1. The Americans do not have literature so to speak. All their literary works come to them from England, or are written according to English taste.

2. This is due to particular and temporary causes and must not prevent us from searching for what the literature natural to democracy is.

3. All ranks are marked and men immobile in their places, literary life like political existence is concentrated in an upper class. From that fixed rules, traditional literary habits, art, delicacy, finished details, taste for style, for form . . .

4. When ranks are mixed, men of talent and writers have diverse origins, a different education, they constantly change, only a little time can be given to the pleasures of the mind. . . . From that, absence of rules, scorn for style, rapidity, fertility, liberty.

5. There is a moment when the literary genius of democracy and that of aristocracy join, short and brilliant period, French literature of the XVIIIth century (YTC, CVf, pp. 14–15).

b. In the *Rubish,* under the title INFLUENCE OF DEMOCRACY ON LITERATURE, the chapter begins in this way: "≠I am speaking about America and America does not yet so to speak have literature, but the subject attracts me and holds me. I cannot pass by without stopping≠. When you enter . . ." (*Rubish,* 1).

Another title of the chapter, still in the *Rubish,* was this one: GENERAL IDEAS ON THE EFFECT PRODUCED BY EQUALITY ON LITERATURE. The initial plan of Tocqueville probably included this sole chapter that, becoming too long, was subsequently divided. The rough drafts of this chapter and of those that follow, up to chapter 18, are found in several jackets; the contents do not always coincide with the title.

The reflections of Tocqueville on literature have given rise to various commentaries: Katherine Harrison, "A French Forecast of American Literature," *South Atlantic Quar-*

First you find a multitude of elementary treatises intended to give the first notion of human knowledge. Most of these works were written in Europe. The Americans reprint them while adapting them to their use. Next comes a nearly innumerable quantity of books on religion, Bibles, sermons, pious stories, controversies, accounts of charitable institutions. Finally appears the long catalogue of political pamphlets: in America, parties, to combat each other, do not write books, but brochures that circulate with an unbelievable rapidity, live for a day and die.[c]

---

terly 25, no. 4 (1926): 350–56; Donald D. Kummings, "The Poetry of Democracies: Tocqueville's Aristocratic Views," *Comparative Literature Studies* 11, no. 4 (1974): 306–19; Reino Virtanen, "Tocqueville on a Democratic Literature," *French Review* 23, no. 3 (1950): 214–22; Paul West, "Literature and Politics. Tocqueville on the Literature of Democracies," *Essays in Criticism* 12, no. 3 (1972): 5–20; Françoise Mélonio and José-Luis Díaz, editors, *Tocqueville et la littérature* (Paris: Presses de l'Université Paris-Sorbonne, 2005).

c. "For these statistical details look in Beaumont" (*Rubish,* 1).

Cf. *Marie,* I, pp. 238–58. Beaumont always showed a more intense interest than Tocqueville in literature. At the time of their voyage in England in 1835, it is Beaumont who questioned J. S. Mill on the relationship between literature and democracy.

Literature./
Democracy./
Conversation with John Mill, 18 June 1835. London./
Question. Up to now I consider democracy as favorable to the material well-being of the greatest number, and from this perspective I am a partisan of it. But a shadow exists in my mind; a doubt troubles me. I do not know if the tendency of democracy is not anti-intellectual; it gives to the greatest number physical well-being; up to a certain point it is even a source of morality for all those whose condition it renders middling, either by destroying great wealth, which corrupts, or by bringing an end to great poverty, which degrades and debases; it also spreads more general, more uniform instruction. There are its benefits; but to what point is it not contrary to the taste for literature, to the development of the advanced sciences, to speculative studies, to intellectual meditations? In order to devote oneself to the love of literature and the pleasures of the mind, leisure is necessary, and who possesses leisure if not the rich? The man who works to live, does he find the leisure to think? Does he have the time, the taste and the ability for it? Isn't it to be feared that at the same time that common instruction spreads among the greatest number, advanced instruction will be abandoned, that the taste for literature will be lost, and that only useful books will be read? that no one will be interested in theories and speculation? that you will think only of application, and no longer of invention?

Amid all of these obscure productions of the human mind appear the more remarkable works of only a small number of authors who are known by Europeans or who should be.[d]

Answer. I believe that the tendency of democracy is diametrically opposed to the fear that you express. Here we see, as an argument in favor of democracy, the impulse that it gives to the taste for letters and intellectual things. It is true that as democracy spreads, the number of those who work in order to exist increases; at the same time the number of persons with leisure decreases. But it is precisely on this fact that we base our belief. We consider it as a fact established by experience that the men who work the most are those who read and think more; while idle men neither read nor think. The man who does nothing and whose whole life is leisure rarely finds the time to do anything. For him, reading is a trial, and three quarters and a half of the rich do not read a volume a year; they are moreover constantly busy with little nothings, with small interests of luxury, dress, horses, wealth, frivolous cares that are distractions rather than occupations. For them it is such a great difficulty to expand their mind for a single instant that writing the least letter seems a trial, reading the least work is an onerous burden (YTC, Beaumont, CX).

d. "<≠These are the works of Mr. Irving, the novels of Mr. Cooper, the eloquent treatises of Doctor Channing≠>" (*Rubish,* 1).
Unpublished travel note from small notebook A:

Books interesting and good to buy:
1. *Stories of American Life,* by American Writers, edited by Mary Russell Mitford (Colburn and Bentley: London, 1831), 3 vols. A worthwhile review is given in *Westminster Review,* April 1831, page 395. They include portrayals of three types: 1. Historical life or life sixty years ago. 2. Border life that is the life of the outer settlements. 3. City life which embraces pictures of masses as they exist at this moment in New York, Philadelphia and the great towns (small notebook A, YTC, BIIa).

Tocqueville does not appear to have read this book.
Tocqueville and Beaumont would have been able to have a conversation with the writer Catherine Maria Sedgwick, of whom they had heard a great deal spoken. But, impatient to reach Boston, they just missed her at Stockbridge (George W. Pierson, *Tocqueville and Beaumont in America,* pp. 349–50). Tocqueville seems to have read the letters of Cooper. In travel notebook E, you read: "Find Cooper's letters" (YTC, BIIa, different reading in *Voyage, OC,* V, 1, p. 65). It probably concerns James Fenimore Cooper, *Notions of the Americans; Picked Up By a Travelling Bachelor* (London: Henry Colburn, 1828), 2 vols.
In an unpublished note (alphabetic notebook A, YTC, BIIa) you find the following list: "Living American writers: Verplank—Paulding—Hall—Stone—Neal—Barker—Willis—Miss Sedgwick." It concerns the authors who are included in the book edited by Mary Russell Mitford, and who are cited in the preface of the work.

Although today America is perhaps the civilized country in which there is least involvement with literature,[e] a large number of individuals is found there who are interested in things of the mind and who make them, if not their whole life's work, at least the attraction of their leisure. But it is England that provides to the latter most of the books that they demand.[f] Nearly all of the great English works are reproduced in the United States. The literary genius of Great Britain still shines its light into the depths of the forests of the New World. There is scarcely a pioneer's cabin where you do not find a few odd volumes of Shakespeare. I recall having read for the first time the feudal drama of Henry V in a log house.[g]

In *Marie* (I, pp. 392–93) Beaumont cites the following American authors: Miss Sedgwick, James Fenimore Cooper, Washington Irving, Jared Sparks, Robert Walsh, Edward Livingston, Daniel Webster, Henry Clay, Edward Everett, and William Ellery Channing. Reino Virtanen has suggested that Channing's *Remarks on National Literature* perhaps influenced the writing of these chapters on literature. See concerning Channing, Reino Virtanen, "Tocqueville and William Ellery Channing," *American Literature*, 22, 1951, pp. 21–28; and "Tocqueville and the Romantics," *Symposium* 13, no. 2 (1959): 167–85. William Ellery Channing, *The Importance and Means of a National Literature* (Edinburgh: Thomas Clark, 1835), 31 pages, claims that the United States does not yet have literature and proposes means to create one.

Tocqueville could as well have been influenced by an article by Philarète Chasles, published under the title "De la littérature dans l'Amérique du Nord," which appeared in the *Revue des deux mondes*, volume III, 1835, pp. 169–202.

e. "The Americans are in the most unfavorable position for having a literature. A new people that each day finds at its disposal the literary works of an ancient people./

Democracy produces a host of bad works; but it does not prevent good ones" (*Rubish*, 1).

f. "Look in all the dictionaries for democracy, you will not find there the word *erudition*"(*Rubish*, 1).

g. I remember that one day, the pioneer was absent, and while awaiting his return, I took one of these volumes, isolated product of a genius of another hemisphere. Having opened it by chance, I fell upon the first part of the drama of Henry V [v: VI]. Time and the overly active curiosity of my hosts had almost destroyed the rest. During this reading I soon lost sight of the sentiment [of (ed.)] all that surrounded me and all the great characters evoked by the poet arose little by little around me. I thought I saw them with their language, their beliefs, their passions, their prejudices, their virtues and their vices.

All the memories of the heroic times of our history assailed me at the same time;

Not only do the Americans go each day to draw upon the treasures of English literature, but also you can truthfully say that they find the literature of England on their own soil.[h] Among the small number of men who are busy in the United States composing works of literature, most are English in content and above all in form. In this way they carry to the middle of democracy the ideas and the literary practices that are current within the aristocratic nation that they have taken as a model. They paint with colors borrowed from foreign mores; almost never representing in its reality the country where they were born, they are rarely popular there.

———————

my imagination filled suddenly with the pomp of feudal society; I saw high turrets, a thousand banners waving in the air; I heard the sound of armor, the burst of clarions, the heavy step of caparisoned war horses. I contemplated for a moment all this mixture of misery and wealth, of strength and weakness, of inequality and grandeur that marked the Middle Ages, and then I opened my eyes and saw myself in my small log cabin built yesterday in the middle of a flowering wilderness that recalled the first days of the world and was inhabited by the descendants of these same Europeans who had become the obscure and peaceful citizens of a democratic republic. I felt gripped, passing my view alternately over these two extreme points of human destiny that I had before me. I was astonished by the immense space that stretched between [them (ed.)] and that humanity had had to cover.

Do you desire to see in all their clarity the extreme mobility and the strange detours of human destiny? Do you want, in a way, to see the raging and irresistible torrent of time flow before your eyes? Go sit down next to the hearth of the American pioneer and there read Shakespeare in the shadow of the virgin forest.

[In the margin] Read the books of Mr. Irving [that (ed.)] have all the merits and all the defects of a translation" (*Rubish,* 1).

h. In a first version:

<≠Mr. Fenimore Cooper borrowed his principal scenes from wild nature and not from democratic forms. He portrayed America as it no longer is, with colors foreign to the America of today. Mr. W. Irving is English in content as well as in form; he excels at representing with finesse and grace scenes borrowed from the aristocratic life of England. He is happy amid old feudal ruins and never borrows> anything from the country where he was born. The writers I am speaking about, despite their talent and the quarrelsome patriotism that they often try to use to *enhance* their efforts in the eyes of their fellow citizens, do not excite more real sympathies in the United States than if they were born in England. Thus, they live as little as they can in the country that they praise to us, and in order to enjoy their glory they come to Europe≠ (*Rubish,* 1).

[Read the books of Mr. W. Irving; there you will only find soft and pale reflections of a fire that is no longer seen and no longer felt {there you will find the qualities and the defects of a translation}].

The citizens of the United States themselves seem so convinced that books are not published for them, that before settling on the merit of one of their writers, they ordinarily wait for him to have been appreciated in England. This is how, in the case of paintings, you willingly leave to the author of the original the right to judge the copy.ʲ

So the inhabitants of the United States do not yet have, strictly speaking, literature. The only authors that I recognize as Americans are journalists. The latter are not great writers, but they speak the language of the country and make themselves heard. I see only foreigners in the others. They are for the Americans what the imitators of the Greeks and the Romans were for us in the period of the renaissance of letters, an object of curiosity, not generally speaking of sympathy. They amuse the mind [<of a few>] and do not act on the mores [<of all>].

I have already said that this state of things was very far from being due only to democracy, and that it was necessary to look for the causes in several particular circumstances independent of democracy.

If the Americans, while still keeping their social state and their laws, had another origin and found themselves transported to another country, I do not doubt that they would have a literature. As they are, I am sure that in the end they will have one; but it will have a character different from the one that shows itself in the American writings of today, one that will be its own. It is not impossible to sketch this character in advance.

I suppose an aristocratic people among whom letters are cultivated [some of this type are found in the world]; the works of the mind, as well as the affairs of government, are regulated there by a sovereign class. Literary life,

j. First version: "America is moreover, taken in mass and despite its efforts to appear independent, still in relation to Europe in the position of a secondary city relative to the capital, and you notice, in its smallest ways of acting, this mixture of pride and servility that is nearly always found in the conduct of the provinces vis-à-vis their capital" (*Rubish*, 1).

like political existence, is concentrated nearly entirely in this class or in those closest to it. This is enough for me to have the key to all the rest.

When a small number of always the same men are involved at the same time in the same matters, they easily agree and decide in common on certain principal rules that must guide each one of them. If the matter that attracts their attention is literature, the works of the mind will soon be subjected by them to a few precise laws that you will no longer be allowed to avoid.

If these men occupy a hereditary position in the country, they will naturally be inclined not only to adopt a certain number of fixed rules for themselves, but also to follow those that their ancestors imposed on themselves; their set of laws will be rigorous and traditional at the same time.

Since they are not necessarily preoccupied with material things, since they have never been so, and since their fathers were not either, they were able over several generations to take an interest in works of the mind. They understood literary art and in the end they love it for itself and take a learned pleasure in seeing that you conform to it.

That is still not all; the men I am speaking about began their life and finish it in comfort or in wealth; so they have naturally conceived the taste for studied enjoyments and the love of refined and delicate pleasures.

In addition, a certain softness of mind and heart that they often contract amid this long and peaceful use of so many worldly goods, leads them to avoid in their very pleasures whatever could be found too unexpected and too intense. They prefer to be amused than to be intensely moved; they want to be interested, but not carried away.[k]

k. Do you want to clarify my thought by examples? Compare modern literature to that of antiquity.

What fertility, what boldness, what variety in our writings! What wisdom, what art, what perfection, what finish in those of the Greeks and Romans!

What causes the difference? I think of the large number of slaves who existed among the ancients, of the small number of masters, of the concentration of power and wealth in a few hands. This begins to enlighten me, but does not yet satisfy me, for the same causes are more or less found among us. Some more powerful reason is necessary. I discover it finally in the rarity and expense of books and the extreme difficulty of reproducing and circulating them. Circumstances, coming to concen-

Now imagine a great number of literary works executed by the men I have just described or for them, and you will easily conceive of a literature where everything is regulated and coordinated in advance. The least work will be meticulous in its smallest details; art and work will be seen in everything; each genre will have particular rules that it will not be free to depart from and that will isolate it from all the others.

The style will seem almost as important as the idea, form as content; the tone will be polished, moderate, elevated. The mind will always have a noble bearing, rarely a brisk pace, and writers will be more attached to perfection than to production.

It will sometimes happen that the members of the lettered class, since they live only with each other and write only for themselves, will entirely lose sight of the rest of the world; this will throw them into the affected and the false; they will make small literary rules for their sole use, which will imperceptibly turn them away from good sense and finally take them away from nature.

By dint of wanting to speak in a way other than common they attain a sort of aristocratic jargon[m] that is hardly less removed from fine language than the dialect of the people.

Those are the natural pitfalls of literature in aristocracies.

Every aristocracy that sets itself entirely apart from the people becomes powerless. That is true in letters as well as in politics.[1]

---

trate the taste for pleasures of the mind in a very small number, formed a small literary aristocracy of the elite within a large political aristocracy" (*Rubish,* 1).

m. Note in the manuscript: "Language of Bensserade and of Voiture. Hôtel de Rambouillet. Novel of Scudéry.

"Some *affected.*

"Others *coarse.*" Tocqueville had probably read P. L. Rœderer, *Mémoire pour servir à l'histoire de la société polie en France* (Paris: Firmin Didot Frères, 1835).

1. *All of this is true above all in aristocratic countries that have been subject to the power of a king for a long time and peacefully.*

When liberty reigns in an aristocracy, the upper classes are constantly obliged to make use of the lower ones; and, by using them, they become closer to them. That often makes something of the democratic spirit penetrate within them. Moreover, among a privileged corps that governs, there develops an energy and habit of enterprise, a taste for movement and noise, that cannot fail to influence all literary works.

Now let us turn the picture around and consider the reverse side.

Let us take ourselves to a democracy whose ancient traditions and present enlightenment make it sensitive to the enjoyments of the mind. Ranks are mixed and confused; knowledge like power is infinitely divided and, if I dare say so, scattered in all directions.

Here is a confused crowd with intellectual needs to satisfy. These new amateurs of the pleasures of the mind have not all received the same education; they do not possess the same enlightenment, they do not resemble their fathers, and at every instant they differ from themselves; for they are constantly changing place, sentiments and fortune. So the mind of each one of them is not linked with that of all the others by common traditions and habits, and they have never had either the power, or the will, or the time to agree among themselves.

It is, however, from within this incoherent and agitated multitude that authors arise, and it is this multitude that distributes profits and glory to the latter.

It is not difficult for me to understand that, things being so, I must expect to find in the literature of such a people only a small number of those rigorous conventions that readers and writers recognize in aristocratic centuries. If it happened that the men of one period fell into agreement on a few, that would still prove nothing for the following period for, among democratic nations, each new generation is a new people. So among these nations, letters can be subjected to strict rules only with difficulty, and it is nearly impossible that they might ever be subjected to permanent rules.

In democracies, all the men who occupy themselves with literature are far from having received a literary education, and, of those among them able to have some smattering of literature, most follow a political career or embrace a profession from which they can turn away only for moments to sample surreptitiously the pleasures of the mind. So they do not make these pleasures the principal charm of their existence; but they consider them as a temporary and necessary relaxation amid the serious work of life. Such men can never acquire sufficiently advanced knowledge of literary art to sense its niceties; the small nuances escape them. Having only a very short time to give to letters, they want to turn it entirely to account. They love books that can be obtained without difficulty, that are quickly read, that do not require learned research to be understood. They demand easy things of beauty that reveal themselves and that can be enjoyed at once; above all they must have the unexpected and the new. Accustomed to a practical, contentious, monotonous existence, they need intense and rapid emotions, sudden insights, striking truths or errors that immediately draw them out of themselves and introduce them suddenly and as if by violence into the middle of the subject.[n]

What more do I need to say about it? And, without my explaining it, who does not understand what is about to follow?

Taken as a whole, the literature of democratic centuries cannot present, as in the time of aristocracy, the image of order, regularity, science and art; form will ordinarily be neglected and sometimes scorned. Style will often appear bizarre, incorrect, overdone and dull, and almost always bold and vehement. Authors will aim for rapidity of execution rather than for perfection of details. Short writings will be more frequent than big books, spirit more frequent than erudition, imagination more frequent than depth. A rough and almost wild strength of thought will reign, and often there will be a very great variety and singular fertility in production. They will try to astonish rather than please, and will strive more to carry passions away than to charm taste.[o]

Writers will undoubtedly be found here and there who would like to take another path, and, if they have superior merit, they will succeed in being read, despite their faults and qualities. But these exceptions will be

n. *"Metaphysics.* Perhaps mystical by spirit of reaction" (*Rubish,* 1).

o. In the manuscript:

<Per[haps (ed.)] here piece B while removing what I say about style a few lines higher?>

B. Men who live in aristocracies have for style, as in general for all forms, a superstitious respect and an exaggerated love. It happens that they value experience and turns of phrase as much as thought. Those who live in democratic countries are on the contrary led to neglect style too much. Sometimes they show an imprudent scorn for it. There are some of them who think themselves philosophers in that and who are often nothing but coarse ignoramuses.

rare, and even those who, in the whole of their work, depart in this way from common practice, will always return to it in some details.P

I have just portrayed two extreme states; but nations do not go suddenly from the first to the second; they arrive there only gradually and through infinite nuances. During the passage that leads a lettered people from one to the other, a moment almost always occurs when as the literary genius of democracies meets that of aristocracies, both seem to want to reign in agreement over the human mind.

Those are transient, but very brilliant periods:q then you have fertility without exuberance, and movement without confusion [liberty in order]. Such was French literature of the XVIIIth century.r

p. "Irving is a model of aristocratic graces.

"Irving must not be considered as an image of democratic literature, but his great success in America proves that democracies themselves are sensitive to great literary merit, whatever it may be" (*Rubish,* 1).

In another place:

> The success of Mr. W. Irving in the United States is a proof of this. I know of nothing more firm and more gracious than the spirit of this author. Nothing more polished than his works. They form a collection of small tableaux painted with an infinite [v: admirable] delicacy. Not only has this particular merit not prevented Mr. Irving from gaining a great reputation in America, but evidently he owes it to this merit alone, for it would be difficult to find any other one in him (*Rubish,* 1).

q. "The most favorable moment for the development of the sciences, of literature and of the arts is when democracy begins to burst into the midst of an aristocratic society. Then you have movement amid order. Then humanity moves very rapidly, but like an army in battle, without breaking ranks and without discipline losing anything to ardor" (*Rubish,* 1).

r. In a letter of 31 July 1834 intended for Charles Stoffels and devoted to literature, Tocqueville formulated the following remarks concerning style:

> Buffon assuredly said something false when he claimed that style was the whole man, but certainly style makes a great part of the man. Show me books that have *remained,* having as sole merit the ideas that they contained. They are few. I do not even know of an example to cite, if not perhaps a few books whose style was of an extreme simplicity; this negative defect does not repulse the reader in an absolute way like the opposite vice. You find that the principal quality of style is to *paint* objects and to make them perceptible to the imagination. I am of the same opinion, but the difficulty is not seeing the goal but attaining it. It is this very desire to put the thought *in relief* that preoccupies all those who are involved in writing today and that makes

most of them fall into such great extravagances. Without having myself a style that satisfies me in any way, I have however studied a great deal and meditated for a long time about the style of others, and I am persuaded of what I am about to say to you. There is in the great French writers, whatever the period from which you take them, a certain characteristic turn of thought, a certain way of seizing the attention of readers that belongs to each of them. I believe that you come to the world with this particular character; or at least I admit that I see no way to acquire it; for if you want to imitate the particular technique of an author, you fall into what painters call pastiches; and if you do not want to imitate anyone, you are colorless. But there is a quality common to all writers; it serves in a way as the basis of their style; it is on this foundation that they each then place their own colors. This quality is quite simply *good sense*. Study all the writers left to us by the century of Louis XIV, that of Louis XV, and the great writers from the beginning of ours, such as Madame de Staël and M. de Chateaubriand, and you will find among all good sense as the base. So what is good sense applied to style? That would take a very long time to define. It is the care to present ideas in the simplest and easiest order to grasp. It is the attention given to presenting at the same time to the reader only one simple and clear point of view whatever the diversity of the matters treated by the book, so that the thought is [not (ed.)] so to speak on two ideas. It is the care to use words in their true sense, and as much as possible in their most limited and most certain sense, in a way that the reader always positively knows what object or what image you want to present to him. I know men so clever that, if you quibble with them on the sense of a sentence, they immediately substitute another one without so to speak changing a single word, each of them being *almost* appropriate for the thing. The former men can be good diplomats, but they will never be good writers. What I also call good sense applied to style is to introduce into *the illustrations* only things comparable to the matter that you want to show. This is better understood by examples. Everyone makes illustrations while speaking, as M. Jourdain made prose; the illustration is the most powerful means to put into relief the matter that you want to make known; but still it is necessary that there is some analogy with the matter, or at least that you understand clearly what type of analogy the author wants to establish between them. When Pascal, after depicting the grandeur of the universe, ends with this famous piece: "The world is an infinite sphere whose circumference is everywhere and whose center is nowhere," the soul is gripped by this image, and however gigantic the idea that it presents, the mind conceives it at the first stroke; the object that Pascal uses for his comparison is familiar; the reader knows perfectly the ordinary dimensions of it and the form; with modifications made by the writer, it becomes however an admirable object of comparison with the universe that extends without end around you like an immense circle whose center you think you occupy wherever you go. Pascal's thought makes (illegible word) so to speak and grasps in an exact and (illegible word) fashion what the mind itself cannot conceive. I do not know why I cited this example. I could have cited thousands of others. In the most innocent, most skillful or most delicate ideas of great writers you always see a foundation of good sense and reason that forms the base. I have allowed myself to go on speaking about this part of style more than

I would go beyond my thought, if I said that the literature of a nation is always subordinated to its social state and political constitution. I know that, apart from these causes, there are several others that give certain characteristics to literary works; but the former seem to me the principal ones.

The connections that exist between the social and political state of a people and the genius of its writers are always very numerous; whoever knows the one is never completely ignorant of the other.

---

others because that is where most of the writers of our time err and that is what makes a jargon of P. L. Courrier [Courier (ed.)] be called their style. . . . If you want to write well, you must above all read, while studying *from the viewpoint of style* those who have written the best. The most useful, without comparison, seem to me to be the prose writers of the century of Louis XIV. Not that you must imitate their *turn,* which is dated, but the base of their style is admirable. There, sticking out, you find all the principal qualities that have distinguished good styles in all centuries (YTC, CIc).

The ideas explained in these chapters scarcely differ from those of Chateaubriand, Sainte-Beuve or La Harpe. Tocqueville's literary tastes always included the classics of the XVIIth and XVIIIth centuries, such as Pascal, Bossuet and Bourdaloue. In 1838, his readings included Rabelais, Plutarch, Cervantes, Machiavelli, Fontenelle, Saint-Evremond and the Koran. See Charles de Grandmaison, "Séjour d'Alexis de Tocqueville en Touraine," *Correspondant,* 114, 1879, p. 933; and the conversation with Senior on literature in *Correspondence and Conversations of Alexis de Tocqueville with Nassau William Senior* (London: H. S. King and Co., 1872), I, pp. 140–43.

CHAPTER 14[a]

Of the Literary Industry[b]

Democracy not only makes the taste for letters penetrate the industrial classes, it introduces the industrial spirit into literature.

[In aristocratic centuries you often take literature as a career, and in the others as a trade.]

In aristocracies, readers are particular and few; in democracies, it is less difficult to please them, and their number is prodigious. As a result, among aristocratic peoples, you can hope to succeed only by immense efforts, and these efforts which can bring a great deal of glory cannot ever gain much money; while among democratic nations, a writer can hope to obtain with-

a. Democracy not only makes the taste for letters penetrate the industrial classes, it introduces the industrial spirit into literature.

Since readers are very numerous and very easy to satisfy because of the absolute need that they have for something new, you can make your fortune by constantly producing a host of new but imperfect works. You thus easily enough attain a small glory and a great fortune.

Democratic literatures for a small number of great writers swarm with sellers of ideas (YTC, CVf, p. 15).

b. On the jacket of the chapter: "Small chapter that seems to me too short (given its merit) and that must, I believe, be combined or even destroyed." In the manuscript you also find a draft of the chapter, but no *rubish* exists for it. The central idea of this chapter, as Reino Virtanen ("Tocqueville and the Romantics," *Symposium* 13, no. 2, 1959, p. 180) has remarked, recalls the article of Sainte-Beuve, "De la littérature industrielle," *Revue des deux mondes*, 19, 1839, pp. 675–91. Cf. *Marie,* I, p. 248.

out much cost a mediocre fame and a great fortune.^{c} For that, he does not have to be admired; it is enough that he is enjoyed.^{d}

The always growing crowd of readers and the continual need that they have for something new assures the sales of a book that they hardly value.

In times of democracy, the public often acts toward authors like kings ordinarily do toward their courtiers; it enriches them and despises them. What more is needed for the venal souls who are born in courts, or who are worthy to live there?

Democratic literatures always swarm with these authors who see in letters only an industry,^{e} and, for the few great writers that you see there, you count sellers of ideas by the thousands.

c. In the draft: "It would be very useful to know what Corneille, Racine and Voiture gained from their works."

d. In the draft:

Not only do the Americans make few books, but also most of their books seem written solely with profit in view. You would say that in general their authors see in literature only an industry and cultivate letters in the same spirit that they clear virgin forests. That is easily understood.

[In the margin: This must probably be deleted, for the Americans cannot present the image of opposites.

If in literature they are subject to the aristocratic genius of the English, as I said previously, how can they present the vices of the literary genius of democracies?

That is not yet clear however.]/

The fault comes in the word *literature*. The Americans do not have literature, but they have books and what I am saying about their books is true.

e. In the draft: "Authors desire money more than in aristocratic centuries because money is everything./

"They earn money more easily because of the multitude of readers./

"And the less they aim for perfection, the more of it they earn."

CHAPTER 15[a]

Why the Study of Greek and Latin Literature Is Particularly Useful in Democratic Societies

What was called the people in the most democratic republics of antiquity hardly resembled what we call the people. In Athens, all citizens took part in public affairs; but there were only twenty thousand citizens out of more than three hundred fifty thousand inhabitants; all the others were slaves and fulfilled most of the functions that today belong to the people and even to the middle classes.

So Athens, with its universal suffrage, was, after all, only an aristocratic republic in which all the nobles had an equal right to government.

a. 1. That the ancient societies always formed true aristocracies, despite their democratic appearance.

2. That their literature was always in an aristocratic state, because of the rarity of books.

3. That their authors show, in fact, very much in relief the qualities natural to those who write in times of aristocracy.

4. That it is therefore very appropriate to study them in democratic times.

5. That does not mean that everyone must be thrown into the study of Greek and Latin.

What is good for literature can be inappropriate for social and political needs.

In democratic centuries it is important to the interest of individuals and to the security of the State that studies are more industrial than literary.

But in these societies there must be schools where one can be nourished by ancient literature.

A few (illegible word) universities and literary (illegible word) would do better for that than the multitude of our bad colleges (YTC, CVf, p. 16).

You must consider the struggle of the patricians and the plebeians of Rome in the same light and see in it only an internal quarrel between the junior members and the elders of the same family. All belonged in fact to the aristocracy and had its spirit.[b]

It must be noted, moreover, that in all of antiquity books were rare and expensive, and that it was highly difficult to reproduce them and to circulate them. These circumstances, coming to concentrate in a small number of men the taste and practice of letters, formed like a small literary aristocracy of the elite within a larger political aristocracy. Also nothing indicates that, among the Greeks and the Romans, letters were ever treated like an industry.

So these peoples, who formed not only aristocracies, but who were also very civilized and very free nations, had to give to their literary productions the particular vices and special qualities that characterize literature in aristocratic centuries.

It is sufficient, in fact, to cast your eyes on the writings that antiquity has left to us to discover that, if writers there sometimes lacked variety and fertility in subjects, boldness, movement and generalization in thought, they always demonstrated an admirable art and care in details; nothing in their works seems done in haste or by chance; everything is

b. [In the margin: To put in the preface when I show the difficulty of the subject.
New state.
Incomplete state.]
It is sufficient to read the *Vies des hommes illustres* of Plutarch to be convinced that antiquity was and always remained profoundly aristocratic in its laws, in its ideas, in its mores [v: opinions], that what was understood by the people of that time does not resemble the people of today, and that the rivalry of plebeians and patricians in Rome compared to what is happening today between the rich and the poor must be considered only as internal quarrels between the elders and the junior members of an aristocracy.
[To the side: that even the democracy of Athens never resembled that of America [v: never could give the idea of the democratic republic].
This idea has been introduced in the chapters on literature and is good there] (YTC, CVk, 1, pp. 37–38).

In March and April 1838, Tocqueville read Plutarch. In his letters to Beaumont, Corcelle and Royer-Collard, he admits that he finds in Plutarch a grandeur of spirit that pleases him and makes him forget the moral meanness of the time in which he lives. Various parts of the manuscript retain traces of this reading.

written for connoisseurs, and the search for ideal beauty is shown constantly. There is no literature that puts more into relief the qualities that are naturally lacking in writers of democracies than that of the ancients. So no literature exists that is more appropriate to study in democratic centuries. This study is, of all, the most appropriate for combatting the literary defects inherent in these centuries; as for their natural qualities, they will arise all by themselves without the need to learn how to acquire them.

Here I must make myself clear.

A study can be useful to the literature of a people and not be appropriate for their social and political needs.

If you persisted stubbornly in teaching only literature in a society where each man was led by habit to make violent efforts to increase his fortune or to maintain it, you would have very polished and very dangerous citizens; for since the social and political state gives them needs every day that education would never teach them to satisfy, they would disturb the State, in the name of the Greeks and the Romans, instead of making it fruitful by their industry.

It is clear that in democratic societies the interest of individuals, as well as the security of the State, requires that the education of the greatest number be scientific, commercial, and industrial rather than literary.

Greek and Latin must not be taught in all schools; but it is important that those destined by their nature or their fortune to cultivate letters, or predisposed to appreciate them, find schools where they can perfectly master ancient literature and be thoroughly penetrated by its spirit. A few excellent universities would be worth more to achieve this goal than a multitude of bad colleges where superfluous studies done badly prevent necessary studies from being done well.

All those who have the ambition to excel in letters, among democratic nations, must be nourished often by the works of antiquity. It is a healthy regimen.

It is not that I consider the literary productions of the ancients as irreproachable. I think only that they have special qualities that can serve marvelously to counterbalance our particular defects. They support us as we lean over the edge.

CHAPTER 16[a]

How American Democracy Has Modified the English Language[b]

If what I have said previously concerning letters in general has been well understood by the reader, he will easily imagine what type of influence the democratic social state and democratic institutions can exercise on language itself, which is the first instrument of thought.

a. 1. Modification that English has experienced in America.

2. Democratic cause of that:

1. Democratic peoples constantly change their words, because among them things are constantly shifting. Thus, great number of new words, character of democratic languages.

2. Character of these new words. Most of them are related to the needs of industry, to the science of administration.

3. Origin of these words. Little of learned etymologies. Some borrowings made from living languages. Above all, gain from itself.

Three means of gaining from itself: 1. Put forgotten terms back into use. 2. Make expressions belonging to a science or to a profession enter into general circulation with a figurative meaning. 3. Give to a word in use an uncommon meaning. That is the most widely used and easiest method, but also the most dangerous. By doubling the meaning of a word in this way, you make it uncertain which one you are leaving aside for it and which one you are giving to it.

4. What makes dialects and *patois* disappear with democratic institutions.

5. What makes all artificial and conventional classifications of words disappear as well in the same period.

6. Why democracy multiplies abstract words, generalizes their use and leads to the abuse of them (YTC, CVf, p. 17).

b. On the jacket of the manuscript: "The review of this chapter was extremely tiring for me; I do not know if this explains why I currently consider the chapter as too long and boring and miss the original draft, fragments of which I will find moreover in the rubish.

"Read this chapter to men of the world and study their impressions."

818

American authors live more, truly speaking, in England than in their own country, since they constantly study English writers and take them daily as models. It is not like this for the population itself; the latter is subjected more immediately to the particular causes that can have an effect on the United States. So you must pay attention not to the written language, but to the spoken language, if you want to see the modifications that the idiom of an aristocratic people can undergo while becoming the language of a democracy.[c]

Educated Englishmen, and judges more competent to appreciate these fine nuances than I am able to be myself,[d] have often assured me that the

c. In the margin: "≠So the language of a people is an excellent indicator for judging their social state, just as knowledge of the social state is sufficient to judge the state of the language in advance.≠"

d. They said that the Americans showed even more propensity than the English for making new words; that when the Americans made a new word, they never looked for its root in learned languages; that they borrowed it from foreign languages or even from their own language by changing the meaning of an already known word or by making a word move from the real meaning to the figurative meaning. These educated Englishmen added that most of these borrowings were made from the vocabulary of artisans, of businessmen, of political men rather than from that of philosophers, so that language had a kind of tendency to become materialized. Finally, they said that the Americans often used indiscriminately the same words in very diverse circumstances; so that the Americans employed on a solemn occasion an expression that the English would have used only in the most ordinary cases and vice versa.

Letter to Mr. Hall (on letter paper, *Rubish*, 1).

The letter to Basil Hall, from which Tocqueville drew this fragment, is found in the library of Princeton University and says this:

Château de Baugy, 19 June 1836./

I cannot thank you enough, Sir, for the letter you kindly sent me on the 4th of this month. I accept with a great deal of gratitude all that it contains of flattery and usefulness. Your opinions on America and on England will always carry a great weight in my view and I love knowing them, even when they do not exactly conform to mine. Controversy between men who esteem one another can only be very profitable. I will prove that your letter pleased me greatly by answering it at great length. I would like my response to engage you in continuing a correspondence to which I attach great value.

You reproach me for having said: *that the interests of the poor were sacrificed in England to those of the rich.* I confess that this thought, explained in so few words, thrown out in passing, without commentaries, is of a nature to present a much more absolute meaning than the one I meant to give it, and my intention has always been to modify it, when I could get to reviewing my work. What I wanted to say principally is that England is a country in which wealth is the *required preliminary* for a host of things that elsewhere you can gain without it. So that in England there is a host of careers that are much more closed to the poor than they are in several other countries. This would still demand a great number of explanations in order to be well understood. I am obliged to set them aside for the moment when I will have the pleasure of seeing you again. For now, I move to a subject that has a more *current* interest for me, which is America.

You find that I have portrayed too favorably the *domestic happiness* of the Americans. As it is very important for me to clarify this delicate point to which I will be obliged to return in my two last volumes, you will allow me, I hope, to submit a few observations to you. I have not claimed that a great tenderness reigned in the interior of households in the United States; I wanted to say that a great deal of order and purity reigned there, an essential condition for the order and tranquillity of political society itself. I believed that came in part from the principles and the character that American women brought to the conjugal union, and it is in this sense that I said that women exercised a great indirect influence on politics. It seemed to me that in the United States more than in any other country that I know, it was acknowledged and regulated by *unanimous consent* that the woman once married devoted herself entirely to her husband and to her children, and that is what made me say that *nowhere had a higher and more just idea of conjugal happiness been imagined.* The extreme purity of morals in marriage seems to me, after all, the first of all the conditions for this happiness, although it is not the only one, and on this point America seems to me to have the advantage even over England. I proved by my conduct the high idea that I have of English women; but if virtue is, as I do not doubt, the general rule for them, this rule seems to me to allow still fewer exceptions on the other side of the Atlantic. Here is my comment on this subject: I *never* heard a thoughtless remark said in the United States about a married woman; American books always assume chaste women; foreigners themselves, whose tongues would not be bound by custom, confess that there is nothing to say about them. I have even met some of them corrupt enough to be distressed by it, and their regret seemed to me the most complete demonstration of the fact. The same unanimity is not seen in England. I met young fools in England who hardly spared the honor of their female compatriots. I saw moralists who complained that the morality of women, principally in the lower classes, was not as great as formerly. Finally, your writers themselves sometimes assume that conjugal faith is violated. All of that does not exist, to my knowledge, in America. But I see myself that I have allowed myself to be carried much too far in my demonstration. I hope that you will see in what precedes only the extreme desire to enlighten myself on a subject that is infinitely important for me to know.

I will answer almost nothing on what you tell me about the Anglican Church. I do not know England well enough to be able to discuss with you the degree of political utility that your church can have. What I want to say is that in general I believe the union of church and State, not harmful to the State, but harmful to the church. I

enlightened classes of the United States differed notably, in their language, from the enlightened classes of Great Britain.[e]

---

have seen too closely among us the fatal consequences of this union not to be afraid that something analogous is happening among you. Now, that is a result that you must try to avoid at all cost, for religion is, in my eyes, the first of all the political guarantees, and I do not see any good that can compensate men for the loss of beliefs.

I thank you very much for taking the trouble to inform me about the idiom of the Americans. This subject has interested me greatly recently, and I want to talk about it with you at greater length since you have assured me that my questions would not bother you.

In the United States I met very well bred Englishmen who made the following remarks to me. They struck me all the more at the moment when they were made to me because I had observed something analogous in the modifications that the French language has undergone during the past one hundred years. They said then that the Americans had still more propensity than the English for making new words, that when they made a new word they never looked for its root in learned languages, that they borrowed it from foreign languages or even from their own language by changing the meaning of an already known word or by making a word move from the real meaning to the figurative meaning. They added that most of these borrowings were made from the language of various industries, that they were taken from the vocabulary of artisans, of businessmen, of political men rather than from that of philosophers, so that the language had a tendency to become materialized, in a way. I do not know, Sir, if I am making myself understood. A long conversation would be necessary to explain what I am forced to put into a few lines. Also I am counting more on your sagacity than on my clarity. These same persons also said that it often happened that the Americans used indiscriminately the same words in very diverse circumstances, so that they employed on a solemn occasion an expression that the English would have used only in the most ordinary cases and vice versa.

Does all of that seem well founded to you? If this scribbling suggests some ideas to you and you would be good enough to share them with me, I will be very obliged to you. And now, Sir, it only remains for me to ask you to excuse my detestable writing—that you will perhaps decipher with difficulty—and to accept the assurance of my most profound consideration.

[signed: Alexis de Tocqueville.]

P. S. If your article appears in the review, I will be very pleased to see it, but believe, Sir, that this circumstance will add nothing to the gratitude that I feel at your having written it.

With the kind permission of Princeton University (General Manuscripts [Misc.] Collection, Manuscripts Division, Department of Rare Books and Special Collections, University Library). The article of Basil Hall cited in the postscript is "Tocqueville on the State of America," *Quarterly Review,* 57, 1836, pp. 132–62.

e. In the margin: "≠ Canada. ≠"

They not only complained that the Americans had put many new words into use; the difference or the distance between the two countries was enough to explain that; but they also complained that these new words were particularly borrowed either from the jargon of parties, or from the mechanical arts, or from the language of business. They added that old English words were often taken by the Americans in a new sense. Finally, they said that the inhabitants of the United States frequently intermingled styles in a singular way, and that they sometimes put together words that, in the language of the mother country, were customarily kept apart. [This is how they happened, for example, to introduce a familiar or common expression into the pomp of a speech.]

These remarks, which were made to me at various times by men who seemed to me to merit belief, led me to reflect upon this subject, and my reflections brought me, by theory, to the same place that they had reached by practice.

In aristocracies, where everything remains at rest, language must naturally share that rest. Few new words are made, because few new things happen; and if you did new things, you would try hard to portray them with known words whose meaning has been fixed by tradition.

If it happens that the human mind there finally stirs by itself, or that enlightenment, penetrating from outside, awakens it, the new expressions that are created have a learned, intellectual and philosophical character that indicates that they do not to owe their birth to a democracy. When the fall of Constantinople made the sciences and letters flow back toward the West [and when the enlightenment of antiquity after being revived in Italy finally penetrated among us], the French language found itself almost all at once invaded by a multitude of new words, all of which had their roots in Greek and Latin. You then saw in France an erudite neologism, which was practiced only by the enlightened classes, and whose effects were never felt by the people or only reached them in the long run.

All the nations of Europe successively presented the same spectacle. Milton alone introduced into the English language more than six hundred words, almost all drawn from Latin, Greek and Hebrew.[f]

---

f. M. de Chateaubriand says in his comments on Milton, I, V, that the latter created

The perpetual movement that reigns within a democracy tends on the contrary constantly to renew the face of language like that of public affairs. Amid this general agitation and this competition of all minds, a great number of new ideas are formed; old ideas are lost or reappear; or they become subdivided into infinite small nuances.

So words are often found there that must go out of use, and others that must be brought into use.

Democratic nations moreover love movement for itself. That is seen in language as well as in politics. Even when they do not need to change words, they sometimes feel the desire to do so.

The genius of democratic peoples shows itself not only in the great number of new words that they put into use, but also in the nature of the ideas that these new words represent.

Among these peoples, the majority makes the law in the matter of language, as in everything else. Its spirit reveals itself there as elsewhere. Now,

---

five to six hundred new words, nearly all drawn from Greek, Hebrew and Latin. Good example of learned neologism./

Consubstantiality, word created or at least recognized and brought to light by the Council of Nice [Nicea (ed.)] in the fourth century to combat Arius.

Transubstantiation, word created in the XVIth century by the adversaries of Luther who wanted to express by [that (ed.)] that the bread of the host changed substance and became the body of Jesus Christ. See *Histoire des variations,* v. 1, p. 113.

Constitutionality, word created by the French Revolution expressing likewise a new idea. Examples of new words that different causes can invent in all times (*Rubish,* 1).

In the margin of the manuscript, Tocqueville notes another example of neologism: "comfortable—English."

Cf. Chateaubriand, *Essai sur la littérature anglaise* (Paris: Charles Gosselin and Furne, 1836), I, pp. 8–9. Tocqueville authorized Henry Reeve, the English translator of his book, to delete the reference to Milton, which the latter considered inaccurate. Reeve finally left it, probably because Tocqueville had informed him that it was already too late to eliminate it from the French edition (*Correspondance anglaise, OC,* VI, 1, pp. 54–57).

During the summer of 1836, which he spent in Switzerland, Tocqueville read *The Prince,* the *History of Florence* and some letters of Machiavelli, the *Complete Works* of Plato and the *Histoire des variations* of Bossuet (the library of the Tocqueville château contains an edition published in Paris in 1730).

the majority is occupied more with public affairs than studies, more with political and commercial interests than with philosophical speculation or literature. Most of the words created or accepted by the majority will bear the mark of these habits; they will serve principally to express the needs of industry, the passions of parties or the details of public administration. Language will expand constantly in that way, while on the contrary it will little by little abandon the terrain of metaphysics and theology.

As for the source from which democratic nations draw their new words and the manner in which they set about to fabricate them, it is easy to say.

Men who live in democratic countries hardly know the language that was spoken in Rome and in Athens, and they do not bother about going back to antiquity in order to find the expression they are lacking. If they sometimes resort to learned etymologies, it is ordinarily vanity that makes them search the content of the dead languages, and not erudition that brings certain words naturally to their minds. It even happens sometimes that it is the most ignorant among them who make the most use of such etymologies. The entirely democratic desire to go beyond your sphere often leads men in democracies to want to enhance a very coarse profession by a Greek or Latin name. The lower an occupation and the more removed from knowledge, the more pompous and erudite is the name. This is how our tightrope walkers have transformed themselves into acrobats and funambulists.

Lacking dead languages, democratic peoples willingly borrow words from living languages; for they communicate constantly among themselves, and the men of different countries willingly imitate each other, because they resemble each other more each day.

But democratic peoples look principally to their own language for the means to innovate. From time to time, they take up in their vocabulary forgotten expressions that they bring to light again, or they take from a particular class of citizens a term that is its own in order to bring the term into the regular language with a figurative meaning; a multitude of expressions that at first belonged only to the special language of a party or a profession thus find themselves brought into general circulation.

The most usual expedient that democratic peoples employ to innovate with regard to language consists of giving an uncommon meaning to an expression already in use. This method is very simple, very quick and very easy. Knowledge is not needed to use it well; and ignorance even facilitates its use. But it makes language run great risks. By doubling the meaning of a word in this way, democratic peoples sometimes make it doubtful which meaning they are leaving aside and which one they are giving to it.

An author begins by turning a known expression a little bit away from its original meaning and after having modified it in this way, he adapts it as well as he can to his subject. Another appears who pulls the meaning in another direction; a third carries it with him along a new path; and since there is no common arbiter, no permanent tribunal that can definitely settle the meaning of the word, the latter remains in a variable situation. As a result, writers almost never have an air of being attached to a single thought; instead they always seem to aim at the middle of a group of ideas, leaving to the reader the trouble of judging which one is hit.

This is an unfortunate consequence of democracy. I would prefer that you sprinkled the language with Chinese, Tartar or Huron words, than to make the meaning of French words uncertain. Harmony and homogeneity are only the secondary beauties of language. There is much more convention in this kind of thing, and you can, if necessary, do without them. But there is no good language without clear terms.[g]

Equality necessarily brings several other changes to language.

In aristocratic centuries, when each nation tends to hold itself apart from all the others and loves to have a physiognomy that is its own, it often happens that several peoples who have a common origin become very foreign to each other, so that, without ceasing to be able to understand each other, they no longer all speak in the same way.

In these same centuries, each nation is divided into a certain number of classes that see each other little and do not mingle; each one of these classes invariably takes on and keeps intellectual habits that belong only to it, and adopts by preference certain words and certain terms that pass afterward

---

g. In the margin, concerning this paragraph: "<To delete, I think.>"

from generation to generation like inheritances. You then find in the same idiom a language of the poor and a language of the rich, a language of commoners and a language of nobles, a learned language and a vulgar language. The more profound the divisions and the more insurmountable the barriers, the more this must be so. I would readily bet that, among the castes of India, language varies prodigiously, and that almost as much difference is found between the language of a pariah and that of a Brahmin as between their forms of dress.

When, on the contrary, men no longer held in their place see each other and communicate constantly, when castes are destroyed, and when classes are renewed and mixed together, all the words of a language are mingled. Those words that cannot suit the greatest number perish; the rest form a common mass from which each person draws more or less haphazardly. Nearly all the different dialects that divided the idioms of Europe are noticeably tending to disappear; there are no *patois* in the New World, and they are disappearing daily in the Old World.[h]

This revolution in the social state influences style as well as language.

Not only does everyone use the same words, but they also get accustomed to employing each of them indiscriminately. The rules that style had created are almost destroyed. You hardly find expressions that, by their nature, seem vulgar, and others that appear refined. Since individuals from various ranks bring with them, to whatever station they rise, expressions and terms that they have used, the origin of words is lost like that of men, and a confusion is developed in language as in society.

I know that in the classification of words rules are found that are not due to one form of society rather than to another, but that derive from the

---

h. In America there is no class which speaks the language in a very delicate and very studied manner, but you do not find a *patois*. The same remark applies to Canada. That is due to several causes, but among others to equality of conditions which, by giving to all men an analogous education, by mixing them together constantly, has had to provide them necessarily with similar forms of language.

We see the same revolution taking place in Europe and above all in France. The *patois* are disappearing as conditions become equal (*Rubish*, 1).

very nature of things. There are expressions and turns which are vulgar because the sentiments that they must express are truly low, and others which are elevated because the objects that they want to portray are naturally very high.

Ranks, by mingling, will never make these differences disappear. But equality cannot fail to destroy what is purely conventional and arbitrary in the forms of thought. I do not even know if the necessary classification which I pointed out above will not always be less respected among a democratic people than among another; because, among such a people, there are no men whose education, enlightenment and leisure permanently dispose them to study the natural laws of language and who make those laws respected by observing them themselves.

I do not want to abandon this subject without portraying democratic languages with a last feature that will perhaps characterize them more than all the others.

I showed previously that democratic peoples had the taste and often the passion for general ideas; that is due to qualities and defects that are their own. This love of general ideas shows itself, in democratic languages, in the continual use of generic terms and abstract words, and by the manner in which they are used. That is the great merit and the great weakness of these languages.[j]

Democratic peoples passionately love generic terms and abstract words, because these expressions enlarge thought and, by allowing many objects to be included in a little space, aid the work of the mind.[k]

---

j. In the margin: "<Perhaps make this into a small chapter having this title: why equality multiplies the number of abstract words, generalizes their use and leads to the abuse of them.

"Probably do so.>"

k. General and abstract terms./

Due to the need to give yourself latitude while speaking either to yourself or to others; to the fear of responsibility; to the need to give yourself latitude to the right and to the left of the point where you are placed. Result of life in a changing, uncertain, agitated time, as a democratic time always is, and of the softness of souls in that same time./

All our impressions turn vague when you approach a moral question; they float

828 THE ENGLISH LANGUAGE

A democratic writer will willingly say in an abstract way *the capable* for capable men, and without getting into details about the things to which this capacity applies. He will speak about *actualities* in order to depict all at once the things that are happening at this moment before his eyes, and he will understand by the word *eventualities* all that can happen in the universe beginning from the moment when he is speaking.

Democratic writers constantly create abstract words of this type, or they take the abstract words of language in a more and more abstract sense.

Even more, to make discourse more rapid, they personify the object of the abstract words and make it act like a real individual. They will say that *the force of things wants the capable to govern.*[m]

I cannot do better than to explain my thought by my own example.

I have often used the word equality in an absolute sense; I have, as well, personified equality in several places, and in this way I have happened to say that equality did certain things or refrained from certain others. You can maintain that the men of the century of Louis XIV would not have spoken in this way; it would never have occurred to the mind of any one of them to use the word equality without applying it to a particular thing, and they would rather have renounced using it than agree to making equality into a living person.

These abstract words that fill democratic languages and that you use

---

between praise and blame. Which comes from the softness of souls that demands little effort from others and requires little from yourself (YTC, CVk, 1, p. 23).

Madame de Staël already complained about the uncontrolled creation of abstract words in Chapter VII of the second part of her *De la littérature* (Paris: Charpentier, 1842), p. 501. La Harpe had done the same.

m. "At the time of the last insurrection of the Greeks against the Turks, a minister [v: orator], having to speak of Greece and not knowing if he had to designate it as a province in revolt or as a free State, took it into his head to call it a locality. An aristocratic language would never have provided such an expedient to politics" (*Rubish,* 1). See René Georgin, "Tocqueville et le langage de la démocratie," *Vie et langage* 17, no. 201 (1968): 740–44; and Laurence Guellec, *Tocqueville et les langages de la démocratie* (Paris: Honoré Champion, 2004).

for the slightest reason without connecting them to any particular fact, enlarge and veil thought. They make the expression more rapid and the idea less clear. But, as regards language, democratic peoples prefer obscurity to labor.

I do not know, moreover, if vagueness does not have a certain secret charm for those who speak and write among these peoples.

Men who live there, since they are often left to the individual efforts of their intellect, are almost always tormented by doubt. Moreover, since their situation changes constantly, they are never held firmly to any one of their opinions by the very immobility of their fortune.

So the men who inhabit democratic countries often have vacillating thoughts; they must have very broad expressions in order to contain them. Since they never know if the idea they express today will suit the new situation that they will have tomorrow, they naturally conceive the taste for abstract terms. An abstract word is like a box with a false bottom; you put the ideas that you want into it, and you take them out without anyone seeing.

[I am so persuaded of the influence that the social state and political institutions of a people exercise on its language, that I think that you could easily succeed in discovering these first facts solely by inspecting the words of the language, and I am astonished that this idea has not been applied more often and more perfectly to the idioms that we know without knowing the men who use or have used them.]

Among all peoples, generic and abstract words form the basis of language; so I am not claiming that you find these words only in democratic languages. I am only saying that the tendency of men, in times of equality, is particularly to augment the number of words of this type, always to take them singly in their most abstract sense, and to use them for the slightest reason, even when the needs of speech do not require it.

CHAPTER 17ᵃ

a. 1. Definition of poetry. Search for and portrayal of the ideal. Object of the chapter. Try to find out if among the actions, sentiments and ideas of democratic peoples, some are found that lend themselves to the ideal and can serve as source of poetry.

2. Democratic peoples have naturally less taste for the ideal because of the passions that bind them constantly to the pursuit of the real.

3. Moreover there are several subjects proper to the portrayal of the ideal that they are lacking.

1. Religions are shaken.
2. They become simplified
3. Men take no further interest in the past.
4. They find with difficulty material for the ideal in the present because they are all small and see each other very clearly.

4. So most of the American [ancient? (ed.)] sources of poetry are drying up, but others are opening.

1. Men of democratic centuries readily take an interest in the future.
2. If individuals are small, society seems [blank (ed.)] to them and lends itself to poetry. Each nation sees itself.
3. The human species is seen and it can be portrayed.
4. There is no complete divinity, but the figure of God is greater and clearer and his place relative to the whole of human affairs is more recognizable.
5. The external man does not lend himself [to poetry (ed.)] but poets descend into the realm of the soul and there they find the sentiments of not just one man in particular, but of man in general to portray; equality brings forth the image of man in general and is interested in him.

Thus democracy does not make all the subjects that lend themselves to the ideal disappear. It makes them less numerous and greater (YTC, CVf, pp. 18–19).

In the RUBISH OF THESE CHAPTERS you find this as well:

Poetry of democracy./
Future of democracy, sole poetic idea of our time. Immense, indefinite idea. Period of renewal, of total change in the social system of humanity. This idea alone throws more poetry into souls than there was in the century of Louis XV and in that of Louis XIV.

It is only the past or the future that is poetic. The present very rarely is. There was nevertheless a great deal of poetry in the present in the Middle Ages. Facts to explain (*Rubish*, 1).

Of Some Sources of Poetry
among Democratic Nations[b]

b. On a jacket that accompanies that of the chapter:

Piece that began the chapter and that must be deleted, I believe, as written in an affected style and above all verbiage./

I would like to portray the influence that democratic institutions exercise in the United States on the poetic genius of man, but beyond the fact that the subject is placed outside of the ordinary circle of my thoughts, a first difficulty stops me.

I do not know if anyone up to now has taken care to provide an uncontested definition of the thing I am attempting to speak about. No one can deny that poetry ≠has not≠ obtained great power over the imagination of men; but who has ever said clearly what poetry was; how many different and often dissimilar things we have gathered under this very name!

[In the margin: Show in a more striking way what is *useful* in poetry. The Romans./

It is not sufficiently understood that men cannot do without poetry./

Poetry and *poetic faculty* to distinguish. Taste for the ideal./

I want to examine not only if democracy leads men to do works of poetry but also if it suggests poetic ideas to them./

The one is not the necessary consequence of the other, for a people can have a great number of poetic ideas and not have the time or the art of writing or the taste for reading. But in general you can say that these two things go together.]

A small rhymed epigram is a work of poetry; a long epic in verse is as well. I see enormous differences between these two productions of the human mind, but they have something similar in the form. I understand that it is to form that the word begins to be attached, and I conclude from it that poetry consists of carefully enclosing the idea in a certain number of syllables symmetrically arranged. But no. I hear that these verses are poetic and that those are not. Some grant that there is poetry in a prose work and others contend that they find no trace of it in a long poem. So poetry rests not only in the form of the thought, but also in the thought itself. It can reside in the two things united or inhabit each one of them separately. So what definitively is poetry? This could become the topic for a dissertation, with which I do not intend to fatigue the reader. So instead of trying to find out what language has wanted to include in the word poetry, I will say what I include in it myself and I will fix the meaning that I give to it in the present chapter.

On a page bearing the title OF POETRY IN AMERICA, you read this first beginning of the chapter: "I often wondered while traveling across the United States if, amid this people exclusively preoccupied by the material cares of life [v: commercial enterprises], among so many mercantile speculations, a single poetic idea would be found, and I believed I recognized several of them that appeared to me eminently to have this character."

Several very different meanings have been given to the word poetry. It would tire readers to try to find out which one of these different meanings is most suitable to choose; I prefer to tell them immediately which one I have chosen.

Poetry, in my view, is the search for and the portrayal of the ideal.[c]

The poet is the one who, by taking away a part of what exists, adding some imaginary features to the picture, and combining certain real circumstances that are not found together, completes, enlarges nature. Thus, the aim of poetry will not be to represent truth, but to embellish it and to offer a higher image to the mind.[d]

Verse will seem to me like the ideal of beauty for language, and in this sense it will be eminently poetic; but in itself alone, it will not constitute poetry.

[<Poetry always takes as the subject of its portraits beings who are really found in nature or who at least live in the imagination of the men to whom it is addressed. It changes, enlarges, embellishes what exists; it does not create what does not exist, and if it attempts to do so, it can still amuse or surprise, but it no longer rouses and becomes the puerile game of an idle imagination.>][e]

I want to find out if, among the actions, sentiments and ideas of democratic peoples, some are found that lend themselves to the imagination of the ideal and that must, for this reason, be considered as natural sources of poetry.

It must first be recognized that the taste for the ideal and the pleasure that is taken in seeing its portrayal are never as intense and as widespread among a democratic people as within an aristocracy.

[In democratic societies the human mind finds itself constantly bound

c. "The greatest proof of the misery of man is poetry. God cannot make poetry; he sees everything clearly" (RUBISH OF THESE CHAPTERS, *Rubish,* 1).

d. "You idealize a small object, you are poetic without being great.

"You represent a great thing in its natural state, you are great or sublime, but not poetic" (*Rubish,* 1).

e. "I will go still further and without limiting the name of poet to writers I will readily agree to extend it to all those who undertake to offer images to men, provided that they represent by them something superior to what is. Raphael will seem to me to merit this title as well as Homer" (RUBISH OF THESE CHAPTERS, *Rubish,* 1).

by the small details of real [v: present] life. That results not only from the fact that all men work, but above all from the fact that they carry out all their works with fervor and I could almost say with love.]^f

Among aristocratic nations, it sometimes happens that the body acts as if by itself, while the soul is plunged into a repose that weighs it down. Among these nations, the people themselves often show poetic tastes, and their spirit sometimes soars above and beyond what surrounds them.^{g}

But, in democracies, the love of natural enjoyments, the idea of something better, competition, the charm of impending success, are like so many spurs that quicken the steps of each man in the career that he has embraced and forbid him from standing aside from it for a single moment. The principal effort of the soul goes in this direction. Imagination is not extinguished, but it devotes itself almost exclusively to imagining the useful and to representing the real.

Equality not only diverts men from portraying the ideal; it decreases the number of subjects to portray.

[You cannot deny that equality [v: democracy], while becoming established among men, does not make a great number of these subjects that lent themselves to the portrayal of the ideal disappear from their view, and does not in this way dry up several of the most abundant sources of poetry.]

Aristocracy, by holding society immobile, favors the steadiness and duration of positive religions, as well as the stability of political institutions.

Not only does it maintain the human spirit in faith, but it disposes it to adopt one faith rather than another. An aristocratic people will always be inclined to place intermediary powers between God and man.

You can say that in this aristocracy shows itself very favorable to poetry. When the universe is populated with supernatural powers that do not fall within the senses, but are discovered by the mind, imagination feels at ease,

f. In the margin: "<This sentence is found word for word, I believe, in *revolutions*. Vary it in one place or the other. The idea is necessary to both.>"

g. In the margin: "<While the middle classes, although they have more leisure, show it almost not at all. From that you can see clearly that it is less the constraint of work that stops the poetic impulse than the spirit that is brought to work.>"

and poets, finding a thousand diverse subjects to portray, find innumerable spectators ready to be interested in their portraits.

In democratic centuries, on the contrary, it sometimes happens that beliefs go drifting away like the laws. Doubt then brings the imagination of poets back to earth and encloses them within the visible and real world.[h]

Even when equality does not shake religions, it simplifies them; it diverts attention from secondary agents in order to bring it principally to the sovereign master.

Aristocracy naturally leads the human mind to the contemplation of the past, and fixes it there. Democracy, on the contrary, gives men a sort of instinctive distaste for what is ancient. In that, aristocracy is very much more favorable to poetry, for things ordinarily enlarge and become obscure as they become more distant; and from this double perspective they lend themselves more to the portrayal of the ideal.

After removing the past from poetry, equality partially removes the present.

Among aristocratic peoples, a certain number of privileged individuals exist, whose existence is so to speak above and beyond the human condition; power, wealth, glory, spirit, delicacy and distinction in all things seem to belong by right to the latter. The crowd never sees them very closely, or does not follow them in detail; there is little that you have to do to make the portrayal of these men poetic.

On the other hand, there exists among these same peoples ignorant, humble and subservient classes; and the latter lend themselves to poetry by the very excess of their coarseness and misery, as the others do by their refinement and their grandeur. Moreover, since the different classes that make up an aristocratic people are very separated from each other and know each other badly, imagination can always, while representing them, add something to or subtract something from the real.

In democratic societies, where men are all very small and very similar,

---

h. "Doubt itself *prosaic* in detail is immensely poetic over all. Byron proved it very well. What poetry in the *why* and the *how* of man in face of God and of nature.

"*Audacious* doubt is eminently democratic" (RUBISH OF THESE CHAPTERS, *Rubish,* 1).

each one, while viewing himself, sees all the others at the same instant. So poets who live in democratic centuries cannot ever take one man in particular as the subject of their portrait; for a subject with mediocre greatness, which you also see clearly on all sides, will never lend itself to the ideal.

Therefore equality, while becoming established on the earth, dries up most of the ancient sources of poetry.

Let us try to show how it finds new ones.

When doubt depopulated heaven and when the progress of equality reduced each man to better known and smaller proportions, poets, not yet imagining what they could put in place of these great subjects that withdrew with aristocracy, turned their eyes toward inanimate nature. Losing heroes and gods from view, they undertook at first to portray rivers and mountains.

That gave birth in the last century to the poetry that was called, par excellence, descriptive.

Some have thought that this embellished portrayal of the material and inanimate things which cover the earth was poetry appropriate to democratic centuries; but I think that is a mistake. I believe that it only represents a period of transition.

I am persuaded that in the long run democracy diverts the imagination from everything that is external to man, in order to fix it only on man.j

Democratic peoples can be very amused for a moment by considering nature; but they get really excited only by the sight of themselves. Here alone are the natural sources of poetry to be found among these peoples, and it may be believed that all poets who do not want to draw upon these sources will lose all sway over the souls of those whom they claim to charm, and will end by no longer having anything except cold witnesses to their transports.

---

j. "Democracy diverts the human mind from the contemplation of external objects in order to concentrate it on itself. 'Man is the most beautiful study of man', Pope said. That is true for all peoples, but there is no more evident truth for a democratic people. Almost the whole of its literature is contained in this single expression" (*Rubish*, 1).

I have demonstrated how the idea of the progress and of the indefinite perfectibility of the human species was appropriate to democratic ages.

Democratic peoples hardly worry about what has been, but they readily dream about what will be, and their imagination has no limits in this direction; it expands and grows without measure.

This offers a vast opening to poets and allows them to move their portrayal far away from what is seen. Democracy, which closes the past to poetry, opens the future.

[≠In democratic centuries poets cannot take as the subject of their portrait a hero or a prince.≠]

Since all the citizens who make up a democratic society are nearly equal and similar, poetry cannot attach itself to any one of them; but the nation offers itself to its brush. The similarity of all individuals, which makes each one of them separately inappropriate for becoming the subject of poetry, allows poets to include them all in the same image and to consider finally the people itself. Democratic nations see their own figure more clearly than all others and this great figure lends itself marvelously to the portrayal of the ideal.

I will easily acknowledge that the Americans[k] do not have poets; I cannot admit as well that they do not have poetic ideas.[m]

Some in Europe are very much interested in the American wilderness, but the Americans themselves hardly think about it. The wonders of inanimate nature leave them indifferent, and so to speak they see the admirable forests that surround them only at the moment when they fall under their blows.[n] Their sight is filled with another spectacle. The American

k. "I cited this example of America not only because America is the particular object of my discourse, but also because I believe that in this it provides me with insights about what must happen among democratic peoples in general" (*Rubish*, 1).

m. Milton, democratic poet./

"Byron *idem./*

"The one is democratic because he drew his generative idea from Christianity.

"The other by the natural impulse of his time" (RUBISH OF THESE CHAPTERS, *Rubish*, 1).

n. "There is until now only a single writer who has felt and could produce this admirable poetry of wild nature such as the wilderness of America reveals to us, and this great poet is not American" (*Rubish*, 1).

people see themselves marching across this wilderness, draining swamps, straightening rivers, populating empty areas, and subduing nature. [Every day they notice their size growing and their strength increasing, and they already perceive themselves in the future leading as absolute masters the vast continent that they have made fruitful and cleared.] This magnificent image of themselves does not only present itself now and then to the imagination of the Americans; you can say that it follows each one of them in the least as well as in the principal of his actions, and that it remains always hovering in his mind.

You cannot imagine anything so small, so colorless, so full of miserable interests, so anti-poetical, in a word, than the life of a man in the United States; but among the thoughts that direct him one is always found that is full of poetry, and that one is like a hidden nerve which gives vigor to all the rest.⁰ [You must not be astonished by this for how could you think that men who do such great things would be entirely devoid of great ideas?]ᴾ

In aristocratic centuries, each people, like each individual, is inclined to hold itself immobile and separate from all the others.

In democratic centuries the extreme mobility of men and their impatient desires make them constantly change place, and make the inhabitants of different countries mingle together, see and hear each other, and borrow from each other. So it is not only the members of the same nation who become similar; nations themselves assimilate, and all together form in the eye of the beholder nothing more than a vast democracy in which each

o. "So I do not fear that democratic peoples lack poetry, but I am afraid that this poetry aims for the gigantesque rather than for grandeur. For it, I fear the influence of their poets more than their timidity, and I am afraid that the sublime there may be several times closer still to the ridiculous than anywhere else" (RUBISH OF THESE CHAPTERS, *Rubish,* 1).

p. In a first draft, this paragraph followed: "≠The sight of what is happening in the United States makes me reflect on democratic peoples in general, and these new reflections modify the opinion that I had had formerly that democracies could not fail to extinguish the poetic genius of man and to substitute for the empire of the imagination that of good sense. That is true, but to a lesser degree than I had believed at first. So I think that there is a kind of poetry within reach of democratic peoples, and I am persuaded that great writers who will be born among them will not fail to see it and to take hold of it≠" (*Rubish,* 1).

citizen is a people. That brings to light for the first time the figure of the human species.

All that relates to the existence of the human species taken as a whole, its vicissitudes, its future becomes a very fertile mine for poetry.[q]

Poets who lived in aristocratic ages made admirable portraits by taking as subjects certain incidents in the life of a people or of a man; but not one of them ever dared to include in his tableau the destinies of the human species, while poets who write in democratic ages can undertake to do so.

At the same time that each person, raising his eyes above his country, finally begins to notice humanity itself, God reveals himself more and more to the human mind in his full and entire majesty.

If in democratic centuries faith in positive religions is often shaky and beliefs in intermediary powers, whatever name you give them, grow dim, men on the other hand are disposed to conceive a much more vast idea of Divinity itself, and the intervention of the divine in human affairs appears to them in a new and greater light.

Seeing the human species as a single whole, they easily imagine that the same design rules over its destinies, and in the actions of each individual, they are led to recognize the mark of this general and constant plan by which God leads the species.[r]

This can also be considered as a very abundant source of poetry that opens in these centuries.

Democratic poets will always seem small and cold if they try to give bodily forms to gods, demons or angels, and try to make them descend from heaven to quarrel over the earth.

But, if democratic poets want to connect the great events that they are relating to the general designs of God for the universe, and, without show-

---

q. Note on the other side of the jacket that contains the *rubish* of the chapter: "In aristocracy, the detail of man poetic. Homer portrays Achilles. In democracy, humanity independently of the particular forms that it can take in certain places and in certain times. Byron, *Childe Harold*, Chateaubriand, *René*" (*Rubish*, 1).

r. "What is more poetic than the *Discours sur l'histoire universelle* of Bossuet? Only God and the human species are present there, however" (*Rubish*, 1).

ing the hand of the sovereign master, cause his thought to be entered into, they will be admired and understood, for the imagination of their compatriots itself follows this road.[s]

You can equally foresee that poets who live in democratic ages will portray passions and ideas rather than persons and actions. [and that they will apply themselves to relating the general features of human passions and ideas rather than those that depend on a time and on a country.[t]

This is easy to understand.]

Language, dress and the daily actions of men in democracies are resistant to the imagination of the ideal. These things are not poetic in themselves, and they would moreover cease to be so, because they are too well known by all those to whom you undertook to speak about them. That forces poets constantly to penetrate below the external surface that the senses reveal to them, in order to glimpse the soul itself. Now there is nothing that lends

---

s. We have had today (22 April 1837) an interesting conversation on poetry.

We all fell into agreement that the intervention of the divinity in human affairs was essentially poetic by nature and particularly necessary to epic poetry.

The discussion turned on the means of making the intervention of the divinity felt today, of making it perceptible.

By common agreement we abandoned mythological divinities, personified passions . . . , as operatic machines that chilled the spectator.

I maintained that today you had equally to avoid using saints, demons and angels, since the spirit of the century was drawn more and more to grasp the idea of the entirely intellectual and non-material action of the divinity on souls, without intermediaries in whom you scarcely believe. But the difficulty arose of making this action, conceived by the mind alone, felt and making this invisible agent seen in the very play of human passions.

Charles [Stoffels? (ed.)] maintained that man was so made that you could never make him conceive of the intervention of the divinity without visible agents. I maintained the opposite, but without being able to develop my thought practically.

[In the margin: Humanitarian poetry.

Poem of man. Human destiny.

Jocelyn. Human condition.

This merits being carefully examined (RUBISH OF THESE CHAPTERS, *Rubish,* 1).

t. "Sensual poetry. Arabs.

Appropriate to democratic peoples" (RUBISH OF THESE CHAPTERS, *Rubish,* 1).

itself more to portraying the ideal than man envisaged in this way in the depths of his non-material nature.[u]

I do not need to travel across heaven and earth to find a marvelous subject full of contrast, of grandeur and infinite pettiness, of profound obscurities and singular clarity, capable at the same time of giving birth to pity, admiration, contempt, terror. I have only to consider myself. Man comes out of nothing, passes through time, and goes to disappear forever into the bosom of God. You see him only for a moment wandering at the edge of the two abysses where he gets lost.

If man were completely unaware of himself, he would not be poetic; for what you have no idea about you cannot portray. If he saw himself clearly, his imagination would remain dormant and would have nothing to add to the picture. But man is revealed enough for him to see something of himself, and hidden enough for the rest to disappear into impenetrable shadows, into which he plunges constantly and always in vain, in order finally to understand himself.[v]

u. In the manuscript, you find in place of this sentence two paragraphs that repeat ideas present in other places of the chapter.

v. Miseries of man./

[In the margin: To put perhaps with sentiments. Transition.

Put somewhere because *good*.

Human will.

In preface probably when I say that I am speaking about the difficulty of the subject.]

If you examine the conduct of men, you easily discover that tastes direct them much more than opinions or ideas.

Where does the instinctive, almost physical sensation that we call taste come from? How is it born, is it supported? Where does it take us and push us? Who knows?

Thus man does not know even the principal motive of his own actions and when, tired of looking for truth in the entire universe, he comes back toward himself, obscurity seems to redouble as he approaches and wants to understand himself.

[In the margin: This text is better.

And when, tired of looking for what makes his fellows act, he tries hard at least to untangle what pushes himself, he still does not know what to believe. He travels across the entire universe and he doubts. He finally comes back toward himself and obscurity seems to redouble as he approaches himself more and wants to understand himself.]

9 March 1836 (YTC, CVk, I, pp. 12–13).

So among democratic peoples, you must not wait for poetry to live by legends, for it to be nourished by traditions and ancient memories, for it to try to repopulate the universe with supernatural beings in whom readers and poets themselves no longer believe, or for it coldly to personify virtues and vices that you can see in their own form. It lacks all these resources; but man remains for it, and that is enough. Human destinies, man, taken apart from his time and country and placed in front of nature and God, with his passions, his doubts, his unprecedented prosperity and incomprehensible miseries, will become for these peoples the principal and almost unique subject of poetry; and this is what you can already ascertain if you consider what has been written by the great writers who have appeared since the world began to turn toward democracy.

Writers who, today, have so admirably reproduced the features of Childe Harold, of René and of Jocelyn[w] did not claim to recount the actions of one man; they wanted to illuminate and enlarge certain still obscure aspects of the human heart.

Tocqueville here is referring to Pascal, very specifically to the fragment on the disproportion of man (*pensée* 390 of the Lafuma edition).

In 1831, he had already written to Ernest de Chabrol a letter with accents of Pascal:

> The more I examine this country and everything, the more I see and the more I am frightened by seeing the few certainties that man is able to acquire in this world. There is no subject that does not grow larger as you pursue it, no fact or observation at the bottom of which you do not find a doubt. All the objects of this life appear to us only like certain decorations of the opera that you see only through a curtain that prevents you from discerning the contours with precision.
>
> There are men who enjoy living in this perpetual half-light; as for me, it tires me out and drives me to despair. I would like to hold political and moral truths as I hold my pen, and doubt besieges me.
>
> Yesterday there was an American who asked me how I classified human miseries; I answered without hesitating that I put them in this order: chronic illnesses, death, doubt. . . . He stopped me and protested; I have reflected about it since and I persist in my classification, but this is enough philosophy (letter of 19 November 1832, YTC, BIa2).

w. Henry Reeve added *Faust* to these examples.

Those are the poems of democracy.

So equality does not destroy all the subjects of poetry; it makes them less numerous and more vast.[x]

---

x. I do not know if poetry such as I have taken care to define it, poetry that does not consist of a particular form but [of (ed.)] a certain kind of ideas, is not among the literary tastes most natural to democracy <because it is enjoyed without preparation and in a moment and it rapidly removes the soul from the middle of the pettiness and monotony of democratic life.

The great images of poetry seize so to [speak (ed.)] the soul without warning; they draw it as if by force far away from its everyday habits.> The enjoyments that poetry provides are more instinctive than reasoned; you enjoy them without preparation, you obtain them for yourself instantaneously. They seize so to speak the soul without warning and draw it as if by force far away from its everyday routine.

What fits democracy better than all that? (RUBISH OF THESE CHAPTERS, *Rubish*, 1).

CHAPTER 18[a]

Why American Writers and Orators Are Often Bombastic[b]

I have often noticed that the Americans, who generally treat matters with a clear and spare language devoid of all ornamentation, and whose extreme simplicity is often common, fall readily into bombast as soon as they want to take up poetic style. They then appear pompous without letup from one end of the speech to the other; and seeing them lavish images at every turn in this way, you would think that they never said anything simply.

The English fall more rarely into a similar fault.

The cause of this can be pointed out without much difficulty.

In democratic societies, each citizen is habitually busy contemplating a very small object, which is himself. If he comes to raise his eyes higher, he then sees only the immense image of society, or the still greater figure of the human species. He has only very particular and very clear ideas, or very general and very vague notions; the intermediate space is empty.

a. 1. Men who live in democracies have only very small ideas that relate to themselves or very general ones. As soon as you take them out of themselves, they want the gigantesque.

2. Their writers give it to them readily because they have similar instincts and as well because they have the democratic taste of succeeding quickly and with little cost.

3. Among democratic peoples poetic sources are beautiful, but rare. They are soon exhausted. And then you throw yourself into the monstrous and the imaginary (YTC, CVf, p. 19).

b. On the jacket of the manuscript: "Perhaps this chapter is too thin to be put separately and should be joined to the preceding one."

So when you have drawn him out of himself, he is always waiting for you to offer him some prodigious object to look at, and it is only at this price that he agrees to keep himself away for a moment from the small complicated concerns that agitate and charm his life.

This seems to me to explain well enough why men of democracies who in general have such narrow affairs, demand from their poets such vast conceptions and portraits so beyond measure.

For their part, writers hardly fail to obey these instincts that they share; they inflate their imagination constantly, and expanding it beyond measure, they make it reach the gigantesque, for which they often abandon the great.

In this way, they hope immediately to attract the eyes of the crowd and to fix them easily on themselves, and they often succeed in doing so; for the crowd, which seeks in poetry only very vast subjects, does not have time to measure exactly the proportions of all the subjects that are presented to it, or taste sure enough to see easily in what way they are disproportionate. The author and the public corrupt each other at the same time.

We have seen, moreover, that among democratic peoples the sources of poetry were beautiful, but not very abundant. You soon end by exhausting them. Finding no more material for the ideal in the real and in the true, poets leave them entirely and create monsters.

I am not afraid that the poetry of democratic peoples may show itself to be timid or that it may stay very close to the earth. I am apprehensive instead that it may lose itself at every moment in the clouds, and that it may finish by portraying entirely imaginary realms. I fear that the works of democratic poets may offer immense and incoherent images, over-charged portraits, bizarre compositions, and that the fantastic beings that have emerged from their mind may sometimes cause the real world to be missed.

CHAPTER 19[a]

Some Observations on the Theater of Democratic Peoples[b]

a. 1. It is in the theater that the literary repercussions of the political revolution first make themselves felt. Spectators are carried away by their secret tastes without having the time to acknowledge it.

2. The literary revolution takes place more suddenly in the theater than elsewhere.

Even in aristocracies the people have their voice in the theater. When the social state becomes democratic, the people become sovereign and overthrow by riot the literary laws of the aristocracy.

3. It is in the theater that the literary revolution is always most visible. The theater puts into relief most of the qualities and all of the defects inherent in democratic literatures.

1. Scorn for erudition. No ancient subjects.
2. Subjects taken from current society and presenting its inconsistencies.
3. Few fixed rules.
4. Style (illegible word) careless.
5. Improbabilities.

4. The Americans show all these instincts when they go to the theater, but they rarely go. Why (YTC, CVf, p. 20).

b. On the jacket of the manuscript:

CH. [perhaps *M* (ed.)] to whom I have just read this chapter (22 December 1838) immediately found 1. that it greatly resembled *literary physiognomy.* 2. that it was a bit serious given the subject. 3. that it would be desirable to introduce more citations and less argumentation./

Doesn't interest begin to tire and isn't this chapter, which is only the development of *literary physiognomy,* too much?

Examine the impression of those who hear it./

I believe, taking everything into account, that this chapter should be deleted.

CH could indicate Charles Stoffels or Ernest de Chabrol. Tocqueville read part of his manuscript to Chateaubriand, but a letter to Beaumont obliges us to place this reading

When the revolution that changed the social and political state of an aristocratic people begins to make itself felt in literature, it is generally in the theater that it is first produced, and it is there that it always remains visible.

The spectator of a dramatic work is in a way taken unprepared by the impression that is suggested to him. He does not have time to search his memory or to consult experts; he does not think about fighting the new literary instincts that are beginning to emerge in him; he yields to them before knowing them.

Authors do not take long to discover which way public taste is thus secretly leaning. They turn their works in that direction; and plays, after serving to make visible the literary revolution that is being prepared, soon end by carrying it out. If you want to judge in advance the literature of a people that is turning toward democracy, study its theater.

Among aristocratic nations themselves, moreover, plays form the most democratic portions of literature. There is no literary enjoyment more accessible to the crowd than those that you experience seeing the stage. Neither preparation nor study is needed to feel them. They grip you amid your preoccupations and your ignorance. When the love, still half crude, for the pleasures of the mind begins to penetrate a class of citizens, it immediately drives them to the theater. The theaters of aristocratic nations have always been full of spectators who do not belong to the aristocracy. It is only in

---

in January 1839. If it concerns *M,* Tocqueville's wife, Mary Mottley, must be considered.

On a loose sheet with the manuscript of the chapter:

Perhaps this chapter should be reduced to only the new ideas that it contains, only recalling all the others in passing.

The new ideas are:

1. It is in the theater that the literary revolution first shows itself.
2. It is there that it is most sudden.
3. It is there that it is always most visible.

the theater that the upper classes have mingled with the middle and lower classes, and that they have agreed if not to accept the advice of the latter, at least to allow them to give it. It is in the theater that the learned and the lettered have always had the most difficulty making their taste prevail over that of the people, and keeping themselves from being carried away by the taste of the people. There the pit has often laid down the law for the boxes.

[So democracy not only introduces the lower classes into the theater, it makes them dominate there.]

If it is difficult for an aristocracy not to allow the theater to be invaded by the people, you will easily understand that the people must rule there as a master once democratic principles have penetrated laws and mores, when ranks merge and minds like fortunes become more similar, and when the upper class loses its power, its traditions and its leisure, along with its hereditary wealth.

So the tastes and instincts natural to democratic peoples as regards literature, will show themselves first in the theater, and you can predict that they will be introduced there with violence. In written works, the literary laws of the aristocracy will become modified little by little in a general and so to speak legal manner. In the theater, they will be overthrown by riots.

[All that I have said in a general way about the literature of democracies is particularly applicable to the works of the theater.]

The theater puts into relief most of the qualities and nearly all the vices inherent in democratic literatures.

Democratic peoples have only very mediocre esteem for learning, and they scarcely care about what happened in Rome and in Athens; they mean for you to talk about themselves, and they ask for the present to be portrayed.

Consequently, when the heroes and mores of antiquity are often reproduced on stage, and care is taken to remain very faithful to ancient traditions, that is enough to conclude that the democratic classes do not yet dominate the theater.

Racine excuses himself very humbly, in the preface of *Britannicus,* for having made Junie enter among the vestal virgins, where, according to Aulu-Gelle, he says, "no one younger than six or older than nine years of age was received." It may be believed that he would not have thought to accuse himself or to defend himself from such a crime, if he had written today.[c]

Such a fact enlightens me not only about the state of literature in the times in which it took place, but also about that of the society itself. A democratic theater does not prove that the nation is democratic; for, as we have just seen, even in aristocracies it can happen that democratic tastes influence the stage. But when the spirit of aristocracy alone rules the theater, that demonstrates invincibly that the whole society is aristocratic, and you can boldly conclude that this same learned and lettered class that directs authors commands citizens and leads public affairs.

It is very rare that the refined tastes and haughty tendencies of the aristocracy, when it governs the theater, do not lead it to make a choice, so the speak, in human nature. Certain social conditions interest it principally, and it is pleased to find them portrayed on the stage; certain virtues, and even certain vices, seem to the aristocracy to merit more particularly being reproduced on stage: it accepts the portrayal of these while it removes all the others from its sight. In the theater, as elsewhere, it only wants to find great lords, and it is moved only by kings. It is the same for styles. An aristocracy willingly imposes certain ways of speaking on authors; it wants all to be said with this tone.

The theater therefore often happens to portray only one of the dimensions of man, or even sometimes to represent what is not found in human nature; it rises above human nature and leaves it behind.

In democratic societies spectators do not have such preferences, and they rarely exhibit similar antipathies; they love to find on stage the confused mixture of conditions, of sentiments and ideas that they find before their eyes. The theater becomes more striking, more popular and more true.

Sometimes, however, those who write for the theater in democracies also go beyond human nature, but in another way than their precursors. By dint of wanting to reproduce minutely the small singularities of the present

---

c. In the margin of a first version that is found in the *rubish* of the chapter:
"Shakespeare, Addison: There where authority does not deign to interfere in the theater" (*Rubish*, 1).

moment and the particular physiognomy of certain men, they forget to relate the general features of the species.

When the democratic classes rule the theater, they introduce as much liberty in the manner of treating the subject as in the very choice of this subject.

The love of the theater being, of all literary tastes, the one most natural to democratic peoples, the number of authors and that of spectators, like that of the performances, increases constantly among these peoples. Such a multitude, composed of such diverse elements and spread over so many different places, cannot accept the same rules and be subject to the same laws. No agreement is possible among very numerous judges who do not know where to meet; each separately makes his judgment. If the effect of democracy is in general to make literary rules and conventions doubtful, in the theater it abolishes them entirely, in order to substitute only the caprice of each author and each public.

It is equally in the theater above all that what I have already said elsewhere in a general way concerning style and art in democratic literatures is revealed. When you read the criticism brought forth by the dramatic works of the century of Louis XIV, you are surprised to see the great esteem of the public for verisimilitude, and the importance that it placed on the fact that a man, remaining always true to himself, did nothing that could not be easily explained and understood. It is equally surprising how much value was then attached to the forms of language and what small quarrels over words were made with dramatic authors.

It seems that the men of the century of Louis XIV attached a very exaggerated value to these details, which are noticed in the study but that elude the stage.[d] For, after all, the principal object of a play is to be presented, and its first merit is to stir emotion. That came from the fact that the spectators of this period were at the same time the readers. Leaving the

---

d. "<What made the men of the century of Louis XIV want to find only princes and kings on the tragic stage was a sentiment analogous to that which made Alexander say, when requested to appear at the Olympic games: I would willingly go if only kings raced there>" (*Rubish,* 1). Tocqueville here takes up a known episode, drawn from the *Life of Alexander* of Plutarch.

performance, they waited at home for the writer, in order to complete their judgment of him.

In democracies, you listen to plays, but you do not read them. Most of those who attend stage plays are not seeking the pleasures of the mind, but the intense emotions of the heart. They are not waiting to find a work of literature, but a spectacle, and provided that the author speaks the language of the country correctly enough to make himself understood and that the characters excite curiosity and awaken sympathy, they are content; without asking anything more of the fiction, they immediately reenter the real world. So style there is less necessary; for on the stage observation of these rules escapes more and more.

As for verisimilitudes, it is impossible to be often new, unexpected, rapid, while remaining faithful to them. So they are neglected, and the public pardons it. You can count on the fact that they will not worry about the roads you have led them along, if you lead them finally to an object that touches them. They will never reproach you for having moved them in spite of the rules.

[Two things must be clearly distinguished.

Complicated intrigues, forced effects, improbability are often due to scorn for art and sometimes to ignorance of it. These faults are found in all theaters that are beginning, and for this reason aristocratic theaters have often provided an example of them, because it is ordinarily aristocracy that leads the youthful period of peoples. The oddities, coarseness and extravagance that are sometimes found in Lope de Vega and in Shakespeare[e] do not prove that these great men followed the natural taste of the aristocracy, but only that they were the first to write for it.[f] Their genius subsequently perpetuated their errors.[g] When a great dramatic author does not purge the stage of the vices that he finds there, he fixes them

e. The *rubish* also names Calderón.

f. "Memoir of Grimm. Deep discussion of what there is of the improbable" (*Rubish,* 1). It perhaps concerns Friedrich M. Grimm, *Nouveaux mémoires secrets et inédits historiques, politiques, anecdotiques et littéraires* . . . , (Paris: Lerouge-Wolf, 1834), 2 vols.

g. Variant in the *rubish:* "This is seen in the renaissance of letters among all peoples even aristocracies. See Lope de Vega, Shakespeare and the French before Corneille. When a great genius . . ." (*Rubish,* 1).

there, and all those who follow imitate those courtiers of Alexander who found it easier to tilt their heads to the side like their master than to conquer Asia.

Democratic writers know in general the conventions of the stage, and the rules of dramatic art, but often they willingly neglect them in order to go faster or to strike more forcefully.]

The Americans bring to full light the different instincts that I have just depicted, when they go to the theater.[h] But it must be recognized that there is still only a small number of them who go. Although spectators and spectacles have prodigiously increased since forty years ago in the United States, the population still goes to this type of amusement only with extreme reticence.

That is due to particular causes that the reader already knows and that it is sufficient to recall to him in two words.

The Puritans, who founded the American republics, were not only enemies of pleasure; they professed in addition an entirely special horror of the theater. They considered it as an abominable diversion, and as long as their spirit reigned unrivaled, dramatic presentations were absolutely unknown among them. These opinions of the first fathers of the colony left profound traces in the mind of their descendants.

The extreme regularity of habits and the great rigidity of mores that are seen in the United States, moreover, have not been very favorable to the development of theatrical art until now.

There are no subjects for drama in a country that has not witnessed great political catastrophes[j] and where love always leads by a direct and easy road to marriage. Men who use every day of the week for making

h. I am moreover obliged to admit, and perhaps it is proper to do so, that in this matter America cannot serve as an example. By what is happening in the United States, it is difficult to judge the direction that the American democracy would give to theatrical art, since the American democracy has so to speak no theaters. Forty years ago I do not think that you would ever have attended a dramatic presentation in this part of the New World. Since then halls for spectacles [v: theaters] have been built in two or three great cities of the Union, but these places of pleasure are closed part of the year and during the rest of the time the native population frequents them little (*Rubish,* 1). Cf. Beaumont, *Marie,* I, pp. 394–96.

j. The manuscript reads: "public catastrophes."

their fortune and Sunday for praying to God do not lend themselves to the comic muse.

A single fact suffices to show that the theater is not very popular in the United States.

The Americans, whose laws authorize freedom and even license of speech in everything, have nonetheless subjected dramatic authors to a kind of censorship.[k] Theatrical presentations can only take place when the administrators of the town allow them. This demonstrates clearly that peoples are like individuals. They give themselves without caution to their principal passions, and then they are very careful not to yield to the impetus of tastes that they do not have.

There is no portion of literature that is tied by tighter and more numerous bonds to the current state of society than the theater.

The theater of one period can never suit the following period if, between the two, an important revolution has changed mores and laws.

The great writers of another century are still studied. But plays written for another public are no longer attended. Dramatic authors of past time live only in books.

The traditional taste of a few men, vanity, fashion, the genius of an actor can for a time sustain or bring back an aristocratic theater within a democracy; but soon it collapses by itself. It is not overthrown; it is abandoned.

k. With a note in the *rubish:* "Ask new clarifications from Niles" (*Rubish,* 1).

CHAPTER 20[a]

Of Some Tendencies Particular to Historians in Democratic Centuries[b]

Historians who write in aristocratic centuries ordinarily make all events depend on the particular will and the mood of certain men, and they readily link the most important revolutions to the slightest accidents. They wisely make the smallest causes stand out, and often they do not see the greatest ones.

Historians who live in democratic centuries show completely opposite tendencies.

Most of them attribute to the individual almost no influence on the destiny of the species, or to citizens on the fate of the people. But, in return, they give great general causes to all the small particular facts. [In their eyes,

---

a. 1. Aristocratic historians attribute all events to a few men. Democratic historians are led to deny the particular influence of men on the destiny of the species and of the people and to search only for general causes. There is exaggeration on both sides. In all events, one part must be attributed to general facts and another to particular influences. But the relationship varies depending on the times. General facts explain more things in democratic centuries and particular influences fewer.

2. Democratic historians are led not only to attribute each fact to a great cause, but also to link facts together and to produce historical systems.

3. Not only are they inclined to contest the power of individuals to lead peoples, but they are easily led to contest the ability of peoples to modify their destinies by themselves and they subject them to a sort of blind fatality (YTC, CVf, p. 21).

One of the titles of the chapter in the *rubish* is: INFLUENCE OF EQUALITY OF CONDITIONS ON THE MANNER OF ENVISAGING AND WRITING HISTORY.

b. On the jacket of the manuscript, in pencil: "Historians of antiquity did not treat history like Mignet and company."

all events are linked together by a tight and necessary chain, and therefore they sometimes end up by denying nations control over themselves and by contesting the liberty of having been able to do what they did.]ᶜ These contrasting tendencies can be explained.

When historians in aristocratic centuries cast their eyes on the world theater, they notice first of all a very small number of principal actors who lead the whole play. These great characters, who keep themselves at the front of the stage, stop their view and hold it; while they apply themselves to uncovering the secret motives that make the latter act and speak, they forget the rest.

The importance of the things that they see a few men do gives them an exaggerated idea of the influence that one man is able to exercise, and naturally disposes them to believe that you must always go back to the particular action of an individual to explain the movements of the crowd.

When, on the contrary, all citizens are independent of each other, and when each one of them is weak, you do not discover any one of them who exercises a very great or, above all, a very enduring power over the mass. At first view, individuals seem absolutely powerless over the mass, and you would say that society moves all by itself by the free and spontaneous participation of all the men who compose it.ᵈ

That naturally leads the human mind to search for the general reason

---

c. In the margin: "<Perhaps to delete. This relates only to the last idea of the chapter.>" Cf. p. 858.

A note in the *Rubish* explains: "This chapter is very closely linked to that on *general ideas*. It must be *combined* there or be kept very *separate* from it" (*Rubish*, 1).

d. "Be careful while treating this subject about wanting to portray *history* and not *historians*, what is happening in the world and not the *manner in which historians* explain it" (*Rubish*, 1).

In the article "Movement of the French Press in 1836," *Revue des deux mondes*, 4th series, X, 1837, pp. 453–98, which Tocqueville utilized for the draft of chapter 2, you find similar affirmations. "It is no longer only a matter," you read on p. 464, "as in the past, of putting in the forefront the figures of great men and of moving into the background the vague and unappreciated action of the masses. Our century, which wants to know everything and which doubts everything, seems to prefer facts and proofs to these striking tableaux in which the art of composition and the wisdom of judgments testify to the power of the writer better than the clutter of citations."

that has been able to strike so many minds all at once in this way and turn them simultaneously in the same direction.[e]

I am very persuaded that, among democratic nations themselves, the genius, the vices or the virtues of certain individuals delay or precipitate the natural course of the destiny of the people; but these sorts of fortuitous and secondary causes are infinitely more varied, more hidden, more complicated, less powerful, and consequently more difficult to disentangle and to trace in times of equality than in the centuries of aristocracy, when it is only a matter of analyzing, amid general facts, the particular action of a single man or of a few men.[f]

The historian soon becomes tired of such a work; his mind becomes lost amid this labyrinth, and, not able to succeed in seeing clearly and in bringing sufficiently to light individual influences, he denies them. He prefers to speak to us about the nature of races, about the physical constitution of a country, or about the spirit of civilization [<great words that I cannot hear said without involuntarily recalling the abhorrence of a vacuum that was

---

e. "<That necessarily leads their minds back toward the search for general causes, about which you always have at least something to say, and often they content themselves with the first one they find>" (*Rubish*, 1).

f. There are two ideas in this chapter which must not be confused.

A people can have its destiny modified or changed by the accidental influence of a powerful man, like Napoleon, I suppose.

Or, as well, by an accident due to chance such as a plague, the loss of a battle . . .

You can refuse to believe in the influence of individuals and believe in that of accidents.

In democratic centuries, the influence of *individuals* is infinitely smaller than in aristocratic centuries, but the influence of *accidents* is not less.

Now, the modern historical system consists of saying not only that individuals cannot modify .-.-.-.- peoples, but also that *accidents* cannot do so. So that the nature of some battle, for example, would not have been able definitively to prevent some nation from succumbing, because there was a sequence of old causes that destined it invincibly to perish.

It is clear that all that I say in the preceding chapter applies to *individuals* and not to *accidents*. This is exaggerated because, when you go back to the origin of accidents, you almost always arrive at *individual* action" (*Rubish*, 1).

attributed to nature before the heaviness of air was discovered>]. That shortens his work, and, at less cost, better satisfies the reader.[g]

M. de Lafayette said somewhere in his *Mémoires*[h] that the exaggerated system of general causes brought marvelous consolations to mediocre public men. I add that it gives admirable consolations to mediocre historians. It always provides them with a few great reasons that promptly pull them through at the most difficult point in their book, and it favors the weakness or laziness of their minds, all the while honoring its depth.

For me, I think that there is no period when one part of the events of this world must not be attributed to very general facts, and another to very particular influences. These two causes are always found; only their relationship differs. General facts explain more things in democratic centuries than in aristocratic centuries, and particular influences fewer. In times of aristocracy, it is the opposite; particular influences are stronger, and general causes are weaker, as long as you do not consider as a general cause the very fact of inequality of conditions, which allows a few individuals to thwart the natural tendencies of all the others.

So historians who try to portray what is happening in democratic societies are right to give a large role to general causes and to apply themselves principally to discovering them; but they are wrong to deny entirely the particular action of individuals, because it is difficult to find and to follow

g. In the margin: "<This is not in perfect agreement with what precedes and draws the mind in another direction. What I say above is that historians prefer looking for general causes than for particular facts. What I say here is that they are content with bad general reasons, which is another idea. My comparison applies only to the last one, for the *heaviness of air* is a general cause, as well as the *abhorrence of a vacuum*. Perhaps delete.>"

h. Marquis de Lafayette, *Mémoires, correspondance et manuscrits du général Lafayette* (Paris: H. Fournier aîné, 1837–1838), 6 vols. In May 1837, Tocqueville received from Corcelle, who was the editor, the first three volumes of this work. It is probable that the author, who did not sympathize with the general, did not read his memoirs (we know that he considered him to be a well-intentioned man but with a *mediocre mind*), and that he found this quotation in the second part of the review done by Sainte-Beuve (*Revue des deux mondes*, 4th series, 15, 1838, pp. 355–81, in which the same quotation appears on page 359).

it [and to content themselves often with great words when great causes elude them].

Not only are historians who live in democratic centuries drawn to giving a great cause to each fact, but also they are led to linking facts and making a system emerge.

In aristocratic centuries, since the attention of historians is diverted at every moment toward individuals, the sequence of events escapes them, or rather they do not believe in such a sequence. The thread of history seems to them broken at every instant by the passage of a man.

In democratic centuries, on the contrary, the historian, seeing far fewer actors and many more actions, can easily establish a relationship and a methodical order among them.

Ancient literature, which has left us such beautiful histories, offers not a single great historical system, while the most miserable modern literatures are swarming with them. It seems that ancient historians did not make enough use of these general theories that our historians are always ready to abuse.

Those who write in democratic centuries have another, more dangerous tendency.

When the trace of the action of individuals or nations becomes lost, it often happens that you see the world move without uncovering the motor. Since it becomes very difficult to see and to analyze the reasons that, acting separately on the will of each citizen, end by producing the movement of the people, you are tempted to believe that the movement is not voluntary and that societies, without knowing it, obey a superior force that dominates them.

Even if you should discover on earth the general fact that directs the particular will of all individuals, that does not save human liberty. A cause vast enough to be applied at the same time to millions of men, and strong enough to bend all of them in the same direction, easily seems irresistible; after seeing that you yielded to it, you are very close to believing that it could not be resisted.

So historians who live in democratic times not only deny to a few citizens the power to act on the destiny of the people, they also take away from peoples themselves the ability to modify their own fate, and subject them either to an inflexible providence or to a sort of blind fatality. According to these historians, each nation is invincibly tied, by its position, its origin, its antecedents, its nature, to a certain destiny that all its efforts cannot change. They make the generations stand together with each other, and, going back in this way, from age to age and from necessary events to necessary events, to the origin of the world, they make a tight and immense chain that envelops the entire human species and binds it.

It is not enough for them to show how facts happened; they like as well to reveal that it could not have happened otherwise. They consider a nation that has reached a certain place in its history, and assert that it has been forced to follow the road that led it there. That is easier than teaching what it could have done to take a better route.[j]

It seems, while reading the historians of aristocratic ages and particularly those of antiquity, that, in order to become master of his fate and govern his fellows, man has only to know how to control himself. You would say, while surveying the histories written in our time, that man can do nothing, either for himself or around him. The historians of antiquity taught how to command; those of our days scarcely teach anything except how to obey. In their writings, the author often appears great, but humanity is always small.

If this doctrine of fatality, which has so many attractions for those who write history in democratic times, by passing from the writers to their readers, in this way penetrated the entire mass of citizens and took hold of the public mind, you can predict that it would soon paralyze the movement of new societies and would reduce Christians to Turks.[k]

I will say, moreover, that such a doctrine is particularly dangerous in this period in which we live; our contemporaries are all too inclined to doubt free will, because each of them feels limited on all sides by his weakness,

j. "I believe that in nearly each instant of their existence nations, like men, are free to modify their fate" (*Rubish*, 1).

k. "Show how the idea of the powerlessness of individuals over the mass leads them to the idea of the powerlessness of the mass over itself and thus leads them to the fatality of the Moslems" (*Rubish*, 1).

but they still readily grant strength and independence to men gathered in a social body. Care must be taken not to obscure this idea, for it is a matter of lifting up souls and not finally demoralizing them.[m]

m. In the *rubish* you find this small chapter on religious eloquence, deleted in the final version:

RELIGIOUS ELOQUENCE OR PREACHING.

.-.-.-.-.- the influence that democracy exercises on works of the human mind, it would probably have been enough for me to reveal how it modifies the language of the pulpit.

[In the margin: Perhaps and even probably delete this chapter. It cannot be applied to America. In America, by exception, religious beliefs are very firm and the language of priests is not a plea in favor of Christianity.]

There is nothing so little variable by their nature as religions and it cannot be otherwise. The true religion rests on absolute truth; other religions claim to be supported by it; so all are immobile, and it is easier to destroy them than to modify them.

This immobility extends to everything that is related to religion no matter how distantly. There is no religious custom so unimportant that it is not more difficult to change [v: destroy] than the constitution of a people.

So when any cause whatsoever leads men to vary style and method in holy things, be sure that this is only one of the last effects of a much more general revolution and that the same cause had already long ago changed the manner of treating all other subjects.

.-.-.-.- Catholic and I enter a church. I see the priest mounting the steps of the pulpit. He is young. He wears priestly vestments, but beyond that there is already nothing of the traditional or of the conventional in his bearing, in his gestures, or in his voice. He doesn't say "My brothers," but "Sirs." He doesn't recite, but he improvises. He does not talk about the growing pain that our sins cause him; our good works do not fill him with ineffable joy. He engages his listener hand to hand, and armed like him, takes him on. He feels that it is no longer a matter of touching us, but of convincing us. He addresses himself not to faith, but to reason; he doesn't impose belief, he discusses it and wants to have it freely accepted. He does not go to search for arguments in the old arsenal of scholastic theology, in the writings of the Doctors, any more than in the decrees of the Popes and the decisions of the Councils. He borrows his proofs from secular science; he draws his comparisons from everyday things; he bases himself on the most general, the clearest and most elementary truths [v: notions] of human philosophy.

He cites the poets and orators of today almost as much as the Fathers of the Church. Rarely does it happen that he speaks Latin, and I cannot prevent myself from suspecting that the *Kyrie Eleison* of the Mass is all the Greek he knows.

Sometimes disorganized, incorrect, incomplete, he is nearly always original, brilliant, unexpected, above all fruitful. Give up reading him, but go to hear him.

If, back in the solitude of your dwelling, you happen to compare the man whom you have just heard with the great Christian orators of past centuries, you will discover, not without terror, what the strange power that moves the world is able to do; and you will understand that democracy, after remaking in passing all the ephemeral [v: changing] institutions of men, finally reaches the things most immobile by their nature, and that, not able to change the substance of Christianity, which is eternal, it at least modifies the language and the form (*Rubish,* 1).

CHAPTER 21[a]

Of Parliamentary Eloquence in the United States[b]

a. 1. The discussions of the English Parliament are led by only a few men, which makes them clear, plain and concise. Why it is not the same in Congress.

1. In aristocratic countries, the members of the legislature study the parliamentary art in advance and for a longer time. This reason is good, but insufficient.

2. The habit of hierarchy and subordination that men have in aristocratic society follows them into the assembly. It is not the same in democratic countries.

3. Aristocratic deputies, all being of considerable importance by themselves, are easily consoled about not playing a role in the assembly and do not want a mediocre one. Democratic deputies have in the country only the rank that they have in the assembly; that necessarily pushes them ahead.

4. They are, moreover, pushed to speak by the voters; and as they depend much more on the voters, they yield to them on this point.

2. That is the petty side of democratic discussions. Here is the great one.

1. Since there are no distinct classes, orators always speak to and about the whole nation.

2. Since they cannot rely on the (illegible word) the privileges of wealth, of corps, or of persons, they are obliged to go back to the general truths provided by the examination of human nature. That gives a great character of grandeur to their eloquence and pushes its effects to the furthest ends of the earth (YTC, CVf, pp. 21–23).

b. There would be two subjects that you could still treat here:

1. The first would consist of finding out if *eloquence* strictly speaking is as natural to democratic assemblies as to others. I do not think so.

2. Why the reports of the Presidents to Congress have always been, until now, so simple, so clear, so noble. This would be more appropriate to the subject" (*Rubish,* 1).

On the first page of a draft of the chapter: "This chapter is an attempt. It probably must be deleted" (*Rubish,* 1). Tocqueville adds in another place: "I believe that nothing must be said about this subject. Since eloquence of the pulpit, which is the most conventional, is modified by democracy, the mind is sufficiently struck by the power of the latter on all types of eloquence" (*Rubish,* 1).

Among aristocratic peoples all men stand together and depend on each other; among all men there is a hierarchical bond by the aid of which each one can be kept in his place and the whole body can be kept in obedience. Something analogous is always found within the political assemblies of these peoples. Parties there line up naturally behind certain leaders, whom they obey by a kind of instinct that is only the result of habits contracted elsewhere. They bring to the small society of the assembly the mores of the larger society.

[In the public assemblies of aristocratic nations there are only a few men who act as spokesmen. All the others assent and keep quiet. Orators speak only when something is useful to the party. They say only what can serve the general interests of the party and they do not needlessly repeat what has already been said. The discussion is clear, rapid and concise.

Breadth and depth are often lacking in the *discussions* of the Parliament of England, but the debate is almost always conducted admirably and speeches are very pertinent to the subject. ≠It is not always so in Congress.≠

I at first believed that this way of treating public affairs came from the long use that the English have of parliamentary life. But it must be clearly admitted that it is due to some other cause, since the Americans, with the same experience, do not follow the same method.

In the democratic countries most accustomed to the representative regime, it often happens that a great number of those who are part of the assemblies have not sufficiently reflected in advance about the suitable way to act there. The reason is that among these peoples public life is rarely a career. You go there by chance; you soon depart. It is a road that you cross and that you do not follow. So to it you bring your natural enlightenment, and not an acquired knowledge.

In aristocratic countries that have had assemblies for a long time, it is not the same. Since there is only a small number of men who can enter national councils, those men apply themselves to becoming part of those councils and study in advance the art of how to conduct themselves there. Since the same men are part of the legislature over a long period of time, they have the time to recognize the methods that best serve the conduct of affairs, and they are always numerous enough to force the new arrivals to conform.

This reason seems good, but it does [not (ed.)] suffice to explain the difference that is noticeable here between the Americans and the English. In the United States, deliberative bodies are so numerous and public assemblies so multiplied that there is no man, who has reached maturity, who has not very often had the occasion to enter into some gathering of this type and who has not been able to see the game. If there are no classes in America that are specially destined for public affairs, all classes get actively involved and constantly think about them. Almost all of even those who remain in private life thus receive a political education. So you must look for a more general and deeper cause than the one indicated above.

Not only do the Americans not always have very precise notions about the parliamentary art, but also they are more strongly inclined to violate the rules of that art when they know them.]

In democratic countries, a great number of citizens often happen to head toward the same point; but each one marches or at least professes to march there only by himself. Accustomed not to regulate his movements except according to his personal impulses, he yields with difficulty to receiving his rules from outside. This taste for and this practice of independence follow him into national councils. If he agrees to associate himself with others for the pursuit of the same plan, he at least wants to remain master of his own way of cooperating in the common success.

That is why, in democratic countries, parties so impatiently endure someone leading them and appear subordinate only when the danger is very great. Even so, the authority of leaders, which in these circumstances can go as far as making parties act and speak, almost never extends to the power of making parties keep quiet.

Among aristocratic peoples, the members of political assemblies are at the same time members of the aristocracy. Each one of them possesses by himself a high and stable rank, and the place that he occupies in the assembly is often less important in his eyes than the one that he fills in the country. That consoles him for not playing a role in the discussion of public affairs, and disposes him not to seek a mediocre role with too much ardor.

In America, it ordinarily happens that the deputy amounts to something only by his position in the assembly. So he is constantly tormented by the need to gain importance, and he feels a petulant desire to bring his ideas fully to light every moment.[c]

He is pushed in this direction not only by his vanity, but also by that of his constituents and by the continual necessity to please them.

Among aristocratic peoples, the member of the legislature rarely has a narrow dependence on voters; for them he is often in some way a necessary representative; sometimes he holds them in a narrow dependency, and if they come finally to refuse him their vote, he easily has himself appointed elsewhere; or, renouncing a political career, he shuts himself up in an idleness that still has splendor.

In a democratic country, like the United States, the deputy hardly ever has an enduring hold on the mind of his constituents. However small the electoral body, democratic instability makes it change face constantly. So it must be captivated every day. He is never sure of them; and if they abandon him, he is immediately without resources; for he does not naturally have a position elevated enough to be easily noticed by those who are not nearby; and, in the complete independence in which citizens live, he cannot hope that his friends or the government will easily impose him on an electoral body that will not know him. So it is in the district that he represents that all the seeds of his fortune are sown; it is from this corner of the earth that he must emerge in order to rise to command the people and to influence the destinies of the world.

Thus, it is natural that, in democratic countries, the members of political assemblies think more about their constituents than about their party, while in aristocracies, they attend more to their party than to their constituents.[d]

c. I do not believe, moreover, that what happens on this point in the United States indicates a general law applicable to all democracies. I believe that there exists at the bottom of the soul of a people a secret disposition that leads it to keep the most capable away from power when it can do so without danger. The people, moreover, when it leads affairs, is like kings who, Montesquieu says, always imagine that their courtiers are their best subjects. Peoples are princes in this. But I believe that this fatal tendency can be combatted naturally by circumstances or artificially by laws, and in America both favor it (*Rubish*, 1).

d. Add that the member of a democratic legislature, just as he does not have the natural taste for parliamentary discipline, does not have a particular interest in sub-

Now, what must be said to please voters is not always what would be suitable for serving well the political opinion that they profess.

The general interest of a party is often that the deputy who is a member never speak about the great public affairs that he understands badly; that he speak little about the small affairs that would hinder the march of the great one; and most often finally, that he keep completely quiet. To maintain silence is the most useful service that a mediocre speaker can render to public matters.

But this is not the way that the voters understand it.

The population of a district charges a citizen to take part in the government of the State, because it has conceived a very grand idea of his merit. Since men appear greater in proportion to being surrounded by smaller objects, it may be believed that the rarer the talents among those represented, the higher the opinion that will be held about the representative. So it often happens that the less the voters have to expect from their deputy, the more they will hope from him; and, however incompetent he may be, they cannot fail to require from him signal efforts that correspond to the rank that they give him.

Apart from the legislator of the State, the voters see also in their representative the natural protector of the district in the legislature; they are not even far from considering him as the agent of each one of those who elected him, and they imagine that he will display no less ardor insisting on their particular interests than on those of the country.

Thus, the voters hold it as certain in advance that the deputy they will choose will be an orator; that he will speak often if he can, and that, in the case where he would have to limit himself, he will at least try hard in his

---

mitting himself to it. In aristocracies, the leaders of parties are often men powerful in themselves, or men who have easily at their disposal all of the party forces. They have in their hands great means to serve and to harm. It frequently happens, for example, that they are in a position to impose their choice on the voters. The party itself, hierarchically organized in the society as in the assembly, can force all the members to cooperate toward a general end that it sets.

In democracies, on the contrary, parties are not better organized outside the assemblies than within. Within parties, there exists a common will to act, but not a government that directs it. So the deputy has truly speaking nothing either to hope or to fear except from his constituents (*Rubish*, 1).

rare speeches to include the examination of all the great affairs of the State along with the account of all the petty grievances that they themselves have complained about; so that, not able to appear often, he shows on each occasion that he knows what to do, and, instead of spouting forth incessantly, he every now and then compresses his remarks entirely into a small scope, providing in this way a kind of brilliant and complete summary of his constituents and of himself. For this price, they promise their next votes.

This pushes into despair honest, mediocre men who, knowing themselves, would not have appeared on their own. The deputy, carried away in this way, speaks up to the great distress of his friends, and, throwing himself imprudently into the middle of the most celebrated orators, he muddles the debate and tires the assembly.

All the laws that tend to make the elected more dependent on the voter therefore modify not only the conduct of the legislators, as I noted elsewhere, but also their language. They influence at the very same time public affairs and the manner of speaking about them.

[I think as well that the more the electoral body is divided into small parts, the more discussions will become droning within the legislative body. You can count on the fact that such a system will fill the assembly with mediocre men[*] and that all the mediocre men whom it sends there will make as many efforts to appear as if they were superior men.]

[*]. Note:

This effect is explained by two very perceptible reasons.

The smaller the electoral district, the more limited is the view of the voter and the more his good choice depends on the chance birth of a capable man near him.

So small electoral circumscriptions will necessarily produce a crowd of mediocre representatives, for the superior men of a nation are not spread equally over the different points of its surface.

The smallness of the electoral body will, moreover, very often prevent voters from choosing those men when by chance they are found near them.

When voters are very numerous and spread over a great area, there is only a small number of them who can have personal relationships with the man they choose, and they elect him because of the merit attributed to him. When they are very few in number, they readily name him because of the friendship that they have for him. The election becomes always an affair of a coterie and often of a family. In an election of this type the superior man loses all of his natural advantages. He can scarcely aspire to stay equal.

There is, so to speak, not a member of Congress who agrees to return home without having given at least one speech, or who bears being interrupted before he is able to include within the limits of his harangue everything that can be said about what is useful to the twenty-four states that compose the Union, and especially to the district he represents. So he puts successively before the minds of his listeners great general truths that he often does not notice himself and that he points out only in a confused way, and small highly subtle particularities that he does not find and explain very easily. Consequently, it often happens that, within this great body, discussion becomes vague and muddled, and it seems to crawl toward the goal that is proposed rather than marching toward it.

Something analogous will always be revealed, I believe, in the public assemblies of democracies.

Happy circumstances and good laws could succeed in drawing to the legislature of a democratic people men much more noteworthy than those who are sent by the Americans to Congress; but you will never prevent the mediocre men who are found in it from putting themselves on public display, smugly and on all sides.

The evil does not appear entirely curable to me, because it is due not only to the regulations of the assembly, but also to its constitution and even to that of the country.

The inhabitants of the United States seem themselves to consider the matter from this point of view, and they testify to their long practice of parliamentary life not by abstaining from bad speeches, but by subjecting themselves courageously to hearing them. They resign themselves to hearing them as if to an evil that experience had made them recognize as inevitable.

[<Some insist that sometimes they are sleeping, but they never grumble.>]

We have shown the petty side of political discussions in democracies; let us reveal the great one.

In YTC, CVk, 1, p. 82, next to this fragment, you find this note: "This should probably be entirely deleted. Constant harping on electoral matters./
"I would in fact delete that.
"To delete."

What has happened for the past one hundred fifty years in the Parliament of England has never caused a great stir outside; the ideas and sentiments expressed by orators have never found much sympathy among the very peoples who found themselves placed closest to the great theater of British liberty, while, from the moment when the first debates took place in the small colonial assemblies of America in the period of the revolution, Europe was moved.[e]

That was due not only to particular and fortuitous circumstances, but also to general and lasting causes.

I see nothing more admirable or more powerful than a great orator discussing great affairs within a democratic assembly. Since there is never a class that has its representatives in charge of upholding its interests, it is always to the whole nation, and in the name of the whole nation that they speak.[f] That enlarges thought and elevates language.[g]

Since precedents there have little sway; since there are no more privileges linked to certain properties or rights inherent to certain bodies or certain men, the mind is forced to go back to general truths drawn from human nature, in order to treat the particular affairs that concern it. Out of that

e. "The English orators of the last century constantly quoted Latin and even Greek at the rostrum.

"Their sons of America quote only Shakespeare, the democratic author par excellence" (*Rubish*, 1).

f. The political discussions of a small democratic people cause a stir in the entire universe. Not only because other peoples, also turning toward democracy, have analogous interests, but also because the political discussions of a democratic people, however small it may be, always have a character of generality that makes them interesting to the human species. They talk about man in general and treat rights that he holds by his nature, which is the same everywhere.

Among aristocratic peoples it is almost always a question of the particular rights of a class, which interests only this class or at most the people among whom the class is found.

This explains the influence of the French revolution even apart from the state of Europe, and in contrast, the slight stir caused by the debates of the English Parliament (*Rubish*, 1).

g. In the margin: "≠I would say something analogous about our time and about ourselves. The debates of our chambers immediately cause a stir in the entire universe and agitate all classes in each country.≠"

is born, in the political discussions of a democratic people, however small it may be, a character of generality that often makes those discussions captivating to the human species. All men are interested in them because it is a question of man, who is everywhere the same.

Among the greatest aristocratic peoples, on the contrary, the most general questions are almost always dealt with by a few particular reasons drawn from the customs of a period or from the rights of a class; this interests only the class in question, or at most the people among whom this class is found.

It is to this cause as much as to the grandeur of the French nation, and to the favorable dispositions of the peoples who hear it, that you must attribute the great effect that our political discussions sometimes produce in the world.

Our orators often speak to all men, even when they are only addressing their fellow citizens.[h]

h. In the *Rubish,* after the rough drafts of these chapters, you find a jacket with these notes:

> [At the head: Influence of equality on education./
> There would have been many things to say about this subject, but I have already so many things in the book, that this one must, I believe, be left aside.]
> Influence of democracy on the education of men or rather their instruction is a necessary chapter. The useful and practical direction that it gives, the change in methods that it brings about. The study of ancient languages, theoretical sciences, speculative studies that they subordinate to other studies.
> To place somewhere in the chapter on *ideas.*
> [To the side: To put a small chapter VI before the large chapter on sciences, literature and the arts, which must be the VIIth.] (*Rubish,* 1).

A draft contains, for the chapter on education, the following plan:

> [As title on the jacket] Influence of democracy on ideas./
> Of academic institutions under democracy.
> An academy having the purpose of keeping minds on a certain path, of imposing a method on them, is contrary to the genius of democracy; it is an aristocratic institution.
> An academy having the goal of making the men who apply themselves to the arts or to the sciences famous and giving them at State expense the comfort and leisure that the democratic social state often denies to them, is an institution that can be not to the taste of a democratic nation, but one that is never contrary to and can some-

times be necessary to the existence of a democracy. It is an eminently democratic institution.

[Inside, on a page] Of the need for paid learned bodies in democracies. This need increases as peoples turn toward democracy.

This truth understood with difficulty by the democracy. Opposite natural inclination that you must combat. The Americans give way to it.

Effect of this: science left to the ordinary encouragement that democracy can provide, that is to say that the men who are working produce only applications, no theories.

[To the side: Ask Monsieur Biot for ideas.]

That the English set about badly to encourage the sciences. They give easy and honorable rest in the hope of work. These things must be proposed as the fruit of work.

Elsewhere: "Of Education in the United States and in democratic countries in general.

"Perhaps I should begin by portraying man in infancy and in the family before leading him to manhood.

"The trouble with this plan is that egoism dominates even the primordial relations" (YTC, CVa, pp. 2–3). Jean-Baptiste Biot, scientist and political writer of legitimist tendencies, was a professor at the Collège de France. On Tocqueville and the question of education after *Democracy,* see Edward Gargan, "The Silence of Tocqueville on Education," *Historical Reflections,* 7, 1980, pp. 565–75.

SECOND PART

Influence of Democracy on the Sentiments of the Americans[a]

a. [As the title] Influence of democracy on sentiments, tastes, or mores./

Ideas that must never be entirely lost from view.

After making known each flaw or each quality inherent in democracy, try to point out with as much *precision* as possible the means that can be taken to attenuate the first and to develop the second. *Example.* Men in democracies are naturally led to concentrate on their interests. To draw them away from their interests as much as possible, to spiritualize them as much as possible, and finally if possible to connect and merge particular interest and general interest, so that you scarcely know how to distinguish the one from the other.

That is the political side of the work that must never be allowed to be entirely lost from view.

But do not do that in a monotonous and tiring way, for fear of boredom, or in too practical and too detailed a way, for fear of leaving myself open to criticism.

Reserve a part of these things for the *introduction of the final chapter* (YTC, CVa, pp. 31–32).

On the back of the jacket of the *Rubish* that contains the drafts of the part on material enjoyments and that bears number X:

First chapters on sentiments./
First system./
Democracy leads men toward the taste for material well-being.
It leads them to commerce, industry, to everything that is produced quickly.
It gives birth to an immoderate desire for happiness in this world.
It favors restlessness of the heart.
Here perhaps spirit of religion (*Rubish*, 1).

871

CHAPTER I[a]

Why Democratic Peoples Show a
More Ardent and More Enduring Love
for Equality Than for Liberty[b]

a. This chapter, one of the best known of *Democracy,* is not found in the manuscript, where you pass directly from the previous chapter (number 19) to the one on individualism (number 20). Nor does it appear in notebook CVf.

A first version of it exists in pages 1 to 14 of notebook CVk, 2. The inclusion in the final version is due to the insistence of Louis de Kergorlay, as is witnessed by this note on the jacket that contains it:

L[ouis (ed.)]. thinks that this piece must *absolutely* appear in the work, either in the current form or by transporting the ideas elsewhere. I believe in fact that he is right. I see that it could be introduced in this way into the present chapter, which would then be divided into three principal ideas:

1. How equality gives the idea and the taste for political liberty.

2. How in the centuries of equality men are much less attached to being free than to remaining equal.

3. How equality suggests ideas and tastes to them that can make them lose liberty and lead them to servitude.

In this way the piece would remain more or less as it is. It would only have to be concluded differently and in such a way as to fit into the general idea of the chapter, more or less like this:

"Thus, love of liberty cannot be the principal passion of men during democratic centuries and it occupies in their heart only the space left for it by another passion."

Before including this section, to see clearly whether all that I say there is not a useless repetition of what I already said in the following sections. I am afraid it is (YTC, CVk, 2, pp. 1–2). See note a for p. 1200.

b. The *rubish* of chapter 10 of this part contains a jacket cover on which you can read: "How equality of ranks suggests to men the taste for liberty [v: equality] and why democratic peoples love equality better than liberty./

"Piece that I will probably make the second section of the chapter and that must be

The first and most intense of the passions given birth by equality of conditions, I do not need to say, is the love of this very equality. So no one will be surprised that I talk about it before all the others.

Everyone has noted that in our time, and especially in France, this passion for equality has a greater place in the human heart every day. It has been said a hundred times that our contemporaries have a much more ardent and much more tenacious love for equality than for liberty; but I do not find that we have yet adequately gone back to the causes of this fact. I am going to try.[c]

––––––––

reexamined with care while reviewing this chapter. 4 September 1838" (*Rubish,* 1). The notes that are found in this jacket belong in large part to the final chapter of the book. In a partial copy from the *Rubish,* they are found precisely with the rough drafts of the fourth part (YTC, CVg, 2, p. 16 and following). Among these notes you find this one:

Some ideas on the sentiment of equality (2 February 1836)./

What must be understood by the sentiment of equality among democratic peoples./

The taste for equality among most men is not: that no one be lower than I, but: that no one be higher than I, which, in practice, can come to the same thing, but which is far from meaning the same thing./

So does a real and true taste for equality exist in this world? Among some elite souls. But you must not base your reasoning on them./

What produced aristocracies? The desire among a few to raise themselves. What leads to democracy? The desire of all to raise themselves. The sentiment is the same; there is only a difference in the number of those who feel it. Each man aims as high as possible, and a level comes about naturally, without anyone wanting to be leveled.

When everyone wants to rise at once, the rule of equality is quite naturally found to be what is most suitable for each man. A thousand runners all have the same goal. Each one burns with the desire of coming in first. For that, it would be good to precede the others in the course. But if I do that, who will assure me that the others will not do so? If there were only five or six who had to run with me, I could perhaps attempt it, but racing with a thousand, you cannot succeed in doing so. What to do? The only means is to prevent anyone from having any privilege and to leave each one to his natural resources. [v: All, however, agree to depart at the same time from the same place.] It is not that they truly love equality, but they are all obliged to resort to it./

To reflect again about all of that (*Rubish,* 1). See note d for p. 1203.

c. First draft of this opening of the chapter:

When conditions are more or less equal among men, each one, feeling independent of his fellows, contracts the habit and the need to follow only his will in his particular

You can imagine an extreme point where liberty and equality meet and merge.

Suppose that all citizens participate in the government and that each one has an equal right to take part in it.

Since no one then differs from his fellows, no one will be able to exercise a tyrannical power; men will be perfectly free, because they will all be entirely equal; and they will all be perfectly equal, because they will be entirely free. Democratic peoples tend toward this ideal.

That is the most complete form that equality can take on earth; but there are a thousand other forms that, without being as perfect, are scarcely less dear to these peoples.

Equality can become established in civil society and not reign in the political world. Everyone can have the right to pursue the same pleasures, to enter the same professions, to meet in the same places; in a word, to live in the same way and to pursue wealth by the same means, without all taking the same part in government.

A kind of equality can even become established in the political world, even if political liberty does not exist. Everyone is equal to all his fellows,

---

actions. This naturally leads the human mind to the idea of political liberty and suggests the taste for it.

Take one man at random from within a democratic people [v: in a country where equality reigns], put him if possible outside of his prejudices, of his interests of the moment, of his memories, so that he gives himself only to the sole interests that the social state suggests to him, and you will discover that among all governments the one that he most easily imagines first and that he loves best is government based on sovereignty of the people.

<So, as the social state of a people becomes democratic, you see the spirit of liberty born within it. These two things generally go together so closely that one makes me consider the other. The attempts that a nation makes to establish liberty within it only teach me that the principle of equality is developing there, and the equality that I see reigning among a people makes me suppose the approach of revolutions.>

So equality of conditions cannot be established among a people without the spirit of liberty being revealed there, and it is never entirely extinguished as long as equality of conditions remains.

Love of political liberty, however, is not the principal passion of these democratic peoples.

You can imagine an extreme point . . . (YTC, CVk, 2, pp. 2–4).

except one, who is, without distinction, the master of all, and who takes the agents of his power equally from among all.

It would be easy to form several other hypotheses according to which a very great equality could easily be combined with institutions more or less free, or even with institutions that would not be free at all.

So although men cannot become absolutely equal without being entirely free, and consequently equality at its most extreme level merges with liberty, you are justified in distinguishing the one from the other.[d]

The taste that men have for liberty and the one that they feel for equality are, in fact, two distinct things, and I am not afraid to add that, among democratic peoples, they are two unequal things.

If you want to pay attention, you will see that in each century, a singular and dominant fact is found to which the other facts are related; this fact almost always gives birth to a generative thought, or to a principal passion that then ends by drawing to itself and carrying along in its course all sentiments and all ideas. It is like the great river toward which all of the surrounding streams seem to flow.

Liberty has shown itself to men in different times and in different forms; it has not been linked exclusively to one social state, and you find it elsewhere than in democracies. So it cannot form the distinctive characteristic of democratic centuries.

The particular and dominant fact that singles out these centuries is equality of conditions; the principal passion that agitates men in those times is love of this equality.

Do not ask what singular charm the men of democratic ages find in living equal; or the particular reasons that they can have to be so stubbornly attached to equality rather than to the other advantages that society presents to them. Equality forms the distinctive characteristic of the period in which they live; that alone is enough to explain why they prefer it to everything else.

d. "<Equality of conditions does not lead to liberty in an irresistible way, but it leads to it; this is our plank of salvation>" (YTC, CVk, 2, p. 6).

But, apart from this reason, there are several others that, in all times, will habitually lead men to prefer equality to liberty.

If a people could ever succeed in destroying by itself or only in decreasing the equality that reigns within it, it would do so only by long and difficult efforts. It would have to modify its social state, abolish its laws, replace its ideas, change its habits, alter its mores. But, to lose political liberty, it is enough not to hold on to it, and liberty escapes.

So men do not hold on to equality only because it is dear to them; they are also attached to it because they believe it must last forever.

You do not find men so limited and so superficial that they do not discover that political liberty may, by its excesses, compromise tranquillity, patrimony, and the life of individuals. But only attentive and clear-sighted men see the dangers with which equality threatens us, and ordinarily they avoid pointing these dangers out. They know that the miseries that they fear are remote, and they imagine that those miseries affect only the generations to come, about whom the present generation scarcely worries. The evils that liberty sometimes brings are immediate; they are visible to all, and more or less everyone feels them. The evils that extreme equality can produce appear only little by little; they gradually insinuate themselves into the social body; they are seen only now and then, and, at the moment when they become most violent, habit has already made it so that they are no longer felt.

The good things that liberty brings show themselves only over time, and it is always easy to fail to recognize the cause that gives them birth.

The advantages of equality make themselves felt immediately, and every day you see them flow from their source.

Political liberty, from time to time, gives sublime pleasures to a certain number of citizens.

Equality provides a multitude of small enjoyments to each man every day. The charms of equality are felt at every moment, and they are within reach of all; the most noble hearts are not insensitive to them, and they are the delight of the most common souls. So the passion to which equality gives birth has to be at the very same time forceful and general.

Men cannot enjoy political liberty without purchasing it at the cost of some sacrifices, and they never secure it except by a great deal of effort. But the pleasures provided by equality are there for the taking. Each one of the small incidents of private life seems to give birth to them, and to enjoy them, you only have to be alive.

Democratic peoples love equality at all times, but there are certain periods when they push the passion that they feel for it to the point of delirium. This happens at the moment when the old social hierarchy, threatened for a long time, is finally destroyed, after a final internal struggle, when the barriers that separated citizens are at last overturned. Men then rush toward equality as toward a conquest, and they cling to it as to a precious good that someone wants to take away from them. The passion for equality penetrates the human heart from all directions, it spreads and fills it entirely. Do not tell men that by giving themselves so blindly to one exclusive passion, they compromise their dearest interests; they are deaf. Do not show them that liberty is escaping from their hands while they are looking elsewhere; they are blind, or rather they see in the whole universe only one single good worthy of desire.

What precedes applies to all democratic nations. What follows concerns only ourselves.

Among most modern nations, and in particular among all the peoples of the continent of Europe, the taste and the idea of liberty only began to arise and to develop at the moment when conditions began to become equal, and as a consequence of this very equality. It was absolute kings who worked hardest to level ranks among their subjects. Among these peoples, equality preceded liberty; so equality was an ancient fact, when liberty was still something new; the one had already created opinions, customs, laws that were its own, when the other appeared alone, and for the first time, in full view. Thus, the second was still only in ideas and in tastes, while the first had already penetrated habits, had taken hold of mores, and had given a particular turn to the least actions of life. Why be surprised if men today prefer the one to the other?[e]

e. Not only are these two things different, but I can easily prove that they are some-

I think that democratic peoples have a natural taste for liberty; left to themselves, they seek it, they love it, and it is only with pain that they see themselves separated from it. But they have an ardent, insatiable, eternal, invincible passion for equality; they want equality in liberty, and if they cannot obtain that, they still want equality in slavery. They will suffer poverty, enslavement, barbarism, but they will not suffer aristocracy.

This is true in all times, and above all in our own. All men and all powers that would like to fight against this irresistible power will be overturned and destroyed by it.[f] In our day, liberty cannot be established without its support, and despotism itself cannot reign without it.

---

times opposed. It is clear for example that men must exercise political rights only to the extent that they are capable of doing so. Without that you would arrive at anarchy, which is only a particular form of tyranny. Now, it is certain that the sentiment of equality is less offended by the subjugation of all to one master, than by the submission of a great number to the government of a few. So the sentiment of equality leads here either to giving (illegible word) rights to everyone, which leads to anarchy, or to giving them to no one, which establishes despotism.

[To the side: "The despot is a distant enemy, the noble is an enemy who touches you."]

You can satisfy the taste of men for equality, without giving them liberty. Often they must even sacrifice a part of the second in order fully to enjoy the first.

So these two things are easily separable.

The very fact that they are not intimately united and that the one is infinitely more precious than the other would make it very easy and natural to neglect the second in order to run after the first./

So let us hold onto liberty with a desperate attachment, let us hold on to it as a good to which all other good things are attached.

[To the side] If, on the one hand, among a democratic people, men are more generally enlightened about their rights, on the other hand, it must be acknowledged that they are less able to defend them, because individually they are very weak and the art of acting in common is difficult and demands institutions that are not provided and an apprenticeship that is not allowed to be undertaken (YTC, CVd, pp. 24–25).

f. [On the jacket of a draft] Equality is not suitable for barbaric peoples; it prevents them from becoming enlightened and civilized./

Idea to introduce perhaps in the chapters on literature or the sciences.

[The beginning is missing (ed.)] and first, I do not believe that in all the ages of the life of peoples a democratic social state must produce the effects that I have just pointed out.

I have never thought that equality of conditions was suitable for the infancy of societies. When men are uncivilized as well as equal, each one of them feels too weak and too limited to look for enlightenment separately and it is almost impossible for all to try to find it at the same time by a common accord.

Nothing is so difficult to take as the first step out of barbarism. I do not doubt that more effort is required for a savage to discover the art of writing than for a civilized man to penetrate the general laws that regulate the world. Now it is not believable that men could ever conceive the need for such an effort without having it clearly shown to them, or that they would make such an effort without grasping the result in advance. In a society of barbarians equal to each other, since the attention of each man is equally absorbed by the first needs and the most coarse interests of life, the idea of intellectual progress can come to the mind of any one of them only with difficulty, and if by chance it is born, it would soon be as if suffocated amid the nearly instructive [instinctive? (ed.)] thoughts to which the poorly satisfied needs of the body always give birth. The savage lacks at the very same time the idea of study and the possibility of devoting himself to it.

I do not believe that history presents a single example of a democratic people who have risen gradually and by themselves toward enlightenment and that is easily understood. We have seen that among a nation where equality and barbarism reign at the same time it was very difficult for an individual to develop his intelligence separately. But if, exceptionally, he happens to do so, the superiority of his knowledge suddenly gives him such a great preponderance over all those who surround him that he does not take long to want to make use of it to put an end to equality to his advantage. So, if peoples {an emerging people} remain democratic, civilization cannot arise within them, and if civilization comes by chance to penetrate among them, they cease to be democratic. I am persuaded that humanity owes its enlightenment to such strokes of fortune, and I ≠ {think that it is in losing their liberty that men acquired the means to reconquer it} ≠ that it is under an aristocracy or under a prince that men still half-savage have gathered the various notions that later would allow them to live civilized, equal and free.

[In the margin: So I think that this same equality of conditions that seems to me very appropriate for precipitating the march of the human mind could prevent it from taking its first steps.]

If I admit that boldness of mind and the taste for general ideas are not necessarily found among peoples whose social state is democratic, I am equally far from claiming that you can hope to find them only there.

There are particular accidents that, among certain peoples, can give a particular impulse to the human mind. Among the accidents, I will put in the first rank the influence that some men exercise over the fate of societies. It seems that Providence, after tracing the various paths that nations can follow and fixing the final end of their course, leaves to individuals the task of slowing or hurrying this march of humanity that they can neither divert nor halt.

Men are found here and there whose vigorous and unyielding minds scoff at the impediments that the social state and laws have formed, and whose minds enjoy pursuing their course even amid the obstacles that are strewn over it.

Such men rarely gain great sway over their fellow-citizens, but in the long run they exercise a powerful influence over their society and they draw the ideas of their descendants in their direction.

When political liberty . . . [interrupted text (ed.)] (YTC, CVk, 1, pp. 18–21).

Of Individualism in Democratic Countries

I have shown how, in centuries of equality, each man looked for his beliefs within himself; I want to show how, in these same centuries, he turns all his sentiments toward himself alone.

*Individualism*ᵇ is a recent expression given birth by a new idea. Our fathers knew only egoism.

a. 1. What individualism is; how it differs from egoism and ends by coming back to it.

2. Individualism is a sickness peculiar to the human heart in democratic times. Why?

1. Democracy makes you forget ancestors.

2. It hides descendants.

3. It separates contemporaries by destroying classes and by making them men independent of each other.

3. So in democratic centuries man is constantly brought back to himself alone and is preoccupied only with himself.

4. It is so above all at the outset of democratic centuries because of the jealousies and hatreds to which the democratic revolution has given birth (YTC, CVf, p. 23).

Tocqueville had thought about beginning the 1840 *Democracy* with this chapter (see note a for p. 697).

b. In the *rubish*, the chapter, which bears the title OF INDIVIDUALISM IN DEMOCRACIES AND OF THE MEANS THAT THE AMERICANS USE TO COMBAT IT, begins in this way: "I am not afraid to use new words when they are necessary to portray a new thing. Here the occasion to do so presents itself. Individualism is a recent expression . . ." (*Rubish*, 1).

The word *individualism,* which seems to echo the *amour propre* (self-love) of Rousseau, was not invented by Tocqueville, but he is largely responsible for its definition and its usage. The word appears for the first time in this volume. James T. Schleifer dated its first use as 24 April 1837 (see note u for pp. 709–10). The novelty of the word must not

Egoism is a passionate and exaggerated love of oneself, which leads man to view everything only in terms of himself alone and to prefer himself to everything.[c]

Individualism is a considered and peaceful sentiment that disposes each citizen to isolate himself from the mass of his fellows and to withdraw to the side with his family and his friends; so that, after thus creating a small society for his own use, he willingly abandons the large society to itself.

Egoism is born out of blind instinct; individualism proceeds from an erroneous judgment rather than from a depraved sentiment. It has its source in failings of the mind as much as in vices of the heart.[d]

Egoism parches the seed of all virtues; individualism at first dries up only the source of public virtues, but, in the long run, it attacks and destroys all the others and is finally absorbed into egoism.

Egoism is a vice as old as the world. It hardly belongs more to one form of society than to another.

---

make us forget that Tocqueville several times used the expression *individual egoism* in a rather similar sense (as in note e of p. 511 in the first volume, and in p. 448, also in the first volume). During his 1835 voyage in England (*Voyage en Angleterre, OC,* V, 2, p. 60), Tocqueville also used another expression to designate almost the same idea. He spoke about the *spirit of exclusion,* a sentiment that "leads each man or each association of men to enjoy its advantages as much as possible by itself all alone, to withdraw as much as possible into its personality and not to allow whomever to see or to put a foot inside." The interesting concept of collective individualism appears only in *L'Ancien Régime et la Révolution* (*OC,* II, 1, p. 158).

Some of Tocqueville's reading, the influence of Kergorlay (who knew Saint-Simonianism well), or the popularization of the word perhaps pushed Tocqueville afterward to use the word *individualism.* In his theory, the term is always accompanied by its opposite, the *spirit of individuality,* which Tocqueville defines in note 2 for p. 1179. Sometimes he also adopts the terms *individual strength, spirit of independence,* and *individual independence.*

Koenrad W. Swart ("Individualism in the Mid-Nineteenth Century, 1826–1860," *Journal of the History of Ideas,* 23, 1962, pp. 77–86) points out that Tocqueville perhaps borrowed the term from Saint-Simon. For a discussion of the ideas of Tocqueville on individualism, see Jean-Claude Lamberti, *Tocqueville et les deux Démocraties* (Paris: PUF, 1983), pp. 217–40, and *La Notion d'individualisme chez Tocqueville* (Paris: PUF, 1970); see James T. Schleifer, *The Making of Tocqueville's "Democracy in America,"* pp. 252–57.

c. In the manuscript: "prefer himself to all others."

d. "≠Egoism, vice of the heart.

"Individualism, of the mind≠" (*Rubish,* 1).

Individualism is of democratic origin, and it threatens to develop as conditions become equal.

Among aristocratic peoples, families remain for centuries in the same condition, and often in the same place. That, so to speak, makes all generations contemporaries. A man almost always knows his ancestors and respects them; he believes he already sees his grandsons, and he loves them. He willingly assumes his duty toward both, and he often happens to sacrifice his personal enjoyments for these beings who are no more or who do not yet exist.

Aristocratic institutions have, moreover, the effect of tying each man closely to several of his fellow citizens.

Since classes are very distinct and unchanging within an aristocratic people, each class becomes for the one who is part of it a kind of small country, more visible and dearer than the large one.

Because, in aristocratic societies, all citizens are placed in fixed positions, some above others, each citizen always sees above him a man whose protection he needs, and below he finds another whose help he can claim.

So men who live in aristocratic centuries are almost always tied in a close way to something that is located outside of themselves, and they are often disposed to forget themselves. It is true that, in these same centuries, the general notion of *fellow* is obscure, and that you scarcely think to lay down your life for the cause of humanity; but you often sacrifice yourself for certain men.[e]

e. Aristocracy, which makes citizens depend on each other, leads them sometimes to great devotion, often to implacable hatreds. Democracy tends to make them indifferent to each other and disposes them to act as if they were alone.

Aristocracy forces man at every moment to go outside of himself in order to attend to others [v: interests other than his own], democracy constantly leads him back toward himself and threatens finally to enclose him entirely within the solitude of his own heart.

If democratic peoples abandon themselves immoderately to this tendency, it is easy to foresee that great evils will result for humanity.

[In the margin] Period of transition. Isolation much more complete. The hatreds of aristocracy and the indifference of democracy are combined. You isolate yourself by instinct and by will (*Rubish,* 1).

In democratic centuries, on the contrary, when the duties of each individual toward the species are much clearer, devotion toward one man [<or
one class>] becomes more rare; the bond of human affections expands and
relaxes.

Among democratic peoples, new families emerge constantly out of nothing, others constantly fall back into nothing, and all those that remain
change face; the thread of time is broken at every moment, and the trace
of the generations fades. You easily forget those who preceded you, and you
have no idea about those who will follow you. Only those closest to you
are of interest.

Since each class is coming closer to the others and is mingling with them,
its members become indifferent and like strangers to each other. Aristocracy
had made all citizens into a long chain that went from the peasant up to
the king; democracy breaks the chain and sets each link apart.

As conditions become equal, a greater number of individuals will be
found who, no longer rich enough or powerful enough to exercise a great
influence over the fate of their fellows, have nonetheless acquired or preserved enough enlightenment and wealth to be able to be sufficient for
themselves. The latter owe nothing to anyone, they expect nothing so to
speak from anyone; they are always accustomed to consider themselves in
isolation, and they readily imagine that their entire destiny is in their hands.

Thus, not only does democracy make each man forget his ancestors, but
it hides his descendants from him and separates him from his contemporaries; it constantly leads him back toward himself alone and threatens finally to enclose him entirely within the solitude of his own heart.[*]

---

[*]. I believe that if I leave the piece that follows on the *period of transition,* it must
simply be put there without making it a separate chapter.

CHAPTER 3

How Individualism Is Greater
at the End of a Democratic Revolution
than at Another Time[a]

It is above all at the moment when a democratic society finally takes form on the debris of an aristocracy, that this isolation of men from each other, and the egoism that follows are most easily seen.

These societies not only contain a great number of independent citizens, they are filled daily with men who, having reached independence only yesterday, are intoxicated with their new power; these men conceive a presumptuous confidence in their strength, and not imagining that from then on they might need to ask for the help of their fellows, they have no difficulty showing that they think only of themselves.

An aristocracy usually succumbs only after a prolonged struggle, during which implacable hatreds are kindled among the different classes. These passions survive victory, and you can follow their traces amid the democratic confusion that follows.[b]

Those among the citizens who were first in the destroyed hierarchy cannot immediately forget their former greatness; for a long time they consider themselves like strangers within the new society. They see in all the men made equal to them by this society, oppressors whose destiny cannot pro-

---

a. On the jacket of the manuscript: "Idea treated further on in the *political* chapters that end the book. Only after examining it in the two places will I be able to see if it must be deleted in one of the two or if it must only be expressed in a different way." This chapter, which is not found on the list of notebook CVf and does not exist in the *Rubish,* bears the number 20bis in the manuscript.

b. "Aristocracies have been seen that protected liberty. But every contested aristocracy becomes tyrannical. This is what is happening to the doctrinaires" (YTC, CVa, p. 1).

voke sympathy; they have lost sight of their former equals and no longer feel tied by a common interest to their fate; so each one, withdrawing apart, thinks he is reduced to being concerned only with himself. Those, on the contrary, who formerly were placed at the bottom of the social ladder, and who had been brought closer to the general level by a sudden revolution, enjoy only with a kind of secret uneasiness their newly acquired independence; if they find at their side a few of their former superiors, they look at them with triumph and fear, and move apart from them.

So it is usually at the beginning of democratic societies that citizens show themselves most disposed to separate themselves.

Democracy leads men not to draw nearer to their fellows; but democratic revolutions dispose them to flee each other and perpetuate within equality the hatreds given birth by inequality.

The great advantage of the Americans is to have arrived at democracy without having to suffer democratic revolutions, and to have been born equal instead of becoming so.[c]

c. Idea to bring very much forward.
[In the margin: Idea to show fully at the head or at the end of the book and also to present in outline in different parts.]
Effects of democracy and particularly harmful effects that are exaggerated in the period of revolution when the democratic social state, mores and laws become established.
Example: democracy has the end of making beliefs less stable, like fortunes and ranks. But at the moment when democracy comes to be established, a shaking of everything occurs that makes doubtful even the notion of good and evil, which is nonetheless the notion that men most easily understand.
That comes not only from {the state of} democracy, but also from the state of revolution. Produced by whatever cause, it will produce effects if not as great at least analogous. A revolution is an accident that temporarily makes all things unstable, and above all it has this effect when it (illegible word) to establish a permanent state whose tendency is in a way to establish instability. The great difficulty in the study of democracy is to distinguish what is democratic from what is only revolutionary. This is very difficult because examples are lacking. There is no European people among whom democracy has settled down, and America is in an exceptional situation. The state of literature in France is not only democratic, but revolutionary.
Public morality, id.
Religious opinions, id.
Political opinions, id. (YTC, CVk, 1, pp. 51–53).

CHAPTER 4[a]

How the Americans Combat Individualism with Free Institutions[b]

Despotism, which, by its nature, is fearful, sees in the isolation of men the most certain guarantee of its own duration, and it ordinarily puts all its efforts into isolating them. There is no vice of the human heart that pleases it as much as egoism: a despot easily pardons the governed for not loving him, provided that they do not love each other.[c] He does not ask them to help him lead the State; it is enough that they do not claim to run it them-

a. 1. Despotism tends to isolate men constantly. So it is particularly dangerous in times when the social state has the same tendency.

2. Liberty is, on the contrary, particularly necessary in these times. Why:

1. By occupying citizens with public affairs, it draws them out of themselves.

2. By making them deal in common with their affairs, it makes them feel their reciprocal dependence.

3. By making the choice of magistrates depend on the public, it gives to all those who have some ambition the desire to serve their fellows in order to merit being their choice.

3. Example of all this drawn from the United States. How the Americans are not only content to combat individualism by creating national liberty, but have also established provincial liberties (YTC, CVf, pp. 23–24).

b. At one moment during the writing, this chapter had as a title: HOW THE AMERICANS COMBAT THE TENDENCIES THAT LEAD MEN TO SEPARATE THEMSELVES BY MUNICIPAL INSTITUTIONS AND THE SPIRIT OF ASSOCIATION (*Rubish,* 1).

"The defect of these chapters is that, in those that follow, I have already treated a part of the effects of individualism, without naming it" (*Rubish,* 1).

c. "The circulation of ideas is to civilization what the circulation of blood is to the human body" (*Rubish,* 1).

selves.^d Those who claim to unite their efforts in order to create common prosperity, he calls unruly and restless spirits; and, changing the natural meaning of words, he calls good citizens those who withdraw narrowly into themselves.^e

d. In the margin: "≠I have made known how, in democratic centuries, each man looked within himself alone for his *beliefs;* I want to show how in these same centuries he turns all his *sentiments* toward himself alone.≠"

e. You must take great notice of the social state of a people before deciding what political laws are suitable for them. When a nation adopts a government whose natural defects are unfortunately in accord with the natural defects of the social state, the nation must expect the latter to grow beyond measure.

Liberty, on the contrary, by creating great common affairs, tends constantly to draw citizens closer together, and it shows them every day in a practical way the tight bond that unites them. Among free peoples, it is the public that distributes honors and power, and it is only by working for the public that you succeed in gaining its favors. So it happens that among these peoples you think about your fellows out of ambition as much as out of disinterestedness, and often you in a way find your interest by forgetting about yourself.

The free institutions that certain peoples can if necessary do without, are therefore particularly necessary to men who are led by a secret instinct constantly to separate themselves from each other and to withdraw within the narrow limits of personal interest.

Despotism . . . [interrupted text (ed.)] (*Rubish,* 1).

In the manuscript this other beginning can be read:

Equality of conditions not only disposes men to be interested only in themselves; it also leads them not to communicate with each other.

In aristocratic countries the members of the upper class get together from time to time for their pleasures, when they have no common affairs.

Among democratic peoples each man, having only a mediocre fortune that he oversees himself, does not have the leisure to seek out the company of his fellows. A great interest must force him to do so.

If the men of democratic countries were abandoned entirely to their natural instincts, they would end up not only by not making use of each other, but by not knowing one another. The circulation of sentiments and ideas would be as if suspended.

[In the margin: <This seems contestable to me for equality suggests a host of restless passions that must necessarily lead men to see each other a great deal even if they are indifferent./

This as well seems contrary to what I said previously that democratic periods were periods when all men came to resemble each other because they saw and heard each other constantly.>]

These are great dangers on which the attention of the legislator must be constantly fixed.

Thus, the vices given birth by despotism are precisely those that equality favors. The two things complement each other and help one another in a fatal way.

Equality places men side by side, without a common bond to hold them. Despotism raises barriers between them and separates them. It disposes them not to think about their fellows and makes indifference into a kind of public virtue.

So despotism, which is dangerous in all times, is to be particularly feared in democratic centuries.[f]

It is easy to see that in these same centuries men have a particular need for liberty.

When citizens are forced to occupy themselves with public affairs, they are necessarily drawn away from the middle of their individual interests and are, from time to time, dragged away from looking at themselves.

From the moment when common affairs are treated together, each man notices that he is not as independent of his fellows as he first imagined, and that, to gain their support, he must often lend them his help.

When the public governs, there is no man who does not feel the value of the public's regard and who does not seek to win it by gaining the esteem and affection of those among whom he must live.

Several of the passions that chill and divide hearts are then forced to withdraw deep into the soul and hide there. Pride conceals itself; scorn dares not to show itself. Egoism is afraid of itself. [You dread to offend and you love to serve.]

Under a free government, since most public functions are elective, the men who feel cramped in private life because of the loftiness of their souls or the restlessness of their desires, sense every day that they cannot do without the population that surrounds them.

It then happens that you think about your fellows out of ambition, and that often, in a way, you find it in your interest to forget yourself. [This

---

f. "Despotism would not only destroy liberty among these people, but in a way society" (*Rubish,* 1).

finally produces within democratic nations something analogous to what was seen in aristocracies.

In aristocratic countries men are bound tightly together by their very inequalities. In democratic countries where the various representatives of public power are elected, men attach themselves to each other by the exertion of their own will, and it is in this sense then that you can say that in those countries election replaces hierarchy to a certain degree.]g h I know that you can raise the objection here of all the intrigues given birth by an election, the shameful means that the candidates often use and the slanders that their enemies spread. Those are occasions of hatred, and they present themselves all the more often as elections become more frequent [≠which never fails to happen in proportion as municipal liberties develop≠].j

These evils are no doubt great, but they are temporary, while the good things that arise with them endure.

The desire to be elected can, for a short while, lead certain men to make war on each other; but this same desire leads all men in the long run to lend each other natural support; and, if it happens that an election accidentally divides two friends, the electoral system draws closer together in a permanent way a multitude of citizens who would always have remained strangers to each other. Liberty creates particular hatreds, but despotism gives birth to general indifference.

g. <If in my mind I wanted to portray with the aid of a physical image how men are connected to each other in aristocracies, I would imagine a chain all of whose links, of unequal shape and unequal thickness, would be passed [along (ed.)] equal spokes that would all end up attached together at the same center.

And if I wanted to understand how they can be connected to each other in democracies, I would imagine a multitude of equal spokes all ending up at the same center, so that, although all turn together, there would never be two of them that touch each other> (*Rubish*, 1).

h. In the margin: "Probably shorten this paragraph. The last sentence of the chapter is the same thing and better."

j. To the side: "<Perhaps this must be deleted, though good. This gives too much of a role to election in free institutions and perhaps in the mind of many readers damages my cause more than serving it.>"

The Americans fought, by means of liberty, against the individualism given birth by equality, and they defeated it.

The law-makers of America did not believe that to cure an illness so natural and so fatal to the social body in democratic times, it was sufficient to grant the nation a single way of representing itself as a whole; they thought, as well, that it was appropriate to give political life to each portion of the territory, in order infinitely to multiply for citizens the occasions to act together, and to make the citizens feel every day that they depend on each other.[k]

This was to behave with wisdom.

The general affairs of a country occupy only the principal citizens. The latter gather together in the same places only from time to time; and, as it often happens that afterward they lose sight of each other, no lasting bonds are established among them. But, when it is a matter of having the particular affairs of a district regulated by the men who live there, the same individuals are always in contact, and they are in a way forced to know each other and to please each other.

You draw a man out of himself with difficulty in order to interest him in the destiny of the entire State, because he poorly understands the influence that the destiny of the State can exercise on his fate. But if it is necessary to have a road pass by the end of his property, he will see at first glance that there is a connection between this small public affair and his greatest private affairs, and he will discover, without anyone showing him, the close bond that here unites particular interest to general interest.

So it is by charging citizens with the administration of small affairs, much more than by giving them the government of great ones, that you

---

k. So the great object of law-makers in democracies must be to create common *affairs* that *force* men to enter into contact with each other.

Laws that lead to this result are useful to all peoples; to democratic peoples they are necessary. Here they increase the well-being of society; there they make society continue to exist, for what is society for thinking beings, if not the communication and connection of minds and hearts?/

That should lead me easily to free institutions that give birth to common *affairs* (*Rubish,* 1).

interest them in the public good and make them see the need that they constantly have for each other in order to produce that good.

You can, by a dazzling action, suddenly capture the favor of a people; but, to win the love and respect of the population that surrounds you, there must be a long succession of small services provided, humble good offices, a constant habit of benevolence and a well-established reputation of disinterestedness.

So local liberties, which make a great number of citizens put value on the affection of their neighbors and of those nearby, constantly bring men back toward each other despite the instincts that separate them, and force them to help each other.

In the United States, the most opulent citizens are very careful not to isolate themselves from the people; on the contrary, they constantly draw closer to them, they readily listen to them and speak with them every day. They know that in democracies the rich always need the poor and that, in democratic times, the poor are attached by manners more than by benefits. The very grandeur of these benefits, which brings out the difference of conditions, causes a secret irritation to those who profit from them; but simplicity of manners has nearly irresistible charms; familiarity of manners seduces and even their coarseness does not always displease.

This truth does not at first sight penetrate the mind of the rich. Usually, they resist it as long as the democratic revolution lasts, and they do not even admit it immediately after the revolution is accomplished. They willingly agree to do good for the people; but they want to continue to hold them carefully at a distance. They believe that is enough; they are wrong. They would ruin themselves in this way without rekindling the heart of the population that surrounds them. It is not the sacrifice of their money that is demanded of them; it is the sacrifice of their pride.[m]

You would say that in the United States there is no imagination that does not exhaust itself inventing means to increase wealth and to satisfy the needs of the public. The most enlightened inhabitants of each district are constantly using their knowledge to discover new secrets appropriate for

---

m. This paragraph and the preceding one are not found in the manuscript.

increasing common prosperity; and, when they have found some, they hasten to give them to the crowd.[n]

While closely examining the vices and weaknesses often shown by those who govern in America, you are astonished by the growing prosperity of the people, and you are mistaken.[o] It is not the elected magistrate who makes the American democracy prosper; but it prospers because the magistrate is elective.[p]

It would be unjust to believe that the patriotism of the Americans and the zeal that each of them shows for the well-being of his fellow citizens has nothing real about it. Although private interest directs most human actions in the United States as well as elsewhere, it does not determine all of them.

I must say that I have often seen Americans make great and true sacrifices for public affairs, and I have observed a hundred times that they hardly ever fail to lend faithful support to each other as needed.

The free institutions that the inhabitants of the United States possess, and the political rights that they use so much, recall constantly, and in a thousand ways, to each citizen that he lives in society. They lead his mind at every moment toward this idea, that the duty as well as the interest of men is to make themselves useful to their fellows; and, as he sees no particular cause to hate them, since he is never either their slave or their master, his heart inclines easily in the direction of benevolence. You first get involved in the general interest by necessity, and then by choice; what was calculation becomes instinct; and by working for the good of your fellow citizens, you finally acquire the habit and taste of serving them.

[When men, unequal to each other, put all their political powers in the hands of one man, that is not enough for them to become indifferent and cold toward each other, because they continue to need each other constantly in civil life.

But when equal men do not take part in government, they almost en-

---

n. In the margin, in pencil: "Not only, but. Ampère."

o. "≠It is not those who are elected to public offices who make democracies prosper, but those who want to be≠" (*Rubish*, 1).

p. In the margin, in pencil: "A connection is desired here. Ampère."

tirely lack the occasion to harm each other or to make use of each other. Each one forgets his fellows to think only of the prince and himself.

So political liberty, which is useful when conditions are unequal, becomes necessary in proportion as they become equal.]q

Many people in France consider equality of conditions as a first evil, and political liberty as a second. When they are forced to submit to the one, they try hard at least to escape the other. As for me, I say that, to combat the evils that equality can produce, there is only one effective remedy: political liberty.

.

q. "When the government [v: sources of power] is found in the population itself and not above it, you feel for the people something of the good and bad sentiments that kings inspire in absolute monarchies; you fear him, you adulate him, and often you love him passionately. Base souls take him as the object of their flattery and lofty ones as the focus of their devotion" (*Rubish*, 1).

CHAPTER 5[a]

Of the Use That Americans Make of Association in Civil Life[b]

I do not want to talk about those political associations by the aid of which men seek to defend themselves against the despotic action of a majority or against the encroachments of royal power. I have already treated this subject elsewhere. It is clear that, if each citizen, as he becomes individually weaker and therefore more incapable of preserving his liberty by himself alone, did not learn the art of uniting with his fellows to defend his liberty, tyranny

a. 1. Here it is not a matter of political associations. I treated this subject in the first work.

2. The Americans are at the very same time the most *democratic* people and the ones who have made the most use of *association*. These two things go together, in fact.

1. In aristocratic countries there are permanent and established associations, composed of a few powerful men and of all those who depend on them.

2. In democratic countries, where all citizens are equal and weak, temporary and voluntary associations must be formed, or civilization is in danger.

3. Not only are industrial associations necessary, but moral and intellectual associations. Why:

1. In order for sentiments and ideas to be renewed and for the human mind to develop, men must act constantly upon each other.

2. Now, in democratic countries, only the government naturally has this power of action. And it exercises it always incompletely and tyrannically.

3. So there associations must come to replace the powerful individuals who in aristocracies take charge of bringing sentiments and ideas to light.

4. *Summary.* In order for men to remain civilized or to become so, the art of association among them must be developed and perfected in the same proportion as equality (illegible word) (YTC, CVf, pp. 24–25).

b. "≠Remark of Édouard: chapter weakly written≠" (*Rubish,* 1).

would necessarily grow with equality.[c] Here it is a matter only of the associations that are formed in civil life and whose aim has nothing political about it.

The political associations that exist in the United States form only a detail amid the immense tableau that associations as a whole present there.

Americans of all ages, of all conditions, of all minds, constantly unite. Not only do they have commercial and industrial associations in which they all take part, but also they have a thousand other kinds: religious, moral, [intellectual,] serious ones, useless ones, very general and very particular ones, immense and very small ones;[d] Americans associate to celebrate holidays, establish seminaries, build inns, erect churches, distribute books, send missionaries to the Antipodes; in this way they create hospitals, prisons, schools. If, finally, it is a matter of bringing a truth to light or of developing a sentiment with the support of a good example, they associate. Wherever, at the head of a new undertaking, you see in France the government, and in England, a great lord, count on seeing in the United States, an association.

---

c. A great publicist of today has said:
   It is not by exterminating the civilized men of the IVth century that the barbarians managed to destroy the civilization of that time. It was enough for them to come between them so to speak and by separating them to make them like strangers to one another.
   [To the side: To finish associations there, to turn G[uizot (ed.)] against himself.]
   It is by a similar path that the men of today could well return to barbarism, if they were not careful.
   [In another place] M. G[uizot (ed.)]. wants to speak about the prevention of *communicating* with rather than about the impossibility of *acting* on each other. These ideas are close but different. In order to *act* on each other, they must first *communicate* with each other. But you can communicate without acting. This is the case of men in democratic countries.
   [To the side: If a government forbid citizens to associate or undertook to take away their taste for doing so, it would behave precisely as the barbarians./
   to communicate-----*newspaper*
   to act-----*association.*] (*Rubish,* 1). See note a of p. 18 of the first volume.

   d. "A thousand types of associations in America. Harmony. C. B. 2. Shaking quakers" (*Rubish,* 1 and YTC, CVa, p. 4).

I found in America some kinds of associations[e] of which, I confess, I had not even the idea, and I often admired the infinite art with which the inhabitants of the United States succeeded in setting a common goal for the efforts of a great number of men, and in making them march freely toward it.

I have since traveled across England, from where the Americans took some of their laws and many of their customs, and it seemed to me that there one was very far from making such constant and skillful use of association.

It often happens that the English individually carry out very great things, while there is scarcely so small an enterprise for which the Americans do not unite. It is clear that the first consider association as a powerful means of action; but the second seem to see it as the only means they have to act.

Thus the most democratic country on earth is, out of all, the one where men today have most perfected the art of pursuing in common the object of their common desires and have applied this new science to the greatest number of things.[f] Does this result from an accident, or could it be that in fact a necessary connection exists between associations and equality?

e. "Three great categories of associations:
"Industrial associations.
"Religious associations. Moral associations: Intellectual."

[In another place] *"Legal* associations, *voluntary* associations: Artificial.
"The government, in some fashion, can well take the place of legal associations, but not of voluntary associations. All of that moreover goes together; *legal* associations teach men about voluntary associations and the latter about legal associations./
"Among voluntary associations also distinguish *political* and *civil* associations" (*Rubish,* 1).

f. Means to take to facilitate the spirit of association.

1. Make the will to associate very easy to carry out.
2. Do yourself only what associations can absolutely not carry out. If, on the contrary, the government marches in the direction of the social state, individualism has no limit. This requires that many nuances be pointed out. For if democratic peoples need more than others to be allowed to do things by themselves, they also sometimes have a greater need than others to have things done for them.
[In the margin: Marvels that democracy can accomplish with the aid of the spirit of association. See the railroads in America. *Revue des deux mondes* (1836).]

Aristocratic societies always contain within them, amid a multitude of individuals who can do nothing by themselves, a small number of very powerful and very rich citizens; each of the latter can by himself carry out great enterprises.

In aristocratic societies, men do not need to unite in order to act, because they are held tightly together.

There, each citizen, rich and powerful, is like the head of a permanent and compulsory association that is composed of all those who are dependent on him and who are made to cooperate in the execution of his plans.

Among democratic peoples, on the contrary, all citizens are independent and weak; they can hardly do anything by themselves, and no one among them can compel his fellows to lend him their help. So they all fall into impotence if they do not learn to help each other freely.[g]

If men who live in democratic countries had neither the right nor the taste to unite for political ends, their independence would run great risks, but they could for a long time retain their wealth and their enlightenment; while, if they did not acquire the custom of associating in ordinary life, civilization itself would be in danger.[h] A people among whom individuals

---

3. Give enlightenment, spread liberty and allow men to solve things by themselves. Comparison with the child that you make walk not in order to have the right to be kept always in leading-strings, but on the contrary to make him able to run all alone someday. But it is not in this way that governments understand it. They treat their subjects more or less as women are treated in China. They force them to wear the shoes of infancy all their lives (*Rubish*, 1).

It is possible that Tocqueville is referring here to the article of Michel Chevalier, "Des chemins de fer comparés aux lignes navigables" (*Revue des deux mondes,* 4th series, 1838, pp. 789–813).

g. "In aristocratic countries, enterprises larger and associations smaller.

"In democratic countries, enterprises smaller and associations larger" (*Rubish,* 1).

h. Civil associations./

[In the margin: Necessary remedy for egoism, more intelligent but more indispensable [and (ed.)] not less natural than sociability.]

Political associations are necessary in democracies as the executive power there is weaker. Without that, the majority is tyrannical.

lost the power to do great things separately without acquiring the ability to achieve them together would soon return to barbarism.

Unfortunately, the same social state that makes associations so necessary to democratic peoples makes them more difficult for them than for all other peoples.

When several members of an aristocracy want to associate, they easily succeed in doing so. As each one of them has great strength in society, the number of members of the association can be very small, and, when the numbers are few, it is very easy for them to know and understand each other and to establish fixed rules.

The same facility is not found among democratic nations, where those in the association must always be very numerous so that the association has some power.

[The liberty to associate is, therefore, more precious and the science of association more necessary among those peoples than among all others and <it becomes more precious and more necessary as equality is greater.>]

I know that there are many of my contemporaries who are not hindered by this. They claim that as citizens become weaker and more incapable, the government must be made more skillful and more active, in order for society to carry out what individuals are no longer able to do. They believe they have answered everything by saying that. But I think they are mistaken.

A government could take the place of a few of the largest American associations, and within the Union several particular states have already

---

Civil associations are useful in aristocratic countries; they are so necessary in democracies that it may be believed that a democratic people among whom civil associations could not form or could form with difficulty would have difficulty not falling into barbarism.

So the legislator in democracies must work hard to favor and to facilitate in all ways the developments of the right of association.

Unfortunately it is a chimera to believe that civil association can undergo great development where political association cannot exist (*Rubish*, 1).

tried to do so. But what political power would ever be able to be sufficient for the innumerable multitude of small enterprises that the American citizens carry out every day with the aid of the association?[j]

It is easy to foresee that the time is coming when man will be less and less able to produce by himself alone the things most common and most necessary to his life.[k] So the task of the social power will grow constantly, and its very efforts will make it greater every day. The more it puts itself in the place of associations, the more individuals, losing the idea of associating, will need it to come to their aid. These are causes and effects that engender each other without stopping. Will the public administration end up directing all the industries for which an isolated citizen cannot suffice?[m] And if a moment finally arrives when, as a consequence of the extreme division of landed property, the land is infinitely divided, so that it can no longer be cultivated except by associations of farm workers, will the head of government have to leave the tiller of the State in order to come to hold the plow?

The morals and intelligence of a democratic people would run no lesser dangers than their trade and industry, if the government came to take the place of associations everywhere.[n]

Sentiments and ideas are renewed, the heart grows larger and the human mind develops only by the reciprocal action of men on each other.

I have demonstrated that this action is almost nil in democratic countries. So it must be created there artificially. And this is what associations alone are able to do.

When the members of an aristocracy adopt a new idea or conceive of a

j. "If these things are no longer done by anyone, the people gradually return to barbarism, and if you charge the great general association, which is called the government, with them, tyranny is inevitable" (*Rubish*, 1).

k. "It is easy to foresee that the day is approaching when men will be forced to associate in order to carry out a portion of the things most necessary to life. *Fourierism*" (*Rubish*, 1).

m. "Commercial associations are the easiest and the first; they are the ones that a government has the most interest in encouraging" (*Rubish*, 1).

n. "In this, as in nearly everything else, the greatest effort of the government must tend toward teaching citizens the art of doing without its help" (*Rubish*, 1).

new sentiment, they place them, in a way, next to them on the great stage where they are themselves, and, in this way exposing those new ideas or sentiments to the sight of the crowd, they introduce them easily into the mind or heart of those who surround them.

In democratic countries only the social power is naturally able to act in this way, but it is easy to see that its action is always insufficient and often dangerous.°

A government can no more suffice for maintaining alone and for renewing the circulation of sentiments and ideas among a great people than for conducting all of the industrial enterprises. From the moment it tries to emerge from the political sphere in order to throw itself into the new path, it will exercise an unbearable tyranny, even without wanting to do so; for government only knows how to dictate precise rules; it imposes the sentiments and ideas that it favors, and it is always difficult to distinguish its counsels from its orders.P

It will be still worse if a government believes itself really interested in having nothing move. It will then keep itself immobile and allow itself to become heavy with a voluntary sleep.

So it is necessary that it does not act alone.

Associations, among democratic peoples, must take the place of the powerful individuals that equality of conditions has made disappear.

As soon as some inhabitants of the United States have conceived of a sentiment or an idea that they want to bring about in the world, they seek each other out, and when they have found each other, they unite. From that moment, they are no longer isolated men, but a power that is seen from afar, and whose actions serve as an example; a power that speaks and to which you listen.

The first time I heard in the United States that one hundred thousand men[*] had publicly pledged not to use strong liquor, the thing seemed to

---

o. "The dominion of the majority is absolute, but it would be too permanent if there were not associations to combat it and to drag it out of its old ways" (*Rubish,* 1).

p. The manuscript says: ". . . to distinguish in it the *teacher from the master.*"

[*]. There are more than that. Look for the figure in the *Penitentiary System.*

me more amusing[q] than serious, and I did not at first see clearly why these citizens, who were so temperate, would not be content to drink water within their families.

I ended by understanding that these hundred thousand Americans, frightened by the progress that drunkenness was making around them, had wanted to give their patronage to temperance. They had acted precisely like a great lord who dressed very plainly in order to inspire disdain for luxury among simple citizens. It may be believed that if these hundred thousand men[r] lived in France, each one of them would have individually addressed the government in order to beg it to oversee the taverns throughout the entire kingdom.

There is nothing, in my opinion, that merits our attention more than the intellectual and moral associations of America. The political and industrial associations of the Americans easily fall within our grasp, but the others escape us; and, if we discover them, we understand them badly, because we have hardly ever seen anything analogous. You must recognize, however, that the intellectual and moral associations are as necessary as the political and industrial ones to the American people, and perhaps more.

In democratic countries, the science of association is the mother science; the progress of all the others depends on the progress of the former.[s]

Among the laws that govern human societies, there is one that seems more definitive and clearer than all the others. For men to remain civilized or to become so, the art of associating must become developed among them and be perfected in the same proportion as equality of conditions grows.

q. The manuscript says: "ridiculous."

r. The manuscript cites: "three hundred thousand."

s. "So I am far from claiming that a democratic government must abandon all important enterprises to the industry of individuals, or even that there is not a certain period in the life of a democratic people when the government must more or less mingle in a great number of enterprises, but I do not believe that in that [interrupted text (ed.)]" (*Rubish*, 1).

[Of the Manner in Which American Governments Act toward Associations]ᵗ

[In England, the State mingles strictly only in its own affairs. Often it even relies on individuals for the task of undertaking and of completing works whose usefulness or grandeur has an almost national appearance.

The English think they have done enough for the citizens by allowing them to give themselves unreservedly to their industry, or by allowing them to associate freely if they need to do so.

The Americans go further: it often happens that they lend to certain associations the support of the State or even charge the State with taking their place.

≠There are works that do not precisely have a national character, but whose execution is very difficult, in which the government takes part in the United States, or that it carries out at its expense. Such a thing is hardly seen in England.≠

That is explained when you consider that, if associations are more necessary in a democratic country, they are at the same time more difficult.

Among an aristocratic people, an association can have very great power and be composed of only a few men. In democratic countries, in order to create a similar association, you must unite a multitude of citizens all with-

---

t. Short unpublished chapter that is found with the manuscript of the chapter:

This chapter contains some good ideas and some good sentences. Nonetheless, I believe it useful to delete it.

1. Because it treats very briefly and very incompletely a very interesting subject that has been treated at great length by others. Among others, Chevalier.
2. Because it gets into the order of ideas of the great political chapters of the end./

Consult L[ouis (ed.)]. and B[eaumont (ed.)]./

It is clear in any case that this chapter is too thin to go alone. It must be deleted or joined to another. Perhaps to the general chapter on associations.

Tocqueville is alluding to Michel Chevalier, author of *Lettres sur l'Amérique du Nord,* 1836.

out defenses, keep them together and lead them. So in aristocratic countries the State can rely on individuals and associations for everything. In democratic countries it cannot do the same.

Those who govern democratic societies are in a very difficult position. If they always want to take the place of great associations, they prevent the spirit of association from developing and they take on a burden that weighs them down; and if they rely only on associations, very useful and often necessary things are not done by anyone.

Men who live in democratic centuries have more need than others to be allowed to do things by themselves, and more than others, they sometimes need things to be done for them. That depends on circumstances.

The greatest art of government in democratic countries consists in clearly distinguishing the circumstances and acting according to how circumstances lead it.

I will say only in a general way that since the first interest of a people of this type is that the spirit of association spreads and becomes secure within it, all the other interests must be subordinated to that one.

So the government [v. social power], even when it lends its support to individuals, must never discharge them entirely from the trouble of helping themselves by uniting; often it must deny them its help in order to let them find the secret of being self-sufficient, and it must withdraw its hand as they better understand the art of doing so.

This is, moreover, not particular to the subject of associations or to democratic times.

The principal aim of good government has always been to make the citizens more and more able to do without its *help*. That is more useful than the help can be.

If men learn in *obedience* only the art of obeying and not that of being free, I do not know what privileges they will have over the animals except that the shepherd would be taken from among them.][u]

---

u. In the margin: "There is the kernel of the thought. There is no correlation between *help* and *obedience*. You can lend help to a man that you do not command."

CHAPTER 6[a]

Of the Relation between Associations and Newspapers[b]

a. 1. When men are independent of one another you can only make a large number of them act in common by persuading each one separately but simultaneously of the utility of the enterprise.

And only a newspaper can thus succeed in putting the same thought in a thousand ears at the same time.

So newspapers are necessary in proportion as conditions are more equal.

2. A newspaper not only suggests the same plan to a large number of men at the same time, it provides them the means to carry out in common the plans that they had conceived themselves.

1. First, it makes them know each other and it puts them in contact.

2. Then, it binds them together; it makes them talk with each other without seeing each other and march in agreement without gathering together.

3. Since newspapers increase with associations, it is easy to understand that the less centralization there is among a people, the more newspapers there must be. For each district then forms a permanent association in which the need for a newspaper makes itself felt much more than when there is only a large national association.

4. Since a newspaper always represents an association, it explains why, the greater equality is and the weaker each individual is, the stronger the press is. The newspaper overpowers each of its readers in the name of all the others (YTC, CVf, pp. 26–27).

b. The *Rubish* contains two jackets with notes and drafts for this chapter. One bears the same title as the chapter; the other bears the following title:

PARTICULAR UTILITY THAT DEMOCRATIC PEOPLES DRAW FROM LIBERTY OF THE PRESS AND IN PARTICULAR FROM NEWSPAPERS./

Chapter scarcely roughed out and *weakly* conceived, to review and perhaps to delete. To put in the middle of associations./

Édouard notes rightly: 1. that the subject of newspapers is of all democratic subjects the one most familiar to the French, that consequently I must hesitate to treat it. 2. that in any case it is too important to treat it accidentally in relation to associations.

905

When men are no longer bound together in a solid and permanent way, you cannot get a large number to act in common, unless by persuading each one whose help is needed that his particular interest obliges him to unite his efforts voluntarily with the efforts of all the others.

That can usually and conveniently be done only with the aid of a newspaper;[c] only a newspaper can succeed in putting the same thought in a thousand minds at the same instant.

A newspaper is an advisor that you do not need to go to find, but which appears by itself and speaks to you daily and briefly about common affairs, without disturbing you in your private affairs.

So newspapers become more necessary as men are more equal and individualism more to be feared. It would diminish their importance to believe that they serve only to guarantee liberty; they maintain civilization.

I will not deny that, in democratic countries, newspapers often lead cit-

---

He proposes that I only show the relation that exists between newspapers and associations. A newspaper is the voice of an association. You can consider it as the soul of the association, the most energetic means that the association uses to form itself. If, on the one hand, there is a connection between the number of associations and equality of conditions, there is a connection between the number of newspapers and that of associations.

An association that has only one newspaper to read is only rough-hewn, but it already exists.

To that I propose to join what I say about how the power of newspapers grows in proportion as conditions become equal./

Associations in democracies can form only from a multitude of weak and humble individuals who do not see each other from far away, who do not have the leisure to seek each other out, or the ability to consult and to agree with each other (in aristocracies, on the contrary, a powerful association can form from a small number of powerful citizens; the latter know each other and they do not need newspapers to consult and to agree with each other). All of these things can take place only because of *newspapers* and in general because of the free publications of the press. So newspapers are necessary in democracies in proportion as associations themselves are necessary (*the central idea is found!*) (*Rubish,* 1).

c. "Make a note to point out that it is a matter here not only of political newspapers, but also and above all of scientific, industrial, religious, moral newspapers . . ." (*Rubish,* 1).

izens to do in common very ill-considered undertakings; but if there were no newspapers, there would be hardly any common action. So the evil that they produce is much less than the one they cure.

A newspaper not only has the effect of suggesting the same plan to a large number of men; it provides them with the means to carry out in common the plans that they would have conceived by themselves.

The principal citizens who inhabit an aristocratic country see each other from far away; and, if they want to combine their strength, they march toward each other, dragging along a multitude in their wake.

It often happens, on the contrary, in democratic countries, that a large number of men who have the desire or the need to associate cannot do so; since all are very small and lost in the crowd, they do not see each other and do not know where to find each other. Along comes a newspaper that exposes to view the sentiment or the idea that came simultaneously, but separately, to each of them. All head immediately for this light, and these wandering spirits, who have been looking for each other for a long time in the shadows, finally meet and unite.

[<In aristocratic countries you group readily around one man, and in democratic countries around a newspaper, and it is in this sense that you can say that newspapers there take the place of great lords.>]

The newspaper has drawn them closer together, and they continue to need it to hold them together.

For an association among a democratic people to have some power it must be numerous. Those who compose it are thus spread over a large area, and each of them is kept in the place that he inhabits by the mediocrity of his fortune and by the multitude of small cares that it requires. They must find a means to talk together every day without seeing each other, and to march in accord without getting together. Thus there is hardly any democratic association that can do without a newspaper.[d]

d. "That also explains the power of newspapers in democracies. They are not naturally stronger than in aristocracies, but they speak amid the universal silence; they act amid the common powerlessness. They take the initiative when no one dares to take it." (*Rubish* PARTICULAR UTILITY THAT DEMOCRATIC PEOPLES DRAW FROM LIBERTY OF THE PRESS AND IN PARTICULAR FROM NEWSPAPERS, *Rubish*, 1).

So a necessary relation exists between associations and newspapers; news-papers make associations, and associations make newspapers; and if it was true to say that associations must multiply as conditions become equal, it is no less certain that the number of newspapers grows as associations multiply.[e]

Consequently America is the only country in the world where at the same time you find the most associations and the most newspapers.

This relationship between the number of newspapers and that of as-sociations leads us to discover another one between the condition of the periodical press and the administrative form of the country, and we learn that the number of newspapers must decrease or increase among a dem-ocratic people in proportion as administrative centralization is more or less great. For among democratic peoples, you cannot entrust the exercise of local powers to the principal citizens as in aristocracies. These powers must be abolished, or their use handed over to a very great number of men. These men form a true association established in a permanent manner by the law for the administration of one portion of the territory, and they need a news-paper to come to find them each day amid their small affairs, and to teach them the state of public affairs. The more numerous the local powers are, the greater is the number of those called by the law to exercise them; and the more this necessity makes itself felt at every moment, the more news-papers proliferate.

It is the extraordinary splitting up of administrative power, much more than great political liberty and the absolute independence of the press, that so singularly multiplies the number of newspapers in America. If all the inhabitants of the Union were voters under the rule of a system that limited their electoral right to the choice of the legislators of the State, they would need only a small number of newspapers, because they could have only a few very important, but very rare occasions to act together; but within the great national association, the law established in each prov-ince and in each city, and so to speak in each village, small associations

e. "Thus the number of newspapers grows not only according to the number of vol-untary associations; it also increases in proportion as the political power [v: administra-tion] becomes decentralized and as the local power passes from the hands of the few into those of all" (*Rubish*, 1).

with the purpose of local administration. The law-maker in this way forced each American to cooperate daily with some of his fellow citizens in a common work, and each of them needs a newspaper to teach him what the others are doing.

I think that a democratic people,[1] who would not have national representation, but a great number of small local powers, would end by having more newspapers than another people among whom a centralized administration would exist alongside an elected legislature. What best explains to me the prodigious development that the daily press has undergone in the United States, is that I see among the Americans the greatest national liberty combined with local liberties of all types.

It is generally believed in France and in England that it is enough to abolish the duties that burden the press in order to increase newspapers indefinitely. That greatly exaggerates the effects of such a reform. Newspapers multiply not only following low cost, but also following the more or less repeated need that a large number of men have to communicate together and to act in common.

I would equally attribute the growing power of newspapers to more general reasons than those that are often used to explain it.

A newspaper can continue to exist only on the condition of reproducing a common doctrine or common sentiment for a large number of men. So a newspaper always represents an association whose members are its habitual readers.

This association can be more or less defined, more or less limited, more or less numerous; but it exists in minds, at least in germ; for that reason alone the newspaper does not die.

This leads us to a final reflection that will end this chapter.

The more conditions become equal, the weaker men are individually,

---

1. *I say a* democratic people. *The administration can be very decentralized among an aristocratic people, without making the need for newspapers felt, because local powers then are in the hands of a very small number of men who act separately or who know each other and can easily see and understand each other.*

the more they allow themselves to go along easily with the current of the crowd and the more difficulty they have holding on alone to an opinion that the crowd abandons.

The newspaper represents the association; you can say that it speaks to each one of its readers in the name of all the others, and the weaker they are individually, the more easily it carries them along.[f]

So the dominion of newspapers must grow as men become more equal.

f. "The press that much more powerful among a democratic people as the spirit of association is less widespread. It is not that it is itself stronger, but that those whom it wants to dominate are weaker" (*Rubish* PARTICULAR UTILITY THAT DEMOCRATIC PEOPLES DRAW FROM LIBERTY OF THE PRESS AND IN PARTICULAR FROM NEWSPAPERS, *Rubish,* 1).

CHAPTER 7[a]

Relations between Civil Associations and Political Associations[b]

a. 1. When men have contracted the habit of associations in civil life, that gives them great facility for associating in political life.

2. Political associations are on their side very powerful for giving men the thought and the art of associating in civil life.

1. Politics provides common interests to a multitude of men at the same time, provides them with natural occasions to associate, which generalizes the theory of association and makes it studied.

2. You can in general become familiar with the theory of association only by risking your money. Associations are the free schools of association.

3. So political associations neutralize in the long run most of the evils that they create. For if they put the tranquillity of the State at risk, they multiply the number of civil associations that favor this tranquillity (YTC, CVf, p. 27).

b. ≠This chapter absolutely needs a general reworking. Its movement is confused and difficult, and several of the ideas that it contains are questionable.≠/

You would say that I come to prove that civil association arises from political association, which is false according to myself, since I say that in countries where political association is *forbidden,* civil association is *rare.*

1. *The first aim* of the chapter is to show that civil association is always weak, lethargic, limited, clumsy wherever political association does not exist. Civil association does not arise from political association any more than the latter from civil association. They develop mutually. In a country where political associations are very numerous, civil associations cannot fail to be so as well, just as men who already have the habit of associating in civil matters have a great facility for associating in politics.

2. *The second objective of the chapter* is to show that a people can have an interest in allowing liberty of political association in order to favor civil association, which is more necessary to its tranquillity than the other is harmful./

There are *free* associations other than *political* associations, but they are not striking.

You can undoubtedly study the laws of association in the *Norman association,* but who thinks of doing so? (*Rubish,* 1).

There is only one nation[c] on earth where the unlimited liberty of associating for political ends is used daily. This same nation is the only one in the world where the citizens have imagined making continual use of the right of association in civil life and have succeeded in gaining in this way all the good things civilization can offer.

Among all peoples where political association is forbidden, civil association is rare.

It is hardly probable that this is a result of an accident; but you must instead conclude from it that there exists a natural and perhaps necessary relationship between the two types of associations.

[≠Men can associate in a thousand ways, but the spirit of association is a whole, and you cannot stop one of its principal developments without weakening it everywhere else.≠]

Some men have by chance a common interest in a certain affair. It concerns a commercial enterprise to direct, an industrial operation to conclude; they meet together and unite; in this way they become familiar little by little with association [and when it becomes necessary to associate for a political end, they feel more inclined to attempt it and more capable of succeeding in doing so.]

The more the number of these small common affairs increases, the more men acquire, even without their knowing, the ability to pursue great affairs together.

Civil associations therefore facilitate political associations; but, on the other hand, political association develops and singularly perfects civil association.

In civil life, each man can, if need be, believe that he is able to be self-sufficient. In politics, he can never imagine it. So when a people has a public life, the idea of association and the desire to associate present themselves each day to the mind of all citizens; whatever natural reluctance men have to act in common, they will always be ready to do so in the interest of a party.

Thus politics generalizes the taste and habit of association; it brings

c. In a first version: ". . . there are only two nations."

about the desire to unite and teaches the art of associating to a host of men who would have always lived alone.

Politics not only gives birth to many associations, it creates very vast associations.

In civil life it is rare for the same interest to attract naturally a large number of men toward a common action. Only with a great deal of art can you succeed in creating something like it.

In politics, the occasion presents itself at every moment. Now, it is only in great associations that the general value of association appears. Citizens individually weak do not form in advance a clear idea of the strength that they can gain by uniting; you must show it to them in order for them to understand it. The result is that it is often easier to gather a multitude for a common purpose than a few men; a thousand citizens do not see the interest that they have in uniting; ten thousand see it. In politics, men unite for great enterprises, and the advantage that they gain from association in important affairs teaches them, in a practical way, the interest that they have in helping each other in the least affairs.

A political association draws a multitude of individuals out of themselves at the same time; however separated they are naturally by age, mind, fortune, it brings them closer together and puts them in contact. They meet once and learn how to find each other always.

You can become engaged in most civil associations only by risking a portion of your patrimony; it is so for all industrial and commercial companies. When men are still little versed in the art of associating and are ignorant of its principal rules, they fear, while associating for the first time in this way, paying dearly for their experience. So they prefer doing without a powerful means of success, to running the dangers that accompany it. But they hesitate less to take part in political associations, which seem without danger to them, because in them they are not risking their own money. Now, they cannot take part for long in those associations without discovering how you maintain order among a great number of men, and by what process you succeed in making them march, in agreement and methodically, toward the same goal. They learn to submit their will to that of all the others, and to subordinate their particular efforts to common action, all things that are no less necessary to know in civil associations than in political associations.

So political associations can be considered as great free schools, where all citizens come to learn the general theory of associations.

So even if political association would not directly serve the progress of civil association, it would still be harmful to the latter to destroy the first.

When citizens can associate only in certain cases, they regard association as a rare and singular process, and they hardly think of it.

When you allow them to associate freely in everything, they end up seeing in association the universal and, so to speak, unique means that men can use to attain the various ends that they propose. Each new need immediately awakens the idea of association. The art of association then becomes, as I said above, the mother science; everyone studies it and applies it.

When certain associations are forbidden and others allowed, it is difficult in advance to distinguish the first from the second. In case of doubt, you refrain from all, and a sort of public opinion becomes established that tends to make you consider any association like a daring and almost illicit enterprise.[1]

1. *That is true, above all, when it is the executive power that is charged with allowing or forbidding associations according to its arbitrary will.*

When the law limits itself to prohibiting certain associations and leaves to the courts the task of punishing those who disobey, the evil is very much less; each citizen then knows in advance more or less what is what; in a way he judges himself before his judges do so, and, avoiding forbidden associations, he devotes himself to permitted associations. All free peoples have always understood that the right of association could be limited in this way. But, if it happened that the legislator charged a man with disentangling in advance which associations are dangerous and which are useful, and left him free to destroy the seed of all associations or to allow them to be born, no one would be able any longer to foresee in advance in what case you can associate and in what other you must refrain from doing so; so the spirit of association would be completely struck with inertia. The first of these two laws attacks only certain associations; the second is addressed to society itself and wounds it. I conceive that a regular government might resort to the first, but I recognize in no government the right to bring about the second.

So it is a chimera to believe that the spirit of association, repressed at one point, will allow itself to develop with the same vigor at all the others, and that it will be enough to permit men to carry out certain enterprises together, for them to hurry to try it. When citizens have the ability and the habit of associating for all things, they will associate as readily for small ones as for great ones. But if they can associate only for small ones, they will not even find the desire and the capacity to do so. In vain will you allow them complete liberty to take charge of their business together; they will only nonchalantly use the rights that you grant them; and after you have exhausted yourself with efforts to turn them away from the forbidden associations, you will be surprised at your inability to persuade them to form the permitted ones.

I am not saying that there can be no civil associations in a country where political association is forbidden; for men can never live in society without giving themselves to some common enterprise. But I maintain that in such a country civil associations will always be very few in number, weakly conceived, ineptly led, and that they will never embrace vast designs, or will fail while wanting to carry them out.

This leads me naturally to think that liberty of association in political matters is not as dangerous for public tranquillity as is supposed, and that it could happen that after disturbing the State for a time, liberty of association strengthens it.[d]

In democratic countries, political associations form, so to speak, the only powerful individuals who aspire to rule the State. Consequently the governments [v. princes] of today consider these types of associations in the same way that the kings of the Middle Ages saw the great vassals of the crown: they feel a kind of instinctive horror for them and combat them at every occasion.

They have, on the contrary, a natural favor for civil associations, because they have easily discovered that the latter, instead of leading the mind of citizens toward public affairs, serve to distract it from these affairs, and by

---

d. According to Jean-Claude Lamberti, Tocqueville is referring here to the law on association of 16 February 1834. *Tocqueville et les deux Démocraties* (Paris: PUF, 1983), p. 104, note 42.

engaging citizens more and more in projects that cannot be accomplished without public peace, civil associations turn them away from revolutions. But the governments of today do not notice that political associations multiply and prodigiously facilitate civil associations, and that by avoiding a dangerous evil, they are depriving themselves of an effective remedy. When you see the Americans associate freely each day, with the purpose of making a political opinion prevail, of bringing a statesman to the government, or of wresting power from another man, you have difficulty understanding that men so independent do not at every moment fall into license.

If, on the other hand, you come to consider the infinite number of industrial enterprises that are being pursued in common in the United States, and you see on all sides Americans working without letup on the execution of some important and difficult plan, which would be confounded by the slightest revolution, you easily conceive why these men, so very busy, are not tempted to disturb the State or to destroy a public peace from which they profit.

Is it enough to see these things separately? Isn't it necessary to find the hidden bond that joins them? It is within political associations that the Americans of all the states, all minds and all ages, daily acquire the general taste for association and become familiar with its use. There they see each other in great number, talk together, understand each other and become active together in all sorts of enterprises. They then carry into civil life the notions that they have acquired in this way and make them serve a thousand uses.

So it is by enjoying a dangerous liberty that the Americans learn the art of making the dangers of liberty smaller.

If you choose a certain moment in the existence of a nation, it is easy to prove that political associations disturb the State and paralyze industry; but when you take the entire life of a people, it will perhaps be easy to demonstrate that liberty of association in political matters is favorable to the well-being and even to the tranquillity of citizens.

I said in the first part of this work: "The unlimited freedom of association cannot be confused with the freedom to write: the first is both less necessary and more dangerous than the second. A nation can set limits on the first without losing control over itself; sometimes it must set limits in order to continue to be in control." And later I added: "You cannot conceal the fact that, of all liberties, the unlimited freedom of association, in political matters, is the last one that a people can bear. If unlimited freedom of association does not make a people fall into anarchy, it puts a people on the brink, so to speak, at every moment."

Thus, I do not believe that a nation is free at all times to allow its citizens the absolute right to associate in political matters; and I even doubt that there is any country in any period in which it would be wise to set no limits to the liberty of association.

A certain people, it is said, cannot maintain peace internally, inspire respect for the laws or establish enduring government, if it does not enclose the right of association within narrow limits. Such benefits are undoubtedly precious, and I conceive that, to acquire or to retain them, a nation agrees temporarily to impose great burdens on itself; but still it is good that the nation knows precisely what these benefits cost it.

That, to save the life of a man, you cut off his arm, I understand; but I do not want you to assure me that he is going to appear as dexterous as if he were not a one-armed man.

CHAPTER 8[a]

How the Americans Combat Individualism by the Doctrine of Interest Well Understood[b]

[I showed in a preceding chapter how equality of conditions developed among all men the taste for well-being, and directed their minds toward the search for what is useful.

Elsewhere, while talking about individualism, I have just shown how this same equality of conditions broke the artificial bonds that united citizens in aristocratic societies, and led each man to search for what is useful to himself alone.

These various changes in the social constitution and in the tastes of humanity cannot fail to influence singularly the theoretical idea that men form of their duties and their rights.][c]

When the world was led by a small number of powerful and rich individuals, the latter loved to form a sublime idea of the duties of man; they took pleasure in professing that it is glorious to forget self and that it is right

a. 1. As men are more equal and more detached from their fellows, the idea of devotion becomes more foreign, and it is more necessary to show how particular interest merges with general interest.

2. This is what is done in America. Not only is the doctrine of interest well understood *openly* professed there, but it is universally admitted.

3. The doctrine of interest well understood is the most appropriate one for the needs of a democratic people, and the moralists of our time should turn toward it (YTC, CVf, p. 28).

b. Former title in the manuscript: OF INTEREST WELL UNDERSTOOD AS PHILO-SOPHICAL DOCTRINE.

c. In the margin, with a bracket indicating this beginning: "Probably delete this."

to do good without interest, just like God. That was the official doctrine of this time in the matter of morality [{moral philosophy}].

I doubt that men were more virtuous in aristocratic centuries than in others, but it is certain that they then talked constantly about the beauties of virtue; they only studied in secret how it was useful. But as imagination soars less and as each person concentrates on himself, moralists become afraid of this idea of sacrifice, and they no longer dare to offer it to the human mind; so they are reduced to trying to find out if the individual advantage of citizens would not be to work toward the happiness of all, and, when they have discovered one of these points where particular interest meets with general interest and merges with it, they hasten to bring it to light; little by little similar observations multiply. What was only an isolated remark becomes a general doctrine, and you believe finally that you see that man, by serving his fellows, serves himself, and that his particular interest is to do good.[d]

[<But this doctrine is not accepted all at once or by all. Many receive a few parts of it and reject the rest. Some *adopt it at the bottom of their hearts and reject it with disdain* before the eyes of the world.>][e]

I have already shown, in several places in this work, how the inhabitants of the United States almost always knew how to combine their own well-being with that of their fellow citizens. What I want to note here is the general theory by the aid of which they succeed in doing so.[f]

---

d. "Democracy *destroys* the instinct for devotion, *reason* for it [devotion] must be found" (*Rubish*, 1).

e. In the margin: "To delete I think./
"These paragraphs seem to Édouard to merit some small development./
"Explain why some affect to despise this theory."

f. Democracy pushes each man to think only of himself; on the other hand, reason and experience indicate that it is sometimes necessary in his own interest to be concerned about others.

The philosophical doctrine of interest well understood as principal rule of human actions has presented itself to the human mind from time to time in all centuries, but in democratic centuries it besieges the human mind and entirely dominates the moral world.

[To the side] The barbarians forced each man to think only of himself; democracy leads them by themselves to want to do so" (*Rubish*, 1).

In the United States, you almost never say that virtue is beautiful. You maintain that it is useful, and you prove it every day. American moralists do not claim that you must sacrifice yourself for your fellows because it is great to do so; but they say boldly that such sacrifices are as necessary to the person who imposes them on himself as to the person who profits from them.g

They have noticed that, in their country and time, man was led back toward himself by an irresistible force and, losing hope of stopping him, they have thought only about guiding him.

So they do not deny that each man may follow his interest, but they strive to prove that the interest of each man is to be honest.

Here I do not want to get into the details of their reasons, which would take me away from my subject; it is enough for me to say that they have persuaded their fellow citizens.

A long time ago, Montaigne said: "When I would not follow the right road because of rectitude, I would follow it because I found by experience that in the end it is usually the happiest and most useful path."h

So the doctrine of interest well understood is not new; but, among the Americans of today, it has been universally admitted; it has become popular; you find it at the bottom of all actions; it pokes through all discussions. You find it no less in the mouths of the poor than in those of the rich.

In Europe the doctrine of interest is much cruder than in America, but at the same time, it is less widespread and above all less evident, and great devotions that are felt no more are still feigned among us every day.

The Americans, in contrast, take pleasure in explaining almost all the

---

g. In aristocratic centuries, you know your interest, but the philosophical doctrine is to scorn it.

In democratic centuries, you maintain that virtue and interest are in agreement.

[To the side] I need America to prove these two propositions, so I must finish rather than begin with it, in order to gather light on this essential point (*Rubish*, 1).

h. A note of the manuscript indicates that this quotation belongs to book II, chapter XVI of the *Essais*. The library of the Tocqueville château had an edition in three volumes dating from 1600.

actions of their life with the aid of interest well understood; they show with satisfaction how enlightened love of themselves leads them constantly to help each other and disposes them willingly to sacrifice for the good of the State a portion of their time and their wealth. I think that in this they often do not do themselves justice; for you sometimes see in the United States, as elsewhere, citizens give themselves to the disinterested and unconsidered impulses that are natural to man; but the Americans hardly ever admit that they yield to movements of this type; they prefer to honor their philosophy rather than themselves.[j]

I could stop here and not try to judge what I have just described. The extreme difficulty of the subject would be my excuse. But I do not want to take advantage of it, and I prefer that my readers, clearly seeing my purpose, refuse to follow me rather than remain in suspense.

Interest well understood is a doctrine not very lofty, but clear and sure. It does not try to attain great objectives, but without too much effort it attains all those it targets. Since the doctrine is within reach of all minds, each man grasps it easily and retains it without difficulty. Accommodating itself marvelously to the weaknesses of men, it easily gains great dominion and it is not difficult for it to preserve that dominion, because the doctrine turns personal interest back against itself and, to direct passions, uses the incentive that excites them.

The doctrine of interest well understood does not produce great devotions; but it suggests small sacrifices every day; by itself, it cannot make a

---

j. Some enlightenment makes men see how their personal interest differs from that of their fellows. A great deal of enlightenment shows them how the two interests often come to merge./

Three successive states:

1. *Ignorance.* Instinctive devotion.
2. *Half-knowledge.* Egoism.
3. *Complete enlightenment.* Thoughtful sacrifice./

There are two ways to make that understood by a people:
1. Experience. 2. Enlightenment.

The most difficult task of governments is not to govern, but to instruct men in governing them[selves (ed.)]./

The worst effect of a bad government is not the evil that it does, but the one that it suggests (*Rubish,* 1).

man virtuous, but it forms a multitude of steady, temperate, moderate, far-sighted citizens who have self-control; and, if it does not lead directly to virtue by will, it imperceptibly draws closer to virtue by habits.[k]

If the doctrine of interest well understood came to dominate the moral world entirely, extraordinary virtues would undoubtedly be rarer. But I also think that then the coarsest depravities would be less common. The doctrine of interest well understood perhaps prevents some men from rising very far above the ordinary level of humanity; but a great number of others who fall below encounter the doctrine and cling to it. Consider a few individuals, it lowers them. Envisage the species, it elevates it.

I will not be afraid to say that the doctrine of interest well understood seems to me, of all philosophical theories, the most appropriate to the needs of the men of our time, and that I see in it the most powerful guarantee remaining to them against themselves. So it is principally toward this doctrine that the mind of the moralists of today should turn. Even if they were to judge it as imperfect, it would still have to be adopted as necessary.

I do not believe, everything considered, that there is more egoism among us than in America; the only difference is that there it is enlightened and here it is not. Each American knows how to sacrifice a portion of his particular interests in order to save the rest. We want to keep everything, and often everything escapes us.

I see around me only men who seem to want to teach their contemporaries, every day by their word and their example, that what is useful is never dishonorable. Will I never finally find some men who undertake to make their contemporaries understand how what is honorable can be useful?

There is no power on earth that can prevent the growing equality of

---

k. "The *beauty* of virtue is the favorite thesis of moralists under aristocracy. Its *utility* under democracy" (*Rubish*, 1).

"Interest well understood is not contrary to the disinterested advance of the good. These are two different things, but not opposite. Great souls for whom this doctrine cannot be enough, pass in a way through it and go beyond it, while ordinary souls stop there" (YTC, CVk, 1, p. 85).

conditions from leading the human mind toward the search for what is useful, and from disposing each citizen to become enclosed within himself.

So you must expect individual interest to become more than ever the principal, if not the sole motivating force of the actions of men; but how each man will understand his individual interest remains to be known.

If citizens, while becoming equal, remained ignorant and coarse, it is difficult to predict to what stupid excess their egoism could be led, and you cannot say in advance into what shameful miseries they would plunge themselves, out of fear of sacrificing something of their well-being to the prosperity of their fellows.[m]

I do not believe that the doctrine of interest, as it is preached in America, is evident in all its parts; but it contains a great number of truths so evident that it is enough to enlighten men in order for them to see them. So enlighten them at all cost, for the century of blind devotions and instinctive virtues is already fleeing far from us, and I see the time drawing near when liberty, the public peace and the social order itself will not be able to do without enlightenment.[n]

---

m. "Utility of provincial institutions in order to create centers of common interest in democracy. National interest is not enough. It is necessary to multiply links, to bring men to see each other, understand each other, and have ideas, sentiments in common" (*Rubish*, 1).

n. Fragment that belongs to the *rubish* of the chapter:

Doctrine of interest./

[To the side: This could be placed as well in sentiments and tastes. To think about it.]

Not very elevated point of view from which the Americans envisage human actions. Doctrine of interest followed elsewhere, *professed* in America. Effort to make it a social doctrine. *Succeeds in fact in making society proceed comfortably, but without grandeur.*

{To put perhaps before or after what I say about religion as political element.}/

This, among the Americans in particular and among democratic peoples in general, is clearly the result: 1. of egoism above all that makes you think only of yourself; 2. of the concentration of the soul in material things.

So this must be treated only after these two ideas are known; this chapter will be only their corollary./

I will first demonstrate that the Americans are led in general to concentrate on their interest and then, that they have made this way of acting into a philosophical theory./

That the legislators of democracies are not able to prevent the establishment and development of this doctrine, that all their effort should be limited to getting the most out of it, to making it so that men have a real interest in doing good, or at least to making this interest clear to all. That is useful in all societies, but very much more useful in those in which men cannot withdraw to the *platonic* enjoyment of doing good and in which they see the other world ready to escape them.

It is equally necessary that men, having reached this point, be enlightened at all cost, for there is enough truth in the notion that man has an interest in doing good, that widespread enlightenment cannot fail to make man discover it.

Proof of this, morality of the well-enlightened man.

Political consequences. Extreme efforts that the legislator must make in democracies to spiritualize man. Particular necessity for religions in democracy; even dogmatic and not very reasonable religions, for lack of anything better. Show heaven even if it is through the worst instruments./

Distinctions to make between the different doctrines of *interest./*

There is a doctrine of interest that consists of believing that you must make the interest of other men yield before your own and that it is natural and reasonable to embrace only the latter. This is an instinctive, crude egoism that hardly merits the name of doctrine.

[In the margin: The doctrine of interest can teach how to live, but not how to die./

The doctrine of interest must not be confused with the doctrine of the *useful*. It is contained in that of the useful, but it is only a part of it.]

There is another doctrine of interest that consists of believing that the best way to be happy is to serve your interest and to be good, honest . . . in a word, that interest well understood requires you often to sacrifice your interest or rather, that to follow your interest over all, you often have to neglect it in detail.

This is a philosophical doctrine that has its value.

[In the margin: Great passions of the *true,* the *beautiful* and the *good*. Analogous things flowing from [the (ed.)] same source, equally rare, producing great men of learning, great men of literature and great virtues.]

There is, finally, a doctrine infinitely purer, more elevated, less material, according to which the basis of actions is duty. Man penetrates divine thought with his intelligence. He sees that the purpose of God is order, and he freely associates himself as much as he is able with this great design. He cooperates with it in his humble sphere, depending on his strength, in order to fulfill his destination and to obey his mandate. There is still personal interest there, for there is a proud and private enjoyment in such points of view and hope for remuneration in a better world; but interest there is as small, as secretive and as legitimate as possible.

Positive religions render this interest more visible; they render these sentiments stronger, more popular. They generally mix the two things in a clever way that facilitates practice. In Christianity, for example, we are told that it is necessary to do good *out of love of God* (magnificent expression of the doctrine that I have just explained) and also to gain eternal life.

Thus Christianity at one end touches the doctrine of interest well understood and at the other the doctrine that I developed afterward and that I could call with Christianity itself, the doctrine of the love of God. In sum, a religion very superior in terms of loftiness to the doctrine of interest well understood because it places interest in the other world and draws us out of this cesspool of human and material interests.

The doctrine of interest well understood can make men honest.

But it is only that of the love of God that makes men virtuous. The one teaches how to live, the other teaches how to die, and how can you make men who do not want to die live well for long?

Why aristocratic peoples are led more than democratic peoples to adopt the second doctrines more than the first.

Class that has material happiness without thinking about it, that can think and is not preoccupied by the trouble to work and to acquire. Another class that by working can scarcely hope to reach material happiness and that turns naturally toward the non-material world.

On the contrary, in democracies each man has just enough material happiness to desire more of it, enough of a chance of gaining it to fix the mind on material happiness or at least that of this world./

Another point of view.

The philosophical doctrine that I spoke about is based on interest.

Religious doctrines are also based on interest.

But there is this great difference between them, that the first places this interest in this world and the others outside of it, which is enough to give actions an infinitely less material and loftier purpose; that the ones out of necessity profess to scorn material goods, while the other, restricting itself to that life, cannot fail to hold material goods in a certain esteem. So although the cause of actions is the same, these actions are very different./

Religions have, by design, made such an intimate union of the doctrine of the love of God and of that of interest, that those who are sincerely devout are constantly mistaken, and it happens that they believe that they are doing actions solely in view of the reward to come, actions that are principally suggested to them by the most pure, most noble and most disinterested instincts of human nature (*Rubish,* 1).

CHAPTER 9[a]

How the Americans Apply the Doctrine of Interest Well Understood in the Matter of Religion[b]

If the doctrine of interest well understood had only this world in view, it would be far from enough; for a great number of sacrifices can find their reward only in the other; and whatever intellectual effort you make to feel the usefulness of virtue, it will always be difficult to make a man live well who does not want to die.

So it is necessary to know if the doctrine of interest well understood can be easily reconciled with religious beliefs.

The philosophers who teach this doctrine say to men that, to be happy in life, you must watch over your passions and carefully repress their excesses; that you cannot gain lasting happiness except by denying yourself

---

a. 1. If the doctrine of interest well understood had only this life in view, it would be far from enough; so we must see if it is not contrary to religions that promote action with the other in view.

2. If you look closely you will see that interest is the motivating force of nearly all religious men, and the lever used by nearly all the founders of religion.

So the doctrine of interest well understood in itself is not contrary to religions, since religions only apply it in another way.

It is easy as well to prove that the men who adopt it are very disposed than [sic] others to submit to religious beliefs and practices.

3. Examples of the Americans (YTC, CVf, pp. 28–29). There is no *rubish* for this chapter.

b. At the first page of the manuscript: "<I am afraid of being superficial and incomplete and commonplace in these two chapters, while there is no matter that requires more knowledge and depth and originality.>"

a thousand passing enjoyments, and that finally you must triumph over yourself constantly in order to serve yourself better.

The founders of nearly all religions adhered more or less to the same language. Without pointing out another path to men, they only placed the goal further away; instead of placing in this world the prize for the sacrifices that they impose, they put it in the other.[c]

Nonetheless, I refuse to believe that all those who practice virtue because of the spirit of religion act only with a reward in view.

I have met zealous Christians who constantly forgot themselves in order to work with more fervor for the happiness of all, and I have heard them claim that they acted this way only to merit the good things of the other world; but I cannot prevent myself from thinking that they are deluding themselves. I respect them too much to believe them.

Christianity tells us, it is true, that you must prefer others to self in order to gain heaven; but Christianity also tells us that you must do good to your fellows out of love of God. That is a magnificent expression; man penetrates divine thought with his intelligence, he sees that the purpose of God is order; he associates freely with this great design; and even while sacrificing his particular interests to this admirable order of all things, he expects no other recompense than the pleasure of contemplating it.

So I do not believe that the sole motivating force of religious men is interest; but I think that interest is the principal means that religions themselves use to lead men, and I do not doubt that it is from this side that they take hold of the crowd and become popular.

So I do not see clearly why the doctrine of interest well understood would put off men of religious beliefs, and it seems to me, on the contrary, that I am sorting out how it brings them closer.

[All the actions of the human mind are linked together, and once man is set by his will on a certain path, he then marches there without wanting to, and he feels himself carried along by his own inertia.]

I suppose that, to attain happiness in this world, a man resists instinct in all that he encounters and coldly considers all the actions of his life, that

c. In the margin: "and that alone is enough to give to religions a great advantage over philosophy . . ."

instead of yielding blindly to the heat of his first desires, he has learned the art of combating them, and that he has become accustomed to sacrificing effortlessly the pleasure of the moment to the permanent interest of his entire life.

If such a man has faith in the religion that he professes, it will hardly cost him anything to submit to the inconveniences that it imposes. Reason itself counsels him to do it, and custom prepared him in advance to endure it.

If he has conceived doubts about the object of his hopes, he will not let himself be stopped easily, and he will judge that it is wise to risk a few of the good things of this world in order to maintain his rights to the immense heritage that has been promised to him in the other.

"To be mistaken in believing the Christian religion true," said Pascal, "there is not much to lose; but what misfortune to be mistaken in believing it false!"[d]

The Americans do not affect a crude indifference for the other life; they do not assume a puerile pride in scorning the perils that they hope to escape.

So they practice their religion without shame and without weakness; but you ordinarily see, even amid their zeal, something so tranquil, so methodical and so calculated, that it seems that it is the reason much more than the heart that leads them to the steps of the altar.[e]

Not only do Americans follow their religion by interest, but they often place in this world the interest that you can have in following religion. In the Middle Ages, priests spoke only about the other life: they hardly worried about proving that a sincere Christian can be a happy man here below.

But American preachers come back to earth constantly, and only with

---

d. To the side: "This thought, which does not seem to me worthy of the great soul of Pascal, sums up perfectly well the state of souls in the countries where reason is becoming enlightened and stronger at the same time that religious beliefs falter." *Pensée* 36 in the Lafuma edition.

e. In the margin: "<So the doctrine of interest well understood can become the ruling philosophy among a people without harming the spirit of religion; but it cannot fail to give the spirit of religion a certain character, and you must expect that, in the soul of the *devout*, it will make the desire to gain heaven predominate over the pure love of God.>"

great pain can they take their eyes away from it. To touch their listeners better, they show them every day how religious beliefs favor liberty and public order, and it is often difficult to know, hearing them, if the principal object of religion is to gain eternal felicity in the other world or well-being in this one.

CHAPTER 10[a]

Of the Taste for
Material Well-Being in America[b]

a. 1. The taste for material well-being is universal in America. Why?

1. In aristocracies, the upper classes, since they have never acquired well-being or feared losing it, readily apply their passions elsewhere and on a more lofty level. Since the lower classes do not have the idea of bettering their lot and are not close enough to well-being to desire it, their imagination is thrown toward the other world.

2. In democratic centuries, on the contrary, each person tries hard to attain well-being or fears losing it. That constantly keeps the soul in suspense on this point (YTC, CVf, p. 29).

First organization of this part of the book in the *Rubish:*

OF THE TASTE FOR MATERIAL ENJOYMENTS IN DEMOCRACIES./

1. Of the taste for material enjoyments in America.

2. Of the different effects that the taste for material enjoyments produces in an aristocracy and in a democracy.

3. Of some bizarre sects that are arising in America.

4. Of restlessness of the heart in America.

5. How the taste for material enjoyments is combined among the Americans with love of liberty and concerns for public affairs.

6. How equality of conditions (or democracy) leads Americans toward industrial professions.

7. How the religious beliefs of the Americans hold within certain limits the excessive taste for material well-being (*Rubish* of chapter 15 of this part, *Rubish,* 1).

b. In the *Rubish* there is a voluminous sheaf bearing the title RUBISH AND IDEAS RELATING TO THE CHAPTERS ON MATERIAL ENJOYMENTS. It contains notes and pages of *rubish* for this chapter and for those that follow, up to and including chapter 18. The *rubish* for this chapter retains another sheaf with this note on the cover:

WHAT MAKES THE LOVE OF RICHES PREDOMINATE OVER ALL OTHER PASSIONS IN DEMOCRATIC CENTURIES./

Chapter to insert in the course of the book, probably before industrial careers./

In America, the passion for material well-being is not always exclusive, but it is general; if everyone does not experience it in the same way, everyone feels it. The concern to satisfy the slightest needs of the body and to provide for the smallest conveniences of life preoccupies minds universally.

Something similar is seen more and more in Europe.

Among the causes that produce these similar effects in two worlds, several are close to my subject, and I must point them out.

When wealth is fixed in the same families by inheritance, you see a great number of men who enjoy material well-being, without feeling the exclusive taste for well-being.

What most strongly holds the human heart is not the peaceful possession of a precious object but the imperfectly satisfied desire to possess it and the constant fear of losing it.

In aristocratic societies the rich, never knowing a state different from their own, do not fear its changing; they scarcely imagine another one. So for them material well-being is not the goal of life; it is a way of living. They consider it, in a way, like existence, and enjoy it without thinking about it.

Since the natural and instinctive taste that all men feel for well-being is thus satisfied without difficulty and without fear, their soul proceeds else-

---

At ambition, what diverts from great ambition, it is the petty ambition for money.

You devote yourself to the petty ambition for money as preliminary to the other and, when you have devoted yourself to it for a long time, you are incapable of moving away from it./

To put I think before material enjoyments. The desire for wealth is close to the desire for material enjoyments, but is distinct.

The only page of the sheaf bears particularly the following notes:

"Regularity. Monotony of life./

"That is not democratic but commercial, or at least it is democratic only in so far as democracy pushes toward commerce and industry.

"There are also religious habits in the middle of that."

In another place: "In aristocracies, even the life of artisans is varied; they have games, ceremonies, a form of worship that serves as a diversion from the monotony of their works. Their body is attached to their profession, not their soul.

"It is not the same thing with democratic peoples" (*Rubish*, 1).

where and attaches itself to some more difficult and greater enterprise that animates it and carries it away.

In this way, in the very midst of material enjoyments, the members of an aristocracy often demonstrate a proud scorn for these very enjoyments and find singular strength when they must finally do without them. All the revolutions that have disturbed or destroyed aristocracies have shown with what ease men accustomed to superfluity were able to do without necessities, while men who have laboriously attained comfort are hardly ever able to live after losing it.[c]

If, from the upper ranks, I pass to the lower classes, I will see analogous effects produced by different causes.

Among nations where aristocracy dominates society and keeps it immobile, the people end by becoming accustomed to poverty as the rich are to their opulence. The latter are not preoccupied by material well-being, because they possess it without difficulty; the former do not think about material well-being, because they despair of gaining it and do not know it well enough to desire it.[d]

c. "≠Byron remarks somewhere that in his voyages, he easily bore and suffered almost without complaint the privations that made his valet despair. The same remark could have been made by a thousand others≠" (*Rubish,* 1). Letter of Byron to his mother, Athens, 17 January 1831; reproduced in *Correspondence of Lord Byron with a Friend* . . . (Paris: A. and W. Calignani, 1825), I, pp. 21–22; the same publishing house published a French version of this text.

d. How the different forms of government can more or less favor the taste for money among men./

Among nations that have an *aristocracy* you seek money because it leads to power. Among nations that have a *nobility* you seek it to console yourself for being excluded from power. It seems that it is among democratic peoples that you have to seek it the least. There as elsewhere, ordinary souls undoubtedly continue to be attached to it; but ambitious spirits take it neither as principal goal and as a makeshift equivalent [? (ed.)].

You object to me in vain that in the United States, which forms a democracy, the love of money is excessive and that in France, where we turn daily toward democracy, love of money is becoming more and more the dominant passion. I will reply that political institutions definitively exercise only a limited influence over the inclinations of the human heart. If love of money is great in France and in the United States, that comes from the fact that in France mores, beliefs and characters are becoming depraved, and that in the United States the material condition of the country presents continual opportunities to the passion to grow rich. In the two countries you love

In these sorts of societies the imagination of the poor is pushed toward the other world; the miseries of real life cramp their imagination; but it escapes those miseries and goes to find its enjoyments beyond.

When, on the contrary, ranks are mingled and privileges destroyed, when patrimonies divide and enlightenment and liberty spread, the desire to gain well-being occurs to the imagination of the poor, and the fear of losing it to the mind of the rich.[e] A multitude of mediocre fortunes is established. Those who possess them have enough material enjoyments to conceive the taste for these enjoyments, and not enough to be content with them. They never obtain these enjoyments except with effort and devote themselves to them only with trepidation.

So they are constantly attached to pursuing or to retaining these enjoyments so precious, so incomplete and so fleeting. [Preoccupied by this sole concern, they often forget all the rest.

It is not the wealth, but the work that you devote to obtaining it for yourself that encloses the human heart within the taste for well-being.][f]

I seek a passion that is natural to men who are excited and limited by the obscurity of their origin or the mediocrity of their fortune, and I find none more appropriate than the taste for well-being. The passion for well-being is essentially a passion of the middle class; it grows and spreads with

---

money not because there are democratic institutions, but even though there are democratic institutions (YTC, CVa, pp. 53–54).

On 28 May 1831, Tocqueville writes from New York to his brother, Édouard:

We are very truly here in another world; political passions here are only on the surface. The profound passion, the only one that profoundly moves the human heart, the passion of every day, is the acquisition of wealth, and there are a thousand means to acquire it without disturbing the State. You have to be very blind in my opinion to want to compare this country to Europe and to adapt to one what suits the other; I believed it before leaving France; I believe it more and more while examining the society in the midst of which I now live; it is a people of merchants who are busy with public affairs when its [sic] work leaves it the leisure (YTC, BIa2).

e. "What makes democratic nations egotistic is not even so much the great number of independent citizens that they contain as the great number of citizens who are constantly reaching independence" (YTC, CVa, pp. 7–8).

f. To the side: "<This sentence is good, but interrupts the flow of the idea.>"

this class; it becomes preponderant with it. From there it gains the upper ranks of society and descends to the people.

I did not meet, in America, a citizen so poor who did not cast a look of hope and envy on the enjoyments of the rich, and whose imagination did not grasp in advance the good things that fate stubbornly refused him.

On the other hand, I never saw among the rich of the United States this superb disdain for material well-being that is sometimes shown even within the heart of the most opulent and most dissolute aristocracies.

Most of these rich have been poor; they have felt the sting of need; they have long fought against a hostile fortune, and now that victory is won, the passions that accompanied the struggle survive it; they remain as if intoxicated amid these small enjoyments that they have pursued for forty years.

It is not that in the United States, as elsewhere, you do not find a fairly large number of rich men who, holding their property by inheritance, possess without effort an opulence that they have not gained. But even these do not appear less attached to the enjoyments of material life. The love of well-being has become the national and dominant taste. The great current of human passions leads in this direction, it sweeps everything along in its wake.g

g. *"Other reason.* In a democratic society the only *visible* advantage that you can enjoy over your fellows is wealth. This explains the desire for *riches,* but not that for *material enjoyments.* These two things are close, but are nonetheless distinct. While it comes to the aid of sensuality here, pride in aristocracies often runs counter to it; you want to distinguish yourself from those who do not have money" (*Rubish,* 1).

CHAPTER 11[a]

Of the Particular Effects Produced by
the Love of Material Enjoyments
in Democratic Centuries[b]

a. When an aristocracy gives itself to the passion for material enjoyments, it aims at extraordinary pleasures; it falls into a thousand excesses that shame human nature and disturb society.

In democratic countries the taste for material enjoyments is a universal passion, constant, but contained. Everyone conceives it and gives himself to it constantly, but it leads no one to great excesses. Everyone seeks to satisfy the slightest needs easily and without cost rather than to obtain great pleasures.

This type of passion for material enjoyments can be reconciled with order and to a certain point with religion and morality. It does not always debilitate souls, but it softens them and silently relaxes their springs of action (YTC, CVf, p. 30).

b. Title in the *rubish:* OF THE DIFFERENT EFFECTS THAT THE TASTE FOR MATERIAL ENJOYMENTS PRODUCES IN AN ARISTOCRACY AND IN A DEMOCRACY.

At another place in the *rubish:* "THAT THE TASTE FOR WELL-BEING AND FOR MATERIAL ENJOYMENTS IN DEMOCRACIES IS MORE TRANQUIL, LEADS TO LESS EXCESS THAN IN ARISTOCRACIES AND CAN BE COMBINED WITH A SORT OF SPIRIT OF ORDER AND MORALITY. 2nd chapter.

"Honest materialism" (*Rubish,* 1). In a letter addressed to an unidentified person, Tocqueville had expressed the same idea in this way:

Author of all these revolutions, carried away himself by the movement that he brought about, the American of the United States ends by feeling pushed by an irresistible need for action; in Europe there are philosophers who preach human perfection; for him, the possible has hardly any limit. To change is to improve; he has constantly before his eyes the image of indefinite perfection that throws deep within his heart an extraordinary restlessness and a great distaste for the present.

Here, the enjoyments of the soul are not very important, the pleasures of imagination do not exist, but an immense door is open for achieving material happiness and each man rushes toward it. In order to reach it, you abandon parents, family, country; you try in the course of one life ten different roads to attain wealth. The same man has been priest, doctor, tradesman, farmer.

I do not know if you live here more happily than elsewhere, but at least you feel

935

You could believe, from what precedes, that the love of material enjoyments must constantly lead the Americans toward disorder in morals, disturb families and in the end compromise the fate of society itself.

But this is not so; the passion for material enjoyments produces within democracies other effects than among aristocratic peoples.

It sometimes happens that weariness with public affairs, the excess of wealth, the ruin of beliefs, the decadence of the State, little by little turn the heart of an aristocracy toward material enjoyments alone. At other times, the power [v. tyranny] of the prince or the weakness of the people, without robbing the nobles of their fortune, forces them to withdraw from power, and by closing the path to great undertakings to them, abandons them to the restlessness of their desires; they then fall heavily back onto themselves, and they seek in the enjoyments of the body to forget their past grandeur.

When the members of an aristocratic body turn exclusively in this way toward material enjoyments, they usually gather at this point alone all the energy that the long habit of power gave them.

To such men the pursuit of well-being is not enough; they require a sumptuous depravity and a dazzling corruption. They worship the material magnificently and seem to vie with one another in their desire to excel in the art of making themselves into brutes.

The more an aristocracy has been strong, glorious and free, the more it will appear depraved, and whatever the splendor of its virtues had been, I dare to predict it will always be surpassed by the brilliance of its vices.[c]

The taste for material enjoyments does not lead democratic peoples to

---

existence less; and you arrive at the great abyss without having had the time to notice the road that you followed.

These men call themselves virtuous; I deny it. They are *steady,* that is all that I am able to say in their favor. They steal from the neighbor and respect his wife, which I can only explain to myself because they love money and do not have the time to make love (Letter of 8 November 1831, YTC, BIa2).

c. "≠I know nothing more deplorable than the spectacle presented by an aristocracy that, losing its power, has remained master of its wealth≠" (*Rubish,* 1).

such excesses.[d] There the love of well-being shows itself to be a tenacious, exclusive, universal passion, but contained. It is not a question of building vast palaces, of vanquishing or of deceiving nature, of exhausting the universe, in order to satisfy better the passions of a man; it is a matter of adding a few feet to his fields, of planting an orchard, of enlarging a house, of making life easier and more comfortable each moment, of avoiding discomfort and satisfying the slightest needs effortlessly and almost without cost. These goals are small, but the soul becomes attached to them; it thinks about them every day and very closely; these goals finish by hiding from the soul the rest of the world, and they sometimes come to stand between the soul and God.

This, you will say, cannot be applied except to those among the citizens whose fortune is mediocre; the rich will show tastes analogous to those that the rich reveal in aristocratic centuries. That I dispute.[e]

Concerning material enjoyments, the most opulent citizens of a democracy will not show tastes very different from those of the people, whether, because having emerged from the people, they really share their tastes, or whether they believe they must submit to them. In democratic societies, the sensuality of the public has taken on a certain moderate and tranquil appearance, to which all souls are obliged to conform. It is as difficult to escape the common rule in its vices as in its virtues.

So the rich who live amid democratic nations aim for the satisfaction of their slightest needs rather than for extraordinary enjoyments; they satisfy a multitude of small desires and do not give themselves to any great disordered passion. They fall therefore into softness rather than debauchery.

This particular taste that the men of democratic centuries conceive for

d. "In aristocracies the taste for material well-being breaks the bonds of society, in democracies it tightens them" (*Rubish,* 1).

e. In the *rubish,* the sentence says: "cannot be applied except to the poor of democracies." On this subject, you read as well the following note: "The remark of Édouard on this point is this:

" 'I am speaking here,' he says, 'only about the *poor* or at most about people who are *well-off,* but there are rich people in democracies and it must be explained why these rich men are also forced to pursue material enjoyments in small ways and share on this point the instincts of the poor.

" '*True remark*' " (*Rubish,* 1).

material enjoyments is not naturally opposed to order; on the contrary, it often needs order to satisfy itself. Nor is it the enemy of regularity of morals; for good morals are useful to public tranquillity and favor industry. Often it even comes to be combined with a sort of religious morality; you want to be as well-off as possible in this world, without renouncing your chances in the other.

Among material goods, there are some whose possession is criminal; you take care to do without them. There are others whose use is allowed by religion and morality; to the latter you give unreservedly your heart, your imagination, your life, and by trying hard to grasp them, you lose sight of these more precious goods that make the glory and the grandeur of the human species.

What I reproach equality for is not carrying men toward the pursuit of forbidden enjoyments; it is for absorbing them entirely in the pursuit of permitted enjoyments.

In this way there could well be established in the world a kind of honest materialism that would not corrupt souls, but would soften them and end by silently relaxing all their springs of action.

CHAPTER 12[a]

Why Certain Americans Exhibit So Excited a Spiritualism[b]

Although the desire to acquire the goods of this world is the dominant passion of the Americans, there are moments of respite when their soul seems suddenly to break the material bonds that hold it and to escape impetuously toward heaven.[c]

In all of the states of the Union, but principally in the half-populated regions of the West, you sometimes meet itinerant preachers who peddle the divine word from place to place.

Entire families, old people, women and children cross difficult places and go through uninhabited woods in order to come from far away to hear them; and when these people have found the preachers, for several days and

a. Although the Americans have as a dominant passion the acquisition of the goods of this world, spiritualism shows itself from time to time among all, and exclusively among some, with singular forms and a fervor that often goes nearly to extravagance.

Camp meetings.

Bizarre sects.

These different effects come from the same cause.

The soul has natural needs that must be satisfied. If you want to imprison it in contemplation of the needs of the body, it ends by escaping and in its momentum it does not stop even at the limits of common sense (YTC, CVf, pp. 30–31).

b. Original title in the *rubish:* OF SOME BIZARRE SECTS THAT ARISE IN AMERICA. See the appendix SECTS IN AMERICA.

c. On the jacket of the manuscript: "Small chapter that must be retained only if someone formally advises me to do so.

"The core of the idea is questionable. Everything considered there were more mystical extravagances in the Middle Ages (centuries of aristocracy) than in America today.

"Moreover, several of these ideas reappear or have already appeared (*I believe*) in the book!"

several nights, while listening to them, they forget their concern for public and private affairs and even the most pressing needs of the body.

[< ≠ America is assuredly the country in the world in which the sentiment of individual power has the most sway. But several religious sects have been founded in the United States that, despairing of moderating the taste for material enjoyments, have gone as far as destroying the incentive of property by establishing community of goods within them. ≠ >]d

You find here and there, within American society, some souls totally filled with an excited and almost fierce spiritualism that you hardly find in Europe. From time to time bizarre sects arise there that try hard to open extraordinary paths to eternal happiness. Religious madness is very common there.

This must not surprise us.

Man has not given himself the taste for the infinite and the love of what is immortal. These sublime instincts do not arise from a caprice of the will; they have their unchanging foundation in his nature; they exist despite his efforts. He can hinder and deform them, but not destroy them.

The soul has needs that must be satisfied; and whatever care you take to distract it from itself, it soon grows bored, restless and agitated amid the enjoyments of the senses.e

If the spirit of the great majority of humanity ever concentrated solely on the pursuit of material goods, you can expect that a prodigious reaction would take place in the souls of some men. The latter would throw themselves frantically into the world of spirits, for fear of remaining hampered in the overly narrow constraints that the body wanted to impose on them.

So you should not be astonished if, within a society that thinks only about the earth, you would find a small number of individuals who wanted

---

d. In the margin: "≠All this shows the weakness of the idea by recalling the *monasteries,* institutions quite differently spiritualist than the small associations that I am speaking about.≠"

e. "≠When I {read the impractical laws of Plato} see Plato in his sublime reveries want to forbid commerce and industry to the citizens and, in order to release them better from coarse desires, want to take away even the possession of their children, I think of his contemporaries, and the sensual democracy of Athens makes me understand the laws of this imaginary republic whose portrait he has drawn for us≠" (*Rubish,* 1).

to look only to heaven. I would be surprised if, among a people solely pre-occupied by its well-being, mysticism did not soon make progress.[f]

It is said that the persecutions of the emperors and the tortures of the circus populated the deserts of the Thebaid; as for me, I think that it was much more the delights of Rome and the Epicurean philosophy of Greece.[g]

If the social state, circumstances and laws did not so narrowly confine the American spirit to the pursuit of well-being, it is to be believed that when the American spirit came to occupy itself with non-material things, it would show more reserve and more experience, and that it would control itself without difficulty. But it feels imprisoned within the limits beyond which it seems it is not allowed to go. As soon as it crosses those limits, it does not know where to settle down, and it often runs without stopping beyond the bounds of common sense.[h]

---

f. "I would not be surprised if the first monasteries to be established in America are trappist monasteries" (*Rubish*, 1).

g. There is in the very nature of man a natural and permanent disposition that pushes his soul despite habits, laws, customs . . . toward the contemplation of elevated and intellectual things.

This natural disposition is found in democracies as elsewhere. And it can even be exalted and perfected there by a sort of reaction to the *material* and the *ordinary* that abound in these sorts of societies.

When society presents elevated and grand points of view, the kinds of souls that I have just spoken about can allow themselves to be caught by and attach themselves to this half-good, instead of detaching themselves entirely from the earth in order to go to find absolute good.

The dissolute orgies of Rome filled the deserts of Thebaid.

K[ergorlay (ed.)]., 13 March 1836 (YTC, CVk, 1, p. 5).

h. "≠If the Americans had a literature this would be even more perceptible. Some would want to escape from monotony by the bizarre, the singular. You could see a mystical literature within a materialistic society./

"Exalted spiritualism. Intellectual orgies.≠" (*Rubish*, 1).

CHAPTER 13[a]

Why the Americans Appear So Restless
Amid Their Well-Being

You still sometimes find, in certain remote districts of the Old World, small populations that have been as if forgotten amid the universal tumult and that have remained unchanged when everything around them moved. Most of these peoples are very ignorant and very wretched; they are not involved in governmental affairs and often governments oppress them. But they usually show a serene face, and they often exhibit a cheerful mood.

I saw in America the most free and most enlightened men placed in the

---

a. Of restlessness of the heart in America. Although the Americans are a very prosperous people, they seem almost always restless and care-ridden; they constantly change places, careers, desires.

That comes principally from these causes:

Equality makes the love of the enjoyments of this world predominate. Now

1. Men who restrict themselves to the pursuit of the enjoyments of this world are always pressed by the idea of the brevity of life. They fear having missed the shortest road that could lead them to happiness.

2. The taste for material enjoyments causes intense desires, but leads easily to discouragement. For the effort that you make to attain the enjoyment must not surpass the enjoyment.

3. Equality suggests a thousand times more desires than it can satisfy. It excites ambition and deceives it. Men can achieve anything, but their individual weakness and competition limit them (YTC, CVf, p. 31).

This chapter appears with the same title OF RESTLESSNESS OF THE HEART IN AMERICA in the *rubish* and manuscript. A page of the *rubish* contains the following note: "Small chapter done with great difficulty. To delete perhaps, but to review in any case. Perhaps in order to avoid the commonplace, I fell into the *forced./*

"Immoderate desire for happiness in this world, that arises from democracy. *Idea to make emerge better from the chapter"* (*Rubish,* 1).

happiest condition in the world; it seemed to me that a kind of cloud habitually covered their features; they appeared to me grave and almost sad, even in their pleasures.[b]

The principal reason for this is that the first do not think about the evils that they endure, while the others think constantly about the goods that they do not have.[c]

It is a strange thing to see with what kind of feverish ardor the Americans pursue well-being, and how they appear tormented constantly by a vague fear of not having chosen the shortest road that can lead to it.[d]

The inhabitant of the United States is attached to the goods of this world, as if he was assured of not dying, and he hastens so much to seize those goods that pass within his reach, that you would say that at every instant he is afraid of ceasing to live before enjoying them. He seizes all of

---

b. I arrived one night in the company of several savages at the house of an American planter. It is the dwelling of a rich planter and at the same time a tavern. You saw reigning there great ease and even a sort of rustic luxury. I was brought into a well-lighted and carefully heated room in which several men of leisure from the neighborhood were already gathered around a table laden with grain whiskey. These men were all more or less drunk, but their drunkenness had a grave and somber character that struck me. They talked painfully about public affairs, about the price of houses, about the hazards of commerce and the cycles of industry. The Indians remained outside, although the night was rainy and they had [only (ed.)] a few bad rags of blankets to cover themselves. They had lighted a large fire and sat around on the humid earth. They spoke happily among themselves. I did not understand the meaning of their speeches, but the noisy bursts of their joy at each instant penetrated the gravity of our banquet (*Rubish*, 1).

c. "The inhabitant of the United States has all the goods of this world within reach, but can grasp none of them without effort" (*Rubish*, 1).

d. "All of that still much more marked in the *revolutionary* period and in *unbelieving* democracies./

"The Americans are *materialistic* by their *tastes*, but they are not by their *ideas*. They ardently pursue the goods of this world, but they have not ceased believing in the existence of another one" (*Rubish*, 1).

them, but without gripping them, and he soon lets them escape from his hands in order to run after new enjoyments.[e]

A man, in the United States, carefully builds a house in which to spend his old age, and he sells it while the ridgepole is being set; he plants a garden and he rents it as he is about to taste its fruits; he clears a field, and he leaves to others the trouble of gathering the harvest. He embraces a profession, and he leaves it. He settles in a place that he soon leaves in order to carry his changing desires elsewhere. If his private affairs give him some respite, he immediately plunges into the whirl of politics. And when, near the end of a year filled with work, he still has a little leisure, he takes his restless curiosity here and there across the vast limits of the United States. He will do as much as five hundred leagues in a few days in order to distract himself better from his happiness.

Death finally intervenes and stops him before he has grown weary of this useless pursuit of a complete felicity that always escapes.

You are at first astounded contemplating this singular agitation exhibited by so many happy men, in the very midst of abundance. This spectacle is, however, as old as the world; what is new is to see it presented by an entire people.

The taste for material enjoyments must be considered as the primary source of this secret restlessness that is revealed in the actions of Americans, and of this inconstancy that they daily exemplify.

The man who has confined his heart solely to the pursuit of the goods of this world is always in a hurry, for he has only a limited time to find them, to take hold of them and to enjoy them. The memory of the brevity of life goads him constantly. Apart from the goods that he possesses, at every instant he imagines a thousand others that death will prevent him from tasting if he does not hurry. This thought fills him with uneasiness, fears,

e. In a first version of the *rubish:*

I met a man in the United States who, after having for a long time hidden great talents in poverty, finally became the wealthiest man of his profession. At the same time in England lived another individual who, following the same career as the first man, had amassed greater wealth. News of it reached the American and this colleague who was on the other side of the ocean troubled his sleep and kept his joy in check (*Rubish,* 1).

and regrets, and keeps his soul in a kind of constant trepidation that leads him to change plans and places at every moment.

If the taste for material well being is joined with a social state in which neither law nor custom any longer holds anyone in his place, it is one more great excitement to this restlessness of spirit; you will then see men continually change path, for fear of missing the shortest road that is to lead them to happiness.

It is easy to understand, moreover, that if the men who passionately seek material enjoyments do desire strongly, they must be easily discouraged; since the final goal is to enjoy, the means to get there must be quick and easy, otherwise the difficulty of obtaining the enjoyment would surpass the enjoyment. So most souls are at the same time ardent and soft, violent and enervated. Often death is less feared than constant efforts toward the same goal.

Equality leads by a still more direct road toward several of the effects that I have just described.

When all the prerogatives of birth and fortune are destroyed, when all the professions are open to everyone, and when you can reach the summit of each one of them on your own, an immense and easy career seems to open before the ambition of men, and they readily imagine that they are called to great destinies.[f] But that is an erroneous view that experience corrects every day. The same equality that allows each citizen to conceive vast hopes makes all citizens individually weak. It limits their strengths on all sides, at the same time that it allows their desires to expand.

Not only are they powerless by themselves, but also they find at each step immense obstacles that they had not at first noticed.

They destroyed the annoying privileges of a few of their fellows; they encounter the competition of all. The boundary marker has changed form rather than place. When men are more or less similar and follow the same road, it is very difficult for any one of them to march quickly and cut through the uniform crowd that surrounds and crushes him.

---

f. In the margin: "<This idea must *necessarily* be found in the chapter on ambition. Do not let it *appear* without reviewing both of them at the same time.>"

This constant opposition that reigns between the instincts given birth by equality and the means that equality provides to satisfy them torments and fatigues souls.g

You can imagine men having arrived at a certain degree of liberty that satisfies them entirely. They then enjoy their independence without restlessness and without fervor. But men will never establish an equality that is enough for them.

Whatever efforts a people may make, it will not succeed in making conditions perfectly equal within it; and if it had the misfortune to arrive at this absolute and complete leveling, there would still be inequality of intelligence that, coming directly from God, will always escape the laws.

No matter how democratic the social state and political constitution of a people, you can therefore count on each of its citizens always seeing near himself several points that are above him, and you can predict that he will obstinately turn his attention solely in their direction. When inequality is the common law of a society, the greatest inequalities do not strike the eye. When all is nearly level, the least inequalities offend it. This is why the desire for equality always becomes more insatiable as equality is greater.h

Among democratic peoples, men easily gain a certain equality; they cannot attain the equality they desire. The latter retreats from them every day, but without ever hiding from their view, and by withdrawing, it draws them in pursuit. They constantly believe that they are about to grasp it, and it constantly escapes their grip. They see it close enough to know its charms, they do not come close enough to enjoy it, and they die before having fully savored its sweet pleasures.

It is to these causes that you must attribute the singular melancholy that the inhabitants of democratic countries often reveal amid their abundance, and this disgust for life that sometimes comes to seize them in the middle of a comfortable and tranquil existence.

Some complain in France that the number of suicides is growing; in

g. The four paragraphs that follow do not appear in the manuscript.

h. "<Envy is a sentiment that develops strongly *only among equals,* that is why it is so common and so ardent in democratic centuries>" (*Rubish,* 1).

America suicide is rare, but we are assured that insanity is more common than anywhere else.

These are different symptoms of the same disease.

Americans do not kill themselves, however agitated they are, because religion forbids them to so do, and because among them materialism does not so to speak exist, although the passion for material well-being is general.

Their will resists, but often their reason gives way.[j]

In democratic times enjoyments are more intense than in aristocratic centuries, and above all the number of those who sample them is infinitely greater; but on the other hand, it must be recognized that hopes and desires are more often disappointed there, souls more excited and more restless, and anxieties more burning.[k]

j. To the side: "<Perhaps remove all of this as too strong.>"

k. Men of democracies are tormented by desires more immense and more unlimited than those of all other men. Their desires generally lead them however to less sustained, less energetic, less persevering actions. The desires have enough power over them to agitate them, to make them lose hope, and not enough to lead them to these great and persevering efforts that bring great and enduring results. They have enough desires to become disgusted with life and to kill themselves, not enough to overcome themselves and to prevail, live and act. They have constantly recurring weak desires, rather than will.

Examine this phenomenon very closely and portray it, probably in the chapter entitled *of restlessness of the heart,* which comes after *material enjoyments,* true cause of what precedes.

12 March 1838 (*Rubish,* 1).

CHAPTER 14[a]

How the Taste for Material Enjoyments Is United, among the Americans, with the Love of Liberty and Concern for Public Affairs

When a democratic State[b] turns to absolute monarchy, the activity that was brought previously to public and private affairs comes suddenly to be concentrated on the latter, and a great material prosperity results for some time; but soon the movement slows and the development of production stops.[c]

a. Liberty is useful for the production of well-being among all peoples, but principally among democratic peoples.

It often happens among these peoples, however, that the excessive taste for well-being causes liberty to be abandoned.

Men there are so preoccupied by their petty private affairs that they regard the attention that they give to great public affairs as a waste of time. That delivers them easily to the despotism of one man or to the tyranny of a party. The Americans offer the opposite example. They concern themselves with public affairs attentively and with the same ardor as with their private interests, which shows clearly that in their mind these two things go together (YTC, CVf, p. 32).

b. The manuscript says "republic."

c. I said in another part of this work the reasons that led me to believe that, if despotism came to be established in a lasting way among a democratic people, it would show itself more ordered and *heavier* than anywhere else. The more I advance into my subject, the more it seems to me that I am finding new reasons to think so.

[In the margin: All of that is weak because these are general truths that do not apply to democratic peoples more than to others. It is the *special* reasons that I must seek.

The *special* reason here would be the *particularly* suffocating nature of despotism among democratic peoples.]

Now, the necessary effect of a despotism of this type is to constrict the imagination of man, to narrow in all ways the limits of his faculties and finally to make him indifferent and as if useless to himself. But perhaps I am exaggerating the danger. Who could believe in such excesses amid the enlightenment of our {Europe} age? So it is claimed. I agree, so I will not speak about the wars undertaken for a particular interest, the misappropriations of public wealth, the plundering by the agents of power, the general uncertainty of private fortunes, things still more fatal to the prosperity of citizens, that are like the usual consequence of the establishment of such a government and whose effect will soon make itself felt on the well-being of the citizens. All these things can be considered as accidents. I want to seek a permanent cause of the evil that I suppose, and I imagine a soft and intelligent despotism that, limiting itself to confiscating liberty, leaves men in possession of all the goods given birth by liberty.

[In the margin: Commerce cannot bear *war;* but the character of democratic despotism is not tyrannical, but minutely detailed and annoying.]

Some maintain that such a government {favors} would save human morality and is, everything considered, more favorable to happiness; I do not believe it. Nonetheless, it can be claimed. But you certainly cannot claim that such a government favors as well the development of material well-being and the acquisition of wealth.

There is a more intimate connection than is thought between political activity and industrial activity. There is nothing that awakens the imagination of a people, that expands the circle of its ideas, that gives it the taste for enterprises of all types and the boldness to execute them, finally that forces citizens to see each other and to enlighten each other mutually with their knowledge, like the concern for public affairs. Men being so disposed, there is no progress that they do not imagine, and, from the simultaneous efforts of all, universal well-being is born.

That is so true that I do not know if you can cite the example of a single manufacturing and commercial people, from the Tyrians to the English, who have not been at the same time a free people. You saw the industrial genius of the Florentines do wonders amid the constantly recurring revolutions that devoured the products of the work of man as they came from his hands. Florence, amid the very excesses of its independence, was rich; it became poor as soon as it wanted to rest under the tranquil and regular government [v: despotism] of the Medicis. So there is a hidden but very close bond between these two things: liberty and industry.[1]

[To the side: Perhaps do not speak about the Florentines, already cited by others on analogous occasions.]

You do not notice this at first. When the absolute authority of a prince follows the government of all, this great human activity that went toward public affairs and private affairs suddenly finds itself concentrated on the second, and for a time, a prodigious impetus and an unparalleled prosperity usually result. But soon movement slows. New ideas cease to circulate with the same rapidity. Men only communicate with each other from time to time, cease counting on their fellows, and end by no longer having confidence in themselves. No longer having the habit or the right to

I do not know if you can cite a single manufacturing and commercial people, from the Tyrians to the Florentines and to the English, who have not been a free people. So there is a close bond and a necessary connection between these two things: liberty and industry.

That is generally true of all nations, but especially of democratic nations.

I showed above how men who live in centuries of equality had a continual need for association in order to obtain nearly all the goods they covet, and on the other hand, I showed how great political liberty perfected and spread widely within their midst the art of association. So liberty, in these centuries, is particularly useful for the production of wealth. You can see, on the contrary, that despotism is particularly the enemy of the production of wealth.

The nature of absolute power, in democratic centuries, is neither cruel nor savage, but it is minutely detailed and irksome. A despotism of this type, although it does not trample humanity underfoot, is directly opposed to the genius of commerce and to the instincts of industry.

Thus the men of democratic times need to be free, in order to obtain more easily the material enjoyments for which they are constantly yearning.

It sometimes happens, however, that the excessive taste that they conceive for these very enjoyments delivers them to the first master who presents himself. The passion for well-being then turns against itself and, without noticing, drives away the object of its desires.

---

act in common in principal matters, they lose as well the practice of associating for secondary ends. The ardor for enterprises becomes dull, the taste for progress becomes less intense. Society marches at first with a more tranquil step, then it stops and finally settles into a complete immobility.

1. To see again concerning this piece something analogous written in England in 1835 (*Rubish*, 1).

In notebook CVa, p. 4, with the date 3 August 1836, there is a copy of a fragment of a letter by Machiavelli on the danger of the streets of Rome during the night. In August 1836, Tocqueville spent his vacation in Switzerland and read Machiavelli's *History of Florence*. See Luc Monnier, "Tocqueville et la Suisse," in *Alexis de Tocqueville. Livre du centenaire* (Paris: CNRS, 1960), pp. 101–13.

There is, in fact, a very perilous transition in the life of democratic peoples.

When the taste for material enjoyments develops among one of these peoples more rapidly than enlightenment and the habits of liberty, there comes a moment when men are carried away, as if beyond themselves, by the sight of these new goods that they are ready to grasp. Preoccupied by the sole concern to make a fortune, they no longer notice the close bond that unites the particular fortune of each one of them to the prosperity of all. There is no need to take away from such citizens the rights that they possess; they willingly allow them to escape. The exercise of their political duties seems to them a tiresome inconvenience that distracts them from their industry. Whether it is a matter of choosing their representatives, coming to the assistance of the authorities, dealing together with common affairs, they lack the time; they cannot waste such precious time on useless works. Those are games for idle men that are not suitable for grave men who are busy with the serious interests of life. The latter believe that they are following the doctrine of interest, but they have only a crude idea of it, and in order to see better to what they call their affairs, they neglect the principal one which is to remain their own masters.

Since the citizens who work do not want to think about public matters, and since the class that could fill its leisure hours by shouldering these concerns no longer exists, the place of the government is as though empty.

If, at this critical moment, a clever man of ambition comes to take hold of power, he finds that the path to all usurpations is open [<and he will have no difficulty turning against liberty the very passions developed or given birth by liberty>].

As long as he sees for a while that all material interests prosper, he will easily be discharged from the rest. Let him, above all, guarantee good order. Men who have a passion for material enjoyments usually find how the agitations of liberty disturb well-being, before noticing how liberty serves to gain it; and at the slightest noise of public passions that penetrates into the petty enjoyments of their private life, they wake up and become anxious; for a long time the fear of anarchy keeps them constantly in suspense and always ready to jump away from liberty at the first disorder.

I agree without difficulty that public peace is a great good, but I do not want to forget that it is through good order that all peoples have arrived at tyranny. It assuredly does not follow that peoples should scorn public peace; but it must not be enough for them. A nation that asks of its government only the maintenance of order is already a slave at the bottom of its heart. The nation is a slave of its well-being, and the man who is to put it in chains can appear.

The despotism of factions is to be feared no less than that of one man.

When the mass of citizens wants only to concern itself with private affairs, the smallest parties do not have to despair of becoming masters of public affairs.

It is then not rare to see on the world's vast stage, as in our theaters, a multitude represented by a few men. The latter speak alone in the name of the absent or inattentive crowd; alone they take action amid the universal immobility; they dispose of everything according to their caprice; they change laws and tyrannize mores at will; and you are astonished to see into what a small number of weak and unworthy hands a great people can fall.

Until now, the Americans have happily avoided all the pitfalls that I have just pointed out; and in that they truly merit our admiration.

There is perhaps no country on earth where you find fewer men of leisure than in America, and where all those who work are more inflamed in the pursuit of well-being. But if the passion of the Americans for material enjoyments is violent, at least it is not blind, and reason, powerless to moderate it, directs it.

An American is busy with his private interests as if he were alone in the world, and a moment later, he devotes himself to public matters as if he had forgotten his private interests. He seems sometimes animated by the most egotistical cupidity and sometimes by the most intense patriotism. The human heart cannot be divided in this manner. The inhabitants of the United States bear witness alternately to such a strong and so similar a passion for their well-being and for their liberty that it is to be believed that these passions unite and blend some place in their soul. The Americans, in fact, see in their liberty the best instrument and the greatest guarantee of their well-being. They love both of these two things. So they do not think that getting involved in public matters is not their business; they believe, on the contrary, that their principal business is to secure by themselves a government that allows them to acquire the goods that they desire, and that does not forbid them to enjoy in peace those they have acquired.

CHAPTER 15[a]

How from Time to Time Religious Beliefs Divert the Soul of the Americans toward Non-Material Enjoyments[b]

[≠However animated the Americans are in the pursuit of well-being, there are moments when they stop and turn away for a moment to think about God and about the other life.≠]

In the United States, when the seventh day of each week arrives, commercial and industrial life seems suspended; all noise ceases. A profound rest, or rather a kind of solemn recollection follows; the soul, finally, regains self-possession and contemplates itself.

During this day, the places consecrated to commerce and industry are deserted; each citizen, surrounded by his children, goes to church; there strange discourses are held forth that do not seem much made for his ears. He hears about the innumerable evils caused by pride and covetousness.

---

a. In America, Sunday and the use made of it interrupt each week the course of purely material thoughts and tastes. It breaks the chain of them. Particular advantages of this.

The democratic social state leads the human mind toward materialistic opinions by sometimes developing beyond measure the taste for well-being. That is a tendency that you must struggle against, just as in aristocratic times you must fight against an opposite excess.

Effect of religions which is to keep spiritualism in honor. So religions are particularly necessary among democratic peoples. What the government of these peoples can do to uphold religions and the spiritualistic opinions that they suggest (YTC, CVf, pp. 32–33).

b. On the jacket of the chapter in the manuscript: "The utility of religions to temper the taste for material enjoyments in democratic centuries has already been *touched* upon in chapter V, but so lightly that I believe that it can be developed here." It concerns chapter V of the first part.

He is told about the necessity to control his desires, about the fine enjoy-ments attached to virtue alone, and about the true happiness that accom-panies it.

Back at home, you do not see him run to his business ledgers. He opens the book of the Holy Scriptures; there he finds sublime or touching por-trayals of the grandeur and the goodness of the Creator, of the infinite magnificence of the works of God, of the elevated destiny reserved for men, of their duties and their rights to immortality.

This is how, from time to time, the American escapes in a way from himself, and how, tearing himself away for a moment from the petty pas-sions that agitate his life and from the transitory interests that fill it, he enters suddenly into an ideal world where everything is great, pure, eternal.

[So I am constantly led to the same subjects by different roads; and I discover more and more the close bond that unites the two parts of my subject.]

In another place in this work, I looked for the causes to which the main-tenance of political institutions in America had to be attributed, and reli-gion seemed to me one of the principal ones. Today, when I am concerned with individuals, I find religion again and notice that it is no less useful to each citizen than to the whole State.

The Americans show, by their practice, that they feel the entire necessity of moralizing democracy by religion. What they think in this regard about themselves is a truth that must penetrate every democratic nation.

I do not doubt that the social and political constitution of a people dis-poses them to certain beliefs and to certain tastes in which they easily abound afterward; while these same causes turn them away from certain opinions and certain tendencies without their working at it themselves, and so to speak without their suspecting it.

All the art of the legislator consists in clearly discerning in advance these natural inclinations of human societies, in order to know where the effort of the citizens must be aided, and where it would instead be necessary to slow it down. For these obligations differ according to the times. Only the end toward which humanity must always head is unchanging; the means to reach that end constantly vary.

[≠There are vices or erroneous opinions that can only be established among a people by struggling against the general current of society. These are not to be feared; they must be considered as unfortunate accidents. But there are others that, having a natural rapport with the very constitution of the people, develop by themselves and effortlessly among the people. Those, however small they may be at their beginning and however rare they seem, deserve to attract the great care of the legislator.≠]ᶜ

If I were born in an aristocratic century, amid a nation in which the hereditary wealth of some and the irremediable poverty of others diverted men from the idea of the better and, as well, held souls as if benumbed in the contemplation of another world, I would want it to be possible for me to stimulate among such a people the sentiment of needs; I would think about finding more rapid and easier means to satisfy the new desires that I would have brought about, and, diverting the greatest efforts of the human mind toward physical study, I would try to excite the human mind in the pursuit of well-being.ᵈ

If it happened that some men caught fire thoughtlessly in the pursuit of wealth and exhibited an excessive love for material enjoyments, I would not become alarmed; these particular traits would soon disappear in the common physiognomy.

Legislators of democracies have other concerns.

Give democratic peoples enlightenment and liberty and leave them alone. They will easily succeed in drawing from this world all the [material] goods that it can offer; they will perfect each one of the useful arts and daily make life more comfortable, easier, sweeter; their social state pushes them naturally in this direction. I am not afraid that they will stop.

---

c. In the margin: "≠To delete this piece perhaps which *slows,* although it clarifies. I have moreover expressed this idea in the first part while speaking about laws.≠"

d. If I had been born in the Middle Ages, I would have been the enemy of superstitions, for then the social movement led there.

But today, I feel indulgent toward all the follies that spiritualism can suggest.

The great enemy is materialism, not only because it is in itself a detestable doctrine, but also because it is unfortunately in accord with the social tendency (*Rubish,* 1).

But while man takes pleasure in this honest and legitimate pursuit of well-being, it is to be feared that in the end he may lose the use of his most sublime faculties, and that by wanting to improve everything around him, he may in the end degrade himself. The danger is there and nowhere else.

So legislators in democracies and all honest and enlightened men who live in democracies must apply themselves without respite to lifting up souls and keeping them pointed toward heaven. It is necessary that all those who are interested in the future of democratic societies unite, and that all in concert make continual efforts to spread within these societies the taste for the infinite, the sentiment for the grand and the love for non-material pleasures.

If among the opinions of a democratic people there exist a few of these harmful theories that tend to make you believe that everything perishes with the body, consider the men who profess them as the natural enemies of the people.

There are many things that offend me in the materialists. Their doctrines seem pernicious to me, and their pride revolts me. If their system could be of some use to man, it seems that it would be in giving him a modest idea of himself. But they do not show that this is so; and when they believe that they have sufficiently established that men are only brutes, they appear as proud as if they had demonstrated that men were gods.[e]

Materialism is, among all nations, a dangerous sickness of the human mind; but it must be particularly feared among a democratic people, because it combines marvelously with the vice of the heart most familiar to these people.

---

e. ≠Baden, 2 August 1836.

Of the pride of the materialists./

There are many things that shock me among the materialists, but the most displeasing in my view is the extreme pride that most of them exhibit. If the doctrine that they profess could be of some use to men, it seems that it would be in inspiring in them a modest idea of themselves and in leading them to humility. But they do not indicate that this is so, and after making a thousand efforts to prove that they are only brutes, they show themselves as proud as if they had demonstrated that they were gods≠" (In the *rubish* of chapter XVII of this part. *Rubish,* 1).

Democracy favors the taste for material enjoyments. This taste, if it becomes excessive, soon disposes men to believe that everything is only matter; and materialism, in turn, finally carries them with an insane fervor toward these same enjoyments. Such is the fatal circle into which democratic nations are pushed. It is good that they see the danger and restrain themselves.

Most religions are only general, simple and practical means to teach men the immortality of the soul. That is the greatest advantage that a democratic people draws from belief, and what makes these beliefs more necessary for such a people than for all others.

So when no matter which religion has put down deep roots within a democracy, be careful about weakening it; but instead protect it carefully as the most precious heritage of aristocratic centuries;[f] do not try to tear men away from their ancient religious opinions in order to substitute new ones, for fear that, during the transition from one faith to another, when the soul finds itself for one moment devoid of beliefs, love of material enjoyments comes to spread and fill the soul entirely.

[I do not believe that all religions are equally true and equally good, but I think that there is none so false or so bad that it would not still be advantageous for a democratic people to profess.]

Assuredly, metempsychosis is not more reasonable than materialism; but if it were absolutely necessary for a democracy to make a choice between the two, I would not hesitate, and I would judge that its citizens risk becoming brutalized less by thinking that their soul is going to pass into the body of a pig than by believing that it is nothing.[g]

The belief in a non-material and immortal principle, united for a time to matter, is so necessary for the grandeur of man, that it still produces beautiful effects even when you do not join the opinion of rewards and punishments with it and when you limit yourself to believing that after

f. To the side: "{Remark by Édouard.}"

g. In the margin: "≠It is above all from there that the piece becomes *weak* because what I say no longer relates exclusively to democracies./

"What follows is a beautiful digression on the general advantages of spiritualisms and nothing more, thrown across the idea of the utility of a religion and of the means for preserving it.≠"

death the divine principle contained in man is absorbed in God or goes to animate another creature.[h]

Even the latter consider the body as the secondary and inferior portion of our nature; and they scorn it even when they undergo its influence; while they have a natural esteem and secret admiration for the non-material part of man, even though they sometimes refuse to submit themselves to its dominion. This is enough to give a certain elevated turn to their ideas and their tastes, and to make them tend without interest, and as if on their own, toward pure sentiments and great thoughts.

It is not certain that Socrates and his school had well-fixed opinions on what must happen to man in the other life; but the sole belief on which they were settled, that the soul has nothing in common with the body and survives it, was enough to give to platonic philosophy the sort of sublime impulse that distinguishes it.

When you read Plato, you notice that in the times prior to him and in his time, many writers existed who advocated materialism. These writers have not survived to our time or have survived only very incompletely. It has been so in nearly all the centuries; most of the great literary reputations are joined with spiritualism. The instinct and the taste of humanity uphold this doctrine; they often save this doctrine despite the men themselves and make the names of those who are attached to it linger on. So it must not be believed that in any time, and in whatever political state, the passion for material enjoyments and the opinions that are linked with it will be able

h. Immortality of the soul./

The need for the *infinite* and the sad experience of the *finite* that we encounter at each step, torments [*sic*] me sometimes, but does not distress me. I see in it one of the greatest proofs of the existence of another world and of the immortality of our souls. From all that we know about God by his works, we know that he does nothing without a near or distant end. This is so true that in the physical world, it is enough for us to find an organ in order to conclude from it in a certain way that the animal that possessed this organ used it in this or that way, and experience comes to prove it. Argument by analogy. I cannot believe that God put in our souls the *organ* of the infinite, if I can express myself in this way, in order to give our soul eternally only to the *finite*, that he gave it the *organ* of hope in a future life, without future life (CVa, p. 57).

to suffice for an entire people.ʲ The heart of man is more vast than you suppose; it can at the same time enclose the taste for the good things of the earth and the love of the good things of heaven; sometimes the heart seems to give itself madly to one of the two; but it never goes for a long time without thinking of the other.ᵏ

j. In a first version you read:

I am moreover very far from believing that men can[not (ed.)] reconcile the taste for well-being that democracy develops and the religious [v: spiritualistic] beliefs that democracy needs. To prove it, I will not use the example of the Americans; their origin sets them aside. But I will cite before all the others that of the English.

The middle classes of England form an immense democracy in which each man is occupied without respite with the concern of improving his lot, and in which all seem devoted to the love of wealth. But the middle classes of England remain faithful to their religious beliefs and they show in a thousand small ways that these beliefs are powerful and sincere [v: true]. England, with its traditions and its memories, is not however relegated to a corner of the universe. Unbelief is next door. The English themselves have seen several of the most celebrated unbelievers arise within it. But the middle classes of England have remained firmly religious until today and are sincere Christians who have produced these industrial wonders that astonish the world.

So the heart of man is . . . (*Rubish,* 1).

A variant from the *Rubish* specifies: "unbelievers. Several have been powerful because of their genius. Hume, Gibbon, Byron" (*Rubish,* 1).

k. To be concerned only with satisfying the needs of the body and to forget about the soul. That is the final outcome to which materialism leads.

To flee into the deserts, to inflict sufferings and privations on yourself in order to live the life of the soul. That is the final outcome of spiritualism. I notice at the one end of this tendency Heliogabalus and at the other St. Jerome.

I would very much want us to be able to find between these two paths a road that would not be a route toward the one or toward the other. For if each of these two opposite roads can be suitable for some men, this middle road is the only one that can be suitable for humanity. Can we not find a path between Heliogabalus and St. Jerome? (*Rubish,* 1).

At another place in the *rubish:*

I proved sufficiently in material tastes that it was to be desired that the taste for well-being did not repress the impulses [of (ed.)] spiritualism of the soul, were it only so that man could obtain for himself those material enjoyments that they [*sic*] desire.

For the subject to be exhausted and my philosophical position clearly established, it would be necessary to be able to add a *small* chapter in which, turning myself away from considering the *fanatical* spiritualists, I would show that in the very interest of

If it is easy to see that, particularly in times of democracy, it is important to make spiritual opinions reign, it is not easy to say what those who govern democratic peoples must do for those opinions to reign.

I do not believe in the prosperity any more than in the duration of official philosophies, and as for State religions, I have always thought that if sometimes they could temporarily serve the interests of political power, they always sooner or later become fatal to the Church.

Nor am I one of those who judge that in order to raise religion in the eyes of the people, and to honor the spiritualism that religion professes, it is good to grant indirectly to its ministers a political influence that the law refuses to them.

[I would even prefer that you gave the clergy a definite power than to allow them to hold an irregular and hidden power. For, in the first case,

---

the soul the body must prosper; I would *rehabilitate the flesh* as the Saint-Simonians said. I would search for this intermediate path between Saint Jerome and Heliogabalus that will always be the great route of humanity.

I would show there

1. That in order to get men to concern themselves with the *needs* of their souls, you must not say to them to neglect the *needs* of the body, for both exist, man being neither a pure *spirit* nor an *animal*, but that the problem to solve is to find a means to reconcile these two needs.

2. *That in itself* it is desirable that sublime virtues do not hide under rags (or at least exceptions that show nothing), that a certain well-being of the body is necessary for the development of the soul, that efforts made by the soul to attain that development are healthy for it, that they give it habits of order, work, that they sharpen its abilities . . ./

In a word, it is necessary to tie this world to the other or one of the two escapes us (*Rubish*, 1).

In a letter of 1843, Tocqueville will repeat the same ideas to Arthur de Gobineau:

Our society has moved away much more from theology than from Christian philosophy. Since our religious beliefs have become less firm and the view of the other world more obscure, morality must show itself more indulgent for material needs and pleasures. It is an idea that the Saint-Simonians expressed, I believe, by saying that it *was necessary to rehabilitate the flesh* (*Correspondance avec Gobineau, OC,* IX, p. 46).

See Joshua Mitchell, *The Fragility of Freedom. Tocqueville on Religion, Democracy and the American Future* (Chicago: University of Chicago Press, 1995).

you at least see clearly the political circle in which priests can act; while in the other, there are no limits at which the imagination of the people must stop, or public misfortunes for which the people will not be tempted to blame the priests.]^m

I feel so convinced of the nearly inevitable dangers that beliefs run when their interpreters mingle in public affairs, and I am so persuaded that Christianity must at all cost be maintained within the new democracies, that I would prefer to chain priests within the sanctuary than to allow them out of it.

So what means remain for authority to lead men back toward spiritualistic opinions or keep them in the religion that suggests these opinions?

What I am going to say is going to do me harm in the eyes of politicians. I believe that the only effective means that governments can use to honor the dogma of the immortality of the soul is to act each day as if they believed it themselves; and I think that it is only by conforming scrupulously to religious morality in great affairs that they can claim to teach citizens to know, love and respect religious morality in little affairs.^n

m. In the *rubish,* the passage continues in this way: "It is rare moreover that you wisely use a precarious and disputed power that you can exercise only in the shadows. For me, I am so persuaded that the spirit of religion must at all cost be maintained within democracies and I feel, on the contrary, so convinced of the nearly inevitable dangers . . ." (*Rubish,* 1).

n. To put after egoism and the material tendency of democracy, when I will say that it is necessary at all cost to throw some non-material ideas, some poetry, some taste for the infinite into the midst of democratic peoples.

Legislators of democracy, if by chance a positive religion exists, respect it, preserve it as a precious flame that is tending to go out, as the most precious heritage of aristocratic centuries . . .

In aristocratic centuries I would work hard to turn the human spirit toward physical studies, in democratic centuries toward the moral sciences. Draw a short parallel between these two tendencies against which you must alternately struggle in order to reveal clearly the higher place at which I position myself and show that I am not a slave to my own ideas (*Rubish,* 1).

How the Excessive Love of Well-Being Can Harm Well-Being[b]

There is more of a connection than you think between the perfection of the soul and the improvement of the goods of the body; man can leave these two things distinct and alternately envisage each one of them; but he cannot separate them entirely without finally losing sight of both of them.

Animals have the same senses that we have and more or less the same desires: there are no material passions that we do not have in common with them and whose germ is not found in a dog as well as in ourselves.

So why do the animals only know how to provide for their first and most crude needs, while we infinitely vary our enjoyments and increase them constantly?

What makes us superior in this to animals is that we use our soul to find the material goods toward which their instinct alone leads them. With man, the angel teaches the brute the art of satisfying himself. Man is capable of rising above the goods of the body and even of scorning life, an idea animals

---

a. "It is the soul that teaches the body the art of satisfying itself. You cannot neglect the one up to a certain point without decreasing the means to satisfy the other" (YTC, CVf, p. 33).

b. "The perfection of the soul serves not only to find new means to satisfy the body, but it also increases the ability that the body has to enjoy.

Idea of L[ouis (ed.)].

"I am persuaded in fact that a man of spirit, imagination, genius, feels material enjoyments a thousand times more when he gives himself to them than a fool, a dull or coarse being" (*Rubish*, 1).

do not even conceive; he therefore knows how to multiply these very advantages to a degree that they also cannot imagine.

Everything that elevates, enlarges, expands the soul, makes it more capable of succeeding at even those enterprises that do not concern it.

Everything that enervates the soul, on the contrary, or lowers it, weakens it for all things, the principal ones as well as the least ones, and threatens to make it almost as powerless for the first as for the second. Thus, the soul must remain great and strong, if only to be able, from time to time, to put its strength and its greatness at the service of the body.

If men ever succeed in being content with material goods, it is to be believed that they would little by little lose the art of producing them, and that they would end by enjoying them without discernment and without progress, like the animals.

CHAPTER 17[a]

How, in Times of Equality and Doubt, It Is Important to Push Back the Goal of Human Actions[b]

In centuries of faith, the final aim of life is placed after life.

So men of those times, naturally and so to speak without wanting to, become accustomed to contemplating over a long period of years an unchanging goal toward which they march constantly, and they learn, by taking imperceptible steps forward, to repress a thousand small passing desires, the better to arrive at the satisfaction of this great and permanent desire that torments them. When the same men want to concern themselves with

a. In centuries of faith, men become accustomed to directing all of their actions in this world with the other in view.

That gives them certain habits and leads them as well to set for themselves very distant goals in life and to march toward them obstinately.

In centuries of unbelief, on the contrary, men are naturally led to want to think only about the next day.

So the great matter for philosophers and for those who govern in the centuries of unbelief and democracy must be to push back the goal of human affairs in the eyes of men. Means that they can use to succeed in doing so (YTC, CVf, pp. 33–34).

b. On the jacket of the *rubish:*

How, in centuries of democracy and doubt, all the effort of the social power must tend toward again giving men the taste for the future./

After *all* the chapters on material enjoyments. Democratic peoples have a general taste for easy and quick enjoyments. That is true of material enjoyments as well as others. So this idea must be treated separately from that of material enjoyments, but it must be treated after, because the predominance of the taste for *material* enjoyments is a great cause of the preeminence of the general taste for current enjoyments (*Rubish,* 1).

earthly things, these habits recur. They readily set for their actions here below a general and certain goal, toward which all their efforts are directed. You do not see them give themselves each day to new attempts; but they have settled plans that they do not grow weary of pursuing.

This explains why religious peoples[c] have often accomplished such enduring things. By concerning themselves with the other world, they found the great secret of succeeding in this one.

Religions give the general habit of behaving with the future in view. In this they are no less useful to happiness in this life than to felicity in the other. It is one of their great political dimensions.

But, as the light of faith grows dim, the view of men narrows; and you would say that each day the goal of human actions appears closer to them.

Once they become accustomed to no longer being concerned about what must come after their life, you see them fall easily back into that complete and brutal indifference about the future that is only too suited to certain instincts of the human species. As soon as they have lost the custom of putting their principal hopes in the long run, they are naturally led to wanting to realize their slightest desires without delay, and it seems that, from the moment they lose hope of living eternally, they are disposed to act as if they had only a single day to exist.

In the centuries of unbelief, it is therefore always to be feared that men will constantly give themselves to the daily whims of their desires and that, renouncing entirely what cannot be acquired without long efforts, they will establish nothing great, peaceful and lasting.

If it happens that, among a people so disposed, the social state becomes democratic, the danger that I am pointing out increases.

[<In aristocracies, the fixity of conditions and the immobility of the social body direct the human mind toward the idea of the future and hold it there.>]

When each man seeks constantly to change place, when an immense competition is open to all, when wealth accumulates and disappears in a few moments amid the tumult of democracy, the idea of a sudden and easy fortune, of great possessions easily gained and lost, the image of chance in

---

c. The manuscript says: "most religious peoples."

all its forms occurs to the human mind. The instability of the social state comes to favor the natural instability of desires. In the middle of these perpetual fluctuations of fate, the present grows; it hides the future that fades away, and men want to think only about the next day.

In these countries where by an unhappy coincidence irreligion and democracy meet, philosophers and those governing must apply themselves constantly to pushing back the goal of human actions in the eyes of men; that is their great concern.

While enclosing himself within the spirit of his century and his country, the moralist must learn to defend himself. May he try hard each day to show his contemporaries how, even amid the perpetual movement that surrounds them, it is easier than they suppose to conceive and to carry out long-term enterprises. May he make them see that, even though humanity has changed appearance, the methods by which men can obtain the prosperity of this world have remained the same, and that, among democratic peoples, as elsewhere, it is only by resisting a thousand small particular everyday desires that you can end up satisfying the general passion for happiness that torments.

The task of those who govern is not less marked out.

At all times it is important that those who govern nations conduct themselves with a view toward the future. But that is still more necessary in democratic and unbelieving centuries than in all others. By acting in this way, the leaders of democracies not only make public affairs prosper, but by their example they also teach individuals the art of conducting private affairs.

Above all they must try hard to banish chance, as much as possible, from the political world.

The sudden and unmerited elevation of a courtier produces only a passing impression in an aristocratic country, because the ensemble of institutions and beliefs usually forces men to move slowly along paths that they cannot leave.

But nothing is more pernicious than such examples offered to the view of a democratic people. Such examples end by hurrying the heart of a democratic people down a slope along which everything is dragging it. So it is principally in times of skepticism and equality that you must carefully avoid having the favor of the people, or that of the prince, granted or denied by chance, take the place of knowledge and services. It is to be hoped that every advance there appears to be the fruit of effort, so that there is no overly easy greatness, and that ambition is forced to set its sights on the goal for a long time before achieving it.

Governments must apply themselves to giving back to men this taste for the future that is no longer inspired by religion and the social state; and without saying so, they must teach citizens every day in a practical way that wealth, fame, and power are the rewards of work; that great successes are found at the end of long desires, and that nothing lasting is gained except what is acquired with pain.

When men become accustomed to foreseeing from a great distance what must happen to them here below, and to finding nourishment in hopes, it becomes difficult for them always to stop their thinking at the precise limits of life, and they are very close to going beyond those limits in order to cast their sight farther.

So I do not doubt that by making citizens accustomed to thinking about the future in this world, you lead them closer little by little, and without their knowing it, to religious beliefs.

Thus, the means that, to a certain point, allows men to do without religion, is perhaps, after all, the only one that remains to us for leading humanity back by a long detour toward faith.

CHAPTER 18[a]

Why, among the Americans, All Honest Professions Are Considered Honorable[b]

Among democratic peoples, where there is no hereditary wealth, each man works in order to live, or has worked, or is born from people who have worked. So the idea of work, as the necessary, natural and honest condition of humanity, presents itself on all sides to the human mind.

Not only is work not held in dishonor among these peoples, it is honored; prejudice is not against work, it is for it. In the United States, a rich man believes that he owes to public opinion the consecration of his leisure to some industrial or commercial operation or to some public duties. He would consider himself of bad reputation if he used his life only for living. It is to avoid this obligation to work that so many rich Americans come to Europe; there, they find the remnants of aristocratic societies among which idleness is still honored.

Equality not only rehabilitates the idea of work, it boosts the idea of work that gains a profit.

a. In America everyone works or has worked. That rehabilitates the idea of work. In America, since fortunes are all mediocre and temporary, the idea of salary is strongly joined with the idea of work.

From the moment when work is honorable and when all work is paid, all professions take on a family resemblance. The salary is a common feature that is found in the physiognomy of all professions (YTC, CVf, p. 34).

b. This chapter and the following, until the end of the second part, do not exist in the manuscript, but appear in notebook CVf. There is *rubish* with the title: "(a. b. c.) Rubish./ WHY DEMOCRACY PUSHES MEN TOWARD COMMERCE AND ALL TYPES OF INDUSTRY AND IN GENERAL TOWARD THE TASTE FOR MATERIAL WELL-BEING. INSTINCTS THAT FOLLOW." There is also *rubish* for the chapter on the industrial aristocracy.

In aristocracies, it is not precisely work that is scorned, it is work for profit. Work is glorious when ambition or virtue alone brings it about. Under aristocracy, however, it constantly happens that the man who works for honor is not insensitive to the allure of gain. But those two desires meet only in the depths of his soul. He takes great care to hide from all eyes the place where they come together. He willingly hides it from himself. In aristocratic countries, there are hardly any public officials who do not pretend to serve the State without interest. Their salary is a detail that they sometimes think little about and that they always pretend not to think about at all.

Thus, the idea of gain remains distinct from that of work. In vain are they joined in point of fact; the past separates them.

In democratic societies, these two ideas are, on the contrary, always visibly united. Since the desire for well-being is universal, since fortunes are mediocre and temporary, since each man needs to increase his resources or to prepare new ones for his children, everyone sees very clearly that gain is, if not wholly, at least partially what leads them to work. Even those who act principally with glory in view get inevitably accustomed to the idea that they are not acting solely for this reason, and they discover, whatever they may say, that the desire to live combines in them with the desire to make their life illustrious.

From the moment when, on the one hand, work seems to all citizens an honorable necessity of the human condition, and when, on the other hand, work is always visibly done, in whole or in part, out of consideration for a salary, the immense space that separated the different professions in aristocratic societies disappears. If the professions are not always similar, they at least have a similar feature.

There is no profession in which work is not done for money. The salary, which is common to all, gives all a family resemblance.

This serves to explain the opinions that the Americans entertain concerning the various professions.

American servants do not believe themselves degraded because they work; for around them, everyone works. They do not feel debased by the idea that they receive a salary; for the President of the United States also works for a salary. He is paid to command, just as they are paid to serve.

In the United States, professions are more or less difficult, more or less lucrative, but they are never noble or base. Every honest profession is honorable.

CHAPTER 19[a]

What Makes Nearly All Americans Tend toward Industrial Professions

I do not know if, of all the useful arts, agriculture is not the one that improves most slowly among democratic nations. Often you would even say that it is stationary, because several of the other useful arts seem to race ahead.

On the contrary, nearly all the tastes and habits that arise from equality lead men naturally toward commerce and industry.[b]

I picture an active, enlightened, free man, comfortably well-off, full of desires. He is too poor to be able to live in idleness; he is rich enough to feel above the immediate fear of need, and he thinks about bettering his lot. This man has conceived the taste for material enjoyments; a thousand

---

a. Democracy not only multiplies the number of workers among different labors, it makes men chose those of commerce and industry.

Nearly all the passions that arise from equality lead in this direction.

Love of material enjoyments.

Desire to enjoy quickly.

Love of games of chance.

In democratic countries, the rich themselves are constantly carried toward these careers. Democracy diverts them from politics. It makes commerce and industry into the most brilliant objects. In democratic countries the rich are always afraid of declining in wealth. Example of the Americans (YTC, CVf, p. 35).

b. *Action.* Equality of conditions leads men toward commerce.

(Idea of L[ouis (ed.)].)

Reaction. Commercial habits, type of commercial morality favorable to the government of democracy. Repress all the overly violent passions of temperaments. No anger, compromise, complicated and compromising [*sic*] interests in times of revolution (*Rubish,* 1).

others abandon themselves to this taste before his eyes; he has begun to give himself to it, and he burns to increase the means to satisfy it more. But life passes, time presses. What is he going to do?

For his efforts, cultivation of the earth promises nearly certain, but slow results. In that way you become rich only little by little and with difficulty. Agriculture is suitable only for the rich who already have a great excess, or for the poor who ask only to live. His choice is made: he sells his field, leaves his home and goes to devote himself to some risky, but lucrative profession.[c]

Now, democratic societies abound in men of this type; and as equality of conditions becomes greater, their number increases.

So democracy not only multiplies the number of workers; it leads men to one work rather than another; and, while it gives them a distaste for agriculture, it directs them toward commerce and industry.[1]

This spirit reveals itself among the richest citizens themselves.

c. Of all the means, the most energetic that you can use to push men exclusively toward love of wealth is the establishment of an aristocracy founded solely on money.

Nearly all the desires that can agitate the human heart are combined in the love of wealth, which becomes like the generative passion and which is seen among the others like the trunk of the tree that supports all the branches.

The taste for money and the ardor for power are then mingled so well in the soul, that it becomes difficult to discern if it is for ambition that men are greedy, or for greed that they are ambitious.

That is what happens in England where someone wants to be rich in order to achieve honors and where someone desires honors as evidence of wealth (*Rubish*, 1).

1. *It has been noted several times that men of industry and men of commerce possessed an immoderate taste for material enjoyments, and commerce and industry were blamed for that; I believe that here the effect has been taken for the cause.*

It is not commerce and industry that suggest the taste for material enjoyments to men, but rather this taste leads men toward industrial and commercial careers, where they hope to be satisfied more completely and more quickly.

If commerce and industry increase the desire for well-being, that results from the fact that every passion becomes stronger as it is exercised more, and grows with all the efforts that you make to satisfy it. All the causes that make the love of the goods of this world predominate in the human heart develop industry and commerce. Equality is one of these causes. It favors commerce, not directly by giving men the taste for trade, but indirectly, by strengthening and generalizing in their souls the love of well-being.

In democratic countries, a man, however wealthy he is assumed to be, is almost always discontent with his fortune, because he finds himself not as rich as his father and is afraid that his sons will not be as rich as he. So most of the rich in democracies constantly dream about the means to acquire wealth, and they naturally turn their sights toward commerce and industry, which seem to them the quickest and most powerful means to gain it. On this point they share the instincts of the poor man without having his needs, or rather they are pushed by the most imperious of all needs: that of not declining.[d]

In aristocracies, the rich are at the same time those who govern. The

d. .-.-.-.- is not by chance that most aristocracies have shown themselves indifferent to the works of industry or enemies to its progress. Underneath prejudice, it is easy to discern something real, which is like its seed.

Commerce often has admirable results in view, but it almost always uses very petty means to attain them.

In aristocracies, it is the same men who have wealth and who hold power, and their business is as much to direct public fortune as to look after their own. Preoccupied by these great matters, they can only with difficulty turn their mind to the run of small affairs that make up commerce, as well as to the minute and almost infinite concerns that commerce requires. So it is to be believed that they would see trade as a wearisome and secondary occupation and would neglect it even when they did not indeed consider it degrading. If some men were found among them who felt a natural taste for industry, they would carefully refrain from devoting themselves to it. For it is useless to resist the dominion of numbers, you never completely escape its yoke; and even within those aristocratic corps that refuse most stubbornly to acknowledge the rights of the national majority, there is a particular majority that governs.

With democracy the connection that united government and wealth disappears. The rich do not know what to do with their leisure; the restlessness of their desires, the extent of their resources, and the taste for great adventures [v: extraordinary things], which are almost always felt by men who stand in some way above the crowd, presses them to action. Only the road to commerce is open to them. In a democracy there is nothing greater or more brilliant than commerce. That is what attracts the attention and the prompting of the public; and all energetic passions are directed toward commerce. Nothing can keep the rich from devoting themselves to it, neither their own prejudices nor those of anyone else.

Since the great fortunes that are seen within a democracy almost always have a commercial origin, those who possess those fortunes have kept the habits or at least the traditions of trade. On the other hand, the rich never make up among a democratic people, as within aristocracies, a corps that has [interrupted text (ed.)] (*Rubish,* 1).

attention that they give constantly to great public affairs diverts them from the small concerns that commerce and industry demand. If the will of one of them is nonetheless directed by chance toward trade, the will of the aristocratic corps immediately bars the route to him; for it is useless to resist the dominion of numbers, you never completely escape its yoke; and, even within those aristocratic corps that refuse most stubbornly to acknowledge the rights of the national majority, there is a particular majority that governs.[2]

In democratic countries, where money does not lead the one who has it to power, but often keeps him away from it, the rich do not know what to do with their leisure.[e] Restlessness and the greatness of their desires, the extent of their resources, the taste for the extraordinary, which are almost always felt by those who stand, in whatever way, above the crowd, presses them to action. Only the road to commerce is open to them. In democracies, there is nothing greater or more brilliant than commerce; that is what attracts the attention of the public and fills the imagination of the crowd; all energetic passions are directed toward commerce. Nothing can prevent the rich from devoting themselves to it, neither their own prejudices, nor those of anyone else. The rich of democracies never form a corps that has its own mores and its own organization; the particular ideas of their class do not stop them, and the general ideas of their country push them. Since, moreover, the great fortunes that are seen within a democratic people almost always have a commercial origin, several generations must pass before those who possess those fortunes have entirely lost the habits of trade.[f]

2. *See the note at the end of the volume.*

e. *"England.*

"≠When it is not those who govern who are rich, but the rich who govern≠" (*Rubish*, 1).

f. Aristocracy of birth and pure democracy form two extremes of the social state of peoples.

In the middle is found the aristocracy of money. The latter is close to aristocracy of birth in that it confers on a small number of citizens great privileges. It fits into democracy in that these privileges can be successively acquired by all. It forms the natural transition between the two things, and you cannot say whether it is ending the rule of aristocracy on earth, or whether it is already opening the new era of democratic centuries (*Rubish*, 1).

Confined to the narrow space that politics leaves to them, the rich of democracies therefore throw themselves from all directions into commerce; there they can expand and use their natural advantages; and it is, in a way, by the very boldness and by the grandeur of their industrial enterprises that you must judge what little value they would have set on industry if they had been born within an aristocracy.

The same remark, moreover, is applicable to all the men of democracies, whether they are poor or rich.

Those who live amid democratic instability have constantly before their eyes the image of chance, and they end by loving all enterprises in which chance plays a role.

So they are all led toward commerce, not only because of the gain that it promises, but by love of the emotions that it gives.

The United States of America has only emerged for a half-century from the colonial dependence in which England held it; the number of great fortunes is very small there, and capital is still rare. But there is no people on earth who has made as rapid progress as the Americans in commerce and industry. They form today the second maritime nation of the world; and, although their manufacturing has to struggle against almost insurmountable natural obstacles, it does not fail to make new gains every day.

In the United States the greatest industrial enterprises are executed without difficulty, because the entire population is involved in industry, and because the poorest as well as the wealthiest citizen readily combine their efforts. So it is astonishing every day to see the immense works that are executed without difficulty by a nation that does not so to speak contain rich men. The Americans arrived only yesterday on the land that they inhabit, and they have already overturned the whole natural order to their profit. They have united the Hudson with the Mississippi and connected the Atlantic Ocean with the Gulf of Mexico, across more than five hundred leagues of the continent that separates these two seas. The longest railroads that have been constructed until now are in America.

But what strikes me most in the United States is not the extraordinary greatness of some industrial enterprises, it is the innumerable multitude of small enterprises.

Nearly all the farmers of the United States have combined some commerce with agriculture; most have made agriculture into a trade.

It is rare for an American farmer to settle forever on the land that he occupies. In the new provinces of the West principally, you clear a field in order to resell it and not to harvest it; you build a farm with the expectation that, since the state of the country is soon going to change due to the increase of inhabitants, you will be able to get a good price.

Every year, a swarm of inhabitants from the North descends toward the South and comes to live in the countries where cotton and sugar cane grow. These men cultivate the earth with the goal of making it produce in a few years what it takes to make them rich, and they already foresee the moment when they will be able to return to their country to enjoy the comfort gained in this way. So the Americans bring to agriculture the spirit of trade, and their industrial passions are seen there as elsewhere.

The Americans make immense progress in industry, because they are all involved in industry at the same time; and for the same reason, they are subject to very unexpected and very formidable industrial crises.

Since they are all engaged in commerce, commerce among them is subject to such numerous and so complicated influences that it is impossible to foresee in advance the difficulties that can arise. Since each one of them is more or less involved in industry, at the slightest shock that business experiences, all particular fortunes totter at the same time, and the State falters.[g]

I believe that the recurrence of industrial crises is an illness endemic among the democratic nations of our day.[h] It can be made less dangerous,

---

g. In the United States, everyone does commerce or has a portion of his fortune placed in commerce. Consequently, you see what is happening at this moment (May 1837) and what will perhaps result from it in the political world.

There is a great part of future humanity to which I must give my attention./

The Americans make immense progress in industry because they are all involved at the same time in industry, and for the same reason, they are subject to very unexpected and very formidable industrial crises (*Rubish*, 1).

h. [In the margin: I do not know if I should include this piece or where I should put it.]

but cannot be cured, because it is not due to an accident, but to the very temperament of these peoples.ʲ

I have shown in this chapter how democracy served the developments of industry. I would have been able to show as well how industry in turn hastened the developments of democracy. For these two things go together and react on each other. Democracy gives birth to the taste for material enjoyments that pushes men toward industry, and industry creates a multitude of mediocre fortunes and develops within the very heart of aristocratic nations a separate class in which ranks are ill defined and poorly maintained, in which people rise and fall constantly, in which leisure is not enjoyed, a separate class whose instincts are all democratic. This class forms for a long time within the very heart of aristocratic nations a kind of small democracy that has its separate instincts, opinions, laws. As the people expands its commerce and its industry, this democratic class becomes more numerous and more influential; little by little its opinions pass into the mores and its ideas into the laws, until finally, having become predominant and so to speak unique, it takes hold of power and directs everything at its will and establishes democracy.

[To the side] All that badly digested (YTC, CVj, 2, pp. 16–17).

j. Fragment of *rubish:*

OF THE RELATION THAT .-.-.- COMMERCE AND INDUSTRY, ON THE ONE HAND, AND ON THE OTHER HAND, DEMOCRACY./

When you examine the direction that industry and democracy give to mores as well as to the minds of men, you are struck by the sight of the great similarity that exists between the effects produced by these two causes.

[In the margin: See in bundle A a good piece by Beaumont on that.]

I want to take as an example the matter that I am treating at this moment (June 1836) which is *the sciences, letters and the arts* (perhaps make good use of this general idea in the article on the sciences and on literature).

When men are engaged in the different commercial and industrial professions, their minds become accustomed to substituting in everything the idea of the useful for that of the beautiful, which leads them to cultivate the applied sciences rather than the theoretical sciences; inexpensive, elementary, productive literature for *finished,* refined literary works; useful building for beautiful monuments.

When conditions become equal and classes disappear, the same instincts arise. Except that instead of being felt by only one part of the nation, they are felt by the generality of citizens.

But these two causes are .-.-.-.-.- perceived separately.

I am first able to imagine very clearly a great industrial class in the middle of an aristocratic people. This class will have its own instincts; and if, as we have seen in England, it is influential in public affairs but without being master of them, it will give a portion of these instincts to all the other classes; and the nation, while keeping the social and political organization that characterizes an aristocracy, will show in part the tastes and the ideas that a democracy displays. This has happened to the English.

But here you will stop me and say: this industrial class is nothing other than a small democracy enclosed within a great aristocracy. Within it equality of conditions, the need to work, etc. reign, which do not reign in the larger society within which it is enclosed. When this class influences the opinions and ways of life of all the other classes, you have an incomplete democracy .-.-.-.- so you cannot cultivate industry without forming a small or large democratic society. When men cultivate industry, they are democratic, and when they are democratic, they necessarily cultivate industry.

I will answer that the men who are occupied with industry can be organized vis-à-vis each other very aristocratically. Which is what happens in a country in which industry is invariably directed by a small number of great capitalists who make the law and a multitude of workers who receive it. But both have nearly the same instincts, as regards the sciences, letters and the arts. So these instincts are due to the types of their occupations much more than to their social state, since the poor man and the rich man equally experience them.

[In the margin: The terms *industry, commerce* are too general. Make them more specific if I want to understand myself.]

From another perspective, could you not imagine a democracy, that is to say a people among whom conditions were more or less equal and among whom the taste for industry would not be found??/

All of this is looking for difficulties that do not exist.

.-.-.-.- the natural sequence of ideas.

When conditions are more or less equal among a people, there is naturally a great number of people who have a mediocre fortune, for [they (ed.)] are not so poor as to despair of bettering their lot and not so rich as to be satisfied with it. They will have enough well-being to know the attractions of well-being, not enough to content themselves with what they have. On the other hand, they will see a thousand ways to alleviate the material misfortunes that they feel, and the more they see the paths to deliver themselves from those misfortunes, the more impatiently will they bear them.

This class will be able to exist, to become strong and numerous among aristocratic nations themselves.[1] But in democracies, it will be dominant; it will be alone so to speak; it will make the laws and opinions.

Now it is clear that this class will be naturally concentrated on the taste for .-.-.-.- enjoyments, on all the instincts described above, and on commerce and industry at the same time. Commerce and industry are not the causes of these instincts, but on the contrary their products. What you can say is that commerce and industry increase these instincts, because every passion grows with all the efforts that you make to satisfy it and the more you concern yourself with it.

[To the side: As the number of mediocre fortunes increases and as the ease of making great fortunes grows, all of this more and more true. America.]

1. Here the example of England. This class that ends by giving its instincts to a people, but that cannot take the aristocratic form away from it. Particular causes such as liberty, maritime commerce, openings to national industries that give this class more intense tastes for well-being (*Rubish,* 1).

CHAPTER 20[a]

How Aristocracy Could Emerge from Industry[b]

a. Of the aristocratic make-up of some of the industries of today.

I showed how democracy favored the development of industry; I am going to show in what roundabout way industry in return leads back toward aristocracy.

It has been discovered in our time that when each worker was occupied only with the same detail, the work as a whole was more perfect.

It has been discovered as well that to do something with less expense, it is necessary to undertake it immediately on a very vast scale.

The first of the two discoveries lowers [v: ruins] and brutalizes the worker. The second constantly raises the master. They introduce the principles of aristocracy into the industrial class.

Now, as society in general becomes more democratic, since the need for inexpensive manufactured objects becomes more general and more intense, the two discoveries above apply more frequently and more rigorously.

So equality disappears from the small society as it becomes established in the large one (YTC, CVf, pp. 35–36).

Several ideas from this chapter come from the book of Viscount Alban de Villeneuve-Bargemont, *Économie politique chrétienne, ou recherches sur la nature et les causes du paupérisme, en France et en Europe* . . . (Paris: Paulin, 1834), 2 vols., which Tocqueville had used for his memoir on pauperism. Chapter XII of the first volume of Villeneuve-Bargemont's book has precisely this title, "The New Feudalism," and contains in germ the principal arguments of this chapter. See note s of p. 81 of the first volume.

b. I do not know where to place this chapter. Three systems:

1. It could perhaps be put in the first volume after the chapter that considers *equality* as the universal fact. It would show the exception and would complete the picture. In this case, it must perhaps be developed a bit.

2. It could perhaps be put before the chapter on salaries. In this case, it will have to be shortened.

3. I think, for the moment, that the best place would be after the chapter where I say that democracy pushes toward industrial careers. It would then be necessary to

I showed how democracy favored the development of industry and immeasurably multiplied the number of industrialists; we are going to see in what roundabout way industry in turn could well lead men toward aristocracy.

It has been recognized that when a worker is occupied every day only with the same detail, the general production of the work is achieved more easily, more rapidly and more economically.

It has been recognized as well that the more an industry was undertaken on a large scale, with great capital and large credit, the less expensive its products were.[c]

These truths have been seen dimly for a long time, but they have been demonstrated in our time. They are already applied to several very important industries, and the smallest industries are successively making use of them.

---

get into the matter a bit differently and bring out the link between this chapter and that which precedes. Something like this:

I said that democracy pushes men toward industry, and industry, such as it seems to want to be constituted today, tends to lead them back toward aristocracy./

Every society begins with aristocracy; industry is subject to this law (*Rubish,* 2).

c. In the margin, in the *rubish:* "<Now, these discoveries must be considered as the two sources from which aristocracy can escape once again to cover the world.> 2 July 1837" (*Rubish,* 2).

There is perhaps no point on which modern critics of Tocqueville are in more agreement than on his ignorance of the changes that took place in America and in Europe during the first half of the XIXth century in matters of industry, of the process of urbanization, and the little attention that he gave to steamboats, canals, railroads and other technical progress. The publication of his travel notes and the book of Seymour Drescher (*Tocqueville and Beaumont on Social Reform,* New York: Harper and Row, 1968) show, however, that his description of Manchester is largely devoted to the results of industrialization and that, far from being unaware of the problem, he knew about it and was preoccupied by it.

If Tocqueville evokes the problem of industrialization only rapidly, it is above all because the purpose of his work, like his anti-materialism, scarcely pushes him there. What interests him is the energy (acquiring money and the taste for material well-being) that creates industry and the effects that it produces (the new manufacturing aristocracy). According to Seymour Drescher again (*Tocqueville and England,* Cambridge, Mass.: Harvard University Press, 1964, pp. 60–61), the friendship of Senior would have had a real influence on Tocqueville's ideas about the economy. See *Voyage en Angleterre, OC,* V, 2, especially pages 67–68 and 78–85.

I see nothing in the political world that should occupy the legislator more than these two new axioms of industrial science.

When an artisan devotes himself constantly and solely to the fabrication of a single object, he ends by acquitting himself of this work with a singular dexterity. But he loses, at the same time, the general ability to apply his mind to directing the work. Each day he becomes more skillful and less industrious, and you can say that in him the man becomes degraded as the worker improves.

What should you expect from a man who has used twenty years of his life making pinheads? And in his case, to what in the future can the powerful human intelligence, which has often stirred the world, be applied, if not to searching for the best way to make pinheads!

When a worker has in this way consumed a considerable portion of his existence, his thought has stopped forever near the daily object of his labor; his body has contracted certain fixed habits that he is no longer allowed to give up. In a word, he no longer belongs to himself, but to the profession that he chose. Laws and mores have in vain taken care to break down all the barriers around this man and to open for him in all directions a thousand different roads toward fortune; an industrial theory more powerful than mores and laws has bound him to an occupation and often to a place in society that he cannot leave. Amid the universal movement, it has made him immobile.

As the principle of the division of labor is more completely applied, the worker becomes weaker, more limited, and more dependent. The art makes progress, the artisan goes backward. On the other hand, as it becomes clearer that the larger the scale of manufacturing and the greater the capital, the more perfect and the less expensive the products of an industry are, very rich and very enlightened men arise to exploit industries that, until then, have been left to ignorant and poor artisans. The greatness of the necessary efforts and the immensity of the results to achieve attract them.

Thus, at the same time that industrial science constantly lowers the class of workers, it raises the class of masters.

While the worker applies his intelligence more and more to the study of a single detail, the master casts his sight every day over a broader whole, and his mind expands in proportion as that of the worker contracts. Soon nothing will be needed by the worker except physical strength without intelligence; the master needs knowledge, and almost genius to succeed. The one more and more resembles the administrator of a vast empire, and the other a brute.

So the master and the worker are not in any way similar here, and every day they differ more. They are no longer held together except as the two end links of a long chain. Each one occupies a place made for him and does not leave it. The one is in a continual, narrow and necessary dependence on the other, and seems born to obey, as the latter to command.

What is this, if not aristocracy?[d]

As conditions become more and more equal in the body of the nation, the need for manufactured objects becomes more general and increases, and an inexpensive price that puts these objects within reach of mediocre fortunes becomes a greater element of success.

So every day more opulent and more enlightened men are found who devote their wealth and their knowledge to industry and who seek, by opening great workshops and strictly dividing labor, to satisfy the new desires that appear on all sides.

Thus, as the mass of the nation turns to democracy, the particular class that is concerned with industry becomes more aristocratic. Men show themselves more and more similar in the nation and more and more different in the particular class, and inequality increases in the small society in proportion as it decreases in the large one.

In this way, when you go back to the source, it seems that you see aristocracy come by a natural effort from the very heart of democracy.

But that aristocracy does not resemble the aristocracies that preceded it.

You will notice first that, applying only to industry and to a few of the

d. "Examine a bit practically the question of knowing how you could re-create an aristocracy of fortunes, bring together (illegible word), give privileges.

"Piece on the impossibility of a new aristocracy, 2nd vol., p. 425" (YTC, CVc, p. 55). This concerns pp. 635–36 of the first volume.

industrial professions, it is an exception, a monstrosity, within the whole of the social state.

The small aristocratic societies formed by certain industries amid the immense democracy of our time include, like the great aristocratic societies of former times, a few very opulent men and a multitude of very miserable ones.

These poor have few means to emerge from their condition and to become rich, but the rich constantly become poor, or leave trade after having realized their profits. Thus, the elements that form the class of the poor are more or less fixed; but the elements that compose the class of the rich are not. Truly speaking, although there are rich men, the class of the rich does not exist; for these rich men have neither spirit nor aims in common, nor shared traditions or shared hopes. So there are members, but not a corps.

Not only are the rich not united solidly with each other, but you can say that there is no true bond between the poor and the rich.

They are not fixed in perpetuity next to each other; at every moment interest draws them closer and separates them. The worker depends in general on the master, but not on a particular master. These two men see each other at the factory and do not know each other elsewhere, and while they touch at one point, they remain very far apart at all others. The manufacturer asks the worker only for his work, and the worker expects from him only a salary. The one does not commit himself to protecting, nor the other to defending, and they are not linked in a permanent way, either by habit or by duty.

The aristocracy established by trade hardly ever settles amid the industrial population that it directs; its goal is not to govern the latter, but to make use of it.

An aristocracy thus constituted cannot have a great hold on those it employs; and if it manages to seize them for a moment, they soon escape. It does not know what it wants and cannot act.

The territorial aristocracy of past centuries was obligated by law, or believed itself obligated by mores, to come to the aid of those who served it and to relieve their miseries. But the manufacturing aristocracy of today, after impoverishing and brutalizing the men it uses, delivers them in times of crisis to public charity to be fed. This results naturally from what precedes. Between the worker and the master, contacts are frequent, but there is no true association.

I think that, everything considered, the manufacturing aristocracy that we see arising before our eyes is one of the harshest that has appeared on the earth; but at the same time it is one of the most limited and least dangerous.

Nonetheless, it is in this direction that the friends of democracy must with anxiety constantly turn their attention; for if permanent inequality of conditions and aristocracy ever penetrate the world again, you can predict that they will come in through this door.

THIRD PART[a]

Influence of Democracy on
Mores Properly So Called

<hr />

a. Action of equality on mores and reaction of mores on equality./

After doing a book that pointed out the influence exercised by equality of conditions on ideas, customs and mores, another one would have to be done that showed the influence exercised by ideas, customs and mores on equality of conditions. For these two things have a reciprocal action on each other. And to take just one example, the comparatively democratic social state of European peoples in the XVIth century allowed the doctrines of Protestantism, based in part on the theory of intellectual equality, to arise and spread; and on the other hand, you cannot deny that these doctrines, once accepted, singularly hastened the leveling of conditions. If I examined separately the first of these influences, without concerning myself with the second, it is not that I did not know and appreciate the extent and the power of the latter. But I believed that in a subject so difficult and so complicated, it was already a lot to study separately one of the parts, to put the parts separately in relief, leaving to more skillful hands the task of exposing the entire tableau to view all at once (YTC, CVk, 1, pp. 48–49). Tocqueville finishes the third part of this volume at Baugy in April 1838.

See Jean-Louis Benoît, *Tocqueville moraliste* (Paris: Honoré Champion, 2004), pp. 309–442.

How Mores Become Milder
as Conditions Become Equal

We have noticed for several centuries that conditions are becoming equal, and we have found at the same time that mores are becoming milder.[b] Are

a. 1. Equality makes mores milder in an *indirect* manner, by giving the taste for well-being, love for peace and for all the professions that need peace.

2. It makes them milder *directly*.

When men are divided into castes, they have a fraternal sentiment for the members of their caste, but they scarcely regard all the others as men. Great (illegible word) and great categories.

When all men are similar, what happens within them alerts them to what must happen in all the others, and they cannot be insensitive to any misery. They are not devoted, but they are mild.

Example of the Americans (YTC, CVf, pp. 36–37).

b. Two peoples have the same origin, they have lived for a long time under the same laws; they have kept the same language and the same habits of life, but they are not similar; what causes that?

[In the margin: At the head of civil society. Transition from political society to civil society. Influence of laws on character.

Influence of democracy in America on mores. Everything is modeled on the people. The rich man must grow up with the people, must travel with them, must take his enjoyments with them. He can scarcely protect himself from them in the refuge of the domestic hearth.

At home the rich man is under permanent suspicion. And he must in a way be poor or once have been poor to aspire to honors.]

The one is eager to change, the past displeases him, the present tires him, only the future seems to him to merit his thought. He scorns age and scoffs at experience. He makes, undoes, remakes his laws without ceasing. Everything changes and is modified by his indefatigable activity, even the earth that supports him. Superiorities of all kinds offend and wound him. He even sees the plebeian privileges of wealth only with disfavor.

these two things only contemporaneous, or does some secret link exist between them, so that the one cannot go ahead without making the other move?

Several causes can work together to make the mores of a people less harsh; but, among all these causes, the most powerful one seems to me to be equality of conditions. So in my view equality of conditions and mores becoming mild are not only contemporaneous events, but also correlative facts.[c]

[≠Equality of conditions leads men toward industrial and commercial professions, which need peace in order for men to devote themselves to those professions. Equality of conditions suggests to men the taste for material enjoyments; it distances them imperceptibly from war and violent

---

His vanity is constantly uneasy. He seeks praise. There is no flattery so small that he does not receive it with joy. If he fails in his efforts to obtain it, he praises himself and becomes intoxicated with the incense that his hands have prepared. The laws are democratic.

The other is prostrated before the past, he mixes everything that comes from antiquity in his idolatry and esteems things not so much because they are good, but because they are old. So he takes care to change nothing in his laws or, if the irresistible march of time forces him to deviate on certain points, there are no ingenious subtleties to which he will not resort in order to persuade himself that he has only found in the work of his fathers what was already there and only developed a thought that had formerly occurred to their minds. Do not hope to get him to acknowledge that he is an innovator; although a very strong logician otherwise, he will agree to go to the absurd rather than admit himself guilty of such a great crime. Full of veneration for superiorities of all kinds, he seems to consider birth and wealth as so many natural and imprescriptible rights [v: privileges] that call certain men to govern society [v. in the margin: wealth as a virtue and birth as an imprescriptible right]. With him, the poor man is scarcely considered as a man. Full, moreover, of an immense pride, he thinks he is sufficiently sure of his grandeur not to ask the common people to acknowledge it, and he judges himself so above praise that he does not need to give it. The laws are aristocratic.

There are men who say that this is the American spirit and I say that it is the democratic spirit. What is taken for the English spirit is the aristocratic spirit (YTC, CVk, I, pp. 14–16). The copyist, Bonnel, indicates that one part of this piece is not in Tocqueville's hand. See p. 437 of the first volume.

c. In the margin: "≠You cannot hide from the fact that the natural place of war would be there, for it is only in the absence of wars or in the manner in which it is conducted that the subject of this chapter is proved.≠"

revolutions. I have already said a portion of these things; I will show the others in the course of this work.^d

Those are the indirect effects of equality of conditions; its direct effects are not less.≠]

When writers of fables want to interest us in the actions of the animals, they give them human ideas and passions. Poets do the same when they speak about spirits and angels.^e No miseries are so deep, or joys so pure that they cannot capture our minds and take hold of our hearts, if we are presented to ourselves under other features.

This applies very well to the subject that occupies us presently.

When all men are arranged in an irrevocable manner, according to their profession, their property and their birth, within an aristocratic society, the members of each class, all considering themselves as children of the same family, experience for each other a continual and active sympathy^f

---

d. Equality of conditions leads citizens toward industrial and commercial professions and makes them love peace, which they need in order to devote themselves to those professions. Equality of conditions thus imperceptibly little by little takes away from the citizens the love of violent emotions and suggests to them the taste for tranquil enjoyments. As conditions become equal, the imagination of men therefore turns imperceptibly away from the cruel pictures offered by war and feeds more readily on the mild images presented by well-being. Human passions are not extinguished, they change objects and become less fierce. Accustomed to the charms of a well-ordered and prosperous life, you are afraid of being saddened by making your fellows suffer and you fear the sight of the pain almost as much as the pain itself.

[In the margin: I do not believe that this piece should be introduced, however to consult./

The things it contains are true and important, but they prevent the unity of the chapter.]

This is how equality of conditions leads indirectly to the mildness of mores. The direct effects are not less.

When writers of fables . . . (YTC, CVk, 1, pp. 5–6).

e. In the margin: "and Milton would never have succeeded in interesting us in the fate of [a blank (ed.)] if he had not given human feelings to the devils and to the angels."

f. *Sympathy./*

It is a democratic word. You have real sympathy only for those similar to you and your equals. The humanity that we notice today is due in part to men being closer to each other. When there were only great lords and men of the people, men were

that can never be found to the same degree among the citizens of a democracy.

But it is not the same with the different classes vis-à-vis each other.

Among an aristocratic people, each caste has its opinions, its sentiments,
its rights, its mores, its separate existence. Thus, the men who compose each
caste are not similar to any of the others; they do not have the same way
of thinking or of feeling, and they scarcely believe that they are part of the
same humanity.

So they cannot understand well what the others experience, or judge the
latter by themselves.

Yet you sometimes see them lend themselves with fervor to mutual aid;
but that is not contrary to what precedes.

These same aristocratic institutions, which had made beings of the same
species so different, had nevertheless joined them by a very close political
bond.

Although the serf was not naturally interested in the fate of the nobles,
he believed himself no less obligated to devote himself to the one among
the nobles who was his leader; and although the noble believed himself of
another nature than the serf, he nonetheless judged that his duty and his
honor forced him to defend, at the risk of his own life, those who lived on
his domains.

It is clear that these mutual obligations did not arise out of natural right,
but political right, and that society obtained more than humanity alone
was able to do. It was not to the man that you believed yourself obliged to
lend support, it was to the vassal or to the lord. Feudal institutions made
very tangible the misfortunes of certain men, not the miseries of the human

---

strangers to each other and above all different; no one could judge by himself what
others felt. So there could not be true sympathy, and mores were hard.

[In the margin: Aristocracy gives birth to great devotions and great hatreds. Democracy leads all men to a sort of tranquil benevolence./

Sympathy *less* but *general*.]

17 October 1836.

These classes were indifferent to each other's fate not because they were *enemies*,
but simply because they were *different*. Sympathy from two Greek words, I believe,
meaning *to feel with* (*Rubish*, 2).

species. They gave to mores generosity rather than mildness, and although they suggested great attachments, they did not give birth to true sympathies; for there are real sympathies only between similar people; and in aristocratic centuries, you see people similar to you only in the members of your caste.

When the chroniclers of the Middle Ages, who all, by their birth or their habits, belonged to the aristocracy, report the tragic end of a nobleman, there are infinite sorrows; while they recount in one breath and without batting an eye the massacre and tortures of the men of the people.

It is not that these writers felt a habitual hatred or a systematic disdain for the people. The war between the various classes of the State had not yet been declared. They obeyed an instinct rather than a passion; as they did not form a clear idea of the sufferings of the poor, they were little interested in their fate.

It was the same with the men of the people, as soon as the feudal bond was broken. These same centuries, which saw so much heroic devotion on the part of the vassals for their lords, had witnessed unheard of cruelties exercised from time to time by the lower classes against the upper classes.g

You must not believe that this mutual insensitivity is due only to the absence of order and enlightenment; for you again find its trace in the following centuries that, even while becoming well-ordered and enlightened, still remained aristocratic.

In the year 1675, the lower classes of Brittany were roused by a new tax. This tumultuous movement was put down with unparalleled atrocity. Here is how Madame de Sévigné, witness to these horrors, informed her daughter about them:

> Aux Rochers, 30 October 1675.
> My heavens, my daughter, how amusing your letter from Aix is! At least reread your letters before sending them. Allow yourself to be caught up in their charm, and with this pleasure, console yourself for the burden you have of writing so many of them. So have you kissed all of Provence? There would be no satisfaction in kissing all of Brittany, unless you loved to smell of wine. [. . . (ed.) . . .] Do you want to know the news from Rennes? [. . . (ed.) . . .] A tax of one hundred thousand *écus* was imposed,

g. In the margin, in pencil: "≠Example, Jacquerie.≠"

and if this amount was not found within twenty-four hours, it would be doubled and would be collected by soldiers. One entire great street was chased away and banished, and the inhabitants were forbidden to come back under pain of death; so that all these miserable people, new mothers, old people, children, wandered in tears outside this city, without knowing where to go, without food or anywhere to sleep. The day before yesterday the violinist who began the dance and the theft of the stamped paper was broken on the wheel; he was quartered, and the four parts were displayed in the four corners of the city. [. . . (ed.) . . .] Sixty bourgeois were taken and tomorrow they will begin to be hanged. This province is a good example to the others, above all to respect governors and the wives of governors, and not to throw stones into their gardens.[1]

Yesterday Madame de Tarente was in her woods in delightful weather. It is not a question of either staying there or eating there. She goes in by the gate and comes out the same way . . .

In another letter she adds:

You talk to me very amusingly about our miseries; we are no longer broken on the wheel so much; one in eight days in order to uphold justice. It is true that hanging now seems refreshing to me. I have an entirely different idea of justice since being in this country. Your men condemned to the galleys seem to me to be a society of honest men who have withdrawn from the world in order to lead a pleasant life.

We would be wrong to believe that Madame de Sévigné, who wrote these lines, was an egotistical and barbarous creature; she passionately loved her children and showed herself very sensitive to the misfortunes of her friends; and we even notice, reading her, that she treated her vassals and her servants with kindness and indulgence. But Madame de Sévigné did not clearly understand what suffering was when you were not a gentleman.

Today, the harshest man, writing to the most insensitive person, would not dare to give himself to the cruel banter that I have just reproduced, and even when his particular mores would permit him to do so, the general mores of the nation would forbid him.

---

1. *To sense the pertinence of this final joke, you must recall that Madame de Grignan was the wife of the Governor of Provence.*

What causes that? Are we more sensitive than our fathers? I do not know; but certainly our sensibility falls on more things.

When ranks are nearly equal among a people, since all men have more or less the same way of thinking and feeling, each one of them can judge in a moment the sensations of all the others; he glances quickly at himself; that is sufficient. So there is no misery that he cannot easily imagine and whose extent is not revealed to him by a secret instinct. Whether it concerns strangers or enemies, imagination immediately puts him in their place. It mingles something personal in his pity, and makes him suffer as the body of his fellow man is torn apart.

In democratic centuries, men rarely sacrifice themselves for each other; but they show a general compassion for all the members of the human species. You do not see them inflict useless evils, and when, without hurting themselves very much, they can relieve the sufferings of others, they take pleasure in doing so; they are not disinterested, but they are mild.

Although the Americans have so to speak reduced egoism to a social and philosophical theory, they have shown themselves no less very open to pity.

There is no country in which criminal justice is administered more benignly than in the United States. While the English seem to want to preserve carefully in their penal legislation the bloody traces of the Middle Ages, the Americans have almost made the death penalty disappear from their legal order.

North America is, I think, the only country on earth where, for the last fifty years, the life of not a single citizen has been taken for political crimes.

What finally proves that this singular mildness of the Americans comes principally from their social state, is the manner in which they treat their slaves.

Perhaps, everything considered, there is no European colony in the New World in which the physical condition of the Blacks is less harsh than in the United States. But slaves there still experience dreadful miseries and are constantly exposed to very cruel punishments.

It is easy to discover that the fate of these unfortunates inspires little pity in their masters, and that they see in slavery not only a fact from which they profit, but also an evil that scarcely touches them. Thus, the same man who is full of humanity for his fellows when the latter are at the same time his equals, becomes insensitive to their sufferings from the moment when equality ceases. So his mildness must be attributed to this equality still more than to civilization and enlightenment.

What I have just said about individuals applies to a certain degree to peoples.

When each nation has its separate opinions, beliefs, laws and customs, it considers itself as forming by itself the whole of humanity, and feels touched only by its own sufferings. If war comes to break out between two peoples so inclined, it cannot fail to be conducted with barbarism.

At the time of their greatest enlightenment, the Romans cut the throats of enemy generals, after dragging them in triumph behind a chariot, and delivered prisoners to the beasts for the amusement of the people. Cicero, who raises such loud cries at the idea of a citizen crucified, finds nothing to say about these atrocious abuses of victory. It is clear that in his eyes a foreigner is not of the same human species as a Roman.[h]

On the contrary, as peoples become more similar to each other, they show themselves reciprocally more compassionate toward their misfortunes, and the law of nations becomes milder.

---

h. Something analogous is seen from one people to another. When peoples are very different from each other, separated by opinions, beliefs, opposite customs, they seem as well to be outside of the same humanity. Moreover, aristocratic sentiments also become established between them. They believe themselves not only different but also superior to each other. That would lead naturally to a law of nations horrible in times of war.

Romans. Jugurtha.

Now wars between peoples are like civil wars in antiquity (*Rubish,* 2).

CHAPTER 2[a]

How Democracy Makes the Habitual Relations of the Americans Simpler and Easier[b]

Democracy does not bind men closely together, but it makes their habitual relationships easier.

Two Englishmen meet by chance at the far ends of the earth; they are surrounded by strangers whose language and mores they hardly know.

[<I think that they are going to run eagerly toward each other. What more is needed to draw men closer in a far-away land than a native land in common?>]

The two men at first consider each other very curiously and with a sort

---

a. In aristocracies based solely on birth, since no one is able to climb or descend, the relationships between men are infrequent, but not constrained.

In aristocracies based principally on money such as the English, aristocratic pride remains, but since the limits of the aristocracy have become doubtful, each man fears that his familiarity will be abused. You avoid contact with someone unknown or you remain icy before him.

When there are no more privileges of birth or privileges of money as in America, men readily mingle and greet each other familiarly (YTC, CVf, p. 37).

b. INFLUENCE OF DEMOCRACY ON AMERICAN SOCIABILITY./

Chapter following those on egoism. Sociability, which is sacrifice in small things, with hope to find it in turn, is very easily understood on the part of beings independent of each other, but equally weak individually, and is not at all contrary to the egoism that I portrayed above./

Good qualities of the Americans. Sociability, lack of susceptibility. See Beaumont, C.N.6 (RUBISH OF THE CHAPTERS ON SOCIABILITY, *Rubish,* 2). The reference to Beaumont also appears in YTC, CVa, p. 30.

of secret uneasiness; then they turn away from each other, or, if they greet each other, they take care to speak only with a restrained and distracted air, and to say things of little importance.[c]

No enmity exists between them, however; they have never seen each other, and reciprocally regard each other as very respectable. So why do they take such care to avoid each other?

We must go back to England in order to understand.

When birth alone, independent of wealth, classifies men, each man knows precisely the place he occupies on the social ladder; he does not try to climb, and is not afraid of descending. In a society organized in this way, men of different castes communicate little with each other; but when chance puts them in contact, they readily become engrossed, without hope or fear of intermingling. Their relationships are not based on equality; but they are not constrained.

When aristocracy of money follows aristocracy of birth, it is no longer the same.

The privileges of a few are still very great, but the possibility of acquiring them is open to all; from that it follows that those who possess them are constantly preoccupied by the fear of losing them or of seeing them shared; and those who do not yet have them want at any cost to possess them, or, if they cannot succeed in that, to appear to possess them, which is not impossible. As the social value of men is no longer fixed by blood in a clear and permanent manner and varies infinitely depending on wealth, ranks always exist, but you no longer see clearly and at first glance those who occupy those ranks.

A hidden war is immediately established among all the citizens; some try hard, by a thousand artifices, to join in reality or in appearance those who are above them; others fight constantly to repulse these men usurping their rights, or rather the same man does both things, and, while he is trying to get into the upper sphere, he struggles without respite against the effort that comes from below.

c. In the margin: "<All of this a bit affected, I think, in imitation of La Bruyère. Read it without warning in order to see the effect.>"

Such is the state of England today, and I think that what precedes must be principally attributed to this state.

Since aristocratic pride is still very great among the English, and since the boundaries of aristocracy have become doubtful, each man fears at every moment that his familiarity will be abused. Not able to judge at first glance what the social situation is of those you meet, you prudently avoid entering into contact with them. You are afraid of forming despite yourself a badly matched friendship by rendering small services; you fear good offices, and you elude the indiscreet recognition of someone unknown as carefully as his hatred.

There are many men who explain, by purely physical causes, this singular unsociability and this reserved and taciturn temperament of the English.[d] I am willing to agree that blood in fact has some role; but I believe that the social state has a much greater one. The example of the Americans proves it.

In America, where privileges of birth have never existed, and where wealth gives no particular right to the one who possesses it, people who do not know each other readily get together in the same places, and find neither advantage nor danger in freely sharing their thoughts. If they meet by chance, they neither seek each other out nor avoid each other; so their encounter is natural, straightforward and open; you see that they neither hope nor fear hardly anything from each other, and that they try no harder to

d. Today the influence exercised by race on the conduct of men is spoken about constantly. The philosophers and men of politics of ancient times have .-.-.-.- race *explains* everything in a word. It seems to me that I easily find why we resort so to this argument that our predecessors did not use.

It is incontestable that the race that men belong to exercises some power over their actions, and on the other hand, it is absolutely impossible to specify what the strength and the duration of this power is; so that you can at will infinitely constrict its action or expand it to everything depending on the needs of the discourse; precious advantages in a time when you expect to reason at little cost, just as you want to grow rich without difficulty.

[In the margin: Some men believe that this reserve of the English comes from the blood. The example of the Americans proves the opposite.]

After a digression for which the reader will, I hope, pardon an author who rarely makes them, I return to my subject (RUBISH OF THE CHAPTERS ON SOCIABILITY, *Rubish*, 2). The manuscript says: "Race in fact has some role, but I believe . . ."

show than to hide the place they occupy. If their countenance is often cold and serious, it is never either haughty or stiff, and when they do not speak to each other, it is because they are not in the mood to speak, and not that they believe that they have a reason to remain silent.

In a foreign country, two Americans are immediately friends, by the very fact that they are Americans. There is no prejudice that drives them apart, and the native land in common brings them together. For two Englishmen the same blood is not enough; the same rank must draw them together.

The Americans notice as well as we this unsociable temperament of the English with each other, and they are no less astonished by it than we ourselves are. But the Americans are attached to England by origin, religion, language, and in part mores; they differ from England only by social state. So it is permissible to say that the reserve of the English derives from the constitution of the country much more than from the constitution of the citizens [<the reserve of the English is not English, but aristocratic>].[*] e

[*]. Form that I believe I have already used; be careful.

e. Relationships of men with each other. Lofty and reserved manners./
   Baden, this 14 August 1836./
   To put with the good effects of a democratic social state./ One of the characteristic and most known traits of the English is the care with which they try to isolate themselves from each other and the perpetual fear that clearly preoccupies them of protecting themselves from contact with men who may occupy a position inferior to the one that they occupy themselves. In a foreign country above all this is carried to an extreme of which we have no idea.

   This fault is infinitely less noticeable in countries in which *an aristocracy of birth* dominates and in those in which *there is no aristocracy at all.*

   In the first, since ranks are never doubtful and since privileges are linked to an inalienable and uncontestable advantage, *that of blood,* each man remains in his place and no one fears meeting an intruder who wants to put himself in your place, or descending without noticing to the lower rank of someone unknown by keeping company with him.

   In the second, since birth or wealth give only slight advantages and do not put the one who possesses them at a very separate or very desirable rank, connection with an inferior is not feared.

   While in an aristocracy constituted on money, like that of England, privileges are very great and the conditions for enjoying them are always doubtful; from that comes this continual terror of doing something that may make you fall in rank.

This fault of the English is due so clearly to institutions and not to *blood* that it shocks the Americans even more than us. Cooper in his journey to Switzerland returns constantly to this *unsociability* of the English, and although he pretends to scorn it, he speaks about it too often not to show how much it offends him.

Nothing is more opposed to continual, free, kindly relationships among men than the frame of mind that I have just talked about (RUBISH OF THE CHAPTERS ON SOCIABILITY, *Rubish,* 2). Tocqueville is referring to *Excursions in Switzerland* by James Fenimore Cooper, published in 1836 in Paris by A.W. Calignani and Co., and by Baudry (see, for example, p. 71 and p. 143 of these editions).

CHAPTER 3[a]

Why the Americans Have So Little Susceptibility in Their Country and Show Such Susceptibility in Ours[b]

The Americans have a vindictive temperament like all solemn and serious-minded peoples. They almost never forget an insult; but it is not easy to insult them, and their resentment is as slow to flare up as to go out.

In aristocratic societies, where a small number of individuals directs everything, the external relationships of men with each other are subject to more or less fixed conventions. Each man then believes that he knows, in a precise way, by what sign it is suitable to show his respect or to indicate his goodwill, and etiquette is a science of which everyone is presumed to be aware.

These customs of the first class then serve as a model for all the other classes, and in addition each one of the latter makes a separate code, to

a. When men of diverse education and fortune meet in the same places, the laws of good manners are no longer fixed; you observe those laws badly vis-à-vis other men and you are not hurt when they are not observed in your regard. That is above all true of free democratic societies in which men, busy together with great affairs, easily forget the outward aspect of actions in order to consider only the actions themselves.

That explains the tolerance and simplicity of the Americans toward each other.

But why are these same Americans intolerant and self-conscious in Europe? Because the remnants of rules and fragments of etiquette remain among us. The Americans, not knowing how to find their bearings in a society so different from theirs, are constantly at a loss, touchy, proud (YTC, CVf, p. 38).

b. On the jacket of the manuscript: "Read this chapter to several people and study whether it has the effect of being *mannered* and *affected*."

which all its members are bound to conform [and finally there is a certain particular ceremonial that is used only between men of different classes].

The rules of good manners thus form a complicated set of laws, which is difficult to master completely, yet from which you are not allowed to deviate without risk; so that each day men constantly are involuntarily exposed to giving or receiving cruel wounds.

But, as ranks fade, as men diverse in their education and birth mix and mingle in the same places, it is almost impossible to agree on the rules of good manners. Since the laws are uncertain, to disobey them is not a crime even in the eyes of those who know them; so you are attached to the substance of actions rather than to the form, and you are at the very same time less courteous and less quarrelsome.

There is a host of small considerations that an American does not care about; he judges that he is not owed them or he supposes that you are unaware that he is owed them. So he does not notice that he is slighted, or he pardons the slight; his manners become less courteous, and his mores simpler and more manly.

This reciprocal indulgence shown by the Americans and this manly confidence that they display result also from a more general and more profound cause.

I already pointed it out in the preceding chapter.

In the United States, ranks differ only very little in civil society and do not differ at all in the political world; so an American does not believe himself bound to give particular considerations to any of his fellows, nor does he think about requiring them for himself. As he does not see that his interest is ardently to seek out the company of some of his fellow citizens, he imagines with difficulty that someone is rejecting his; not despising anyone because of condition, he does not imagine that anyone despises him because of the same reason, and until he has clearly noticed the insult, he does not believe that someone wants to offend him.

The social state [v: equality] naturally disposes the Americans not to become easily offended in small things. And, on the other hand, the democratic liberty that they enjoy finally makes this indulgence pass into the national mores.

Political institutions in the United States constantly put citizens of all classes in contact and force them to follow great enterprises together. Men thus occupied hardly have the time to think about the details of etiquette, and moreover they have too much interest in living together harmoniously to stop over those details. So they become easily accustomed to considering, in the men they meet, sentiments and ideas rather than manners, and they do not allow themselves to be excited over trifles.

I noticed many times that, in the United States, it is not an easy thing to make a man understand that his presence is bothersome. To reach that point, indirect paths are not always sufficient.

I contradict an American at every point, in order to make him sense that his speeches fatigue me; and at every instant I see him make new efforts to persuade me; I keep a stubborn silence, and he imagines that I am reflecting profoundly on the truths that he is presenting; and when finally I suddenly escape from his pursuit, he assumes that a pressing matter calls me elsewhere. This man will not comprehend that he exasperates me unless I tell him so, and I will be able to save myself from him only by becoming his mortal enemy.

What is surprising at first is that this same man transported to Europe suddenly becomes punctilious and difficult to deal with [<he attaches himself stubbornly to the slightest details of etiquette and often he even creates imaginary ones that apply only to him>], to the point that often I have as much difficulty in not offending him as I found in displeasing him. These two so different effects are produced by the same cause.

Democratic institutions in general give men a vast idea of their country and of themselves.

The American leaves his country with his heart puffed up with pride. He arrives in Europe and notices first that we are not as preoccupied as he imagined with the United States and with the great people that inhabits them. This begins to upset him.[c]

He has heard it said that conditions are not equal in our hemisphere. He notices, in fact, that among the nations of Europe, the trace of ranks

c. "Because with a great deal of national pride, they are still not sure about the rank that they hold among nations, and because claiming the first rank, they *are not* sure that it is granted to them" (*Rubish*, 2).

is not entirely erased; that wealth and birth retain uncertain privileges that are as difficult for him to ignore as to define. This spectacle surprises him and makes him uneasy, because it is entirely new to him; nothing that he has seen in his country helps him to understand it. So he is deeply unaware of what place it is suitable to occupy in this half-destroyed hierarchy, among those classes that are distinct enough to hate and despise each other, and close enough for him to be always ready to confuse them. He is afraid of putting himself too high, and above all of being ranked too low; this double danger constantly troubles his mind and continually hinders his actions, like his conversation.

Tradition taught him that in Europe things ceremonial varied infinitely depending on conditions; this memory of another time really disturbs him, and he fears all the more not gaining the considerations that are due to him since he does not know precisely what they consist of. So he is always walking like a man surrounded by traps; society for him is not a relaxation, but a serious work. He weighs your slightest moves, questions your looks and carefully analyzes all your words, for fear that they contain some hidden allusions that injure him. I do not know if there has ever been a country gentleman more punctilious than he in the matter of good manners; he works hard to obey the least laws of etiquette himself, and he does not put up with anyone neglecting any of those laws in his regard; he is at the very same time full of scruples and demands; he would like to do enough, but is afraid of doing too much, and as he does not know very well the limits of either, he holds himself in an uneasy and haughty reserve.

This is still not all, and here is another twist of the human heart.

An American speaks every day about the admirable equality that reigns in the United States; he boasts out loud about it concerning his country; but he is secretly distressed about it concerning himself, and he aspires to show that, as for him, he is an exception to the general order that he advocates.

You hardly meet an American[d] who does not want to be connected a bit

---

d. You find, with the manuscript of the chapter, a jacket on which you read: "RUBISH THAT I LEAVE WITH THE CHAPTER IN ORDER TO EXAMINE IT ONE LAST TIME." Inside Tocqueville specifies: ". . . an American {of New England} who . . ."

by his birth to the first settlers of the colonies, and, as for branches of the great families of England, America seemed to me totally covered by them.

When an opulent American comes to Europe, his first concern is to surround himself with all the riches of luxury; and he is so afraid that someone will take him for a simple citizen of a democracy that he twists and turns in a hundred ways in order to present before you every day a new image of his wealth. He usually finds lodging in the most conspicuous area of the city; he has numerous servants who surround him constantly. [Still he will notice that he is badly served and frequently gets worked up against these people who become familiar with their masters.]

I heard an American complain that, in the principal *salons* of Paris, you met only mixed society. The taste reigning there did not seem pure enough to him, and he adroitly let it be understood that in his opinion, manners there lacked distinction. He was not used to seeing wit hide in this way under common forms.

Such contrasts should not be surprising. [The same cause gives birth to them.]

If the trace of old aristocratic distinctions were not so completely erased in the United States, the Americans would appear less simple and less tolerant in their country, less demanding and less ill-at-ease in ours.

CHAPTER 4[a]

Consequences of the Three Preceding Chapters

When men feel a natural pity for each other's misfortunes, when easy and frequent relationships draw them closer each day without any susceptibility dividing them, it is easy to understand that they will, as needed, mutually lend each other their aid. When an American asks for the help of his fellows, it is very rare for the latter to refuse it to him, and I have often observed that they grant it to him spontaneously with great zeal.

If some unforeseen accident takes place on the public road, people rush from all directions to the one who is the victim; if some great unexpected misfortune strikes a family, the purses of a thousand strangers open without difficulty; modest, but very numerous gifts come to the aid of the family's misery.

It frequently happens, among the most civilized nations of the globe, that someone unfortunate finds himself as isolated in the middle of the crowd as the savage in the woods; that is hardly ever seen in the United States. The Americans, who are always cold in their manners and often crude, hardly ever appear insensitive, and, if they do not hasten to offer their services, they do not refuse to render them.

All of this is not contrary to what I said before regarding individualism. I even see that these things, far from being in conflict, are in agreement.

---

a. Men of democracies naturally show pity for each other; having frequent and easy relationships together, not easily becoming irritated with each other, it is natural that they like to help each other in their needs. This is what happens in the United States. In democracies great services are rarely accorded, but good offices are rendered constantly. It is that a man appears devoted to service, but all are willing to help (YTC, CVf, pp. 38–39). There is no *rubish* for this chapter.

Equality of conditions, at the same time that it makes men feel their independence, shows them their weakness; they are free, but exposed to a thousand accidents, and experience does not take long to teach them that, although they do not habitually need the help of others, some moment almost always occurs when they cannot do without that help.

We see every day in Europe that men of the same profession readily help each other; they are all exposed to the same evils; that is enough for them to try mutually to protect themselves from those evils, however hard or egotistical they are elsewhere. So whenever one of them is in danger, and when, by a small temporary sacrifice or a sudden impulse, the others can shield him, they do not fail to attempt it. It is not that they are profoundly interested in his fate; for if, by chance, the efforts that they make to help him are useless, they immediately forget him and return to themselves; but a sort of tacit and almost involuntary agreement has been made between them, according to which each one owes to the others a momentary support that, in his turn, he will be able to ask for himself.

Extend to a people what I say about only a class, and you will understand my thought.

There exists, in fact, among all the citizens of a democracy, a convention analogous to the one that I am talking about; everyone feels subject to the same weakness and to the same dangers, and their interest, as well as their sympathy, makes it a law for them to lend each other mutual assistance as needed.

The more similar conditions become, the more men exhibit this reciprocal disposition for mutual obligation.

In democracies, where great services are scarcely accorded, good offices are rendered constantly. It is rare that a man appears devoted to service, but all are willing to help.

CHAPTER 5[a]

How Democracy Modifies the Relationships of Servant and Master

An American,[b] who had traveled for a long time in Europe, said to me one day:

---

a. 1. Character of domestic service in aristocratic centuries.

1. Servants form a separate class that has its gradations, its prejudices, its public opinion.

2. The perpetuity and immobility of classes make it that there are families of servants who remain for centuries next to families of masters. From that arises a confusion of sentiments, opinions, and interests between them.

3. In that time it is easy to obtain a respectful, prompt and easy obedience, because each master presses on the will of his servants with all the weight of the aristocracy.

2. Character of democratic domestic service. No devoted loyalty, but an exact obedience arising not from a general superiority of the master over the servant, but from a contract freely accepted.

3. Transitional domestic service, where everything is confused. The master wants to find in his servants the devoted loyalty that arose from the aristocratic social state, and the servants do not even want to grant the obedience that they promised (YTC, CVf, pp. 39–40). In the *rubish* you find traces of a first chapter bearing the title: THE MASTER AND THE TENANT FARMER IN DEMOCRACIES.

b. Conversation with Mr. Robinson, an American engineer of great talents. 22 March 1837./

[In the margin: Perhaps introduce this conversation in the text.]

Mr. Robinson told me that the English treated their servants with a contempt, a haughtiness and with absolute manners that singularly surprised an American.

On the other hand, he remarked that the French often used with their domestics a familiarity and a courtesy that did not seem less extraordinary to him. He had heard a lady say to a domestic who informed her about the execution of an order: I am very much obliged, so and so. This form seems strange to him. I see some French, he added, call a porter, Monsieur. It is something I could never do.

The English treat their servants with a haughtiness and with absolute manners that surprise us; but, on the other hand, the French sometimes use a familiarity with theirs, or reveal in their regard a courtesy that we cannot imagine. You would say that they are afraid of giving orders. The position of superior and inferior is badly kept.

This remark is correct, and I have made it myself many times.[c]

I have always considered England as the country in the world where, today, the bond of domestic service is the tightest and France the country on earth where it is most loose. Nowhere has the master appeared to me higher or lower than in these two countries.

The Americans are placed between these extremes.

That is the superficial and apparent fact. We must go much further in order to discover its causes.

We have not yet seen societies in which conditions were so equal that neither rich nor poor were found, and consequently, neither masters nor servants.

Democracy does not prevent these two classes of men from existing; but it changes their spirit and modifies their relationships.

[It is easy to see that all classes that compose a society are so naturally bound together that all must move at the same time or remain immobile. It is enough to hold one of them in place for all the others to stop by themselves.

So from the moment when I find a caste of perpetual masters composed of the same families, I understand without difficulty that there exists a caste

---

This same Mr. Robinson, said finally: in the United States domestic servants believe themselves obliged to do only what is in the contract. They are very independent and little .-.-.-.- relationships with the master, the position of superior and inferior is always kept.

This conversation gets very much, it seems to me, into the meaning of my chapter (*Rubish,* 2). The person speaking to Tocqueville is unidentified.

c. In the margin: "<If this remark is correct, the American of the preceding chapter was therefore not wrong. Clearly to delete either this or the sentence from the other chapter. That jumps out.>"

of servants formed in the same way, and I foresee that this perpetuity is going to produce similar effects from both sides.]d

Among aristocratic peoples, servants form a particular class that does not vary any more than that of the masters. A fixed order does not take long to arise; in the first as in the second, you soon see a hierarchy, numerous classifications, marked ranks, and the generations follow each other without the positions changing. Servants and masters are two societies superimposed on each other, always distinct, but governed by analogous principles.e

This aristocratic constitution influences the ideas and mores of the servants scarcely less than those of the masters, and although the effects may be different, it is easy to recognize the same cause.

Both form small nations amid the large one; and in the end, in their midst, certain permanent notions about right and wrong are born. The different actions of human life are seen in a particular light that does not change. In the society of servants as in that of the masters, men exercise a great influence on each other. They acknowledge fixed rules, and lacking a law, they encounter a public opinion that directs them; well-regulated habits and an order reign there.

These men, whose destiny is to obey, undoubtedly do not understand glory, virtue, integrity, honor, in the same way as the masters. But they have developed a glory, virtues, and an integrity of servants, and they imagine, if I can express myself in this way, a sort of servants' honor.[1]

Because a class is low, you must not believe that all those who are part

---

d. In the margin: "<Good sentence, but to delete. This piece must be pruned rather than added to.>"

e. "In a society all classes go together. They all move at the same time or all remain immobile. When a single class becomes immobile all the others stop by themselves.

I stop the wheel of a clock and everything stops" (*Rubish*, 2).

1. *If you come to examine closely and in detail the principal opinions that direct these men, the analogy appears still more striking, and you are astonished to find among them, as well as among the most haughty members of a feudal hierarchy, pride of birth, respect for one's ancestors and descendents, scorn for the inferior, fear of contact, taste for etiquette, for the traditions of antiquity.*

of it have a base heart. That would be a great error. However inferior the class may be, the man who is first in it and who has no idea of leaving that class, finds himself in an aristocratic position that suggests to him elevated sentiments, a noble pride and a respect for himself, which makes him fit for great virtues and uncommon actions.

Among aristocratic peoples, it was not rare to find, in the service of the great, noble and vigorous souls who bore servitude without feeling it, and who submitted to the will of their master without fearing his anger.

But it was hardly ever like this in the lower ranks of the domestic class. [<The first were placed higher in the scale of beings than the modern servant, the second fell below.>] You conceive that the one who holds the lowest place of a hierarchy of valets is very low.

The French had created a word expressly for this lowest of the servants of the aristocracy. They called him a lackey.

[<≠The lackey was this man abandoned by fate who was born, lived, died in a hereditary shame, despised and laughed at by all.≠>]

The word lackey served as an extreme word, when any other was missing, to represent human baseness; under the old monarchy, when you wanted at some moment to portray a vile and degraded being, you said of him that he had the *soul of a lackey.* That alone sufficed. The meaning was complete and understood.[f]

Permanent inequality of conditions not only gives servants certain particular virtues and certain particular vices; it also places them in a particular position vis-à-vis the masters.

Among aristocratic peoples, the poor man is trained, from birth, with the idea of being commanded. In whatever direction he turns his eyes, he immediately sees the image of hierarchy and the sight of obedience.

[If this man, prepared in this way, consecrates himself to the service of one of his fellows, he will not fail to bring to this particular state the general

---

f. In the margin: "≠When Mirabeau, this democrat still so full of the striking vices and virtues of the aristocracy, wanted to portray in his energetic style a cowardly and nasty being [interrupted text (ed.)].≠"

notions that the view of society suggests to him. <≠The image of the large society will be reproduced in the small one.≠>]g

So in countries where permanent inequality of conditions reigns, the master easily obtains from his servants a prompt, complete, respectful and easy obedience, because the latter revere in him, not only the master, but the class of masters. He presses on their will with all the weight of the aristocracy.

He commands their actions; to a certain degree he even directs their thoughts. The master, in aristocracies, often exercises, even without his knowing it, a prodigious sway over the opinions, habits, and mores of those who obey him; and his influence extends very much further than even his authority.h

In aristocratic societies,j not only are there hereditary families of valets, as well as hereditary families of masters; but also the same families of valets remain, over several generations, at the side of the same families of masters (they are like parallel lines that never meet or separate); this prodigiously modifies the mutual relationships of these two orders of persons.

Thus, although, under aristocracy, the master and the servant have between them no mutual resemblance; although fortune, education, opinions, rights place them, on the contrary, at an immense distance on the scale of beings, time nevertheless ends up binding them together. A long community of memories ties them together, and, however different they may be, they assimilate; while, in democracies, where they are naturally almost the same, they always remain strangers to each other. [A few slight differences in conditions separate men, great permanent differences bind them together.]

So among aristocratic peoples, the master comes to envisage his servants

g. In the margin: "<*Perhaps delete this.*>"
h. Variant: "<Not only does he direct them without difficulty in everything that relates to him, but his influence extends to the entire ensemble of their actions. His example or his lessons naturally lead their minds toward certain beliefs and open their hearts, as he pleases, to certain tastes. He modifies in a thousand ways their ideas and their mores, and even when he ceases to be their master, he remains in a way their tutor.>"
j. The manuscript says: "In aristocratic centuries . . ."

like an inferior and secondary part of himself, and he often interests himself in their fate, by a final effort of egoism.

On their side, the servants are not far from considering themselves from the same point of view, and they sometimes identify with the person of the master, so that they finally become an accessory, in their own eyes, as in his.

In aristocracies, the servant occupies a subordinate position that he cannot leave; near him is found another man, who holds a superior rank that he cannot lose. On the one hand, obscurity, poverty, obedience forever; on the other, glory, wealth, command forever. These conditions are always different and always close, and the bond that unites them is as durable as are the conditions.

In this extreme, the servant ends by becoming disinterested in himself; he turns away from himself; he deserts himself in a way, or rather he transfers himself entirely to his master; there he creates an imaginary personality. He cloaks himself with satisfaction with the riches of those who command him; he takes pride in their glory, raises himself with their nobility, and feeds constantly on a borrowed grandeur, on which he sometimes puts more value than those who possess it fully and truly.

There is something at once touching and ridiculous in such a strange confusion of two existences.

These passions of masters carried into the souls of valets take the natural dimensions of the place that they occupy; they shrink and become lower. What was pride with the first becomes childish vanity and miserable pretension with the others. The servants of a great nobleman usually show themselves very particular about what is owed to him, and they are more attached to his least privileges than he is.

You still sometimes meet among us one of those old servants of the aristocracy; he outlives his race and will soon disappear with it.[k]

k. In the margin: "≠Caleb.≠"
In the *rubish:* "Caleb. The portrait of this man could only be drawn in an aristocratic country and can only be understood in a country that was so. The Americans will never know what Caleb means" (*Rubish,* 2).

In the United States I saw no one who resembled him. Not only do the Americans not know this man, but you have great difficulty making them understand that he exists. They find it hardly less difficult to conceive it than we ourselves have to imagine what a slave was among the Romans, or a serf in the Middle Ages. All of these men are in fact, although to different degrees, the products of the same cause. Together they withdraw far from our sight and flee daily into the obscurity of the past with the social state that gave them birth.

Equality of conditions makes new beings of the servant and of the master, and establishes new relationships between them.

When conditions are nearly equal, men constantly change place; there is still a class of valets and a class of masters; but it is not always the same individuals, or above all the same families that compose it; and there is not more permanence in command than in obedience.

Servants, not forming a separate people, do not have customs, prejudices or mores that are their own; you do not notice among them a certain turn of spirit or a particular way of feeling; they know neither the vices nor the virtues of a condition, but they share the enlightenment, ideas, sentiments, virtues and vices of their contemporaries; and they are decent or knavish just as the masters are.

Conditions are no less equal among the servants than among the masters.

As you do not find marked ranks or permanent hierarchy in the class of servants, you must not expect to find the baseness and the grandeur that are displayed in the aristocracies of valets as well as in all the others.

I never saw in the United States anything that could have reminded me of the idea of the elite servant, an idea of which we in Europe have kept

---

In another place: "I have sometimes met Caleb amid the ruins of our aristocratic society" (*Rubish,* 2). This concerns Balderstone Caleb, the faithful and devoted servant of the landowner of Ravenswood in *The Bride of Lammermoor* of Walter Scott.

When he reread this chapter in September 1839, Tocqueville found it too theoretical. He asked Ampère to provide him with some examples, something the latter seems not to have done (*Correspondance avec Ampère, OC,* XI, pp. 129–31).

the memory; but neither did I find in the United States the idea of the lackey. The trace of the one as well as the other is lost there.

In democracies, servants are not only equal among themselves; you can say that they are, in a way, equal to their masters.

This needs to be explained in order to make it well understood.

At every instant, the servant can become the master and aspires to become so; the servant is not therefore a man different from his master.

So why does the first have the right to command and what forces the second to obey? The temporary and free agreement of their two wills. They are not naturally inferior to each other; they become so temporarily only as a result of the contract. Within the limits of this contract, one is the servant and the other the master; outside, they are two citizens, two men.

What I beg the reader to understand well is that this is not only the notion that the servants themselves form of their state. The masters consider domestic service in the same light, and the precise limits of command and obedience are as well fixed in the mind of the one as in that of the other.[m]

m. In the drafts you find several pages on the relations of master and servant. They are contained in a jacket with the title: CHAPTER 4, SOME IDEAS RELATIVE TO THE INFLUENCE EXERCISED ON THE MORES OF THE AMERICANS BY THEIR PHILO-SOPHICAL METHOD (YTC, CVk, 2, p. 29).

On one of these pages in this jacket you can read:

[In the margin: It is clear that this entire piece beginning here and ending at the bottom of sheet 5 can only with difficulty be included in the consequences of just the philosophical method of the Americans. To reexamine./

This fits into another order of ideas. To equality of conditions itself which makes the servant higher and the master lower than in Europe, and not to the philosophical consequences that result from this equality. To put in the place where I will see general causes.

To keep but to transfer I think to another place this entire piece up to *in aristocratic countries . . .*]

If, after examining the relationships of the son with the father, I consider those of the servant with the master, I no longer discover any analogy between the Americans and the English.

England is assuredly the country in the world where the two men are placed the farthest from each other, and America the place on earth where they are the closest and yet the most independent of each other.

When most citizens have for a long time attained a more or less similar condition, and when equality is an old and accepted fact, public understanding, never influenced by the exceptions, assigns in a general way to the value of man certain limits above or below which it is difficult for any man to remain for long.

In vain do wealth and poverty, command and obedience put accidentally great distances between two men; public opinion, which is founded on the usual order of things, brings them closer to the common level and creates between them a sort of imaginary equality, despite the real inequality of their conditions.

This omnipotent opinion ends up penetrating the souls even of those whose interest could fortify them against it; it modifies their judgment at the same time that it subjugates their will.

At the bottom of their souls, the master and the servant no longer see a profound dissimilarity between them, and they neither hope nor fear ever to find one. So they are without disdain and without anger, and they find themselves neither humble nor proud when they look at each other.

The master judges that the contract is the only source of his power, and the servant finds in it the only cause of his obedience. They do not argue with each other over the reciprocal position that they occupy; instead each one easily sees his own position and sticks to it. [You do not see arising between these two men ardent or deep affections, but as they have <constantly a limited need for each other, they look upon each other with a sort of tranquil benevolence.>]

In our [{democratic}] armies, the soldier is more or less taken from the same classes as the officers and can reach the same posts; outside of military ranks, the soldier considers himself as perfectly equal to his leaders, and he is in fact; but when in military service, he has no difficulty obeying, and

---

That is due to several causes that I want to seek although interest in my subject does not absolutely oblige me to do so.

When among a people you find a very small number of great fortunes, a small number of destitute situations, and a multitude of comfortable fortunes, the result would seem to have to be that the rich feel stronger there and the poor weaker than anywhere else, but it is not so. When most citizens have attained . . . (YTC, CVk, 2, pp. 30–31). See note a of p. 696.

his obedience, although voluntary and well-defined, is no less prompt, clear and easy.

This gives an idea of what happens in democratic societies between the servant and the master.

It would be insane to believe that there could ever arise between these two men any of those ardent and deep affections that are sometimes lit within aristocratic domestic service, or that striking examples of devotion should be seen to appear.

In aristocracies, the servant and the master see each other only from time to time, and they often speak only by intermediary. But they usually depend closely on one another.

Among democratic peoples, the servant and the master are very close; their bodies are constantly in contact, their souls do not mingle; they have shared occupations, they almost never have shared interests.

Among these peoples, the servant always considers himself as a passer-by in the house of his masters. He has not known their ancestors and will not see their descendants; he has nothing lasting to expect from them. Why would he confuse his existence with theirs, and from where would this singular self-abandonment come? The reciprocal position has changed; the relationship must do so.

I would like to be able to support all that precedes with the example of the Americans; but I cannot do so without carefully distinguishing peoples and places.

In the south of the Union, slavery exists. So all that I have just said cannot apply.

In the North, most servants are emancipated slaves or the sons of those emancipated. These men occupy a disputed position in public esteem; the law brings them closer to the level of their master, mores stubbornly push them away. They themselves do not clearly discern their place, and they appear almost always insolent or cringing.

But, in these same provinces of the North, particularly in New England, you find a fairly large number of whites who consent, in return for a salary, to subject themselves temporarily to the will of their fellows. I have heard it said that the servants usually fulfill the duties of their condition with exactitude and intelligence, and that, without believing themselves naturally inferior to the one who is giving them orders, they easily submit to obeying him.

It seemed to me that those servants brought to their service some of the manly habits given birth by independence and equality. Once having chosen a hard condition, they did not look for indirect ways to escape from it, and they respect themselves enough not to refuse to their masters an obedience that they have freely promised.

On their side, the masters demand of their servants only faithful and strict execution of the contract; they do not ask them for respect; they do not claim their love or their devotion; it is enough to find them punctual and honest.

So it would not be true to say that, under democracy, the relationships of servant and master are disorderly; they are organized in another manner; the rule is different, but there is a rule.

I do not have to search here if this new state that I have just described is inferior to that which preceded, or if it is only different. It is enough for me that it is well-ordered and fixed; for what is most important to find among men is not a certain order, but order.

But what will I say about those sad and turbulent periods during which equality is being founded amid the tumult of a revolution, while democracy, after being established in the social state, is still struggling with difficulty against prejudices and mores?

The law and, in part, opinion already proclaim that no natural and permanent inferiority exists between servant and master. But this new faith has not yet deeply penetrated the mind of the latter, or rather his heart rejects it. In the secrecy of his soul, the master still considers that he is a particular and superior species; but he does not dare to say so, and he allows himself to be drawn trembling toward the standard level. His command becomes at the very same time timid and hard; already he no longer feels for his servants the protective and benevolent sentiments that always arise from a long-standing, uncontested power, and he is astonished that having himself changed, his servant changes. He wants his servant, who is only so to speak passing through domestic service, to contract regular and permanent habits, to show himself satisfied with and proud of a servile position, from which he must sooner or later emerge; he wants his servant to devote himself to a man who can neither protect nor ruin him, and to become attached finally, by an eternal bond, to beings who resemble him and who do not last any longer than he does.

Among aristocratic peoples, it often happens that the condition of domestic service does not debase the souls of those who submit to it, because they do not know and do not imagine any others, and because the prodigious inequality that is exhibited between them and the master seems to them the necessary and inevitable result of some hidden law of Providence.

Under democracy, the condition of domestic service has nothing degrading about it, because it is freely chosen, temporarily adopted, because public opinion does not condemn it, and because it creates no permanent inequality between the servant and the master.[n]

But, during the passage from one social condition to another, a moment almost always comes when the minds of men vacillate between the aristocratic notion of subjection and the democratic notion of obedience.

Obedience then loses its morality in the eyes of the one who obeys; he no longer considers it as an obligation in a way divine, and he does not yet see it in its purely human aspect; in his eyes it is neither holy or just, and he submits to it as to a degrading and useful fact.

At that moment, the confused and incomplete image of equality presents itself to the mind of the servants; they do not at first discern if it is in the very condition of domestic service or outside of it that this equality to which they have a right is found, and at the bottom of their hearts they revolt against an inferiority to which they have subjected themselves and from which they profit. They consent to serve, and they are ashamed to obey [<and while the masters still refuse to acknowledge equality outside of domestic service, the second want to find it even within these very limits>]; they love the advantages of servitude, but not the master, or, to say it better, they are not sure if they should not be the masters, and they are disposed to consider the one who commands them as the unjust usurper of their right.

n. In the margin, with a bracket that includes this paragraph and one part of the preceding one: "<This is, I believe, the return of an idea already expressed in the chapter. See.>"

That is when you see in the house of each citizen something analogous to the sad spectacle that political society presents. A hidden and internal war goes on constantly between always suspicious and rival powers. The master shows himself ill-willed and soft, the servant ill-willed and intractable; the one wants to shirk constantly, by dishonest limitations, the obligation to protect and to pay, the other wants to shirk the obligation to obey. Between them the reins of domestic administration hang loose, and each one tries hard to seize them. The lines that divide authority from tyranny, liberty from license, right from fact, seem in their eyes muddled and confused, and no one knows precisely what he is, or what he can do, or what he should do.

Such a state is not democratic, but revolutionary.º

o. At the end of the manuscript:

Opinion of Louis on the chapter./
    Praise.
    The chapter contains a very large number of new ideas. The style is good.
    Criticism.
    The first pages do not grab the mind of the reader. In general all of the *aristocratic domestic service* is of less intense interest than the rest. That is due not to the fact that the ideas are known, but to the theoretical way of presenting them.
    According to Louis, I have made the *moral* condition of the servant in aristocracy worse than it was. But is he right?
    The same reproach applies, although to a lesser degree, to the whole piece.
    It is done to please philosophical minds. It does not get down enough to the level of ordinary minds. The subject is such however to interest all minds. It is a chapter that all readers will like to read and will believe themselves able to understand. So it must be put within their reach or in relief, and it can be done so only by getting a bit into facts, examples, details and by keeping myself less in abstractions than I do.
    In summary this chapter is a very good piece that must be kept with the idea that it needs to be revised./
    The general order of the piece must be kept./
    Observation of Édouard.
    He finds the piece good, but he thinks that new efforts must be made to put in relief my ideas relative to *democratic domestic service,* to fix more firmly by stylistic artifices the mind of the reader on this point, to bring out better than I do what is gained and what is lost in this new state.
    Édouard would like me to use more the example of the Americans to demonstrate, by example, what should happen in a society where the master and the domestic servant find themselves together in the same electoral college.
    The difficulty is that I know only very imperfectly what they want me to say.

CHAPTER 6ᵃ

How Democratic Institutions and Mores Tend to Raise the Cost and Shorten the Length of Leases

What I said about servants and masters applies to a certain point to landowners and tenant farmers. The subject merits, however, to be considered separately.

In America, there are, so to speak, no tenant farmers; every man owns the field that he cultivates.

It must be recognized that democratic laws tend powerfully to increase the number of landowners and to decrease that of tenant farmers. Nonetheless, what is happening in the United States must be attributed much less to the new institutions of the country than to the country itself. In America land costs little, and everyone becomes a landowner easily. The land yields little, and its products can be shared by a landowner and a tenant farmer only with difficulty.

a. In aristocracies farm rents are paid not only in money, but in respect, in affection, in services. Under democracy they are paid only in money.

Since a permanent bond no longer exists between families and the land, the landowner and the tenant farmer are strangers who meet by chance to discuss a matter.

Since fortunes are becoming divided, the landowner always has a desire to acquire and fears losing. He rigorously stipulates everything to which he has a right.

The landowner and the tenant farmer have analogous habits of mind and an analogous social situation. Between two equal citizens in straitened circumstances, the object of a rental contract cannot be anything other than money.

When you have one hundred tenant farmers, you readily make pecuniary sacrifices to gain their goodwill. You do not care about the goodwill of a single tenant farmer.

When democracy has made the idea of instability penetrate all minds, you have an instinctive horror for a contract, even an advantageous one, that has to last a long time (YTC, CVf, pp. 40–41).

So America is unique in this as in other things; and it would be an error to take it as an example.

I think that in democratic countries as well as in aristocracies, landowners and tenant farmers will be found; but landowners and tenant farmers will not be bound together in the same way.

In aristocracies, farm rents are paid not only in money, but also in respect, in affection and in services. In democratic countries, they are paid only in money.[b] When patrimonies divide and change hands, and when the permanent relationship that existed between families and the land disappears, it is no longer anything except chance that puts the landowner and the

---

b. There are no drafts of this chapter in the *Rubish*. In the manuscript, on the other hand, you find a jacket with various notes and fragments. The first page specifies:

"Pieces that began the chapter and that I believe must be deleted; they had the purpose of explaining what happened under aristocracy. I was afraid that this perpetual return to two social states was monotonous.

"To review one last time." This jacket contains another version of the chapter, identical enough, except for the beginning:

In aristocracies in which great estates exist and in which custom and law fix the ownership of these estates in the same families, the landowner, by renting his fields, does not have as his only goal, or even sometimes as his principal goal, to enrich himself. Several other concerns share his soul. The tenant farmers with whom he deals are not strangers in his eyes. Their ancestors lived with his; his children will grow up amid theirs. They are tied to him and he to them by a long chain of memories and hopes. So the landowner wants to have his rights not only to the rent that they promised him, but also to their respect and their love; and he thinks that he owes it to himself not to impose obligations which are too hard on these men among whom he lives every day and whose well-being or miseries are necessarily before his eyes; and he is able to do so, for he enjoys an immense superfluity.

The richest and most powerful landowner of an aristocratic country cannot do without zealous friends and faithful servants, tenants ready to serve him. All those men are like instruments by the aid of which he seizes the surrounding population and handles it as he wills. It is through them that he succeeds in enjoying the greatest non-material advantages that wealth assures. Thus their support must be bought.

So in an aristocratic country the price of lands [v: tenant farms] is not paid only in money, but in respect, in affection, in services.

It ceases to be so as patrimonies are divided, as fortunes become equal, as the bond that united the upper and the lower classes comes to loosen <and as the relationship that existed between political power and possession of the land comes to disappear.>

When patrimonies . . .

tenant farmer in contact. They join together for a moment to debate the conditions of the contract, and afterward lose sight of each other. They are two strangers brought together by interest who rigorously discuss a matter that concerns only money.

As property is divided and wealth is dispersed here and there over the whole surface of the country, the State fills with men whose old wealth is in decline and with the newly rich whose needs increase faster than their resources. For all of them, the least profit is of consequence, and no one among them feels disposed to allow any one of his advantages to escape, or to lose any portion whatsoever of his income.

Since ranks are mingling and the very greatest as well as the very smallest fortunes are becoming rarer, there is less distance every day between the social condition of the landowner and that of the tenant farmer; the one does not naturally have an undisputed superiority over the other. Now, between two equal men in straitened circumstances, what can the subject of a rental contract be, if not money?[c]

A man whose property is an entire district and who owns one hundred small farms understands that it is a matter of winning the hearts of several thousand men at the same time; this seems to him to merit his efforts. To attain such a great objective, he easily makes sacrifices.

The one who owns a hundred acres is not burdened by such concerns; it is hardly important for him to win the particular goodwill of his tenant.

An aristocracy does not die like a man, in a day. Its principle is destroyed slowly deep within souls, before being attacked in the laws. So a long time before war breaks out against an aristocracy, you see the bond that until then united the upper classes to the lower loosen little by little. Indifference and scorn betray one side; jealousy and hate, the other. Relations between the poor and the rich become rarer and less mild; the cost of leases rises. It is not yet the result of the democratic revolution, but it is the sure sign of it. For an aristocracy that has allowed the heart of the people to escape

---

c. "In the work of Candolle on the subjects of gold and silver, there are on the long leases of feudal times curious remarks that prove that leases *rise* and *become shorter* as equality increases. As conditions become equal, the costs of leases rise" (YTC, CVa, p. 31).

definitively from its hands, is like a tree with dead roots; the higher it is, the more easily is it toppled by the winds.

For fifty years, the cost of farm rents has grown prodigiously, not only in France, but in most of Europe. The singular progress made by agriculture and industry during the same period is not enough, in my mind, to explain this phenomenon. You must resort to some other more powerful and more hidden cause. I think that this cause must be sought in the democratic institutions that several European peoples have adopted and in the democratic passions that more or less agitate all the others.

I have often heard great English landowners congratulate themselves that, in our times, they draw much more money from their estates than their fathers did.[d]

Perhaps they are right to be pleased; but certainly they do not know what they are pleased about. They think they are making a clear profit, and they are only making an exchange. It is their influence that they are giving up for cash; and what they gain in money, they are soon going to lose in power.

There is still another sign by which you can easily recognize that a great democratic revolution is being accomplished or is being prepared.

In the Middle Ages, nearly all the land was rented in perpetuity, or at least at very long term. When you study the domestic economy of that time, you see that leases of ninety-nine years were more frequent than those of twelve years are today.

Everyone believed then in the immortality of families; conditions seemed fixed forever, and the whole society appeared so immobile that no one imagined that anything ever had to move within it.

---

d. Inside the jacket of the manuscript that contains the drafts:

In aristocracies, the clauses of the lease are generally debated between a poor man to whom necessity has taught the importance of the smallest details, and a rich man who is accustomed to seeing everything broadly and to scorning small gains. The one treats the affair with all the fierceness given by need, and the other with the nonchalance suggested in such matters by a great superfluity. It is easy to foresee that the interest of the rich man must succumb in this unequal struggle.

In democracy, on the contrary, the landowner and the tenant bring the same needs and same desires.

In centuries of equality, the human mind takes a different turn. It easily believes that nothing is unchanging. The idea of instability possesses it.

In this frame of mind, the landowner and the tenant himself feel a sort of instinctive horror for long-term obligations; they fear being limited one day by an agreement that they profit from today. They vaguely expect some sudden and unforeseen change in their condition. They are afraid of themselves; they fear that, when their taste changes, they will be distressed by not being able to leave what was the object of their desires, and they are right to fear it; for in democratic centuries, what is most changeable, amid the movement of things, is the heart of man.

CHAPTER 7[a]

Influence of Democracy on Salaries

Most of the remarks that I made previously, when talking about servants and masters, can be applied to masters and workers.[b]

a. Democracy has a general and permanent tendency to bring the worker and master closer and to equalize their profits more and more.

[In the margin: Chapter that it is not certain that I will include.]

This is the general rule, but in industry, such as it is constituted today in some of its parts, the opposite is seen.

That is an exceptional fact, but very formidable and that much more formidable as it is exceptional (YTC, CVf, p. 41).

On the jacket of the manuscript:

The question of knowing whether I should let this chapter remain is still doubtful and needs to be asked of B[eaumont (ed.)]. and L[ouis (ed.)]./

The subject can seem known and yet redundant because of chapter 34 quarto where the matter is already treated./

This chapter has the disadvantage of posing the greatest question of our time without even trying to resolve it. You are disappointed after reading it.

Chapter 34 quarto corresponds to chapter 20 of the second part of volume II, on the industrial aristocracy.

b. What I say about the servant always more or less applies to the worker. But democracy tends, more and more, to isolate the latter from the master, and while separating him from the master, to raise him to the same level.

Tendency of democracy to raise salaries, to make the worker share in the profits.

How in the current state of commercial science and habits there is an opposite tendency that accumulates capital in the hands of a few great manufacturers and reduces the workers to the greatest dependency and to the most extreme poverty.

That this tendency is already noticeable in the United States, although in a much less pronounced way than in France, and above all in England. To find out why? That it is there .-.-.-.-.-.- democracy that fills the world. It is the only door open in the future to the re-formation of an aristocratic society.

As [<{conditions become equal}; as ranks blend and>] the rules of social hierarchy are less observed, while the great descend, the small rise and
poverty as well as wealth ceases to be hereditary, you see the distance that
separates the worker from the master decrease every day in fact and in
opinion.

The worker conceives a higher idea of his rights, of his future, of himself;
a new ambition, new desires fill him, new needs assail him. At every moment, he casts eyes full of covetousness on the profits of those who employ
him; in order to come to share them, he tries hard to set his work at the
highest price, and he usually ends by succeeding in doing so.

[Thus equality of conditions tends to lead to the gradual elevation of
salaries, and in turn, the elevation of salaries constantly increases equality
of conditions. So the slow and progressive augmentation of salaries seems
to me one of the general laws that govern democratic societies.

But, in our times, a great and unfortunate exception presents itself.

I showed in the first part of this work how *a few* of the principles of
aristocracy, after being chased away from political society found refuge in
the industrial world. This profoundly modifies, but only in *some* points,
the general truth that I announced above.]^c

In democratic countries, as elsewhere, most industries are conducted at
little cost by men not placed by wealth and enlightenment above the common level of those they employ. These entrepreneurs of industry are very
numerous; their interests differ; [their number varies and is constantly re-

---

Democracy pushes toward commerce and commerce remakes an aristocracy.

This danger cannot be averted except by the discovery of means (associations or
others) by the aid of which you could do commerce without accumulating as much
capital in the same hands.

Immense question.

I believe that I would do well to touch upon these questions, to cast the most
penetrating glance that I could at them, but without stopping there. They demand
a book themselves (*Rubish,* 2).

c. In the margin: "<Perhaps instead of putting the general ideas separately in the first
volume, they should energetically and in a few words be explained here. The more I
think about it, the more I am of this opinion. I am leaving the notes for this part nearby.>"

newed] so they cannot easily agree among themselves and combine their efforts.

On the other side, almost all the workers have some assured resources that allow them to refuse their services when someone does not want to give them what they consider as just payment for their work.

In the continual struggle that these two classes wage over salaries, strength is therefore divided; successes alternate.

It is even to be believed that in the long run the interest of the workers must prevail; for the high salaries that they have already gained make them less dependent every day on their masters, and the more independent they are, the more easily they can gain an increase in salaries.

I will take as example the industry that today is still the most practiced among us, as among nearly all the nations of the world: the cultivation of the land.

In France, most of those who rent their services to cultivate the soil themselves possess a few parcels, which if necessary, allow them to subsist without working for others. When the latter come to offer their hands to the great landowner or to a neighboring farmer, and they refuse to give them a certain salary, they withdraw to their small domain and wait for another occasion to present itself.[d]

I think that by taking these things as a whole, you can say that the slow and progressive elevation of salaries is one of the general laws that govern democratic societies. As conditions become more equal, salaries rise, and the higher salaries are, the more equal conditions become.

But, in our times, a great and unfortunate exception is found.

---

d. The four paragraphs that follow are missing in the manuscript. In their place you find the following paragraph:

But there are in our times *certain* very important industries that must from the start be undertaken as *large,* with great capital, numerous relationships and a great credit, in order to pursue them profitably. In these industries, the master provides at *great* expense the raw material and the tools; the workers give only their *labor.* You understand from the first that the industrial entrepreneurs should necessarily expect great profits, for without that, they would remain idle and would not risk their acquired wealth for a small gain.

As it is necessary to be already . . .

I showed, in a preceding chapter,[e] how aristocracy, chased from political society, withdrew into certain parts of the industrial world, and there established its dominion under another form.

This powerfully influences the level of salaries.[f]

As it is necessary to be already very rich in order to undertake the great industries I am talking about, the number of those who undertake them is very small. Being few, they can easily be in league with each other, and set the price that they please for work.[g]

e. In a first version, in the *rubish,* you find here this note: "This chapter is the [blank (ed.)] of the first volume. It was not found in the edition of 1834 [*sic*] and was only inserted since" (*Rubish,* 2).

f. "All societies that are born begin by organizing themselves aristocratically. Industry is subject to this law at this moment.

"Industry today shows all the advantages and all the disadvantages inherent in aristocracy."

"June 1838" (YTC, CVk, 1, p. 12). See note b of p. 980.

g. 1. Why can I call the constitution of a certain industry aristocratic?

2. Why does this constitution tend to drive down salaries? What it has of aristocratic.

It can only be exercised by a small number of men, because in order to profit from this industry, you must have great capital, a great credit, very extensive relationships.

It places a few owners called manufacturers opposite a multitude of proletarians called workers who work in the factory as the agricultural population cultivated the land three centuries ago, without spirit of ownership and without gradual participation in the profits./

No permanent bond between poor and rich./

The poor become rich with difficulty, but the rich become poor easily, and if they remained rich, they would not always be in contact with the same poor./

.-.-.-.- Since the manufacturers are very few, they can easily come to an agreement and pay only a certain price for work and, if anyone refuses the conditions they propose, they can wait without ruining themselves. While the workers can reach such an agreement only with difficulty; and they die of hunger if they do not succeed in their project at the first blow./

Moreover, these are labors of a particular type that give to the body special habits that make it unsuitable to something else./

What it has of democratic.

Wealth accumulated in this way does not establish family. It forms an exception in the general system and does not take long to submit to the common law. There

Their workers are, on the contrary, in very great number, and the quantity grows constantly; for extraordinary prosperity arrives from time to time during which salaries rise beyond measure and attract the surrounding population to manufacturing. Now, once men have entered this career, we have seen that they cannot come out of it, because they do not take long to contract the habits of body and mind that make them unsuited to any other labor.[h] These men in general have little enlightenment, industry and resources; so they are almost at the mercy of their master. When competition or other fortuitous circumstances make the gains of the latter decrease, he can restrict their salaries almost at will, and easily regain from them what fortune has taken away from him.

If by common agreement they refuse work, the master, who is a rich man, can easily wait, without ruining himself, until necessity leads them back to him; but they must work every day in order to live, for they have hardly any other property except their hands. Oppression has already for a long time impoverished them, and they are easier to oppress as they become poorer. It is a vicious circle from which they can in no way emerge.

[Thus, while in the rest of society ranks mingle each day and conditions become closer, an immense distance, greater every day, separates the servant and the master here. Their position, their future, their tastes, their mores differ profoundly. Nothing in their lot is similar. Between these two men, contact is purely material; their souls do not know each other. <The master has only a confused idea of the needs, the sufferings and the joys of the worker. So he can feel for him only a little sympathy; in his eyes, the worker is not his fellow, not even his neighbor, for Christian charity hardly warms

---

are great manufacturing fortunes, but there are no manufacturing families, nor even a manufacturing class that has its separate spirit, traditions, tastes.

If the children of the rich manufacturer constantly fall back into the crowd, every day out of the crowd arise men who take their place; thus there is never any classification or immobility in the social body, which forms nonetheless the characteristics (*Rubish*, 2).

h. "In a textile mill, on the contrary, the worker is a poor devil who owns only his hands and who needs them every day" (*Rubish*, 2).

hearts in our time.> So in these industries, the master finds himself with regard to his workers in a position analogous to the one formerly occupied by the great landed proprietor vis-à-vis the agricultural class. With this difference, nonetheless, that the aristocracy based on trade establishes no solid bond of memory, affection, and interest with the population that surrounds it; that it hardly ever settles in a permanent manner amid the surrounding population and that its goal is not to govern that population, but to make use of it.]ʲ

So you should not be astonished if salaries, after sometimes rising suddenly, go down here in a permanent way, while in other professions, the cost of labor, which in general grows only little by little, increases constantly.

This state of dependence and misery in which a part of the industrial population finds itself in our time is an exceptional fact contrary to all that surrounds it; but for this very reason, there is no fact more serious, or one that better deserves to attract the particular attention of the legislator; for it is difficult, when the whole society moves, to hold one class immobile, and it is difficult, when the greatest number constantly open new roads to fortune, to make a few endure their needs and their desires in peace.

---

j. In the margin: "<I am afraid that I said almost the same things in the same words in another place. *To verify.* >"

CHAPTER 8[a]

Influence of Democracy on the Family [b]

I have just examined how, among democratic peoples, and in particular among the Americans, equality of conditions modifies the relationships of citizens with each other.

a. After showing how equality modified the relationships of citizens, I want to penetrate further and show how it acts on the relationships of family members.

The father in the aristocratic family is not only the author of the family, he is its political head, the pontiff. . . .

Democracy destroys everything political and conventional that there was in his authority, but it does not destroy this authority; it only gives it another character.

The magistrate has disappeared, the father remains.

The same thing with brothers, the artificial bond that united brothers in the aristocratic family is destroyed. The natural bond becomes stronger.

This is applicable to all associations based on natural sentiments. Democracy relaxes social bonds, it tightens natural bonds (YTC, CVf, pp. 41–42).

b. On a jacket containing the manuscript of this chapter:

This chapter seems to me to contain some good things, but it was done by fits and starts, languidly and slowly. It demands to be reviewed all at once in order for the thought to circulate more easily. Review the *rubish* carefully./

Development a bit didactic and a bit heavy. If I could delete the *aristocratic* as much as possible and allow the *mind* of the reader to re-do what I remove. That would be much better."

Note in the *rubish:* "The difficulty is that I do not know well what the intimate relationships of father and sons and of brothers among themselves are in America and that I can hardly speak except about France. I believe these relationships not hostile, but very cold in America" (*Rubish,* 2). On the family as antidote to the "democratic disease" see F. L. Morton, "Sexual Equality and the Family in Tocqueville's *Democracy in America,*" *Canadian Journal of Political Science* XVII, no. 2 (1984): 309–24; and Laura Janara, *Democracy Growing Up. Authority, Autonomy and Passion in Tocqueville's "Democracy in America"* (Albany: State University of New York Press, 2002).

I want to penetrate further, and enter the bosom of the family. My goal here is not to look for new truths, but to show how facts already known are related to my subject.

Everyone has noticed that in our time new relationships have been established among the different members of the family, that the distance that formerly separated the father from his son has diminished, and that paternal authority has been, if not destroyed, at least altered.

Something analogous, but still more striking, is seen in the United States.

In America, the family, taking this word in its Roman and aristocratic sense, does not exist.[c] Some remnants are found only during the first years following the birth of the children. The father then exercises, without opposition, the domestic dictatorship that the weakness of his sons requires and that their interest, as well as his incontestable superiority, justifies.[d]

---

c. Former beginning of the chapter in the *rubish:*

There is a perpetual reaction of mores on the mind and of the mind on mores.

If you carefully studied the private [v: interior and exterior] life of the Americans, you would not fail to discover in a multitude of details the more or less distant effects of the philosophical method that they have adopted.

But such a study would take me too far away. I want to limit myself to providing a small number [of (ed.)] examples. I will show a few links, the detached mind of the reader will grasp the chain.

When men have accepted as general principle that it is good to judge everything by yourself, taking the opinion of others as information and not as rule, the relationship of the father with his children, of the master with his servants, and generally of the superior with the inferior finds itself changed.

[In the margin: Religion is a refuge where the human mind rests.

Politics forms an arena in which in the United States the majority, despite its desires, binds it and tires it out by its very inaction.]

Nothing is more visible than this in America.

In the United States, the family . . .

This fragment belongs to the single sheet found in a jacket on which you can read on the cover: "<S>

"It would be good to leave this small chapter after philosophical method in order to show its consequences. I would say at the end that what I had said about the relationship of the father and the sons extends to that of servants and masters and in general to all superiors and inferiors, as we will see elsewhere. This chapter is good" (*Rubish,* 2).

d. The manuscript says "legitimates."

But from the moment when the young American approaches manhood, the bonds of filial obedience loosen day by day. Master of his thoughts, the young American is soon master of his conduct. In America, there is no adolescence strictly speaking. Coming out of childhood, the man is revealed and begins to follow his own path.

You would be wrong to believe that this happens following a domestic struggle, in which the son gained, by a kind of moral violence, the liberty that his father refused to him. The same habits, the same principles that push the son to seize independence, dispose the other to consider the use of that independence as an incontestable right.

So you notice in the first none of these wild passions, full of hatred, that agitate men for a long time after they have escaped from an established power. The second does not feel those regrets, full of bitterness and anger, that usually outlast the deposed power. The father saw from afar the limits at which his authority had to expire; and when time has brought him to those limits, he abdicates without difficulty. The son foresaw in advance the precise period when his own will would become his rule, and he takes hold of liberty without rushing and without effort, as a good that he is due and that no one seeks to take away from him.[1]

---

1. *The Americans, however, have not yet imagined, as we have in France, removing from fathers one of the principal elements of power, by taking away from them their liberty to dispose of their property after death. In the United States, the right to make out your will is unlimited.*

In that as in all the rest, it is easy to notice that, if the political legislation of the Americans is much more democratic than ours, our civil legislation is infinitely more democratic than theirs. That is easily understood.

The author of our civil legislation was a man who saw his interest in satisfying the democratic passions of his contemporaries in everything that was not directly and immediately hostile to his power. He willingly allowed a few popular principles to rule property and govern families, provided that you did not want to introduce them into the conduct of the State. While the democratic torrent filled the civil laws, he hoped to keep himself easily sheltered behind the political laws. This view is at the same time full of cleverness and egoism; but such a compromise could not last. For, in the long run, political society cannot fail to become the expression and the image of civil society; and it is in this sense that you can say that there is nothing more political among a people than the civil legislation.[e]

e. In the manuscript this note appears above, at the word "path." At this place you find, instead, this other note:

Pieces that probably must be put in notes at the bottom of the pages of this chapter./

Note (B)./

I know that something analogous to what I have just said shows itself in England, one of the countries in the world where until today aristocracy has preserved the most dominion, and paternal authority the least power. From this juxtaposition you could conclude that the sentiment of independence in children is more English than democratic, and that it is due less to the habits of equality that have been contracted in the United States than to the political liberty that reigns there.

I do not think that it is so.

The bonds that hold together the various elements of the family seem to me still much less tight among the Americans than among the English, and they loosen visibly among the latter as their laws and their mores become more democratic. The result, it seems to me, is that if it is true that a certain sentiment of independence can exist within a family without equality reigning in the State, at least it must be recognized that democracy favors and develops it.

You must not forget, moreover, that England is a very aristocratic country in the middle of which a great number of democratic ideas have circulated from time immemorial and whose laws have always been intermingled with some institutions appropriate only to democracy.

What is the sovereign rule of public [v: national] opinion to which all the English of the last [century (ed.)] constantly declared that you must submit, if not a still obscure notion of the democratic dogma of the sovereignty of the people?

What does this general principle mean that the money of those paying taxes, whoever they are, can only be taxed when the latter have themselves or by their representatives voted the tax, if not the explicit recognition of the democratic right of all to participate in the government?

If I glance generally at English society, I see clearly that the aristocracy leads the State and directs the provinces, but if I look within the administration of the parishes, I discover that there at least the entire society governs itself; I see that everything comes from it [v: the people] and returns to it.[1] I notice officers who, freely elected by the universality of citizens, are occupied with the poor, inspect the roads, direct the affairs of the church, administer in an almost sovereign way common property. The authority created in this way is very limited, I admit, but it is essentially democratic. Expand the circle of attributions and you will believe yourself suddenly transported to one of the towns of Massachusetts {New England}.

These *reflections,* which came in relation to a detail, could serve to explain many important things that are happening at this moment before our eyes.

So nothing that is taking place today among the English is an entirely new development. The English are not creating democracy, they are expanding in England the democratic spirit and democratic customs.

(1) <Here a note. Ask Reeve.>

It is perhaps useful to demonstrate how these changes that took place in the family are closely tied to the social and political revolution that is finally being accomplished before our eyes.[f]

There are certain great social principles that a people apply everywhere or allow to subsist nowhere.

In countries organized aristocratically and hierarchically, power never addresses itself directly to the whole of the governed. Since men depend on each other, you limit yourself to leading the first ones. The rest follow. This applies to the family, as to all associations that have a head. Among aristocratic peoples, society knows, strictly speaking, only the father. It holds onto the sons only by the hands of the father; it governs him and he governs them. So the father has not only a natural right. He is given a political right to command. He is the author and the sustainer of the family; he is also its magistrate.

In democracies, where the arm of the government goes to find each man in particular in the middle of the crowd in order to bend him separately to the common laws, there is no need for such an intermediary; the father is, in the eyes of the law, only a citizen older and richer than his sons.

When most conditions are very unequal, and when inequality of conditions is permanent, the idea of the superior grows in the imagination of men; should the law not grant him prerogatives, custom and opinion concede them to him.[g] When, on the contrary, men differ little from each other and do not always remain dissimilar, the general notion of the superior

---

See the letter of Henry Reeve to Tocqueville (London, 29 March 1836, YTC, CVa, pp. 41–44); published by James T. Schleifer in "Tocqueville and Centralization: Four Previously Unpublished Manuscripts," *Yale University Library Gazette* 58, nos. 1–2 (1983): 33–36; and Tocqueville's response (*Correspondance anglaise, OC,* VI, 1, pp. 29–30).

f. The following paragraph replaces this passage of the manuscript: "Thus at the same time that great changes are taking place today in society, changes no less great are taking place in the family.

"It is perhaps useful to demonstrate how these two things are connected and to show what the causes and the limits are of the democratic revolution that is finally being accomplished before our eyes."

g. In the margin: "<Should this sentence be included?/

"The great power that the father exercises in aristocratic countries takes its source not only in a law and in a custom. The spirit {the ensemble} of all the customs and all the laws comes to his aid.>"

becomes weaker and less clear; in vain does the will of the legislator try hard to place the one who obeys far below the one who commands; mores bring these two men closer to each other and draw them every day toward the same level.

So if I do not see, in the legislation of an aristocratic people, particular privileges accorded to the head of the family, I will not fail to be assured that his power is very respected and more extensive than within a democracy; for I know that, whatever the laws, the superior will always seem higher and the inferior lower in aristocracies than among democratic peoples.

When men live in the memory of what was rather than in the preoccupation with what is, and when they are much more concerned about what their ancestors thought than about trying to think for themselves, the father is the natural and necessary bond between the past and the present, the link where these two chains end and join together.[h] In aristocracies, the father is therefore not only the political head of the family; he is the organ of traditions, the interpreter of customs, the arbiter of mores. You listen to him with deference; you approach him only with respect, and the love that you give him is always tempered by fear.

When the social state becomes democratic, and men adopt as general principle that it is good and legitimate to judge everything for yourself while taking ancient beliefs as information and not as a rule, the power of opinion exercised by the father over the sons, as well as his legal power, becomes less great.

The division of patrimonies that democracy brings contributes perhaps more than all the rest to changing the relationships of father and children.

When the father of the family has little property, his son and he live constantly in the same place and are busy together with the same work.

h. "I saw a commune in France in which the inhabitants did not go to church on Sunday. But they filled the cemetery on All Souls' Day; their beliefs revived suddenly at the memory of the family members they had lost; and they felt the need to pray for them, even when they forgot to do it for themselves.

"To put in the place where I say that democracy makes the sentiments of family milder. If I must say so, a touching tableau can be made there in a few words" (YTC, CVk, 1, p. 18).

Habit and need draw them closer and force them to communicate with each other at every moment; so a sort of familial intimacy cannot fail to be established between them, which makes authority less absolute, and which is badly adapted to external forms of respect.[j]

Now, among democratic peoples, the class that possesses these small fortunes is precisely the one that empowers ideas and shapes mores. It at the same time makes its opinions, like its will, prevail everywhere, and even those who are most inclined to resist its commands end up letting themselves be led by its examples. I have seen fiery enemies of democracy who had their children address them with *tu* [the familiar form].

Thus, at the same time that power is escaping from aristocracy, you see disappear what there was of [the] austere, conventional and legal in paternal power, and a kind of equality becomes established around the domestic hearth.

I do not know if, everything considered, society loses with this change; but I am led to believe that the individual gains. I think that as mores and laws are more democratic, the relationships of father and son become more intimate and milder; rule and authority are encountered less often; confidence and affection are often greater, and it seems that the natural bond tightens, while the social bond loosens.

In the democratic family, the father exercises hardly any power other than the one that you are pleased to grant to the tenderness and experience of an old man. His orders would perhaps be unrecognized; but his advice is usually full of power. If he is not surrounded by official respect, his sons at least approach him with confidence. There is no recognized formula for speaking to him; but he is spoken to constantly and readily consulted every day. The master and the magistrate have disappeared; the father remains.

It is sufficient, to judge the difference between these two social states on this point, to skim through the domestic correspondence that aristocracies

j. In a variant: "The relationships of a rich man with his family are rare and solemn. He only appears surrounded by a sort of domestic pomp; his sons see him only from afar. Business, pleasures, a tutor and valets separate him from them. Now, in aristocracy, the rich form a separate corps and a permanent association, and they regulate customs as well as laws."

have left us. The style is always correct, ceremonial, rigid, and so cold that the natural warmth of the heart can hardly be felt through the words.

There reigns, in contrast, in all the words that a son addresses to his father, among democratic peoples, something free, familiar, and tender at the same time that reveals at first glance that new relationships have been established within the family.

[Here, moreover, as elsewhere, the democratic revolution is accompanied and sometimes followed by great excesses.

When the barriers that separated the different members of the family go down, before new limits are yet fixed and well-known, it often happens that the father and the children mix in a kind of unnatural equality and gross familiarity. The father is then no longer a tender, *but* grave and a bit austere friend; he is a joyful companion of pleasure and sometimes a vile comrade of debauchery. He does not work to elevate the reason of his sons to the level of his. To please them better, he reduces his maturity to the level of their juvenile passions.

This is anarchy and corruption, and not democracy.]k

An analogous revolution modifies the mutual relationships of the children.

In an aristocratic family, as well as in aristocratic society, all the places are marked. Not only does the father there occupy a separate rank and enjoy immense privileges; the children themselves are not equal to each other; age and gender fix irrevocably for each his rank and assure him certain prerogatives. Democracy overturns or reduces most of these barriers.

In the aristocratic family, the eldest of the sons, since he inherits the greatest part of the property and almost all the rights, becomes the head and to a certain point the master of his brothers. Greatness and power are his; mediocrity and dependence are theirs. Nonetheless, it would be a mistake to believe that, among aristocratic peoples, the privileges of the eldest were advantages to him alone, and that they excited around him only envy and hate.

k. In the margin: "<Piece not to include, I believe, because it reproduces in a monotonous way the idea of the transitional period that is found in several chapters and notably in the preceding chapter.>"

The eldest usually tries hard to obtain wealth and power for his brothers, because the general splendor of the house is reflected on the one who represents it; and the younger brothers try to facilitate all the enterprises of the eldest, because the grandeur and strength of the head of the family make him more and more able to elevate all the branches.

So the various members of the aristocratic family are very tightly bound together; their interests go together, their minds are in agreement; but it is rare that their hearts understand each other.

Democracy also joins the brothers to each other; but it goes about it in another way.

Under democratic laws, the children are perfectly equal, consequently independent; nothing necessarily draws them closer together, but also nothing pushes them apart; and since they have a common origin, grow up under the same roof, are the object of the same concerns, and since no particular prerogative differentiates or separates them, you see arising easily among them the sweet and youthful intimacy of childhood. With the bond thus formed at the beginning of life, occasions for breaking that bond hardly present themselves, for fraternity draws them closer each day without hampering them.

So it is not by interests, it is by the community of memories and the free sympathy of opinions and tastes that democracy attaches brothers to each other. It divides their inheritance, but it allows their souls to blend.

The sweet pleasure of these democratic mores is so great that the partisans of aristocracy themselves allow themselves to adopt it, and after enjoying it for a time, they are not tempted to return to the respectful and cold forms of the aristocratic family. They willingly keep the domestic habits of democracy, provided that they can reject its social state and its laws. But these things go together, and you cannot enjoy the first without undergoing the others.

What I have just said about filial love and fraternal tenderness must be understood about all the passions that spontaneously have their sources in nature itself.

When a certain way of thinking or of feeling is the product of a particular state of humanity, once this state changes, nothing remains. Thus, the law can tie two citizens very closely together; once the law is abolished, they separate [and again become strangers]. There was nothing tighter than the knot that joined the vassal to the lord in the feudal world. Now these two men no longer know each other. The fear, the recognition and the love that formerly bound them have disappeared. You do not find a trace of them.

But it is not so with the natural sentiments of the human species. It is rare that the law, by trying hard to bend those sentiments in a certain way, does not weaken them, that by wanting to add to them, the law does not take something away from them, and that, left to themselves, those sentiments are not always stronger.

Democracy, which destroys or obscures nearly all the old social conventions and prevents men from stopping easily at new ones, makes most of the sentiments that arise from these conventions disappear entirely. But it only modifies the others, and often it gives them an energy and a sweetness that they did not have.

I think that it is not impossible to contain in a single sentence the entire meaning of this chapter and of several others that precede it. Democracy loosens social bonds, but it tightens natural bonds. It brings family members closer together at the same time that it separates citizens.

[This in my view is one of the most incontestable advantages of democratic institutions. When men are naturally strangers [v: far apart], it can be good to draw them toward each other and tie them together in an artificial way. But when they are naturally close and keep together, the science of the legislator rarely adds to their union and can harm it.]m

m. In the margin: "<That is not the place.>"

CHAPTER 9[a]

Education of Young Girls in the United States[b]

There have never been free societies without morals, and as I said in the first part of this work, it is the woman who molds the morals. So everything that influences the condition of women, their habits and their opinions, has a great political interest in my view.[c]

a. "Liberty of young girls in the United States.

"Firmness and coldness of their reason. They have pure morals rather than chaste minds.

"The Americans wanted them to regulate themselves. They made a constant appeal to their individual reason.

"Democratic education necessary to keep women from the dangers that arise from democratic mores" (YTC, CVf, p. 42). The ideas of this chapter appear almost literally in *Marie* (I, pp. 18–32). Tocqueville had already sketched the general features of the chapter on American women in a letter of 28 November 1831 to his sister-in-law, Émilie (YTC, BIa2). The question had been considered as well at the time of his conversations with Lieber and Gallatin (non-alphabetic notebooks 1, 2 and 3, YTC, BIIa, and *Voyage, OC,* V, 1, pp. 61 and 93).

b. On the jacket which contains the manuscript: "Perhaps join 43 and 44 in the same chapter." This chapter bears number 43 in the manuscript. Number 44 corresponds to the following chapter. The notes and drafts of this chapter and the following ones are scattered in several jackets of the *Rubish.*

c. At first this chapter began thus:

Nothing struck me more [v: I was strongly] [In the margin: <I have already said that several times.>] in America than the condition of women and I ask permission of the reader to stop a few moments at this subject. There have never been free societies without morals, and, as I said in the first part of this work, it is the woman who molds the morals. So everything that influences the condition of women, their habits and their opinions, has a great political interest in my view.

The Protestant religion professes higher esteem for the wisdom of man than Catholicism does. It shows a much greater confidence in the light of individual reason.

Protestantism is a democratic doctrine that preceded and facilitated the establish-

Among nearly all the Protestant nations, young girls are infinitely more in control of their actions than among Catholic peoples.

This independence is still greater in Protestant countries that, like England, have kept or acquired the right to govern themselves. Liberty then penetrates the family by political habits and by religious beliefs.

In the United States, the doctrines of Protestantism come to combine with a very free constitution and a very democratic social state; and nowhere is the young girl more quickly or more completely left to herself.

A long time before the young American girl has reached nubile age, she begins to be freed little by little from maternal protection; she has not yet entirely left childhood when already she thinks by herself, speaks freely and acts alone; the great world scene is exposed constantly before her; far from trying to hide it from her view, it is laid bare more and more every day before her sight, and she is taught to consider it with a firm and calm eye. Thus, the vices and perils presented by society do not take long to be revealed to her; she sees them clearly, judges them without illusion and faces them without fear; for she is full of confidence in her strength, and her confidence seems shared by all those who surround her.

So you must almost never expect to find with the American young girl this virginal guilelessness amid awakening desires, anymore than these naïve and ingenuous graces that usually accompany the European girl in the passage from childhood to youth. It is rare that the American, whatever her age, shows puerile timidity and ignorance. Like the European young girl, she wants to please, but she knows the cost precisely. If she does not give

---

ment of social and political equality. Men have, if I can say so, made democracy pass by heaven before establishing it on earth.

The practical differences of these different religious theories make themselves seen principally by the way in which the education of women is directed. For it is always in the circle of the family and domestic affairs that religion exercises the most dominion.

[In the margin, with a bracket that includes the last three paragraphs and the following three: <Probably delete this. It is dangerous ground on which I should go only by necessity.>]

Among nearly all . . .

herself to evil, at least she knows about it; she has pure morals, rather than a chaste mind.

I was often surprised and almost frightened by seeing the singular dexterity and happy boldness with which the American young girls knew how to direct their thoughts and their words amid the pitfalls of a lively conversation; a philosopher would have stumbled a hundred times on the narrow path that they traveled without accident and without difficulty.

It is easy in fact to recognize that, even amid the independence of her earliest youth, the American girl never entirely ceases to be in control of herself; she enjoys all permitted pleasures without abandoning herself to any one of them, and her reason never relinquishes the reins, although it often seems to let them hang loosely.[d]

In France, where we still mix in such a strange way the debris of all the ages in our opinions and in our tastes, it often happens that we give women a timid, secluded and almost monastic education, as in the time of aristocracy; and we then abandon them suddenly, without guide and without help, amid the disorders inseparable from a democratic society.

The Americans are in better harmony with themselves.

They have seen that, within a democracy, individual independence could not fail to be very great, youth precocious, tastes badly restrained, custom changeable, public opinion often uncertain or powerless, paternal authority weak and marital power in question.[e]

In this state of things, they judged that there was little chance of being able to repress in the woman the most tyrannical passions of the human heart, and that it was surer to teach her the art of combatting them herself. As they could not prevent her virtue from often being in danger, they wanted her to know how to defend her virtue, and they counted more on the free effort of her will than on weakened or destroyed barriers. So instead of keeping her distrustful of herself, they try constantly to increase her

d. In the margin, beside an earlier version: "<≠Philosophers have argued among themselves for six thousand years to determine the precise limits that separate licentiousness from an innocent liberty, but here is a young girl who seems to have discovered this precise [v: delicate] point by herself and who settles herself there.≠>"

e. In the manuscript you find the word "limited."

confidence in her own strength. Having neither the possibility nor the desire to keep the young girl in a perpetual and complete ignorance, they hastened to give her a precocious knowledge of everything. Far from hiding the corrupt things of the world from her, they wanted her to see them first and train herself to flee them, and they preferred to guarantee her honesty than to respect her innocence too much.[f]

Although the Americans are a strongly religious people, they did not rely on religion alone to defend the virtue of the woman; they sought to arm her reason. In this, as in many other circumstances, they followed the same

---

f. On a sheet of the manuscript which bears the title *"Rubish"*:

≠Moreover you would be wrong to believe that in the United States reason alone is relied on to guide and assure the first steps of the young girl [in the margin: the general independence of the mind and the Christian faith on certain specific dogmas].

I said elsewhere how in democracies the spirit of religion and the spirit of liberty were marvelously combined. This idea constantly presents itself to me without my seeking it, and I find it at each turn of my subject.

In America religious belief has for a long time become a public opinion. It reigns despotically on the mind [v: intelligence] of the majority and uses democracy itself to limit the errors of democratic liberty in the moral world.

The Americans have made incredible efforts to get individual independence to regulate itself and it is only when they have finally arrived at the farthest limits of human strength that they have finally called religion to their aid and have had themselves sustained in its arms.≠

[In the margin: This entire page seems to me of the sort to be deleted. I have already spoken many times about the effects of religion. I will speak yet again about it when it concerns mores. ≠This last idea, moreover, makes the mind suddenly and disagreeably enter a path for which it is not prepared.≠]

In a rough draft of the *Rubish* the fragment continues in this way:

Thus, in whatever direction I turn my subject, I always notice the same objects at the end of the course that I want to follow. Always I see American liberty relying on faith and marching in concert with it. Thus I arrive by a new road at the point that I had already reached in another part of this work, and I conclude at this time as then that if nations subjected to an aristocracy or to a despot can, if need be, do without religious beliefs without ceasing to form a society, it cannot be the same for republican and democratic peoples; and that if the first must want to believe in order to find an alleviation for their miseries, the second need to believe in order to exist (RUBISH OF THE CHAPTER ON THE REGULARITY OF MORES, *Rubish,* 2).

method. They first made incredible efforts to get individual independence to regulate itself, and it is only after arriving at the farthest limits of human strength, that they finally called religion to their help [and made it sustain them in its arms].g

I know that such an education is not without danger; nor am I unaware that it tends to develop judgment at the expense of imagination, and to make honest and cold women rather than tender wives and amiable companions to man. If society is more tranquil and better ordered because of it, private life often has fewer charms. But those are secondary evils that must be faced because of a larger interest. Having come to the point where we are, we are no longer allowed to make a choice. A democratic education is needed to protect the woman from the perils with which the institutions and mores of democracy surround her.

[Fragment of *rubish* that was to have served to link this chapter to the one following.

[The beginning is missing (ed.)] her family? To each she addresses a word, a smile, a look. Young men who met her in a public gathering approach her; and while walking, she converses familiarly with them. By the freedom of all her movements, you easily find that nothing in her actions should surprise those who see her or trouble herself. Liberty and at the same time the discreet reserve of her words show that, despite her young age, she has already ceased to see the world through the virginal veil of first innocence and that, if she has not yet learned at her expense to know human perversity, the example of others has at least been enough to teach her about it. Do not be afraid that the flow of a lively conversation will lead her beyond the limits of propriety; she is the mistress of her thought like all the rest, and she knows how to hold herself easily within the narrow space that separates innocent banter from licentious speech. Philosophers have argued among themselves for six thousand years to determine the precise point where virtue ends and vice begins, but here is a young girl who seems to have known how to separate them at first glance. Constantly, you see her approach with assurance these formidable limits that she almost never crosses.

g. In the margin: "<Must that be left?>"

Do you want more? Do you desire to know her better still? Follow her in these brilliant circles where, perhaps alone, she is going this evening. There you will be able to contemplate her in the full use of her independence and in all the splendor of triumph. That is where she enjoys beyond measure, you could almost say that she abuses without regret, the triple dominion given by spirit, youth and beauty. She carries along in her wake, she enlivens those around her. You say to her that she is beautiful, and she does not try to hide that she is pleased to receive these tributes that admiration lavishes on her. Some come forward to listen to her, others draw her aside in order to enjoy alone the pleasure of hearing her. She speaks about literature, politics, clothes, morals, love, religion, the fine arts, following the occasion of the moment and her desires. Sometimes she herself seems intoxicated by her own words.

But then where is her father? Enclosed in a dusty corner of his house, he is calculating . . . [large blank (ed.)]

And her mother? Her mother consecrates every instant to the care of a still young family; perhaps at this moment she is breast-feeding a twelfth infant just sent to her by Providence. The one, like the other, is little concerned about the actions of their daughter. Do not conclude that they are indifferent to her fate; they trust more in her precocious reason than in their surveillance.

<I am in truth sorry to find fortuitously a connection between something as gracious and as light as the emerging coquetry [v: innocent liberty] of a young girl and a matter as grave and as austere as philosophy, but the necessity of my subject forces me.

So I think, since it must be said, that it is in the philosophical method of the Americans that you must seek one of the first causes of this great liberty left to youth by a common [v: tacit] agreement.

The inhabitants of the United States have accepted in a general manner that it was good not to chain the human mind by precedents and customs, that you must not bind the mind to form or enslave it to means, but that to a certain point it must be left to its natural independence, and you must allow each person to march toward truth by his own path.

Starting from this doctrine, they are not afraid to base society on foundations unknown to their predecessors. They have imposed new rules on comm[erce (ed.)] and uncovered new resources for human industry.

It is by virtue of this same doctrine that young American girls remain themselves and can without shame obey the free impulses of their nature in everything that is not criminal.>

It is true that in America the independence of the woman becomes lost . . . (In the jacket entitled TO PROFIT FROM THE IDEAS OF THIS CHAPTER (IF I HAVE NOT ALREADY DONE IT) BY SEEING AGAIN THE CHAPTERS ON THE WOMAN, *Rubish,* 2).]

How the Young Girl Is Found Again in the Features of the Wife

In America, the independence of the woman becomes irretrievably lost amid the bonds of marriage. If the young girl is less restrained there than anywhere else, the wife submits to the most strict obligations. The one makes the paternal home a place of liberty and pleasure, the other lives in the house of her husband as in a cloister.[b]

These two conditions so different are perhaps not so contrary as you suppose, and it is natural that American women pass by the one in order to reach the other.

Religious peoples and industrial nations have a particularly serious idea of marriage. The first consider the regularity of the life of a woman as the best guarantee and the most certain sign of the purity of her morals. The others see in it the sure proof of the order and the prosperity of the house.

The Americans form at the very same time a Puritan nation and a commercial people; so their religious beliefs, as well as their industrial habits,

---

a. The American woman makes the house of her parents a place of liberty and pleasure. She leads a monastic life in the house of her husband.

These two conditions so different are less contrary than you imagine. American women pass naturally by the one in order to reach the other.

It is in the independence of their first youth and in the manly education that they then received that they have acquired the experience, the power over themselves and the (illegible word) with which they submit without hesitation and without complaint to the exigencies of the marriage state (YTC, CVf, p. 43).

b. To the side, in a first version: "An analogous spectacle is seen in England, with this difference nonetheless that the young girl there is less free and the woman less constrained than in the United States."

lead them to require from the woman an abnegation of herself and a continual sacrifice of her pleasures to her business, which it is rare to ask of her in Europe. Thus, an inexorable public opinion reigns in the United States that carefully encloses the woman in the small circle of domestic interests and duties, and that forbids her to go beyond it.[c]

Coming into the world, the young American woman finds these notions firmly established; she sees the rules that derive from them; she does not take long to be convinced that she cannot escape one moment from the customs of her contemporaries without immediately endangering her tranquillity, her honor and even her social existence, and in the firmness of her reason and in the manly habits that her education gave her, she finds the energy to submit.

You can say that it is from the practice of independence that she drew the courage to endure the sacrifice without struggle and without complaint, when the moment has come to impose it on herself.

The American woman, moreover, never falls into the bonds of marriage as into a trap set for her simplicity and ignorance. She has been taught in advance what is expected of her, and it is by herself and freely that she puts herself under the yoke. She courageously bears her new condition because she has chosen it.

As in America paternal discipline is very lax and the conjugal bond is very strict, it is only with circumspection and with fear that a young girl incurs it. Premature unions are scarcely seen. So American women marry only when their reason is trained and developed; while elsewhere most women begin to train and to develop their reason only in marriage.

I am, moreover, very far from believing that this great change that takes place in all the habits of women in the United States, as soon as they are married, must be attributed only to the constraint of public opinion. Often they impose it on themselves solely by the effort of their will.

When the time has arrived to choose a husband, this cold and austere

---

c. "From the moment when the world becomes commercial, the household is nothing more than a house of commerce, a name of a firm. K[ergorlay (ed.)]" (In the *rubish* of the chapter on the family, *Rubish,* 2).

reason, which the free view of the world has enlightened and strengthened, indicates to the American woman that a light and independent spirit in the bonds of marriage is a matter of eternal trouble, not of pleasure; that the amusements of the young girl cannot become the diversions of the wife, and that for the woman the sources of happiness are in the conjugal home. Seeing in advance and clearly the only road that can lead to domestic felicity, she takes it with her first steps, and follows it to the end without trying to go back.

This same vigor of will that the young wives of America display, by bowing suddenly and without complaint to the austere duties of their new state, is found as well in all the great trials of their life.

There is no country in the world where particular fortunes are more unstable than in the United States. It is not rare that, in the course of his existence, the same man climbs and again descends all the degrees that lead from opulence to poverty.

The women of America bear these [sudden] revolutions with a tranquil and indomitable energy. You would say that their desires narrow with their fortune, as easily as they expand.

Most of the adventurers who go each year to people the uninhabited areas of the west belong, as I said in my first work,[d] to the old Anglo-American race of the North. Several of these men who run with such boldness toward wealth already enjoyed comfort in their country. They lead their companions with them and make them share the innumerable perils and miseries that always signal the beginning of such enterprises. I often met at the limits of the wilderness young women who, after being raised amid all of the refinements of the great cities of New England, had passed, almost without transition, from the rich homes of their parents to a badly sealed hut in the middle of a wood. Fever, solitude, boredom had not broken the main springs of their courage. Their features seemed altered and faded, but their view was firm. They appeared at once sad and resolute.

d. See p. 458 of the first volume.

I do not doubt that these young American women had amassed, in their first education, this internal strength that they then used.

So the young girl in the United States is still found in the features of the wife; the role has changed, the habits differ, the spirit is the same.

How Equality of Conditions Contributes to Maintaining Good Morals in America

There are philosophers and historians who have said, or implied, that women were more or less severe in their morals depending on whether they lived farther from or closer to the equator. That is getting out of the matter cheaply, and in this case, a globe and a compass would suffice to resolve in an instant one of the most difficult problems that humanity presents.

I do not see that this materialistic doctrine is established by the facts.

The same nations have shown themselves, in different periods of their history, chaste or dissolute. So the regularity or the disorderliness of their

---

a. Climate, race and religion are not enough to explain the great regularity of morals in the United States.

You must resort to the social and political state.

How democracy favors the regularity of morals.

1. It prevents disorderliness before marriage, because you can always marry.

2. It prevents it afterward.

1. Because you have loved and chosen each other and because it is to be believed that you suit each other.

2. Because if you were mistaken, public opinion no longer accepts that you fail to fulfill freely accepted commitments.

3. Other causes:

1. Continual occupation of men and women.

2. Nature of these occupations that removes the taste as well as the time to give themselves without restraint to their passions.

4. Why what is happening in Europe and in France is contrary to this, and this makes our morals become more lax as our social state more democratic (YTC, CVf, pp. 43–44).

morals is due to a few changeable causes, and not only to the nature of the country, which did not change.

I will not deny that, in certain climates, the passions that arise from the mutual attraction of the sexes are particularly ardent; but I think that this natural ardor can always be excited or restrained by the social state and the political institutions.

Although the travelers who have visited North America differ among themselves on several points, they all agree in noting that morals there are infinitely more severe than anywhere else.

It is clear that, on this point, the Americans are very superior to their fathers, the English. A superficial view of the two nations is enough to show it.[b]

In England, as in all the other countries of Europe, public spite is constantly brought to bear on the weaknesses of women. You often hear philosophers and statesmen complain that morals are not regular enough, and literature assumes it every day.

---

b. Good morals./

Democracy is favorable to good morals, even apart from religious beliefs. This is proved in two ways:

1. In England, same beliefs, but not the same morals. Recall on this subject the remark that I made in a letter to Basil Hall in which I said that, without allowing myself to judge alone the morals of American women and English women, I was however led to believe the first superior to the second. In America, no one allows himself to say a single word about the honor of women. Foreigners themselves keep quiet about it. I have even seen some corrupt enough to regret the purity of morals. All books, even novels, assume chaste women. In England, the dandies talk about getting lucky, philosophers complain that the morality of women is decreasing, foreigners tell racy escapades and books (illegible word) leave it to be assumed.

2. An aristocracy without beliefs (like that of France, for example, or that of England under Charles II). Nothing more excessive .-[you (ed.)].- then see what .-[the (ed.)].- aristocracy can do when it goes in the same direction as passions. The French aristocracy even when it was enlightened was still infinitely less regular than the American democracy.

[In the margin] Horrible excesses of the Roman aristocracy. See Properce (*Rubish,* 2). The letter to Basil Hall is cited in note d of p. 819.

In America, all books, without excepting novels, assume women to be chaste, and no one tells racy escapades.

This great regularity of American morals is undoubtedly due in part to the country, to race, to religion.c But all these causes, which are found elsewhere, are still not enough to explain it. For that you must resort to some particular reason.

This reason appears to me to be equality and the institutions that derive from it.

Equality of conditions does not by itself alone produce regularity of morals; but you cannot doubt that it facilitates and augments it.

Among aristocratic peoples, birth and fortune often make men and women beings so different that they can never succeed in uniting. Passions draw them together, but the social state and the ideas that the social state suggests prevent them from joining in a permanent and open way. From that a great number of fleeting and clandestine unions necessarily arise. Nature compensates in secret for the constraint that the laws impose.

The same thing does not happen when equality of conditions has made all the imaginary or real barriers that separate the man from the woman fall. There is then no young woman who does not believe herself able to become the wife of the man she prefers; this makes disorderliness in morals before marriage very difficult. For, whatever the credulity of passions, there is hardly any way for a woman to be persuaded that someone loves her when he is perfectly free to marry her and does not do so.

The same cause acts, although in a more indirect manner, in marriage.

Nothing serves better to legitimate illegitimate love in the eyes of those who feel it or in the eyes of the crowd who contemplate it, than forced unions or unions made by chance.[1]

---

c. "≠A believing democracy will always be more regular in its morals than a believing aristocracy≠" (*Rubish*, 2).

1. *It is easy to be convinced of this truth by studying the different literatures of Europe.*

When a European wants to retrace in his fiction a few of the great catastrophes that appear so often among us within marriage, he takes care to excite in advance the pity of the reader by showing him beings who are badly matched or forced together. Although for a long time

In a country where the woman always freely exercises her choice, and where education has made her able to choose well, public opinion is unrelenting about her faults.

The rigor of the Americans arises in part from that. They consider marriage as an often onerous contract, but one by which you are nonetheless bound strictly to execute all the clauses, because you were able to know them in advance and you enjoyed complete liberty not to commit yourself to anything.[d]

What makes fidelity more obligatory makes it easier.

In aristocratic countries the purpose of marriage is to join property rather than persons; consequently it sometimes happens that the husband is chosen while in school and the wife while in the care of a wet-nurse. It is not surprising that the conjugal bond that holds the fortunes of the two married individuals together allows their hearts to wander at random. That flows naturally from the spirit of the contract.

When, on the contrary, each person always chooses his own companion, without anything external hindering or even guiding him, it is usually only

our morals have been softened by a great tolerance, it would be difficult to succeed in interesting us in the misfortunes of these characters if the author did not begin by excusing their failing. This artifice does not fail to succeed. The daily spectacle that we witness prepares us from afar to be indulgent.

American writers cannot make such excuses credible in the eyes of their readers; their customs, their laws refuse to do so and, having no hope of making disorderliness amiable, they do not portray it. It is, in part, to this cause that the small number of novels published in the United States must be attributed.

d. Fragment at the end of the chapter:

To put in the place where I examine in general if democracy leads to disorderliness. Somewhere near page 3./

It sometimes happens that in democracies men seem more corrupt than among aristocratic nations, but here you must be very careful not to be fooled by an appearance.

Equality of conditions does not make men immoral, but when men are immoral at the same time that they are equal, the effects of immorality are shown more easily on the outside.

For, among democratic peoples, since citizens have almost no action on each other, no one takes charge of maintaining order in the society or of keeping human passions in a certain external order.

Thus equality of conditions does not create the corruption of morals, but sometimes it exposes it.

similarity of tastes and ideas that draw the man and the woman closer; and this same similarity holds and settles them next to one another.

Our fathers had conceived a singular opinion in regard to marriage.

As they had noticed that the small number of marriages by inclination that took place in their time had almost always had a disastrous outcome, they had concluded resolutely that in such matters it was very dangerous to consult your own heart. Chance seemed more clear-sighted than choice.

It was not very difficult to see, however, that the examples they had before their eyes proved nothing.[e]

I will remark first that, if democratic peoples grant to women the right to choose freely their husbands, they take care in advance to provide their minds with the enlightenment, and their wills with the strength, that can be necessary for such a choice; while the young women who, among aristocratic peoples, escape furtively from paternal authority in order to throw themselves into the arms of a man whom they have been given neither the time to know nor the capacity to judge, lack all of these guarantees. You cannot be surprised that they make bad use of their free will, the first time that they use it; or that they fall into such cruel errors when, not having received democratic education, they want to follow, in marrying, the customs of democracy.

But there is more.

When a man and a woman want to come together across the inequalities of the aristocratic social state, they have immense obstacles to overcome. After breaking or loosening the bonds of filial obedience, they have to escape, by a final effort, the rule of custom and the tyranny of opinion; and when finally they have reached the end of this hard undertaking, they find themselves like strangers in the middle of their natural friends and close relatives; the prejudice that they overcame separates them from these friends and relatives. This situation does not take long to drain their courage and to embitter their hearts.

So if it happens that spouses united in this way are at first unhappy, and

---

e. "There is no man so powerful that he is able to struggle successfully for long against the whole of the customs and the opinions of his contemporaries, and reason will never be right against everyone" (*Rubish*, 2).

then guilty, it must not be attributed to the fact that they freely chose each other, but rather to the fact that they live in a society that does not accept such choices.

You must not forget, moreover, that the same effort that makes a man depart violently from a common delusion almost always carries him beyond reason; that, to dare to declare a war, even a legitimate one, against the ideas of your century and your country, the spirit must have a certain fierce and adventurous disposition, and that men of this character, whatever direction they take, rarely attain happiness and virtue. And, to say so in passing, this is what explains why, in the most necessary and most holy of revolutions, so few moderate and honest revolutionaries are found.

That, in an aristocratic century, a man dares by chance to consult, concerning the conjugal union, no other preferences than his particular opinion and his taste, and that disorderliness of morals and misery do not subsequently take long to enter his household, must not therefore be surprising. But, when this same way of acting is the natural and usual order of things, when the social state facilitates it, when paternal power goes along with it and when public opinion advocates it, you must not doubt that the internal peace of families becomes greater and that conjugal faith is better kept.

Nearly all the men of democracies follow a political career or exercise a profession, and on the other hand, the mediocrity of fortunes obliges the woman there to enclose herself every day within the interior of her house, in order to preside herself, and very closely, over the details of domestic administration.

All these distinct and forced labors are like so many natural barriers that, separating the sexes, make the solicitations of the one rarer and less intense, and the resistance of the other easier.

It is not that equality of conditions can ever succeed in making men chaste; but it gives to the disorderliness of their morals a less dangerous character. Since no one then has any longer either the leisure or the occasion to attack the virtues that want to defend themselves, you see at the very same time a great number of courtesans and a multitude of honest women.[f]

f. If that gets to the point that women give themselves to the first one who comes

Such a state of things produces deplorable individual miseries, but it does not prevent the social body from being in good form and strong; it does not destroy the bonds of family and does not enervate national mores. What puts society in danger is not great corruption among a few, it is the laxity of all. In the eyes of the legislator, prostitution is less to fear than love affairs.

This tumultuous and constantly fretful life, which equality gives to men, not only diverts them from love by removing the leisure to devote themselves to it; it also turns them away by a more secret, but more certain road.

All the men who live in democratic times contract more or less the intellectual habits of the industrial and commercial classes; their minds take a serious, calculating and positive turn; they willingly turn away from the ideal in order to aim for some visible and immediate goal that presents itself as the natural and necessary object of desires. Equality does not in this way destroy imagination; but it limits it and allows it to fly only by skimming over the earth.g

No one is less of a dreamer than the citizens of a democracy, and you hardly see any who want to give themselves to these idle and solitary con-

---

along without defending themselves, a horrible corruption can result, but it can also happen that you do not attack women from whom you expect some resistance.

It then happens that there is a multitude of streetwalkers [v: courtesans] and honest women.

[In the margin: Men always have the time to make love, but not courtship./

Man always attacks no matter what you do. The important thing is that women defend themselves well] (RUBISH OF THE CHAPTERS ON THE WOMAN, *Rubish,* 2).

g. Love in democracies./

Sentiment rarer but when .-.-.-.- more disorderly, freer from all rules than in aristocracies.

The greatest love during the century of Louis XIV stopped before certain facts, certain rules of language, certain ideas that would not stop it today.

[In the margin: See the Romans, the conversations of that time./

A certain moderation of language reigns amid the disorder of the senses.]

I am speaking here only about the barrier that customs present to it and not about the barrier that virtue presents. The latter is found in all social forms. It weakens or widens only when the core of mores is altered (RUBISH OF THE CHAPTERS ON THE WOMAN, *Rubish,* 2).

templations that ordinarily precede and that produce the great agitations of the heart.

They put, it is true, a great value on gaining for themselves the kind of profound, regular and peaceful affection that makes the charm and the security of life; but they do not readily run after the violent and capricious emotions that disturb and shorten it.

I know that all that precedes is completely applicable only to America and cannot, for now, be extended in a general way to Europe.

During the half-century that laws and habits have with an unparalleled energy pushed several European peoples toward democracy, you do not see that among these nations the relations of man and woman have become more regular and more chaste. The opposite even allows itself to be seen in some places. Certain classes are better regulated; general morality seems more lax. I will not be afraid to note it, for I feel myself no better disposed to flatter my contemporaries than to speak ill of them.

This spectacle must be distressing, but not surprising.

The happy influence that a democratic social state can exercise on the regularity of habits is one of those facts that can only be seen in the long run. If equality of conditions is favorable to good morals, the social effort, which makes conditions equal, is very deadly to them.[h]

During the fifty years that France has been undergoing transformation, we have rarely had liberty, but always disorderliness. Amid this universal confusion of ideas and this general disturbance of opinions, among this incoherent mixture of the just and the unjust, of the true and the false, of the right and the fact, public virtue has become uncertain, and private morality unsteady.

But all revolutions, whatever their objective or their agents, have at first produced similar effects. Even those that ended by tightening the bond of morals began by loosening it.

h. "<I hardly doubt that the democratic movement of today has contributed to the loosening that we witness, but this seems to me due particularly to our democracy and not to democracy in general>" (*Rubish*, 2).

So the disorders that we often witness do not seem to be an enduring fact. Already strange signs herald it.

There is nothing more miserably corrupt than an aristocracy that keeps its wealth while losing its power, and that, reduced to vulgar enjoyments, still possesses immense leisure. The energetic passions and great thoughts that formerly had animated it then disappear, and you hardly find anything else except a multitude of small gnawing vices that attach themselves to the aristocracy like worms to a cadaver.[j]

No one disputes that the French aristocracy of the last century was very dissolute; while ancient habits and old beliefs still maintained respect for morals in the other classes.

Nor will anyone have any difficulty coming to agreement that, in our time, a certain severity of principles shows itself among the debris of this same aristocracy, while disorderliness of morals has seemed to spread in the middle and inferior ranks of society. So that the same families that appeared, fifty years ago, the most lax, appear today the most exemplary, and that democracy seems to have made only the aristocratic classes moral.[k]

[There are men who see in this fact a cause for fears about the future.

I find in it a reason for hope.]

The Revolution, by dividing the fortunes of the nobles, by forcing them

j. "Take away their power and they tear down all the rest themselves. In their obscene rest, they no longer cultivate even the intellectual tastes that embellished the glorious leisure of their fathers. But most plunge into a gross well-being and console themselves with horses and dogs for not being able to govern the State" (YTC, CVc, p. 54).

"They will be like the Jews among the Christian nations of the Middle Ages [v: after the destruction of the temple], but different from the Jews on one point; they will not perpetuate themselves [v: like them they will await a Messiah who will not come]" (YTC, CVc, p. 60). This same note appears on the back of the jacket of the *rubish* SOCIABILITY OF THE AMERICANS. See note c of pp. 1263–64.

k. "Corc[elle (ed.)]. advises me (12 August 1837) to explain my thought when I say that the loosening of morals is greater today than fifty years ago, and to make some distinctions .-.-.-. which such a judgment does not seem .-.-.-. correct.

"His advice seems to me very difficult to follow in the text, whose rapidity does not allow me to stop, but it can be done in a note at the bottom of the page" (RUBISH OF THE CHAPTERS ON THE WOMAN, *Rubish,* 2). The Corcelles stayed at the Tocqueville château from the end of July to mid-August 1837 (see *Correspondance avec Corcelle, OC,* XV, 1, p. 81).

to occupy themselves assiduously with their affairs and with their families, by enclosing them with their children under the same roof, finally by giving a more reasonable and more serious turn to their thoughts, suggested to them, without their noticing it themselves, respect for religious beliefs, love of order, of peaceful pleasures, of domestic joys and of well-being; while the rest of the nation, which naturally had these same tastes, was carried toward [added: moral] disorderliness by the very effort that had to be made in order to overturn the laws and political customs.

The old French aristocracy suffered the consequences of the Revolution, and it did not feel the revolutionary passions, or share the often anarchic impulse that it produced; it is easy to imagine that it experiences in its morals the salutary influence of this revolution even before those who brought it about.

So it is permissible to say, although at first view it seems surprising, that, today, it is the most anti-democratic classes of the nation who best show the type of morality that it is reasonable to expect from democracy.

I cannot prevent myself from believing that, when we will have gained all the effects of the democratic revolution, after emerging from the tumult that arose from it, what is true today only of a few will little by little become true of all.

CHAPTER 12[a]

How the Americans Understand the Equality of Man and of Woman[b]

I showed how democracy destroyed or modified the various inequalities given birth by society; but is that all, and does democracy not succeed finally

a. "1. The man and the woman mingle less in America than anywhere else.

"2. Marital authority is strongly respected.

"3. The Americans have, however, tried much harder than we have done in Europe to raise the woman to the level of the man, but it is in the intellectual and moral world" (YTC, CVf, p. 44).

b. In notebook CVk, 2 (pp. 14–25), a copy of the chapter contains this initial note: "Chapter such as I revised it, but without being able to be satisfied about it in this form any more than the other. The fact is that I no longer understand anything; my mind is exhausted. (October 1839).

"Have the two versions copied and submit them to my friends" (YTC, CVk, 2, p. 14). On the jacket of the manuscript, in pencil:

It must be condensed more. Remark of *Ampère* and *Édouard*./

The same thing is noted in England. Comes from the Germanic and Protestant notion, but stronger in America because of the democratic layer. Good to say according to Ampère./

The above ideas are original only from the perspective that they are due to aristocracy or to democracy. As for portraits, they are drawn in other authors, principally Madame de Staël./

Make more clearly felt and seen the systems called *emancipation* of the woman. Do not assume that the reader knows them. This will add something piquant much [*sic*] to the chapter. Cite even, either in a note or in the text, the extravagant ideas of the Saint-Simonians and others on this point.

Tocqueville finished this chapter at the end of August 1837. The Beaumonts, who passed several days with the Tocquevilles in Normandy, approved this chapter that Tocqueville read to them.

in acting on this great inequality of man and woman, which has seemed, until today, to have its eternal foundation in nature?

I think that the social movement that brings closer to the same level the son and the father, the servant and the master, and in general, the inferior and the superior, elevates the woman and must more and more make her the equal of the man.

But here, more than ever, I feel the need to be well understood; for there is no subject on which the coarse and disorderly imagination of our century has been given a freer rein.

There are men in Europe who, confusing the different attributes of the sexes, claim to make the man and the woman beings, not only equal, but similar.[c] They give to the one as to the other the same functions, impose the same duties on them, and grant them the same rights; they mix them in everything, work, pleasures, public affairs. It can easily be imagined that by trying hard in this way to make one sex equal to the other, both are degraded; and that from this crude mixture of the works of nature only weak men and dishonest women can ever emerge.

This is not how the Americans understood the type of democratic equality that can be established between the woman and the man.[d] They thought that, since nature had established such a great variation between the physical and moral constitution of the man and that of the woman, its clearly indicated goal was to give a different use to their different faculties; and they judged that progress did not consist of making almost the same things out of dissimilar beings, but of having each of them fulfill his task to the best possible degree. The Americans applied to the two sexes the great principle of political economy that dominates industry today. They carefully divided the functions of the man and the woman, in order that the great work of society was better accomplished.

---

c. In the margin: "<In Europe women do not try to become perfect in their line, but to encroach upon ours.>"

d. Variation in the manuscript: ". . . and man. <In America no one has ever imagined joining the sexes in the same careers or making them contribute in the same way to social well-being, and no one that I know has yet found that the final consequence of democratic institutions and principles was to make the woman independent of the man and to transform her into jurist, judge or warrior.>"

America is the country in the world where the most constant care has been taken to draw clearly separated lines of action for the two sexes, and where the desire has been that both marched with an equal step, but always along different paths. You do not see American women lead matters outside of the family, conduct business, or finally enter into the political sphere; but you also do not find any who are forced to give themselves to the hard work of plowing or to any one of the difficult exercises that require the development of physical strength. There are no families so poor that they make an exception to this rule.[e]

If the American woman cannot escape the peaceful circle of domestic occupations, she is, on the other hand, never forced to leave it. [<She has been enclosed in her home, but there she rules.>]

The result is that American women, who often show a male reason and an entirely manly energy, conserve in general a very delicate appearance, and always remain women by manners, although they reveal themselves as men sometimes by mind and heart.

Nor have the Americans ever imagined that the consequence of democratic principles was to overturn marital authority and to introduce confusion of authority into the family.[f] They thought that every association, to be effective, must have a head, and that the natural head of the conjugal association was the man. So they do not deny to the latter the right to direct his companion; and they believe that, in the small society of husband and wife, as in the great political society, the goal of democracy is to regulate necessary powers and to make them legitimate, and not to destroy all power. [The Americans have, however, drawn the man and the woman closer than any other people, but it is only in the moral order.]

This opinion is not particular to one sex and contested by the other.

I did not notice that American women considered conjugal authority as

e. "≠All that is equally true of England, although to a lesser degree. This separation of man and woman exists in several countries of Europe and above all in England, but no where is it as well-marked≠" (YTC, CVk, 2, p. 16). See note j of p. 1066.

f. "Stand up somewhere against divorce and say what I heard repeated in the United States, that it gave rise to more evils than it cured" (*Rubish,* 2).

a happy usurpation of their rights, or that they believed that it was de-grading to submit to it. I seemed to see, on the contrary, that they took a kind of glory in the voluntary surrender of their will, and that they located their grandeur in bending to the yoke themselves and not in escaping it. That, at least, was the sentiment expressed by the most virtuous; the others kept silent, and you do not hear in the United States the adulterous wife noisily claim the rights of woman, while trampling her most holy duties under foot.

It has often been remarked that in Europe a certain disdain is found even amid the flatteries that men lavish on women; although the European man often makes himself the slave of the woman, you see that he never sincerely believes her his equal.[g]

In the United States, women are scarcely praised; but it is seen every day that they are respected.

American men constantly exhibit a full confidence in the reason of their companion, and a profound respect for her liberty. They judge that her mind is as capable as that of man of discovering the naked truth, and her heart firm enough to follow the truth; and they have never sought to shelter the virtue of one more than that of the other from prejudices, ignorance or fear.[h]

It seems that in Europe, where you submit so easily to the despotic rule of women, you nonetheless refuse them some of the greatest attributes of the human species [added: while obeying them], and that you consider them as seductive [v: inferior] and incomplete beings; and, what you cannot find too astonishing, women themselves finish by seeing themselves in the same light, and they are not far from considering as a privilege the ability that is left to them to appear frivolous, weak and fearful. American women do not demand such rights.

---

g. In the margin: "This is shown—Education."

h. "Although the Americans do not make their daughter fight in the gymnasium as was formerly practiced in Sparta, you can no less say that they gave them a male edu-cation, since they teach them to use in a manly way reason, which is *the greatest attribute of man.* The exercises of Greece only tended to make the woman as strong as the man. They do not try to fortify their body, but to make their soul firm" (RUBISH OF THE CHAPTERS ON THE WOMAN, *Rubish,* 2).

You would say, on the other hand, that as regards morals, we have granted to the man a kind of singular immunity; so that there is as it were one virtue for him, and another one for his companion; and that, according to public opinion, the same act may be alternatively a crime or only a failing.

The Americans do not know this iniquitous division of duties and rights. Among them, [purity of morals in marriage and respect for conjugal faith are imposed equally on the man and on the woman and] the seducer is as dishonored as his victim.

It is true that American men rarely show to women these attentive considerations with which we enjoy surrounding them in Europe; but they always show, by their conduct, that they assume them to be virtuous and delicate; and they have such a great respect for their moral liberty that in their presence each man carefully watches his words, for fear that the women may be forced to hear language that wounds them. In America, a young girl undertakes a long journey, alone and without fear.j

The legislators of the United States, who have made nearly all the provisions of the penal code milder, punish rape with death; and there is no crime that public opinion pursues with a more inexorable ardor. This can be explained: since the Americans imagine nothing more precious than the honor of the woman, or nothing so respectable as her independence, they consider that there is no punishment too severe for those who take them away from her against her will.

In France, where the same crime is struck by much milder penalties, it is often difficult to find a jury that convicts. Would it be scorn for modesty or scorn for the woman? I cannot prevent myself from believing that it is both.

Thus, the Americans do not believe that man and woman have the duty or the right to do the same things, but they show the same respect for the role of each one of them, and they consider them as beings whose value is equal, although their destinies differ. They do not give the courage of the woman the same form or the same use as that of the man; but they never

---

j. In the margin: "All this, says Ampère, is Germanic and not democratic. It is found in Germany and in England, as well as in America."

doubt her courage; and if they consider that the man and his companion should not always use their intelligence and their reason in the same way, they judge, as least, that the reason of the one is as certain as that of the other, and her intelligence as clear.[k]

So the Americans, who have allowed the [<natural>] inferiority of the woman to continue to exist in society, have with all their power elevated her, in the intellectual and moral world, to the level of the man; and in this they seem to me to have understood admirably the true notion of democratic progress. [They have not imagined for the woman a greatness similar to that of the man, but they have imagined her as great as the man, and they have made her their equal even when they have kept the necessary right to command her.]

As for me, I will not hesitate to say it: although in the United States the woman hardly leaves the domestic circle, and although she is, in certain respects, very dependent, nowhere has her position seemed higher to me; and if, now that I am approaching the end of this book, in which I have shown so many considerable things done by the Americans, you asked me to what I think the singular prosperity and growing strength of this people must be principally attributed, I would answer that it is to the superiority of their women.[m]

k. "Piece of Pascal on the greatness of the different orders, p. 93 [98? (ed.)]" (With the notes of the chapter on mores, *Rubish,* 2). The edition used by Tocqueville has not been identified.

m. "≠Say clearly somewhere that the women seem to me very superior to the men in America≠" (*Rubish,* 2).

How Equality Divides the Americans Naturally into a Multitude of Small Particular Societies[b]

You would be led to believe that the ultimate consequence and necessary effect of democratic institutions is to mix citizens in private life as well as in public life, and to force them all to lead a common existence [<to mingle them constantly in the same pleasures and in the same affairs.

Some of the legislators of antiquity had tried it and the Convention attempted it in our times.>]

That is to understand in a very crude and very tyrannical way the equality that arises from democracy.

There is no social state or laws that can make men so similar that education, fortune and tastes do not put some difference between them, and if different men can sometimes find it in their interest to do the same things in common, you must believe that they will never find their pleasure in doing so. So they will always, whatever you do, slip out of the hand of the

---

a. In aristocratic countries, each class forms like a great natural friendship that obliges men to see and to meet each other.

When there are no longer any classes that inevitably hold a certain number of men together, there is nothing more than whim, instinct, taste that draws them together, which multiplies particular societies infinitely.

The Americans who mingle constantly with each other in order to deal with common affairs, set themselves carefully apart with a small number of friends in order to enjoy private life" (YTC, CVf, p. 45).

b. Variant of the title on the jacket of the manuscript: HOW DEMOCRACY [v: EQUALITY] AFTER DESTROYING THE GREAT BARRIERS THAT SEPARATED MEN, DIVIDES THEM INTO A MULTITUDE OF SMALL PARTICULAR SOCIETIES.

legislator; and escaping in some way from the circle in which you try to enclose them, they will establish, alongside the great political society, small private societies, whose bond will be the similarity of conditions, habits and mores.

In the United States, citizens do not have any preeminence over each other; they owe each other reciprocally neither obedience nor respect; they administer justice together and govern the State, and in general they all join together to deal with the matters that influence the common destiny; but I never heard it said that anyone claimed to lead them all to amuse themselves in the same way or to enjoy themselves mixed haphazardly together in the same places.

The Americans, who mingle so easily within political assemblies and courtrooms, on the contrary, separate themselves with great care into small very distinct associations, in order to enjoy the pleasures of private life all by themselves. Each one of them readily recognizes all of his fellow citizens as his equals, but he receives only a very small number among his friends and guests.

That seems very natural to me. As the circle of public society expands, it must be expected that the sphere of private relations will narrow; instead of imagining that the citizens of new societies are going to end up living in common, I am afraid indeed that they will finally end up by forming nothing more than very small cliques.

Among aristocratic peoples, the different classes are like vast enclosures which you cannot leave and which you cannot enter. The classes do not communicate with each other; but within the interior of each one of them, men inevitably talk to each other every day. Even when they do not naturally suit each other, the general affinity of the same condition draws them closer.[c]

---

c. When men classed within an aristocracy are all part of a hierarchy, each one, at whatever place in the social chain where he is located, finds above and below him one of his fellows with whom he is in daily contact. He judges that his interest as well as his duty is to serve these two men in all encounters. But he remains a stranger and almost an enemy to all the others.

They finish by believing that all men are not part of the same humanity.

It is not a complete insensitivity, it is a (illegible word) sensitivity (YTC, CVa, pp. 6–7).

But, when neither law nor custom takes charge of establishing frequent and habitual relations between certain men, the accidental similarity of opinions and propensities decides it; which varies particular societies infinitely.

In democracies, where citizens never differ much from one another and are naturally so close that at each instant they can all blend into a common mass, a multitude of artificial and arbitrary classifications is created by the aid of which each man tries to set himself apart, for fear of being dragged despite himself into the crowd.

It can never fail to be so; for you can change human institutions, but not man. Whatever the general effort of a society to make citizens equal and similar, the particular pride of individuals will always try to escape from the level, and will want to form somewhere an inequality from which he profits.

In aristocracies, men are separated from each other by high immobile barriers; in democracies, they are divided by a multitude of small, nearly invisible threads, which break at every moment and change place constantly.

Thus, whatever the progress of equality, a large number of small private associations among democratic peoples will always be formed amid the great political society. But none of them will resemble, in manners, the upper class that directs aristocracies.

CHAPTER 14[a]

Some Reflections on American Manners[b]

There is nothing, at first view, that seems less important than the external form of human actions, and there is nothing to which men attach more

a. Manners come from the very heart of mores and sometimes result as well from an arbitrary convention between certain men.

Men of democratic countries do not naturally have grand manners because their life is limited.

Moreover, they do not have studied manners because they cannot agree on the establishment of the rule of savoir-faire. So there is always incoherence in their manners, above all as long as the democratic revolution lasts.

That aristocratic manners disappear forever with aristocracy, that not even the taste or the idea of them is preserved.

You must not be too distressed about it, but it is permitted to regret it (YTC, CVf, p. 45).

The manuscript of this chapter contains another version of the beginning, contained in a jacket that explains: "Piece that began the chapter which I removed because it seemed to me to get back into often reproduced deductions of ideas, but which I must have copied and read." This fragment, with the exception of the description of aristocratic society (reproduced in note f) is not very different from the published version.

Tocqueville began the writing of this chapter at the beginning of the month of September 1837. "Here I am at *manners,* a very difficult subject for everyone, but particularly for me, who finds himself ill at ease in the small details of private life. Consequently I will be brief. I hope in about a week to have finished and to be able to get into the great chapters that end the book" (*Correspondance avec Corcelle, OC,* XV, 1, p. 86).

b. On the jacket of the manuscript: "Courtesy, civility. Neglected words that must be used by going over it again."

On the jacket of the *rubish:* "To reexamine with more care than the other *rubish.* A fairly large number of ideas that I was not able to express at first are found here in germ or in development.

"Courtesy, civility, civil: words that I have neglected" (*Rubish,* 2).

In another place: "I do not think that it is unworthy of the gravity of my subject to

value; they become accustomed to everything, except living in a society that does not have their manners. So the influence that the social and political state exercises on manners is worth the trouble to be examined seriously.[c]

---

examine the influence that democracy can exercise on manners. Form influences more than you think the substance of human actions" (*Rubish*, 2).

c. If after having considered the relationships that exist between the superior and the inferior, I examine the relations of equals among themselves, I discover facts analogous to those that I pointed out above.

There are a thousand means indeed to judge the social state and political laws of a people once you have well understood what the various consequences are that flow naturally from these two different things. The most trivial observations of a traveler can lead you to truth on this point as well as the searching remarks of philosophers. Everything goes together in the constitution of moral man as well as in his physical nature, and just as Cuvier, by seeing a single organ, was able to reconstruct the whole body of the entire animal, someone who would know one of the opinions or habits of a people would often be able, I think, to conceive a fairly complete picture of the people itself.

If an ignorant (illegible word) of the Antipodes told me that, in the country that he has just traveled across, certain rules of politeness are observed as immutable laws and that the least actions of men there are subjected to a sort of ceremonial from which no one can ever depart, I will not be afraid to assert that I already know enough about it to assert that the inhabitants of the country that he is speaking to me about are divided among themselves in a profound and permanent way by different and unequal conditions.

When the human mind is delivered from the shackles that inequality of conditions imposed on it, it does not fail to attach a certain cachet of individual originality to its least as to its principal conceptions.

I accept without difficulty that men change their laws [v: constitution] more readily than the customs of etiquette and that they modify the general principles of their morals more easily than the external form of their words. I know that innovations usually begin with the important classes of things before arriving at the least important. But finally they arrive there, and after overturning the dominion of the rule in politics, in sciences, in philosophy, the human mind escapes from it in the small actions of every day.

It is impossible to live for a time in the United States without discovering that a sort of chance seems to preside in social relationships. Politeness is subjected to laws less fixed, less detailed, more arbitrary, less complicated than in Europe. It is in some way improvised each day (illegible word), each man following the utility of the moment. More value is attached there to the intention of pleasing than to the means that are used to do so. Custom, tone, example influence the actions of men, but they do not link their conduct to them in as absolute a manner as in the civilized portions of the Old World.

It would be good to insert here a small portrait in the manner of *Lettres persanes* or of *Les Caractères* of La Bruyère. But I lack the facts. [They (ed.)] must be taken from France.

You notice something analogous among us in Europe.

Manners generally come from the very heart of mores; and sometimes they result as well from an arbitrary convention between certain men. They are at the same time natural and acquired.

When men see that they are first without question and without difficulty; when every day they have before their eyes the great matters that occupy them, leaving the details to others, and when they live with a wealth that they did not acquire and they are not afraid of losing, you easily imagine that they feel a sort of superb disdain for the petty interests and material

---

[In the margin: Perhaps the notes of Beaumont will provide [some (ed.)].]

Among the nations of Europe where a great inequality of conditions still reigns, most of the small daily relationships of men with each other continue to be subjected to fixed and traditional rules that give society, despite the changes that are taking place within it, an unchanging aspect. On the contrary, among peoples whose social state is already very democratic, the exceptions to this rule become so numerous every day that it is difficult to say if the rule exists or where it is found.

So if you see each man dress himself more or less as he pleases, speak or keep quiet as he desires, accept or reject generally received formulations, subject himself to the rule of fashion or escape from it with impunity, if each man escapes in some way from common *practice* and easily gets himself exempted, do not laugh; the moment has come to think and to act. These things are trivial, but the cause that produces them is serious. *You have before your eyes the slightest symptoms of a great illness.* Be sure that when each man believes himself entitled to decide alone the form of an item of clothing or the proprieties of language, he does not hesitate to judge all things by himself, and when the small social conventions are so badly observed, count on the fact that an important revolution has taken place in the great social conventions.

So these indications alone should be enough for you to understand that a great revolution has already taken place in human societies, that it is good from now on to think about tightening the social bond which on all sides is trying to become looser, and that, no longer able to force all men to do the same things, a means must be found to lead them to want to do so (YTC, CVk, 2, pp. 33–37).

You find this note in the *rubish:*

There is in the bundle entitled: *Detached piece on the philosophical method of the Americans* . . . ideas and sentences that I should make use of when I review the chapters relative to the relationships of the son with the children [*sic*], of the servant with the master . . ./

Idem when I arrive at the customs of society. *In fine* good piece./

Idem at the chapter on revolutions. Note at the head of the piece entitled new sources of beliefs./

26 November 1838 (*Rubish*, 2).

cares of life, and that they have a natural grandeur in thought that words and manners reveal.

In democratic countries, manners usually have little grandeur, because private life in them is very limited. Manners are often common, because thought has only a few opportunities to rise above the preoccupation with domestic interests.[d]

True dignity of manners consists of always appearing in your place, neither higher, nor lower;[e] that is within reach of the peasant as of the prince. In democracies all places seem doubtful; as a result, it happens that manners, which are often arrogant there, are rarely dignified. Moreover, they are never either very well-ordered or very studied.[f]

d. To put with manners./
 August 1837.
 How under democracy citizens, although perfectly equal civilly and politically, having daily relationships and no ideas of preeminence over each other, divide themselves however into distinct societies for the charm and usefulness of life, according to their education and their fortune.
 That the continual jumble and meeting in the same places for the same enjoyments of dissimilar men is a crude notion of equality (*Rubish,* 2).

e. "I believe that good taste like beauty has its foundation in nature itself. It is or is not, apart from the will of men; but the natural rules in the matter of good taste can only be collected and put in order by a select society, enlightened enough and small enough in number always to hold onto the rules that it acknowledged at one time as the best. So there is something conventional in matters of taste, whereas there is hardly any convention possible under democracies" (*Rubish,* 2).

f. So an aristocratic class not only has grand manners, but it also has well-ordered and studied manners. Although the form of human actions originally emerged there, as elsewhere, from the substance of sentiments and ideas, it ended over time by being independent of sentiments and ideas; and custom there finally became an invisible and blind force that constrains different beings to act in an analogous manner and gives all of them a common appearance.
 Among the multitude of all the small particular societies into which the great democratic body is divided, there is not a single one that presents a similar tableau.
 There are rich men in a democracy, but there is no rich class. You find powerful men there, but not powerful families, or those that have habitually, over several generations, hereditarily had before their eyes the great spectacle of grandeur; if by chance there are a few of this kind, they are not naturally or solidly attached to each other and do not form a separate body within the general society. So they cannot

Men who live in democracies are too mobile for a certain number of them to succeed in establishing a code of savoir-faire and to be able to make sure that it is followed. So each man there acts more or less as he likes, and a certain incoherence in manners always reigns, because manners conform to the individual sentiments and ideas of each man, rather than to an ideal model given in advance for the imitation of all.

Nonetheless, this is much more apparent at the moment when aristocracy has just fallen than when it has been destroyed for a long time.

The new political institutions and the new mores then gather in the same places men still made prodigiously dissimilar by education and habits and often force them to live together; this makes great colorful mixtures emerge at every moment. You still remember that a precise code of politeness existed; but you no longer know either what it contains or where it is to be found. Men have lost the common law of manners, and they have not yet decided to do without it; but each one tries hard to form a certain arbitrary and changing rule out of the debris of former customs; so that manners have neither the regularity nor the grandeur that they often exhibit among aristocratic peoples, nor the simple and free turn that you sometimes notice in democracy; they are at the very same time constrained and unconstrained.

That is not the normal state.

When equality is complete and old, all men, having more or less the same ideas and doing more or less the same things, have no need to agree or to copy each other in order to act and to speak in the same way; you constantly see a multitude of small dissimilarities in their manners; you do not notice any great differences. They never resemble each other perfectly, because they do not have the same model; they are never very dissimilar,

---

regulate in a detailed and invariable way the external actions of their members. If they had the will to do so, time is lacking. For each day they are themselves swept along, in spite of their efforts, in the democratic movement that sweeps everything along.

Fragment contained in the jacket of the manuscript to which note a for p. 1262 makes reference.

because they share the same condition. At first view, you would say that the manners of all Americans are exactly the same. It is only when considering them very closely that you notice the particularities by which they all differ.[g]

The English have made much fun of American manners; and what is peculiar is that most of those who have given us such an amusing portrait belonged to the middle classes of England, to whom this same portrait very much applies. So that these merciless detractors usually offer the example of what they are blaming in the United States; they do not notice that they are scoffing at themselves, to the great delight of the aristocracy of their country.[h]

Nothing harms democracy more than the external form of its mores. Many men would readily become accustomed to its vices, who cannot bear its manners.

I cannot, however, accept that there is nothing to praise in the manners of democratic peoples.

Among aristocratic nations, all those who are near the first class usually try hard to resemble it, which produces very ridiculous and very insipid imitations. If democratic peoples do not possess the model of grand manners, they at least escape from the obligation of seeing bad copies every day.

In democracies, manners are never as refined as among aristocratic peoples; but they also never appear as crude. You hear neither the gross words of the populace, nor the noble and select expressions of the great lords. There is often triviality in the mores, but not brutality or baseness.

[If it is true that the men who live among these peoples scarcely ever offer to render small services, they readily oblige you in your needs; manners are less polite than in aristocracies and more benevolent.]

I said that in democracies a precise code regarding savoir-faire cannot evolve. This has its disadvantage and its advantages. In aristocracies, the

g. "You can say however that customs, mores are more well-ordered in the United States than in France. That results from Puritan opinions that *order* life and from commercial habits that *direct* it" (*Rubish,* 2).

h. Perhaps Tocqueville is alluding to Basil Hall.

rules of propriety impose on each man the same appearance; they make all the members of the same class similar, despite their particular propensities; they adorn the natural and hide it. Among democratic peoples, manners are neither as studied nor as well-ordered; but they are often more sincere. They form like a light and poorly woven veil, through which the true sentiments and individual ideas of each man are easily seen. So the form and the substance of human actions there often have an intimate rapport, and, if the great tableau of humanity is less ornate, it is more true. This is why, in a sense, you can say that the effect of democracy is not precisely to give men certain manners, but to prevent them from having manners.

You can sometimes find again in a democracy some of the sentiments, passions, virtues and vices of aristocracy, but not its manners. The latter are lost and disappear forever, when the democratic revolution is complete.[j]

It seems that there is nothing more durable than the manners of an aristocratic class; for it still preserves them for some time after having lost its property and its power; nor anything as fragile, for scarcely have they disappeared than any trace of them is no longer found, and it is difficult to say what they were from the moment that they are no more. A change in the social state works this wonder; a few generations are enough.

The principal features of aristocracy remain engraved in history when aristocracy is destroyed, but the light and delicate forms of its mores disappear from the memory of men, almost immediately after its fall. Men cannot imagine them once they are no longer before their eyes. They escape without men seeing or feeling it. For, in order to feel the type of refined pleasure obtained by the distinction and the choice of manners, habit and education must have prepared the heart, and the taste for manners is easily lost with the practice.

Thus, not only can democratic peoples not have the manners of aristocracy, but they do not conceive or desire them; they do not imagine them;

---

j. "In democracies *individuals* very distinguished in taste and manners can be found, but such a *society* [v: class] is never found" (*Rubish*, 2).

the manners of aristocracy are, for democratic peoples, as if they had never been.

[You would be wrong to believe that the model of aristocratic manners can at least be preserved among a few remnants of the old aristocracy. The members of a fallen aristocracy can indeed preserve the prejudices of their fathers, but not their manners.]

Too much importance must not be attached to this loss; but it is permitted to regret it.[k]

I know that more than once it has happened that the same men have had very distinguished mores and very vulgar sentiments; the interior of courts has shown enough that great appearance could often hide very base hearts. But, if the manners of aristocracy did not bring about virtue, they sometimes ornamented virtue itself. It was not an ordinary spectacle to see a numerous and powerful class, in which all of the external actions of life seemed, at every instant, to reveal natural nobility of sentiments and thoughts, refinement and consistency of tastes, and urbanity of mores.

---

k. ≠It is often by necessity as much as by taste that the rich [v: the upper classes] of democracies copy the people's ways of acting. ≠ In the United States the most opulent citizens show haughty manners only in the intimacy of their home [v: are very careful not to flaunt their grandeur]. . . . They readily listen to them [the people (ed.)], and constantly speak to them.

The rich of democracies draw toward them the poor man and attach him to themselves by manners more than by benefits. The very greatness of the benefits, which brings to light the difference of conditions, causes a secret irritation in those who profit from them. But simplicity of manners has nearly irresistible charms. Their familiarity inveigles, and even their crudeness does not always displease. This truth penetrates only very slowly the mind of the rich.

[In the margin: They go out constantly to mingle with the people. They readily listen to them and speak to them every day in the countries of Europe that turn to democracy.]

They usually understand it only when it is too late to make use of it. They agree to do good to the men of the people, but they want to continue to hold them carefully at a distance. They believe that is enough, but they are wrong. They would ruin themselves in this way without warming the heart of the population that surrounds them. It is not the sacrifice of their money that is asked of them, it is that of their pride.

[In the margin: They resist it as long as the revolution lasts and they accept it only a long time after it has ended.]

26 September 1839 [1837? (ed.)] (YTC, CVk, 1, pp. 6–7).

The manners of aristocracy gave beautiful illusions about human nature; and, although the tableau was often false, you experienced a noble pleasure in looking at it.[m]

m. *Democracy. Manners.*

In France the elegant simplicity of manners is hardly found except among men belonging to old families; the others show themselves either very affected or very vulgar in their way of acting. That comes, I think, from the state of revolution in which we are still. It is a time of crisis that must be borne. Amid the confusion that reigns in all things, *new* men do not know precisely what must be done in order to distinguish themselves from the crowd. Some believe that the best means to show yourself superior is to be rude and forward; others think that on the contrary you must be particular about even the least details for fear of betraying your common origin at some point. Both are anxious about the results of their efforts, and their agitation betrays itself constantly amid their simulated assurance. Men who, on the contrary, have had a long habit of being without question and by heredity the first are not anxious about these things. They have a natural ease, and they attain without thinking about it the goal toward which the others tend, most often without being able to attain it. A time will come, I hope, when there will be among us a fixed and settled model of what is suitable and in good taste, and each man will conform to it without difficulty. Then to all well-bred men will happen what happened formerly within the aristocracy, when there was a certain code of proprieties to which each man submitted without discussing it and so to speak without knowing it.

You see that my tendencies are always democratic. I am a partisan of democracy without having any illusion about its faults and without failing to recognize its dangers. I am even all the more so as I believe that I see both more clearly, because I am profoundly convinced that there is no way to prevent its triumph, and that it is only by marching with it and by directing its progress as much as possible that you can decrease the evils it brings and produce the good things that it promises (*Rubish,* 2). This fragment is written on the writing paper of Tocqueville.

CHAPTER 15[a]

Of the Gravity of Americans and Why It Does Not Prevent Them from Often Doing Thoughtless Things[b]

The men who live in democratic countries do not value those sorts of unsophisticated, turbulent and crude diversions to which the people devote themselves in aristocracies; they find them childish or insipid. They show scarcely more taste for the intellectual and refined amusements of the aristocratic classes; they must have something productive and substantial in their pleasures, and they want to mix material enjoyments with their joy.

In aristocratic societies, the people readily abandon themselves to the impulses of a tumultuous and noisy gaiety that abruptly tears them away from the contemplation of their miseries; the inhabitants of democracies do not like to feel drawn violently out of themselves in this way, and they always lose sight of themselves with regret. To these frivolous transports, they prefer the grave and silent relaxations that resemble business affairs and do not cause them to forget them entirely. [In this sense you can say that gambling is an entirely democratic pastime.]

There is an American who, instead of going during his moments of leisure to dance joyously in the public square, as the men of his profession

---

a. "The Americans are grave because they are constantly occupied by serious things, and they are thoughtless because they have only an instant of attention to give to each one of those things" (YTC, CVf, p. 46).

b. The *rubish* indicates that in the beginning the chapter was divided into three distinct chapters:

1. Gravity of the Americans.
2. Amusements in democracies.
3. Why democratic peoples despite their gravity act thoughtlessly (*Rubish,* 2).

continue to do in a great part of Europe, withdraws alone deep within his house to drink. This man enjoys two pleasures at once: he thinks about his trade, and he gets drunk decently at home.c

[≠I have visited peoples very ignorant, very miserable and completely strangers to their own affairs; to me, they appeared, in general, joyous. I have traveled across a country whose inhabitants, enlightened and rich, directed themselves in everything; I always found them grave and often sad [v: worried and taciturn].≠]

I believed that the English formed the most serious nation that existed on earth, but I saw the Americans, and I changed my opinion.d

[≠The inhabitant of the United States has an austere appearance, something anxious and preoccupied reigns in his look; his manner is constrained and you easily see that he never opens to external impressions anything except the smallest part of his soul. He is sometimes somber and always grave.≠]

I do not want to say that temperament does not count for much in the character of the inhabitants of the United States. I think, nonetheless, that the political institutions contribute to it still more.

I believe that the gravity of the Americans arises in part from their pride. In democratic countries, the poor man himself has a high idea of his personal value. He views himself with satisfaction and readily believes that others are looking at him. In this frame of mind, he carefully watches his words and his actions and does not let himself go, for fear of disclosing what he lacks. He imagines that, in order to appear dignified, he must remain grave.

But I notice another more intimate and more powerful cause that instinctively produces among the Americans this gravity that astonishes me.

Under despotism, peoples give themselves from time to time to outbursts of a wild joy; but, in general, they are cheerless and reserved, because they are afraid.

In absolute monarchies, which custom and mores temper, peoples often

c. Originally, the first chapter ended here.
d. "There is also something *Puritan* and *English* in this gravity of the Americans./ "Gravity that is often due to an absence of serenity in the soul" (*Rubish,* 2).

display an even-tempered and lively mood, because having some liberty and great enough security, they are excluded from the most important cares of life; but all free peoples are grave, because their minds are habitually absorbed by the sight of some dangerous or difficult project.

It is so above all among free peoples who are constituted as democracies. Then, in all classes, an infinite number of men is found who are constantly preoccupied by the serious matters of government, and those who do not think about directing the public fortune give themselves entirely to the concern of increasing their private fortune. Among such a people, gravity is no longer particular to certain men; it becomes a national habit.

You speak about the small democracies of antiquity, whose citizens came to the public square with crowns of roses, and who spent nearly all their time in dances and in spectacles. I do not believe in such republics any more than that of Plato; or, if things happened there as we are told, I am not afraid to assert that these so-called democracies were formed out of elements very different from ours, and that they had with the latter only the name in common.

[<As for me, I cannot prevent myself from believing that a people will be more serious as its institutions and its mores become more democratic.>]

It must not be believed, however, that amid all their labors, the men who live in democracies consider themselves to be pitied; the opposite is noticed. There are no men who value their conditions as much as those men do. They would find life without savor, if you delivered them from the cares that torment them, and they are more attached to their concerns than aristocratic peoples to their pleasures.

[Although the Americans are more serious than the English, you meet among them far fewer melancholy men.[e] Among a people where all citizens work, there are sometimes great anxieties, miseries and bitter distresses, but not melancholy.]

e. "No melancholy in America. Idea to treat separately afterward.
"[In the margin] Louis" (*Rubish*, 2).

I wonder why the same democratic peoples, who are so grave, sometimes behave in so thoughtless a way.[f]

The Americans, who almost always maintain a steady bearing and a cold manner, nonetheless allow themselves often to be carried very far beyond the limits of reason by a sudden passion or an unthinking opinion, and it happens that they seriously commit singular blunders.

This contrast should not be surprising.

[<Amid the tumult and the thousand discordant noises that are heard within a democracy, sometimes the voice of truth becomes lost.>]

There is a sort of ignorance that arises from extreme publicity. In despotic States, men do not know how to act, because they are told nothing; among democratic nations, they often act haphazardly, because the desire has been to tell them everything. The first do not know, and the others forget. The principal features of each tableau disappear for them among the multitude of details.

You are astonished by all the imprudent remarks that a public man sometimes allows himself in free States and above all in democratic States, without being compromised by them; while, in absolute monarchies, a few words that escape by chance are enough to expose him forever and ruin him without resources.

That is explained by what precedes. When you speak in the middle of a great crowd, many words are not heard, or are immediately erased from the memory of those who hear; but in the silence of a mute and immobile multitude, the slightest whispers strike the ear.

In democracies, men are never settled; a thousand chance occurrences make them constantly change place, and almost always something unexpected and, so to speak, improvised reigns in their life. Consequently they are often forced to do what they learned badly, to speak about what they scarcely understand, and to give themselves to work for which a long apprenticeship has not prepared them.

In aristocracies, each man has only a single goal that he pursues constantly. But among democratic peoples, the existence of man is more com-

---

f. The third chapter began with this paragraph.

plicated; it is rare that the same mind there does not embrace several things at once, and often things very foreign to each other. Since he cannot understand all of them well, he easily becomes satisfied with imperfect notions.

When the inhabitant of democracies is not pressed by his needs, he is at least by his desires; for among all the goods that surround him, he sees none that is entirely out of his reach. So he does everything with haste, contents himself with approximations, and never stops except for a moment to consider each of his actions.

His curiosity is at once insatiable and satisfied at little cost, for he values knowing a lot quickly, rather than knowing anything well.

He hardly has time, and he soon loses the taste to go deeper.

Thus, democratic peoples are grave, because their social and political state leads them constantly to concern themselves with serious things; and they act thoughtlessly, because they give only a little time and attention to each one of these things.

The habit of inattention must be considered as the greatest vice of the democratic mind.

CHAPTER 16[a]

Why the National Vanity of the Americans Is More Anxious and More Quarrelsome Than That of the English[b]

All free peoples take pride in themselves, but national pride does not appear among all in the same manner.

The Americans, in their relationships with foreigners, seem impatient with the least censure and insatiable for praise. The slightest praise pleases them, and the greatest rarely is enough to satisfy them; they badger you every moment to get you to praise them; and, if you resist their insistent demands, they praise themselves. You would say that, doubting their own merit, they want to have its picture before their eyes at every instant. Their vanity is not only greedy, it is anxious and envious. It grants nothing while constantly asking. It seeks compliments and is quarrelsome at the same time.

a. The national vanity of the English is measured and haughty, it neither grants or asks anything.

[In the margin: Chapter perhaps to delete.]

That of the Americans seeks compliments, is quarrelsome and anxious.

On this point, English mores have taken the turn of ideas of the aristocracy which, possessing incalculable and inalienable advantages, enjoys them with insouciance and with pride.

The Americans have equally transferred the habits of their private vanity to their national vanity (YTC, CVf, p. 46).

b. On the jacket of the manuscript: "I do not know if this chapter should be kept. The eternal comparison is found there. Moreover, I have said analogous things elsewhere, particularly in the first work, relating to the vanity that democratic institutions give to the Americans. *America is a country of liberty,* vol. II, pp. 115 and 116." Tocqueville is alluding to the part devoted to public spirit in the United States, pp. 116–21 of the 1835 edition (pp. 384–89 of the first volume of this edition).

I say to an American that the country that he inhabits is beautiful; he replies: "It is true, there is no country like it in the world!" I admire the liberty enjoyed by the inhabitants and he answers me: "What a precious gift liberty is! But there are very few peoples who are worthy to enjoy it." I remark on the purity of morals that reigns in the United States: "I imagine," he says, "that a foreigner, who has been struck by the corruption that is seen in all the other nations, is astonished by this spectacle." I finally abandon him to self-contemplation; but he returns to me and does not leave until he has succeeded in making me repeat what I have just said to him. You cannot imagine a patriotism[c] more troublesome and more talkative. It tires even those who honor it.[d]

It is not like this with the English. The Englishman calmly enjoys the real or imaginary advantages that in his eyes his country possesses. If he grants nothing to other nations, he also asks nothing for his own. The disapproval of foreigners does not upset him and their praise hardly gratifies him. He maintains vis-à-vis the entire world a reserve full of disdain and ignorance. His pride does not need to be fed; it lives on itself.[e]

That two peoples, who not long ago sprang from the same stock, appear so opposite to each other in the manner of feeling and speaking, is remarkable.

In aristocratic countries, the great possess immense privileges, on which their pride rests, without trying to feed on the slight advantages that are

c. "Patriotism, reasoned egoism" (YTC, CVa, p. 4).

d. I recall that one day in New York, I found myself in the company of a young American woman, daughter of a man whose discoveries in the art of navigation will be famous forever. I had noticed her [v: M. F. was no less remarkable] because of her extreme flirtatiousness as much as for her stunning beauty. Now, I happened one day to allow myself to say to her while laughing that she was worthy to be a French woman. Immediately her gaze became severe; the engaging smile that was usually on her lips suddenly vanished. Full of indignation, she gave me the most ridiculous and the most amusing look of a prude {that I had ever seen in my life} and wrapped herself in an impassive dignity. Do not think that what offended her so much was to be flirtatious; she would have readily accepted condemnation on this point; it was to be not completely American (*Rubish*, 2). It probably concerned Julia Fulton (see George W. Pierson, *Tocqueville and Beaumont in America*, p. 142).

e. To the side: "<It is the aristocracy that on this point has given the turn to the ideas and habits of the English nation.>"

related. Since these privileges came to them by inheritance, they consider them, in a way, as a part of themselves, or at least as a natural right, inherent in their person. So they have a calm sentiment of their superiority; they do not think about praising prerogatives that everyone notices and that no one denies to them. They are not surprised enough by them to speak about them. They remain immobile in their solitary grandeur, sure that everyone sees them without their trying to show themselves, and sure that no one will undertake to take their grandeur away from them.

When an aristocracy leads public affairs, its national pride naturally takes this reserved, unconcerned and haughty form, and all the other classes of the nation imitate it.

When on the contrary conditions differ little, the least advantages have importance. Since each man sees around him a million men who possess all the same or analogous advantages, pride becomes demanding and jealous; it becomes attached to miserable nothings and defends them stubbornly.

In democracies, since conditions are very mobile, men almost always have recently acquired the advantages they possess; this makes them feel an infinite pleasure in putting them on view, in order to show to others and to attest to themselves that they enjoy those advantages; and since, at every instant, these advantages can happen to escape them, they are constantly alarmed and work hard to demonstrate that they still have them. Men who live in democracies love their country in the same way that they love themselves, and they transfer the habits of their private vanity to their national vanity.

The anxious and insatiable vanity of democratic peoples is due so much to the equality and to the fragility of conditions, that the members of the proudest nobility show absolutely the same passion in the small parts of their existence where there is something unstable or disputed.

An aristocratic class always differs profoundly from the other classes of the nation by the extent and the perpetuity of its prerogatives; but sometimes it happens that several of its members differ from each other only by small fleeting advantages that they can lose and gain every day.

We have seen the members of a powerful aristocracy, gathered in a capital or in a court, argue fiercely over the frivolous privileges that depend on the caprice of fashion or on the will of the master. They then showed toward one another precisely the same puerile jealousies that animate the men of democracies, the same ardor to grab the least advantages that their equals disputed with them, and the same need to put on view to all the advantages that they enjoyed.

If courtiers ever dared to have national pride, I do not doubt that they would show a pride entirely similar to that of democratic peoples.

How the Appearance of Society in the United States Is at the Very Same Time Agitated and Monotonousᵇ

It seems that nothing is more appropriate for exciting and feeding curiosity than the appearance of the United States. Fortunes, ideas, laws vary constantly there. You would say that immobile nature itself is mobile, so much is it transformed every day under the hand of man.

In the long run, however, the sight of so agitated a society seems monotonous, and after contemplating for a while a tableau so changeable, the spectator becomes bored.

Among aristocratic peoples, each man is more or less fixed in his sphere; but men are prodigiously dissimilar; they have essentially different passions, ideas, habits and tastes. Nothing stirs, everything varies.

In democracies, on the contrary, all men are similar and do more or less similar things. They are subject, it is true, to great and continual vicissi-

---

a. "The appearance of American society is agitated because men and things constantly change place. It is monotonous because all the changes are similar.

"There is in America truly speaking only a single passion, love of wealth, which is monotonous. For this passion to be satisfied, small regular and methodical actions are needed, which is also monotonous" (YTC, CVf, pp. 46–47).

b. The jacket of the chapter bears this date: "≠4 January 1838.≠" It contains three loose sheets contained in a jacket on which you read: "RUBISH OF THE CHAPTER ENTITLED: HOW THE APPEARANCE OF SOCIETY IN THE UNITED STATES AND THE LIFE OF MEN IS [*sic*] AT THE VERY SAME TIME AGITATED AND MONOTONOUS./

"This rubish contains more things than usual to see again." Despite Tocqueville's remark, the notes do not present many differences with the chapter. The other *rubish* also contains notes and drafts of this chapter.

tudes; but, since the same successes and the same reverses recur continually, only the name of the actors is different; the play is the same. The appearance of American society is agitated, because men and things change constantly; and it is monotonous, because all the changes are the same.

The men who live in democratic times have many passions; but most of their passions end in the love of wealth or come from it. That is not because their souls are smaller, but because then the importance of money is really greater.[c]

When fellow citizens are all independent and indifferent, it is only by paying that you can obtain the cooperation of each one of them; this infinitely multiplies the use of wealth and increases its value.

Since the prestige that was attached to ancient things has disappeared, birth, state, profession no longer distinguish men, or scarcely distinguish them; there remains hardly anything except money that creates very visible differences between them and that can put a few of them beyond comparison. The distinction that arises from wealth is increased by the disappearance and lessening of all the other distinctions.

c. Among all the passions of the Americans there is one that the influence of the social state has made predominate over all the others and has so to speak made unique. I am speaking about the love of wealth. The inhabitant of the United States has put his energy and his boldness in the service of this passion, which I would not be afraid to call central since in America all the movements of the soul end up there. Now, love of wealth[1] has this singular character that, however disordered it is, it needs order and *rules* to be satisfied. It is methodical even in the greatest deviations. So the same passion that leads the American, at every moment, to risk his fortune, his reputation, his life in order to gain well-being, forces him to subject himself to laborious and peaceful habits and *binds* his actions to certain precise and detailed *rules* that do not vary. It is by a succession of small, regular and uniform actions that [he (ed.)] arrives at opulence or ruin and despair, and you can say, although at first it seems surprising, that *it is* the very violence of his desires that contributes more than anything else to making his existence monotonous. His passions disturb and compromise his life, but do not make it varied.

(1) Édouard observes rightly that it is not all love of wealth and among all people who have this character, but in certain circumstances and among certain nations, among certain men, and that that must be made apparent (*Rubish*, 2).

Among aristocratic peoples, money leads to only a few points on the vast circumference of desires; in democracies, it seems to lead to all.

So love of wealth, as principal or accessory, is usually found at the bottom of the actions of Americans; this gives all their passions a family air, and does not take long to make the tableau tiring.

This perpetual return of the same passion is monotonous; the particular procedures that this passion uses to become satisfied are monotonous as well.

In a sound and peaceful democracy, like that of the United States, where you cannot become rich either by war, or by public employment, or by political confiscations, love of wealth directs men principally toward industry. Now, industry, which often brings such great disturbances and such great disasters, can nonetheless prosper only with the aid of very regular habits and by a long succession of small, very uniform actions. Habits are all the more regular and actions more uniform as the passion is more intense. You can say that it is the very violence of their desires that makes the Americans so methodical. It disturbs their soul, but it makes their life orderly.

What I say about America applies, moreover, to nearly all the men of our times. Variety is disappearing from the human species; the same ways of acting, thinking and feeling are found in all the corners of the world.[d] That happens not only because all peoples are frequenting each

d. Originality./
    Perhaps to put with monotony./
    It is necessary to be different from your fellows in order to envisage the world in another way [v: to think differently from them].
    It is necessary to feel strong and independent from them in order to *dare* to act in your own way and to follow alone your own path [v: to show what you think].
    These two *conditions* are found only where *conditions* are very unequal, and where men exist who are powerful enough by themselves to *dare* to show without fear what distinguishes them from the rest of men and sometimes to glory in it.
    The result is that originality of mind and manners [v: of ideas and of actions] is much more common among aristocratic peoples than among others, above all among aristocratic peoples who enjoy {great} {political} liberty. The political state then allows the differences given birth by the social state to be shown.

other more and are copying each other more faithfully, but also because in each country men, putting aside more and more the ideas and sentiments particular to a caste, to a profession, to a family, come simultaneously to what is closest to the constitution of man, which is everywhere the same.[e] They thus become similar, although they do not imitate each other. They are like travelers spread throughout a large forest in which all roads lead to the same point. If all see the central point at the same time and turn their steps in this direction, they come imperceptibly closer to one another, without seeking each other, without seeing each other, without knowing each other, and finally they will be surprised to see themselves gathered in the same place.[f] All peoples who take as the aim of their studies and their imitation, not a particular man, but man himself, will end up by meeting with the same mores, like these travelers at the center point.

Among such a people originality ends by becoming a national habit that is found afterward among the individuals of all ranks.[1]

Each man ends by contracting the habit of following in everything his personal *impulses,* and originality becomes a trait of the national physiognomy that is found among all individuals.

There is no man who gives more prominence to individual [v: capricious] mood and who pushes singularity closer to peculiar ways and extravagance than the English. There are none ≠of them≠ who depart less from the common road than the Americans. <The most powerful confine themselves there as narrowly as the least.>

But the Americans and the English have the same origin. The social state alone makes the difference.

20 April 1838.

1. Can you say that originality is a habit? (YTC, CVk, 1, pp. 8–9).

e. After the prejudices of profession, caste, family have disappeared in order to yield to generative and general ideas, men are still divided by the prejudices of nation, which present the final obstacle to the boldness and generalization of thought, but this classification of human thought by nation cannot endure for long if several nations adopt a democratic social state at the same time. Since all these nations then take man himself as goal of their inquiry and since man is the same everywhere, a multitude of their ideas ends up by being similar, not because they imitate each other (which often happens), but because they are simultaneously coming closer to the same thing without consulting about it.

[In the margin] The destruction of small sovereignties and the destruction of castes and of aristocratic ranks produce analogous effects; from them result a generalization of thought and a greater boldness to conceive new thoughts (*Rubish,* 2).

f. "<This central point in philosophy is the study of man>" (*Rubish,* 2).

CHAPTER 18[a]

Of Honor in the United States and in Democratic Societies[1]

It seems that men use two very distinct methods in the public judgment that they make about the actions of their fellows: sometimes they judge

---

a. Honor derives from the particular needs of certain men. Every particular association has its honor.

This proved by feudal honor, applicable to American honor.

What must be understood by American honor.

1. It differs from feudal honor by the nature of its prescriptions.

2. It differs from it also by the number of its prescriptions, by their clarity, their precision; the power with which it makes them followed.

That more and more true as citizens become more similar and nations more alike (YTC, CVf, p. 47).

The drafts of this chapter are found in three different jackets. Two of them bear the same title as the chapter; the third bears the following title: "WHY MEN ARE MORE UNCONCERNED ABOUT THEIR HONOR IN DEMOCRACIES. To *examine separately.* Subtle and perhaps false idea."

In pencil on the first page of an old version: "<The chapter is a bit too theoretical. General impression of Édouard>" (*Rubish*, 2). In the beginning, the ideas on honor seem to have belonged to the chapters on the army (see note b of pp. 1170–71).

1. *The word* honor *is not always taken in the same sense in French.*

1. *It means first the esteem, the glory, the consideration that you get from your fellows; it is in this sense that you say* win honor.

2. *Honor also means the ensemble of rules by the aid of which you obtain this glory, this esteem, and this consideration. This is how you say* that a man has always conformed strictly to the laws of honor; that he has forfeited honor. *While writing the present chapter, I have always taken the word* honor *in this last sense.*

[The reader will perhaps find this note superfluous, but when your language is poor, you must not be miserly with definitions.]

them according to the simple notions of the just and the unjust, which are spread over the whole earth; sometimes they assess them with the aid of very particular notions that belong only to one country and to one period. Often it happens that these two rules differ; sometimes they conflict with each other, but never do they merge entirely or cancel each other out.[b]

Honor, in the time of its greatest power, governs the will more than belief, and men, even if they submit without hesitation and without murmuring to its commandments, still feel, by a kind of obscure but powerful instinct, that a more general, more ancient and more holy law exists, which they sometimes disobey without ceasing to know it. There are actions that have been judged upright and dishonoring at the same time. The refusal of a duel has often been in this category.

I believe that you can explain these phenomena other than by the caprice of certain individuals and certain peoples, as has been done until now.

[The whim of men enters into it only partly.]

Humanity feels permanent and general needs, which have given birth to moral laws; to their disregard all men have naturally attached, in all places and in all times, the ideas of blame and shame. They have called *doing evil* to evade them, *doing good* to submit to them.[c]

Established as well, within the vast human association, are more restricted associations, which are called peoples, and amid the latter, others smaller still, which are called classes or castes.

Each one of these associations forms like a particular species within the

b. On the jacket of the manuscript: "The capital vice of this entire chapter, what makes it sound *false,* is that I give to honor a unique source while it has several. Honor is without doubt based on particular needs arising either from the social and political state, or from the physical constitution and climate. It arises as well, whatever I say, from the whim of men.

"Whim has a part, but it is the smallest.

"<Baugy, 27 January 1838.>"

c. "There are certain general rules that are necessary to the existence and to the well-being of human societies whatever the time, the place, the laws; individual conscience points these rules out to all men and public reason forces them to conform to them. Voluntary obedience to each of these general laws is virtue" (YTC, CVk, 1, pp. 58–59).

human race; and although it does not differ essentially from the mass of men, it holds itself a little apart and feels needs that are its own. These are the special needs that modify in some fashion and in certain countries the way of envisaging human actions and the esteem that is suitable to give to them.[d]

The general and permanent interest of humanity is that men do not kill each other; but it can happen that the particular and temporary interest of a people or of a class is, in certain cases, to excuse and even to honor the homicide.[e]

d. I must be careful, Éd[ouard (ed.)] told me, not to destroy in this way the (illegible word) of virtue and to bring the mind of the reader to the conclusion that virtue is not always necessary, or even useful to men. To reflect on that./

I fear being too absolute by saying that honor comes from the special needs of a special society, and that consequently it is always useful and often necessary for its existence, which would legitimize in a way all its immoralities and its extravagances to the detriment of virtue. To say that honor is explained by the special constitution of associations, that is incontestable, but to add that it is *necessary* for their existence, isn't that to go too far in a multitude of cases?

There is in honor an element different from the needs and the interests of those who conceive it. That seems to me at least very probable upon examination.

[To the side: Use the Blacks to prove how the point of honor can become intense (illegible word) powerful, as soon as the social state departs from nature.]

Religion, climate, race must influence the notions of honor. Perhaps it would be necessary to grant a part to all of that. My idea would only be more correct, by becoming less general and less absolute.

Let us never lose sight of the fact that honor is the ensemble of opinions relating to the judgment of human actions, in view of the glory or the shame that our fellows attach to them. This forms a radical difference between honor and virtue, apart from all the other differences.

[To the side] Say somewhere that an extraordinary honor announces an extraordinary social state and vice versa. That generalizes the past in a useful way (YTC, CVk, 1, pp. 61–62).

e. There is an idea that crosses my mind at every instant; I must finally try to look at it one moment and confront it.

I fear that the outcome of my chapter is that true and false, just and unjust, good and evil, vice and virtue are only relative things depending on the perspective from which you see them, a result that I would be very upset to reach, for I believe it false; and in addition such an opinion would be in clear contradiction to the ensemble of my opinions. I am at this moment too tired of my subject to see these questions clearly, but I must come back to them with a fresh mind./

[In the margin: Good and evil exist apart from the blame or the praise of certain

Honor is nothing other than this particular rule based on a particular condition, with the aid of which a people or a class distributes blame or praise.[f]

There is nothing more unproductive for the human mind than an abstract idea. So I hasten to run toward facts. An example will cast light on my thought.

I will choose the most extraordinary type of honor that has ever appeared in the world, and the one that we know the best: aristocratic honor born

---

men and even of humanity. What I am looking for here is not what is good or evil in an absolute way, but what men praise or blame. This is capital.

How, moreover, to define evil, if not what is harmful to humanity, and good what is useful to it?

Where is our (three illegible words)?

I do not want to say that there is no absolute good in human actions, but only that the particular interests of certain men can lead them to attribute arbitrarily to certain actions a particular value, and that this value becomes the rule of those who act with praise or blame in view, that is, by *honor.*]

To act by *virtue,* that is to do what you believe good without other motive than the pleasure of doing it and the idea of complying with a duty. To act by *honor,* that is to act not with absolute good or evil in view, but in consideration of what our fellows think of it and of the shame or the glory that will result from it.

The rule of the first man is within himself, it is *conscience.*

The rule of the other is outside, it is *opinion.*

The goal of this chapter is to show the origin and the effects of this opinion (YTC, CVk, 1, pp. 62–63).

f. The recompense of the man who follows honor is more assured and more immediate than *that of the one who follows virtue. That is why men have never taught [that (ed.)] virtue* is in view of God and of yourself, *honor in view of opinion.* Why? So that you can place in the other world the recompense of those who submit to the *laws of honor.* Judgment, discernment, spiritual effort are necessary for virtue; only memory is necessary to conform to honor.

[In the margin: Honor, visible rule, *convenient for actions, less perfect,* more sure./

Sometimes finally the rule makes an action indifferent in the eyes of virtue into a matter of glory or of shame. Virtue, flexible; honor, inflexible] (YTC, CVk, 1, p. 60).

within feudal society. I will explain it with the aid of what precedes, and I will explain what precedes by it.[g]

I do not have to search here when and how the aristocracy of the Middle Ages was born, why it separated itself so profoundly from the rest of the nation, what had established and consolidated its power. I find it in place, and I seek to understand why it considered most human actions in such a particular light.

What strikes me first is that in the feudal world actions were not always praised or blamed by reason of their intrinsic value, but that sometimes they happened to be valued solely in relation to the author or the subject of the actions, which is repugnant to the general conscience of humanity. So certain actions that dishonored a nobleman were indifferent on the part of the commoner; others changed character depending on whether the person who suffered them belonged to the aristocracy or lived outside of it.

When these different opinions were born, the nobility formed a separate body, in the middle of the people, whom it dominated from the inaccessible heights to which it had withdrawn. To maintain this particular position that created its strength, it not only needed political privileges; it had to have virtues and vices for its exclusive use [in order to continue to distinguish itself in all things from what was outside or below it].

That some particular virtue or some particular vice belonged to the nobility rather than to commoners; that some particular action was neutral when it involved a villein or blameworthy when it concerned a nobleman, that is what was often arbitrary; but that honor or shame was attached to the actions of a man depending on his condition, that is what resulted from the very constitution of an aristocratic society. That was seen, in fact, in all the countries that had an aristocracy. As long as a single vestige of it remains, these singularities are still found: to seduce a young woman of color hardly harms the reputation of an American man; to marry her dishonors him.[h]

g. A draft of what follows exists in YTC, CVk, 1 (pp. 64–73). Tocqueville noted on the jacket: "Review carefully these variants [illegible word] *this 25 October 1839.*

"Piece that I reworked so laboriously that I fear that I have ruined it.

"October 1839" (YTC, CVk, 1, p. 64).

h. Édouard considers it of the greatest [importance? (ed.)] to include this./

In certain cases, feudal honor prescribed vengeance and stigmatized pardoning insults; in others it imperiously commanded men to master themselves; it ordered forgetting self. It did not make a law of humanity or of gentleness; but it praised generosity; it valued liberality more than benevolence; it allowed someone to enrich himself by games of chance, by war, but not by work; it preferred great crimes to small gains. Greed revolted it less than avarice, violence often pleased it, while guile and treason always appeared contemptible to it.

These bizarre notions were not born solely out of the caprice of those who had conceived them.

A class that has succeeded in putting itself above and at the head of all the others, and that makes constant efforts to maintain itself at this supreme rank, must particularly honor the virtues that have grandeur and brilliance, and that can be easily combined with pride and love of power. Such a class

---

It is impossible that there is not something useful to draw from the opinions of the Americans on Blacks and from the opinion suggested to them by the presence of Blacks.

In the South of the United States:

It is shameful to become familiar with a Black, to receive one at home even though he is free and rich, unspeakable to marry one.

It is not shameful to mistreat one, to seduce one. A host of actions, rebuked when they concern a white, are not suppressed by public opinion when they concern a Black. There are certain virtues and certain vices that are thought to be principally appropriate to him.

In the same portion of the Union, it is glorious to be idle, to be a duelist, a good horseman, a good hunter, to be magnificent in manners, opulent, generous, not to let others be disrespectful to you, to be very susceptible to insults, to keep your word scrupulously, little esteem for industry.

These are in a word the opinions of the aristocracy of the Middle Ages (the opposite of what is seen in the North, so that from one side aristocratic honor, from the other democratic) modified and softened by these causes.

It is not a warrior aristocracy.

Its position gives it the taste for the acquisition of wealth and for agriculture.

Its intimate connection with the North suggests to it many opinions not in harmony with the social state and that it would not have if it was isolated.

The absence of hierarchy in its ranks./

The difficulty of making use of all of that is that what I have just said constitutes an aristocratic honor and that, as to America, my goal and my interest is to get imperceptibly into democratic honor. That is, however, very interesting and could perhaps be placed at the head of *America* (*Rubish*, 2).

is not afraid of upsetting the natural order of conscience, in order to put these virtues above all the others. You even conceive that it readily raises certain bold and brilliant vices above peaceful and modest virtues. It is in a way forced to do so by its condition.

[≠These singular opinions arise naturally from the singularities of the social state.≠]

Before all virtues and in the place of a great number of them, the nobles of the Middles Ages put military courage [while they considered fear as the most shameful and most irreparable of weaknesses].

That too was a singular opinion that arose necessarily from the singularity of the social state.

Feudal aristocracy was born by war and for war; it had found its power in arms and it maintained it by arms; so nothing was more necessary for it than military courage; and it was natural that the aristocracy glorified it above all the rest. So everything that exhibited military courage externally, even if it were at the expense of reason and humanity, was approved and often commanded by the aristocracy. The whim of men was found only in the detail.

That a man regarded receiving a slap on the cheek as an enormous insult and was obliged to kill in single combat the man who had lightly struck him in this way, that was arbitrary; but that a nobleman could not receive an insult peacefully and was dishonored if he allowed himself to be struck without fighting, that sprang from the very principles and needs of a military aristocracy.

So it was true, to a certain point, to say that honor had capricious aspects; but the caprices of honor were always confined within certain necessary limits. This particular rule, called honor by our fathers, is so far from seeming to me an arbitrary law, that I would easily undertake to connect its most incoherent and most bizarre prescriptions to a small number of fixed and invariable needs of feudal societies.

If I followed feudal honor into the field of politics, I would not have any more difficulty explaining its workings.

The social state and political institutions of the Middle Ages were such that national power never directly governed the citizens. National power did not so to speak exist in their eyes; each man knew only a certain man whom he was obliged to obey. It was by the latter that, without knowing it, all the others were attached. So in feudal societies, all public order turned on the sentiment of fidelity to the very person of the lord. That destroyed, you fell immediately into anarchy.

Fidelity to the political head was, moreover, a sentiment whose value all the members of the aristocracy saw every day, for each one of them was at the same time lord and vassal and had to command as well as obey.

To remain faithful to your lord, to sacrifice yourself for him as needed, to share his good or bad fortune, to help him in his undertakings whatever they were, such were the first prescriptions of feudal honor in political matters. The treason of the vassal was condemned by opinion with an extraordinary severity. A particularly ignominious name was created for it; it was called a *felony*.

[≠Fidelity to the feudal head becomes {on the contrary, a kind of religion}.≠]

You find, on the contrary, in the Middle Ages only a few traces of a passion that animated ancient societies [≠and that reappeared among modern ones as the feudal world was transformed.≠]. I mean patriotism.ʲ The very noun patriotism is not old in our language.[2]

---

j. Of patriotism.
   (How to link this to democracy?)
   [In the margin: Parallel of ancient and modern patriotism.
      The Romans and the Americans, real, profound, dogmatic, simple, rational, egoistic, superficial, talkative.]
   To judge patriotism, it must not be taken when it acts in the direction of the passions that serve it as a vehicle, but on the contrary when it must struggle against those same passions. When I see the French people rushing to the borders in 1792, I am in doubt about whether they came to defend France or the Revolution that assured the triumph of democracy [v: equality]. But when in Rome the Senate goes as a body before Varro, man of the people, raised by the caprice of the people to the Consulate, and thanks him for not having lost hope in the country, I see into the bottom of hearts and I no longer doubt.
   I do not claim that the patriotism that is combined with an interest of party is a thing without value. I am only saying that to judge it well, it must be reduced to itself. Everything that shakes the human heart and calls it beyond the material interests of life, and raises it above fear of death is a great thing (YTC, CVk, 1, pp. 13–14).

2. *The word* patrie *itself is found among French authors only after the XVIth century.*

Feudal institutions concealed country from view; they made love of it less necessary. They caused the nation to be forgotten while making you passionate about one man. Consequently you do not see that feudal honor ever made it a strict law to remain faithful to your country.

It is not that love of country did not exist in the hearts of our fathers; but it formed a kind of weak and obscure instinct, which became clearer and stronger as classes were destroyed and [≠political≠] power was centralized.

This is clearly seen in the contrasting judgments that the peoples of Europe bring to the different facts of their history, depending on the generation that judges them. What principally dishonored the High Constable de Bourbon in the eyes of his contemporaries is that he bore arms against his king; what dishonors him most in our eyes is that he waged war on his country. We stigmatize his actions as much as our ancestors, but for other reasons.

I have chosen feudal honor to clarify my thought, because feudal honor has more marked and better features than any other. I could have taken my example from elsewhere; I would have reached the same end by another road.[k]

k. I have only wanted to examine among feudal peoples solely the opinions of the aristocratic class. But if I had descended into the detail of these complicated societies ≠and if I had contemplated separately the different classes that formed the social body≠, I would have found (illegible word) an analogous spectacle.

In each one of the classes ≠of feudal society≠ as well as within the aristocracy reigned in fact a public opinion that distributed in a sovereign way praise and blame according to a rule that it had created for its own use {and that was not always} consistent . . .

[In the margin: ≠All of this is not necessary in itself, but slows and hinders the movement of the piece. To have it copied separately and probably to delete (illegible word).

Ideas to introduce somewhere in the portrait of the feudal world.≠]

The particular condition of the men who composed these classes suggested to them a particular esteem for certain human actions and a very special scorn for certain others, and it led them to attach to some of their actions glory or shame, according to a measure that was their own. In that time, opinions, although aristocratic, colored more or less all human opinions; it was easy, however, to recognize a bourgeois honor, one of villeins, one of serfs, like an honor of nobles. Each one of them differed from aristocratic honor in its rules and was similar to it in its cause and in its objective (YTC, CVk, 1, pp. 71–72).

Although we know the Romans less well than our ancestors, we none-theless know that there existed among them, in regard to glory and dis-honor, particular opinions that did not flow only from general notions of good and evil. Many human actions there were considered in a different light, depending on whether it concerned a citizen or a foreigner, a free man or a slave; certain vices were glorified, certain virtues were raised above all others.

"Now in that time," says Plutarch in the life of Coriolanus, "valor was honored and valued in Rome above all other virtues. What attests to this is that it was called *virtus,* the very noun for virtue, attributing the name of the common type to a particular species. So much so that virtue in Latin was just like saying valor." Who does not recognize in that the particular need of that singular association formed to conquer the world?

Each nation will lend itself to analogous observations; for, as I said above, every time that men gather together in a particular society, a code of honor becomes immediately established among them, that is to say an ensemble of opinions that is proper to them about what must be praised or blamed; and these particular rules always have their source in the special habits and special interests of the association.

That applies, in a certain measure, to democratic societies as to others. We are going to find the proof of it among the Americans.[3]

You still find scattered, among the opinions of the Americans, a few detached notions of the ancient aristocratic honor of Europe. These tra-ditional opinions are in very small number; they have weak roots and little power. It is a religion of which you allow a few temples to continue to exist, but in which you no longer believe.

Amid these half-obliterated notions of an exotic honor, appear a few new opinions that constitute what could today be called American honor.

I have shown how the Americans were pushed incessantly toward com-

---

3. *I am speaking here about the Americans*[m] *who inhabit the countries where slavery does not exist. They are the only ones who can present the complete image of a democratic society.*
    m. In the drafts: "I am speaking principally about the Americans of New England and of the states without slaves" (*Rubish,* 2).

merce and industry. Their origin, their social state, their political institutions, and the very place that they inhabit draw them irresistibly in this direction. So they form, at present, an almost exclusively industrial and commercial association, placed at the heart of a new and immense country that its principal purpose is to exploit. Such is the characteristic feature that, today, most particularly distinguishes the American people from all the others.

All the peaceful virtues that tend to give a regular bearing to the social body and tend to favor trade must therefore be especially honored among this people, and you cannot neglect them without falling into public scorn.

All the turbulent virtues that often give brilliance, but even more often give trouble to a society, occupy on the contrary a subordinate rank in the opinion of this same people. You can neglect them without losing the esteem of your fellow citizens, and you would perhaps risk losing it by acquiring them.

The Americans make no less an arbitrary classification of the vices.

There are certain tendencies, blameworthy in the eyes of the general reason and of the universal conscience of humanity, that find themselves in agreement with the particular and temporary needs of the American association; and it condemns them only weakly, sometimes it praises them. I will cite particularly the love of wealth and the secondary tendencies that are connected to it. In order to clear, to make fruitful, to transform this vast uninhabited continent that is his domain, the American must have the daily support of an energetic passion; this passion can only be the love of wealth; so the passion for wealth has no stigma attached to it in America, and provided that it does not go beyond the limits assigned to it by public order, it is honored. The American calls a noble and estimable ambition what our fathers of the Middle Ages named servile cupidity; in the same way the American gives the name of blind and barbaric fury to the conquering fervor and warrior spirit that threw our fathers into new battles every day.

In the United States, fortunes are easily destroyed and rise again. The country is without limits and full of inexhaustible resources. The people have all the needs and all the appetites of a being who is growing, and whatever efforts he makes, he is always surrounded by more goods than he is able to grasp. What is to be feared among such a people is not the ruin of a few individuals, soon repaired, it is the inactivity and indolence of all. Boldness in industrial enterprises is the first cause of its rapid progress, its strength, its grandeur. Industry is for it like a vast lottery in which a small number of men lose every day, but in which the State wins constantly; so such a people must see boldness with favor and honor it in matters of industry. Now, every bold enterprise imperils the fortune of the one who devotes himself to it and the fortune of all those who trust in him. The Americans, who make commercial temerity into a kind of virtue, cannot, in any case whatsoever, stigmatize those who are daring.

That is why in the United States such a singular indulgence is shown for the merchant who goes bankrupt; the honor of the latter does not suffer from such an accident. In that, the Americans differ, not only from European peoples, but from all the commercial nations of today; but then, in their position and their needs, they do not resemble any of them.

In America, all the vices that are of a nature to alter the purity of morals and to destroy the conjugal union are treated with a severity unknown to the rest of the world. That contrasts strangely, at first view, with the tolerance that is shown there on other points. You are surprised to meet among the same people a morality so lax and so austere.

These things are not as inconsistent as you suppose. Public opinion, in the United States, only mildly represses love of wealth, which serves the industrial greatness and prosperity of the nation; and it particularly condemns bad morals, which distract the human mind from the search for well-being and disturbs the internal order of the family, so necessary to the success of business. So in order to be respected by their fellows, Americans are forced to yield to regular habits. In this sense you can say that they put their honor in being chaste.

American honor agrees with the old honor of Europe on one point: it puts courage at the head of virtues, and makes it the greatest of moral necessities for man; but it does not envisage courage in the same way.

In the United States, warrior valor is little prized; the courage that is known the best and esteemed the most is the one that makes you face the furies of the Ocean in order to arrive earliest in port, bear without complaint the miseries of the wilderness, and its solitude, more cruel than all the miseries; the courage that makes you almost insensitive to the sudden reversal of a fortune painfully acquired, and immediately suggests new efforts to build a new one. Courage of this type is principally necessary for the maintenance and the prosperity of the American association, and it is particularly honored and glorified by it. You cannot show yourself lacking in it, without dishonor.

I find a final feature; it will really put the idea of this chapter into relief.

In a democratic society, like that of the United States, where fortunes are small and poorly assured, everyone works, and work leads to everything. That has turned the point of honor around and directed it against idleness.

I sometimes met in America rich young men, enemies by temperament of all difficult effort, who were forced to take up a profession. Their nature and their fortune allowed them to remain idle; public opinion imperiously forbid it to them, and they had to obey.[n] I have often seen, on the contrary, among European nations where the aristocracy still struggles against the torrent that carries it along, I have seen, I say, men goaded constantly by their needs and their desires who remain idle in order not to lose the esteem of their equals, and who subject themselves more easily to boredom and want than to work.

Who does not see in these two so opposite obligations two different rules, both of which emanate nonetheless from honor?

What our fathers called honor above all was, truly speaking, only one of its forms. They gave a generic name to what was only a type. [If the aristocratic honor of the Middle Ages had more marked features and a physiognomy more extraordinary than all that had preceded and followed it, that was only because it was born amidst the most exceptional social state that ever existed and the one most removed from the natural and ordinary condition of humanity. Never in fact, in our western world, had men been separated by so many artificial barriers and felt more particular

n. To the side: "<The question is to know if I must say only that about America. I believe that the reader expects more and would be surprised.>"

needs.]° So honor is found in democratic centuries as in times of aristocracy. But it will not be difficult to show that in the former it presents another physiognomy.

Not only are its prescriptions different, we are going to see that they are fewer and less clear and that its laws are followed with less vigor.

A caste is always in a much more particular situation than a people. There is nothing more exceptional in the world than a small society always composed of the same families, like the aristocracy of the Middle Ages, for example, and whose objective is to concentrate and to hold enlightenment, wealth and power in its hands exclusively and by heredity.

Now, the more exceptional the position of a society is, the more numerous are its special needs, and the more the notions of its honor, which correspond to its needs, increase.

So the prescriptions of honor will always be fewer among a people that is not divided into castes, than among another. If nations come to be established where it is difficult even to find classes, honor will be limited there to a small number of precepts, and those precepts will be less and less removed from the moral laws adopted by the generality of humanity.

Thus the prescriptions of honor will be less bizarre and fewer in a democratic nation than in an aristocratic one.

They will also be more obscure; that results necessarily from what precedes.

Since the characteristic features of honor are less numerous and less singular, it must often be difficult to discern them.

There are still other reasons.

Among the aristocratic nations of the Middle Ages the generations succeeded each other in vain; each family was like an immortal and perpetually immobile man;ᴾ ideas varied scarcely more than conditions.

o. In the margin: "Piece to delete probably. To see again."
p. To the side: "<Good sentence, but which is, I believe, found elsewhere.>"

So each man had always before his eyes the same objects, which he envisaged from the same point of view; little by little he saw into the slightest details, and his perception could not fail, in the long run, to become clear and distinct. Thus, not only did the men of feudal times have very extraordinary opinions that constituted their honor, but also each one of these opinions was shaped in their minds in a clear-cut and precise way.

It can never be the same in a country like America, where all the citizens are in motion; where society, itself changing every day, changes its opinions with its needs. In such a country, you catch a glimpse of the rule of honor; you rarely have the leisure to consider it intently.

Were society immobile, it would still be difficult to fix the meaning that must be given to the word honor.

In the Middle Ages, since each class had its honor, the same opinion was never accepted simultaneously by a very great number of men, which allowed giving it a fixed and precise form; all the more so since all those who accepted it, all having a perfectly identical and very exceptional position, found a natural disposition to agree on the prescriptions of a law that was made only for them alone.

Honor thus became a complete and detailed code in which everything was foreseen and ordered in advance, and which presented a fixed and always visible rule to human actions. Among a democratic nation like the American people, where ranks are mixed and where the entire society forms only a single mass, all of whose elements are analogous without being entirely the same, you can never exactly agree in advance about what is allowed and forbidden by honor.

There exist indeed, within this people, certain national needs that give birth to common opinions in the matter of honor; but such opinions never present themselves at the same time, in the same manner and with equal force to the mind of all the citizens; the law of honor exists, but it often lacks interpreters.

The confusion is even still greater in a democratic country like ours,q in which the different classes that composed the old society, starting to mingle

q. The manuscript says: "... among a people in which the different classes ..."

without yet being able to blend, bring to each other every day the various and often contradictory notions of their honor; in which each man, following his caprices, abandons one part of the opinions of his fathers and holds onto the other; so that amid so many arbitrary measures, a common rule can never be established. It is nearly impossible then to say in advance what actions will be honored or stigmatized. These are miserable times, but they do not last.

Among democratic nations, honor, not being well defined, is necessarily less powerful; for it is difficult to apply with certainty and firmness a law that is imperfectly known.[r] Public opinion, which is the natural and sovereign interpreter of the law of honor, not seeing distinctly in which direction it is appropriate to tip blame or praise, only delivers its judgment with hesitation. Sometimes it happens that it contradicts itself; often it remains immobile and lets things happen.

[≠The law of honor, were it clear, would still be weak among democratic peoples by the sole fact that its not very numerous prescriptions are few. For the principal strength of a body of laws comes from the fact that it extends at the same time to a multitude of matters and, every day in a thousand diverse ways, bends the human mind to obedience. A law that provides for just a few cases and that is only applied here and there is always feeble.

Now, the prescriptions of honor are always more numerous and less detailed to the extent that classes, not being as close to each other, have fewer interests apart from the mass and fewer particular needs.≠]

The relative weakness of honor in democracy is due to several other causes.

In aristocratic countries, the same honor is never accepted except by a certain, often limited number of men, always separated from the rest of their fellows. So honor easily mixes and mingles, in the minds of those men,

---

r. "<Delicate idea and a little subtle but true at bottom. To include./
"The pleasure that honor gives is an intellectual and moral enjoyment that must lose its value like all the others of this type in democratic centuries, even if the notions of honor did not become fewer and more confused>" (In the jacket WHY MEN . . . , *Rubish*, 2).

with the idea of all that distinguishes them. It appears to them like the distinctive feature of their physiognomy; they apply its different rules with all the ardor of personal interest, and if I can express myself in this way, they bring passion to obeying it.

This truth manifests itself very clearly when you read the customary laws of the Middle Ages, on the point of legal duels.[s] You see there that the nobles were bound, in their quarrels, to use the lance and the sword, while the villeins used the cudgel with each other, "it being understood," the laws add, *that the villeins have no honor.*" That did not mean, as we imagine today, that those men were dishonorable; it meant only that their actions were not judged by the same rules as those of the aristocracy.[t]

---

s. The duel. Why the duel diminishes as nations become more democratic. The progress of public reason is not a sufficient cause. The duel is the sanction of the law of civility. When the law becomes uncertain and is almost abolished, it ceases by itself. But it remains a means of vengeance.

[In the margin: Almost purposeless efforts of the legislators of today who want to destroy the duel. The duel is attacked by a general cause more powerful than legislation, and that cause alone is strong enough to destroy it.]

.-.-.-.-.-.-.-

No one fights in the United States for conventional insults, but for insults that are considered as mortal in the eyes of reason, such as the subornation of a woman or of a girl, for example. And then they fight to the death. The custom of the duel must tend to disappear everywhere military aristocratic honor is disappearing. So what I said in the preceding chapter explains sufficiently why the custom of the duel is gradually growing weaker among modern peoples and particularly among democratic nations. But there are still other reasons, and were the duel held in honor by the opinion of these peoples it would still be more difficult to find the occasion to fight a duel.

Great number of those to whom it would be necessary to answer.

Uncertainty of the insult. The duel no longer keeps order. Men do not kill each other and (illegible word) to take (illegible word); the duel for conventional insult must first disappear, then finally the duel for real insult, rarer duel and more cruel. Example: United States of the South. States of the North.

Here they still fight, there they do almost nothing more than go to court.

The Americans fight when the Romans murdered (YTC, Cva, pp. 51–52). During the judicial year 1828 or 1829, Tocqueville gave a speech on the duel (André Jardin, *Alexis de Tocqueville*, p. 75). Beaumont dedicated a long commentary to duels in *Marie* (I, pp. 370–77).

t. This paragraph is not found in the manuscript.

What is astonishing, at first view, is that, when honor reigns with this full power, its prescriptions are in general very strange, so that it seems to be obeyed better the more it appears to diverge from reason; from that it has sometimes been concluded that feudal honor was strong, because of its very extravagance.

These two things have, in fact, the same origin; but they are not derived from each other.

Honor is bizarre in proportion as it represents more particular needs felt by a smaller number of men; and it is powerful because it represents needs of this type. So honor is not powerful because it is bizarre; but it is bizarre and powerful because of the same cause.

I will make another remark.

Among aristocratic peoples, all ranks differ, but all ranks are fixed; each man occupies in his sphere a place that he cannot leave, and in which he lives amid other men bound around him in the same way. So among these nations, no one can hope or fear not being seen; there is no man placed so low who does not have his stage, and who can, by his obscurity, escape from blame or from praise.

In democratic States, on the contrary, where all citizens are merged in the same crowd and are constantly in motion, public opinion has nothing to hold on to; its subject disappears at every instant and escapes.[u] So honor will always be less imperious and less pressing; for honor acts only with the public in mind, different in that from simple virtue,[v] which lives on its own and is satisfied with its testimony.

u. \<Public opinion, which is the sovereign judge in the matter of honor, is often uncertain. It does not discern clearly\> for it is difficult to apply with certainty and firmness a rule that is only imperfectly known. So public opinion, which is the natural and sovereign interpreter of honor, almost always strikes while hesitating and often its voice is lost amid the thousand discordant noises that arise on all sides, and since it constantly changes interpreters you always imagine that its decision is not without appeal (In the jacket WHY THE MEN . . . , *Rubish,* 2).

v. Montesquieu spoke about our honor and not about honor./
   Virtue. More perfect rule, less easy to follow./
   We must never lose sight of this capital difference between virtue and honor, that

virtue leads men to want to do good for the pleasure of the good, that is at least its claim, while honor, by its own admission, has for principal and almost unique goal to be seen and approved. It is always a bit of a theatrical virtue.

All of my deduction of ideas does not, up to now, provide me with the reason for this (*Rubish,* 2).

On the jacket of the manuscript you read: "Read what Montesquieu wrote on honor, books III, IV and XXVIII." A jacket of the *rubish* of this chapter bears the following note: "In these *rubish* there are several good ideas that I left behind and that it would be good to reexamine." This jacket contains two unpublished letters. The first is a letter of M. Feuillet, of the Royal Institute, to Hervé de Tocqueville, in which he mentions that he has not been able to find a treatise on the dispositions of the preconception of honor and that he recommends reading the *Encyclopédie* and books III, IV, and XXVIII of *L'Esprit des lois*. The second is a letter from Hervé de Tocqueville to his son, that we reproduce here in full:

Paris, 17 January 1838.

I received your letter the evening before yesterday, my good friend. I went yesterday morning to see M. Feuillet. He asked me for twenty-four hours to research the documents that could enlighten you. You will see from his response, which I am sending to you, that he found nothing. I am going to try to gather from my memory something that may in part compensate for it.

Honor can be defined as the sentiment that leads to sacrificing everything to escape the scorn of your fellows, even life, even on some occasions virtue and religion.

In the article of the *Encyclopédie* cited by M. Feuillet you find the following definition: "The sentiment of esteem for yourself is the most delightful of all, but the most virtuous man is often overwhelmed by the weight of his imperfection and seeks in the looks, in the bearing of men, the expression of an esteem that reconciles him with himself.

"From that two kinds of honor, that which is based within ourselves, on what we are; that which is in others, based on what they think of us.

"In the man of the people, honor is the esteem that he has for himself, and his right to the esteem of the public derives from his exactitude in observing certain laws established by prejudices and by custom.

"Of these laws, some conform to reason, others are opposed to it. Honor among the most civilized nations can therefore be attached sometimes to estimable qualities and actions, often to destructive practices, sometimes to extravagant customs, sometimes even to vices.

"But why is this changing honor, almost always principal in governments, always so bizarre? Why is it placed in puerile or destructive practices? Why does it sometimes impose duties condemned by nature, purified reason and virtue? And why in certain times is it particularly attributed to certain qualities, certain actions, and in other times to actions and to qualities of an opposite type?

"The great principle of utility of David Hume must be recalled: it is utility that always decides our esteem. But certain qualities, certain talents are at various times more or less useful. Honored at first, they are less so afterward.

"If the communal status of women is not established, conjugal fidelity will be their honor. Since it is not believed that a woman can fail in fidelity to a respectable man, the honor of the husband depends on the chastity of his wife."

Such is the summary of the article from the *Encyclopédie* relating to the subject that concerns you. There is a profound sense in the sentence that relates the establishment and maintenance of the various types of honor to utility. In fact there existed in the old monarchy first a general honor and a special one for each profession. General honor consisted of abstaining from all that merits scorn. Special honor was inseparable from virtue and from integrity among magistrates, tradesmen, merchants. Only in the military profession could honor be outside of virtue, act apart from it and sometimes in opposition to it.

As civilization advanced, the aberrations of military honor penetrated the middle class and little by little extended to the lowest ranks. Currently it is understood differently in many respects. But the prejudice that an insult must be washed away by blood has survived. This is how a murderer believes he can erase the shame of his crime and attenuate it in fact by suicide, which is an additional crime.

I am going to speak about special honors. 1. That of the nobility. It obliged the nobility to devote itself to the service of the State in the profession of arms, to sacrifice for the State its life and if needed its fortune. The gentleman guilty of a crime was not dishonored if he was beheaded. Another punishment dishonored him and his descendants.

He could not marry inappropriately without failing in honor. Nonetheless, in the XVIIIth century, wealth was accepted in order to compensate for birth.

He could not exercise the mechanical arts, or do commerce. Only in Brittany, he put down his sword, went to do maritime commerce and, upon returning, took up his sword again. His quality of nobleman was as if suspended during his absence.

I believe that the nobleman could not subscribe to letters of exchange without staining his honor. He could indeed not pay suppliers, but the word bankruptcy would have dishonored him. It was the same if he did not pay gambling debts, wagers and other debts with written proof of indebtedness.

He had to be sensitive to insults and disposed to demand satisfaction. From that the proverb: being contradicted is worth being struck with the sword. A blow could be expiated only by the death of one of the two combatants. The refusal to fight and even hesitation to accept a duel caused dishonor. But also, the dishonor that should have accompanied a lot of blameworthy actions was erased by the duel. You remained guilty before the law and conscience, but ceased to be so according to honor.

It goes without saying that every base action took away honor. Moreover, there was, I believe, neither code nor court. Opinion judged, and it was more or less severe. When it had condemned, the stain was permanent. The unfortunate whom it had reached was obliged to hide himself to avoid awful affronts. Louis XIV had in truth created the court of the Marshals of France which exercised a certain jurisdiction as

If the reader has well grasped all that precedes, he must have understood that there exists, between inequality of conditions and what we have called honor, a close and necessary connection that, if I am not wrong, had not yet been clearly pointed out. So I must make a final effort to bring it clearly to light.[w]

---

regards honor, but I believe it concerned itself above all with the causes of duels. M. Feuillet promised me to do research on this subject. In sum, the nobleman was more dishonored than the commoner for actions that would have stained the honor of the latter. You saw yourself as dishonored by a blow of the sovereign because you could not demand satisfaction from him.

The honor of the magistrate was something else entirely. A duel would have dishonored him. His honor consisted of integrity, decency of conduct, a quiet life and a busy existence.

The tradesman was not dishonored if he refused to fight. His honor consisted of running his company well, of the clarity of his enterprises, exactitude in fulfilling his engagements, his fidelity, integrity in supplies.

There more or less, my good friend, is all that I can say on this subject. All that formerly existed has left a trace that you can see. Only honor was much more delicate and punctilious than it is now. Material interests invade the ground of honor and you allow many things that would have made you blush formerly, and that in all ranks and in all classes.

Cold is always hard and I am concerned about you. Tell Marie that I thank her for her letter. I have begun to answer her. I do not have the time to finish today. Kiss her for me and tell her to kiss you for me.

A thousand tender regards to Édouard and his family. A thousand friendly greetings from mother Guermarquer.

If I get new information, I will send it immediately./

The man declared dishonored by opinion was forced by his fellows, colleagues or comrades to give his resignation.

In January 1838, Kergorlay, on a visit to Baugy for four days, probably helped Tocqueville in drafting this chapter. The author wrote to Beaumont on 18 January: "Louis has just spent four days here; I was at that moment *tangled* in a system of ideas from which I could not extricate myself. It was a true intellectual cul-de-sac, which he got me out of in a few hours. This boy has in him a veritable mine from which he alone cannot and does not know how to draw" (*Correspondance avec Beaumont, OC,* VIII, 1, p. 279). The papers of the heirs of Tocqueville contain a manuscript from Kergorlay on honor with this commentary from the author: "Very remarkable piece by Louis de Kergorlay. To see again, if I do a second edition."

w. <If the reader has clearly grasped all that precedes, he must have understood that there exists a singular correlation between inequality of conditions and what we have called honor. These are two facts that derive necessarily from each other.

As conditions become equal within a people and as the citizens become more equal

A nation takes up a separate position within humanity. Apart from certain general needs inherent in the human species, it has its own particular interests and needs. Immediately established within the nation in the matter of blame and praise are certain opinions that are its own and that its citizens call honor.

Within this same nation, a caste becomes established, which, separating itself in turn from all the other classes, contracts particular needs, and the latter, in turn, give rise to special opinions.[x] The honor of this caste, bizarre mixture of the particular notions of the nation and of the still more particular notions of the caste, will diverge as far as you can imagine from the simple and general opinions of men. We have reached the extreme point; let us go back.

Ranks mingle, privileges are abolished. Since the men who compose the nation have again become similar and equal, their interests and their needs blend, and you see successively vanish all the singular notions that each caste called honor; honor now derives only from the particular needs of the nation itself; it represents its individuality among peoples.

If it were finally allowed to suppose that all races were blended and that all the peoples of the world had reached the point of having the same interests, the same needs, and of no longer being different from each other by any characteristic feature, you would cease entirely to attribute a conventional value to human actions; everyone would envisage them in the same light; the general needs of humanity, which conscience reveals to every man, would be the common measure. Then, you would no longer find in this world anything except the simple and general notions of good and evil, to which would be linked, by a natural and necessary bond, the ideas of praise and blame.

---

and more similar, honor does not disappear, but it becomes less strange in its precepts, less absolute and less powerful> (*Rubish,* 2).

x. In the margin: "<Here this eternal question presents itself. *Is it opinion that gave birth to fact or fact, opinion?*>"

Thus finally to contain in a single formula my whole thought, it is the dissimilarities and the inequalities of men that created honor; it grows weaker as these differences fade away, and it would disappear with them.^{y}

y. On a sheet at the end of the manuscript:

To copy separately./
   Of all religions, the one that has most considered the human species in its unity and has had most in view in its laws the general needs of humanity, leaving aside social state, laws, times and places, is the Christian religion.
   So Christian peoples have always been and will always be very constrained in using honor whatever honor may be. It is [what (ed.)] has been the weakness of Christianity in certain periods and among certain peoples, but that is also what has established its general strength and what assures its perpetuity./
   This reflection came to me today, 11 February, while reading the *Imitation*. This book was written amid all the prejudices of honor of the Middle Ages and in the country where honor reigned most despotically, and the book combats them all. It is true that Thomas d'A. [Thomas Kempis (ed.)] sometimes, according to me, forgets the general principles of Christianity in order to start at the particular duties of the religious state and on this point you could say that he combats the notions of aristocratic honor with those of monastic honor.

CHAPTER 19[a]

Why in the United States You Find So Many Ambitious Men and So Few Great Ambitions[b]

The first thing that strikes you in the United States is the innumerable multitude of those who seek to leave their original condition; and the second is the small number of great ambitions which stand out among this universal movement of ambition.[c] There are no Americans who do not

a. The democratic revolution must be clearly distinguished from democracy.

As long as the revolution lasts, ambitions are very great, but they become small when the revolution has ended.

Why:

When democracy does not prevent ambitions from being born, it at least gives them a particular character.

What this character is.

That we must try in our time to purify and to regulate ambition, but we have to be afraid of hindering it too much and impoverishing it (YTC, CVf, pp. 47–48).

b. "The chapter should rather be entitled *of the greatness of desires*" (*Rubish*, 2).

c. In the *rubish:*

Ambition in democracies./

[In the margin: A great part ideas of Louis.]

When you examine this subject attentively, you arrive at thinking this:

Democracy immensely augments the number of ambitious men and decreases the number of great ambitions. It makes all men aim a bit beyond where they are; it prevents almost anyone from aiming very far.

The cause of that is in equality of conditions. Equality of conditions and the absence of classifications gives all men the ability to change their position; these same causes prevent any man from being naturally and reasonably led to aim for a very elevated situation.

Kings think naturally of conquering kingdoms, the nobleman of governing the State or of acquiring glory. Placed very high, these great goals are close to them; and their situation as well as their taste pushes them naturally to seize them. The poor aim to acquire a mediocre fortune. Men who have a mediocre fortune aim to become

appear to be devoured by the desire to rise; but you see hardly any who seem to nourish very vast hopes or to aim very high. All want constantly to acquire property, reputation, power; few envisage all these things on a large scale. And at first view that is surprising, since you notice nothing, either in the mores or in the laws of America, that should limit desires and prevent them from taking off in all directions.d

----

rich. These goals are not as great as the first if you consider them in an absolute way; from a relative point of view they are not smaller. The desires that lead men toward the first and toward the second are the same.

≠Sometimes, however, within democracies immense ambitions are born, for what happens to the human body in savage life happens there. All the children who are born weak die there, those who survive become very strong men. The strength that made them conquer the first obstacles, pushes them very much farther.≠

This, moreover, is applicable only to established and peaceful democracies. In democracies in revolution ambitions are numerous and great; equality of conditions allows each man to change place, and fortune puts temporarily within reach of each man the greatest places. This is what has made some think in a general way that democracies push men toward great ambitions. The exception has been taken for the rule. France has served as an example for everything in order to prove the first proposition. This idea is correct in a general way only when you apply it to an army. The democratic principle introduced into an army cannot fail to create there a multitude of great ambitions and to push men toward prodigious things. An army at war is nothing else than a society in revolution. So what I have said above occasionally about society always applies to an army./

Review all of these ideas, reflect about them well before accepting them. Know if what I call a state of revolution is not after all the natural state of democracies.

If what I am saying is true, the consequences to draw from it would be important and of several sorts. A sort of weakening would result in all sentiments, and even in ideas; the source of great thoughts, of heroic tastes would be not dried up, but diminished. The remedy to that (*Rubish,* 2).

The *rubish* of this chapter contains the letter of 2 February 1838 of Tocqueville to Kergorlay and the response of Kergorlay dated 6 January, but clearly from the month of February of the same year. Tocqueville questions the recipient of his letter about the increase of small and great ambitions in democracies. Kergorlay answers that democracies increase small ambitions, but that he can say nothing about great ones. These two letters are published in the *Correspondance avec Kergorlay, OC,* XIII, 2, pp. 12–18.

d. On a sheet of the manuscript:

The generative idea of this chapter remains of doubtful truth for two reasons among others:

It seems difficult to attribute this singular state of things to equality of conditions [{democracy}]; for, at the moment when the same equality became established among us, it immediately caused almost limitless ambitions to develop.[e] I believe, however, that it is principally in the social state and democratic mores of the Americans that the cause of what precedes must be sought.

Every revolution magnifies the ambition of men. That is above all true of the revolution that overthrows an aristocracy.[f]

[The revolution that finally creates a democratic social state must be clearly distinguished from the democratic social state itself.

When a powerful aristocracy disappears suddenly amid the popular waves raised against it, it is not only men who change place; laws, ideas, mores are renewed; the entire world seems to change appearance. The old order on which humanity rested finally collapses and a new order comes to light. The authors and the witnesses of these wonders, while contemplating them, feel as if transported beyond themselves; the grandeur of the things that are taking place before their eyes and by their hands expands their soul and fills it with vast thoughts and immense desires.

Ambition then takes on an audacious and grandiose character. It appears sometimes disinterested, often sublime. That is due not to the social state of the people, but to the singular revolution that it is undergoing.][g]

---

1. The governmental machine is so powerful in democratic centuries that the one who succeeded in holding it in his hand can easily imagine immense projects.

2. Since all men are more or less similar, you can hope to be understood by all at the same time and to act on all, which must expand thought and raise the heart.

e. "Is it very sure that if the American statesmen had a great power they would not have a great ambition?/
"Ambition is desire to act on your fellows, to command them" (*Rubish*, 2).

f. "It is clear that if I succeeded in presenting as an absolute truth that equality *destroys ambition* and prevents *revolutions,* I would contradict a great part of my own ideas previously put forward.

"So I must be very careful there and stick with the possibility of the thing" (*Rubish,* 2).

g. In the margin: "≠All of that upon reading seems to me a bit the amplification of a man who is groping along. Style of improvisation.≠

"Read all of that to Beaumont before deleting it entirely."

Since the old barriers that separated the crowd from fame and power have fallen suddenly, an impetuous and universal upward movement takes place toward these long desired splendors whose enjoyment is finally allowed. In this first exaltation of triumph, nothing seems impossible to anyone. Not only do desires have no limits, but the power to satisfy them has hardly any. Amid this general and sudden renewal of customs and laws, in this vast confusion of all men and all rules, citizens rise and fall with an unheard-of rapidity, and power passes so quickly from hand to hand that no one should despair of seizing it in his turn.

You must remember clearly, moreover, that the men who destroy an aristocracy lived under its laws; they saw its splendors and allowed themselves, without knowing it, to be penetrated by the sentiments and the ideas that the aristocracy had conceived. So at the moment when an aristocracy dissolves, its spirit still hovers over the mass, and its instincts are conserved for a long time after it has been vanquished.

So ambitions always appear very great, as long as the democratic revolution endures; after it has finished, it will still be the same for some time.

The recollection of the extraordinary events that they have witnessed does not fade in one day from the memory of men. The passions that revolution had suggested do not disappear with it.[h] The sentiment of insta-

---

h. Our civil troubles have brought to light men who, by the immensity of their *genius* and of their crimes, have remained in the picture of the past like deformed but gigantesque masses that constantly and from all sides attract the sight of the crowd.

[In the margin: *19 September 1837.*

2 v.

Perhaps to mores strictly speaking.

Depraved ambition.

To ambition perhaps.]

From that is born among us a sort of depraved taste and dishonest admiration for everything that diverges in whatever fashion from the ordinary dimensions of humanity. You want to escape the common rule, no matter where. Not able to be different by your acts, you seek at least to make yourself extraordinary by your manners; if you do not do great things, you at least say bizarre things; and often, after you have failed to be a hero, you do not scorn becoming a remarkable rogue.

bility is perpetuated amid order. The idea of the ease of success outlives the strange vicissitudes that have given it birth. Desires remain very vast, while the means to satisfy them diminishes every day. The taste for great fortunes subsists, even though great fortunes become rare, and you see taking fire on all sides disproportionate and unfortunate ambitions that burn secretly and fruitlessly in the heart that harbors them.

Little by little, however, the last traces of the struggle fade; the remnants of the aristocracy finally disappear. You forget the great events that accompanied its fall; rest follows war, the dominion of rules is reborn within the new world; desires become proportionate to means; needs, ideas and sentiments become linked together; men finally come to the same level; democratic society is finally established.

If we consider a democratic people having reached this permanent and normal state, it will present to us a spectacle entirely different from the one that we have just contemplated, and we will be able to judge without difficulty that, if ambition becomes great while conditions are becoming equal, it loses this characteristic when they are equal.

Since great fortunes are divided and knowledge is widespread, no one is absolutely deprived of enlightenment or of property; since privileges and disqualifications of classes are abolished, and since men have forever broken the bonds that held them immobile, the idea of progress presents itself to the mind of each one of them; the desire to rise is born at the same time in all hearts; each man wants to leave his place. Ambition is the universal sentiment.

But, if equality of conditions gives some resources to all citizens, it prevents any one among them from having very extensive resources; this necessarily encloses desires within rather narrow limits.

Since men of genius have been glorious and powerful despite the disorder of their lives, many men imagine that, lacking genius, disorder suffices [for (ed.)] leading them to glory and to greatness.

The French Revolution in its inexhaustible fertility produced only a single Mirabeau, but today you see swarming a multitude of small disagreeable Mirabeaus who, lacking the talents of their model, succeed already too well in copying his vices (YTC, CVk, 1, pp. 1–2).

So among democratic peoples, ambition is ardent and continuous, but it cannot habitually aim very high; and life ordinarily is spent there ardently coveting small objects that you see within your reach.j

What above all diverts men of democracies from great ambition is not the smallness of their fortune, but the violent effort that they make to improve it every day. They force their soul to use all its strength in order to do mediocre things, which cannot soon fail to limit its view and to circumscribe its power. They could be very much poorer and remain greater.

The small number of opulent citizens who are found within a democracy do not make an exception to this rule. A man who rises by degrees toward wealth and power contracts, in this long effort, habits of prudence and restraint which he cannot afterward give up. You do not gradually enlarge your soul like your house.k

An analogous remark is applicable to the sons of this same man. They

---

j. What must above all be pointed out in the chapter on ambition is not that ambition is *naturally small* or aims at first very low, but [that (ed.)] it is *easy to tire* by obstacles.

The *softness* of souls makes it so that when a goal can be obtained only with much effort and time, you give up obtaining it and limit yourself to a goal less grand but easier to attain. I have not made this idea come out enough, idea which is however capital and presents applications without number. That is how, at the moment (April 1838) when I am dealing with the army, I see clearly that in democracies the soldier would very much want to be made an officer, but for that it would be necessary to study, to impose efforts on himself, to run dangers that put him off. He prefers to await the end of his time, to return to his fields and to work very quietly toward obtaining well-being for himself.

[In the margin: Ambition is no longer *moderate* but *effeminate*.

It is not ambition which is small, it is courage./ Ambition is *vulgar* rather than *small. Vulgar,* there is the true word of the chapter.]

The officer on his part would find it excellent to have the salary, the power and the general consideration, and he sees nothing that prevents him absolutely from reaching them. But for that an energy of will, a brilliance, a splendor that costs him something would be necessary. He prefers to reach the time of his retirement far from danger and to go to live in his village without working.

This is what explains the picture of Lamoricière.

All this shows my idea with a new face that must be made into one of the principal ideas of the chapter (*Rubish,* 2).

k. On the side: "<All that is perhaps a bit high and mighty.>" The same observation is also found in the *rubish.*

are born, it is true, in a high position, but their parents were humble; they grew up amid sentiments and ideas which are difficult for them to escape later; and it is to be believed that the sons will inherit at the same time the instincts of their father and his property.

It can happen, on the contrary, that the poorest offspring of a powerful aristocracy exhibits a vast ambition, because the traditional opinions of his race and the general spirit of his caste still sustain him for some time above his fortune.

What also prevents the men of democratic times from easily devoting themselves to the ambition for great things is the time that they foresee must pass before they are able to embark upon them. "A great advantage of quality," Pascal said, "is to put a man, at eighteen or twenty years of age, in as strong a position as another man would be at fifty; this is thirty years gained without difficulty."m Those thirty years are usually lacking for the ambitious men of democracies. Equality, which allows each man the ability to reach everything, prevents him from growing up quickly.

In a democratic society, as elsewhere, there are only a certain number of great fortunes to make; and because the careers that lead to them are open to each citizen without distinction, the progress of all must indeed slow down. Since the candidates appear more or less the same, and since it is difficult to make a choice from among them without violating the principle of equality, which is the supreme law of democratic societies, the first idea that presents itself is to make all march with the same step and to subject them all to the same tests.

So as men become more similar and as the principle of equality penetrates institutions and mores more peacefully and profoundly, the rules for advancement become more inflexible, advancement slower; the difficulty of quickly attaining a certain degree of grandeur increases.

By hatred of privilege and by overabundance of choices, you come to the point of forcing all men, whatever their size, to pass through the same channel, and you subject them all without distinction to a multitude of small preliminary exercises, in the middle of which their youth is lost and

m. It refers to *pensée* 193 of the Lafuma edition.

their imagination grows dim; so that they despair of ever being able to enjoy fully the advantages that you offer to them; and when they are finally able to do extraordinary things, they have lost the taste for them.

In China, where equality of conditions is very great and very ancient, a man passes from one public office to another only after being subjected to a competitive examination. This test is found at each step of his career, and the idea of it has entered the mores so well that I remember reading a Chinese novel in which the hero, after many vicissitudes, finally touches the heart of his mistress by doing well on an examination. Great ambitions breathe badly in such an atmosphere.

What I say about politics extends to everything; equality produces the same effects everywhere; wherever the law does not undertake to regulate and to slow the movement of men, competition suffices.

In a well-established democratic society, great and rapid rises are therefore rare; they form exceptions to the common rule. It is their singularity that makes you forget their small number.

The men of democracies end up catching sight of all these things; in the long run they notice that the legislator opens before them a limitless field, in which everyone can easily take a few steps, but which no one can imagine crossing quickly. Between them and the vast and final object of their desires, they see a multitude of small, intermediary barriers, which they must clear slowly; this sight fatigues their ambition in advance and discourages it. So they renounce these distant and doubtful hopes, in order to seek less elevated and easier enjoyments close to them. The law does not limit their horizon, but they narrow it themselves.

I said that great ambitions were more rare in democratic centuries than in times of aristocracy;[n] I add that, when, despite natural obstacles, great ambitions are born, they have another physiognomy.

n. "<Democratic nations produce great things rather than great men>" (*Rubish*, 2).

In the *rubish* of the following chapter: "Democracy suggests a few immoderate ambitions, without check, without limit, of a boldness and an imprudence without parallel (like that of Thiers), such as you hardly ever see in aristocratic centuries; but in general it gives rise to a multitude of small, vulgar, commonplace ambitions and diminishes the number of great proportionate ambitions" (*Rubish*, 2).

In aristocracies, the course of ambition is often extensive; but its limits are fixed. In democratic countries, it moves usually in a narrow field; but if it happens to go beyond those limits, you would say that there is no longer anything that limits it. Since men there are weak, isolated and changing, and since precedents there have little sway and laws little duration, resistance to innovations is soft and the social body never seems very sound or very settled. So that, when those who are ambitious once have power in hand, they believe they are able to dare anything; and when power escapes them, they immediately think about overturning the State in order to regain it.º

That gives to great political ambition a violent and revolutionary character, which is rare to see, to the same degree, in aristocratic societies.

A multitude of small, very judicious ambitions, out of which now and then spring a few great, badly ordered desires: such usually is the picture presented by democratic nations. A measured, moderate and vast ambition is hardly ever found there.ᴾ

o. "Charles XII had a great aristocratic ambition; Napoleon, a great democratic ambition.

"Each one is vast in a way.

"[To the side] The one wanted above all to make his triumphs talked about, the other to enjoy them" (*Rubish*, 2).

In a variant of these same notes, in another place in the *rubish*, Tocqueville adds: "There was something of the *parvenu* in the ambition of Napoleon" (Rubish, 2).

p. M. Guizot, in his article on religion inserted in the *Université catholique* for the month of M[arch (ed.)] 1838 says:

"Never has ambition been more impatient and more widespread. Never have so many hearts been prey to such a thirst for all goods, for all pleasures. Arrogant pleasures and coarse pleasures, thirst for material well-being and for intellectual vanity, taste for activity and for softness, adventures and idleness: everything seems possible, and desirable, and accessible to all. It is not that passion is strong, nor man disposed to make much effort for the satisfaction of his desires. He wants feebly, but he desires immensely. . . . The world has never seen such a conflict of weak wills, of fantasies, of claims, of demands, never heard such a noise of voices being raised all together to claim as their right what they lack and what pleases them. And it is not toward God that these voices are being raised. Ambition is at the same time widespread and lower."

[On the back] *Weak wills*, this term is precious and expresses well one of my thoughts. You have an immense and weak will because everything seems open and permitted; you do not have a firm will because soon the obstacles are revealed. Ap-

I showed elsewhere by what secret strength equality made the passion for material enjoyments and the exclusive love of the present predominate in the human heart; these different instincts mingle with the sentiment of ambition and tinge it, so to speak, with their colors.

I think that the ambitious men of democracies are preoccupied less than all the others by the interests and judgments of the future; the present moment alone occupies them and absorbs them. They rapidly complete many undertakings rather than raising a few very enduring monuments; they love success much more than glory. What they ask above all from men is obedience. What they want above all is dominion. Their mores almost always remain less elevated than their condition; this means that very often they bring very vulgar tastes to an extraordinary fortune, and that they seem to have risen to sovereign power only in order to gain more easily for themselves small and coarse pleasures.

I believe that today it is very necessary to purify, to regulate and to adjust the sentiment of ambition, but that it would be very dangerous to want to impoverish it and to curb it beyond measure. You must attempt in advance to set extreme limits for it, which you will never allow it to surpass; but you must take care not to hinder its impetus too much within the allowed limits.

I admit that I fear boldness much less, for democratic societies, than mediocrity of desires; what seems to me most to fear is that, amid the small incessant occupations of private life, ambition may lose its impetus and its grandeur; that human passions may become calmer and lower at the same time, so that each day the bearing of the social body may become more tranquil and less elevated.

So I think that the heads of these new societies would be very wrong to want to put the citizens to sleep in a happiness that is too smooth and

---

pearance and reality are always opposite. The social state awakens ambition and puts it to sleep, gives great desires and finally leads you to be content with little.

[In the margin] Precious new deduction to include, deduction which explains very well this evident phenomenon of democracies. *Immense* ambition and *petty* rich men (*Rubish,* 2). It refers to François Guizot, "Of Religion in Modern Societies," *Université catholique* 5, no. 27 (March 1838): 231–40. The passage cited is found on p. 232.

peaceful, and that it is good that they sometimes give them difficult and perilous things to do, in order to elevate ambition there and to open a theater to it.q

Moralists complain constantly that the favorite vice of our period is pride.

That is true in a certain sense: there is no one, in fact, who does not believe himself worth more than his neighbor and who agrees to obey his superior. But that is very false in another sense; for this same man, who cannot bear either subordination or equality, nonetheless despises himself to the point that he believes himself made only for appreciating vulgar pleasures. He stops willingly at mediocre desires without daring to embark upon high undertakings; he scarcely imagines them.

So far from believing that humility must be recommended to our contemporaries, I would like you to try hard to give them a more vast idea of themselves and of their species;r humility is not healthy for them; what they lack most, in my opinion, is pride. I would willingly give up several of our small virtues for this vice.

[In a jacket with the manuscript of the chapter:

> Piece of the end that I am not very sure of having correctly deleted. Have it copied and read./
>> I must not yet despair of combining this with the original version./
>> Seeing the general movement of ambition that today torments all men and the senseless passions that often agitate them, there are many men who suppose that the principal business of the legislator in democratic

---

q. "A word that M. Thiers said to me one day in 1837 must not be lost from view: the bourgeois do great things when they are not led in a bourgeois way" (*Rubish*, 2).

r. "The great objective of a democratic government must be to give its subjects *great reasonable* ambitions" (*Rubish*, 2).

In another place of the *rubish:* "Utility that there can be in favoring philosophical doctrines that elevate in a general manner the notion of the human species and keep the human spirit at a certain proud height, like the dogma of the immortality of the soul, of the predestination of man to a better world, of his high position in the chain of being.

Philosophical humility is worth nothing in democratic centuries" (*Rubish*, 2).

centuries is to extinguish ambition and to narrow their desires. This seems true to me only to a certain measure.

It is in fact very important in those times to give fixed and visible limits to ambition.

<I am led to believe that among democratic nations it can be useful to entrust sovereign power to only a single family in order for sovereign power not to appear each day within reach of every man.>

I think that among democratic nations more than among all others it is important carefully to contain powers, however great they may be, within known and unsurpassable limits before which immoderate imaginations stop in advance. I imagine that you must work harder than elsewhere to make the constitution of the country seem strong and un-changing [v: unassailable] and, where the law fails, to make public opin-ion secure enough to raise an immobile barrier against unrestrained passions.

Thus, I understand that among democratic peoples it is particularly necessary to limit great ambition, but I believe that it would be dangerous to hinder its impetus too much within the allowed limits.

I admit straight on that I fear the boldness of desires much less for future generations than the mediocrity of desires. What, according to me, is principally to fear in the coming centuries is that in the midst of the small, incessant and tumultuous occupations of life, ambition may lose its impetus and its grandeur; that human passions may become exhausted and lower and that each day the appearance of humanity may become more peaceful and less elevated.

If, therefore, the legislators of the new world want men to remain at the level attained by our fathers and to go beyond it, they must take great care not to discourage the sentiment of ambition too much.

So instead of excessively plunging citizens into the contemplation of their particular interests so that they more easily abandon the direction of the State to their leaders, it is important to tear them away from themselves often in order to occupy them with public affairs and, if possible, to sub-stitute the love of fame and the taste for great things for the passion for well-being.

I think as well that in democratic societies you must be very careful not to imprison rare virtues too narrowly within the ordinary rules; it is good there to prepare in advance great places which, by great talents and by great

efforts, you can imagine reaching quickly and where you can imagine acting with independence.

This is what occurs naturally with liberty, and nothing shows its necessity better when conditions are equal.

Free institutions constantly force men to forget the petty affairs of individuals in order to preoccupy them with the great interests of peoples;
they elevate ambition and open a theater for it.

An absolute prince who becomes established within a people among
whom conditions are equal {democratic} is always obliged, in order to have
his power excused, to limit himself in the choice of his agents, to subject
advancement to fixed and invariable rules, to profess an exaggerated respect for equality of rights, for there is no power in the world which is
able to make a democratic people bear at the same time tyranny and
privilege.

A self-governing nation never allows itself to be imprisoned by such
fetters, and its omnipotent will constantly creates, despite customs and
laws, great quick fortunes which leave vast hopes for ambition.

So may the legislators of today seek to purify and to regulate ambition,
but may they take care not to want to diminish it too much.

Ambition must be given an honest, reasonable and great end, not
extinguished.

≠The more I consider what is coming in the future, the more I think
that from now on the great goal of the legislator must be to regulate and
to adjust ambition, rather than to diminish it.

So there is nothing that seems more appropriate to the new social state
than liberties in a monarchy, an hereditary prince and great elective
powers.≠]

CHAPTER 20[a]

Of Positions Becoming an Industry among Certain Democratic Nations

[I have talked about how as conditions become equal the sentiment of ambition spreads.

That is seen among all peoples whose social state is becoming democratic, but among them all ambition does not use the same means to satisfy itself.]

In the United States, as soon as a citizen has some enlightenment and some resources, he seeks to enrich himself in commerce and industry, or he buys a field covered with forest and becomes a pioneer. All that he asks of the State is not to come to disturb him in his labors and to ensure the fruit of those labors.

Among most European peoples, when a man begins to feel his strength and to expand his desires, the first idea that occurs to him is to gain a public post.[b] These different results, coming from the same cause, are worth our stopping a moment here to consider.

a. Among all democratic peoples, the number of ambitions is immense.

But among all, ambition does not take the same paths.

In America, every man seeks to raise himself by industry or commerce.

In France, as soon as [he has (ed.)] the desire to raise himself above his condition, he asks for a public post.

Princes favor this tendency, and they are wrong. For since the number of positions that they can give has a limit, and since the number of those who desire positions increases without limits, princes must necessarily soon find themselves before a people of discontented place seekers (YTC, CVf, p. 48). On the jacket of the manuscript of the chapter, you read: "10 March 1838. Baugy."

b. In a former version: "I have heard it said that in Spain as soon as a man felt himself in an analogous position, the first idea that occurred to him was to gain a public post and that, if he was not able to succeed in doing so, he remained idle" (Rubish, 2).

When public offices are few, badly paid, unreliable, and on the other hand, industrial careers are numerous and productive, the new and impatient desires that arise every day from equality are led from all directions toward industry and not toward administration.

But if, at the same time that ranks are becoming equal, enlightenment remains incomplete or spirits timid, or commerce and industry, hampered in their development, offer only difficult and slow means to make a fortune, citizens, losing hope of improving their lot by themselves, rush tumultuously toward the head of the State[c] and ask his help. To make themselves more comfortable at the expense of the public treasury seems to them to be, if not the only path open to them, at least, the easiest path and the one most open to all for leaving a condition that is no longer enough for them. The search for positions becomes the most popular of all industries.

It must be so, above all, in large, centralized monarchies, in which the number of paid officials is immense and the existence of the office holders is adequately secure, so that no one loses hope of obtaining a post there and of enjoying it peacefully like a patrimony.[d]

I will not say that this universal and excessive desire for public office is a great social evil; that it destroys, within each citizen, the spirit of independence and spreads throughout the entire body of the nation a venal and servile temper; that it suffocates the manly virtues; nor will I make the observation that an industry of this type creates only an unproductive activity and agitates the country without making it fruitful: all of that is easily understood.

But I want to remark that the government that favors such a tendency risks its tranquillity and puts its very life in great danger.

I know that, in a time like ours, when we see the love and respect that was formerly attached to power being gradually extinguished, it can appear necessary to those governing to bind each man more tightly by his interest, and that it seems easy to them to use his very passions to keep him in order and in silence; but it cannot be so for long, and what can appear for a certain

---

c. At first: ". . . toward the power of the State." In the margin: "<I do not like this word 'power,' vague and new.>"

d. In the margin, in a first draft from the *Rubish:* "Spain, great proof of this. "United States, no. A thousand channels for ambition" (*Rubish,* 2).

period as a cause of strength becomes assuredly in the long run a great cause of trouble and of weakness.

Among democratic peoples, as among all others, the number of public posts ends by having limits; but among these same peoples, the number of ambitious men has no limits; the number increases constantly, by a gradual and irresistible movement, as conditions become equal; the number reaches its limit only when men are lacking.

So when ambition has no outlet except the administration alone, the government necessarily ends by encountering a permanent opposition; for its task is to satisfy with limited means, desires that multiply without limits. You have to be well aware that, of all the peoples of this world, the one most difficult to contain and to lead is a people of place seekers. Whatever the efforts made by its leaders, they can never satisfy such a people, and you must always fear that it will finally overturn the constitution of the country and change the face of the State, solely for the need to open up positions.[e]

[<≠It is very insane to want to contain in a single streambed the always swelling torrent of human ambitions. It would be wiser in my opinion to divide up the mass and to separate it into a thousand various channels.>

I am persuaded on my part that in a democratic society the interest of

---

e. When a man succeeds in rising by industrial careers . . . he generally makes a thousand others and sometimes the whole nation profit from his rise. He establishes an enduring situation in the country.

When, on the contrary, a man succeeds in rising by public offices, his rise serves only himself. It does not even offer anything stable for him. It takes all independence away from him. Finally it prevents, for example, other abilities from being directed elsewhere. This state of things is very unfortunate for the government itself, considering it apart from the nation. For individual ambition in democracies has no limits, and the number of positions to give ends by having limits. When all democratic ambition concentrates on positions, a government must always expect a terrible, always permanent opposition. A people of place seekers makes revolutions in order to have vacant positions when all those that exist are already filled. *Industrial* (I am using this word lacking anything better) ambition can often come to the support of public stability. Ambition for positions in a democracy can only tend toward upheavals (*Rubish,* 2).

those governing as well as that of the governed is to multiply private careers infinitely. ≠]

The princes of our times, who work hard to draw toward themselves alone all the new desires aroused by equality, and to satisfy them, will therefore finish, if I am not mistaken, by regretting being engaged in such an enterprise; they will discover one day that they have risked their power by making it so necessary, and that it would have been more honest and more sure to teach each one of their subjects the art of being self-sufficient.

CHAPTER 21[a]

Why Great Revolutions Will Become Rare[b]

a. "This chapter would take a very long time to analyze; since I lack time, I leave it." (YTC, CVf, p. 49).

On 15 May 1838 Tocqueville read this chapter to Corcelle and Ampère. The latter, noticing the influence of Rousseau and the tone of the Great Century, could not prevent himself from noting his sadness at seeing the turn that Tocqueville's thought takes here (*Correspondance avec Ampère, OC,* XI, pp. xvi–xvii).

The theory of revolutions has had little commentary to this day. See Melvin Richter, "Tocqueville's Contribution to the Theory of Revolution," in C. Friedrich, ed., *Revolution* (New York: Atherton, 1966), pp. 75–121; and Irving Zeitlin, *Liberty, Equality and Revolution in Alexis de Tocqueville* (Boston: Little, Brown, 1971).

b. On the jacket of the manuscript:

OF REVOLUTIONARY PASSIONS AMONG DEMOCRATIC PEOPLES./

≠WHY THE AMERICANS SEEM SO AGITATED AND ARE SO IMMOBILE./

WHY THE AMERICANS MAKE SO MANY INNOVATIONS AND SO FEW REVOLUTIONS./≠

Take care while going over this chapter to point out better that I am speaking about a final and remote state and not about the times of transition in which we are still. That is necessary in order not to appear paradoxical./

Baugy, end of March 1838.

At the end of the chapter in the manuscript:

Note to leave at the head of the chapter. The spirit of the chapter must absolutely comply with it./

I can say very well, without putting myself in contradiction with myself, that equality does not lead men to *great and sudden revolutions.*

But I cannot say, without giving the lie to a thousand passages of this book and of the one that precedes it, that the natural tendency of equality is to make men *immobile.*

Nor is that true.

Equality leads man to continual *small changes* and pushes him away from *great revolutions;* there is the truth.

A people who has lived for centuries under the regime of castes and classes arrives at a democratic social state only through a long succession of more or less painful transformations, with the aid of violent efforts, and after numerous vicissitudes during which goods, opinions and power rapidly change place.

Even when this great revolution is finished, you see the revolutionary habits that it created still continue to exist, and profound agitation follows it.

Since all of this occurs at the moment when conditions are becoming equal, you conclude that a hidden connection and a secret bond exist between equality itself and revolutions, so that the one cannot exist without the others arising.

On this point, reasoning seems in agreement with experience.

Among a people where ranks are nearly equal no apparent bond unites men and holds them firmly in their place. No one among them has the permanent right or the power to command, and no one's condition is to obey; but each man, finding himself provided with some enlightenment and some resources, can choose his path and walk apart from all his fellows.

The same causes that make citizens independent of each other push them each day toward new and restless desires, and goad them constantly.

So it seems natural to believe that, in a democratic society, ideas, things and men must eternally change forms and places, and that democratic centuries will be times of rapid and constant transformations.

What is true as well is that a multitude of these small movements that are taken for progress are not.

Man goes back and forth in place.

All that I can add is that there is such a political state that, combining with equality and profiting from this fear of revolutions natural to democratic peoples, would be able to make them entirely stationary./

Hic.

In democratic societies, revolutions will be less *frequent,* less *violent* and less *sudden* than you believe.

Perhaps it can even happen that society there becomes *stationary.*

There is the clear idea that must emerge from the chapter. More would be too much; less, too little.

Is that the case in fact? Does equality of conditions lead men in a habitual and permanent way toward revolutions? Does it contain some disturbing principle that prevents society from becoming settled and disposes citizens constantly to renew their laws, their doctrines and their mores? I do not believe so. The subject is important; I beg the reader to follow me closely.[c]

Nearly all the revolutions that have changed the face of peoples have been made in order to sanction or to destroy inequality. Take away the secondary causes that have produced the great agitations of men, you will almost always arrive at inequality. It is the poor who have wanted to steal the property of the rich, or the rich who have tried to put the poor in chains. So if you can establish a state of society in which each man has something to keep and little to take, you will have done a great deal for the peace of the world.

I am not unaware that, among a great democratic people, there are always very poor citizens and very rich citizens; but the poor, instead of forming the immense majority of the nation as always happens in aristocratic societies, are small in number, and the law has not tied them together by the bonds of an irremediable and hereditary misery.

The rich, on their side, are few and powerless; they do not have privileges that attract attention; their wealth itself, no longer incorporated in and represented by the land, is elusive and as if invisible. Just as there are no longer races of the poor, there are no longer races of the rich; the latter emerge each day from within the crowd, and return to it constantly. So they do not form a separate class that you can easily define and despoil; and since, moreover, the rich are attached by a thousand secret threads to the mass of their

---

c. I must be very careful in all of this chapter because everything I say about the difficulty of revolutions depends prodigiously on the nature of political institutions. That will leap to the attention of the reader and he must not believe that he has discovered what I have not seen.

It is incontestable that autocracy, combining itself with equality of conditions, will make the most steady and the most somnolent of governments, but I do not know if you can say as much about equality combining with political liberty. I believe it nonetheless, everything considered and once permanent and peaceful equality has been established, but perhaps it will be necessary to make the distinction (*Rubish,* 2).

fellow citizens, the people can scarcely hope to strike them without hitting themselves. Between these two extremes of democratic societies, is found an innumerable multitude of almost similar men who, without being precisely rich or poor, possess enough property to desire order, and do not have enough property to arouse envy.

Those men are naturally enemies of violent movements; their immobility keeps at rest everything above and below them, and secures the social body in its settled position.

It isn't that those same men are satisfied with their present fortune, or that they feel a natural horror for a revolution whose spoils they would share without experiencing its evils; on the contrary, they desire to become rich with unequaled ardor; but the difficulty is to know from whom to take the wealth. The same social state that constantly suggests desires to them contains those desires within necessary limits. It gives men more liberty to change and less interest in changing.[d]

Not only do men of democracies not naturally desire revolutions, but they fear them.

There is no revolution that does not more or less threaten acquired property. Most of those who inhabit democratic countries are property owners; they not only have properties; they live in the condition in which men attach the highest value to their property.[e]

If you attentively consider each one of the classes that compose society, it is easy to see that in no class are the passions that arise from property more ruthless and more tenacious than among the middle class.

Often the poor hardly worry about what they possess, because they suffer from what they lack much more than they enjoy the little that they have. The rich have many other passions to satisfy than that of wealth, and besides, the long and difficult use of a great fortune sometimes ends by making them as if insensitive to its sweet pleasures.

But the men who live in a comfort equally removed from opulence and

---

d. The manuscript includes in this place the reference to note a. See note z for p. 1152.

e. "There is no country in which I saw as much horror for the theory of agrarian law than in the United States" (*Rubish,* 2).

from misery put an immense value on their property. Since they are still very close to poverty, they see its rigors close up, and fear them; between poverty and them, there is nothing except a small patrimony on which they soon fix their fears and their hopes. At every instant, they become more interested in their property because of the constant concerns that it gives them, and they become attached to it because of the daily efforts that they make to augment it. The idea of giving up the least part of it is unbearable to them, and they consider its complete loss as the greatest of misfortunes. Now, it is the number of these ardent and anxious small property owners that equality of conditions increases incessantly.

Thus, in democratic societies, the majority of citizens does not see clearly what it could gain from a revolution, and it feels at every instant and in a thousand ways what it could lose.[f]

I said, in another place in this work, how equality of conditions pushed men naturally toward industrial and commercial careers, and how it increased and diversified property in land; finally I showed how equality of conditions inspired in each man an ardent and constant desire to augment his well-being. There is nothing more contrary to revolutionary passions than all these things.

f. On a loose sheet at the end of the manuscript of the chapter:

Material bond./

I wonder how, when citizens differ in opinion on so many points as they do among most democratic peoples, it happens nonetheless that a certain material order is established easily enough among them, and I explain it to myself.

In proportion as conditions become equal, the material order becomes a positive and visible interest for more individuals at the same time. Since everyone has something to lose and since no one has much to gain from great changes, it is tacitly agreed not to change beyond a certain measure. This is how the division of property moderates the spirit of *change* to which it gave birth. On the one hand, it pushes men toward innovations of all types; on the other, it holds them within the limits of certain innovations.

In democracies the natural taste of citizens perhaps leads them to *disturb* the State, but concern for their interest prevents them from doing so. These democratic societies are always agitated, rarely overturned. In aristocracies, on the contrary, where the opinions of men are naturally more similar and conditions as well as interests more different, a small event can lead to confusion in everything.

Perhaps here what I said about personal property.

A revolution, in its final result, can happen to serve industry and commerce; but its first effect will almost always be[g] to ruin the industrialists and the merchants, because it cannot fail, first of all, to change the general state of consumption and to reverse temporarily the relation that existed between production and needs.

Moreover, I know nothing more opposed to revolutionary mores than commercial mores. Commerce is naturally hostile to all violent passions. It loves moderation, takes pleasure in compromises, very carefully flees from anger. It is patient, flexible, ingratiating, and it resorts to extreme means only when the most absolute necessity forces it to do so. Commerce makes men independent of each other; it gives them a high idea of their individual value; it leads them to want to conduct their own affairs, and teaches them to succeed in doing so; so it disposes them to liberty, but distances them from revolutions.

[≠Thus the effects of equality of conditions are diverse. Equality, making men independent of each other, puts them at full liberty to innovate and at the same time gives them tastes which need stability in order to be satisfied.≠]

In a revolution, the owners of personal property[h] have more to fear than all the others; for on the one hand, their property is often easy to seize, and

g. The manuscript says: "will be always."

h. "I said elsewhere that democracy pushed men toward commerce and industry and tended to augment personal wealth.

"Commercial habits in return are very favorable to the maintenance of democracy. Habit of repressing all too violent passions. Moderation. No anger. Compromises. Complicated and compromising interests in times of revolution.

"As for the effects of property in land, see note (m.n.o.)" (*Rubish*, 2).

Personal wealth (m.n.o.)./

How democracy tends to augment personal wealth. How it gives men a distaste for slow industries such as the cultivation of the land and pushes them toward commerce.

Political consequences of this. Idea of Damais: the man rich in capital in land risks in revolutions only his income; the man rich in personal capital risks, on the contrary, his entire existence. The one is much [more (ed.)] hostile to every appearance of trouble than the other. Many other consequences to draw from that. To look closely at this (YTC, CVa, p. 52).

on the other hand, at every moment it can disappear completely. This is less to be feared by owners of landed property who, while losing the income from their lands, hope at least throughout the vicissitudes, to keep the land itself. Consequently you see that the first are much more frightened than the second at the sight of revolutionary movements.

So peoples are less disposed to revolutions as personal property is multiplied and diversified among them and as the number of those who possess personal property becomes greater.

Moreover, whatever profession men embrace and whatever type of property they enjoy, one feature is common to all.

No one is fully satisfied with his present fortune, and everyone works hard every day, by a thousand diverse means, to augment it. Consider each one among them at whatever period of his life, and you will see him preoccupied with some new plans whose goal is to increase his comfort; do not speak to him about the interests and rights of humanity; this small domestic enterprise absorbs all of his thoughts for the moment and makes him wish to put public agitations off to another time.

That not only prevents them from making revolutions, but turns them away from wanting to do so. Violent political passions have little hold on men who have in this way attached their entire soul to the pursuit of well-being. The ardor that they give to small affairs calms them down about great ones.

It is true that from time to time in democratic societies enterprising and ambitious citizens arise whose immense desires cannot be satisfied by following the common path. These men love revolutions and call them forth; but they have great difficulty bringing them about, if extraordinary events do not come to their aid.

You do not struggle effectively against the spirit of your century and country; and one man, however powerful you suppose him to be, has difficulty getting his contemporaries to share sentiments and ideas that the whole of their desires and their sentiments reject. So once equality of conditions has become an old and uncontested fact and has stamped its character on mores, you must not believe that men easily allow themselves to rush into dangers following an imprudent leader or a bold innovator.

It is not that they resist him in an open way, with the aid of intelligent contrivances, or even by a premeditated plan to resist. They do not fight him with energy; sometimes they even applaud him, but they do not follow him. To his ardor, they secretly oppose their inertia; to his revolutionary instincts, their conservative interests; their stay-at-home tastes to his adventurous passions; their good sense to the flights of his genius; to his poetry, their prose. With a thousand efforts, he arouses them for one moment, and soon they escape him; and as if brought down by their own weight, they fall back. He exhausts himself, wanting to animate this indifferent and inattentive crowd, and he finally sees himself reduced to impotence, not because he is vanquished, but because he is alone.

I do not claim that men who live in democratic societies are naturally immobile; I think, on the contrary, that within such a society an eternal movement reigns and that no one knows rest; but I believe that men there become agitated within certain limits beyond which they hardly ever go. They vary, alter, or renew secondary things every day; they take great care not to touch principal ones. They love change; but they fear revolutions.

Although the Americans are constantly modifying or repealing some of their laws, they are very far from exhibiting revolutionary passions. By the promptness with which they stop and calm themselves down when public agitation begins to become threatening, even at the moment when passions seem the most excited, it is easy to discover that they fear a revolution as the greatest of misfortunes, and that each one among them is inwardly resolved to make great sacrifices to avoid it. There is no country in the world where the sentiment of property shows itself more active and more anxious than in the United States, and where the majority shows less of a tendency toward doctrines that threaten to alter in any manner whatsoever the constitution of property.j

j. The Americans constantly change their opinions in detail, but they are more invincibly attached to certain opinions than any other people on earth. This [is (ed.)] a singularity that is very striking at first view and that can only be understood by thinking about the difficulty that men have in acting upon each other in democracies and in establishing entirely new beliefs in the minds of a great number of men.

[On the back] Great revolutions in *ideas,* very rare events under democracies. Great revolutions in *facts,* something rarer still (*Rubish,* 2).

I have often remarked that theories that are revolutionary by their nature, in that they can only be realized by a complete and sometimes sudden change in the state of property and persons, are infinitely less in favor in the United States than in the great monarchies of Europe. If a few men profess them, the mass rejects them with a kind of instinctive horror.

I am not afraid to say that most of the maxims that are customarily called democratic in France would be proscribed by the democracy of the United States. That is easily understood. In America, you have democratic ideas and passions; in Europe, we still have revolutionary passions and ideas.

If America ever experiences great revolutions, they will be brought about by the presence of Blacks on the soil of the United States: that is to say that it will be not equality of conditions, but on the contrary inequality of conditions that gives birth to them.

When conditions are equal, each man willingly becomes isolated within himself and forgets the public. If the legislators of democratic peoples did not seek to correct this fatal tendency or favored it, with the thought that this tendency diverts citizens from political passions and thus turns them away from revolutions, they could themselves end up producing the evil that they want to avoid. And a moment could arrive when the disorderly passions of a few men, making use of the unintelligent egoism and faint-heartedness of the greatest number, would end up forcing the social body to undergo strange vicissitudes.

In democratic societies,[k] hardly any one other than small minorities desires revolutions; but minorities can sometimes make them.[m]

k. The manuscript says: "In democratic centuries . . ."
m. In an aristocratic country two or three powerful individuals join together and make a revolution. Among a democratic people millions of independent men must agree and associate in order to attain the same goal, which is that much more difficult since among these peoples the State is naturally more skilled and stronger and individuals more powerless and weaker than anywhere else.

Thus equality not only removes from men the taste for revolutions, to a certain point it takes the power away from them (*Rubish*, 2).

I am not saying that democratic nations are safe from revolutions; I am only saying that the social state of these nations does not lead them to, but rather distances them from revolutions. Democratic peoples, left to themselves, do not easily become engaged in great adventures; they are carried toward revolutions only unknowingly; they sometimes undergo revolutions, but they do not make them. And I add that, when they have been permitted to acquire enlightenment and experience, they do not allow them to be made.[n]

I know well that in this matter public institutions themselves can do a great deal; they favor or restrain the instincts that arise from the social state. So I am not maintaining, I repeat, that a people is safe from revolution for the sole reason that, within it, conditions are equal; but I believe that, whatever the institutions of such a people, great revolutions there will always be infinitely less violent and rarer than is supposed; and I easily foresee such a political state that, combining with equality, would make society more stationary [<and more immobile>] than it has ever been in our West.

What I have just said about facts applies in part to ideas.

Two things are astonishing in the United States: the great mobility of most human actions and the singular fixity of certain principles. Men stir constantly, the human mind seems almost immobile.

Once an opinion has spread over the American soil and taken root, you could say that no power on earth is able to eradicate it. In the United States the general doctrines in matters of religion, philosophy, morals, and even of politics, do not vary, or at least they are only modified after a hidden

---

A note at the end of the manuscript explains:

There are two remarks of Édouard that I must make use of.

1. In political revolutions: in aristocracies it is the majority that has an interest in revolutions. In democracies, the minority. That is implied several times. Say it clearly.
2. In intellectual revolutions. All men, having a certain smattering of everything, imagine that they have nothing new to learn or to learn from anyone.

n. To the side of a first version in the rough drafts:
"Perhaps here Athens and Florence./
"In this matter I would very much like people to stop citing to us, in relation to everything, the example of the democratic republics of Greece and Italy . . ." (*Rubish*, 2).

and often imperceptible effort;° the crudest prejudices themselves fade only with an inconceivable slowness amid the friction repeated a thousand times between things and men.

I hear it said that it is in the nature and in the habits of democracies to change sentiments and thoughts at every moment. That is perhaps true of small democratic nations,[*] such as those of antiquity [added: or of the Middle Ages], which were gathered all together in the public square and then stirred up at the pleasure of an orator. I saw nothing similar within the great democratic people that occupies the opposite shores of our ocean. What struck me in the United States was the difficulty experienced in disabusing the majority of an idea that it has conceived and in detaching the majority from a man that it adopts. Writings or speeches can hardly succeed in doing so; experience alone achieves it in the end; sometimes experience must be repeated.P

This is astonishing at first view; a more attentive examination explains it.

[<≠It is ideas that, most often, produce facts, and in turn facts constantly modify ideas.≠>]

I do not believe that it is as easy as you imagine to uproot the prejudices of a democratic people; to change its beliefs; to substitute new religious, philosophical, political and moral principles for those that were once established; in a word, to make great and frequent intellectual revolutions. It

o. "In metaphysics and in morals and in religion, authority seems to me more necessary and less offensive than in politics, in science and in the arts./

"If equality of con.-.-t.-ons [conditions? (ed.)] combined with autocracy, I think that the most immobile state of things that we have seen until now in our Europe would result" (*Rubish*, 2).

[*]. Show in a note there, in two words, that these were not democracies. Idle men.

p. In the margin:

Show how what was called *democracy* in antiquity and in the Middle Ages had no real analogy with what we see in our times./

In Florence no middle class. Capitalists. Workers. No agricultural class. Manufacturing and dense population.

The same cause makes them conceive false opinions and makes them obstinately keep their false opinions. They adopt such opinions because they do not have the leisure to examine them carefully and they keep them because they do not want to take the trouble and the time to review them.

is not that the human mind is idle there; it is in constant motion; but it exerts itself to vary infinitely the consequences of known principles and to discover new consequences rather than to seek new principles. It turns back on itself with agility, rather than rushing forward by a rapid and direct effort; it extends its sphere little by little by continuous and quick small movements; it does not shift ground suddenly.

Men equal in rights, in education, in fortune, and to say everything in a phrase, of similar condition, necessarily have almost similar needs, habits and tastes. Since they see matters in the same way, their mind is inclined naturally toward analogous ideas, and although each one of them can withdraw from his contemporaries and create his own beliefs, they end up, without knowing it and without wanting to, by finding themselves all with a certain number of common opinions.

[The intellectual anarchy of democratic societies is more apparent than real. Men differ infinitely on questions of detail, but on the great principles they are in agreement.]

The more attentively I consider the effects of equality on the mind, the more I am persuaded that the intellectual anarchy of which we are witnesses is not, as some suppose, the natural state of democratic peoples.q I believe that the intellectual anarchy must instead be considered as

q. On a sheet at the end of the manuscript of the chapter:

I must take great care not to fall into the improbable and the paradoxical and to appear to be conjuring up ghosts.

Equality of conditions, giving individual reason a complete independence, must lead men toward intellectual anarchy and bring about continual revolutions in human opinions.

This is the first idea that presents itself, the common idea, the most likely idea at first view.

By examining things more closely, I discover that there are limits to this individual independence in democratic countries that I had not seen at first and which make me believe that beliefs must be more *common* and more *stable* than we judge at first glance.

That is already doing a great deal to lead the mind of the reader there.

But I want to aim still further and I am going even as far as imagining that the final result of democracy will be to make the human mind too immobile and human opinions too stable.

an accident particular to their youth, and that it shows itself only during the period of transition when men have already broken the old bonds that tied them together, and still differ prodigiously by origin, education and mores; so that, having retained very diverse ideas, instincts and tastes, nothing prevents them any longer from bringing them forth. The principal opinions of men become similar as conditions become alike. Such seems to me to be the general and permanent fact; the rest is fortuitous and fleeting.[r]

I believe that rarely, in a democratic society, will a man come to imagine, at a single stroke, a system of ideas very removed from the one that his contemporaries have adopted; and if such an innovator appeared, I imagine that he would at first have great difficulty making himself heard and still more making himself believed.[s]

When conditions are almost the same, one man does not easily allow himself to be persuaded by another. Since all see each other very close up, since together they have learned the same things and lead the same life, they

---

This idea is so extraordinary and so removed from the mind of the reader that I must make him see it only in the background and as an hypothesis.

Note in the rough drafts:

This idea that the democratic social state is anti-revolutionary so shocks accepted ideas that I must win over the mind of the reader little by little, and for that I must begin by saying that this social state is less *revolutionary* than is supposed. I begin there and by an imperceptible curve I arrive at saying that there is room to fear that it is not revolutionary enough. True idea, but which would seem paradoxical at first view.

[To the side] Finish and do not begin with intellectual revolutions. The perfection of the logical order would require beginning there, since facts arise from ideas; but if I put my fears about the stationary state after social and political revolutions, I would be thought *far-fetched* and would not be understood. After intellectual revolutions that will be understood (*Rubish*, 2).

r. "Perhaps distinguish the democratic *social state* from democratic *political institutions, equality of conditions* from *democracy* strictly speaking.

"The one leads to stability, the other to revolutions.

"[To the side] Equality of conditions with free institutions is still not a revolutionary constitution; combined with monarchy, it is the most naturally immobile of all states" (*Rubish*, 2).

s. In the margin: "Because the opinions of men are naturally similar, is it a reason for those opinions not to undergo a revolution?"

are not naturally disposed to take one among them as a guide and to follow him blindly; you hardly believe your fellow or your equal on his word.

It is not only confidence in the enlightenment of certain individuals that becomes weak among democratic nations; as I said elsewhere, the general idea of the intellectual superiority that any man can gain over all the others does not take long to grow dim.

As men become more alike, the dogma of the equality of minds insinuates itself little by little in their beliefs, and it becomes more difficult for an innovator, whoever he may be, to gain and to exercise a great power over the mind of a people. So in such societies, sudden intellectual revolutions are rare; for if you cast your eyes over the history of the world, you see that it is much less the strength of an argument than the authority of a name that has produced the great and rapid mutations of human opinions.

Note, moreover, that since the men who live in democratic societies[t] are not attached by any bond to each other, each one of them must be persuaded. While in aristocratic societies it is enough to be able to act on the mind of a few; all the others follow. If Luther had lived in a century of equality, and if he had not had lords and princes as an audience, he would perhaps have had more difficulty changing the face of Europe.

It is not that the men of democracies are naturally very convinced of the certitude of their opinions and very firm in their beliefs; they often have doubts that no one, in their view, can resolve. It sometimes happens in those times that the human mind would willingly change position; but, since nothing either pushes it strongly or directs it, it oscillates in place and does not move.[1]

t. The manuscript says: "democratic centuries."

1. *If I try to find out what state of society is most favorable to great intellectual revolutions, I find that it is found somewhere between the complete equality of all citizens and the absolute separation of classes.*

Under the regime of castes, the generations succeed each other without men changing place; some expect nothing more, others hope for nothing better. Imagination falls asleep amid this

When the confidence of a democratic people has been won, it is still a great matter to gain its attention. It is very difficult to make the men who live in democracies listen, when you are not talking to them about themselves.[u] They do not listen to the things that you say to them, because they are always very preoccupied with the things that they are doing.

There are, in fact, few idle men among democratic nations. Life there passes amid movement and noise, and men there are so occupied with acting that little time remains to them for thinking. What I want to note above all is that not only are they occupied, but they are passionate about their occupations. They are perpetually in action, and each one of their actions absorbs their soul; the heat that they bring to their affairs prevents them from catching fire about ideas.

I think that it is very difficult to excite the enthusiasm of a democratic people for any theory whatsoever that does not have a visible, direct and immediate connection to the daily conduct of life. So such a people does not easily abandon its ancient beliefs. For it is enthusiasm that hurls the human mind out of beaten paths and that creates great intellectual revolutions like great political revolutions.

Thus democratic peoples have neither the leisure nor the taste to go in search of new opinions. Even when they come to doubt those they possess, they nevertheless maintain them because it would require too much time

---

silence and this universal immobility, and the very idea of movement no longer occurs to the human mind.

When classes have been abolished and conditions have become almost equal, all men move constantly, but each one of them is isolated, independent and weak. This last state differs prodigiously from the first; it is, however, analogous on one point. Great revolutions of the human mind are very rare there.

But between these two extremes of the history of peoples, an intermediary age is found, a glorious and troubled period, when conditions are not so fixed that intelligence is asleep, and when conditions are unequal enough that men exercise a very great power over each other's mind, and that a few can modify the beliefs of all. That is when powerful reformers arise and when new ideas suddenly change the face of the world.

u. In the manuscript: ". . . when you are not talking to them about what has a visible and direct connection to the daily conduct of life, they ordinarily appear very distant. Their minds constantly escape you."

and investigation for them to change their opinions; they keep them, not as certain, but as established.

There are still other and more powerful reasons that are opposed to a great change taking place easily in the doctrines of a democratic people. I have already pointed it out at the beginning of this book.

If, within such a people, individual influences are weak and almost non-existent, the power exercised by the mass on the mind of each individual is very great. I have given the reasons for it elsewhere. What I want to say at this moment is that you would be wrong to believe that this depended solely on the form of government, and that the majority there had to lose its intellectual dominion with its political power.

In aristocracies men often have a greatness and a strength that is their own. When they find themselves in contradiction with the greatest number of their fellows, they withdraw within themselves, sustain and console themselves apart. It is not the same among democratic peoples. Among them, public favor seems as necessary as the air that you breathe, and to be in disagreement with the mass is, so to speak, not to live. The mass does not need to use laws to bend those who do not think as it does. It is enough to disapprove of them. The sentiment of their isolation and of their powerlessness overwhelms them immediately and reduces them to despair.

Every time that conditions are equal, general opinion presses with an immense weight on the mind of each individual; opinion envelops, directs and oppresses it; that is due to the very constitution of the society much more than to its political laws. As all men resemble each other more, each one feels more and more weak in the face of all. Not finding anything that raises him very far above them and that distinguishes him from them, he mistrusts himself as soon as they fight him; not only does he doubt his strength, but he also comes to doubt his right, and he is very close to acknowledging that he is wrong, when the greatest number assert it. The majority does not need to constrain him; it convinces him.[v]

So in whatever way you organize the powers of a democratic society and

---

v. In the margin: "<The majority does not need political power to make life unbearable to the one who contradicts it.>"

balance them, it will always be very difficult to believe in what the mass rejects and to profess what it condemns.

This marvelously favors the stability of beliefs.

When an opinion has taken root among a democratic people and has become established in the mind of the greatest number, it then subsists by itself and perpetuates itself without effort, because no one attacks it. Those who had at first rejected it as false end by receiving it as general, and those who continue to combat it at the bottom of their hearts reveal nothing; they are very careful not to become engaged in a dangerous and useless struggle.

It is true that, when the majority of a democratic people changes opinion, it can at will bring about strange and sudden revolutions in the intellectual world; but it is very difficult for its opinion to change, and almost as difficult to notice that it has changed.

It sometimes happens that time, events or the individual and solitary effort of minds, end by shaking or by destroying a belief little by little without anything being outwardly visible. It is not fought openly. Men do not gather together to make war on it. Its partisans leave it quietly one by one; but each day a few abandon it, until finally it is shared only by a small number.

In this state, it still reigns.

Since its enemies continue to be silent, or communicate their thoughts only surreptitiously, they themselves are for a long time unable to be sure that a great revolution has taken place, and in doubt they remain immobile. They observe and they are silent. [<They still tremble before the power that no longer exists and yield in a cowardly way to an imaginary authority.>] The majority no longer believes; but it still has the appearance of believing, and this empty phantom of public opinion is enough to chill innovators and to keep them in silence and respect.

[≠That is seen in all centuries but particularly in democratic centuries.

Take liberty of the press away from a democratic nation and the human mind falls asleep.≠]

We live in a period that has seen the most rapid changes take place in the mind of men. It could happen, however, that soon the principal human opinions will be more stable than they have been in the preceding centuries of our history; this time has not come, but perhaps it is approaching.

As I examine more closely the natural needs and instincts of democratic peoples, I am persuaded that, if equality is ever established in a general and permanent way in the world, great intellectual and political revolutions will become very difficult and rarer than we suppose.[w]

Because the men of democracies appear always excited, uncertain, breathless, ready to change will and place, [<thoughts, careers]> you imagine that they are suddenly going to abolish their laws, to adopt new beliefs and to take up new mores. You do not consider that, if equality leads men to change, it suggests to them interests and tastes that need stability in order to be satisfied; it pushes them and, at the same time, stops them; it spurs them on and ties them to the earth; it inflames their desires and limits their strength.

This is what is not revealed at first. The passions that push citizens away from each other in a democracy appear by themselves. But you do not notice at first glance the hidden force that holds them back and gathers them together.

Will I dare to say it amid the ruins that surround me? What I dread most for the generations to come is not revolutions.[x]

If citizens continue to enclose themselves more and more narrowly within the circle of small domestic interests and to be agitated there without respite, you can fear that they will end by becoming as if impervious to these great and powerful public emotions that disturb peoples, but which develop and renew them. When I see property become so mobile, and the love of property so anxious and so ardent, I cannot prevent myself from fearing that men will reach the point of regarding every new theory as a danger, every innovation as an unfortunate trouble, every social progress as a first step toward a revolution, and that they will refuse entirely to move

w. "I understand by great revolutions changes that profoundly modify the social state, the political constitution, the mores, the opinions of a people" (*Rubish*, 2).

x. "Will I dare to say it? What I dread most for the generations to come is not great revolutions, but apathy" (*Rubish*, 2).

for fear that they would be carried away. I tremble, I confess, that they will finally allow themselves to be possessed so well by a cowardly love of present enjoyments, that the interest in their own future and that of their descendants will disappear, and that they will prefer to follow feebly the course of their destiny, than to make, if needed, a sudden and energetic effort to redress it.

You believe that the new societies are going to change face every day, and as for me, I fear that they will end by being too invariably fixed in the same institutions, the same prejudices, the same mores; so that humanity comes to a stop and becomes limited; that the mind eternally turns back on itself without producing new ideas; that man becomes exhausted in small solitary and sterile movements, and that, even while constantly moving, humanity no longer advances.

[At the end of the manuscript of this chapter:

This piece interrupted the natural course of ideas. Put it in a note.[y]

<It is not only the results of revolutions that frighten democratic peoples. The extreme violence of revolutionary methods is repugnant to them.>[*]

I showed how equality of conditions, by making men alike, interested them mutually in their miseries and made their mores milder.

These habits of private life are found again in public life and prevent political passions [v: hatreds] from being too cruel and too implacable.

Here you must not confuse revolutions that are made to establish equal-

---

y. In the margin: "<Where to place this idea which is necessary, but which can only be introduced with difficulty into an argument without interrupting it?

"R: In a note.

"Democracy not only distances men from revolutions by their interests but also by their tastes.>" The indications in the manuscript show that this piece should have been placed immediately before "I am not unaware . . ."

[*]. Is that true in a general way? What is more favorable to revolutionary methods than this maxim that the individual is nothing, society everything? What social state better permits giving yourself to those methods and applying them than the one in which the individual is in fact so weak that you can crush him with impunity?

ity with those that take place after equality is established, and you must be very careful about applying to the second the character of the first.

Revolutions that are made to establish equality are almost always cruel because the struggle takes place between men who are already equal enough to be able to make war on each other and who are dissimilar enough to strike each other without pity.[z]

This harshness of sentiments no longer exists from the moment when citizens have become equal and alike. Among a democratic people the general and permanent mildness of mores imposes a certain restraint on the most intense political hatreds. Men willingly allow a revolution to go as far as injustice, but not as far as cruelty. The confiscation of property is repugnant to them, the sight of human blood is offensive to them; they allow you to oppress, but they do not want you to kill.

This softening of political passions is seen clearly in the United States. America is, I believe, the only country in the world where for the last fifty years not a single man has been condemned to death for a political offense. There have, nonetheless, been a few great political crimes; there has been no scaffold. It is true that several times in the United States and above all in more recent times, you have seen the population give itself to horrible excesses against Blacks and concerning slavery. But even that proves what I am asserting. The political passions of the Americans become barbaric only when an aristocratic institution is found (this is good but has already been said previously).]

z. In the margin:

<What makes democratic revolutions milder is that the interests that they engage are or seem less great. Men are always cruel when their passions are violently excited by a great interest. This could be of use to me as a transition.>

(a) The same reason that causes men to have less interest in making great revolutions in democratic centuries than in others makes revolutions there milder and less complete. For what contributes most to inflame passions and to push them toward violence is the greatness of the goal that they pursue.

There is still another reason. I showed . . . [interrupted text (ed.)]"

CHAPTER 22[a]

Why Democratic Peoples Naturally Desire Peace and Democratic Armies Naturally Desire War

The same interests, the same fears, the same passions that divert democratic peoples from revolutions distance them from war; the military spirit and the revolutionary spirit grow weaker at the same time and for the same reasons.[b]

---

a. "What I said in the preceding chapter explains why democratic peoples naturally love peace.

"Democratic armies naturally love war, because in these armies ambition is much more general and more (illegible word) than in all others, and because in times of peace advancement is more difficult.

"These opposite dispositions of the people and of the army make democratic societies run great dangers.

"Remedies indicated for averting these dangers" (YTC, CVf, p. 49).

In the *Rubish,* all the manuscripts belonging to the chapters on war are gathered in the same jacket with the title: INFLUENCE OF EQUALITY ON WARRIOR PASSIONS. Initially the titles of the chapters were the following:

MILITARY SPIRIT. [Chapter 22]

HOW A DEMOCRATIC ARMY COULD CEASE TO BE WARLIKE AND REMAIN TUR-BULENT. [This section constitutes the current chapter 22.]

WHICH CLASS IN THE DEMOCRATIC ARMY IS THE MOST NATURALLY WARLIKE AND REVOLUTIONARY. [Chapter 23]

RUBISH OF CHAPTER 4. [Chapter 24]

INFLUENCE OF EQUALITY ON MILITARY DISCIPLINE. [Chapter 25]

RUBISH OF CHAPTER 6. [Chapter 26]

Tocqueville finished drafting these chapters at the end of the month of April 1838.

"The objection which presents itself to all these chapters is that I do not have a sufficient *personal* knowledge of the matter" (*Rubish,* 2).

b. At this place you find in the manuscript a reference to note (a). In the *rubish,* a

1153

The ever-increasing number of property owners friendly to peace, the development of personal wealth, which war so rapidly devours, this leniency of morals, this softness of heart, this predisposition toward pity that equality inspires, this coldness of reason that makes men hardly sensitive to the poetic and violent emotions which arise among arms, all these causes join together to extinguish military spirit.

I believe that you can accept as a general and constant rule that, among civilized peoples, warrior passions will become rarer and less intense, as conditions will be more equal.

War, however, is an accident to which all peoples are subject, democratic peoples as well as others. Whatever taste these nations have for peace, they must clearly keep themselves ready to repulse war, or in other words, they must have an army.

Fortune, which has done such distinctive things to favor the inhabitants of the United States, placed them in the middle of a wilderness where they have, so to speak, no neighbors. A few thousand soldiers are sufficient for them, but this is American and not democratic.

Equality of conditions, and the mores as well as the institutions that derive from it, do not release a democratic people from the obligation to maintain armies, and its armies always exercise a very great influence on its fate. So it is singularly important to inquire what the natural instincts are of those who compose its armies.

Among aristocratic peoples, among those above all in which birth alone determines rank, inequality is found in the army as in the nation; the officer is the noble, the soldier is the serf. The one is necessarily called to command, the other to obey. So in aristocratic armies, the ambition of the soldier has very narrow limits.

---

jacket bears the notation "Piece that originally was inserted at sign (a) and that must not be definitively deleted except after consultation.

"To have copied after reestablishing page 2, which I took out for another use." This jacket contains ideas that already appear in the chapter. A copy, reproduced in YTC, CVk, 1, pp. 89–91, bears this commentary: "Piece copied separately; I must pay attention to it at the final examination./

"Piece that originally began the chapter. I removed it as extending and reproducing ideas if not entirely similar, at least very analogous to those contained in the preceding chapter. To see again" (YTC, CVk, 1, p. 89).

Nor is that of the officers unlimited.

An aristocratic body is not only part of a hierarchy; it always contains an internal hierarchy; the members who compose it are placed some above the others, in a certain way that does not vary. This one is naturally called by birth to command a regiment, and that one a company; having reached the extreme limits of their hopes, they stop on their own and remain satisfied with their lot.

There is first of all one great cause that in aristocracies tempers the desire of the officer for advancement.

Among aristocratic peoples, the officer, apart from his rank in the army, still occupies an elevated rank in society; the first is almost always in his eyes only an accessory to the second; the noble, by embracing the career of arms, obeys ambition less than a sort of duty that his birth imposes on him. He enters the army in order to employ honorably the idle years of his youth, and in order to be able to bring back to his household and to his peers a few honorable memories of military life; but his principal objective there is not to gain property, consideration and power; for he possesses these advantages on his own and enjoys them without leaving home.

In democratic armies, all the soldiers can become officers, which generalizes the desire for advancement and extends the limits of military ambition almost infinitely.

On his side, the officer sees nothing that naturally and inevitably stops him at one rank rather than at another, and each rank has an immense value in his eyes, because his rank in society depends almost always on his rank in the army.

Among democratic peoples, it often happens that the officer has no property except his pay, and can expect consideration only from his military honors. So every time he changes offices, he changes fortune and is in a way another man. What was incidental to existence in aristocratic armies has thus become the main thing, everything, existence itself.

Under the old French monarchy,[c] officers were given only their title of

---

c. Under the old regime and still currently in England generals were called by their nobility. Today, they are given only their military title. This small change in the conventions of language is sufficient to indicate that a great revolution has taken place in the constitution of society and in that of the army.

Within democratic armies, the desire to advance is almost universal; it is ardent, tenacious, continual; it increases with all the other desires, and is extinguished only with life. Now, it is easy to see that, of all the armies of the world, those in which advancement must be slowest in time of peace are democratic armies. Since the number of ranks is naturally limited, the number of competitors almost innumerable, and the inflexible law of equality bears on all, no one can make rapid progress, and many cannot budge. Thus the need to advance is greater, and the ease of advancing less than elsewhere.[d]

---

title of nobility. In France they are given only their military title. There is a great political revolution mixed with this revolution in the conventions of language.

They count on their salary to live, on their military cross, on their ranks to appear, shine . . . , even more, all can equally attain everything. When a great prince said to young soldiers that the baton of Maréchal de France could be found in the knapsack of each one of them, he was only translating into an energetic and original form the common thought (*Rubish*, 2).

d. Democratic army./

L[ouis (ed.)]. said to me today (17 March 1837) about the army of Africa some damning things if they are true, which I still doubt to the extent that he said.

He told me that this army was not very warlike, that you had all the difficulty in the world making it fight, that the soldier thought only about finishing his time and returning to France, the officer thought only about reaching with the least danger possible the time of his retirement, that the softness there was surprising, that the regiments arrived in Africa only grudgingly, that there they took part in expeditions only grudgingly and that in the expeditions they exposed themselves as little as they could.

He claims that the army presented the same spectacle at Anvers, and he adds that if we enter into war with Europe we will without fail be defeated.

[In the margin: L[ouis (ed.)]. fell into agreement that nothing similar was seen before 1830.]

It seems to me that I am able to conclude from all that he said that the principal causes of this state of things could be reduced to this:

1. Disorganization caused by the Revolution of 1830. A great number of good subjects dismissed or retiring.

All of the ambitious men contained in a democratic army therefore wish vehemently for war, because war empties places and finally allows violation of the right of seniority, which is the only privilege natural to democracy.

We thus arrive at this singular consequence that, of all armies, the ones that most ardently desire war are democratic armies, and that, among peoples, those who most love peace are democratic peoples; and what really makes the thing extraordinary is that it is equality which produces these opposite effects simultaneously.

Citizens, being equal, conceive daily the desire and discover the possibility of changing their condition and of increasing their well-being; that disposes them to love peace, which makes industry prosper and allows each

---

2. Moral effect caused by this revolution. The soldier not only inferior to the civilian, which must be so, but beaten by the civilian who has suddenly become a better soldier than he is.

3. Old remnants of the Empire with which the regiments were inundated. Old non-commissioned officers who have been made officers. Four hundred battalions created and disbanded almost immediately, forming afterward an immense mass of officers which stops advancement. Almost all the lower ranks occupied by old men. In a word, the disorder of a great revolution without the movement and the impetus that it causes. It has been disorganizing without creating anything.

4. General deterioration of morals resulting from the deceptions that followed 1830, of the baseness of the government, of tricks, of the cult of cleverness. . . . This deterioration makes itself felt in the army as elsewhere. *Civilians* sell their conscience and *military men* seek to save their skin.

5. The inferior condition in which the army is found. The officer is paid little; he is taken from the secondary classes and not mixed with the upper classes; he is not received in society; he is inferior in education and in enlightenment. The civilization of the army is very inferior to that of the country. The officer is abased in all ways in his own eyes and becomes a stranger to the great sentiments and to the great thoughts that cause great things. This inferiority of the army has increased since 1830 when the aristocratic element of the army disappeared.

The first four causes that I have just talked about are accidental and transitory, but it is not sure that the fifth is not due profoundly to the state of a democratic army in peace, and it necessitates attracting my most serious attention (In the *Rubish* HOW A DEMOCRATIC ARMY COULD CEASE TO BE WARLIKE AND REMAIN TURBULENT). Certain ideas of these chapters are already found in a letter of 10 November 1836 to Kergorlay (*Correspondance avec Kergorlay, OC,* XIII, 1, pp. 416–17).

man to push his small enterprises tranquilly to their end; and from the other side, this same equality, by augmenting the value of military honors in the eyes of those who follow the career of arms, and by making honors accessible to all, makes soldiers dream of battlefields. From both sides, the restlessness of heart is the same, the taste for enjoyments is as insatiable, ambition is equal; only the means to satisfy it is different.

These opposing predispositions of the nation and of the army make democratic societies run great dangers.

When the military spirit deserts a people, the military career immediately ceases to be honored, and men of war fall to the lowest rank of public officials. They are little esteemed and no longer understood. Then the opposite of what is seen in aristocratic centuries happens. It is no longer the principal citizens who enter the army, but the least. Men give themselves to military ambition only when no other is allowed. This forms a vicious circle from which it is difficult to escape. The elite of the nation avoids the military career, because this career is not honored; and it is not honored, because the elite of the nation no longer enters it.

[≠Although the military man has in general a better-regulated and milder existence in democratic times than in all the others, he nonetheless experiences an unbearable uneasiness there; his body is better nourished, better clothed, but his soul suffers.≠]

So you must not be astonished if democratic armies often appear restless, muttering, and poorly satisfied with their lot, even though the physical condition there is usually very much milder and discipline less rigid than in all the others. The soldier feels himself in an inferior position, and his wounded pride ends by giving him the taste for war, which makes him necessary, or the love of revolutions, during which he hopes to conquer, weapons in hand, the political influence and the individual consideration that others deny him.

The composition of democratic armies makes this last danger very much to be feared.

In democratic society, nearly all citizens have some property to preserve; but democratic armies are led, in general, by proletarians. Most among them have little to lose in civil disturbances. The mass of the nation naturally fears revolutions more than in centuries of aristocracy; but the leaders of the army fear them much less.

Moreover, since among democratic peoples, as I have said before, the wealthiest, most educated, most capable citizens hardly enter the military career, it happens that the army, as a whole, ends up becoming a small nation apart, in which intelligence is less widespread and habits are cruder than in the large nation. Now, this small uncivilized nation possesses the weapons, and it alone knows how to use them.

What, in fact, increases the danger that the military and turbulent spirit of the army presents to democratic peoples is the pacific temperament of the citizens; there is nothing so dangerous as an army within a nation that is not warlike; the excessive love of all the citizens for tranquillity daily puts the constitution at the mercy of soldiers.

So you can say in a general way that, if democratic peoples are naturally led toward peace by their interests and their instincts, they are constantly drawn toward war and revolutions by their armies.

Military revolutions, which are almost never to be feared in aristocracies, are always to be feared in democratic nations. These dangers must be ranked among the most formidable of all those that their future holds; the attention of statesmen [v: of good citizens] must be applied unrelentingly to finding a remedy for them.

When a nation feels itself tormented internally by the restless ambition of its army, the first thought that presents itself is to give war as a goal for this troublesome ambition.

I do not want to speak ill of war; war almost always enlarges the thought of a people and elevates the heart. There are cases where it alone can arrest the excessive development of certain tendencies that arise naturally from equality, and where war must be considered as necessary for certain inveterate illnesses[e] to which democratic societies are subject.

---

e. In the manuscript: ". . . as a necessary remedy for certain moral illnesses . . ."

War has great advantages; but it must not be imagined that war decreases the danger that has just been indicated. It only defers it, and it comes back more terrible after the war, for the army bears peace much more impatiently after having tasted war. War would only be a remedy for a [democratic] people who always wanted glory.

[Napoleon often let it be understood that he would have willingly stopped in the middle of his triumphs if the passions of his soldiers had not, so to speak, compelled him to throw himself constantly into new endeavors.]^f

I foresee that all the warrior princes who arise within great democratic nations will find that it is much easier for them to conquer with their army than to make the army live in peace after the victory. There are two things that a democratic people will always have a great deal of difficulty doing: beginning a war and ending it.^g

If, moreover, war has particular advantages for democratic peoples, on the other hand it makes them run certain dangers that aristocracies do not have to fear to the same degree. I will cite only two of them.

If war satisfies the army, it hinders and often drives to despair that innumerable crowd of citizens whose small passions daily need peace to be satisfied. So it risks bringing about in another form the disorder that it should prevent.

There is no long war that, in a democratic country, does not put liberty at great risk. It is not that you must fear precisely to see, after each victory, conquering generals seize sovereign power by force, in the manner of Sylla or of Caesar.^h The danger is of another kind. War does not always deliver democratic peoples to military government; but it cannot fail to increase immensely, among these peoples, the attributions of the civil government;

---

f. "<That was not due to a particular disposition of his soldiers, but to the very constitution of his army.>/
   "<Such an idea never occurred to the mind of Frederick II or that of Louis XIV>" (*Rubish*, 2).
   g. "When a democracy makes war, it must do it admirably, because the entire desire of amelioration that torments all individuals turns toward ranks, salaries, glory. War is then nourished by all the possible industries that it destroys" (*Rubish*, 2).
   h. In a first version of the *rubish*, he adds: "or of Bonaparte" (*Rubish*, 2).

it almost inevitably centralizes in the government's hands the direction of all men and the use of everything. If it does not lead suddenly to despotism by violence, it goes there softly by habits.ʲ

    j. War bringing about and cementing the union of the clerk and the soldier./
      It is by this path that I must arrive at this idea:
      At first paint administrative tyranny preparing and establishing itself under the government whose general forms are liberal.
      Then an accident, among others, war, giving the opportunity to concentrate the higher powers and leading to the union cited above.
      [To the side: Military monarchy becomes established in this way, not by brutal, violent, irregular military power, but on the contrary, by regular, plain, clear, absolute military power, society having become an army, and the military before all the others, not as a *warrior,* but as master and *administrator.* The warrior will always be at the second rank in democratic societies, *capital idea.*]
      That will be striking, because the danger is not imaginary.
      Reread the chapter on the military spirit at that point.
      10 April 1838 (YTC, CVj, 2, pp. 10–11).

In another draft:

    War unites many wills in the same end; it suggests very energetic and very noble passions; it creates enthusiasm, elevates the soul, suggests devotion. In these regards war gets into the health of a democratic people, which without war could collapse indefinitely.
      But to make war, a very energetic and almost tyrannical central power must be created; it must be allowed many arbitrary or violent acts. The result of war can put in the hands of this power the liberty of the nation, always badly guaranteed in democracies, above all in emerging democracies.
      War, which can be good from time to time when a people is strongly and long organized democratically, must therefore be avoided with great care during the entire period of transition.
      M. Thiers told me one day last year (1836): "War will show the weakness of democratic governments; it will cover them with confusion and will force peoples, out of the sentiment of their preservation, to put their affairs back into a few hands. War cannot fail to make understood the insufficiency of the government of journalists and of lawyers," he added.
      M. L'Ad., one of the ardent and unintelligent partisans of M. Thiers, said the other day (18 April) in front of me that representative government was a sad thing; that liberty of the press notably would be incompatible with our security, if we were at war, and that at the first general war it would have to be suppressed.
      All that shows why those who aim for despotism must desire war and why in fact they desire it and push for it (YTC, CVd, pp. 14–15).

All those who seek to destroy liberty within a democratic nation should know that the surest and shortest means to succeed in doing so is war. That is the first axiom of the science.

A remedy seems to offer itself when the ambition of officers and of soldiers comes to be feared; it is to increase the number of places available, by augmenting the army. This relieves the present evil, but mortgages the future even more.

To augment the army can produce a lasting effect in an aristocratic society, because in these societies military ambition is limited to a single type of men, and stops, for each man, at a certain limit; so that you can manage to satisfy almost all of those who feel military ambition.

But among a democratic people, nothing is gained by increasing the army, because the number of ambitious men always increases in exactly the same proportion as the army itself. Those whose wishes you have fulfilled by creating new posts are immediately replaced by a new crowd that you cannot satisfy, and the first soon begin to complain again; for the same agitation of spirit that reigns among the citizens of a democracy shows itself in the army;[k] what men want there is not to gain a certain rank, but always to advance. If the desires are not very vast, they are reborn constantly. So a democratic people that augments its army only softens, for a moment,

---

In the same notebook you find, a bit before, this other note on the same subject:

There are two ways to arrive at despotism by liberty:
  Two systems:
  Local liberties--------no great liberty.
  Great liberty---------no local liberties.
  D'Argenson----------Thiers.
I want to say it not for the instruction of governments, which have nothing to learn in this matter, but for that of peoples (YTC, CVd, pp. 48–49).

Tocqueville is referring very probably to the ideas on decentralization set forth by Argenson in *Considérations sur le gouvernement ancien et présent de la France* (Amsterdam, 1784), in particular chapters 6, 7, and 8.

k. In the margin: "<When I see a democratic people, out of fear of men of war, augment the number of places in the army, I cannot prevent myself from thinking of the Romans of the decadence who bought peace with the barbarians and soon found them again the following year more enterprising and more numerous.>"

the ambition of men of war; but soon it becomes more formidable, because those who feel it are more numerous.[m]

I think, for my part, that a restless and turbulent spirit is an evil inherent in the very constitution of democratic armies, and that we must give up on curing it. The legislators of democracies must not imagine finding a military organization that by itself has the strength to calm and to contain men of war; they would exhaust themselves in vain efforts before attaining it.

It is not in the army that you can find the remedy for the vices of the army, but in the country.

Democratic peoples naturally fear trouble and despotism. It is only a matter of making these instincts into thoughtful, intelligent and stable tastes. When citizens have finally learned to make peaceful and useful use of liberty and have felt its benefits; when they have contracted a manly love of order and have voluntarily yielded to the established rule, these same citizens, while entering into the career of arms, bring these habits and these mores to the army without knowing it and as if despite themselves. The general spirit of the nation, penetrating the particular spirit of the army, tempers the opinions and the desires that arise from the military state, or by the omnipotent force of public opinion, it suppresses them. Have enlightened, well-ordered, steady and free citizens, and you will have disciplined and obedient soldiers.

Every law that, while repressing the turbulent spirit of the army, would tend to diminish, within the nation, the spirit of civil liberty and to obscure

---

m. The more I reflect on this the more I think that it is by armies that democracies will perish, that that is the great danger of modern times, the chance for *democratic* despotism for the future. Difficulty of cutting down on a democratic army when it exists. Difficulty of not having an army when the neighbors have one. Near impossibility of not being dragged into war or into seditions if armed.

To work on this fact. There are great truths there to put into relief./

29 September 1836.

You find on the same page this other note, which seems to be later: "Periods of transition. Ease of pushing democratic peoples toward war, of seizing power by arms. Danger to which you must always have your eyes open. Thiers" (*Rubish*, 2).

the idea of law and of rights would therefore go against its purpose. It would favor the establishment of a military tyranny much more than it would harm it.

After all, and no matter what you do, a great army within a democratic people will always be a great danger; and the most effective means of decreasing this danger will be to reduce the army; but it is a remedy that not all peoples are able to use.[n]

n. On a page of the manuscript, next to a variant of the paragraphs that finish the chapter: "Two things to do:

"1. Make the men who enter the army be penetrated by the advantages of order and of liberty.

"2. Give to the citizens a moral or material power that allows them to contain the soldiers as needed."

CHAPTER 23[a]

Which Class, in Democratic Armies, Is the Most Warlike and the Most Revolutionary

It is the essence of a democratic army to be very numerous, relative to the people who furnish it; I will talk about the reasons further along.

On the other hand, the men who live in democratic times scarcely ever choose the military career.

So democratic peoples are soon led to renounce voluntary recruitment in order to resort to compulsory enlistment.[b] The necessity of their condition obliges them to take this last measure, and you can easily predict that all will adopt it.

Since military service is compulsory, the burden is shared indiscriminately and equally by all citizens. That again follows necessarily from the condition of these peoples and from their ideas. The government can more or less do what it wants provided that it addresses itself to everyone at the

---

a. In democratic armies, soldiers, having to spend only a little time in the service, and being drawn to it in spite of themselves, never completely take on the spirit of the army. These are the ones who remain citizens the most. The officers on the contrary, since they are someone in society only because of their military rank, become entirely attached to the army and can become like strangers to the country. Their turbulent spirit is often weakened, however, by the stability and the sweet pleasures of the situation already acquired.

These reasons are not found to temper the restless ambition of the non-commissioned officers. The latter form the really military and revolutionary element of democratic armies (YTC, CVf, pp. 49–50).

b. "The natural tendency of a democratic people is to have an army of mercenaries" (*Rubish*, 2).

same time; it is the inequality of the burden and not the burden itself that ordinarily makes you resist.

Now, since military service is common to all citizens, the clear result is that each of them remains in the service only a few years.

Thus in the nature of things the soldier is in the army only in passing, while among most aristocratic nations, the military state is a profession that the soldier takes or that is imposed on him for life.

This has great consequences. Among the soldiers who make up a democratic army, some become attached to military life; but the greatest number, brought in spite of themselves into the service and always ready to return to their homes, do not consider themselves seriously engaged in the military career and think only about getting out of it. The latter do not contract the needs and only half-share the passions that arise from this career. They comply with their military duties, but their soul remains attached to the interests and the desires that occupied it in civilian life. So they do not take on the spirit of the army; instead they bring into the army the spirit of the society and preserve it there. Among democratic peoples, it is the simple soldiers who most remain citizens; national habits retain the greatest hold and public opinion the most power over them. It is through the soldiers above all that you can hope to make the love of liberty and respect for rights, which you knew how to inspire among the people themselves, penetrate into a democratic army. The opposite happens among aristocratic nations, in which the soldiers end up having nothing at all in common with their fellow citizens, living among them like strangers and often like enemies.

In aristocratic armies, the conservative element is the officer, because the officer alone has kept close ties to civilian society and never gives up the will to resume sooner or later his position there; in democratic armies, it is the soldier and for entirely similar reasons.

It often happens, on the contrary, that in these same democratic armies, the officer contracts tastes and desires entirely separate from those of the nation. That is understandable.

Among democratic peoples, the man who becomes an officer breaks all the ties that attached him to civilian life; he emerges from it forever and he has no interest in returning to it. His true country is the army, since he is nothing except by the rank that he occupies there; so he follows the fortune of the army, grows or declines with it, and it is toward the army alone that from now on he directs his hopes. Since the officer has needs very distinct from those of the country, it can happen that he ardently desires war or works for a revolution at the very moment when the nation aspires most to stability and peace.

Nonetheless there are causes that temper the warrior and restless temperament in him. If ambition is universal and continuous among democratic peoples, we have seen that it is rarely great there. The man who, coming out of the secondary classes of the nation, has arrived, through the lower ranks of the army, at the rank of officer, has already taken an immense step. He has entered into a sphere superior to the one he occupied within civilian society, and he has acquired rights there that most democratic nations will always consider as inalienable.[1] He stops willingly after this great effort, and thinks about enjoying his conquest. The fear of compromising what he possesses already softens in his heart the desire to acquire what he does not have. After having overcome the first and the greatest obstacle that stopped his progress, he resigns himself with less impatience to the slowness of his march. This cooling of ambition increases as, rising higher in rank, he finds more to lose from risks. If I am not mistaken, the least warlike as well as the least revolutionary part of a democratic army will always be the head.

What I have just said about the officer and the soldier is not applicable to a numerous class that, in all armies, occupies the intermediary place between them; I mean the non-commissioned officers.

This class of non-commissioned officers, which before the present century had not yet appeared in history, is henceforth called, I think, to play a role.

Just like the officer, the non-commissioned officer has broken in his thought all the ties that attached him to civilian society; just like him, he

---

1. *The position of the officer is, in fact, much more secure among democratic peoples than among the others.*[c] *The less the officer is worth by himself, the more valuable rank is comparatively, and the more the legislator finds it just and necessary to assure its enjoyment.*

c. The manuscript says: ". . . than within aristocracies."

has made the military life his career and, more than the officer perhaps, he has turned all of his desires solely in this direction; but unlike the officer he has not yet reached an elevated and solid place where it is permissible for him to stop and to breathe comfortably, while waiting to be able to climb higher.

By the very nature of his functions that cannot change, the non-commissioned officer is condemned to lead an obscure, narrow, uneasy and precarious existence. So far he sees only the perils of the military life. He knows only privations and obedience, more difficult to bear than the perils. He suffers all the more from his present miseries, because he knows that the constitution of society and that of the army allow him to free himself from these miseries; from one day to the next, in fact, he can become an officer. Then he commands, has honors, independence, rights, enjoyments; not only does this object of his hopes seem immense to him, but before grasping it, he is never sure of attaining it. There is nothing irrevocable about his rank; he is left each day entirely to the arbitrariness of his leaders; the needs of discipline require imperatively that it be so. A slight fault, a caprice, can always make him lose, in a moment, the fruit of several years of work and efforts. Until he has reached the rank he covets, he has therefore done nothing.[d] Only then does he seem to enter into the career. With a man thus incited constantly by his youth, his needs, his passions, the spirit of his times, his hopes and his fears, a desperate ambition cannot fail to catch fire.

So the non-commissioned officer wants war, he wants it always and at any price, and if you refuse him war, he desires revolutions which suspend the authority of the rules; in the midst of these revolutions he hopes, by means of confusion and political passions, to expel his officer and take his place; and it is not impossible for him to bring about revolutions, because he exercises a great influence over the soldiers by shared origins and habits, even though he differs greatly from them by passions and desires.

You would be wrong to believe that these various predispositions of the

d. The manuscript of the chapter ends here. In the margin, with a bracket that goes from the beginning of the paragraph to this place: "All of this is the weak part of the piece. Developed and yet incomplete."

officer, of the non-commissioned officer and of the soldier depend on a time or a country. They will appear in all periods and among all democratic nations.

In every democratic army, it will always be the non-commissioned officer who will least represent the pacific and regular spirit of the country, and the soldier who will best represent it. The soldier will bring to the military career the strength or the weakness of national mores; there he will manifest the faithful image of the nation. If the nation is ignorant and weak, he will allow himself to be carried away to disorder by his leaders, without his knowing or despite himself. If the nation is enlightened and energetic, he will keep them in order himself.

CHAPTER 24[a]

What Makes Democratic Armies Weaker
Than Other Armies While Beginning
a Military Campaign and More Formidable
When the War Is Prolonged[b]

a. 1. A democratic army is more unsuited than another to war after a long peace.

1. Because all the officers in all the ranks are old there.

2. Because they have allowed themselves to be penetrated by the malaise of the national mores.

3. Because they have fallen morally below the level of the people.

2. A democratic army is more formidable than another after a long war.

1. Because, since competition is immense and since the war pushes each man forcibly into his place, you always end by discovering great men of war.

2. Because war, having destroyed all the peaceful industries, becomes the sole industry, so that toward it alone are turned all the ambitious and restless desires that arise from equality.

Of military discipline in democratic armies (YTC, CVf, pp. 50–51).

Former titles of the chapter in the manuscript: "≠WHY A DEMOCRATIC PEOPLE RISKS MORE THAN ANOTHER TO BE CONQUERED DURING THE FIRST MILITARY CAMPAIGNS.≠/

"WHY THE CHANCES FOR A DEMOCRATIC ARMY INCREASE AS THE WAR CONTINUES./

"EFFECTS PRODUCED BY A LONG PEACE AND A LONG WAR ON A DEMOCRATIC ARMY."

b. The soldier./

Modification of the soldier in democracies./

Military discipline. Relationship of the soldier and of the officer. Driving force of actions./

Reaction of this on the sentiment of honor. An aristocratic body of officers formulates arbitrary laws of honor./

[Note, which seems later] Of honor in general in American society. That a democratic society can have virtue, but not what we call honor. Honor is an arbitrary

Every army that begins a military campaign after a long peace risks being defeated; every army that has waged war for a long time has great chances to win: this truth is particularly applicable to democratic armies.

In aristocracies, the military life, being a privileged career, is honored even in times of peace. Men who have great talents, great enlightenment and a great ambition embrace it; the army is, in everything, at the level of the nation; often it even surpasses it.

We have seen how, on the contrary, among democratic peoples, the elite of the nation moves little by little away from the military career in order to seek, by other roads, consideration, power and above all wealth. After a long peace, and in democratic times periods of peace are long, the army is always inferior to the country itself. War finds it in this state;[c] and until war has changed it, there is a danger for the country and for the army.

I showed how, in democratic armies and in times of peace, the right of seniority is the supreme and inflexible law for advancement. That follows

---

law, a convention that needs to be minutely detailed and interpreted by a body of arbiters.

[In the margin: Honor is an aristocratic convention relative to the manner in which you must envisage human actions./

What I have to say about honor seems to me too important to be said in relation to other things.]

Precede this with an oratorical turn. If I am understood, I am assured of not hurting anyone. But I am afraid of not being able to make myself easily understood (*Rubish*, 2).

c. In the manuscript:

<But war does not take long to change it.

As the military spirit awakens to the noise of arms, as great national dangers draw all eyes toward the army, as great fortunes suddenly occur on the fields of battle, the military life rises in the esteem of men and the most immense and boldest ambitions turn toward it.

This revolution is inevitable, but it cannot take place in a moment; and there is a danger for the army and for the State until it is accomplished.>

[In the margin] ≠To delete I think because it is not *necessary* there and is necessary further along.

French of the XIXth century.≠

not only, as I said, from the constitution of these armies, but also from the very constitution of the people, and will always be found.

Moreover, since among these peoples the officer is something in the country only because of his military position, and since he draws all his consideration and all his comfort from it, he only withdraws or is excluded from the army at the very end of life.

The result of these two causes is that when, after a long peace, a democratic people finally takes up arms, all the leaders of its army are found to be old men. I am not speaking only about the generals, but about the subordinate officers, most of whom have remained immobile, or have been able to move only step by step. If you consider a democratic army after a long peace, you see with surprise that all the soldiers are not far from childhood and all the leaders are in their waning years; so that the first lack experience; and the second, vigor.

That is a great cause of reverses; for the first condition to conduct war well is to be young; I would not have dared to say it, if the greatest captain of modern times had not said so.

These two causes do not act in the same way on aristocratic armies.

Since you advance there by right of birth much more than by right of seniority, you always find in all the ranks a certain number of young men who bring to war all the first energy of body and soul.

Moreover, as men who seek military honors among an aristocratic people have an assured position in civilian society, they rarely wait in the army for the approach of old age to surprise them. After devoting to the career of arms the most vigorous years of their youth, they withdraw and go to spend the remainder of their mature years at home.

A long peace not only fills democratic armies with old officers, it also gives to all the officers habits of body and mind that make them little suited to war. The man who has lived for a long time amid the peaceful and half-hearted atmosphere of democratic mores yields with difficulty at first to the hard work and austere duties that war imposes. If he does not absolutely lose the taste for arms, he at least takes on ways of living that prevent him from winning.

Among aristocratic peoples, the softness of civilian life exercises less influence on military mores, because among these peoples the aristocracy leads the army. Now, an aristocracy, however immersed in delights it may be, always has several other passions than that of well-being, and it readily makes the temporary sacrifice of its well-being in order to satisfy those passions better.

I showed how in democratic armies, in times of peace, the delays in advancement are extreme. The officers at first bear this state of things with impatience; they become agitated, restless and despairing; but in the long run, most of them resign themselves to it. Those who have the most ambition and resources leave the army; the others, finally adjusting their tastes and their desires to their mediocre lot, end up considering the military life from a civilian perspective. What they value most about it is the comfort and the stability that accompany it; on the assurance of this small fortune, they base the entire picture of their future, and they ask only to be able to enjoy it peacefully.

Thus, not only does a long peace fill democratic armies with old officers, but it often gives the instincts of old men even to those who are still at a vigorous age.[d]

I have equally shown how among democratic nations, in times of peace, the military career was little honored and not much followed.

This public disfavor is a very heavy burden that weighs on the spirit of the army. Souls are as if bent down by it; and when war finally arrives, they cannot regain their elasticity and their vigor in a moment.

A similar cause of moral weakness is not found in aristocratic armies.

d. In the margin:

<Perhaps here this idea (I do not believe so).

This troublesome influence of peace makes itself much less felt in aristocratic armies because the officers who are found there, having an assured well-being before entering the career of arms, are only seeking reputation, the sole good that they are lacking. This same need is felt by them at all times. The length of peace does not weaken it and war, no matter when it occurs, always seems to them the best occasion to satisfy it.>

[<Among aristocratic peoples the career of arms is always honored, whatever the current of public opinion might otherwise be.>] Officers there never find themselves lowered in their own eyes and in those of their fellows, because apart from their military grandeur, they are great by themselves.

If the influence of peace made itself felt in the two armies in the same way, the results would still be different.

When the officers of an aristocratic army have lost the warrior spirit and the desire to raise themselves by the profession of arms, they still keep a certain respect for the honor of their order and an old habit of being first and giving the example. But when the officers of a democratic army no longer have love of war and military ambition, nothing remains.

So I think that a democratic people who undertakes a war after a long peace risks being defeated much more than another; but it must not allow itself to be easily demoralized by reverses, for the chances of its army increase with the very duration of the war.

When war, by continuing, has finally torn all citizens away from their peaceful labors and made all their small undertakings fail, it happens that the same passions that made them attach so much value to peace turn toward arms. War, after destroying all industries, becomes itself the great and sole industry, and then the ardent and ambitious desires given birth by equality are directed from all sides toward it alone. This is why these same democratic nations that are so hard to drag onto the field of battle sometimes do such prodigious things there, once you have finally succeeded in having them take up arms.

As war more and more draws all eyes toward the army, as you see it create in a short time great reputations and great fortunes, the elite of the nation takes up the career of arms; all the naturally enterprising, proud and warlike spirits produced not only by the aristocracy, but by the entire country, are drawn in this direction.

Since the number of competitors for military honors is immense, and since war pushes each man roughly into his place, great generals always end up being found. A long war brings about in a democratic army what a revolution brings about in the people itself. It breaks the rules and makes all the extraordinary men appear suddenly. The officers whose soul and body have become old during the peace are pushed aside, retire or die. In their place presses a crowd of young men whom the war has already hardened and whose desires it has expanded and inflamed. The latter want to grow greater at any price and constantly; after them come others who have the same passions and the same desires; and after those, others still, without finding any limits except those of the army. Equality allows ambition to all, and death takes care of providing chances to all ambitions. Death constantly opens ranks, empties places, closes and opens careers.

There is, moreover, a hidden connection between military mores and democratic mores that war exposes.

Men of democracies naturally have the passionate desire to acquire quickly the goods that they covet and to enjoy them easily. Most of them adore chance and fear death much less than pain. In this spirit they conduct commerce and industry; and this same spirit, carried by them onto the fields of battle, leads them readily to risk their lives in order to assure, in one moment, the rewards of victory. No greatness is more satisfying to the imagination of a democratic people than military greatness, a brilliant and sudden greatness that is obtained without work, by risking only your life.

Thus, while interest and tastes move the citizens of a democracy away from war, the habits of their soul prepare them to wage war well; they easily become good soldiers as soon as you have been able to tear them away from their affairs and their well-being.

If peace is particularly harmful to democratic armies, war therefore assures them advantages that other armies never have; and these advantages, although not very noticeable at first, cannot fail, in the long run, to give them victory.[e]

An aristocratic people who, fighting against a democratic nation, does not succeed in destroying it immediately with the first military campaigns, always greatly risks being defeated by it.

---

e. In the margin: "≠I had had the idea of introducing there chapter 'a' but that would interrupt the thread of the discourse.≠" Chapter "a" is the one that follows.

CHAPTER 25[a]

Of Discipline in Democratic Armies

It is a very widespread opinion, above all among aristocratic peoples, that the great social equality that reigns within democracies makes the soldier independent of the officer in the long run and thus destroys the bond of discipline.

It is an error. There are, in fact, two types of discipline that must not be confused.

When the officer is the noble and the soldier the serf; the one the rich man, and the other the poor man; when the first is enlightened and strong, and the second ignorant and weak, it is easy to establish between these two men the closest bond of obedience. The soldier has yielded to military discipline before entering the army, so to speak, or rather military discipline is only a perfecting of social servitude. In aristocratic armies, the soldier ends up easily enough being as though indifferent to everything except to the order of his leaders. He acts without thinking, triumphs without ardor, and dies without complaining. In this state, he is no longer a man, but more a very fearsome animal trained for war.

Democratic peoples must give up hope of ever obtaining from their soldiers this blind, scrupulous, resigned and totally constant obedience that aristocratic peoples impose on their soldiers without difficulty. The state of society does not prepare their soldiers for it; democratic peoples risk losing their natural advantages by wanting to gain that obedience artificially.

a. As has been pointed out, in notebook YTC, CVf, p. 51, this chapter was part of the preceding one. In the jacket of the *rubish* you find this note: "Chapter too small and of too little importance to be alone, but I do not know what to combine it with./
"I am not sure that it is not mediocre" (*Rubish,* 2).

Among democratic peoples, military discipline must not try to obliterate the free impulse of souls; it can only aspire to direct it; the obedience that it creates is less exact, but more impetuous and more intelligent. Its root is in the very will of the man who obeys; it rests not on his instinct alone, but on his reason; consequently discipline often grows tighter on its own as danger makes it more necessary. The discipline of an aristocratic army readily relaxes in war, because this discipline is based on habits, and because war disturbs these habits. The discipline of a democratic army, on the contrary, becomes firmer before the enemy, because each soldier then sees very clearly that to conquer he must remain silent and obey.

The peoples who have done the most considerable things by war have known no other discipline than the one I am talking about. Among the ancients, only free men and citizens, who differed little from each other and were accustomed to treating each other as equals, were received in the armies. In this sense, you can say that the armies of antiquity were democratic, although they came from the aristocracy; consequently in those armies a sort of fraternal familiarity reigned between the officer and the soldier. You will be convinced by reading Plutarch's *Lives of the Great Captains.* The soldiers there speak constantly and very freely to their generals, and the latter listen willingly to the speeches of their soldiers and respond to them. It is by these words and these examples, much more than by compulsion and punishments that they lead them. You would say they were companions as much as leaders.

I do not know if Greek and Roman soldiers ever perfected to the same degree as the Russians[b] the small details of military discipline; but that did not prevent Alexander from conquering Asia, and Rome, the world.

---

b. In a version of the drafts: ". . . the Russians or the English . . ." (*Rubish,* 2).

CHAPTER 26ᵃ

Some Considerations on War
in Democratic Societies

[<War exercises such a prodigious influence on the fate of all peoples that you will pardon me, I hope, for not abandoning the subject that deals with it without trying to exhaust it.>]

When the principle of equality develops not only in one nation, but at the same time among several neighboring nations, as is seen today in Europe, the men who inhabit these various countries, despite the disparity of languages, customs and laws, are nevertheless similar on this point that they equally fear war and conceive the same love for peace.[1] In vain does

a. All democratic peoples are similar in the love of peace. All are equally led to commerce by equality, and commerce links their interests so that they cannot hurt their neighbor without harming themselves. So wars are rare. But they are great because these two peoples cannot set about to make war on a small scale.

Since men are similar, only numbers decide, from that the obligation for large armies. Thus armies seem to grow as the military spirit fades.

Great changes take place as well in the manner of making war.

A democratic people can more easily than another conquer and be conquered (illegible word). Why you always march on the capitals. Why civil wars become very difficult (YTC, CVf, pp. 51–52).

On the jacket of the chapter: "≠Perhaps all that will be to delete./

Chapter to look at again closely, done a bit too hastily.≠"

The idea that decentralization hinders the rapidity of reaction but increases the capacity of resistance is already found set forth in a letter of 1828 to Beaumont. This letter comments at length on the *History of England* of John Lingard (*Correspondance avec Beaumont, OC,* VIII, 1, p. 53).

1. *The fear that European peoples show for war is not only due to the progress that equality*

ambition or anger arm princes; a sort of apathy and universal benevolence pacifies them in spite of themselves and makes them drop the sword from their hands. Wars become rarer.

As equality, developing at the same time in several countries, simultaneously pushes the men who inhabit them toward industry and commerce, not only are their tastes similar, but also their interests mingle and become entangled, so that no nation can inflict harm on others that does not come back on itself, and all end by considering war as a calamity almost as great for the victor as for the defeated.

Thus, on the one hand, it is very difficult in democratic centuries to bring peoples to fight with each other, but, on the other hand, it is almost impossible for two of them to make war in isolation. The interests of all are so intertwined, their opinions and their needs so similar, that no people can keep itself at rest when the others are agitated. So wars become rarer; but when they arise, they are on a field more vast.

Democratic peoples who are neighbors do not become similar only on a few points, as I have just said; they end by resembling each other in nearly everything.[2]

---

has made among them; I do not need, I think, to point it out to the reader. Apart from this permanent cause, there are several accidental ones that are very powerful. I will cite, before all the others, the extreme weariness that the wars of the Revolution and of the Empire have left.

2. That comes not solely from the fact that peoples have the same social state, but from the fact that this same social state is such that it leads men naturally to imitate each other and to blend.

When citizens are divided into castes and into classes, not only do they differ from each other, but also they have neither the taste or the desire to become alike; each man, on the contrary, seeks more and more to keep intact his own opinions and habits and to remain himself. The spirit of individuality is very robust.

When a people has a democratic social state, that is to say that neither castes nor classes exist within it any longer and that all citizens there are more or less equal in enlightenment and in property, the human spirit heads in the opposite direction. Men are similar, and moreover they suffer in a way from not being similar. Far from wanting to preserve what can still make each one of them different, they ask only to lose that singularity in order to blend into the common mass, which alone in their eyes represents right and strength. The spirit of individuality is almost destroyed.

Now this similitude of peoples has very important consequences concerning war.

When I ask myself why the Helvetic confederation of the XVth century made the largest and most powerful nations of Europe tremble, while today its power is in exact proportion to its population, I find that the Swiss have become similar to all the men who surround them, and those men to the Swiss; so that, since numbers alone make the difference between them, victory necessarily belongs to the biggest battalions. One of the results of the democratic revolution taking place in Europe is therefore to make the force of numbers prevail on every battlefield, and to compel all the small nations to become incorporated into the large ones, or at least to take part in the policy of the latter.[c]

In times of aristocracy, even those who are naturally similar aspire to create imaginary differences between them. In times of democracy, even those who naturally are not alike ask only to become similar and copy each other, so much is the spirit of each man always carried along by the general movement of humanity.

Something similar makes itself noticed as well from people to people. Two peoples would have the same aristocratic social state; they would be able to remain very distinct and very different, because the spirit of aristocracy is to become more individual. But two neighboring peoples could not have the same democratic social state without immediately adopting similar opinions and mores, because the spirit of democracy makes men tend to assimilate.[b]

b. In the manuscript, this note is part of the text and continues in this way:

. . . to assimilate. <≠In centuries of inequality each nation takes great care therefore to keep itself apart and to remain distinct, while in centuries of equality all nations come closer together, follow each other and help each other.

The democratic social state, coming to be established at the same time among several peoples, makes all citizens there more or less similar and this same social state makes them all individually weak. Two causes which powerfully facilitate <in these same periods> the birth and the consolidation of great empires. For the first gives to the latter countries a natural propensity to live in common and the second allows forcing them to do so [v: prevents them from separating from each other] once you have succeeded in uniting them. Thus you can say in a *general* way that, as the social state of men becomes more democratic, small nations tend to disappear and large ones are established, which makes wars become rarer and embrace a larger space.≠>

c. Baden, 5 August 1836.
I wondered today to myself why certain small peoples of Europe such as the Swiss for example had formerly played such a great role, while today their power had be-

[≠This must necessarily make wars rarer and greater.

This resemblance that the citizens of different peoples have with each other has still many other consequences.≠]

Since the determining factor for victory is numbers, the result is that each people must with all its efforts strain to bring the most men possible onto the field of battle.

When you could enroll under the colors a type of troops superior to all the others, such as the Swiss infantry or the French cavalry of the XVIth century, you did not consider that you had the need to levy very large armies; but it is not so when all soldiers are equally valuable.

The same cause that gives birth to this new need also provides the means to satisfy it. For, as I said, when all men are similar, they are all weak. The social power is naturally much stronger among democratic peoples than anywhere else. So these peoples, at the same time that they feel the desire to call all the male population to arms, have the ability to assemble them there; this means that, in centuries of equality, armies seem to grow as the military spirit fades.[d]

In the same centuries, the manner of making war is also changed by the same causes.

---

come in exact proportion to their number and their strength, so that while the confederation of the XVth century made the greatest continental powers tremble, today there is no people of Europe having four or five million inhabitants that cannot in the long run oppress Switzerland, which has only two.

The reason is that the Swiss have become more or less similar in everything to the peoples who are around them and the latter to the Swiss, so that, since numbers alone make the difference between them, to the biggest battalions necessarily belongs victory.

One of the results of the great democratic revolution that is taking place among peoples as well as between individuals will therefore have as a final result to make the force of numbers prevail everywhere and to deliver small nations without hope to the tyranny of large ones [v: they are forced to become incorporated into the large ones or to take part in their policy] (*Rubish*, 2).

d. In the margin: "<Comfort does not prevent the military from fighting but it prevents the bourgeois from taking up arms.>"

Machiavelli[e] says in his book *The Prince* "that it is much more difficult to subjugate a people who have a prince and barons for leaders than a nation which is led by a prince and slaves." Let us put, in order not to offend anyone, public officials in the place of slaves and we will have a great truth, very applicable to our subject.

It is very difficult for a great aristocratic people to conquer its neighbors and to be conquered by them. It cannot conquer them, because it can never gather all its forces and hold men together for a long time; and it can never be conquered, because the enemy finds everywhere small centers of resistance that stop it. I will compare war in an aristocratic country to war in a country of mountains; the defeated find at every instant the occasion to rally in new positions and to hold firm there.

e. Machiavelli in his horrible work *The Prince* expresses a true and profound idea when he says in chapter IV that among principalities those that are governed by a *prince and slaves* must be clearly distinguished from those that are governed by a *prince and barons.*

The first, he says, are difficult to conquer because you cannot find within them subjects powerful enough to aid the conquest, and because the sovereign who governs them can easily gather all the forces of the empire against you.

Conquest accomplished, the same reasons allow you to preserve it easily.

The second are easy to penetrate because it is not difficult to win over a few of the great men of the kingdom. But does the conqueror want to hold on? He experiences all sorts of difficulties. It is not enough for him to extinguish the race of the prince; a crowd of powerful lords will always remain who will put themselves at the head of the malcontents, and since it is impossible for him to make every one content and to destroy those powerful lords, he will soon be chased away.

Machiavelli explains in this way the ease that Alexander had establishing himself on the throne of Darius and the difficulty that has always been encountered in conquering France.

Machiavelli who after all is only a superficial man, clever at discovering secondary causes, but from whom great general causes escape, touches there accidentally and without seeing it one of the great political consequences that clearly follow from a democratic or aristocratic social state.

Democratic States in fact make very much greater efforts to defend themselves than others, but once beaten and conquered, there is less of a remedy than among aristocratic nations.

To this cause you must equally attribute the difficulty of making long civil wars among democratic peoples.

As democratic peoples become more democratic you can count on the fact that civil wars there will become rarer and shorter. This is what explains the length of wars as regards religion, unless in a democratic country there are provinces strongly constituted, in which case there will be foreign wars in the form of civil war (*Rubish*, 2).

Precisely the opposite makes itself seen among democratic nations.

The latter easily bring all their available forces to the field of battle, and when the nation is rich and numerous, it easily becomes victorious; but once it has been defeated and its territory has been penetrated, few resources remain to it, and if it gets to the point of having its capital taken, the nation is lost. That is very easily explained; since each citizen is individually very isolated and very weak, no one can either defend himself or offer a point of support to others. In a democratic country only the State is strong; since the military strength of the State is destroyed by the destruction of its army and its civil power paralyzed by the taking of its capital, the rest forms nothing more than a multitude without rule and without strength that cannot struggle against the organized power that attacks it. I know that you can reduce the danger by creating liberties and, consequently, provincial entities, but this remedy will always be insufficient.

Not only will the population then no longer be able to continue the war, but it is to be feared that it will not want to try.

[≠The greatest difficulty that a democratic population finds is not to defend itself with weapons in hand, but to want to defend itself in such a way. ≠]ᶠ

According to the law of nations adopted by civilized nations, wars do not have as a purpose to appropriate the goods of individuals, but only to seize political power. Private property is destroyed only accidentally and in order to attain the second objective.

When an aristocratic nation is invaded after the defeat of its army, the nobles, although they are at the same time the rich, prefer to continue to defend themselves individually rather than to submit; for if the conqueror remained master of the country, he would take away their political power to which they are even more attached than to their property; so they prefer combat to conquest, which is for them the greatest misfortune, and they easily carry the people with them, because the people have contracted the long custom of following and obeying them, and besides have almost nothing to risk in war.

---

f. In the margin: "≠Bad in form but the idea of transition good. ≠"

In a nation where equality of conditions reigns,[g] each citizen takes, on the contrary, only a small part in political power, and often takes no part at all; on the other hand, everyone is independent and has property to lose; so that there conquest is feared much less and war much more than among an aristocratic people. It will always be very difficult to cause a democratic population to take up arms when war is brought to its territory.[h] This is why it is necessary to give to these peoples rights and a political spirit that suggests to each person some of the interests that cause nobles to act in aristocracies.

It is very necessary that princes and other leaders of democratic nations remember: only the passion and the habit of liberty can, with advantage, combat the habit and the passion of well-being. I imagine nothing better prepared for conquest, in case of reverses, than a democratic people who does not have free institutions.

Formerly you began military campaigns with few soldiers; you fought small battles and conducted long sieges. Now you fight great battles, and as soon as you can march freely ahead, you race toward the capital in order to end the war with one blow.

Napoleon, it is said, invented this new system. It did not depend on one man, whoever he was, to create such a system. The manner in which Napoleon made war was suggested to him by the state of society of his time, and it succeeded for him because it was marvelously suited to this state and because he put it to use for the first time. Napoleon is the first to have traveled at the head of an army the path to all the capitals. But it is the ruin of feudal[j] society that had opened this road to him. It is to be believed that, if this extraordinary man had been born three centuries ago, he would not have gathered the same fruits from his method, or rather he would have had another method.

g. The manuscript says: "In a democratic nation."

h. "Difficulty of making a democratic people take up arms.

"That is true in all democratic countries, but above all in democratic countries that do not have free institutions" (*Rubish,* 2).

j. The manuscript says: "But it is the progress of equality of conditions that had opened it."

I will add only one more word about civil wars, for I am afraid of tiring the patience of the reader.

Most of the things I have said concerning foreign wars apply with stronger reason to civil wars [<and it is there above all that the strength of the State and the weakness of individuals are revealed>]. Men who live in democratic countries do not naturally have the military spirit; they sometimes take it on when they are dragged, despite themselves, onto the fields of battle. But to rise up by himself, in a body, and to expose himself willingly to the miseries that war and above all civil war bring, is a choice that the man of democracies does not make. Only the most adventurous citizens agree to throw themselves into such a risk; the mass of the population remains immobile.

Even when the mass of the population would like to act, it does not easily succeed in doing so; for it does not find within it ancient and well-established influences to which it wishes to submit, no already known leaders to gather the malcontents, to regulate and to lead them; no political powers placed below the national power, which effectively come to support the resistance put up against the nation's power.

In democratic countries, the moral power of the majority is immense, and the material forces at its disposal are out of proportion with those that, at first, it is possible to unite against it. The party in the majority's seat, which speaks in its name and uses its power, triumphs therefore, in one moment and without difficulty, over all particular resistances. It does not even allow them the time to be born; it crushes them in germ.

So those who, among these peoples, want to make a revolution by arms, have no other resources than to seize unexpectedly the already functioning machine of the government, which can be carried out by a surprise attack rather than by a war; for from the moment when a war is official, the party which represents the State is almost always sure to win.

The only case in which a civil war could arise would be the one in which, the army being divided, one portion raised the banner of revolt and the other remained faithful. An army forms a very tightly bound and very hardy small society which is able to be self-sufficient for a while. The war could be bloody, but it would not be long; for either the army in revolt would draw the government to its side just by showing its strength or by its first victory, and the war would be over; or the battle would begin, and the portion of the army not supported by the organized power of the State would soon disperse on its own or be destroyed.

So you can accept, as a general truth, that in the centuries of equality, civil wars will become much rarer and shorter.[3]

3. *It is well understood that I am speaking here about* single *democratic nations and not about confederated democratic nations. In confederations, since the preponderant power always resides, despite fictions, in the government of the state and not in the federal government, civil wars are only disguised foreign wars.*

FOURTH PART[a]

a. Plan of this part in a draft:

General influence of democratic ideas and mores on government./

≠1. How democratic ideas favor the establishment of a centralized government.
2. How id. mores do id.
3. Particular causes, but related to the great democratic cause, that can lead there.
4. Type of despotism to fear. Here show administrative despotism and the manner in which it could successively take hold≠ of private life. Dangers of this state.
5. Remedies. Here all that I can say on association, aristocratic persons, liberty, great passions . . ./

Last chapter./

1. New affirmation of the irresistible march of democracy.
2. *General* judgment of this new state.
3. Nations can turn it to good or to detestable account and they hang in the balance (YTC, CVk, 1, pp. 73–74).

Plan of the chapter in the *rubish:*

General idea of the last chapter./
To do well, this chapter must fit together well with those that precede, which are:

1. *Ambition,* in which I show the sentiment of ambition *universal* and *small.*
2. *Revolutions,* in which I show that great revolutions will be rare.
3. The *army,* in which I show the restlessness and habitual discontent of democratic armies.

I believe that what would have to be done now would be this:

1. Show how the human mind plunges on all sides among democratic peoples into the idea of *unity,* of *uniformity.*
2. Show afterward how that idea leads to administrative despotism.
[To the side: A fact certainly new in our hemisphere, for if I am not mistaken the thing has existed for two thousand years in the Antipodes.]

3. Necessity of upholding human individuality. Union of liberty and equality. Separation of the revolutionary element.

[To the side: Here idea of aristocratic persons.]/
These are three ideas that follow each other well.

This is found in a jacket placed with the *rubish* of the chapter on material well-being (chapter 10 of the second part). The jacket bears this commentary: "How equality of ranks suggests to men the taste for liberty and for equality. Why democratic peoples love equality better than liberty./

"Piece from which I will probably have to make the second section of the chapter and that must be carefully reexamined while reviewing this chapter. 4 September 1838" (*Rubish*, 1).

The drafts reproduced in notebook CVd bear this commentary at the head:

Ideas and fragments that all relate more or less to the great chapter entitled: How the ideas and the sentiments suggested by equality influence the political constitution./
Sketch of the final chapter./
Individualism. Natural [Material (ed.)] enjoyments./
Perhaps put a part of all that in the chapter on sentiments that favor the concentration of power.

Particularly what I say about the taste for material enjoyments, and individualism. The piece.

More probably place in the work a chapter on *material enjoyments* and *individualism,* pieces of this section which merit being kept (28 July 1838).

1bis. 1. Summary of the book. That equality of conditions is an irresistible, accomplished fact, which will break all those who want to struggle against it. This above all true when equality (illegible word).

[To the side: Order of ideas of this chapter.

2. Equality of conditions suggests equally to men the taste for *liberty* and the taste for *equality.*

But the one is a *superficial* and *passing* taste. The other a *tenacious* and ardent passion.]

2. That despotism can hope to succeed in becoming established only by respecting equality and by flattering democratic tendencies.

3. How a government that aspires to despotism must set about doing so and the opportunities that the ideas, the habits and the instincts of democracy provide for it.

I. Why democratic peoples are naturally led to the centralization of power.

Theory of centralization presents itself naturally to the mind of men when equality exists.

Difficulty of knowing to whom to return intermediary powers. Jealousy of the neighbor. All this increased by revolutions.

II. Democratic taste for material well-being which leads men to become absorbed in searching for it or in enjoying it.

Of the Influence That Democratic Ideas and Sentiments Exercise on Political Society[b]

III. Individualism which makes each man want to be occupied only with himself.

4. Since the government is, in this way, master of everything, it only needs *war* to destroy even the shadow of liberty.

1. Facility that it also finds in the democratic social state for that.

2. By this means, which will establish despotism, despots will be successively overturned. Picture analogous to that at the end of the Roman empire.

Aristocracy of men of war.

Having reached this point, you can hope to see the end of a tyrant, but not that of tyranny.

[To the side: Opposing view to all (illegible word).

1. To unite the spirit of liberty to the spirit of equality.

2. To separate the spirit of equality from the revolutionary spirit. Why the revolutionary spirit is more natural to democratic peoples and more (illegible word). Particular necessity in these democratic centuries for the spirit of equality. In democratic centuries, you must be scrupulous, extraordinarily respectful on this point] (YTC, CVd, pp. 1–3).

This part is missing in notebook CVf.

b. In the manuscript: "Do only a single chapter from all of that beginning with the foreword (a) and then divided into sections." This fourth part forms one single chapter in the manuscript and bears the number 60. The conclusion, which constitutes the last chapter, bears the number 61. Apart from the drafts of the chapter, there exist various drafts contained in jackets and bearing the following titles: UNITY, CENTRALIZATION, ADMINISTRATIVE DESPOTISM; NOTES OF THE CHAPTER; RELATIVE TO THE IDEA OF UNITY; IDEAS WHICH I CAN HOPE TO USE; and THOUGHTS TO ADD ON THE INFLUENCE EXERCISED BY DEMOCRATIC IDEAS ON THE FORMS OF GOVERNMENT.

In July 1838 (*OCB,* VII, pp. 167–68), Tocqueville writes to his brother, Édouard, that he is working on the last part of his book and that this is composed of two short chapters. At the end of the month of August, he notes that he has already finished the draft of the first version; on October 1 he begins to work on the last chapter. Writing the draft and revision will take an entire year, and the two initial chapters will be replaced by a total of eight chapters. The quantity of notes and drafts testifies to Tocqueville's efforts to finish the part that he considered the most important of his work.

The manuscript and the drafts seem to indicate that the first chapter of this part was added at the end, and that the second and third chapters formed only one in the first drafts.

After having shown the ideas and the sentiments suggested by equality, I would badly fulfill the purpose of this book if, while concluding, I did not show what general influence these same sentiments and these same ideas can exercise on the government of human societies.

To succeed in doing that, I will often be obliged to retrace my steps. But I hope that the reader will not refuse to follow me when roads that he knows lead him toward some new truth.

CHAPTER I

Equality Naturally Gives Men the Taste for Free Institutions

Equality, which makes men independent of each other, makes them contract the habit and the taste to follow only their will in their personal actions. This complete independence, which they enjoy continually vis-à-vis their equals and in the practice of private life, disposes them to consider all authority with a discontented eye, and soon suggests to them the idea and the love of political liberty. So men who live in these times march on a natural slope that leads them toward free institutions. Take one of them at random; go back, if possible, to his primitive instincts; you will discover that, among the different governments, the one that he conceives first and that he prizes most, is the government whose leader he has elected and whose actions he controls.[a]

Of all the political effects that equality of conditions produces, it is this love of independence that first strikes our attention and that timid spirits fear even more; and we cannot say that they are absolutely wrong to be afraid, for anarchy has more frightening features in democratic countries than elsewhere.[b] Since citizens have no effect on each other, at the instant

a. In the manuscript: ". . . government based on the principle of sovereignty of the people."

b. What to do to combine the spirit of equality and the spirit of liberty and make liberty reign amid a leveled society.

This part is the most important for me./

The hydra of anarchy is the sacramental phrase of all the enemies of liberty. The cowardly, the corrupt, the servile try to outdo each other in repeating it. The weak and the honest say it also.

It is a monster that I must look in the face. For it is after all the great enemy of my ideas. What I want to bring along and to convince are honest souls. Well! The

when the national power that keeps them all in their place becomes absent, it seems that disorder must immediately be at its height and that, with each citizen on his own, the social body is suddenly going to find itself reduced to dust.

I am convinced nevertheless that anarchy is not the principal evil that democratic centuries must fear, but the least.

---

latter, at the point we have reached, are not afraid of despotism. They tremble before the hydra of anarchy. The fact is that there exists today a singular phenomenon for which we must account.

[To the side: It is honest men led by rogues who have always enslaved the world.

They do not see that in this way they are preparing habits, ideas, laws for all types of despotism, that of all or of one man. These men who today ask of power only to save them from anarchy resemble those drowning men who cling to a dead body and drag it away with them. By violent and reactionary laws, by the violation of existing laws, by the absence of laws, they destroy the ideas of the just and the unjust, of the permissible and the forbidden, of the legal and the illegal, and they thus open the door to all anarchical tyrannies. They are the pioneers of anarchy.]

Liberty and *power* gradually become weaker and each one in its own way. They are two exhausted and stiff old men who struggle with each other without either one winning, because their weaknesses, not their strengths, are equal; and grappling with each other, they roll together in the same dust.

Thus, those who say that liberty is weak are right. Those who maintain that power is weak are also right. What to conclude from that? Fix all the force of my mind on that.

[To the side: I believe, moreover, that the same symptoms presented themselves before the temporary or definitive enslavement of all peoples.]

To show that arbitrary and anti-liberal measures will not save us from the hydra of anarchy and to demonstrate that legal and liberal measures will not lead there, that is what we must above all work hard to do.

What modern nation (three illegible words) despotism, and how to break despotism without anarchy. Despotism is party to anarchy.

[To the side] What to think of the future of an unfortunate country in which there is an honest and pure man who says that he is not concerned about its posterity, but about himself; who says that country in the general sense is a word, that he very much wants the country to be and to remain free, provided that his fortune and his life remain sure, but that rather than putting these things in dogma [danger (ed.)], tyranny seems better to him; who says that he prefers a permanent, meddlesome, civilizing despotism to a temporary anarchy? And what to hope for his century when the other honest and pure men who surround the former approve his language? This is [illegible word] the sad spectacle that I had today, 7 February 1837 (YTC, CVd, pp. 16–18).

Equality produces, in fact, two tendencies: one leads men directly to independence and can push them suddenly as far as anarchy; the other leads them by a longer, more secret, but surer road toward servitude.

Peoples easily see the first and resist it; they allow themselves to be carried along by the other without seeing it; it is particularly important to show it.

As for me,[c] far from reproaching equality for the unruliness that it inspires, I praise it principally for that. I admire equality when I see it deposit deep within the mind and heart of each man this obscure notion of and this instinctive propensity for political independence. In this way equality prepares the remedy for the evil to which it gives birth. It is from this side that I am attached to it.

c. "As for me, I consider this taste for natural independence as the most precious present that equality has given to men" (YTC, CVk, 2, pp. 45–46).

CHAPTER 2[a]

That the Ideas of Democratic Peoples in Matters of Government Naturally Favor the Concentration of Powers[b]

a. Order of this section.

The theoretical and philosophical idea of government among democratic peoples is uniformity and centralization.

[To the side: That democratic peoples imagine liberty only in the form of a great assembly of representatives with *strong* and *regulative* executive power.]

Diverse instincts which lead democratic peoples to love centralization of power.

1. Difficulty of knowing to whom to deliver provincial administration.

2. The noble having disappeared, incapacity of local [v: new] men, ignorance, above all at the beginning.

3. Envy of the neighbor. Sentiments above all visible when aristocracy has long reigned in a country

4. That a despot in *embryo* must loudly profess these doctrines, favor and approve interests.

≠5. Establish only a sole representative assembly, a strong and regulative executive power. ≠

5. Establish only national representation, next to it an executive power which would be more or less subject to it, but which would be *strong, inquisitorial, regulative.*

[To the side: Among democratic peoples, it is not impossible that a government is centralizing and popular at the same time, and it can go so far as calling itself centralizing and liberal, and it is not impossible that it is believed.]

6. Individualism, material enjoyments (YTC, CVd, pp. 31–32).

b. Titles on the jacket that contains the manuscript: "WHAT IDEAS MEN NATURALLY CONCEIVE IN THE MATTER OF GOVERNMENT IN CENTURIES OF EQUALITY./

"HOW THE IDEAS THAT NATURALLY PRESENT THEMSELVES TO MEN IN CENTURIES OF EQUALITY LEAD THEM TO CONCENTRATE ALL POWERS."

[The principal notions that men form in the matter of government are not entirely arbitrary. They are born in each period out of the social state, and the mind receives them rather than creating them.]ᶜ

The idea of secondary powers, placed between the sovereign and the subjects, presented itself naturally to the imagination of aristocratic peoples, because these powers included within them individuals or families that birth, enlightenment, wealth kept unrivaled and that seemed destined to command. This same idea is naturally absent from the minds of men in centuries of equality because of opposite reasons; you can only introduce it to their minds artificially, and you can only maintain it there with difficulty; while without thinking about it, so to speak, they conceive the idea of a unique and central power that by itself leads all citizens.

In politics, moreover, as in philosophy and in religion, the minds of democratic peoples receive simple and general ideas with delight. They are repulsed by complicated systems, and they are pleased to imagine a great nation all of whose citizens resemble a single model and are directed by a single power.

After the idea of a unique and central power, the one that presents itself most spontaneously to the minds of men in centuries of equality is the idea of a uniform legislation. As each one of them sees himself as little different from his neighbors, he understands poorly why the rule that is applicable to one man would not be equally applicable to all the others. The least privileges are therefore repugnant to his reason. The slightest dissimilarities in the political institutions of the same people wound him, and legislative uniformity seems to him to be the first condition of good government.

I find, on the contrary, that the same notion of a uniform rule, imposed equally on all the members of the social body, is as if foreign to the human mind in aristocratic centuries. It does not accept it, or it rejects it.

These opposite tendencies of the mind end up, on both sides, by becoming such blind instincts and such invincible habits, that they still direct actions, in spite of particular facts. Sometimes, despite the immense variety

---

c. To the side: "Be careful that this does not too much resemble the opening regarding *honor.*"

of the Middle Ages, perfectly similar individuals were found; this did not prevent the legislator from assigning to each one of them diverse duties and different rights. And, on the contrary, in our times, governments wear themselves out in order to impose the same customs and the same laws on populations that are not yet similar.

As conditions become equal among a people, individuals appear smaller and society seems larger; or rather, each citizen, having become similar to all the others, is lost in the crowd, and you no longer notice anything except the vast and magnificent image of the people itself.[d]

This naturally gives men of democratic times a very high opinion of the privileges of the society and a very humble idea of the rights of the individual.[e] They easily agree that the interest of the one is everything and that the interest of the other is nothing. They grant readily enough that the power that represents the society possesses much more enlightenment and wisdom than any one of the men who compose it, and that its duty, as well as its right, is to take each citizen by the hand and to lead him.[f]

If you really want to examine our contemporaries closely, and to penetrate to the root of their political opinions, you will find a few of the ideas that I have just reproduced, and you will perhaps be astonished to find so much agreement among men who are so often at war with each other.

---

d. Note to the side of a first version: "Perhaps all these ideas, which seem to me clear and even too evident, will seem too metaphysical, and perhaps it will be necessary to put them within the reach of the ordinary reader by more detailed explanations?" (*Rubish*, 2).

e. *"To show better* also how in the United States the state breaks individuals and even organized groups of men [*corps*] with a prodigious ease, since the idea of individual rights there is weaker and more obscure than in England." Jacket, THOUGHTS TO ADD ON THE INFLUENCE EXERCISED BY DEMOCRATIC IDEAS ON THE FORMS OF GOVERNMENT (*Rubish*, 2).

f. A note in the manuscript: "Can introduce piece (a) there."

This piece (a) specifies: "<A unique and central government [v: power] charged with dispensing the same laws to the entire State and with regulating in the same way each one of those who inhabit it, an intelligent, far-sighted and strong administration that enlightens, aids, constantly directs individuals, such is the ideal that in democratic times will always occur by itself to the imagination of men as soon as they come to think about government.>"

The Americans believe that, in each state,[TN8] social power must emanate directly from the people; but once this power is constituted, they imagine, so to speak, no limits for it; they readily recognize that it has the right to do everything.

As for the particular privileges granted to cities, to families or to individuals, they have lost even the idea. Their minds have never foreseen that the same law could not be applied uniformly to all the parts of the same state and to all the men who inhabit it.

[≠In Europe we reject the dogma of sovereignty of the people that the Americans accept; we give power another origin.≠][g]

These same opinions are spreading more and more in Europe; they are being introduced within the very heart of nations that most violently reject the dogma of sovereignty of the people. These nations give power a different origin than the Americans; but they envisage power with the same features. Among all nations, the notion of intermediary power is growing dim and fading.[h] The idea of a right inherent in certain individuals is disappearing rapidly from the minds of men; the idea of the all-powerful and so to speak unique right of society is coming to take its place. These ideas take root and grow as conditions become more equal and men more similar; equality gives birth to them and they in their turn hasten the progress of equality.[j]

TRANSLATOR'S NOTE 8: In this paragraph and in the next one, and in note e for p. 1196 and note a for p. 1206, the translator has repeated the pattern followed in the first volume. Where Tocqueville seems clearly to be referring to the American states, the translator has dropped the uppercase for state. Elsewhere, the uppercase is retained: State.

g. In the margin: "<These opinions have not been borrowed by the Americans from their fathers the English, for at the period of the establishment of the colonies, the English, no more than other Europeans, had not yet conceived of such opinions. Still today they have adopted them only in part. They introduce them only in our times, but with difficulty and as conditions become less different and men more similar.>"

h. In the margin: "<The problem with all this is that it seems to me to anticipate section IV, which I will be able to judge only when I am there. If so, it would be necessary to stop at the end of page 2 and make this chapter the head of the following chapter which would then be titled: *How the ideas* and the sentiments . . .>" Page 2 of the manuscript ends at the paragraph that begins thus: "If you really want to examine . . ."

j. On a loose sheet in the manuscript:

I listen to those among my fellow citizens who are most hostile to popular forms and I see that, according to them, the public administration must get involved in almost

In France, where the revolution I am speaking about is more advanced than in any other people of Europe, these same opinions have entirely taken hold of the mind. When you listen attentively to the voices of our different parties, you will see that there is not one of them that does not adopt them. Most consider that the government acts badly; but all think that the government must act constantly and put its hand to everything. Even those who wage war most harshly against each other do not fail to agree on this point. The unity, ubiquity, omnipotence of the social power, the uniformity of its rules, form the salient feature that characterizes all the political systems born in our times. You find them at the bottom of the most bizarre utopias.[k] The human mind still pursues these images when it dreams.

If such ideas present themselves spontaneously to the mind of individuals, they occur even more readily to the imagination of princes.

While the old social state of Europe deteriorates and dissolves, sovereigns develop new beliefs about their abilities and their duties; they understand for the first time that the central power that they represent can and must, by itself and on a uniform plan, administer all matters and all men. This opinion, which, I dare say, had never been conceived before our time by the kings of Europe, penetrates the mind of these princes to the deepest

---

everything and that it must impose the same rules on all. To regulate, to direct, to compel citizens constantly in principal affairs as well as in the least, such for them is its role. I go from there to those who think that all authority must come immediately from the people, and I hear the same discourse coming from them; and I return finally doubting if the most violent adversaries of the government are not more favorable to the concentration of powers than the government itself [v: if the exclusive friends of liberty are not more favorable to the centralization of power than its most violent adversaries].

k. See note b of p. 727.

level; it remains firm there amid the agitation of all the other opinions.[m]
[A few perceive it very clearly, everyone glimpses it.][n]

So the men of today are much less divided than you imagine; they argue constantly in order to know into which hands sovereignty will be placed; but they agree easily about the duties and about the rights of sovereignty. All conceive the government in the image of a unique, simple, providential and creative power.

All the secondary ideas in political matters are in motion; that one remains fixed, inalterable; it never changes.[o] Writers and statesmen adopt it; the crowd seizes it avidly; the governed and those who govern agree about pursuing it with the same ardor; it comes first; it seems innate.

So it does not come from a caprice of the human mind, but it is a natural condition of the present state of men.

m. Order of ideas already followed./

1. Idea of a uniform legislation.
2. Idea of a unique power.
3. Immense idea of social right, very thin idea of individual right.
4. Confirmation of what precedes by the *ideas*[1] of the Americans, of the English, of the French . . . in the matter of government.

(1) Be very careful that it is not a matter of showing what is happening among these peoples, but the *ideas* that they are forming in the matter of government" (RELATIVE TO THE IDEA OF UNITY IN GENERAL, *Rubish,* 2).

n. In the margin: "≠This sentence excludes the preceding one. Either the one or the other must be removed.≠"

o. Note in the margin in a first version: "Perhaps here all the ultra-unitary extravagances, Saint-Simonianism . . ." (*Rubish,* 2).

CHAPTER 3

That the Sentiments of Democratic Peoples Are in Agreement with Their Ideas for Bringing Them to Concentrate Power[a]

If, in centuries of equality, men easily perceive the idea of a great central power, you cannot doubt, on the other hand, that their habits and their sentiments dispose them to recognize such a power and to lend it sup-

---

a. The idea of all this chapter is simple.

Equality gives birth to two tendencies:

1. One which takes men to *liberty.*

2. The other which distances men from *liberty* and leads them to *servitude.*

Liberty and *servitude* coming from *equality.* There is the idea of the chapter. *Equality* comes only as source of *liberty* and of *servitude./*
Now.

To know what makes men love *equality* more than *liberty;* it is a closely connected, but very distinct idea; for men could prefer equality to liberty, without equality being what pushed them toward servitude.

The comparison of the love of equality and the love of liberty is worth being made. But here it hinders the natural movement of the mind./

Make it a separate chapter which I will introduce afterward where I can (*Rubish,* 2).

It is possible that certain ideas on centralization set forth in this chapter and the following had their origin in the observations made by Tocqueville in England. In 1835, particularly, Tocqueville believed he had found in England a tendency toward centralization that he thought likely for the ensemble of democracies. The Poor Law and conversations with Mill and Reeve seem to have in part confirmed his theory for him (*Voyage en Angleterre, OC,* V, 2, pp. 22, 26, 49, and 53); also see Seymour Drescher, *Tocqueville and England* (Cambridge, Mass.: Harvard University Press, 1964).

On 8 July 1838, when he began this last part, Tocqueville asked Beaumont for examples about centralization. Beaumont's answer is lost (*Correspondance avec Beaumont, OC,* VIII, 1, pp. 311–12).

port.[b] The demonstration of this can be done in a few words, since most of the reasons have already been given elsewhere.

Men who inhabit democratic countries, having neither superiors, nor inferiors, nor habitual and necessary associates, readily fall back on themselves and consider themselves in isolation. I have had the occasion to show it at great length when the matter was individualism.

So these men never, except with effort, tear themselves away from their particular affairs in order to occupy themselves with common affairs; their natural inclination is to abandon the care of these affairs to the sole visible and permanent representative of collective interests, which is the State.

Not only do they not naturally have the taste for occupying themselves with public matters, but also they often lack time to do so. Private life is so active in democratic times, so agitated, so full of desires, of work, that hardly any energy or leisure is left to any man for political life.

It is not I who will deny that such inclinations are not invincible, since my principal goal in writing this book has been to combat them. I maintain only that, today, a secret force develops them constantly in the human heart, and that it is enough not to stop them for those inclinations to fill it up.

I have equally had the occasion to show how the growing love of well-being and the mobile nature of property made democratic peoples fear material disorder. The love of public tranquillity is often the only political passion that these peoples retain, and it becomes more active and more powerful among them, as all the others collapse and die; that naturally disposes citizens to give new rights constantly to or to allow new rights to be taken by the central power, which alone seems to them to have the interest and the means to defend them from anarchy while defending itself.[c]

---

b. "≠I see clearly how the fear of revolutions leads men to give great prerogatives to power in general, but not how it leads them to centralize power.≠" (*Rubish*, 2).

c. *7 March 1838. Unity, centralization.*

However animated you are against unity and the governmental unity that is called centralization, you cannot nonetheless deny that unity and centralization are

[<For they do not see around them either individual or corps that is by itself strong enough and lasting enough to defend itself and to defend them.>]

Since, in centuries of equality, no one is obliged to lend his strength to his fellow, and no one has the right to expect great support from his fellow, each man is independent and weak at the very same time. These two states, which must not be either envisaged separately or confused, give the citizen of democracies very contradictory instincts. His independence fills him with confidence and pride among his equals, and his debility makes him, from time to time, feel the need for outside help which he cannot expect from any of his equals, since they are all powerless and cold. In this extreme case, he turns his eyes naturally toward this immense being that alone rises up amidst the universal decline. His needs and, above all, his desires lead him constantly toward this being, and he ends by envisaging it as the sole and necessary support for individual weakness.[1]

---

the most powerful means to do quickly, energetically, and in a given place, very great things.

That reveals one of the reasons why in democratic centuries centralization and unity are loved so much. The character of these centuries is love of rapid and easy enjoyments and indifference about the future. In the eyes of all the public men of those times, centralization is the means of attaining quickly and without difficulty the results that they desire.

Thus equality gives birth to the idea of unity and the same equality suggests the taste for it (*Rubish*, 2).

1. *In democratic societies, only the central power has some stability in its position and some permanence in its enterprises. All the citizens are stirring constantly and becoming transformed. Now, it is in the nature of every government to want gradually to enlarge its sphere. So it is very difficult that in the long run the latter does not manage to succeed, since it acts with a fixed thought and a continuous will on men whose position, ideas and desires vary every day.*

Often it happens that the citizens work for it without wanting to do so.

Democratic centuries are times of experiments, of innovation and of adventures. A multitude of men is always engaged in a difficult or new enterprise that they are pursuing separately without being burdened by their fellows. The former very much accept, as a general principle, that the public power must not intervene in private affairs, but, by exception, each one of them desires that it helps him in the special matter that preoccupies him and seeks to draw the action of the government in his direction, all the while wanting to restrain it in all others.

Since a multitude of men has this particular view at the same time on a host of different

This finally makes understandable what often occurs among democratic peoples, where you see men, who endure superiors with such difficulty, patiently suffer a master, and appear proud and servile at the very same time.

The hatred that men bring to privilege increases as privileges become rarer and smaller, so that you would say that democratic passions become more inflamed at the very time when they find the least sustenance.[d] I have already given the reason for this phenomenon. No inequality, however great, offends the eye when all conditions are unequal; while the smallest dissimilarity seems shocking amid general uniformity; the sight of it becomes more unbearable as uniformity is more complete. So it is natural that love of equality grows constantly with equality itself; by satisfying it, you develop it.

This immortal and more and more burning hatred, which animates democratic peoples against the least privileges, singularly favors the gradual concentration of all political rights in the hands of the sole representative of the State. The sovereign, necessarily and without dispute above all cit-

---

matters, the sphere of the central power expands imperceptibly in all directions, even though each one of them wishes to limit it. So a democratic government increases its attributions by the sole fact that it lasts. Time works for it; it profits from all accidents; individual passions help it even without their knowing, and you can say that a democratic government becomes that much more centralized the older the democratic society is.

d. This proposition that *hatred of inequality is that much greater as inequality is less* is well proved by what happened among aristocratic peoples themselves within the interior of each class. The nobles were not jealous of the king, but of those among them who rose above the others, and they called loudly for equality. As long as the bourgeois were different from the nobles, they were not jealous of the nobles, but of each other; and if we get down to the bottom of our heart, won't we all be appalled to see that envy makes itself felt there above all in regard to our neighbors, our friends and our near relations? You are not jealous of those people because they are neighbors, friends and relations, but because they are our fellows and our equals.

The hatred of inequality in proportion as inequality is less is therefore a truth in all times and applicable to all men (NEW IDEAS RELATIVE TO DEMOCRATIC SENTIMENTS THAT FAVOR CENTRALIZATION, *Rubish,* 2).

izens, does not excite the envy of any one of them, and each one believes that all the prerogatives that he concedes to the sovereign are taken away from his equals.

[<In centuries of equality, each man, living independent of all of his fellows, becomes accustomed to directing his private affairs without constraint. When these same men are united in common, they naturally conceive the idea of and the taste for administering themselves by themselves. So equality leads men toward administrative decentralization, but creates at the same time powerful instincts which turn them away from it.>]ᵉ

The man of democratic centuries obeys only with an extreme repugnance his neighbor who is his equal; he refuses to acknowledge in him an enlightenment superior to his own; he mistrusts his neighbor's justice and regards his power with jealousy; he fears and despises him; he loves to make him feel at every instant the common dependence that they both have on the same master.

Every central power that follows these natural instincts loves equality and favors it; for equality [(of conditions)] singularly facilitates the action of such a power, extends it and assures it.

You can say equally that every central government adores [legislative] uniformity; uniformityᶠ spares it from the examination of an infinity of details with which it would have to be concerned, if the rule had to be made for men, rather than making all men indiscriminately come under the same rule. Thus, the government loves what the citizens love, and it naturally hates what they hate. This community of sentiments, which, among democratic nations, continually unites in the same thought each individual and the sovereign power, establishes between them a secret and permanent sym-

---

e. In the margin: "≠Perhaps keep this for the place where I will speak about *liberal* instincts created by equality.≠"

f. "Pantheism.

"Saint-Simonianism." (In the *Rubish* RELATIVE TO THE IDEA OF UNITY IN GENERAL, *Rubish*, 2.)

"Saint-Simonian theory and other democratic theories. Pantheism. Agreement of the governmental and radical press on this point." (In the jacket that bears the title: "UNITY, CENTRALIZATION, ADMINISTRATIVE DESPOTISM./

"Mixture of administrative and judicial power./

"23 March 1838" *Rubish*, 2.)

pathy. You pardon the government its faults in favor of its tastes; public confidence abandons the government only with difficulty amid its excesses and its errors, and returns as soon as it is called back. Democratic peoples often hate the agents of the central power; but they always love this power itself. [<Because they consider it as the most powerful instrument that they could use as needed to help them make everyone who escapes from the common rule come back to it.>

I said that in times of equality the idea of intermediary powers set between simple individuals and the government did not naturally present itself to the human mind. I add that men who live in these centuries envisage such powers only with distrust and submit to them only with difficulty.]

Thus, I have come by two different roads to the same end. I have shown that equality suggested to men the thought of a unique, uniform and strong government. I have just shown that it gives them the taste for it; so today nations are tending toward a government of this type. The natural inclination of their mind and heart leads them to it, and it is enough for them not to hold themselves back in order to reach it.

I think that, in the democratic centuries that are going to open up, individual independence and local liberties will always be a product of art. Centralization will be the natural government.

CHAPTER 4[a]

a. Appendix of section.—Section IV./
   Ideas of the chapter.

1. *When liberty has existed before equality,* it establishes habits that are opposed to the excessive development of the central power.

2. *When equality has developed rapidly with the aid of a revolution,* the taste for intermediary powers disappears more quickly. Centralization becomes necessary in a way.

3. Revolution makes hatred and jealousy of the neighbor more intense and leads either the upper or the lower classes to want to centralize.

4. Enlightenment and ignorance.

5. War.

6. Disorder.

7. Democratic nature of the central power.

[In the margin: New ideas.

1. Extraordinary talents.

2. Two ideas relative to revolutions and which have not been treated there.

3. When a people has been formed from several peoples, like the Americans.

≠4. When democratic society is ancient, the permanent ambition of the g[overnment (ed.)] gives it the advantage in the long run, because of the shifting desires of the citizens and of the multitude of (illegible word) into which they are constantly throwing themselves.≠]

The entire vice of this chapter seems to me to reside in this:

1. Definitively, the greatest number and the principal ones of the particular reasons that I give are connected with the particular accident of a *revolution.* So it would be necessary to put them separately and to announce in advance that I am going to deal with this order of particular causes. It is worth the trouble.

2. It would be necessary to put *those causes* in a better order so that the mind would pass better from one to the other.

It is on these two points that I must make a final effort while reviewing one last time.
   6 November 1839 (YTC, CVk, 1, pp. 74–76).

On a page of drafts:

Note applicable to all the sections, but principally to section III./
   I do not believe that in all this chapter and particularly in this section I have made

Of Some Particular and Accidental Causes That End up Leading a Democratic People to Centralize Power or That Turn Them Away from Doing So[b]

sufficient use of America because of the preoccupation that I had that the principal goal of the chapter was to speak about Europe and to Europe. But even with this goal, perhaps it is necessary to show better what is happening in America. I showed a glimpse of it in several places, but perhaps it would be worth more, instead of *spreading* America around as I have done, to gather it together at one point and show:

1. That we must distinguish between the Union and the states. The national element finding itself only in the *state*.

2. To show or rather to recall in what way the state is more centralized than the monarchies of Europe and in what way less centralized. The government more, the administration less. There are pages of my first work to reread and perhaps to cite. .-.[what (ed.)].- makes administrative centralization less great in America than in Europe despite equality.

If I do not make the reader see America clearly, he will perhaps be invincibly opposed to my ideas, because seen in a haze and considered roughly, America seems in fact to provide an opposite argument.

Reflect on all that while reviewing (*Rubish*, 2).

b. In the drafts:

Other causes or particular causes that can favor centralization./

To introduce this in the preceding chapters or to put it in a supplementary chapter./

[In the margin: ≠Perhaps show how the Americans have escaped excessive centralization of powers with the help of *favorable particular causes*.

Separation of colonies.

No foreign wars.

Few internal troubles.

Habits of local government.

Principles of aristocratic liberty without mixture of aristocracy.

Idea of rights without hatreds that lead to violating rights./

≠1. Superior men who all believe they have an interest in centralization.

2. Passions of all political men which lead to centralization.

3. Superficial minds.≠

3. External danger.

4. Internal troubles.[a]

5. Hatred of the remnants of an aristocracy. England.

If all democratic peoples are carried instinctively toward centralization of powers, they are led there in an unequal manner. It depends on particular circumstances that can develop or limit the natural effects of the social state. These circumstances are in very great number; I will only speak about a few.

Among men who have lived free for a long time before becoming equal, the instincts that liberty gave combat, up to a certain point, the tendencies suggested by equality; and although among those men the central power increases its privileges, the individuals there never entirely lose their independence.

But when equality happens to develop among a people who have never known or who, for a long time, have no longer known liberty, as is seen on the continent of Europe, and when the old habits of the nation come to combine suddenly and by a sort of natural attraction with the new habits and doctrines that arise from the social state, all powers seem to rush by themselves toward the center; they accumulate there with a surprising rapidity, and the State all at once attains the extreme limits of its strength, while the individuals allow themselves to fall in a moment to the lowest degree of weakness.

The English who came, three centuries ago, to establish a democratic society in the wilderness of the New World were all accustomed in the mother country to take part in public affairs; they knew the jury; they had freedom of speech and freedom of the press, individual liberty, [added: independent courts], the idea of right and the custom of resorting to it. They carried these

---

[(a) All centralizing geniuses love war and all warrior minds love centralization.]

6. Democratic origin of the sovereign; people or prince.

≠7. Social state that becomes democratic without absolute monarchy and without free habits, under the aegis and by the favor of the central power.

8. Hatred of the neighbor increased by the aristocratic notion of the neighbor.

9. Difficulty of finding local governments when aristocracy chased away.≠

<10. Centralization increases by itself by *enduring*. Government becomes more capable and individuals more incapable.>

≠11. Little enlightenment in the people, which delivers more and more to the power≠] (*Rubish*, 2).

free institutions and these manly mores to America, and these institutions and mores sustained them against the invasions of the State.

Among the Americans, it is therefore liberty that is old; equality is comparatively new. The opposite happens in Europe where equality, introduced by absolute power and under the eyes of the kings, had already penetrated the habits of the people long before liberty entered their ideas.

I have said that, among democratic peoples, government naturally presented itself to the human mind only under the form of a unique and central power, and that the notion of intermediary powers was not familiar to it. That is particularly applicable to democratic nations that have seen the principle of equality triumph with the aid of a violent revolution. Since the classes that directed local affairs [<served as intermediary between the sovereign and the people>] disappear suddenly in this tempest, and the confused mass that remains still has neither the organization nor the habits that allow it to take in hand the administration of these same affairs, you see nothing except the State itself which can take charge of all the details of government. Centralization becomes in a way a necessary fact.[c]

Napoleon [{the national Convention}][d] must be neither praised nor

c. "In our time a famous sect has appeared that claimed to centralize all the forces of society in the same hands.

"[Further along, on the same page] If someone had spoken to me about the doctrines of the Saint-Simonians without letting me know the time or the country that saw them arise, I dare to affirm that I would have said without fear that they had been born in a democratic century [v: country]" (NOTES OF THE CHAPTER, *Rubish,* 2).

d. Financial centralization, and that one includes all the others, was established in France by the Convention, 5 September 1794, on a report of Cambon who, applying to finances the great principle of the unity and of the indivisibility of France, declared that in the future there would be only one budget, as there was only one State.

The excess of this principle forced it to be abandoned in the year IV and forced departmental budgets to be done.

But since then we have not ceased and still do not cease to remove sums from these budgets in order to carry them over to the budget of the State, that is to say that little by little we return more and more to the financial system created abruptly by the Convention. We see, adds the *Journal des débats,* which provided me with these details (6 March 1838) that the movement of administrative centralization continues, since the budget of the State swells and the departmental budget decreases (YTC, CVk, 2, p. 42).

blamed for having concentrated in his hands alone all administrative powers; for, after the abrupt disappearance of the nobility and of the upper
bourgeoisie, these powers came to him by themselves; it would have been
as difficult for him to reject them as to take them. [<He must be reproached
for the tyrannical use that he often made of his power, rather than for his
power.>]ᵉ Such a necessity has never been felt by the Americans, who, not
having had a revolution and being from the beginning governed by themselves, have never had to charge the State with temporarily serving them as
tutor.ᶠ

Thus, among a democratic people, centralization develops not only according to the progress of equality, but also according to the manner in
which this equality is established.ᵍ

Tocqueville is referring here to discussions on the law on departmental attributions
that had taken place in the Chamber of Deputies in the month of March 1838. The
details cited belong to the session of 6 March, reproduced in the *Journal des débats* the
next day.

e. In the margin: "≠This sentence is too much because here it is only a matter of
administrative centralization.≠"

f. .-.-.- In France, Napoleon was in the matter .-.-[of (ed.)].-.- centralization the
accident, but the real and permanent cause was this sudden destruction of the upper
{administrative} classes.

Those whose education, wealth, habits and memories naturally enabled them to
conduct provincial affairs disappear; and with the confused mass that remained, still
not having either enlightenment, or organization, or mores which could allow it to
direct these same affairs, to whom would this same concern necessarily revert, if not
to the central power? So centralization has been a necessary fact. That is true; the
error is to say that it must be an eternal fact.

[To the side] I put a child under my guardianship; is this to say that I must keep
him under my rule at manhood? (UNITY, CENTRALIZATION, ADMINISTRATIVE
DESPOTISM, *Rubish*, 2).

g. The two great disadvantages of centralization are these: 1. In the long run it prevents more undertakings and improvements than it can produce. 2. It delivers all of
the social existence to a power that, becoming indolent or tyrannical, can end by
plunging the nation into impotence or servitude.

These two dangers are distant and .-.-.- disclose even .-.-.-

The good that centralization produces, the order, the regularity, the uniformity so
adored by democratic peoples, are, on the contrary, noticed and appreciated right
away by these same minds.

How would its cause not be popular? (THOUGHTS TO ADD ON THE INFLUENCE
EXERCISED BY DEMOCRATIC IDEAS ON THE FORMS OF GOVERNMENT, *Rubish*, 2).

[When conditions have become equal among a nation only following a long and difficult social effort, the sentiments that led to the democratic revolution and those given birth by it subsist for a long time after the revolution. The memory of privileges is joined with the privileges themselves. The trace of former ranks is perpetuated. The people still see the destroyed remnants with hatred and envy, and the nobles envisage the people with terror. You find former adversaries around you on both sides, and you outdo each other throwing yourselves into the arms of the government for fear of falling under the oppression of your neighbors.

This is how the political tendencies that equality imparts are that much stronger among a people as conditions have been more unequal and as equality has had more difficulty becoming established.

The Americans arrived equal on the soil that they occupy. They never had privileges of birth or fortune to destroy. They naturally feel no hatred of some against others. So they subject themselves readily to the administration of those close at hand, because they neither hate nor fear them.][h]

At the beginning of a great democratic revolution, and when the war between the different classes has only begun, the people try hard to centralize public administration in the hands of the government, in order to tear the direction of local affairs away from the aristocracy. Toward the end of this same revolution, on the contrary, it is ordinarily the vanquished aristocracy which attempts to deliver to the State the direction of all [{local}] affairs, because it fears the petty tyranny of the people, who have become its equal and often its master.

Thus, it is not always the same class of citizens that applies itself to increasing the prerogatives of power; but as long as the democratic revolution lasts, a class, powerful by numbers or by wealth, is always found in the nation that is led to centralize the public administration by special passions and particular interests, apart from hatred of the government of the neighbor, which is a general and permanent sentiment among democratic peoples. You can see today that it is the lower classes of England that work

h. This fragment constitutes an independent sheet of the manuscript. Tocqueville's indications allow us to think that it would have been placed here.

with all their strength to destroy local independence and to carry the administration of all points from the circumference to the center, while the upper classes try hard to keep this same administration within its ancient limits. I dare to predict that a day will come when you will see an entirely opposite spectacle.[j]

What precedes makes it well understood why, among a democratic people who has arrived at equality by a long and difficult social effort, the social power must always be stronger and the individual weaker than in a democratic society where, from the beginning, citizens have always been equal. This is what the example of the Americans finally proves.

The men who inhabit the United States have never been separated by any privilege; they have never known the reciprocal relation of inferior and master, and since they do not fear and do not hate one another, they have never known the need to call upon the sovereign to direct the details of their affairs.[k] The destiny of the Americans is singular; they took from the aristocracy of England the idea of individual rights and the taste for local liberties; and they were able to preserve both, because they did not have to combat aristocracy.

If in all times enlightenment is useful to men for defending their in-

---

j. "When you examine all the laws that .-.-.- in England for the past fifty years and above all during recent years, you will see that all more or less have a tendency toward centralization and uniformity. That is enough for me to conclude that the great democratic revolution that today shapes the world is proceeding constantly among the English people, in spite of the obstacles that oppose it and despite the wealth and the men that the aristocracy still possesses there" (RELATIVE TO THE IDEA OF UNITY IN GENERAL, *Rubish,* 2).

k. On this point the Americans, whatever their errors and their faults, deserve to be praised. They have well earned humanity's gratitude. They have shown that the democratic social state and democratic laws did not have as a necessary result the degeneration of the human race.

I am very content to have found this idea because I believe it correct and because it is the only way to make *America* appear a final time in my last chapters, which really relate only to France.

[To the side] In America the State is a great deal, but the individual is something. Less than in England, but more than in France. He has rights, a strength of individuality less respected than among the English, more than among us (UNITY, CENTRALIZATION, ADMINISTRATIVE DESPOTISM, *Rubish,* 2).

dependence, that is above all true in democratic centuries. It is easy, when all men are similar, to establish a unique and omnipotent government; instincts are sufficient. But men need a great deal of intelligence, science and art, in order to organize and to maintain, in the same circumstances, secondary powers, and in order to create, amid the independence and individual weakness of citizens, free associations able to struggle against tyranny without destroying order [{and in order to replace the individual power of a few families with free associations of citizens}].

So concentration of powers and individual servitude will grow, among democratic nations, not only in proportion to equality, but also by reason of ignorance.[m]

It is true that, in centuries less advanced in knowledge, the government often lacks the enlightenment to perfect despotism, as the citizens lack the enlightenment to escape it. But the effect is not equal on the two sides.

However uncivilized a democratic people may be, the central power that directs it is never completely without enlightenment, because it easily attracts what little enlightenment there is in the country, and because, as needed, it goes outside to seek it. So among a nation that is ignorant as well as democratic, a prodigious difference between the intellectual capacity of the sovereign power and that of each one of its subjects cannot fail to manifest itself. The former ends by easily concentrating all powers in its hands.

m. Centralization./

There are two types of decentralization.

One that is in a way instinctive, blind, full of prejudices, devoid of rules, that is born from the desire of small localities to be independent.

There is another one that is reasoned, enlightened, that knows its limits.

These two decentralizations are at the two ends of civilization. In the middle is a central power [that is] energetic, intelligent, that claims [doubtful reading (ed.)] to be able to do everything by itself and that manages, after a fashion, to do so.

Baden, 14 August 1836 (UNITY, CENTRALIZATION, ADMINISTRATIVE DESPOTISM, *Rubish*, 2).

The administrative power of the State expands constantly, because only the State is skillful enough to administer.[n]

Aristocratic nations, however little enlightened you suppose them, never present the same spectacle, because enlightenment there is distributed equally between the prince and the principal citizens.

The Pasha who reigns today over Egypt found the population of the country composed of very ignorant and very equal men, and to govern it he appropriated the science and the intelligence of Europe. The particular enlightenment of the sovereign thus coming to combine with the ignorance

---

n. On accidental causes./

After the place where I show the government as the necessary heir to the old powers when they are suddenly destroyed.

Every time that a great revolution agitates a people, it gives birth within it to a host of new relationships, interests and needs, and you feel on all sides the need for a power that comes to regulate these relationships, guarantee these interests, satisfy these needs. That gives great opportunities to the government that this revolution has established to expand the circle of its action well beyond the old limits and to create a multitude of new attributions that none of the abolished powers had had. That is that much easier for the government because, amid this renewal of all things, the citizens are full of uncertainty, ignorance and fear, not seeing clearly enough.

So when equality is established with the help of and amid a great revolution it happens that the government immediately (two illegible words) its prerogatives not only because of equality of conditions, but also because of the revolution (which makes conditions equal) (YTC, CVj, 2, p. 13).

Page 14 of this same notebook contains an identical fragment.
After this passage, you read:

This includes two ideas:

1. Current existence is more complicated than the life of the former aristocratic societies. Consequently the social power must get involved in more things.

2. Equality is a new fact that puts the individual vis-à-vis the government in a state of uncertainty, ignorance and weakness, which delivers him naturally to the latter. Transitory thing which at this moment plays an immense role (illegible word)./

Another idea of L[ouis (ed.)].

Men without belief give themselves easily to the direction of the power because they are overwhelmed by the weight of their liberty. Man cannot bear independence in all things and the extreme liberty of his mind leads him to curb his actions.

Very debatable truth.

Talk more about all that with L[ouis (ed.)] (YTC, CVj, 2, pp. 14–15).

and the democratic weakness of his subjects, the farthest limit of centralization has been attained without difficulty, and the prince has been able
to make the country into his factory and the inhabitants into his workers.º

I believe that the extreme centralization of political power ends by en-
ervating society and thus by weakening the government itself in the long
run. But I do not deny that a centralized social force is able to execute easily,
in a given time and at a determined point, great enterprises.P That is above
all true in war, when success depends much more on the ease that you find
in bringing all your resources rapidly to a certain point, than even on the
extent of those resources. So it is principally in war that peoples feel the
desire and often the need to increase the prerogatives of the central power.
All warrior geniuses love centralization, which increases their forces, and
all centralizing geniuses love war, which obliges nations to draw all powers
into the hands of the State. Thus, the democratic tendency which leads

o. "Unity. Centralization./

"Supply myself with an article on Egypt published in the *Revue des deux mondes* of
1 March 1838 and in which someone admires greatly that the Pasha has made himself
the proprietor and the unique industrialist of his country, and in which it is implied that
something approaching this or analogous could perhaps be tried in France."

"Symptoms of the time" (UNITY, CENTRALIZATION, ADMINISTRATIVE DESPO-
TISM, *Rubish*, 2).

".-.-.- centralization of the Pasha of Egypt which proves that when conditions are
once equal, the idea of a central and uniform government presents itself as well in a
period of incomplete civilization as in one of advanced civilization. I do not even know
if centralization is not rather an idea of medium civilization than of very advanced civilization" (IDEAS TO ADD ON THE INFLUENCE EXERCISED BY DEMOCRATIC IDEAS
ON THE FORMS OF GOVERNMENT, *Rubish*, 2).

p. That among democratic nations, above all those that are not commercial, the State
must be involved in more *enterprises* than in others./

Nuance to observe in that. If the State itself takes charge of everything, it finishes
by throwing individuals into nothingness. If it takes charge of nothing, it is to be
feared that it will not be able to emerge from it. Nuances very delicate, difficult to
grasp. Position that is very easy to abuse. English system of not getting involved in
anything. Aristocratic system. Liberty gives the desire and the idea of doing great
things, and individuals powerful enough to do them easily by associating. American
system in which the State encourages and does not share in the activities of enterprises, loans money, grants land, does nothing by itself (with the drafts of chapter 5
of the second part, on association in civil life, *Rubish*, 1).

men constantly to multiply the privileges of the State and to limit the rights of individuals is much more rapid and more continuous among democratic peoples who are subject by their position to great and frequent wars, and whose existence can often be put in danger, than among all others.

I have said how the fear of disorder and the love of well-being imperceptibly led democratic peoples to augment the attributions of the central government, the sole power that seems to them by itself strong enough, intelligent enough, stable enough to protect them against anarchy. I hardly need to add that all the particular circumstances that tend to make the state of a democratic society disturbed and precarious increase this general instinct and lead individuals, more and more, to sacrifice their rights to their tranquillity.

So a people is never so disposed to increase the attributions of the central power than when emerging from a long and bloody revolution that, after tearing property from the hands of its former owners, has shaken all beliefs, filled the nation with furious hatreds, opposing interests and conflicting factions. The taste for public tranquillity then becomes a blind passion, and citizens are subject to becoming enamored with a very disordered love of order.

I have just examined several accidents, all of which contribute to aiding the centralization of power. I have not yet spoken about the principal one.

The first of all the accidental causes which, among democratic peoples, can draw the direction of all affairs into the hands of the sovereign is the origin of the sovereign himself and his inclinations.

Men who live in centuries of equality love the central power naturally^q and willingly expand its privileges; but if it happens that this same

q. *Superior men* who all want to centralize. Accidental cause, the more democracies encounter such men, the more centralized they will become.

All the extraordinary men.

All the extraordinary talents go in this direction. Extraordinary talents in other times are often a cause of restlessness for the people among whom they are found. They create wars, divisions, violence, tyranny. But beyond that, in democracies, they

power faithfully represents their interests and exactly reproduces their instincts, the confidence that they have in it has hardly any limits, and they believe that they are granting to themselves all that they are giving away.[r]

Drawing administrative powers toward the center will always be less easy[s] and less rapid with kings who are still attached at some point to the old aristocratic order than with new princes, self-made men, who seem to be tied indissolubly to the cause of equality by birth, prejudices, instincts and habits. I do not want to say that the princes of aristocratic origin who live in the centuries of democracy do not seek to centralize. I believe that they apply themselves to that as diligently as all the others. For them, the only advantages of equality are in this direction; but their opportunities are fewer, because the citizens, instead of naturally anticipating their desires, often lend themselves to those desires only with difficulty. In democratic societies, centralization will always be that much greater as the sovereign is less aristocratic: there is the rule.

----

always create centralization, because centralization is an admirable means of action that is clearly conceived and easily obtained only at that time.

I will say as much about all the extraordinary men who come to be born from time to time among these peoples.

All will love centralization and will seek to expand it, and it will be that much greater as they appear in greater number (YTC, CVk, 1, pp. 76–77).

r. [In the margin: Ease of succeeding when the power does not give rise to fear about equality./

January 1837.]

What must be done in order to take hold of despotic power among democratic peoples and in the centuries of democratic transition. Ease of turning democratic passions against their goal, to cause liberty to be sacrificed to the blind love of equality and to the *revolutionary* passions that it brings about. To place somewhere toward the end of the volume and perhaps at the end after war (YTC, CVk, 2, p. 56).

s. Variant in the manuscript: ". . . will always be more easy, more rapid and greater among democratic nations that live as a republic than among those that obey a monarch, and under new dynasties than under the old, and it will never meet fewer obstacles than under princes who have emerged from a low position, self-made men, who by their origin, their prejudices, their interests and their habits seem intimately tied to the cause of equality. You can say in a general way that in democratic societies centralization will always be that much greater as the sovereign is less aristocratic."

[I do not believe in the hereditary and imprescriptible rights of princes, and I know how difficult it is to maintain the old families of kings in the midst of new ideas. Ancient dynasties have some particular advantages in centuries of equality, however, that I want to acknowledge.]^t

t. That, before everything, in order for a power to be able to arrive at tyranny among a democratic people, it must have come from the people and must at every occasion flatter the sentiment of equality.

Centralization. Individualism. Material enjoyment./

What precedes opens the way for me.

I want to find out by what condition despotism could establish itself among a democratic people and show how it could use the ideas and the sentiments that arise from equality. To struggle at the same time against the spirit of equality and the spirit of liberty would be folly, but they can be divided. Thus the great problem that the despots of our time and those of the centuries to come will have to have daily in view [interrupted text (ed.)].

From now on, those who will want to create absolute power by aristocracy or aristocracy by absolute power will be great fools, you can affirm it from today.

So what is necessary first for a power [v: government], so that it is possible for it to aspire to tyranny in a longer or shorter time?

I am not afraid to say it, a popular [v: plebeian] origin. It must, by its prejudices, its instincts, its memories, its interests, be intensely favorable to equality. Those are the primary qualities, without which, skill and even genius would be of no use to it to succeed, and with which, vices would be enough.

If it happened that this same man had a bold, brilliant, fertile mind, that he was without restraint in his passions as without limits in his desires, and that he himself naturally shared the democratic inclinations and vices, faults, opinions, which he wanted to use, I do not doubt that he would soon make himself formidable to liberty, and I do not know what the limits of his fortune would be if he added to all of these advantages that of being a bastard [v: if he joined to all of these advantages that of coming from the ranks of the people, his success would be even more probable].

[To the side: Debatable theorem.]

The first concern and the principal affair (of a government or of a man who aims for tyranny) must be to interest the dominant passion of the century in his favor. He can be wasteful, arbitrary, even cruel; it is not sure that he (illegible word) as long as he is not assumed to be aristocratic. But were he the opposite of all these things, he will assuredly perish if it is half-suspected that he is aristocratic. It is possible that in this, favorable circumstances serve him.

If by chance there exists within a democratic people a party, a class, or even a man who in the eyes of the public represents the principle of the inequality of conditions, that is a fortunate accident from which a government that aims for omnipotence must hasten to profit. Let it first exercise its emerging strength on the former; let it do

When an old race of kings directs an aristocracy, since the natural prejudices of the sovereign are in perfect accord with the natural prejudices of the nobles, the vices inherent in aristocratic societies develop freely and find no remedy. The opposite happens when the offshoot of a feudal branch is placed at the head of a democratic people. The prince is inclined each day by his education, his habits and his memories, toward sentiments that inequality of conditions suggests; and the people tend constantly, by its social state, toward the mores to which equality gives birth. So it often happens that the citizens seek to contain the central power, much less as tyrannical than as aristocratic; and that they firmly maintain their independence, not only because they want to be free, but above all because they intend to remain equal. [It is in this sense that you can say that old dynasties lead aristocratic peoples to despotism and democratic nations to liberty.

<It is difficult for such a struggle to last for long without leading to a revolution, but as long as it lasts, you cannot deny that it powerfully serves the political education of the democracy.>]

A revolution that overturns an old family of kings, in order to place new men at the head of a democratic people, can temporarily weaken the central power; but however anarchic it seems at first, you must not hesitate to predict that its final and necessary result will be to expand and to assure the prerogatives of this very power.

---

against them its apprenticeship for tyranny. It can attempt it without danger. Two great results gained from the same blow. On the one hand, it proves in this way its hatred for aristocracy; {on the other} it accustoms the people to illegality and familiarizes them with arbitrariness and violence. How to suspect a power that emerges from our ranks, that represents us to ourselves, that acts for us and in our name, in the matter that is most in our hearts; that loves what we love, hates what we hate and strikes what we cannot reach? Won't there be time to take precautions when it tries finally to turn against us the weapon that has been entrusted to it? The nation closes its eyes to that and falls asleep.

[With a bracket that includes the last two paragraphs: To delete.]

This reveals the type of utility that a democratic people can draw from ancient dynasties. When an ancient family of kings directs an aristocracy . . . (YTC, CVd, pp. 32–36); you find a draft of this fragment in YTC, CVd, pp. 37–41).

The first, and in a way the only necessary condition for arriving at centralization of the public power in a democratic society is to love equality or make people believe that you do. Thus, the science of despotism, formerly so complicated, is simplified; it is reduced, so to speak, to a unique principle.[u]

u. The manuscript proposes two other conclusions:

As for me, when I consider the growing weakness of the men of today, their love [v: passion] for equality which increases with their powerlessness, and the type of natural instinct that seems on all sides to carry them without their knowledge toward servitude, I do not dare ask God to inspire in citizens love of liberty, but I beg Him at least to give to the sovereigns [v: princes] who govern them the taste for aristocracy. This would be enough to save human independence.

In another place:

Last words of section IV./
    Moreover, it must very much be believed, liberty, in order to become established and to be maintained, has no less need than despotism to appear as friend of equality. I beg the partisans of liberty to understand it well and to consider that to appear always as a friend of equality, there [is (ed.)] only one sure means worthy of them; it is to be so; it is to attach themselves to equality by the mind if not by the heart.

CHAPTER 5

That among the European Nations of Today the Sovereign Power Increases Although Sovereigns Are Less Stable[a]

If you come to reflect on what precedes, you will be surprised and frightened to see how, in Europe, everything seems to contribute to increasing indefinitely the prerogatives of the central power and each day to make individual existence weaker, more subordinate and more precarious.

The democratic nations of Europe have all the general and permanent tendencies that lead the Americans toward centralization of powers, and moreover they are subject to a multitude of secondary and accidental causes that the Americans do not know. You would say that each step that they take toward equality brings them closer to despotism.

It is enough to look around us and at ourselves to be convinced of it.

During the aristocratic centuries that preceded ours, the sovereigns of Europe had been deprived of or had let go of several of the rights inherent in their power. Not yet one hundred years ago, among most European nations, almost independent individuals or bodies were found that administered justice, called up and maintained soldiers, collected taxes, and often even made or explained the law. Everywhere the State has, for itself alone, taken back these natural attributions of sovereign power; in everything that relates to government, it no longer puts up with an intermediary between it and the citizens, and it directs the citizens by itself in general affairs. I

a. Title in the drafts: THAT CENTRALIZATION IS THE GREATEST DANGER FOR THE DEMOCRATIC NATIONS OF EUROPE (*Rubish,* 2).

am very far[b] from censuring this concentration of power; I am limiting myself to showing it.

In the same period, a great number of secondary powers existed in Europe that represented local interests and administered local affairs. Most of these local authorities have already disappeared; all are tending rapidly to disappear or to fall into the most complete dependency. From one end of Europe to the other, the privileges of lords, the liberties of cities, the provincial administrations are destroyed or are going to be.

Europe has experienced, for a half-century, many revolutions and counter-revolutions that have moved it in opposite directions.[c] But all these movements are similar on one point: all have shaken or destroyed secondary powers. Local privileges that the French nation had not abolished in countries conquered by it have finally succumbed under the efforts of the princes who defeated France. These princes rejected all the novelties that the [French] Revolution had created among them, except centralization. It is the only thing that they have agreed to keep from it.

What I want to note is that all these diverse rights that in our time have been successively taken away from classes, corporations, men, have not served to raise new secondary powers on a more democratic foundation, but have been concentrated on all sides in the hands of the sovereign. Everywhere the State arrives more and more at directing by itself the least citizens and at alone leading each one of them in the least affairs.[1]

b. The manuscript says: "I am far from censuring . . ."

c. "The greatest originality of my chapter is in this idea, still a bit confused, that shows *two revolutions* operating almost in opposite directions. The one that tends to give to the central power a new origin, new tastes, to detach it from aristocracy. . . .

"And the other that constantly increases its prerogatives" (*Rubish*, 2).

1. *This gradual weakening of the individual in the face of society manifests itself in a thousand ways. I will cite among others what relates to wills.*

In aristocratic countries, a profound respect is usually professed for the last will of men. That goes sometimes, among the ancient peoples of Europe, even as far as superstition; the social power, far from hindering the caprices of the dying man, lent its strength to the least of them; it assured him of a perpetual power.[d]

Nearly all the charitable establishments of old Europe were in the hands of individuals or of corporations; they have all more or less fallen into dependence on the sovereign, and in several countries they are governed by the sovereign. It is the State that has undertaken almost alone to give bread to those who are hungry, relief and a refuge to the sick, work to those without it; it has made itself the almost unique repairer of all miseries.

Education, as well as charity, has become a national affair among most of the peoples of today. The State receives and often takes the child from the arms of its mother in order to entrust it to its agents; it is the State that takes charge of inspiring sentiments in each generation and providing each generation with ideas. Uniformity reigns in studies as in all the rest; there diversity, like liberty, disappears each day.

Nor am I afraid to advance that, among nearly all the Christian nations of today, Catholic as well as Protestant, religion is threatened with falling into the hands of the government.[e] It is not that sovereigns show themselves very eager to fix dogma themselves;[f] but more and more they are taking hold of the will of the one who explains dogma; they take away from the cleric his property, assign him a salary, deflect and use for their sole profit the influence that the priest possesses; they make him one of their officials

---

When all living men are weak, the will of the dead is less respected. A very narrow circle is drawn around it, and if it happens to go outside of it, the sovereign annuls or controls it. In the Middle Ages, the power to make out your will had, so to speak, no limits. Among the French of today, you cannot distribute your patrimony among your children without the State intervening. After having dictated the entire life, it still wants to regulate the final act.

d. "See piece of Beaumont on property in England and above all on the immense place that the last will and testament occupies. 2nd volume of *L'Irlande*.

"Individual power of the man. Very important aristocratic character which manifests itself very strongly in what is related to the will" (with drafts of the chapter that follows, *Rubish,* 2).

e. The manuscript says: "all religions tend to become national."

f. "Ultra-unitary movement of the clergy. Symptoms of the time. Reread Lacordaire./

"Intellectual centralization. Idea of unity which pushed man as far as the last refuges of individual originality" (NOTES OF THE CHAPTER, *Rubish,* 2).

and often one of their servants, and with him they penetrate to the deepest recesses of the soul of each man.[2]

But that is still only one side of the picture.

Not only has the power of the sovereign expanded, as we have just seen, into the entire sphere of old powers; this is no longer enough to satisfy it; it overflows that sphere on all sides and spreads over the domain that until now has been reserved to individual independence. A multitude of actions which formerly escaped entirely from the control of society has been subjected to it today, and their number increases constantly.[g]

Among aristocratic peoples, the social power usually limited itself to directing and to overseeing citizens in everything that had a direct and visible connection to the national interest; it willingly abandoned them to their free will in everything else. Among these peoples, the government seemed often to forget that there is a point at which the failings and the miseries

---

2. *As the attributions of the central power augment, the number of officials who represent it increases. They form a nation within each nation and, since the government lends them its stability, they more and more replace the aristocracy among each nation.*

Nearly everywhere in Europe, the sovereign [power] dominates in two ways: it leads one part of the citizens by the fear that they feel for its agents, and the other by the hope that they conceive of becoming those agents.

g. Nothing can delight the imagination of an ambitious man more than the image of a unique power that, with a word, can put an entire people on alert and move it from one place to another. That seems admirable above all in times like ours when we are so impatient to enjoy, and when we want to gain great enjoyments only by means of small efforts.

[To the side: Perhaps move to accidental causes.]

You can predict that nearly all the ambitious and capable minds that a democratic country contains will apply themselves without let-up to expanding the attributions of the social power, because all hope to direct it one day. It is a waste of time to want to demonstrate to those men [that (ed.)] extreme centralization <agglomeration> of powers can harm the State, since they centralize for themselves.

In democratic countries, you find only very honest or very mediocre men who occupy themselves with setting some limits for the central power. The first are rare and the second can do nothing.

In democratic countries, the people are led not only by their tastes to concentrate power, but also by the passions of all the citizens.

[To the side] Perhaps move to accidental causes (*Rubish*, 2). See p. 1293.

of individuals compromise universal well-being, and that sometimes preventing the ruin of an individual must be a public matter.

Democratic nations of our time lean toward an opposite extreme.

It is clear that most of our princes do not want only to direct the whole people; you would say that they consider themselves responsible for the actions and for the individual destiny of their subjects,[h] that they have un-

---

h. When men all depend more or less on each other, it is enough for the government to lead the principal ones among them in order for the rest to follow.

But when they are all equal and independent, society must in a way be occupied separately with each citizen and guide him.

So it is natural and necessary that the attributions of the government be more numerous and more detailed in a democratic country than in an aristocratic country (IDEAS THAT I CAN HOPE TO USE, *Rubish,* 2).

You find also in a copy of the drafts these two pieces on the same subject:

Centralization./

I have just pointed out in which conditions alone despotism could impose itself on democratic peoples; it remains for me to show the means that it can use.

[To the side: Too didactic.]

I consider a democratic people abstractly from its antecedents, and I conceive that it will always be more difficult to establish a local liberty there than among an aristocratic nation. No one has a visible right to command. No one has leisure, general ideas, enlightenment.

So a long education is always required to make democratic localities able to govern themselves.

But if I consider a democratic people at a certain point of its existence, the difficulty is very much greater.

[To the side: When aristocracy has just been destroyed and when democracy is not yet *trained* and *elevated,* to whom to give the local power?]

Among peoples, some reach democracy by liberal institutions, as the English will do; others by absolute power, as we have done.

This changes the conditions of the problem.

In the first case, when aristocracy loses its power, all its successors are ready to take its place. And even in this case, centralizing tendency. Say a word about the English and show that they are not centralizing with an interest in good administration, but with a democratic interest.

In the second, the sole possible heir to aristocracy is royal power. The only question is knowing if it will always preserve the inheritance (YTC, CVd, pp. 41–42).

Centralization./

Centralization is that much more absurd as the government is more truly representative. When the minister is occupied for six months with attacking and defending

dertaken to lead and to enlighten each one of them in the different acts of his life, and as needed, to make him happy despite himself.[j]

On their side, individuals more and more envisage the social power in the same way; they call it to their aid in all their needs, and at every moment they set their sight on it as on a tutor or on a guide.

I assert that there is no country in Europe in which the public administration has not become not only more centralized, but also more inquisitorial and more detailed; everywhere it penetrates more than formerly into private affairs; it regulates in its own way more actions and smaller actions, and every day it establishes itself more and more beside, around and above each individual in order to assist him, advise him and constrain him.[k]

----

himself in the chambers, how can he have the time to direct all the provincial interests with which he is charged? The care [illegible word] the responsibility for it comes necessarily to a clerk. Now, what superior guarantee is offered by the wisdom of a clerk compared to that of local magistrates?

4 April 1837 (YTC, CVd, p. 31).

j. Tocqueville seems to refer to the well-known passage of chapter VII of the first book of *Contrat social.* Rousseau, *Œuvres complètes* (Paris: Pléiade, 1964), III, p. 364.

k. A centralized administration, but slow and fond of red tape and paperwork./

.-.-.- in the session of 2 .-.- March 1838 after praising the administration of m[ines (ed.)] .-.- at the top of his voice, he complained however that its members do not visit, as they ought to do, all the mines that are subject to their inspection and are crushed under all the red tape and paperwork. As if a centralized administration could ever completely meet its program, and as if it was not by its *essence* fond of red tape and paperwork. This last thing above all follows very closely.

From the moment when everything comes from a center, the director of the machine, who can see nothing by himself, but who must know everything, needs to have innumerable accounts sent to him, to *sheck* [*check* (ed.)] one employee by another. In a great centralized administration a hierarchy is needed, that is to say a .-.-.-.- of order and correspondence. Those are the needs. The passions are still much more fond of red tape and paperwork. The permanent inclination of the minister is to want to do everything and to know everything and to order everything, which necessitates still much more correspondence than need does.

And the offices that rule the minister have an interest in drawing everything toward him, which is to say toward them. They have the same passions as the minister does, and they never have, as he does, the political and general point of view that can curb these passions.

So a centralized administration is by its nature slow and fond of writing. It can have great advantages, but this disadvantage is certain./

Formerly, the sovereign lived from the revenue of his lands or from tax income. It is no longer the same today now that his needs have grown with his power. In the same circumstances in which formerly a prince established a new tax, today we resort to a loan. Little by little the State thus becomes the debtor of most of the rich, and it centralizes in its hands the largest capital.[m]

It attracts the smallest capital in another way.

As men mingle and conditions become equal, the poor man has more resources, enlightenment and desires. He conceives the idea of bettering his lot, and he seeks to succeed in doing so by savings. So savings give birth each day to an infinite number of small accumulations of capital, slow and successive fruits of work; they increase constantly. But the greatest number would remain unproductive if they stayed scattered. That has given birth to a new philanthropic institution which will soon become, if I am not mistaken, one of our greatest political institutions. Charitable men conceived the thought of gathering the savings of the poor and utilizing the

---

The obligation of dealing with all affairs without seeing each other *necessitates* infinite paperwork./

Édouard told me something correct: that fondness for red tape and paperwork was that much greater as the affair was smaller. A great affair is dealt with in Paris. People see each other, come to an understanding, become interested. But in order to understand why a *commune* wants to sell six feet of land, infinite paperwork is required, for people cannot see each other and no one takes an interest (UNITY, CENTRALIZATION, ADMINISTRATIVE DESPOTISM, *Rubish,* 2).

Tocqueville is referring to the discussion on the administration of mines which had taken place in the Chamber in March 1838 (see the *Journal des débats* of 21 March 1838). After the floods of the mines of Rive-de-Gier, the government had presented to the Chamber a proposed law in which it required, under penalty of expropriation, the execution of certain measures on the part of the owners of mines in case of danger. The deputies opposed to the proposed law defended the liberty of the owner by relying on article 7 of the law of 21 April 1810, which considered mines as a common property whose conveying and expropriation fell into the domain of the ordinary principles of civil law. See, further on, Tocqueville's note 5.

m. In 1837, Tocqueville had asked Beaumont to bring back to him from England all types of brochures and information on the Scottish savings banks, destined for the drafting of the second part of his *Mémoire sur le paupérisme*. The information gathered by Beaumont confirmed Tocqueville in his fear of a state centralization as regards savings (*Correspondance avec Beaumont, OC,* VIII, 1, pp. 185, 191, 193, and 196).

earnings. In some countries, these benevolent associations have remained entirely distinct from the State; but in almost all they tend visibly to merge with it, and there are even a few in which the government has replaced them and undertaken the immense task of centralizing the daily savings of several million workers in a single place and of turning those savings to good account by its hands alone.

Thus, the State draws to itself the money of the rich by borrowing, and by savings banks it disposes as it wills of the pennies of the poor. The wealth of the country rushes constantly toward it and into its hand; wealth accumulates there all the more as equality of conditions becomes greater [{the country is more democratic}]; for among a democratic nation, only the State inspires confidence with individuals, because only it alone seems to them to have some strength and some duration.[3]

Thus, the sovereign power does not limit itself to directing public fortune; it also gets into private fortunes;[n] it is the leader of each citizen and often his master, and moreover, it becomes his steward and his cashier.

Not only does the central power alone fill the entire sphere of old powers, expand and go beyond it, but it moves there with more agility, strength and independence than it ever did formerly.

All the governments of Europe have in our time prodigiously perfected administrative science;[o] they do more things, and they do each thing with

3. *On the one hand, the taste for well-being augments constantly, and the government takes hold more and more of all the sources of well-being.*

So men go by two diverse paths toward servitude. The taste for well-being turns them away from getting involved in the government, and the love of well-being makes them more and more narrowly dependent on those who govern.

n. "Opinion of Michel de Bourges (23 March 1838) to ponder: I seem here to want to strengthen beyond measure the principle of property which according to my political principles is always defended strongly enough. That leads to reflection because it seems that all the men of today, whatever their origin and point of departure, royalists and republicans, democrats or fiery enemies of democracy, unite in the principle of unity, and from there run in common toward servitude" (UNITY, CENTRALIZATION, ADMINISTRATIVE DESPOTISM, *Rubish,* 2). It probably concerns an extract from the debate on mines to which note 5 of p. 1234 refers.

o. This theory, so vaunted, so accepted today, and now self-sustaining [word fragment], of the exact division of judicial and administrative powers must be examined once and for all, head on and very closely. This theory is spoken about only with

more order, rapidity and with less expense; they seem to enrich themselves constantly with all the enlightenment which they have taken from individuals. Each day the princes of Europe hold their delegated agents in a more narrow dependence, and they invent new methods to direct them more closely and to oversee them with less difficulty. It is not enough for them to conduct all affairs by their agents; they undertake to direct the conduct of their agents in all their affairs; so that the public administration depends not only on the same power, it draws itself more and more into the same place and becomes concentrated in fewer hands. The government centralizes its actions at the same time that it increases its prerogatives: double cause of strength.

When you examine the constitution that the judicial power formerly had among most of the nations of Europe, two things are striking: the independence of this power and the extent of its attributions.

Not only did the courts of justice decide nearly all the quarrels among individuals; in a great number of cases, they served as arbiters between each individual and the State.

---

respect; it is the holy ark. Let us pierce this covering; let us dare to discuss what is believed as a religion; let us see the naked truth and face to face.

That it is true in a general way that judicial and administrative powers must be distinct is incontestable.

But is it important for the salvation of the State and for good administration that the judicial system and the executive power are never combined in the same acts? That is what I do not believe. You start from a good principle, but you push it to the absurd. The intervention of the judicial power in the acts of the administrative power seems to me often useful and sometimes so necessary that I do not imagine liberty possible without that.

Perhaps this question must be gone into more deeply by me here, but beyond that, it merits a particular, detailed, practical examination on my part for France. This must be for me one of the first works after this book. For I believe that the principal hazard for the future is there. It is incontestable that the administrative power is *inevitably* called to play a more important and more multifarious role in the centuries which begin than previously.

[In the margin: the *Conseil d'État* is something, but not enough, and it would be nothing without liberty of the press.]

The entire question is to know if you can combine the guarantees of liberty with the necessary action of administrative power.

You cannot stop the development of this power, but you can give it some counterbalances/ (UNITY, CENTRALIZATION, ADMINISTRATIVE DESPOTISM, *Rubish,* 2).

I do not want to speak here about the administrative and political attributions that the courts had usurped in some countries, but about the
judicial attributions that they possessed in all. Among all the peoples of
Europe, there were and there still are many individual rights, most related
to the general right of property, which were placed under the safeguard of
the judge and which the State could not violate without the permission of
the former.

It is this semi-political power which principally distinguished the courts
of Europe from all the others; for all peoples have had judges, but all have
not given judges the same privileges.

If we now examine what is happening among the democratic nations of
Europe which are called free, as well as among the others, we see that on
all sides, alongside these courts, other more dependent ones are being created, whose particular purpose is to decide in exceptional instances the li-
tigious questions that can arise between the public administration and the
citizens. The old judicial power is left with its independence, but its jurisdiction is narrowed, and more and more the tendency is to make it only
an arbiter between particular interests.P

p. Two tendencies to distinguish:
  1. One that tends to concentrate all powers in the State.
  2. The other that tends to concentrate the exercise of all powers in the executive./

Tendency to free the administrative power from all judicial control./
Among all peoples the judicial power appears as the support for individual independence, and everywhere that its attributions decrease, the existence of the individual [v: of particulars] becomes precarious.
  It is from there, I believe, that the question must be engaged. There is today a clear
tendency to rid the sovereign power of the judge (*Rubish,* 2).

In another jacket:

French centralizers use the word *State* in a peculiar way. Often this difference alone
separates us.
  The State, they say, in the century in which we are and in those into which we are
entering, must get involved in many things. Agreed. But by *State* they almost always
mean the *executive* power alone, acting without the cooperation or the guarantee of
the legislative and judicial powers. It is here that we no longer agree.
  The State must indeed have great prerogatives among democratic peoples, but the
executive power must not exercise them alone and without control, in order for liberty
to be saved and for the individual not to disappear entirely before the social power.

The number of these special courts increases constantly, and their at-tributions grow. So the government escapes more every day from the ob-ligation to have its will and its rights sanctioned by another power. Not able to do without judges, it wants, at least, to choose its judges itself and to hold them always in its hand; that is to say, between it and individuals, it places still more the image of justice rather than justice itself.q

Thus, it is not enough for the State to draw all affairs to itself; it also ends more and more by deciding all of these by itself without control and without recourse.[4]

There is among the modern nations of Europe one great cause that, apart from all those that I have just pointed out, contributes constantly to expand the action of the sovereign power or to augment its prerogatives; we have not taken enough notice of it. This cause is the development of industry, which the progress of equality favors.r

---

[To the side: You see without fear the government increase its *civil* privileges, as if it were not on the latter that political influence sooner or later rests. I would believe the future of liberty more assured with a government that would have many political rights and few civil rights than with a government that would have few political rights and many civil rights.

Civil rights means nothing. The word escapes me, but the thought is there] (UNITY, CENTRALIZATION, ADMINISTRATIVE DESPOTISM, *Rubish*, 2). See note d of p. 1223.

q. The manuscript says: ". . . but not justice itself."

4. *On this subject in France there is a strange sophism. When a trial between the admin-istration and an individual arises, we refuse to submit its examination to an ordinary judge, in order it is said, not to mix administrative power and judicial power. As if it were not mixing these two powers and mixing them in the most dangerous and most tyrannical fashion to clothe the government with the right to judge and to administer at the same time.*

r. 1. General reasons that cause the progress of industry to make the central power progress:

1. Nature of the property and of the industrial class that most naturally occupies the government.

2. Creation of new goods and persons.

2. Particular and European reasons:

1. Ancient prejudice against the property and the class.

Facts that support these arguments (*Rubish,* 2).

[<The goods created by industry are rightly regarded by all enlightened nations as particularly appropriate to be taxed. Thus, as industry develops, you see new taxes arise, and these taxes are in general more complicated, more difficult and more exacting to collect than all the others.[s]

It must be remarked on the other hand that . . .>][t]

Industry usually gathers a multitude of men in the same place; it establishes new and complicated relationships among them. It exposes them to great and sudden shifts between abundance and poverty, during which public tranquillity is threatened. It can happen finally that these works compromise the health and even the lives of those who profit from them or of those who devote themselves to them. Thus, the industrial class has more need to be regulated, supervised and restrained than all the other classes, and it is natural that the attributions of the government grow with it.

This truth is generally applicable; but here is what relates more particularly to the nations of Europe.

In the centuries that have preceded those in which we live, the aristocracy possessed the land and was able to defend it. So landed property was surrounded by guarantees, and its owners enjoyed a great independence. That created laws and habits that have been perpetuated despite the division of lands and the ruin of the nobles; and today the landowners and farmers are still, of all citizens, those who escape most easily from the control of the social power.

In these same aristocratic centuries, where all the sources of our history are found, personal property had little importance and its owners were despised and weak; the industrialists formed an exceptional class in the middle of the aristocratic world. Since they did not have assured patronage, they were not protected, and often they were not able to protect themselves.[u]

s. "Perhaps be infinitely more rapid in this piece. Tell the facts without explaining them. They are present to the readers because they are French facts" (*Rubish*, 2).

t. In the margin: "<All this applies only to indirect taxes, and indirect taxes do not strike only industrial products. The thought is therefore obscure and partly false.>"

u. "As industry develops you see growing with it a class of men who live only on the

So it became a habit to consider industrial property as a property of a particular nature, which did not merit the same guarantees as property in general, and to consider the industrialists as a small, separate class in the social order, whose independence had little value, and as a class that it was fitting to abandon to the regulatory passion of princes. If, in fact, you open the codes of the Middle Ages, you are astonished to see how, in these centuries of individual independence, industry was constantly regulated by kings, up to the smallest details; on this point, centralization is as active and as detailed as it could be.

Since this time, a great revolution has taken place in the world; industrial property, which was only in germ, has developed; it covers Europe; the industrial[v] class has expanded; it has enriched itself from the remnants of all the others; it has grown in number, in importance, in wealth; it grows constantly; nearly all those who are not part of it are connected to it, at least at some point; after having been the exceptional class, it threatens to become the principal class and, so to speak, the sole class;[w] but the political ideas and habits to which it formerly gave birth have remained. These ideas and these habits have not changed, because they are old, and then because they are in perfect harmony with the new ideas and general habits of the men of our times.[x]

---

salary of every day and who can only find in the accumulation of salary the means to conquer their independence and to change their lot little by little. This class has always existed in the world, but its development is new. It is already numerous; it threatens to become innumerable" (*Rubish*, 2).

v. "I believe that *industrialist* must be understood as every man who gains money by the aid of a mechanical art, such as iron worker, carpenter, and finally manufacturer.

"I do not believe that merchants, who only buy and sell, can be put in the number of industrialists.

"[To the side: What do I mean by industrial property?

"You see clearly what an industrialist is, but what is an industrial property?]

"Farmers are certainly not there and, with more reason, tenant farmers" (*Rubish*, 2).

w. In the margin: "<The democratic class par excellence.>"

x. "<To govern the men of our times, new vices and new virtues are needed>" (*Rubish*, 2).

So industrial property does not augment its rights with its importance. The industrial class does not become less dependent by becoming more numerous; but you would say, on the contrary, that it carries despotism within it, and that despotism expands naturally as it develops.[5]

And in another place: "Ideas to keep, to treat, but I do not know where and how to make them enter into my classifications./

"What astonishes me in man is not so much the weakness that he exhibits against a multitude of natural enemies, as the manner in which he obeys a kind of invisible power that hides in himself."

[In the margin:

To put *perhaps* in the place where I will be able to depict the incessant though somewhat thwarted march of the modern world.]

There are centuries when men are always led toward the same points, from whatever direction they are pushed and wherever they seem to want to go. You see them one moment rush forward along an opposite path, and when they have broken all the barriers that were set against them and that they can breach, they stop by themselves and retrace their steps.

Sometimes a government wants to compel them to adopt certain opinions and certain customs. They shudder and resist. And when they have triumphed over their masters, they do alone what someone wanted to prescribe for them; and they succumb to a hidden force within their own breast that acts without their knowing.

There are times when great virtues or great talents are necessary in order to act upon a people and to dominate it; there are others when great vices suffice almost alone.

In order to act upon an honest people and dominate it, great virtues or great talents are necessary. In order to produce the same effect on a corrupt nation, great vices can suffice (YTC, CVa, pp. 33–34).

5. *I will cite a few facts in support of this. It is in the mines that the natural sources of industrial wealth are found. As industry developed in Europe, as the product of the mines became a more general interest and their good exploitation more difficult because of the division of property that equality brought, most sovereigns claimed the right to own the resources of the mines and to oversee the work; this had not been seen for properties of another type.*

The mines, which were individual properties subject to the same obligations and provided with the same guarantees as other landed property, thus fell into the public domain. It is the State that exploits them or that grants concessions; owners are transformed into users; they hold their rights from the State and, moreover, the State almost everywhere claims the power to direct them; it draws up rules for them, imposes methods on them, subjects them to a habitual surveillance, and if they resist, an administrative court dispossesses them; and the public ad-

ministration transfers their privileges to others; so that the government possesses not only the mines, it holds all the miners in its hand.

As industry develops, however, the exploitation of old mines increases. New ones are opened. The population of the mines spreads and grows larger. Every day, the sovereigns expand their domain under our feet and populate it with their servants.[y]

y. Unity, centralization, administrative despotism./

Discussion relative to the mines of Gier (2 .-.- March 1838) have just suggested to me.—[the (ed.)].—following ideas:

The new world will see *industrial property* augment incessantly. That is indeed the new property par excellence, the democratic property.

Now, I see clearly the means by which the government takes hold of the direction and of the *management* of this property and in this way augments its influence in proportion as this property develops. It does not lack pretexts and even reasons for that.

[In the margin: Begin by showing how the government itself will become a great industrialist, will do immense enterprises in industry, at the same time that it becomes the master and the director of all the other industrialists. It attracts all the industrial capital by great enterprises and by centralized savings banks.]

The first reason is that this type of property, just coming into existence so to speak, is [not (ed.)] defended like all the others by an old respect for custom and allows itself to be regulated much more.

But there are reasons of detail of which I am going to detail a few. Coal, iron and minerals in general are the great sources of commercial wealth. These riches were formerly patrimonial. The top carried ownership of the bottom. The government, putting forward this plausible enough reason that such riches are more national than individual, dispossesses the one who holds them, unless he exploits them, and grants them to others (decree of 1810). Great abuses have taken place since in the practice of concession. The government claims to oblige the new owners, who are nothing more in its eyes than concessionaires, to exploit as it wants, to do the work that it indicates, or it takes back the concession and gives it to another.[1] All this immense population that owns or exploits the mines, a population constantly growing in number and above all in importance, becomes by a single deed composed of administrative *agents* and nothing more. The government not owning the mines, but the miners.

1. [All that will be appropriate, and even just, if the judicial power were introduced there. Its absence causes the whole evil. The principle of the absolute and continuous division of the administrative and judicial power is irreconcilable with the *liberty* and the *prosperity* of the State. If the administration does not get involved in this commercial property, public prosperity is in danger; and liberty, if it alone is involved in it. The problem to resolve is to unite them.]

Other example. The owners of land along the river do not agree on what to do to guarantee the banks of the river. The government forces them to associate in order to do the necessary work in common. Nothing better. But it directs the association and forces it to save the land. So it has all the riverside residents in its hands. But that gets away from commercial property which I want .-.-.-

[In the margin: Bonaparte said in 1810 concerning .-.-.- by dint of multiplying the obstacles, you make France take big steps toward tyranny. That you saw a prefect prevent the building of a house because the owner refused to .-.-.- his plan. It was only a matter of the rules of the .-.-.- He added: the concessionaire must only be despoiled of his property when he himself agrees to cede it. There is no difference from this perspective between a mine and a farm. Napoleon does not deny that the concessionaire be subjected to conditions, he only wants the non-compliance with these conditions not to carry the loss of the concession. Courts will sentence, he says, the concessionaire to executing them, as is practiced in regard to other contracts.]

.-.-.-.-.-.- there are immense commercial enterprises that in civilized countries cannot be carried out without the authorization of the social power, administration or legislature. Such particularly are the great works that necessitate the destruction of particular properties and that must respond to a public need, such as toll road, canal, bridge, port. . . . This gives an opening to the same argument as for the mines. The State, having granted concessions, claims to have the right to direct and, if someone does [not (ed.)] obey its directives, to dispossess. And among the social powers, it is the administration alone that claims the right in order not to mix legislative and administrative powers, and it wants to do it alone in order not to mix the administrative and judicial powers.

In England it is Parliament that authorizes. See in the work of Simon the charter of the railroad of Birmingham.

So that apart from the canals, roads, bridges that it owns, builds or directs by its agents, it is master of those who own, make or direct all the others.

Third example.

Among democratic peoples all commercial enterprises of some value can be carried out only by associations, but association is a means of which you .- .- to abuse. A collective owner is a new being that merits less consideration than individual owners who have been known since the beginning of the world and that at the same time is more frightening because it is more powerful. Under the pretext of gathering capital for a useful enterprise, the credulity of the public is misled, and capital is amassed in order to turn it to the profit of the inventor of the project. Society must be protected against such a trap. The remedy is to charge the administration with examining in advance the bases of the association and to grant or to refuse the right to associate, which puts in the hands of the government the most active passions and the most energetic needs of future generations. For, I repeat, commercial property is called to become the first and the most important of all.

I go further and I would be very .-.-.-.- not a step further, and if after having obtained the right to authorize .-.-.- association, you soon asked me for the right to direct them, if not in all cases, at least in a great number, with the threat of withdrawing the authorization for associating in case of refusal. So that after having put

In proportion as the nation becomes more industrial, it feels a greater need for roads, canals, ports and other works of a semi-public nature, which facilitate the acquisition of wealth; and in proportion as the nation is more democratic, individuals experience more difficulty in executing such works, and the State more ease in doing them. I am not afraid to assert that the manifest tendency of all the sovereigns of our time is to undertake alone the execution of such enterprises; in that way, they enclose populations each day within a more narrow dependence.

On the other hand, as the power of the State increases and as its needs augment, the State itself consumes an always greater quantity of industrial products, which it fabricates ordinarily in its arsenals and its factories. In this way, in each kingdom, the sovereign power becomes the greatest industrialist;[z] it draws to and retains in its service a prodigious number of engineers, architects, mechanics and artisans.[a]

---

in its hands all those who have the desire to associate, you would also put there all those who have associated, that is to say, nearly the entire society in democratic centuries.

You would leave free only non-commercial property, which every day loses its importance, and individual commercial property, which cannot have any importance among democratic nations.

Again, if you reached the owners of this latter by a thousand regulations .-.-.- of public utility that the administration promulgates, interprets and applies alone without recourse [variant: in the name of order, of the healthiness of morals, of tranquillity, of public prosperity or in the interest of even those you coerce]" (UNITY, CENTRALIZATION, ADMINISTRATIVE DESPOTISM, *Rubish,* 2).

During his journey to England in 1835, Tocqueville already remarked: "The necessity of introducing the judicial power into the administration is one of these *central* ideas to which I am led by all my research about what has allowed and can allow men to have political liberty" (*Voyage en Angleterre, OC,* V, 2, p. 68).

The idea is found again in *L'Ancien régime et la Révolution.* In chapter 4 of the second book (*OC,* II, 1, p. 125), after having spoken about the number of special courts and of the judicial rights of the *intendant,* he concluded: "The intervention of the judicial system in the administration harms only affairs, while the intervention of the administration in the judicial system depraves men and tends to make them at the very same time revolutionary and servile."

z. "Double movement:

"The government draws closer to industry and takes hold of the smallest industrialists.

"Private industry becomes bigger and enters into the sphere of power./

"And the government descends into the sphere of private industry" (*Rubish,* 2).

a. "*Equality* is the great fact of our time.

It is not only the first of industrialists; it tends more and more to make itself the leader or rather the master of all the others.[b]

Since citizens have become weak while becoming more equal,[c] they can do nothing in industry without associating; now, the public power naturally wants to place these associations under its control.

It must be recognized that these kinds of collective beings, which are called associations, are stronger and more formidable than a simple individual can be, and that they have less responsibility than the latter for their own actions; the result is that it seems reasonable to allow to each one of them less independence from the social power than would be allowed for an individual.

Sovereigns have that much more inclination to act in this way since it suits their tastes. Among democratic peoples it is only by association that

---

"Industrial *development* the second.

"Both augment the power of the government, or rather both are only one" (*Rubish*, 2).

b. Yesterday (26 February 1836) I met M. Polonceau. I had a very interesting conversation with him.

He spent twenty years in the administration of bridges and roads, was chief engineer there, and has more or less retired since that time. He is an active, innovative, perhaps imprudent spirit, which the *esprit de corps* could not tame. He perhaps speaks with animosity about the administration of which he was part, but he says very interesting and, I believe, generally very true things, about the taste of this administration for established things, principally established by it, about its efforts to impede everything that does not come from it, about its determination not to adopt fixed rules that would limit it, about its interminable delays, its expensive habits, its preferences, its little taste for publicity.

He told me that to know its organization and to appreciate its spirit I must study:

1. The decree of organization given in 1811.
2. The collection of annual reports on bridges and roads (YTC, CVa, pp. 57–58).

c. In the manuscript:

. . . more equal, they are obliged to unite together constantly even for industrial works of an entirely private nature. Industry cannot fail to develop in a democratic country without giving birth to an infinite number of associations. ≠These associations are so many new persons whose rights have not yet been well established and who enter into the world at a period when the idea of the rights of individuals is weak and that of the sovereign very extensive. You have a great facility≠ and these associations fall naturally under the control of the public power.

the resistance of citizens to the central power can come about; consequently the latter never sees associations that are not under its control except with disfavor; and what is very worth noting is that, among democratic peoples, citizens often envisage these same associations, which they need so much, with a secret sentiment of fear and jealousy which prevents them from defending them. The power and the duration of these small particular societies, amid the general weakness and instability, astonishes them and worries them, and citizens are not far from considering as dangerous privileges the free use that each association makes of its natural powers.

All these associations that are arising today are, moreover, so many new persons, for whom time has not consecrated rights and who enter into the world at a period when the idea of particular rights is weak, and when the social power is without limits; it is not surprising that associations lose their liberty at birth.

Among all the peoples of Europe, there are certain associations that can be formed only after the State has examined their statutes and authorized their existence. Among several, efforts are being made to extend this rule to all associations. You see easily where the success of such an undertaking would lead.

If the sovereign power had once the general right to authorize, on certain conditions, associations of all types, it would not take long to claim that of overseeing them and of directing them, so that the associations would not able to evade the rule that it had imposed on them. In this way, the State, after making all those who desire to associate dependent on it, would make all those who have associated dependent as well, that is to say, nearly all the men who are alive today.

The sovereign powers thus appropriate more and more, and put to their use the greatest part of this new force that industry creates today in the world. Industry leads us, and they lead industry.[d]

d. What happened at the end of the 1837 session for railroads, and the way in which nearly everyone fell into agreement that the government must take charge of everything, is characteristic and shows clearly the slope that carries us, friends and enemies of liberty, toward the centralization of all powers in the hands of the government and the introduction of its hand into all affairs.

Those men are very foolish to believe that while giving a government immense *civil* attributions, they will easily put fetters on it in the field of politics, and to think that a man {charged} with handling by himself alone all the financial resources of a great people, with putting millions of workers into motion, with executing works of all types upon which national prosperity and life are based, will not be master of all the rest when he wants to be.

This 30 June 1837.

The language of the newspaper the *Siècle* has for a month been characteristic because this newspaper is conspicuously in the hands of Odilon Barrot and of the liberal and democratic opposition of the left.

If it is a matter of public works in general, it wants the government to take charge of them alone, to dragoon masses of workers, to bring them sometimes from one side, sometimes from another.

As for the railroads in particular, the government must above all take charge of them, for such an undertaking would give too much power to individuals and would grant them immense privileges. Moreover, it would be necessary to grant different concessions, so that the great French unity and uniformity would not be altered.

There is nothing, including the mines, that, according to the *Siècle* (27 June 1837), the government must not exploit. *Why,* it says, *would the State not claim the exploitation of the underground domain, instead of conceding it freely to the privileged?*

Do you see how democratic passions adapt here marvelously well to the increases of central power and how democratic instincts and prejudices go complacently before tyranny provided that unity and equality are sheltered?/

I cannot prevent myself from admiring the simplicity of those who believe that you can without disadvantage increase the civil rights of the government provided that you do not increase its political power, as if . . . [interrupted text (ed.)] (Fragment on writing paper, UNITY, CENTRALIZATION, ADMINISTRATIVE DESPOTISM, *Rubish,* 2).

In the same jacket you also find these explanations:

Ideas relative to centralization, to blend into the final chapter./

M. Thiers said to me today (27 May 1837) regarding the commission for the railroad from Lyon to Marseille that he had ended by convincing *all* the members of the commission that great public works must always be done in France at State *expense* and by its agents.

Do not forget that when I speak about the ultra-centralizing tendency of our times" (YTC, CVd, p. 30).

M. Thiers, in the session of .-.-.- January 1838, said (see *Siècle* of that day).

Without doubt Spain did not enter into the c.-.- of 92 and 93. Spain did not build scaffolds as in France; the terror was what it could be in the peninsula, in a country without centralization, without unity. So no scaffold, but the cutting of throats.

The comment is good, to keep (UNITY, CENTRALIZATION, ADMINISTRATIVE DESPOTISM, *Rubish,* 2).

[As for those who still work alone in the industrial world, their number and above all their importance is constantly decreasing; and for a long time, moreover, the government has exercised the right to regulate them as it pleases and has imposed on them each day new laws of which the government itself alone is the administrator and the interpreter.

<≠Perhaps you will find that I have expanded too much on this last part. Its importance will be my excuse.

The progress of equality and the development of industry are the two greatest facts of our times.

I wanted to show how both contributed to enlarge the sphere of the central power and to restrict individual independence each day within the narrowest limits.≠>]e

I attach so much importance to all that I have just said that I am tormented with the fear of having detracted from my thought by wanting to make it clearer.

So if the reader finds that the examples cited to support my words are insufficient or badly chosen; if he thinks that in some place I have exaggerated the progress of the social power, and that on the contrary I have limited beyond measure the sphere in which individual independence still moves, I beg him to abandon the book for a moment and to consider in his turn by himself the matters that I have undertaken to show him. Let him examine attentively what is happening each day among us and beyond us; let him question his neighbors; let him finally consider himself; I am very much mistaken if he does not arrive, without a guide and by other paths, at the point where I wanted to lead him.

[He will discover that the various rights that today have been successively wrested from classes, corporations, men, instead of serving to raise new secondary powers on another more democratic foundation, have almost all collected in the sole hands of the sovereign, that everywhere the public administration has become more clever, more intelligent and stronger, that the individual has become more isolated, more inexperienced, and weaker relative to the public administration, and that finally the State, whatever

---

e. In the margin: "<≠These two facts are closely related to each other, for it is enough to enlighten equal men for them to tend all by themselves toward industry.≠>"

its representative, has placed itself more every day next to and above each citizen in order to instruct him, guide him, aid him and constrain him.]^f

He will notice that, during the half-century that has just gone by, centralization has grown everywhere in a thousand different fashions. Wars, revolutions, conquests have served its development; all men have worked to increase it.^{g} During this same period, when men have with a prodigious rapidity succeeded each other at the head of affairs, their ideas, their interests, their passions have varied infinitely; but all have wanted to centralize in some ways. The instinct for centralization has been like the sole immobile point amid the singular mobility of their existence and their thoughts.^{h}

And when the reader, after examining this detail of human affairs, will want to embrace the vast picture as a whole, he will remain astonished.

On the one hand, the firmest dynasties are shaken or destroyed; on all sides peoples escape violently from the dominion of their laws; they destroy

f. To the side: "<This said above. Is it better there?>"

g. It concentrates in its hand great public functions that were wrongly separated from it, such as the preparation of all types of general laws,

> customs,
> the collection of taxes,
> the central direction of the judicial system,
> the army, the police,
> the direction of great local affairs that by their greatness have a general interest,
> the supervision of all [interrupted text (ed.)] (*Rubish*, 2).

h. ≠To uphold the individual in the face of the social power whatever it is, to preserve for him something of his independence, of his strength, of his originality, such must be the continual effort of all the friends of humanity in democratic centuries. Just as in democratic [aristocratic (ed.)] centuries, it was necessary to magnify society and to reduce the individual.

Were I alone in saying that, I would not remain silent.≠

[To the side: This must go in the peroration of section V.

Question of dynasty, secondary question.]

Centralization must grow constantly because it results from instincts that do not change. Men succeed each other in power; their passions, their interests, their ideas vary; but all, either voluntarily or involuntarily, centralize, because by centralizing, they obey, without knowing it, an instinct that is immobile. Amid the singular mobility of their thoughts and of their existence, it is the only permanent and durable thing that is in power today.

[In the margin] 27 February 1838 (YTC, CVk, 2, pp. 41–42).

or limit the authority of their lords or of their princes; all the nations that are not in revolution seem at least restless and unsettled; the same spirit of revolt animates them. And, on the other, in this same time of anarchy and among these same peoples so unruly, the social power constantly increases its prerogatives; it becomes more centralized, more enterprising, more absolute, more extensive. The citizens fall under the control of the public administration at every instant; they are carried imperceptibly and as if without their knowledge to sacrifice to the public administration some new parts of their individual independence, and these same men who from time to time overturn a throne and trample kings underfoot, bow more and more, without resistance, to the slightest will of a clerk.

So therefore, two revolutions seem to be taking place today in opposite directions: one continually weakens power, and the other constantly reinforces it. In no other period of our history has it appeared either so weak or so strong.

But when you finally come to consider the state of the world more closely, you see that these two revolutions are intimately linked to each other, that they come from the same source, and that, after having had a different course, they finally lead men to the same place.

I will not be afraid again to repeat one last time what I have already said or pointed out in several places of this book. We must be very careful about confusing the very fact of equality with the revolution that finally introduces it into the social state and into the laws; that is the reason for nearly all the phenomena that astonish us.

All the ancient political powers of Europe, the greatest as well as the least, were established in the centuries of aristocracy, and they more or less represented or defended the principle of inequality and of privilege. To make the new needs and interests suggested by growing equality prevail in the government, it was therefore necessary for the men of our times to overturn or restrain the ancient powers. That has led them to make revolutions and has inspired in a great number of them this wild taste for disorder and for independence to which all revolutions, whatever their objective, always give birth.

I do not believe that there is a single country in Europe where the development of equality has not been preceded or followed by some violent changes in the state of property and of persons, and almost all these changes have been accompanied by a great deal of anarchy and license, because they were done by the least civilized portion of the nation against the portion that was most civilized.

From that have come the two opposite tendencies that I previously showed. As long as the democratic revolution was in its heat, the men occupied with destroying the ancient aristocratic powers that fought against it appeared animated by a great spirit of independence; and as the victory of equality became more complete, they abandoned themselves little by little to the natural instincts that arose from this same equality, and they reinforced and centralized the social power. They had wanted to be free in order to be able to make themselves equal; and as equality became more established with the help of liberty, it made liberty more difficult for them.

These two states have not always been successive. Our fathers have shown how a people could organize an immense tyranny within itself at the very moment when it escaped from the authority of the nobles and braved the power of all the kings, teaching the world at the same time the way to conquer its independence and to lose it.

The men of today notice that the old powers are collapsing on all sides; they see all the old influences dying, all the old barriers falling; that disturbs the judgment of the most able; they pay attention only to the prodigious revolution which is taking place before their eyes, and they believe that humanity is going to fall forever into anarchy. If they considered the final consequences of this revolution, they would perhaps imagine other fears.

As for me, I do not trust, I confess, the spirit of liberty which seems to animate my contemporaries; I see well that the nations of today are turbulent; but I do not find clearly that they are liberal, and I am afraid that at the end of these agitations, which make all thrones totter, sovereigns will find themselves stronger than they were [I am afraid finally that in this century of license, everything is being prepared for the enslavement of the generations to come].

CHAPTER 6

What Type of Despotism
Democratic Nations Have to Fear[a]

I had noticed during my stay in the United States that a democratic social state similar to that of the Americans could offer singular opportunities for the establishment of despotism,[b] and I had seen on my return to Europe how most of our princes had already made use of the ideas, sentiments and

a. What the character of military despotism would be if it came to be established among a democratic people.

Idea to treat either at *military spirit* or at *administrative despotism.* Probably at the first. To blend into a chapter rather than to treat separately.

I see two places for this.

1. The first is after what I said about the turbulent spirit of the army, about its habitual discontent, about the place that it occupies in society. I could show these sentiments leading the army to seize the government. I would then say in what spirit it would govern.

2. Here is the second place: after painting administrative despotism, I could ask myself if it would not be changed for the worse by its combination with military government (something possible). I would prove that things would hardly be worse. I would then pass to the combination of this same despotism with sovereignty of the people and I would prove that things would hardly be better.

3. Finally couldn't I place this idea separately (illegible word)? (YTC, CVj, 2, pp. 9–10).

b. *"Despotism,* tyrannical, arbitrary and absolute government of only one man (or of only one power must be added).

"The principle of despotic States is that only one man governs there entirely according to his will, having absolutely no other laws than that of his caprices. *Encyclopédie.* This was written before we had seen the despotism of an assembly under the Republic."

In another place in the *rubish:* "This word *despotism* is unfortunate because its old meaning does not exactly correspond to the new meaning that I want to give it" (*Rubish,* 2).

needs that arose from that social state, in order to expand the circle of their power.

That led me to believe that Christian nations would end perhaps by suffering some oppression similar to that which weighed formerly on several of the peoples of antiquity.[c]

A more detailed examination of the subject and five years of new meditations have not lessened my fears, but they have changed their object.

We have never in past centuries seen a sovereign so absolute and so powerful that he undertook to administer by himself, and without the help of secondary powers, all the parts of a great empire; there is none who attempted to subject all his subjects indiscriminately to the details of a uniform rule, or who descended to the side of each one of his subjects in order to rule over him and to lead him. The idea of such an undertaking had never occurred to the human mind, and if a man ever happened to imagine it, the insufficiency of enlightenment, the imperfection of administrative procedures, and above all the natural obstacles that inequality of conditions created would have soon stopped him in the execution of such a vast design.

We see that in the time of the greatest power of the Caesars, the different peoples who inhabited the Roman world had still kept diverse customs and mores. Although subjected to the same monarch, most of the provinces were administered separately; they were full of powerful and active municipalities, and although all the government of the empire was concentrated in the hands of the emperor alone, and although he remained always, as needed, the arbiter of all things, the details of social life and of individual existence ordinarily escaped his control.

The emperors possessed, it is true, an immense power without counterbalance, which allowed them to give themselves freely to their bizarre inclinations and to use the entire strength of the State to satisfy them; they

---

c. To the side: "<Perhaps place this here:

"Those, I said, who think to rediscover the monarchy of H[enri (ed.)]. IV or L[ouis (ed.)]. XIV seem very blind to me. As for me, when I consider the state which several European nations have already reached and toward which all the others are tending, I feel myself led to believe that among them there will soon no longer be a place except for democratic liberty or for the tyranny of the Caesars.>" Tocqueville cites here p. 511 of the first volume.

often happened to abuse this power in order arbitrarily to take away a citizen's property or his life. Their tyranny weighed prodigiously on a few; but it did not extend to a great number; it was tied to a few great principal matters and neglected the rest; it was violent and limited.[d]

d. 7 March 1838.

I said in the first part of this book that the new societies could well finally arrive at something similar to what we saw at the fall of the Roman empire. There is no longer any middle ground, I said, between the government of all and the tyranny of the Caesars.

Four years of new meditations made me consider the same matter from another point of view and convinced me that if men are enslaved, they will be so in an entirely new fashion and will exhibit a spectacle for which the past has not prepared us.

There was something of the great, of the colossal in the Roman tyranny, of the aristocratic, the magnificent, of the master of slaves, of the barbaric, of the pagan. All things that cannot habitually be found in a civilized and democratic society.

New society, regular, peaceful, ruled with art and uniformity, mixture of college, seminary, regiment, asleep rather than chained in the arms of clerks and soldiers, bureaucratic tyranny, fond of red tape, very repressive of all impulse, destroying the will for great things in germ, but mild and regular, equal for all. A sort of paternity without the purpose of bringing the children to manhood.

That is the real and original picture. That of the first volume was declamatory, common, hackneyed and false (*Rubish*, 2).

To reflect.

If, instead of the disordered despotism of the army rabble, idea already known, it would not be better to introduce here the portrait of a regulated despotism in which everything happens with as much order, meticulousness, and tyranny as in a barracks.

If instead of that I adopt the ancient idea of military despotism, there is at least a new notion to show.

It is military despotism following *revolution and democratic anarchy*, becoming established in a time when everything has been overturned and when nothing has yet settled down in positions, habits, ideas, tastes, when everything is in question, when the limits of the just and the unjust are abolished, when even the limits of practice and custom no longer exist, when we are accustomed to everything, when we expect anything in advance, when nothing is absolutely unforeseen and everything possible.

[To the side] Perhaps the image of the barracks could be placed after that as the port, the definitive state (YTC, CVd, pp. 15–16).

On the different types of despotism in the work of Tocqueville, see James T. Schleifer, *The Making of Tocqueville's "Democracy in America,"* pp. 147–56, 179–85. Roger Boesche, "The Prison, Tocqueville's Model for Despotism," *Western Political Quarterly* 33, no. 4 (1980): 550–63, established some points of similarity between the despotism of Tocqueville and his idea of the prison.

It seems that, if despotism came to be established among the democratic nations of today, it would have other characteristics; it would be more extensive and milder, and it would degrade men without tormenting them.

I do not doubt that, in centuries of enlightenment and equality such as ours, sovereigns might have succeeded more easily in uniting all public powers in their hands alone, and in penetrating more habitually and more deeply into the circle of private interests, than any of those of antiquity were ever able to do. But this same equality, which facilitates despotism, tempers it; we have seen how, as men are more similar and more equal, public mores become more humane and milder; when no citizen has a great power or great wealth, tyranny lacks, in a way, opportunity and theater. Since all fortunes are mediocre, passions are naturally contained, imagination limited, pleasures simple. This universal moderation moderates the sovereign himself and stops within certain limits the disordered impulse of his desires.

Apart from these reasons drawn from the very nature of the social state, I could add many others that would take me beyond my subject; but I want to keep myself within the limits that I have set for myself.

Democratic governments will be able to become violent and even cruel in certain moments of great agitation and great dangers; but these crises will be rare and passing.

When I think about the petty passions of the men of our times, about the softness of their mores, about the extent of their enlightenment, about the purity of their religion, about the mildness of their morality, about their painstaking and steady habits, about the restraint that they nearly all maintain in vice as in virtue, I am not afraid that they will find in their leaders tyrants, but rather tutors.

So I think that the type of oppression by which democratic peoples are threatened will resemble nothing of what preceded it in the world; our contemporaries cannot find the image of it in their memories. I seek in vain myself for an expression that exactly reproduces the idea that I am forming of it and includes it; [<the thing that I want to speak about is new, and men have not yet created the expression which must portray it.>] the old words of despotism and of tyranny do not work. The thing is new, so I must try to define it, since I cannot name it.[e]

I want to imagine under what new features despotism could present itself to the world; I see an innumerable crowd of similar and equal men who spin around restlessly, in order to gain small and vulgar pleasures with which they fill their souls.[f] Each one of them, withdrawn apart, is like a stranger to the destiny of all the others; his children and his particular friends form

e. The despotism that I fear for the generations to come has no precedent in the world and lacks a name. I will call it administrative despotism[1] for lack of anything better. <I would call it paternal if it aimed at making men free and if it set a limit for itself like paternity.>

[To the side: To be completely true, it is necessary to make it understood that equality can, it is true, lead as far as a violent and cruel oppression because of the weakness of individuals, but that is a rare and exceptional event. The ordinary course is one that I am pointing out.]

If you attentively examine all the tyrannies known in history, you see that they have all consisted of a more or less unlimited power entrusted to one or several men and which they used violently against a few. It was by its violence rather than by its *generality* that this tyranny made itself conspicuous.

[In the margin: It is in this portrait that all the originality and the depth of my idea resides. What I have at the end of my first work was hackneyed and superficial.]

(1) <Apply myself to finding a name for it. That is important> (*Rubish,* 2).

This difficulty in finding new words recalls Montesquieu who, in the foreword of *L'Esprit des lois* (*Œuvres complètes,* Paris: Pléiade, 1951, II, p. 227), writes: "I had new ideas; it was very necessary to find new words, or to give new meanings to old ones."

On the origins of paternal despotism, see Rousseau, chapter IV, book I, of the *Contrat social* and his *Discours sur l'origine et les fondements de l'inégalité parmi les hommes* (*Œuvres complètes,* Paris: Pléiade, 1964, III, p. 182).

f. Liberty in the very midst of these diversions is always serious. But there is nothing so joyful as despotism. The sight of human miseries, the unhappy are its natural enemies. It loves on the contrary to find the image of joy everywhere in its path, and it is pleased with games and spectacles. However timid it is by its nature, it does not fear the excesses of a licentious gaity; and the foulest voluptuous pleasures do not frighten it. No one desires more than it does that peoples enjoy themselves, provided that they think only about enjoying themselves; and it willingly intoxicates them with pleasures so that they do more easily without happiness (YTC, CVd, p. 12).

In a similar fragment, on p. 13 of the same notebook, this sentence is found: "Only novice despots are enemies of joy. Free governments seek to give men happiness rather than pleasure" (YTC, CVd, p. 13). The *rubish* contains an identical passage.

for him the entire human species;ᵍ as for the remainder of his fellow citizens, he is next to them, but he does not see them; he touches them without feeling them; he exists only in himself and for himself alone, and if he still has a family, you can say that at least he no longer has a country.ʰ

Above those men arises an immense and tutelary power that alone takes charge of assuring their enjoyment and of looking after their fate. It is absolute, detailed, regular, far-sighted and mild. It would resemble paternal power if, like it, it had as a goal to prepare men for manhood; but on the contrary it seeks only to fix them irrevocably in childhood; it likes the citizens to enjoy themselves, provided that they think only about enjoying themselves.ʲ It works willingly for their happiness; but it wants to be the

g. In the margin: "<Perhaps narrow this tableau. See the effect that it produces when reading.>"

h. In the margin: "<See if this is not found *word for word* at individualism; that the idea was there would not be important.

"Very useful here, try to leave it.>"

j. Note in the manuscript:

Idea that revolutions and anarchy could be combined with this sort of administrative despotism. Days of anarchy in years of despotism. Revolutions always short and not very profound, but perhaps frequent. Palace revolutions that I can easily distinguish from great revolutions, the near impossibility of which I depicted above. These are not revolutions truly speaking. Idea to introduce somewhere in this chapter. Because our contemporaries fear disorder much more than servitude, they must be struck from that side.

A draft comments:

To fight despotism I am obliged to prove that it leads to anarchy. If it led only to itself, it would perhaps be followed willingly.

[In the margin: Continuation of note (B. B.).

Perhaps at the type of despotism which threatens us./

If you could believe in a tranquil and stable despotism, that is to say, in the worst of all, my cause would be lost./

A singular state, ours, in which we have had at the same time too little liberty and license, too little authority and tyranny!/

For a people who has come to the state that I suppose, anarchy, license are possible accidents, even probable ones, but despotism is the normal condition.]

Anarchy is not a lasting state, despotism is. Apathy where we find ourselves leads it is true to anarchy and to despotism. But I can say nonetheless that it leads to despotism because despotism is the final state. Can't this be disputed? And is it not permissible to believe that, in a country in which you would have equality of conditions

unique agent for it and the sole arbiter; it attends to their security, provides for their needs, facilitates their pleasures, conducts their principal affairs, directs their industry, settles their estates, divides their inheritances;[k] how can it not remove entirely from them the trouble to think and the difficulty of living?

This is how it makes the use of free will less useful and rarer every day; how it encloses the action of the will within a smaller space and little by little steals from each citizen even the use of himself.[m] Equality has prepared men for all these things; it has disposed men to bear them and often even to regard them as a benefit.

---

without rooted free institutions, you could go perpetually from anarchy to despotism and from despotism to anarchy without ever settling down? No, despotism would finish by taking root, growing and finally covering the whole country with its harmful shadow.

If that is true, it must be said. It would be an order of ideas that could be developed with advantage and with coloring.

You could believe that equality gives too much taste for independence for despotism to be lasting, and too few habits of independence and means of defending it for liberty to be lasting./

I believe, after all, that all the movement of my (illegible word), which is the tendency of democratic societies toward despotism, is true and must remain, but it must be *amply* inserted somewhere that this tendency does not exclude a great deal of anarchy before and during this gradual but not *continuous* march toward despotism. Equality, without rooted free institutions, leading to anarchy almost as energetically as to despotism (YTC, CVk, 2, pp. 48–49).

k. Toward the end of the manuscript of the chapter: "≠The aristocracy of England is the only one that knows how to defend itself and that has offered liberty to men at the cost of equality; it will fall, but it will fall slowly, and with glory.≠"

m. There are men who have no will to distinguish themselves from their fellows; there are others who have, on the contrary, a permanent and continual will to do so. There are others finally who make only small efforts in order to raise themselves above the earth and who immediately fall back. The latter are the unhappiest of all; for they have the troubles of ambition without having the dubious pleasures of it.

All of man is in the will. His entire future is hidden there as in a germ that the first ray of good fortune comes to make fruitful. There are women who put qualities of character before everything, because those qualities provide the tranquillity of every day, and for those women the idea of happiness does not go beyond the tranquillity and peace of the household. Women of that kind recall to me those men who prefer the type of social paralysis given by despotism to the agitation and the great emotions of liberty. Both hold the same place in my estimation (YTC, CVa, p. 56).

After having thus taken each individual one by one into its powerful hands, and having molded him as it pleases, the sovereign power extends its arms over the entire society; it covers the surface of society with a network of small, complicated, minute, and uniform rules, which the most original minds and the most vigorous souls cannot break through to go beyond the crowd; it does not break wills, but it softens them, bends them and directs them; [<≠in certain moments of great passions and great dangers, the sovereign power becomes suddenly violent and arbitrary. Habitually it is moderate, benevolent, regular and humane≠>] it rarely forces action, but it constantly opposes your acting; it does not destroy, it prevents birth; it does not tyrannize, it hinders, it represses, it enervates, it extinguishes, it stupifies, and finally it reduces each nation to being nothing more than a flock of timid and industrious animals, of which the government is the shepherd.[n]

I have always believed that this sort of servitude, regulated, mild and peaceful, of which I have just done the portrait, could be combined better than we imagine with some of the external forms of liberty, and that it

n. On a loose sheet of the manuscript:

Centralization./
    Show well that the administrative despotism that I am speaking about is independent of representative, liberal or revolutionary institutions, in a word, of political power; that whether the political world is led by an absolute king, by one or several assemblies, whether it is contested in the name of liberty or of order, whether it even falls into anarchy, whether it becomes weak and is divided, the action of the administrative power will be neither less continuous nor less strong, nor less overwhelming.
    [To the side: The man or class that puts the administrative machine in motion can change without the machine changing. You can argue in order to know who will hold the instrument of tyranny, but the instrument remains the same.]
    It is a true distinction and one very important to make in order to dispel the cloud that exists in the mind of the reader every time that you threaten with tyranny the men of today who live amid anarchy and who see political power vacillate or become weak./
    [To the side: A great political anarchy and an overwhelming administrative despotism./
    4 May 1838.]

would not be impossible for it to be established in the very shadow of the sovereignty of the people.°

o. So you can say that for democratic peoples centralization is an innate idea. Not only will this monstrous concentration of all the social [v: political] powers in the same hands not shock the natural ideas of democratic peoples as regards government, but it will favor several of the secret instincts and the most lively tastes that equality [v: their social state] suggests.

Equality of conditions suggests naturally to men an intense and constant taste for material well-being. I said so elsewhere. I have also shown in another place how, as equality became greater, each man, finding himself more independent and more separated from his fellows, felt more disposed to *consider* himself (this word implies a contradiction with what precedes on the innate idea of centralization) separately and to live in isolation.

Those are powerful instruments of tyranny for whoever knows how to use them.

Far from combating these natural tendencies of a democratic social state, a government which aims for absolute power will work with all its power to make them irresistible, and it will inflame the passions that liberty should moderate or extinguish. There exist in the south of Europe petty princes whose tyranny is so touchy and so irksome that the life of the most inoffensive citizens [v: the most servile and the most peaceful souls are] was saddened and made uncomfortable by it. Those princes are, if I am not mistaken, clumsy despots. They bring to the execution of their designs more zeal than light, and they do not know that in the centuries in which we are living men are more disposed to bear that you violate their rights than their comforts.

[To the side: Two consequences of the taste for material well-being for a despot to look after: 1. Softening of souls which causes you no longer to have a taste for the highest pleasures that liberty provides; 2. Effort of the whole human spirit toward the acquisition of well-being, which causes you no longer to have the time to give yourself to those pleasures.]

The clever man who seeks to establish absolute power among a democratic nation will demand only one thing from the citizens: that they do not get involved in the government and contract none of the habits that can in the long run lead men to get involved in it. But he will also work hard to make civil life as independent, as prosperous, as easy as it can be without political liberty. He will facilitate material well-being with all his power; he will honor it, he will glorify it each day in the eyes of the crowd, and pushing with all his power the souls that are naturally inclined toward solely the enjoyments of the senses, he will turn them away from the most beautiful works and the most noble pleasures of man.

Among democratic peoples men have little leisure; they are all naturally very occupied with their private affairs and only impatiently do they bear being turned away from them. The concern for common interests distracts and fatigues them; the sovereign power appears and unburdens them. Do not believe that it intends to oppress them in this way; it is relieving them. It carefully organizes the time of which they

[I suppose that a democratic nation, after destroying within it all the secondary powers, establishes in its midst a very inquisitorial, very extensive, very centralized, very powerful executive power, that it confers on this power the right to conduct all the details of public affairs and to lead a part of private affairs, that it put [*sic*] individuals in a strict and daily dependence on this power, but that it makes this executive power itself depend on an elected legislature which, without governing, traces the principal rules of the government.

<I go still further and I suppose that the administration, instead of being

------

make such good use, and removes from them the troubles and the worries of government in order to deliver them entirely to concerns about their private fortunes.

So the State is full of solicitude for the happiness of the citizens, but it wants to be the unique agent and the sole (illegible word) of it. It is the State that takes care of providing their security, facilitating their pleasures, directing the principal affairs; the State itself creates roads, digs canals, directs industries, divides inheritances. It may even be able to plow the earth and finally take away from each man even the difficulty of living!

Equality of conditions has prepared men for all these things; it has disposed them to bear them and often even to regard them as a good.

This is how, aiding itself sometimes with the vices of men, sometimes with their weaknesses, often with their inexperience, the central power little by little and without effort takes hold of the entire life of a democratic people. It does not tear their rights away from them; their rights are abandoned to it. It does not do violence to mores [v: sentiments]; it does not overturn ideas, but it gently directs both toward servitude.

Here it is, acknowledged arbiter of everything. Society does nothing for itself, and it does everything. Divided from his fellows, each citizen thinks only of himself. The source of public virtues has dried up.

[What will the first tyrant who is coming be called? I do not know, but he is approaching. What is still missing for this deceptive symbol of public order to disappear and for a profound and incurable disorder to be revealed?

What more is needed for this sublime authority, for this visible providence that we have established among us to be able to trample underfoot the most holy laws, do violence as it pleases to our hearts and walk over our heads? War. Peace has prepared despotism, war establishes it.

[In the margin: Not only as a consequence of victory, but war alone by the need for power and for concentration that it creates.

A new aristocracy of soldiers is the only one that seems to me still practical.]] (YTC, CVd, pp. 3–4, 8–9, 9–10, 10–12).

There are several variants of these passages in the same pages. In another place, Tocqueville repeats: "When I said that there was no more aristocracy possible, I was mistaken; you can still have the aristocracy of men of war" (YTC, CVd, p. 26).

alongside the legislative chambers, is in the very legislature, as was seen in France at the time of the Convention, so that the same elected power makes the law and executes it even in its smallest details.>

All that means, if I am not mistaken, that after allowing the sovereign power as a master to direct each citizen [v: particular wills] and to bend him every day as it pleases, the sovereign itself is subjected from time to time to the general will [*volontés générales:* (Translator)] of the nation.]

Our contemporaries are incessantly tormented by two hostile passions: they feel the need to be led and the desire to remain free. Unable to destroy either the one or the other of these opposite instincts, they work hard to satisfy both at the same time. They imagine a unique, tutelary, omnipotent power, but elected by the citizens. They combine centralization[p] and sovereignty of the people. That gives them some relief. They console themselves about being in tutelage by thinking that they have chosen their tutors themselves. Each individual endures being bound, because he sees that it is not a man or a class, but the people itself that holds the end of the chain.

In this system, the citizens emerge for a moment from dependency in order to indicate their master, and return to it.[q]

p. The French believe that centralization is French. They are wrong; it is democratic and I dare to predict that all peoples whose social state will be the same and who follow only the instincts that this social state suggests will arrive at the point where we are./

Destroy classes, equalize ranks, make men similar, and you will see power become centralized as if by itself, whatever the country, the genius of the people or the state of enlightenment. Particular circumstances will be able to hasten the natural movement or slow it down, but not stop it or create an opposite one.

[To the side: Contained within certain limits, centralization is a necessary fact, and I add that it is a fact about which we must be glad./

A strong and intelligent central power is one of the first political necessities in centuries of equality. Acknowledge it boldly] (*Rubish,* 2).

Already in 1828, in an already quoted letter to Gustave de Beaumont, Tocqueville said of Edward I: "He reestablished order and made good civil laws which, as you know, often make people forget about good political laws" (*Correspondance avec Beaumont, OC,* VIII, 1, p. 55).

q. "<This is seen above all today in the nations of Europe, still half filled with liberal passions that arose from the struggle with aristocracy, working hard to find a form of

There are many men today who accommodate themselves very easily to this type of compromise between administrative despotism and sovereignty of the people, and who think they have guaranteed the liberty of individuals when it is to the national power that they deliver that liberty. That is not enough for me. The nature of the master is much less important to me than the obedience.

I will not deny, however, that such a constitution is infinitely preferable to one that, after concentrating all powers, would put them in the hands of an unaccountable man or body. Of all the different forms that democratic despotism could take, the latter would assuredly be the worst.

When the sovereign is elected or closely supervised by a legislature truly elected and independent, the oppression that it can make individuals suffer is sometimes greater; but the oppression is always less degrading because each citizen, when he is being hindered and when he is reduced to powerlessness, can still imagine that by obeying he is only submitting to himself, and that it is to one of his desires that he is sacrificing all the rest.[r]

I understand equally that, when the sovereign represents the nation and depends on it, the strength and the rights that are taken from each citizen do not serve only the leader of the State, but profit the State itself, and that individuals gain some advantage from the sacrifice of their independence that they have made to the public.

[I understand also that when public opinion draws certain limits and can keep the sovereign power within them, tyranny properly speaking is

---

government that at the same time satisfies the love that they still have for independence and the new instincts that make them tend toward servitude>" (Note in the drafts that could also refer to another part of the chapter, *Rubish,* 2).

r. In the margin: "<I do not know if, everything considered, this is still not the best course that you can reasonably hope from equality and the only type of liberty that it is capable of allowing to men.>"

And a little further along: "<All the end of the chapter starting from here seems to me to come to an end too abruptly. All the more because that is the most vulnerable side and the most interesting side of the entire book.>"

little to be feared, or at least it can never become general. Thus it is not the tyranny of the social power that is the most to fear, but its regular use.]ˢ

To create a national representation in a very centralized country, is therefore to diminish the evil that extreme centralization can produce, but not to destroy it.ᵗ

s. In the margin: "<This is not relevant because I have already ruled out the idea of tyranny above.>"

t. Title on a jacket:

That the instinct of democratic peoples is to want one great assembly of its representatives rather than secondary assemblies. That a government that aims at tyranny among a democratic people can tolerate a great general representation {(it is often obliged to do so)}, but must never allow secondary assemblies {(which is usually easy for it)}.

[Within the jacket] Unique assembly./

If I were secretly a friend of absolute power and were, however, forced to grant my country the forms of liberty, I would seek first to untangle among free institutions those that a democratic people imagines the best, that it requires with the most authority, and that its leaders cannot refuse to it without danger; I would soon discover that what it asks above all, still less by reasoning than by instinct, is one general assembly of its representatives. All the rest seems doubtful or indifferent to it, but this first axiom of its politics seems principal and almost unique to it. So I would hasten to yield to this irresistible desire of an emerging democracy.

I would allow the free will of all the citizens to be represented in one assembly, but I would want it to express itself only there. I would grant independence for great affairs; I would keep despotism for small ones, so that if I were forced to tolerate liberty in the laws, I would at least prevent liberty from becoming established in habits.

[In the margin: So I would limit myself to making a magnificent exception to the general rule of servitude, following this principle of logic that the exception proves the rule and confirms it.]

≠So I would allow the deputies of the whole country to deliberate on peace and war, regulate the finances of the State, its prosperity, its industry, its life, but I would prevent at all cost the inhabitants [v: representatives] of a *canton* from having the liberty to settle things among themselves.≠

A great legislative body placed at the center of a democratic people manifests the present independence of this people, but it cannot ever guarantee its future independence.

Since it is at the very same time provided with a great material strength and an immense moral power, since it alone has the right to speak in the general silence, since it alone can act amid the universal weakness, it feels itself above all the laws; it is free

I see clearly that, in this way, individual intervention is kept in the most important affairs; but it is no less suppressed in the small ones and the particular ones.[u] We forget that it is dangerous, above all, to enslave men

---

from all the rules and sheltered from all points of resistance. So it bends wills as it wishes, abolishes rights, alters or changes mores. And if it comes finally to be destroyed or to destroy itself, the habits of servility that it created survive it.

[To the side: You bring to the national representation men who have received no preliminary and in a way primary education in the representative system; they appear ignorant, undisciplined, indecisive, confused; you then say that it is the representative system which is worth nothing and you distance yourself from it.

All that I see and hear since my arrival in Paris (April 1837) shows me that in a lively way.]

To concentrate all the political life of a people in one assembly is to give to liberty only a single head and to expose it to perishing with one blow.

So as long as a free institution of this nature remains isolated, it always leaves fair hopes to despotism; it is an evil that carries its remedy with it (YTC, CVd, pp. 45–48).

There are other versions of this paragraph in CVd, pp. 48–52. Following the coup d'état of Louis-Napoleon Bonaparte, Tocqueville will abandon all political activity. In February 1852, he writes to a friend, with an entirely similar tone:

I have refused any type of candidacy for the next elections, not wanting to have the appearance of taking seriously the parody of a free government that is going to be played. You know that the new assembly is nothing because it has no publicity and can only reject the budget without being able to amend it, and you have learned undoubtedly that the candidates who would want to oppose those of the government cannot either speak to the voters, or write to them, or form committees, or travel across the country without risk of being arrested; that in a word the new power pursues its plan to govern with the aid of the peasants and the soldiers, borrowing from democracy only its worst principle, the brutal strength of numbers, the universal vote amid the silence and the darkness that despotism creates. You understand that it is better to write books than to get involved in such a mess (Letter of Tocqueville to Milnes, 9 February 1852. With the kind permission of Trinity College, Cambridge. Houghton papers, 25/209).

u. In the margin:

<Perhaps begin this page with this sentence:

I see citizens who gather together to constitute and regulate in common a sole and unique power that represents them all and to which each one of them delivers the care of his particular interests and which he charges with exercising all rights.

In this way, something of individual intervention is preserved in the most important and most general affairs, but it is suppressed entirely in the small ones and the particular ones. We forget . . .>

in the detail. I would, for my part, be led to believe liberty less necessary in the great things than in the least, if I thought that the one could ever be assured without possessing the other.

Subjection in small affairs manifests itself every day and makes itself felt indiscriminately by all citizens. It does not drive them to despair; but it thwarts them constantly and leads them to relinquish the use of their will [and finally to give up on themselves]. It thus extinguishes their spirit little by little, and enervates their souls; while the obedience that is due only in a small number of very grave, but very rare circumstances, displays servitude only now and then, and makes it weigh only on certain men. In vain will you charge these same citizens, whom you have made so dependent on the central power, with choosing from time to time the representatives of this power; this use so important, but so short and so rare, of their free will, will not prevent them from losing little by little the ability to think, to feel and to act by themselves, and from thus falling gradually below the level of humanity.^{v}

I add that they will soon become incapable of [properly] exercising the great and sole privilege remaining to them. Democratic peoples who have introduced liberty in the political sphere, at the same time that they increased despotism in the administrative sphere, have been led to very strange peculiarities.^{w} If small affairs, in which simple good sense can suf-

---

v. The Americans have avoided these first dangers of democratic infancy. Although they have granted immense rights to society, they have not sacrificed the individual to it. They have left to the latter, outside of the political world, a great *security* and a great *independence.* They have not given the government the same *civil privileges,* and they have not put it beyond the reach and the control of the judicial power by requiring in a stupid manner as we the necessity of the division of powers (UNITY, CENTRALIZATION, ADMINISTRATIVE DESPOTISM, *Rubish,* 2).

w. Note at the end of the manuscript of the chapter:

Their pet hobby is to want to combine the greatest political independence with the greatest administrative dependence.

I would do well, I believe, to hit this prejudice straight on, to say something analogous to the above sentence, to say that that comes from tugging in opposite directions. We tend toward liberty and toward servitude at the same time; we want to combine them, although they cannot be combined. Not able to be free, we want at least to be oppressed in the name of the people.

fice, must be managed, they consider that the citizens are incapable of it; if it is a matter of the government of the whole State, they entrust these citizens with immense prerogatives; they make them alternately the playthings of the sovereign and its masters, more than kings and less than men. After having exhausted all the different systems of election, without finding one that suits them, they are surprised and still search; as if the evil that they notice were not due to the constitution of the country much more than to that of the electoral body.

It is, in fact, difficult to imagine how men who have entirely given up the habit of directing themselves, could succeed in choosing well those who should lead them; and it cannot be believed that a liberal, energetic and wise government can ever come out of the votes of a people of servants.[x]

A constitution that would be republican at the head, and ultra-monarchical in all the other parts has always seemed to me an ephemeral monster. The vices of those who govern and the imbecility of the governed

---

x. Unity, centralization./

We believe we are making a clever and sufficient concession by allowing these same men, almost entirely deprived of their free will in every day actions, to unite now and then to choose one of the three great powers. In other words, after refusing to them the right to direct their own affairs, we concede to them the privilege of governing the State.

[To the side: The idea opposite is good. If I want to strike minds by the picture of *administrative despotism,* I must move away as little as possible from *what we see before our eyes.* A tyranny of the Caesars was a bogeyman that cannot make anyone afraid, although at bottom that is not so unreasonable as we think. I must not aim to say the most complete truth, but the most easily grasped and the most useful.]

This is a very insufficient and very dangerous remedy.

A national assembly named by such voters cannot fail to be *revolutionary* or *servile.*

It is a great foolishness to hope to make a strong, liberal, energetic and wise government emerge from a people of servants./

6 April 1838 (*Rubish,* 2).

On another page, Tocqueville adds: "I cannot prevent myself from considering this form of government as transitory. It leads necessarily to institutions truly [v: more] liberal or to the non-accountable despotism of one man" (*Rubish,* 2).

would not take long to lead them to ruin; and the people, tired of its representatives and of itself, would create freer institutions, or would soon return to stretching out at the feet of a single master.[y]

y. "Those who believe they are able to stop for long at a government which is republican at its head and ultra-monarchical at its tail, *chambers* and a *centralized administration,* are great fools. But the thing can go for a while in this way. Portray it in the place where I do the portrait of democratic despotism.

"22 June" (*Rubish,* 2).

CHAPTER 7ᵃ

Continuation of the Preceding Chapters

I believe that it is easier to establish an absolute and despotic government among a [democratic] people where conditions are equal than among another, and I think that, if such a government were once established among such a people, not only would it oppress men, but in the long run it would rob from each of them some of the principal attributes of humanity.ᵇ

So despotism seems to me particularly to be feared in democratic ages.

a. The jacket that contains the manuscript of the chapter also contains Tocqueville's working manuscript and a copy of the entire chapter written in his hand. You can read on the jacket: "Continuation of the preceding chapter./

"[In pencil] I bet that M. de C[hateaubriand? (ed.)]. did not understand this chapter. "20 minutes."

In the plan for the fourth part included in *Rubish*, 1 (contained in a jacket that is found with the drafts of the chapter on material enjoyments and that bears the title HOW EQUALITY OF RANKS SUGGESTS TO MEN THE TASTE FOR LIBERTY AND FOR EQUALITY), the chapter on the type of despotism is followed by another with the title WHAT MUST BE DONE TO TURN ASIDE THIS DANGER. Tocqueville notes to the side of the title: "This title contains the idea, but not the expression that this idea must have. The title drafted in this way would be too ambitious. It would promise more than I can keep."

The same idea is found on the jacket that contains the manuscript: "This title means nothing at all, but all those that I want to put in its place mean too much. The only real title would be: What must be done to avoid the evils that I point out in the preceding chapters. But such a title would announce much more than the chapter can hold; in such a case, it is better to be useless than ambitious."

b. "The social state separates men, the political state must draw them closer./

"The social state gives them the taste for well-being [v: inclines them toward the earth], the political state must raise them up by giving them great ideas and great emotions" (*Rubish*, 2).

I would, I think, have loved liberty in all times; but I feel myself inclined to adore it in the times in which we live.

I am persuaded, on the other hand, that in the centuries which we are entering, all those who try to base liberty on privilege and on aristocracy will fail. All those who want to attract and keep authority within a single class will fail. There is today no sovereign power clever enough and strong enough to establish despotism by reestablishing permanent distinctions among its subjects;c nor is there any legislator so wise and so powerful who

---

c. From now on the atmosphere that surrounds us will be democratic, you will be able to breathe only on condition of taking up your position there.

There show how the members of the aristocracy can without haste and without delay, without pride and without servility, draw closer to the people and, abandoning the memories of another time, take a place in the present time . . .

Then add.

As for those who will want to hold themselves aside, hoping to escape in this way the common destruction and to preserve for other times the elements of an aristocracy, they will soon discover that life is tiring and difficult for them. Surrounded by hostile prejudices, the butt of suspicions, forced to breathe on all sides the air of hatred, objects of pity and envy at the same time, more strangers in the country where they were born than the traveler who comes to find shelter under their roof, they will be like the Jews after the destruction of the temple; like [them (ed.)], they will constantly await a Messiah who must not come. But they will differ from the Jews on one point; they will not perpetuate themselves. An aristocracy in vain wants to outlive its grandeur and to preserve itself intact amid the ruin of the institutions that it established; it cannot succeed. And if its enemies are powerless to accomplish its ruin, it will soon take charge itself of accomplishing it. Careers that gain honors and glory are closed to its members, and they refuse to embrace professions that give or preserve wealth. So they are as if struck with immobility amid the universal movement; among a people in which all work, they are reduced to an idleness so complete that you have never seen any thing like it. Within the most aristocratic [democratic (ed.)] societies this immense and useless leisure overwhelms them. A restless boredom devours them. Since they cannot obtain the most noble pleasures of men, they seek the tumultuous and coarse enjoyments that tear them violently away from themselves, and they console themselves with horses and dogs for not being able to govern the State. They have neither the courtesy nor the energy of their ancestors; they have only preserved their pride. And you are astonished by the unimaginable sterility of the races most fruitful in great men./

At every moment the law of inheritances comes to surprise a few among them amid these obscene and unworthy leisure activities and throws them into obscurity and poverty. The solitude then becomes more profound around those who remain, the isolation more frightening, the discouragement more complete every day; a name

is able to maintain free institutions if he does not take equality as first principle and as symbol. So all those among our contemporaries who want to create or to assure the independence and dignity of their fellows must appear as friends of equality; and the only means worthy of them of appearing so is to be so: the success of their holy enterprise depends on it.[d]

Thus, it is not a matter of reconstructing an aristocratic society, but of making liberty emerge from within the democratic society in which God makes us live.

---

is lost, a precious memory fades, the trace of several generations gone by disappears. New families come out of the void into which the first descend. Power, wealth and glory have forever passed into other hands.

I am profoundly convinced that it is no less impossible to establish a new aristocracy than to preserve the ruins of the former aristocracy. For my part, I cannot understand the fears that are inspired among the friends of democracy, openly or in secret, by those who intend to re-create to a certain measure ranks, privileges, hereditary rights, permanent influences. Such men are dangerous only to themselves. They only compromise the cause that they embrace and the conservative doctrines that they mix with it.

The current of the century is against them, and the day when finally they want seriously to raise the dike that is to contain it, they will immediately be swept away forever by it. So democracy has henceforth nothing to fear from its adversaries. It is from within that its corrupters and its masters will come. I do not see how its reign could be prevented from becoming established, but I easily discover what must be done to make it detestable./

What is the danger?

To flatter the feelings of democratic hate and envy and to gain power in this way.

To give equality lavishly, to take away liberty in return (YTC, CVc, pp. 55–58).

F. D. often repeats that an aristocracy is a command staff. That is a good definition. An aristocracy is not a body by itself all alone, but the head of a body. Reduced to itself it can still do brilliant things, but not great and lasting things.

This comparison of an aristocracy to a command staff was found with a rigorous exactitude in 1792. The officers being all gathered on the right of the Rhine, the soldiers remained on the left bank. This was the final demonstration of what I said above, the most striking image of the state of French society (YTC, CVa, pp. 52–53). The same idea appears in YTC, CVc, p. 55.

d. In the margin of the copy of the chapter, in pencil: "I strongly persist in asking deletion."

These two first truths seem to me simple, clear and fertile, and they lead me naturally to consider what type of free government can be established among a people in which conditions are equal.

It results from the very constitution of democratic nations and from their needs that, among them, the power of the sovereign must be more uniform, more centralized, more extensive, more penetrating, more powerful than elsewhere.[e] Society there is naturally more active and stronger; the individual, more subordinate and weaker. The one does more; the other less; that is inevitable.[f]

So in democratic countries you must not expect the circle of individual independence ever to be as wide as in countries of aristocracy. But that is not to be desired; for among aristocratic nations, society is often sacrificed to the individual, and the prosperity of the greatest number to the grandeur of a few.

It is at the very same time necessary and desirable that the central power that directs a democratic people be active and powerful. It is not a matter of making it weak or indolent, but only of preventing it from abusing its agility and strength.[g]

e. "In democratic societies not only is the government stronger (illegible word) than the citizens, but also it alone has duration, foresight, extended plans, profound calculations. It surpasses the citizens as much in quality as in strength. At the next-to-last chapter. 1 September 1838" (YTC, CVk, 1, p. 23).

f. In the margin: "Men who live in centuries of equality are naturally isolated and powerless; it is only by the artificial and temporary combination of their efforts that they can attain great objectives."

g. Notes on a page at the end of the manuscript of the chapter:

Necessity of a strong government, because of the weakness or the destruction of all the other social bonds that could allow a society to march all alone and to contain disorder within certain limits./

Remove all political government from an aristocracy, annul entirely the national, central power, a certain order will still be maintained there, because, exercising a certain influence on each other, individuals hold together, have the habit of immobility and keep in their place for a long time, without the political power getting involved.

[To the side] *Another idea* to recall here. Among democratic peoples only the government has stability, duration, extended plans, views of the future, can follow extended undertakings, all things necessary to the well-being of nations which have such a long life. Everything is unstable and fleeting among democratic peoples, outside of the government.

What contributed the most to assure the independence of individuals in aristocratic centuries is that the sovereign power did not take charge alone of governing and administering the citizens; it was obliged to leave a part of this concern to the members of the aristocracy; so that the social power, always divided, never weighed entirely and in the same way on every man.[h]

Not only did the sovereign power not do everything by itself, but most of the officers who acted in its place, since they drew their power from the fact of their birth and not from it, were not constantly in its hand. It could not at any moment create them or destroy them, depending on its caprices, and bend them all uniformly to its least desires. That also guaranteed the independence of individuals.

I also understand that today you cannot resort to the same means, but I see democratic procedures that replace them.[j]

The same idea is expressed in a rough draft:

I confess that the government among democratic peoples is easier and more convenient than in democracies [aristocracies (ed.)], but is it better? That is the question. Is the first merit of a government to work easily? If that was so, what better than despotism and what worse than liberty? What more stable than the one? You establish it one day and it works for a thousand years. What more fragile than the other? What efforts to establish it, what (illegible word) work to (illegible word) it. See however the result of the one and the other. So the ideal of perfection must be sought elsewhere (YTC, CVk, 2, p. 54).

h. You are astonished at first sight by the respect that is still witnessed today for *domanial property* and the little respect that is shown for *industrial property*.[1] That comes from the fact that domanial property .- [is (ed.)] .- ancient property, the property of aristocratic centuries and that the principles that protected it in these centuries (principles deriving from the social state) have left profound traces in the mores. While for industrial property, modern and democratic property, you give yourself to the instincts natural to democracy, which are to substitute the State for the individual and constantly to break the latter under the feet of the mass.

  1. Those two terms are not in natural opposition, but I do not have the time to clarify my thought (*Rubish*, 2).

j. Remedies to democracy indicated in the course of the book, to gather together perhaps in the first or final chapter.

  [In the margin: Try to arrive at the same conclusion by another path than in political society.]

Instead of giving to the sovereign alone all the administrative powers that were taken from the corporation or from the nobles, you can entrust a part of them to secondary bodies formed temporarily out of simple citizens; in this way, the liberty of individuals will be surer, without their equality being less.

The Americans, who are not as attached as we to words, have kept the name of county for the largest of their administrative districts; but they have in part replaced the county by a provincial assembly[k] [chosen freely by the inhabitants themselves].[m]

I will admit without difficulty that in a period of equality like ours, it would be unjust and unreasonable to institute hereditary officials; but nothing prevents substituting for them, to a certain measure, elected officials. Election is a democratic expedient that assures the independence of the official vis-à-vis the central power, as much as and more than heredity can do among aristocratic peoples.

Aristocratic countries are full of rich and influential individuals who know how to be self-sufficient and who are not easily or secretly oppressed; and the latter keep power within the general habits of moderation and restraint [<while in democratic countries each citizen taken in isolation cannot offer any resistance and does not ever succeed in

---

Necessity of not giving omnipotence to the majority in order not to lose the liberty to act which results naturally from a democratic social state.

Necessity of introducing liberty among a democratic people in order to give it the necessary movement toward things of the mind.

Pour out enlightenment lavishly in democratic nations in order to elevate the tendencies of the human mind. Democracy without enlightenment and liberty would lead the human species back to barbarism.

Necessity of beliefs in order to immaterialize the lives of democratic peoples. Democratic peoples can be grasped only by them. Religion is an almost non-material interest which gives celestial thoughts./

Do not adopt one social principle *alone* however good it seems.

Do not use one form of government *alone*. Stay away from acridity [unity? (ed.)] (YTC, CVk, 2, pp. 54–55).

k. "Only provincial institutions can make the democratic instinct of liberty a habit" (YTC, CVd, p. 19).

m. This fragment is found in the copy of the chapter.

attracting the eyes of the public to the evils that tyranny makes him suffer.>]

I know well that democratic countries do not naturally present similar individuals; but there you can artificially create something analogous.

I believe firmly that you cannot establish an aristocracy[n] again in the world; but I think that simple citizens by associating together can constitute very wealthy, very influential, very strong beings, in a word aristocratic persons.[o]

[<Thus, in whatever direction I look, I discover association as the most powerful remedy for the evils with which equality threatens us.>]

n. "As for me, all that I wish for my country is that those who aim for despotism there aim at the same time for aristocracy" (YTC, CVd, p. 25).

o. In a jacket with rough drafts of the chapter which bears the title IDEA OF ARIS-TOCRATIC PERSONS:

.-.-.-.-.-.-

Possibility of creating within a democratic people *aristocratic persons,* means of uniting in part the advantages of the two systems.

What I mean by aristocratic persons are permanent and legal associations such as cities, *cantons,* departments, or voluntary and temporary associations such as, I suppose, in literature, the Norman association; in industry, the company of *Messageries;* in politics, the society "Aide-toi le ciel t'aidera." These associations are cited as examples and not as models.

This would have one part of the advantages of aristocracy properly speaking without its disadvantages.

That would not establish permanent inequality and .-.- the injustices that .-.-.- ; it would not elevate .-.- certain men above .-.- all the rest . . .

It would create powerful individuals capable of great efforts, of vast projects, of firm resistance; it would bind men together in another way, but as tightly as aristocracy. It would make the species greater and would elevate thought. . . . (*Rubish,* 2).

On the question of associations for Tocqueville, see: Renato Cavallaro, "Dall'individualismo al controllo democratico: aspetti del pensiero di Alexis de Tocqueville sull'associazionismo volontario," *Critica Sociologica,* 28, 1973–1974, pp. 99–125; William H. George, "Montesquieu and De Tocqueville and Corporative Individualism," *American Political Science Review* 16, no. 1 (1922): 10–21; Georges Gojat, "Les corps intermédiaires et la décentralisation dans l'oeuvre de Tocqueville," in *Libéralisme, traditionalisme, décentralisation* (Paris: Armand Colin, 1952), pp. 1–43; and José María Sauca Cano, *La ciencia de la asociación de Tocqueville* (Madrid: Centro de Estudios Constitucionales, 1995).

In this manner several of the greatest political advantages of aristocracy would be obtained, without its injustices or its dangers. A political, industrial, commercial, or even scientific and literary association is an enlightened and powerful citizen whom you cannot bend at will or oppress in the shadow, and who, by defending its particular rights against the demands of power, saves common liberties.

In times of aristocracy, each man is always bound in a very tight way to several of his fellow citizens, so that you cannot attack the former without the others running to his aid. In centuries of equality, each individual is naturally isolated; he has no hereditary friends whose help he can require, no class whose sympathies for him are assured; he is easily set apart, and he is trampled underfoot with impunity.P Today, a citizen who is oppressed has therefore only one means of defending himself; it is to address himself to the whole nation, and if it is deaf to him, to humanity; he has only one means to do it, it is the press. Thus liberty of the press is infinitely more precious among democratic nations than among all others; it alone cures most of the evils that equality can produce. Equality isolates and weakens men; but the press places beside each one of them a very powerful weapon, which the weakest and most isolated can use. Equality takes away from each individual the support of those close to him; but the press allows him to call to his aid all his fellow citizens and all those similar to him. Printing hastened the progress of equality, and it is one of its best correctives.

I think that men who live in aristocracies can, if necessary, do without liberty of the press; but those who inhabit democratic countries cannot do so. [<For the latter, between independence and servitude, I see hardly anything except the press.>] To guarantee the personal independence of the latter, I do not trust great political assemblies, parliamentary prerogatives, the proclamation of sovereignty of the people.

All these things, up to a certain point, fit with individual servitude; but

p. In the margin: "The entire style of this chapter is defective and to review, but the thoughts are so difficult that at this moment I can only concern myself with them."

this servitude cannot be complete if the press is free. The press is, par excellence, the democratic instrument of liberty.

I will say something analogous about the judicial power.[q]

It is the essence of the judicial power to occupy itself with particular interests and to fix its eyes on the small matters that are exposed to its view; it is also the essence of this power not to come by itself to the help of those who are oppressed, but to be constantly at the disposal of the most humble man among them. The latter, however weak you suppose him to be, can always force the judge to listen to his complaint and to respond to it: that results from the very constitution of the judicial power.

So such a power is especially applicable to the needs of liberty, in a time when the eye and the hand of the sovereign are introduced constantly into the most minute details of human actions, and when individuals, too weak to protect themselves, are too isolated to be able to count on the help of those like them. The strength of the courts has been, in all times, the greatest guarantee that can be offered to individual independence, but that is true above all in democratic centuries; particular rights and interests are always in danger there, if the judicial power does not grow and expand as conditions become equal.

Equality suggests to men several tendencies very dangerous for liberty, and the legislator must always keep his eyes open to them. I will only recall the principal ones.

Men who live in democratic centuries do not easily understand the utility of forms;[r] they feel an instinctive disdain for them. I spoke about the reasons for this elsewhere. Forms excite their scorn and often their hatred. Since they usually aspire only to easy and present enjoyments, they throw themselves impetuously toward the object of each one of their desires; the least delays lead them to despair. This temperament, which they bring to political life, sets them against forms which slow or stop them each day in some of their desires.

q. In the margin: "The weaker individuals are, the stronger the courts must be."

r. With the rough drafts of this chapter, you find a fragment on forms, poorly drafted, and which seems to be in the hand of Louis de Kergorlay. See note u of p. 1273 and note g of p. 750. A note in the *rubish* mentions: "I had a good conversation with Louis about this entire subject; look at it again" (*Rubish*, 2).

This disadvantage that men of democracies find in forms is, however, what makes the latter so useful to liberty, their principal merit being to serve as a barrier between the strong and the weak, those who govern and the governed, to slow the first and to give to the second the time for them to figure things out. Forms are more necessary as the sovereign power is more active and more powerful and as individuals become more indolent and more feeble. Thus democratic peoples naturally need forms more than other peoples, and naturally they respect them less.[s] That merits very serious attention.

There is nothing more miserable than the superb disdain of most of our contemporaries for questions of forms; for today the smallest questions of forms have acquired an importance that they had not had until now. Several of the greatest interests of humanity are connected with it.

I think that, if the statesmen who lived in aristocratic centuries could sometimes scorn forms with impunity and often rise above them, those who lead peoples today must consider the least form with respect and neglect it only when an imperious necessity forces them to do so. In aristocracies, you had superstition for forms; we must have an enlightened and thoughtful cult of them.

Another instinct very natural to democratic peoples, and very dangerous, is that which leads them to scorn individual rights and to take them into little account.

Men are in general attached to a right and show it respect by reason of its importance or of the long use that they have made of it. Individual rights which are found among democratic peoples are ordinarily of little importance, very recent and very unstable; that means that they are often easily sacrificed and violated almost always without regrets.

Now it happens that, in this same time and among these same nations in which men conceive a natural scorn for the rights of individuals, the

s. "All peoples who have done great things for liberty have had the taste [v: the faith] and I could almost say superstition for forms./
"Forms are not liberty, but they are its body" (*Rubish,* 2).

rights of the society expand naturally and become stronger; that is to say that men become less attached to particular rights, at the moment when it would be most necessary to keep them and to defend the few of them that remain.[t]

So it is above all in the democratic times in which we find ourselves that the true friends of liberty and of human grandeur must, constantly, stand up and be ready to prevent the social power from sacrificing lightly the particular rights of some individuals to the general execution of its designs. In those times no citizen is so obscure that it is not very dangerous to allow him to be oppressed, or individual rights of so little importance that you can surrender to arbitrariness with impunity. The reason for it is simple. When you violate the particular right of an individual in a time when the human mind is penetrated by the importance and the holiness of the rights of this type, you do harm only to the one you rob. But to violate such a right today is to corrupt the national mores profoundly and to put the entire society at risk, because the very idea of these kinds of rights tends constantly among us to deteriorate and become lost.

[<I find as well and for entirely similar reasons that in democratic centuries, above all, sovereigns must watch themselves with the greatest care in order to repress the natural tendency which leads them to sacrifice a

---

t. [The beginning is missing (ed.)] that the confidence in the idea of the right of reason that is spreading each day, do you not notice that each day the idea of fact and of force replaces it, and what is the final and legitimate representative of force, if not the soldier?

[To the side: Do you not see that with equality without liberty we are marching toward a singular servitude and toward an inevitable barbarism? And if you see all these things, what are you doing?]

Do you not see that opinions are dividing more quickly than patrimonies, that each man is enclosing himself narrowly within his own mind, like the farm laborer in his field?

[To the side: Do you not see that souls are falling lower and that the love of liberty, this great and noble passion of man, is deserting him?]

That egoism is constantly taking on new strength without acquiring new light?

The idea of right which is being extinguished.

That sentiments become more individual each day, and that soon men will be more separated by their beliefs than they have ever been by inequality of conditions? (YTC, CVd, pp. 19–20).

particular right, however small it is, to the general execution to their designs.>]

There are certain habits, certain ideas, certain vices that belong to the state of revolution, and that a long revolution cannot fail to engender and to generalize, whatever its character, its objective and its theater are.

When whatever nation has several times in a short expanse of time changed leaders, opinions and laws, the men who compose it end by contracting the taste for movement and by becoming accustomed to all movements taking place rapidly and with the aid of force. They then naturally conceive a contempt for forms, whose impotence they see every day, and only with impatience do they bear the dominion of rules, which have been evaded so many times before their eyes.

Since the ordinary notions of equity and morality no longer suffice to explain and justify all the novelties to which the revolution gives birth each day, you latch onto the principle of social utility, you create the dogma of political necessity; and you become readily accustomed to sacrificing particular interests without scruples and to trampling individual rights underfoot, in order to attain more promptly the general goal that you propose.

These habits and these ideas, which I will call revolutionary,[u] because all revolutions produce them, manifest themselves within aristocracies as well

---

u. Definition of revolutionary spirit:
    taste for rapid changes,
    use of violence to bring them about,
    tyrannical spirit,
    contempt for forms,
    contempt for acquired rights,
    indifference about the means in view of the end, doctrine of the useful,
    satisfaction given to brutal appetites./
    The revolutionary spirit which everywhere is the greatest enemy of liberty and is such above all among democratic peoples, because there is a natural and secret bond between it and democracy. It takes its source in the natural faults of democracy and scorns them.
    A revolution can sometimes be just and necessary; it can establish liberty, but the revolutionary spirit is always detestable and can never lead to anything except to tyranny (*Rubish*, 2).

as among democratic peoples; but among the first they are often less powerful and always less durable, because there they encounter habits, ideas, flaws and failings that are contrary to them. So they fade away by themselves as soon as the revolution is finished, and the nation returns to its former political ways. It is not always so in democratic countries, where it is always to be feared that revolutionary instincts, becoming milder and more regular without dying out, will gradually turn into governmental mores and administrative habits.[v]

So I do not know of a country in which revolutions are more dangerous than democratic countries, because, apart from the accidental and passing evils that revolutions can never fail to produce, they always risk creating permanent and, so to speak, eternal ones.

I believe that there are honest acts of resistance and legitimate rebellions [v. revolutions]. So I am not saying, in an absolute way, that men of democratic times must never make revolutions; but I think that they are right to hesitate more than all the others before undertaking them, and that it is better for them to bear many of the inconveniences of the present state than to resort to such a perilous remedy.

I will conclude with a general idea that includes within it not only all the particular ideas that have been expressed in this present chapter, but also most of those that this book has the purpose of putting forth.

[What was above all to be feared formerly is no longer to be feared and new dangers have arisen that our fathers did not know.][w]

In the centuries of aristocracy that preceded ours, there were very powerful individuals and a very feeble social authority. The very image of society was obscure and was constantly lost amid all the different powers that governed the citizens. The principal effort of the men of that time had to be to proceed to make the social power greater and to fortify it, to increase and to assure its prerogatives, and on the contrary, to restrict individual independence within more narrow limits, and to subordinate particular interest to the general interest.

v. In the margin of the copy: "<Where the passing sentiments that revolution suggests find themselves in sympathy with the permanent sentiments that equality gives.>"
w. In the margin of the copy: "Perhaps delete that?"

Other dangers and other concerns await the men of today.

Among most modern nations, the sovereign power, whatever its origin, its constitution and its name, has become almost omnipotent, and individuals fall more and more into the final degree of weakness and dependency.

Everything was different in the old societies. Unity and uniformity were found nowhere. In our societies, everything threatens to become so similar, that the particular figure of each individual will soon be lost entirely in the common physiognomy. Our fathers were always ready to abuse this idea that particular rights are worthy of respect, and we are naturally led to exaggerate this other, that the interest of one individual must always yield before the interest of several.

The political world is changing; from now on we must seek new remedies for new evils.

To fix for the social power extensive, but visible and immobile limits; to give to individuals certain rights and to guarantee to them the uncontested enjoyment of these rights; to preserve for the individual the little of independence, of strength and of originality that remain to him; to raise him up beside society and sustain him in the face of it: such seems to me to be the first goal of the legislator in the age we are entering.[x]

It could be said that the sovereigns of today only seek to create great things with men. I would like them to think a bit more about creating great men, to attach less value to the work and more to the worker,[y] and

---

x. "I would very much like you to tell me what makes the grandeur of man if it is not man himself./

"Who the devil does it concern except each one of us?" (*Rubish*, 2).

y. They limit themselves to wanting society to be great; I, man; they are interested in an ideal being, without a body; I, in God's creature, in my fellow man./

They attach more value to the work; I, to the worker./

To raise up and to make the individual greater, constant goal of great men in democratic centuries./

This 29 January 1838 (*Rubish*, 2).

Another rough draft expresses the same thought:

How will we be able to understand each other? I seek to live with dignity and honor, and you only seek to live.

to remember constantly that a nation cannot long remain strong when each man is individually weak, and that we have not yet found either social forms or political combinations that can create an energetic people by bringing together faint-hearted and soft citizens.[z]

I see among our contemporaries two opposite but equally fatal ideas.

Some see in equality only the anarchical tendencies that it engenders. They fear their free will; they are afraid of themselves.

The others, in smaller number, but better enlightened, have another view. Alongside the road that, starting at equality, leads to anarchy, they have finally found the path that seems to lead men invincibly toward servitude; they bend their soul in advance to this necessary servitude; and despairing of remaining free, they already adore at the bottom of their heart the master who must soon come.

The first abandon liberty because they consider it dangerous; the second because they judge it impossible.

If I had had this last belief, I would not have written the work that you

---

What you fear most from the democratic social state are the political troubles that it brings forth, and me, that is what I fear least about it. You dread democratic liberty, and I democratic despotism.

These men who, similar to domestic animals, worry little about having a master provided that the master feeds them, and who seek in life only to live.

[In the margin: Many men consider democratic civil laws as an evil and democratic political laws as another and the greatest evil; but I say that the one is the sole remedy that you can apply to the other.

All the idea of my politics is in this remark] (YTC, CVk, 2, pp. 53–54).

z. The manuscript and the copy of the chapter finish here. In the margin of the manuscript you find this note:

I can and perhaps I must stop here. I see vaguely, however, that there would be something more, and more striking to add, for finally I am still speaking in all that precedes only about the interest of society and not about that of the individual himself. Now, is not all the grandeur of man in the grandeur of the individual rather than in the grandeur of society, which is an ideal being produced from the mind of man? Society is made for the individual and not the individual for society. By what a strange reversal of things would you arrive at sacrificing the individual with the view of favoring society, and what singular detachment from himself would lead this last to acquiesce in such an attempt?

have just read; I would have limited myself to bemoaning in secret the destiny of my fellow men.

I wanted to put forth in full light the risks that equality makes human independence run, because I believe firmly that these risks are the most formidable as well as the least foreseen of all those that the future holds.[a] But I do not believe them insurmountable.

The men who live in the democratic centuries that we are entering naturally have the taste for independence.[b] Naturally they bear rules with impatience: the permanence of even the state they prefer wearies them. They love power; but they are inclined to scorn and to hate the one who exercises it, and they easily escape from between his hands because of their smallness and their very mobility.

These instincts will always be found, because they emerge from the core of the social state which will not change. For a long time they will prevent any despotism from being able to become established, and they will provide new weapons to each new generation that wants to fight in favor of the liberty of men.

So let us have for the future this salutary fear that makes us vigilant and combative, and not this sort of soft and idle terror that weakens and enervates hearts.[c]

a. The great men of paganism have often willingly sacrificed to false gods [v: idols] in which they did not believe, because they knew that peoples could imagine only under this crude image the idea of the divinity, one and supreme, belief in which is necessary to humanity.

In the same way statesmen, who know that legality is not *order* [v: is only the external form of order and not order], must however honor it [v: bend their knees before it] as the only permanent image of order that can be grasped by the organs of the common people [*vulgarius*] (*Rubish*, 2).

b. Idea of the [blank (ed.)] to show that the taste for *independence* is natural to men in times of equality and why; but that it is a secondary taste almost always subordinate to the taste for *power;* that this natural tendency toward liberty is however our anchor of salvation; that it is by developing it and by making it practical and manly that you can hope to obtain all the good of equality without its evils (YTC, CVk, 2, p. 49).

c. "It is a matter above all of proving that it is with the help of *liberty* that you can hope to prevent *license.* Everything is there. Fear must be put on the side of liberty if you want to succeed" (YTC, CVk, 2, pp. 52–53).

CHAPTER 8[a]

General View of the Subject[b]

a. In the first box of the *Rubish* (*Rubish,* 1), with the chapter on material enjoyments, in a jacket bearing the title HOW EQUALITY OF RANKS SUGGESTS TO MEN THE TASTE FOR LIBERTY AND FOR EQUALITY, you find this note: "Perhaps finish by a chapter entitled GENERAL VIEW OF THE SUBJECT, in which I recall the fatal march of equality. Perhaps here I will show that it is only by democracy that you can attenuate the evils of democracy, the impossibility and the danger of the government of the middle classes, the necessity to aim firmly for the government of all by all." (*Rubish,* 1). In the second box of the *Rubish,* the rough drafts and notes of this chapter are accompanied by various papers contained in a jacket that has as a title OF THE MANNER IN WHICH THE AMERICAN GOVERNMENTS ACT VIS-À-VIS ASSOCIATIONS. Tocqueville noted to the side: "I propose to delete this chapter." The ideas of these pages are found in different places in the last chapters.

b. [On a jacket: Last chapter. General view of the subject./

General appraisal of the effects of equality./

I can [only (ed.)] approach this summary frankly and grandly, otherwise it would seem out of place and incomplete. I must show myself wanting to reduce the entire picture that I have just painted to a narrow frame, setting aside details, or closing my eyes to them, no longer occupying myself with America, which opened the path to me; and after thus preparing the reader for something very general and with very few details, to keep the piece: I look at my country . . .

To begin by recalling the march of the four volumes.]

Capital and principal idea./

Influence of democracy on human morality.

Medium morality, perhaps in the view of God.

Interest which gains, men not virtuous, but steady.

Final chapter. I think. All of man is there./

Chapter too vast, too thorny. To refrain probably.

[On the following page] A final chapter.

Less individual independence, more national strength.

Less independence, more security.

Less independence of the sovereign, more independence of the subjects.

[On the following page] I do not believe in the definitive organization of the government of the middle classes, and if I believed it possible, I would oppose myself to it.

Before leaving forever the course that I have just covered, I would like to be able to encompass with a last look all the various features that mark the face of the new world, and finally to judge the general influence that equal-

---

Idea to put in the place where I show again the fatal march of equality.

[Here we omit several paragraphs (ed.).]

[On the following page] Finish the book by a great chapter that tries to summarize all the *democratic* subject and to draw from it *oratorically* the consequences for the world and in particular for Europe and us. Maxims of *conciliation,* of resignation, of union with the march of Providence, complete impartiality.

A simple and solemn movement, like the subject./

Capital idea.

That it is necessary to draw yourself out of particular points of view in order to place yourself, if possible, in general points of view that do not depend on either times or places. Penetrate as deeply as possible into the thought of God and judge from there.

[On the following page] Use democracy to moderate democracy. That is the sole path of salvation that is open to us. Discern the sentiments, the ideas, the laws that, without being hostile to the principles of democracy, without being naturally incompatible with democracy, can however correct its unfortunate tendencies and, while modifying it, become incorporated with it.

Beyond that everything is foolish and imprudent (YTC, CVk, 2, pp. 50–52).

In Tocqueville's papers you find these other plans:

Presumed order of the last chapter.

1. Summary of the four volumes.

2. Why democracy, certain sides of which a (illegible word), can be the best state in the eyes of God.

3. From now on democracy has nothing to fear except itself.

4. *Bad* and *good* democracy and if it must be *assured.*

It is from its ranks that its masters and its destroyers will come. It has nothing to fear from its enemies, but from its children (YTC, CVc, pp. 59–60).

Last chapter.

I said when beginning that the march of equality was irresistible. I believe it more and more. Movement of the rest of Europe as democratic by kings, as ours by the people. There is only one aristocracy that knows how to defend itself, that of England. All the others form command staffs without armies.

General fact flowing from the development of equality . . .

More honesty, fewer virtues.

Each man smaller, more ignorant, weaker, humanity greater, stronger, more knowledgeable.

Smaller individual efforts, a greater general result.

Less tranquillity, more power (YTC, CVk, 1, p. 4).

ity must exercise on the fate of men; but the difficulty of such an enterprise stops me; in the presence of such a great matter, I feel my sight fail and my reason falter.[c]

This new society, which I have sought to portray and which I want to judge, has only just been born. Time has not yet set its form; the great revolution that created it is still going on, and in what is happening today, it is nearly impossible to discern what must pass away with the revolution itself, and what must remain after it.

The world that is rising is still half caught in the ruins of the world that is falling, and amid the immense confusion presented by human affairs, no one can say which old institutions and ancient mores will remain standing and which will finally disappear.

Although the revolution that is taking place in the social state, the laws, the ideas, the sentiments of men, is still very far from being finished, already you cannot compare its works with anything that has been seen previously in the world. I go back century by century to the most distant antiquity; I notice nothing that resembles what is before our eyes. Since the past no longer clarifies the future, the mind moves in shadows.

But amid this picture so vast, so new, so confused, I already glimpse a few principal features which are becoming apparent and I point them out.

I see that the good and the bad are distributed equally enough in the world. Great wealth disappears; the number of small fortunes increases; desires and enjoyments multiply; there is no more extraordinary prosperity or irreversible poverty. Ambition is a universal sentiment; there are few vast ambitions. Each individual is isolated and weak; society is agile, far-sighted and strong; individuals do small things and the State immense ones.

Souls are not energetic; but mores are mild and legislation humane. If little great devotion, few very high, very brilliant, and very pure virtues are

---

c. In the margin: "<I cast my eyes over my country and I see there a universal transformation. I widen my view, I carry it by degrees to the extreme limits of the vast space occupied on the globe by the European race; everywhere I am struck by an analogous spectacle. Among all peoples, ancient institutions and ancient mores have disappeared or are disappearing in order to give place to something different. Everything that exists today [interrupted text (ed.)].>"

found, habits are steady, violence is rare and cruelty almost unknown. The lives of men become longer and their property more secure. Life is not very ornate, but very comfortable and very peaceful. There are few very delicate and very coarse pleasures, little courtesy in manners and little brutality in tastes. You scarcely find very learned men or very ignorant populations. Genius becomes rarer and enlightenment more common. The human mind is developed by the small combined efforts of all men, and not by the powerful impulse of a few of them. There is less perfection, but more fecundity in works. All the bonds of race, class, country are loosening; the great bond of humanity is tightening.[d]

If among all these various features, I seek the one that seems to me the most general and the most striking, I come to see that what is noticeable in fortunes reappears again in a thousand other forms. Nearly all the extremes become softer and are blunted; nearly all the salient points are worn away to make way for something middling, which is at the very same time less high and less low, less brilliant and less obscure than what was seen in the world.[e]

I run my eyes over this innumerable crowd composed of similar beings, in which nothing either rises or falls. The spectacle of this universal uniformity [and of this mediocrity] saddens me and chills me, and I am tempted to regret the society that is no more.

d. In the margin: "<This picture seems good enough to me, but it is incomplete. It perhaps contains some useless things, and there are some necessary ones to .-.-. To complete it, it is necessary to have gone through the whole book.>"

e. It is necessary to find in some part of the work, in the foreword or the last chapter, the idea of the *middle* that has been so dishonored in our times. Show that there is a firm, clear, voluntary way to see and to grasp the truth between two extremes. To conceive and to say that the truth is not in an absolute system.

[In the margin: I do not like the middle to be taken between grandeur and baseness, between courage and fear, between vice and virtue. But I like the middle between two opposite *excesses.*]

Dare to say somewhere the idea of L[ouis (ed.)]. that a difference must be made between absolute affirmation [v: certitude] and Pyrrhonism, that the system of probabilities is the only true one, the only *human* one, provided that probability causes you to act as energetically as certitude.

All that is poorly said, but the germ is there (YTC, CVk, 1, pp. 41–42).

When the world was filled with very great and very small, very rich and very poor, very learned and very ignorant, [very fortunate and very miserable] men, I turned my eyes away from the second to fix them only on the first, and the latter delighted my sight. But I understand that this pleasure arose from my weakness; it is because I cannot see all that surrounds me at the same time that I am allowed to choose in this way and to separate, among so many objects, those that it pleases me to consider. It is not the same for the all-powerful and eternal Being, whose eyes necessarily take in the whole of things, and who sees all of humanity and each man distinctly, though at the same time.

It is natural to believe that what most satisfies the sight of this creator and preserver of men, is not the singular prosperity of a few, but the greatest well-being of all; so what seems to me decline, is in his eyes progress; what hurts me, agrees with him. Equality is perhaps less elevated; but it is more just, and its justice makes its grandeur and its beauty.

I try hard to enter into this point of view of God, and from there I seek to consider and to judge human things.[f]

No one, on the earth, can yet assert in an absolute and general way that the new state of societies is superior to the old state; but it is already easy to see that it is different.

There are certain vices and certain virtues that were attached to the constitution of aristocratic nations and that are so contrary to the genius of the new peoples that you cannot introduce those vices and virtues among them. There are good tendencies and bad instincts that were foreign to the first that are natural to the second; ideas that occur by themselves to the imagination of the first and that the mind of the second rejects. They are like two distinct humanities, each of which has its particular advantages and disadvantages, its good and its evil which are its own.[g]

So you must be very careful about judging the societies that are being

f. "Who knows if, in the eyes of God, the beautiful is not the useful?" (YTC, CVa, p. 41).

g. "You must not aim to make democratic peoples as similar as possible to aristocratic nations, but to gain for them as much as possible the type of grandeur and prosperity that is appropriate to them" (*Rubish*, 2).

born by the ideas that you have drawn from those that are no longer. That would be unjust, for these societies, differing prodigiously from each other, are not comparable.

It would be scarcely more reasonable to ask of the men [v. democratic peoples] of today the particular virtues that resulted from the social state of their ancestors, since this social state itself has fallen, and since in its fall it swept away in a confused way all the good and all the bad that it carried with it.

But these things are still poorly understood today.

I notice a great number of my contemporaries who undertake to make a choice among the institutions, the opinions, the ideas that arose from the aristocratic constitution of the former society; they would willingly abandon some, but they would still like to retain others and carry them with them into the new world.

I think that those men use up their time and their strength in an honest and sterile work.

It is no longer a matter of retaining the particular advantages that inequality of conditions gains for men, but of assuring the new advantages that equality can offer them.[h] We must not aim to make ourselves similar to our fathers, but to work hard to attain the type of grandeur and happiness that is appropriate to us.

As for me, having reached the final end of my journey, I discern from afar, but all at once, all the various matters that I had contemplated sepa-

h. Equality of conditions, the absence of classes . . . are evils you say. It belittles human nature, establishes the mediocre in everything. Perhaps you are right.

Do you know a means to cure the evil by the opposites, that is to say by the reestablishment or even the maintaining of inequality, the permanent classification of men? No. At the very bottom of your heart you do not believe in the possibility of all these things.

But admitting that equality of conditions is an invincible fact, you contest its consequences in the political world; and you attack liberty and call despotism to your aid, and seek to assure present security at the expense of future races.

And it is here that you are clearly wrong. For there is only democracy (by this word I mean self-government) that can diminish and make bearable the inevitable evils of a democratic social state.

5 September 1837 (YTC, CVk, 2, p. 53).

rately while going along, and I feel full of fears and full of hopes.j I see great dangers that it is possible to avert, great evils that can be avoided or limited; and I become more and more confirmed in this belief that, to be honest and prosperous, it is still enough for democratic nations to want to be so.

I am not unaware that several of my contemporaries have thought that here below peoples are never masters of themselves, and that they obey necessarily I do not know what insurmountable and unintelligent force that arises from previous events, from race, from soil, or from climate.k

j. I see two distinct roads that open at the same time before the men of today. They touch at first, but as they get farther from the common point of departure, they move away from each other and an immense space between them is found at the end. The one leads to liberty and the other leads to servitude. And as you march along one or along the other, liberty becomes greater and servitude heavier. Each day that the space separating them expands, it is more difficult to cross it to find the good road again. Peoples have not yet reached the place where they must choose between these two paths. But all are getting closer to it. An irresistible force is pushing them there. I already see the first advancing. The others follow the first at unequal distances.

Although I may be the last one in this holy league, if it is forming, I am content.

Some push them toward chaos, the others drag them, little by little and without noticing, perhaps, toward the most stupefying of all servitudes. The nations hesitate, become disturbed and falter . . .

Oh! Who will open the way, who will carry the new banner, who will give his name to this glorious dawning. One man, whoever he may be, cannot do it, but an association of men could do so. Association of disinterested, honest or enterprising men (illegible word) sentiments . . . I will be distressed by them, but let me be allowed to say that I am not afraid of them.

As for my opinions on all the others, I do not defend myself; the public is the judge.

[On another page] I said at the beginning of this long work that peoples (vol. 1, p. 90) could draw two great political consequences from the democratic social state, that these consequences differed prodigiously from each other, but that they both emerged from the same fact. Here I am at the end of my course, and I feel myself more firm in this belief (YTC, CVd, pp. 20–22). Tocqueville is referring to the last paragraphs of chapter III of the first part of the first volume (p. 90).

k. Idea of *necessity,* of fatality. Explain how my system differs essentially from that of Chiquet [Mignet (ed.)] and company. Do a satirical portrait of the latter without naming individuals. Show that without claiming to be [a (ed.)] genius who embraces the necessities of the political order, there is a great weakness of mind and a great distaste for work. Explain how my system is perfectly compatible with human liberty.

Those are false and cowardly doctrines that can produce only weak men and pusillanimous nations. Providence has created humanity neither entirely independent nor completely slave. It traces around each man, it is true, a fatal circle out of which he cannot go; but within its vast limits, man is powerful and free; so are peoples.[m]

The nations of today cannot make conditions among them not be equal; but it depends on them whether equality leads them to servitude or liberty, to enlightenment or barbarism, to prosperity or misery.[n]

Apply these general ideas to democracy.

That is a very beautiful piece to place at the head or the tail of the work.

[In the margin: You have not reproached me as I anticipated for seeming to fall into the *mania* of the century. But I reproach myself for it because I do not want to fall into it. You absolve me, and I accuse myself. I wake up every morning obeying a general and eternal law that I did not know the night before.

Unfortunately, there are some of those laws] (YTC, CVa, pp. 58–59).

And in the same line:

To be very careful in the preliminary or final chapter to make it clearly understood that I am not exclusive in my point of view. Many particular causes like climate, race, religion influence the ideas and the sentiments of men, independently of the social state.

[To the side: The progress of enlightenment (illegible word), principal idea that I have constantly found on my road and at which I have not wanted to stop.]

The particular purpose of this book is not to deny these influences, but to put into relief the particular influence of the social state.

January 1838 (YTC, CVk, 1, pp. 47–48).

m. "I am profoundly convinced that democracy can be regulated and organized; it is not something easy, but it is something that can be done, and I add that it is the only thing left to do" (YTC, CVd, p. 19).

n. "A man is never *master* of his destiny because death can come to seize him in the execution of his wisest plans, but a people, which does not perish, remains always master of itself" (*Rubish*, 2).

Notes

Page 975

There are, however, aristocracies that have engaged in commerce with ardor and cultivated industry with success. The history of the world provides several striking examples. But in general it must be said that aristocracy is not favorable to the development of industry and of commerce. Only aristocracies of money are an exception to this rule.

Among the latter there is hardly any desire that does not need wealth to be satisfied. The love of wealth becomes, so to speak, the great highway for human passions. All the other passions lead to it or cross it.

The taste for money and the thirst for consideration and power then blend so well in the same souls that it becomes difficult to discern if it is out of ambition that men are greedy, or if it is out of greediness that they are ambitious. This is what happens in England, where you want to be rich in order to attain honors, and where you desire honors as the manifestation of wealth. The human spirit is then gripped on all sides and swept toward commerce and industry, which are the shortest roads that lead to opulence.

Moreover, this seems to me an exceptional and transitory fact. When wealth has become the only sign of aristocracy, it is very difficult for the rich to maintain themselves in power alone and to exclude all the others.

Aristocracy of birth and pure democracy are at the two extremes of the social and political state of nations; in the middle is found the aristocracy of money:[a] the latter is close to the aristocracy of birth in that it confers

a. "≠The aristocracy of money does not seem lasting to me. This form of society has something at the very same time of both aristocracy and democracy, and it leads from the one to the other by a more or less slow but inevitable march≠" (YTC, CVk, 1, p. 86).

great privileges on a small number of citizens; it is close to democracy in that the privileges can be successively acquired by all; it often forms like a natural transition between these two things, and you cannot say if it brings the reign of aristocratic institutions to an end, or if it already opens the new era of democracy.

Page 1050

I find in the journal of my trip the following piece, which will completely reveal the trials to which the women of America who agree to accompany their husbands into the wilderness are subjected. There is nothing that commends this picture to the reader except its great truth.[b]

. . . From time to time we came across new clearings. All these establishments were similar. I am going to describe the one where we stopped this evening; it will leave me with a picture of all the others.

The small bell that the pioneers carefully hang around the necks of the animals in order to find them in the woods announced to us from afar the approach to a clearing; soon we heard the sound of the ax that fells the trees of the forest. As we approach, signs of destruction announce to us the presence of civilized man. Cut branches cover the road; trunks half-charred by fire or mutilated by the ax still stand upright along our passage. We continue our march and we come to a woods in which all the trees seem to have been stricken by sudden death; in the middle of the summer, they present nothing more than the image of winter; examining them more closely we notice that in their bark a deep circle has been traced that, stopping the circulation of the sap, did not take long to make them die; we learn that this, in fact, is how the pioneer usually begins. Not able, during the first year, to cut all the trees that cover his new property, he sows corn under their branches and, by killing them, he prevents them from shading his crop. After this field, an incomplete beginning, a first step of civilization in the wilderness, we suddenly notice the cabin of the landowner; it is placed in the center of a ground more carefully cultivated than the rest, but

b. See pp. 1314–16 of Appendix II.

where man still sustains an unequal struggle against the forest. There the trees are cut, but not uprooted; their trunks still cover and clutter the ground that they formerly shaded. Around these dried-up remains, wheat, oak shoots, plants of all types, grasses of all kinds grow jumbled together and increase together on an intractable and half-wild ground. At the center of this vigorous and varied vegetation arises the house of the pioneer, or as it is called in this country, the *log house*. Like the field that surrounds it, this rustic dwelling announces a new and hurried work; its length does not seem to us to exceed thirty feet; its height, fifteen; its walls as well as the roof are formed from tree trunks not squared off, between which moss and earth have been placed to prevent the cold and the rain from penetrating the interior.

Since night was approaching, we determined to go to ask the owner of the *log house* for shelter.

At the sound of our steps, the children who were rolling around amid the debris of the forest get up precipitously and flee toward the house as if frightened at the sight of a man, while two large half-wild dogs, ears upright and muzzles elongated, emerge from their cabin and come growling to cover the retreat of their young masters. The pioneer himself appears at the door of his dwelling; he casts a rapid and searching glance at us, signals to his dogs to come back into the house; he serves as their example himself without showing that our sight excites his curiosity or his concern.

We enter the *log house*. The interior does not recall the cabins of the peasants of Europe; you find more of the superfluous and less of the necessary.

There is only a single window at which hangs a muslin curtain; on a hearth of beaten earth crackles a great fire that lights up the whole interior of the building; above this hearth you notice a beautiful rifle with a grooved barrel, a deer skin, eagle feathers; to the right of the chimney a map of the United States is spread which the wind flaps and agitates by coming through the chinks in the wall; near it, on a shelf made from a rough-hewn plank, are placed a few volumes. I notice the Bible, the first six cantos of Milton and two plays of Shakespeare. Along the walls are placed trunks instead of armoires; in the center is found a crudely worked table, whose feet, made from wood still green and with the bark still on, seem to have grown by themselves out of the earth on the spot occupied by the table; I see on this table a teapot of English porcelain, some silver spoons, a few chipped cups and some newspapers.

The master of this dwelling has the angular features and slender limbs that distinguish the inhabitant of New England; it is clear that this man was not born in the wilderness where we meet him; his physical constitution is enough to announce that his first years were spent within an intellectual society, and that he belongs to this restless, reasoning and adventurous race that does coldly what only the ardor of the passions explains and which subjects itself for a time to uncivilized life the better to conquer and to civilize the wilderness.

When the pioneer sees that we are crossing the threshold of his dwelling, he comes to meet us and extends his hand, as is the custom; but his physiognomy remains rigid; he speaks first to interrogate us about what is happening in the world, and when he has satisfied his curiosity, he becomes silent; you would think him fatigued by troublesome individuals and by chatter. We interrogate him in turn, and he gives us all the information we need; then he occupies himself without eagerness but diligently with providing for our needs. Seeing him devote himself in this way to these kind attentions, why, despite ourselves, do we feel our gratitude cool? It is because he, while exercising hospitality, seems to be submitting to a painful necessity of his fate; he sees a duty that his position imposes on him, not a pleasure.

At the other end of the room is seated a woman who is rocking a young child on her knees. She nods to us without interrupting herself. Like the pioneer, this woman is in the prime of life; her appearance seems superior to her condition; her dress still announces even now a barely extinguished taste for finery; but her delicate limbs seem weakened; her features are tired; her eyes gentle and serious. You see spread over her whole physiognomy a religious resignation, a profound peace of the passions, and I do not know what natural and tranquil steadfastness that meets all the evils of life without fearing them or defying them.

Her children crowd around her; they are full of health, excitement, and energy; they are true sons of the wilderness. Their mother from time to time gives them looks full of melancholy and joy. To see their strength and her weakness, you would say that she has exhausted herself by giving them life, and that she does not regret what they have cost her.

The house inhabited by the emigrants has no interior wall or attic. Into the single room that it contains, the entire family comes to find shelter at night. This dwelling by itself alone forms like a small world; it is the ark of civilization lost amid an ocean of leaves. One hundred steps further the eternal forest spreads its shadow and the wilderness begins again.

Page 1052

It is not equality of conditions that makes men immoral and irreligious. But when men are immoral and irreligious at the same time as being equal, the effects of immorality and irreligion occur in the open easily because men have little influence on each other and because no class exists that can take charge of keeping order in society. Equality of conditions never creates corruption of morals, but sometimes it allows it to happen.

Pages 1085–87

If you put aside all those who do not think and those who dare not say what they think, you will still find that the immense majority of Americans seem satisfied with the political institutions that govern them; and in fact, I believe that they are. I regard this cast of public opinion as an indication, but not as a proof of the absolute goodness of American laws. National pride, the satisfaction given by the laws to certain dominant passions, fortuitous events, unnoticed vices, and more than all of that the interest of a majority that silences those who oppose it, can for a long time delude an entire people as well as one man.

See England in the whole course of the XVIIIth century. Never did a nation lavish more praise on itself; no people was ever more perfectly content with itself; everything then was good in its constitution, everything there was irreproachable, even its most visible faults. Today a multitude of Englishmen seems to be busy only with proving that this constitution was defective in a thousand places. Who was right, the English people of the last century, or the English people of today?

The same thing happened in France. It is certain that under Louis XIV the great mass of the nation was passionate about the form of government that then ruled society. They are very much mistaken who believe that the French character of that time was debased. In that century in France, there could be servitude in certain respects, but the spirit of servitude was certainly not found. The writers of the time felt a sort of real enthusiasm in raising the royal power above all others, and there was no one, even including the obscure peasant in his cottage, who did not take pride in the glory of the sovereign and who did not die with joy while crying: "Long live the King!" These same forms have become odious to us. Who was wrong, the French of Louis XIV, or the French of today?

So it is not only on the predispositions of a people that you must rely in order to judge its laws, since from one century to another they change, but on more elevated grounds and a more general experience.

The love that a people shows for its laws proves only one thing: that you must not hasten to change them.

Page 1169

In the chapter to which this note relates I have just shown one danger; I want to point out another rarer one, but one that, if it ever appeared, would be very much more to fear.

If the love of material enjoyments and the taste for well-being that equality naturally suggests to men, while taking hold of the spirit of a democratic people, came to fill them entirely, national mores would become so antipathetic to the military spirit that armies themselves would perhaps end up loving peace despite the particular interest that leads them to desire war. Placed in the middle of this universal softness, soldiers would come to think that it was indeed better to rise gradually, but comfortably and without efforts, in peace, than to buy a rapid advancement at the cost of the strains and the miseries of camp life. In this spirit, the army would take up arms without zeal and would use them without energy; it would allow itself to be led to the enemy rather than marching there by itself.

You must not believe that this pacific inclination of the army would distance it from revolutions, for revolutions, and above all military revolutions, which are usually very quick, often carry great risks, but do not require extended efforts; they satisfy ambition at less cost than war; in revolutions you only risk your life, to which the men of democracies are less attached than to their comforts.

There is nothing more dangerous for the liberty and the tranquillity of a people than an army that is afraid of war, because, no longer seeking its grandeur and its influence on the fields of battle, it wants to find them elsewhere. So it could happen that the men who compose a democratic army would lose the interests of the citizen without gaining the virtues of the soldier, and that the army would cease to be warlike without ceasing to be turbulent.

I will repeat here what I already said above. The remedy for such dangers is not in the army, but in the country. A democratic people that maintains manly mores will always as needed find warrior mores in its soldiers.

Page 1200

Men put the grandeur of the idea of unity in the means; God, in the end; the result is that this idea of grandeur leads us to a thousand petty things. To force all men to march with the same step, toward the same purpose, that is a human idea. To introduce an infinite variety in actions, but to combine them so that all these actions lead by a thousand paths toward the accomplishment of a great design, that is a divine idea.

The human idea of unity is almost always sterile; that of God, immensely fruitful. Men think to attest to their grandeur by simplifying the means. It is the purpose of God which is simple, His means vary infinitely.[c]

c. "Every uniform rule is necessarily tyrannical because men are never alike" (UNITY, CENTRALIZATION, ADMINISTRATIVE DESPOTISM, *Rubish,* 2).

Page 1206

A democratic people is not only led by its tastes to centralize power; the passions of all those who lead it push it there constantly.

You can easily predict that almost all of the ambitious and capable citizens contained within a democratic country will work without let-up to expand the attributions of the social power, because all hope to direct it one day. It is a waste of time to want to prove to those men that extreme centralization can harm the State, since they are centralizing for themselves.

Among the public men of democracies, there are hardly any men except those who are very disinterested or very mediocre who want to decentralize power. The first are rare and the others powerless.

Page 1247

I have often asked myself what would happen if, amid the softness of democratic mores and as a result of the restless spirit of the army, a military government was ever established among some of the nations of today.

I think that the government itself would not be far from the portrait that I drew in the chapter to which this note relates, and that it would not reproduce the savage features of the military oligarchy.

I am persuaded that in this case there would be a kind of fusion between the habits of the clerk and those of the soldier. The administration would take on something of the military spirit, and the military some of the practices of the civil administration. The result of this would be a regular, clear, plain, absolute command; the people made into the image of the army, and society kept like a barracks.

Page 1260–61

You cannot say in an absolute and general way that the greatest danger of today is license or tyranny, anarchy or despotism. Both are equally to be feared and can emerge as easily from the same single cause, which is *general apathy*, fruit of individualism; this apathy means that the day when the executive power gathers some strength, it is able to oppress, and that the day after, when a party can put thirty men in the field, the latter is equally able to oppress. Since neither the one nor the other is able to establish anything lasting, what makes them succeed easily prevents them from succeeding for long. They arise because nothing resists them, and they fall because nothing sustains them.

What is important to combat is therefore much less anarchy or despotism than apathy, which can create almost indifferently the one or the other.

APPENDIX I

Journey to Lake Oneida[a]

On July 8, 1831, at sunrise, we left the small village called Fort Brewerton, and we began to advance toward the northeast.

About one mile from the house of our host, a path opens in the forest; we hastened to take it. The heat was beginning to become uncomfortable. After a windy night had followed a morning without any cool breeze. Soon we found ourselves sheltered from the rays of the sun and in the middle of one of these deep forests of the New World whose somber and wild majesty grips the imagination and fills the soul with a sort of religious terror.

How to paint such a spectacle? On a marshy terrain where a thousand small streams, not yet imprisoned by the hand of man, run and are lost in liberty, nature has scattered pell-mell and with an incredible profusion the seeds of nearly all the plants that creep on the earth or rise above the soil.

Over our heads was spread as it were a vast dome of greenery. Under this thick veil and amid the humid depths of the woods, the eye saw an immense confusion; a sort of chaos. Trees of all ages, foliage of all colors, herbs, fruits, flowers of a thousand species, intermingled, intertwined in the same places. Generations of trees have followed each other there with-

---

a. *Journey to Lake Oneida* and *A Fortnight in the Wilderness* were written by Tocqueville during his journey in America. If he had not wanted to publish them, it was because he was concerned about not entering into competition on this point with Beaumont. *Journey to Lake Oneida* was published for the first time by Beaumont in *Œuvres et correspondance inédites d'Alexis de Tocqueville, OCB,* V, pp. 161–71. It has recently been included in *Voyages en Sicile et aux États-Unis, OC,* V, 1, pp. 336–41. Tocqueville presented a first version in a letter of 25 July 1831 to his sister-in-law, Alexandrine (reproduced with some modifications in *OCB,* VII, pp. 39–45). The family archives contain a copy of the text in the hand of Mary Mottley and corrected by Tocqueville. The episode also appears in *Marie,* II, pp. 45–46 and 329.

out interruption for centuries, and the earth is covered with their remains. Some seem struck down yesterday; others, already half settled into the earth, present nothing more than a hollow and flat surface; others finally are reduced to dust and serve as fertilizer for their last shoots. In the midst of them a thousand diverse plants hasten to emerge in their turn. They slip between these immobile cadavers, creep along their surface, penetrate beneath their withered bark, lift up and scatter their powdery remains.[b] It is like a struggle between death and life. Sometimes, we happened to encounter an immense tree that the wind had uprooted, but the rows are so close together in the forest that, despite its weight, it was not able to make it to the ground. It still balanced its dry branches in the air.

A solemn silence reigned amid this solitude; you saw only a few or no animated creatures, man was missing and yet it was not a desert. Everything, on the contrary, showed a productive force in nature unknown elsewhere; everything was activity; the air seemed impregnated with an odor of vegetation. It seemed as if you heard an internal noise that revealed the work of creation and as if you saw sap and life circulating in always open channels.

It was amid this imposing solitude and in the light of an uncertain day that we walked for several hours, without hearing any noise other than that made by our horses trampling underfoot the leaves piled up by several winters or pushing with difficulty through the dry branches that covered the path. We kept silent ourselves, our souls were filled with the grandeur and the novelty of the spectacle. Finally we heard the echo of the first blows of an ax which announced in the distance the presence of a European. Felled trees, burned and blackened trunks, some plants useful to the life of man sown amid a confused mixture of a hundred various remnants, led us to the habitation of the pioneer. At the center of a rather narrow circle drawn

b. Several of these sentences are found word for word in the *Democracy*. Cf. pp. 37–38 and 459–61 of the first volume.

around it by iron and fire arose the crude house of the forerunner of European civilization. It was like the oasis in the middle of the desert.

After conversing a few moments with the inhabitant of this place, we resumed our course and a half-hour later we arrived at a fisherman's cabin built on the very shores of the lake that we were coming to visit.

Lake Oneida is situated in the middle of low hills and at the center of still respectable forests. A belt of thick foliage surrounds it on all sides, and its waters moisten the roots of trees that are reflected in its transparent and tranquil surface. The isolated cabin of a fisherman rose alone on its shores. Moreover, no sail appeared on its entire surface; you did not even see smoke rise above its woods, for the European, without having completely taken possession of its banks, had already approached closely enough to exile the numerous and warlike tribe that had once given the lake its name.

About one mile from the shore on which we stood were two islands, oval in form and of equal length. These islands are covered by a wood so thick that it entirely conceals the earth that supports it; you would say two clumps of trees floating peacefully on the surface of the lake.

No road passes near this place; you do not see in these regions great industrial establishments, or places famous for their picturesque beauty. Yet it was not chance that had led us close to this solitary lake. It was on the contrary the goal and the end of our journey.

Already many years ago, a book entitled *Journey to Lake Oneida* had fallen into my hands.[c] The author told about a young Frenchman and his

---

c. Sophie von la Roche, *Erscheinungen am See Oneida* (Leipzig: H. Gräff, 1798), 3 vols. Tocqueville, who tried to learn German on several occasions, probably had a rudimentary knowledge of this language only when he was preparing the *Old Regime*. He must have read the abridged version of the book of Sophie von la Roche, which was published in French by Joachim Heinrich Campe with the title *Voyage d'un Allemand au Lac Onéida*, as part of the collection *Bibliothèque géographique et instructive des jeunes gens, ou recueil de voyages* . . . (Paris: J. E. Gabriel Dufour, 1803), X, pp. 1–170. See Victor Lange, "Visitors to Lake Oneida, An Account of the Background of Sophie von la Roche's novel 'Erscheinungen am See Oneida,' " *Symposium* 2, no. 1 (1948): 48–78. It is not the only time that the reading of a novel pushed Tocqueville to travel. The reading

wife, chased from their country by the storms of our first Revolution, who had come to seek a refuge on one of the islands that the lake surrounds with its waters.[d] There, separated from the entire universe, far from the tempests of Europe, and rejected by the society that gave them birth, these two unfortunates lived for each other, consoled each other in their misfortune.

The book had left a deep and lasting mark on my soul. Whether this effect on me was due to the talent of the author, to the real charm of events, or to the influence of age, I could not say; but the remembrance of the two French inhabitants of Lake Oneida had not faded from my memory. How many times had I not envied the tranquil delights of their solitude. The domestic happiness, the charms of the married state, love itself mingling in my mind with the image of the solitary island where my imagination had created a new Eden. This story, told to my traveling companion, had deeply moved him in turn. We often happened to talk about it, and we always ended up repeating either with laughter or with sadness: happiness in the world exists only on the shores of Lake Oneida. When events that were impossible for us to foresee posted us both to America, this memory returned to us with more force. We promised ourselves to go to visit our two French compatriots if they still existed, or at least to travel over to their dwelling-place. Admire here the strange power of the imagination over the mind of man; these wild places, this silent and immobile lake, these islands covered with greenery did not strike us as new objects; on the contrary, we seemed to see once again a place where we had passed part of our youth.

We hurried to enter the fisherman's cabin. The man was in the woods. An old woman lived there alone. She came limping to greet us at the doorway of her house. "What do you call this green island that arises a mile from here in the middle of the lake?" we said to her. "It is called French-

---

of *Kenilworth* by Walter Scott will be the origin of an evening excursion and of an account very similar to this one. See note e of p. 799 of the second volume.

Certain passages of this account recall the fifth promenade of [Rousseau's] *Rêveries du promeneur solitaire.*

d. "For a bit of powder and lead, they bought the island from the Indians." Letter of Tocqueville to his sister-in-law, Alexandrine (Batavia, 25 July 1831), YTC, BIa2, and *OCB*, VII, p. 40.

man's island," she answered. "Do you know why it has been given that name?" "I am told it was named this because of a Frenchman who, many years ago, came there to live." "Was he alone?" "No, he brought his young wife with him." "Do they still live in this place?" "Twenty-one years ago, when I came to settle in this place, the French were no longer on the island."[e] I recall that I had the curiosity to go to visit it. This island that appears so wild to you from here was then a beautiful place; its interior was carefully cultivated, the house of the French was placed in the middle of an orchard, surrounded by fruits and flowers. A large vinestock climbed up its walls and then surrounded it on all sides, but without an inhabitant, the house had already fallen into ruins. "So what became of the two French?" "The woman died, the man abandoned the island, and we don't know what became of him since." "Could you entrust us with the boat that is tied by your door in order to cross the part of the lake that separates us from the island?" "Very willingly, but it is a long way to row and the work is hard for men who are not used to it, and besides what could you see of interest in a place that has become wild again?"

Since we hastened, without answering her, to put the dingy in the water, she said, "I see what it is, you want to buy this island; the soil is good and land is not yet expensive in our district." We answered her that we were travelers. "Then," she started again, "you are undoubtedly relatives of the Frenchman, and he charged you with visiting his property." "Even less," we replied, "we do not even know his name."[f] The good woman shook her head with incredulity and we, maneuvering the oars, began to advance rapidly toward Frenchman's island.

During this short crossing, we kept a profound silence; our hearts were full of sweet and painful emotions. As we approached, it made less sense to us that this island could have been inhabited once, so wild were its sur-

e. In his letter to Alexandrine, Tocqueville writes instead: "and they were still there when we ourselves came, now twenty-two years ago, to live in this place." *Ibid.,* p. 41.

f. Devatines, Desvatins, De Wattines, Vatine, and others, depending on the different versions of the story. André Jardin and George Pierson (*Lettres d'Amérique,* p. 94, note 3) believe him to be a member of the family La Croix de Watines.

roundings. Little was needed for us to believe ourselves the victims of a false report. Finally we reached its bank, and slipping under the immense branches that the trees projected over the lake, we began to penetrate further. We first crossed a circle of century-old trees that seemed to defend the approach to the place. Beyond the rampart of foliage we suddenly discovered another sight. A sparse undergrowth and a young cluster of trees filled the whole interior of the island. In the forests that we had crossed in the morning, we had often seen man struggling, hand to hand, against nature, and succeeding, though with difficulty, to remove its energetic and wild character in order to bend it to his laws. Here, on the contrary, we saw the forest reclaiming its dominion, marching once again toward the conquest of the wilderness, defying man and making the fleeting traces of his victory disappear rapidly.

It was easy to recognize that a diligent hand had once cleared the place now occupied in the center of the island by the young generation of trees that I spoke about. You did not find old trunks spread over the debris. Everything there, on the contrary, smacked of youth. It was clear that the surrounding trees had grown offshoots in the middle of the abandoned fields, weeds had grown in the place that formerly supported the crop of the exile, brambles and parasitic plants had come to retake possession of their former domain. Scarcely here and there did you find the trace of a fence or the sign of a field. For an hour we tried unsuccessfully to find a few vestiges of the abandoned house in the foliage of the woods and amid the undergrowth that cluttered the ground. This rural luxury that the wife of the fisherman had just described to us, the lawn, the flowerbed, the flowers, the fruits, these products of civilization that an ingenious tenderness had introduced into the middle of a wilderness, all had disappeared with the beings who had lived there. We were going to give up our effort, when we noticed an apple tree half dead of old age; this began to put us on the track. Near there a plant that we at first took for a creeper climbed along the highest trees intertwining with their slender trunks or hanging like a garland of foliage from their branches; examining it more closely, we recognized a vinestock. Then we were able to judge with certainty that we were on the very emplacement chosen, forty years ago, by our two unfortunate compatriots to make their last refuge. But barely by digging in the thick bed of leaves that covered the soil, were we able to find a few remnants falling into rot that in a bit of time would have ceased to exist. As for the very remains of the woman who was not afraid to exchange the delights of civilized life for a tomb in a deserted island of the New World, it was impossible for us to find a trace. Had the exile left this precious trust in the wilderness? Had he, on the contrary, carried it to the place where he himself ended his life? No one could tell us that.

Perhaps those who will read these lines will not imagine the sentiments that they recount and will treat them as exaggeration and chimera? But I will say nonetheless that, with our hearts full of emotion, agitated by fears and hopes, and animated by a sort of religious sentiment, we devoted ourselves to this minute research and pursued the traces of these two beings whose name, family and, in part, whose story were unknown to us. They attracted our attention only because they had felt in these very places the sufferings and joys that have their source in all hearts and are therefore of interest to all hearts.g

Is there a misery greater than that of this man!

Here is an unfortunate man whom human society has offended; his fellows have rejected, banished him and forced him to renounce their company and then to flee from them into the wilderness. A single being attached herself to his steps, followed him into seclusion, came to dress the wounds of his soul and to substitute for the joys of the world the most penetrating emotions of the heart. There he is reconciled to his destiny. He has forgotten revolutions, parties, cities, his family, his rank, his fortune; he finally breathes. His wife dies. Death comes to strike her and it spares him. Unfortunate man! What is to become of him? Is he going to remain alone in the wilderness? Will he return to a society where he has been forgotten for a long time? He is no longer made either for seclusion or for the world; he would no longer know how to live either with men or without them; he is neither a savage nor a civilized man; he is nothing but a remnant similar to those trees of the American forest that the wind has had the strength to uproot, but not to pull down; he is upright, but he is no longer living.

g. ". . . despite its natural beauty, this island by itself was of only slight interest to me; but a man had lived there, and this man was French, unfortunate and proscribed!" Beaumont, *Marie*, II, p. 329.

After traveling across the island in all directions, after visiting its slightest remnants, and after listening to the icy silence that now reigns beneath its shadows, we retook the road to the continent.[h]

Not without regret, I saw the vast rampart of greenery fade into the distance. It had for so many years known how to defend the two exiles against the European's bullet and the savage's arrow, but it was not able to hide their cottage from the invisible blows of death.[j]

h. On July 8, 1831, returning from his journey to Frenchman's Island, Tocqueville wrote: "What most intensely interested and moved me, not only since I have been in America, but also since I have traveled, is this trip." Pocket notebook 1, YTC, BIIa, and *Voyage, OC,* V, 1, p. 162. The emotion seems to have been so profound that henceforth solitude and melancholy would always be associated in the mind of Tocqueville with the American *wilderness.*

j. George W. Pierson, in *Tocqueville and Beaumont in America* (pp. 197–205), shows that the true history of the two French is far from the romantic version that Tocqueville learned about. The accounts of various travelers who met them indicate that the two French had arrived in America in 1786, and not at the time of the French Revolution, and that they had moved to Oneida only after being ruined in various enterprises. For some time, they inhabited the island with their three children and, far from enjoying their condition, everything leads us to believe that, on the contrary, they hoped for nothing other than to return to France. Their little appreciation for the inhabitants of the country seems to have put them on bad terms with their neighbors. They seem in the end to have found the money necessary to go back to France.

Tocqueville and Beaumont were not able to stop themselves from preferring the version of Sophie von la Roche. Like the French of this story, they left France after a revolution; their future was equally uncertain. What event could occur during their absence that would force them to become exiles in America? How not to let yourself be captivated by a drama that has as a setting an island and American nature, great and wild? Can we blame Tocqueville for having embellished the story and for having dreamed so romantically about the remains of the young French woman?

"Does the man who no longer lives have some appreciable advantage over the man who has never been?" Tocqueville asked himself in *Visit to Kenilworth.* "They both exist only by the will of those who are occupied with them. If the fictional being is more attractive than the real being, why would he occupy their thought less?" (YTC, CXIb12, and *OCB,* VII, p. 119).

APPENDIX 2

A Fortnight in the Wilderness[a]

Written aboard the steamboat "Superior."
Begun the first of August 1831.

One of the things that most intensely piqued our curiosity when coming to America was to travel across the farthest limits of European civilization and, if time permitted, even to visit a few of those Indian tribes that have preferred to flee into the most untamed wilderness than to yield to what whites call the delights of the life of society. But it is more difficult than you think to find the wilderness today. From New York, as we advanced toward the northwest, the goal of our journey seemed to flee before us. We traveled through some places famous in the history of the Indians; we encountered valleys that they named; we crossed rivers that still carry the name of their tribes, but everywhere the hut of the savage has given way to the house of the civilized man. The woods had fallen; the uninhabited places took on life.

We seemed, however, to follow in the footsteps of the natives. People said to us, ten years ago they were here; there, five years ago; there, two years ago. In the place where you see the most beautiful church of the village, a person told us, I cut down the first tree of the forest. Here, another told

---

a. Beaumont published *A Fortnight in the Wilderness* in the December 1, 1860, issue of the *Revue des deux mondes,* pp. 565–606. He included it afterward in his edition of the works of Tocqueville (*OCB,* V, pp. 173–258). In the new edition of the works, the text appears in the volume of the notes of the American journey (*OC,* V, 1, pp. 342–87). Also see Beaumont, *Marie,* II, pp. 56–91.

We have used the copy that exists at Yale (YTC, BIIIa), which contains variants of the version published by Beaumont.

us, the great council of the Iroquois confederation took place. "And what has become of the Indians," I said? "The Indians," our host replied, "they are beyond the Great Lakes, I do not know where. It is a race that is becoming extinct; they are not made for civilization: it kills them."

Man becomes accustomed to everything. To death on the fields of battle, to death in hospitals, to kill and to suffer. He gets used to all sights. An ancient people, the first and the legitimate master of the American continent, melts away daily like snow in the rays of the sun and disappears before your eyes from the surface of the earth. In the same areas and in its place, another race increases with a still more surprising rapidity. By this race forests fall, swamps are drained; lakes like seas, immense rivers vainly resist its triumphant march. Uninhabited places become villages, villages become cities. The daily witness to these marvels, the American sees nothing in all of that to astonish him. This unbelievable destruction, this still more surprising increase seems to him the usual course of the events of this world. He becomes accustomed to it as if to the immutable order of nature.

Thus, always in search of savages and of the wilderness, we traveled across the 360 miles that separate New York from Buffalo.

The first object that struck our eyes was a large number of Indians who had gathered that day in Buffalo to receive payment for the lands they had surrendered to the United States.

I do not believe I have ever felt a more complete disappointment than at the sight of these Indians. I was full of memories of M. de Chateaubriand[b] and of Cooper, and I expected to see, in the natives of America,

---

b. It was at Oneida Castle that the travelers had seen Indians for the first time. Some among them had run after their coach asking for alms. "We met the last among them on our route" writes Tocqueville to his mother about the Indians; "they ask for alms and are as inoffensive as their fathers were formidable." YTC, BIa2, and *OCB*, VII, p. 38. See Beaumont, *Lettres d'Amérique*, p. 94.

Tocqueville had elsewhere described Atala as follows:

Concerning this, do you know what Atala or someone like her is? I must give you the description so that you can judge her resemblance to the one of *M. de Chateaubriand*. Atala is an Indian woman of a very dark *café au lait* color, whose straight and shining hair falls perfectly straight to the small of her back. She usually has a large, almost

savages on whose face nature had left the trace of some of those lofty virtues that the spirit of liberty brings forth. I thought I would find in them men whose bodies had been developed by hunting and war and who would lose nothing by being seen naked. You can judge my astonishment by comparing this portrait with the one that is about to follow:

The Indians that I saw that night were small in stature; their limbs, as much as you could judge them under their clothing, were spindly and a bit wiry; their skin, instead of presenting a tint of reddish copper, as is commonly believed, was of a bronze so dark at first glance it seemed to be very close to that of mulattos. Their black and shining hair fell with a singular straightness onto their necks and shoulders. Their mouths were in general

---

aquiline nose, a wide mouth equipped with gleaming teeth and two large black eyes that in daylight are quite similar to those of a cat at night. Do not think that with this natural beauty she neglects her appearance. Not at all. First of all, around her eyes, she draws a black stripe; then underneath, a beautiful red stripe; then, a blue one; then, a green one; until her face resembles a rainbow. Then she hangs from each ear a kind of set of Chinese bells that weighs a half-pound. In addition, those who are the most *worldly* put through their nostrils a large ring of tin that hangs over their mouths and produces the most gracious effect. They also add a necklace composed of large discs on which various wild animals are carved. Their garment consists of a type of cloth tunic that falls a little below their knees. They are usually draped with a blanket that at night serves as their bed. You are still not at the end of the portrait. The style in the woods is to walk pigeon-toed. I do not know if it is more unnatural than to walk with the feet pointed outward; but our European eyes get used to this kind of beauty with difficulty. Do you imagine that to achieve this effect the Indian woman binds her feet from childhood, so that at twenty years of age, the two tips of her feet face each other while walking. Then she elicits all compliments and is reputed to be among the most *fashionable*. All that I know is that I would not want to take the place of Chactas near her for all the gold in the world. The Indian men are, moreover, better than their women. They are large, strapping young men, built like stags and with their agility. They have a charming expression when they smile and resemble devils incarnate when they are angry (letter to the vicomtesse Hippolyte de Tocqueville, Albany, 7 September 1831, YTC, BIa2).

Beaumont was of the same opinion: "I do not know up to now where M. de Chateaubriand took the type for his Atala. I see a few Indian men who are fairly good in their person, but the women are frightful and repulsive." Letter to Ernest de Chabrol (2 August 1831), *Lettres d'Amérique*, p. 114.

inordinately large, the facial expression ignoble and nasty. Their physiognomy proclaimed their profound depravity that only a long abuse of the benefits of civilization can give. You would have said men belonging to the lowest population of our great European cities. And yet they were still savages. With the vices that they got from us, was mingled something of the barbaric and uncivilized that made them a hundred times still more repulsive. These Indians did not carry weapons. They were covered by European clothes, but they did not use them in the same way we did.[c] You saw that they were not used to them and still found themselves imprisoned in their folds. With the ornaments of Europe, they joined products of a barbaric luxury, feathers, enormous earrings and shell necklaces. The movements of these men were rapid and disorderly, their voices shrill and discordant, their looks restless and savage. At first sight, you would have been tempted to see in each one of them only a beast of the forest to which education had been quite able to give the appearance of a man, but that had nonetheless remained an animal. These weak and depraved creatures belonged, however, to one of the most famous tribes of the former American world. We had before us, and it is pitiful to say so, the last remnants of the celebrated Confederation of the Iroquois whose manly wisdom was no less known than their courage and who for a long time held the balance between the two greatest European nations.

You would be wrong, however, to want to judge the Indian race on the basis of this ill-formed example, this lost offshoot of a wild tree that had grown up in the mire of our cities. That would be to repeat the error that we committed ourselves and that we had the occasion to recognize later.

That evening we left the city and a little distance from the last houses we saw an Indian lying along the road. It was a young man. He was motionless and we thought he was dead. A few stifled groans that escaped painfully from his chest let us know that he was still alive and was fighting one of those dangerous bouts of drunkenness caused by brandy. The sun had

---

c. "Some were covered with blankets; some women [with] pants and hats; some men with women's clothing" (alphabetic notebook A, 20 July 1831, YTC, BIIa, and *Voyage, OC*, V, 1, p. 224).

already set; the ground was becoming more and more damp. Everything announced that this unfortunate young man would give up his last breath there, unless he were helped. It was the time when the Indians left Buffalo to go back to their village; from time to time a group of them happened to pass by near us. They approached, brutally turned over the body of their compatriot in order to see who he was and then began to walk again without deigning to respond to our comments. Most of these men were drunk themselves. Finally a young Indian woman came along who at first seemed to approach with a certain interest. I thought that it was the wife or the sister of the dying man. She looked at him attentively, called his name out loud, felt his heart and, being assured that he was alive, tried to draw him out of his lethargy. But since her efforts were futile, we saw her become furious with this inanimate body that lay before her. She struck his head, twisted his face with her hands, trampled on him. While abandoning herself to these acts of ferocity, she let out inarticulate and wild cries that, at this time, still seem to reverberate in my ears. Finally we believed that we had to intervene, and we ordered her peremptorily to withdraw. She obeyed, but we heard her let out a burst of barbaric laughter as she went away.

Back in the city, we told several people about the young Indian. We spoke about the imminent danger to which he was exposed; we even offered to pay his expenses at an inn. All of that was futile. We couldn't get anyone to get involved. Some said to us: These men are used to drinking to excess and to sleeping on the ground. They do not die of such accidents. Others asserted that probably the Indian would die; but you read this half-expressed thought on their lips: What is the life of an Indian? That, deep down, was the general sentiment. Amidst this society so well-ordered, so prudish, so full of morality and virtue, you find a complete insensitivity; a sort of cold and implacable egoism when it concerns the natives of America. The inhabitants of the United States do not hunt the Indians with hounds and horn as the Spanish of Mexico did. But it is the same ruthless sentiment that animates the European race here as well as everywhere else.

How many times in the course of our travels did we not meet honest city dwellers who said to us in the evening, calmly seated in a corner of their home: Each day the number of Indians is decreasing. It isn't that we often wage war on them, but the brandy that we sell to them at a low cost removes more of them every year than we could do with our arms. This world belongs to us, they added; God, by denying its first inhabitants the ability to become more civilized, destined them in advance to an inevitable destruction. The true owners of the continent are those who know how to make the most of its riches.

Satisfied with his reasoning the American goes to church where he hears a minister of the Gospel repeat to him that men are brothers and that the eternal being, who made them all on the same model, gave to all of them the duty to help one another.

*   *   *   *   *

On July 19 at ten o'clock in the morning we boarded the steamboat *Ohio,* taking us toward Detroit. A very strong breeze blew from the northwest and gave the waters of Lake Erie all the appearance of the agitation of ocean waves. To the right spread a limitless horizon, to the left we kept close to the southern coasts of the lake which we often approached close enough to hear voices. These coasts were perfectly flat and differed from those of all the lakes that I had had the occasion to visit in Europe. Nor did they resemble the shores of the sea. Immense forests shaded them and formed a sort of thick and rarely broken belt around the lake.[d] From time to time, however, the country suddenly changes appearance. Coming around a woods, you notice the elegant spire of a church steeple, houses sparkling with whiteness and cleanliness, shops. Two steps further, the primitive and seemingly impenetrable forest regains its sway and again its foliage is reflected in the waters of the lake.

Those who have traveled throughout the United States will find in this picture a striking emblem of American society. Everything there is abrupt

---

d. "I believe that in one of my letters, I complained that you found hardly any more forest in America; I must make amends here. Not only do you find forest and woods in America; but the entire country is still only a vast forest, in the middle of which some clearings have been made." Letter of Tocqueville to his mother (Auburn, 17 July 1831), YTC, BIaI, and *OCB,* VII, pp. 36–37.

and unexpected; everywhere extreme civilization and nature abandoned to itself are found together and, in a way, face to face. It is not what you imagine in France. As for me, in my traveler's illusions—and what class of men does not have its own—I imagined something entirely different. I had noticed that in Europe, the more or less isolated state in which a province or a city was found, its wealth or its poverty, its small or large size exercised an immense influence on the ideas, the mores, the whole civilization of its inhabitants and often put the difference of several centuries between the various parts of the same territory.

I thought it was so with more reason in the New World, and that a country, populated in an incomplete and partial manner as America, had to present all the conditions of existence and offer the image of society across all the ages. So America, according to me, was the only country in which you could follow step by step all the transformations that the social state imposed on man and in which it was possible to see those transformations like a vast chain that descended link by link from the opulent patrician of the cities to the savage of the wilderness. There, in a word, I expected to find the entire history of humanity enclosed within a few degrees of longitude.

Nothing is true in this picture. Of all the countries in the world, America is the least appropriate for providing the spectacle that I was coming to find there. In America, still more than in Europe, there is only a single society.[e] It can be rich or poor, humble or brilliant, commercial or agricultural, but everywhere it is composed of the same elements. The leveling effect of an equal civilization has passed over it. The man that you have left in the streets of New York, you will find again in the middle of the nearly impenetrable wilderness; the same clothing, same spirit, same language, same habits, same pleasures. Nothing rustic, nothing naive, nothing that feels like the wilderness, nothing that even resembles our villages. The reason for this singular state of things is easy to understand. The portions of the territories populated earliest and most completely have achieved a high level of civilization, instruction has been lavished there profusely, the spirit of equality [{the republican spirit}] has given a singularly uniform color to the internal habits of life. Now, note it well, these are precisely the same men who go

e. See p. 491 of the first volume.

each year to populate the wilderness. In Europe, each man lives and dies on the soil where he was born. In America, nowhere do you find representatives of a race that has multiplied in the wilderness after living there for a long time, unknown to the world and left to its own efforts. Those who inhabit these isolated places arrived there yesterday. They came with the mores, the ideas, the needs of civilization. They yield to savage life only what the imperious nature of things requires of them. From that the most bizarre contrasts result. You pass without transition from the wilderness to the street of a city, from the most wild scenes to the most pleasant pictures of civilized life. If night surprises you, do not force yourself to take shelter at the foot of a tree; you have a great chance of arriving in a village where you will find everything, even including French fashions and caricatures of boulevards. The merchant of Buffalo and of Detroit is as well supplied as that of New York; the mills of Lyons work for the one as for the other. You leave the main roads, you plunge along paths hardly cleared. You finally see a cleared field, a cabin made of logs half-hewn where daylight enters only by a narrow window; you finally believe you have reached the dwelling of the American peasant. Error. You penetrate the cabin that seems to be the home of all miseries, but the owner of this place wears the same clothes as you; he speaks the language of the cities. On the crude table are books and newspapers; the owner himself hastens to take you inside in order to know exactly what is happening in old Europe and to ask you for an accounting about what has struck you the most in his country. He will draw on paper a military campaign plan for the Belgians, and will teach you gravely what remains to be done for the prosperity of France. [≠He hastens to draw you away from the dramas of his country in order to talk to you about old Europe. He will say to you that the Poles have won [lost? (ed.)] at Ostrolenka and will inform you that a majority of one hundred votes has just destroyed the heredity peerage in the hereditary monarchy of France.≠] You would think you are seeing a rich landowner who has come to live temporarily for a few nights at a hunting camp. And in fact, the log cabin is for the American only a momentary shelter, a temporary concession made to the necessity of circumstances. When the fields that surround it are entirely in production and when the new owner has the leisure to occupy himself with the pleasant things of life, a house more spacious and more appropriate to his needs will replace the *log house* and will serve as a shelter for the numerous children who one day will also go off to create a dwelling in the wilderness.

But, to come back to our journey, we navigated with difficulty all day long in sight of the coasts of Pennsylvania and later those of Ohio. We stopped for a moment at Presqu'île, today Erie. That is where the canal from Pittsburgh will end. By means of this work, whose complete execution is, they say, easy and now certain, the Mississippi will communicate with the River of the North and the riches of Europe will circulate freely across the five hundred leagues of land that separate the Gulf of Mexico from the Atlantic Ocean.

In the evening, the weather having become favorable, we headed rapidly toward Detroit by crossing the middle of the lake. The following morning, we were in sight of the small island called *Middle Sister* near where, in 1814, Commodore Perry won a famous naval victory over the English.

A little later, the even coasts of Canada seemed to approach rapidly and we saw the Detroit River opening before us and, appearing in the distance, the walls of Fort Malden. This place, founded by the French, still bears numerous traces of its origin. The houses have the form and the placement of those of our peasants. In the center of the hamlet arises the Catholic church tower surmounted by a cock. You would say a village around Caen or Evreux. While we considered, not without emotion, this image of France, our attention was diverted by the sight of a singular spectacle. To our right, on the river bank, a Scottish soldier mounted guard in full uniform. He wore the uniform that the fields of Waterloo have made so famous. The feathered cap, the jacket, nothing was missing; the sun made his uniform and his weapons glisten. To our left, and as if to provide a parallel for us, two entirely naked Indians, their bodies gaudy with colors, their noses pierced by rings, arrived at the same moment on the opposite bank. They climbed into a small bark canoe in which a blanket formed the sail. Abandoning this fragile, small boat to the work of the wind and current, they darted like an arrow toward our vessel, which they went around in an instant. Then they went calmly to fish near the English soldier who, still glistening and immobile, seemed placed there like the representative of the brilliant and armed civilization of Europe.

We arrived at Detroit at three o'clock. Detroit is a small city of two or three thousand souls that the Jesuits founded in the middle of the woods in 1710 and that still contains a large number of French families.

We had crossed the entire State of New York and done one hundred leagues on Lake Erie; this time we touched upon the limits of civilization, but we did not know at all where we needed to head. To find out was not something as easy as you may believe. To travel through nearly impenetrable forests, to cross deep rivers, to face pestilential swamps, to sleep exposed to the dampness of the woods, these are the efforts that the American imagines without difficulty if it is a matter of earning a dollar; for that is the point. But that someone would do similar things out of curiosity, this does not occur to his mind. Add that living in the wilderness, he prizes only the work of man. He will gladly send you to visit a road, a bridge, a beautiful village. But that you attach a value to great trees and to a beautiful solitude, that is absolutely beyond him.[f]

So nothing is more difficult than to find someone able to understand you. You want to see the forest, our hosts said smilingly to us; go straight ahead of you, you will find what you want. In the vicinity there are as a matter of fact new roads and well-cleared paths. As for the Indians, you will see too many of them in our public squares and in our streets; there is no need to go farther for that. Those Indians at least are beginning to become civilized and have a less savage appearance. We didn't take long to realize that it was impossible to obtain the truth from them by frontal assault and that we had to *maneuver.*

So we went to the official charged by the United States with the sale of the still unoccupied lands covering the district of Michigan; we presented ourselves to him as men who, without having a well-fixed intention of settling in the country, could nonetheless have a long-term interest in knowing the price of the lands and their situation. Major Biddle,[g] which was the

---

f. See chapter 17 of the first part of this volume, especially pp. 835–37.

g. John Biddle (1792–1859). Graduate of Princeton University, Captain during the

name of the official, understood marvelously this time what we wanted to do and immediately launched into a host of details that we listened to eagerly. This part, he says to us, showing us on the map the St. Joseph river, which after long twistings and turnings, discharges into Lake Michigan, seems to be the most suitable for meeting your plans; the land is good there; some beautiful villages have already been established, and the road that leads there is so well maintained that every day public coaches travel it. Good! we said to ourselves; we now know where we should not go unless we want to visit the wilderness by postal coach. We thanked Mr. Biddle for his advice and asked him, with an air of indifference and a kind of scorn, what was the portion of the district where until now the current of emigration made itself least felt. "Over here," he says to us, without giving more value to his words than we to our question, "toward the northwest. Toward Pontiac and in the area surrounding this village some quite beautiful settlements have been recently founded. But you must not think about settling farther away; the country is covered by an almost impenetrable forest that extends endlessly toward the northwest, where you find only wild beasts and Indians. The United States plans to open a road there shortly; but as yet it has only been started and stops at Pontiac. I repeat to you, it is a part that you must not think about." We again thanked Mr. Biddle for his good counsel and we left determined to do exactly the opposite.[h] We were beside

---

War of 1812, charged with the sale of lands at Detroit and later delegate of the territory to Congress, from 1829 to 1831, president of the constitutional convention in 1835. See *Early History of Michigan with Biographies* . . . (Lansing: Thorp & Godfrey, 1888); and *Michigan Biographies* (Lansing: The Michigan Historical Commission, 1924), 2 vols.

   h. I went to see in Detroit the public officer charged with the sale of lands, or of the *land-office,* and he gave me the following details.

   Since the ice melted, that is from the month of last May, the time when the Lake became navigable, until the first of July, about 5,000 new settlers (this is the English word, we do not have the exact equivalent) arrived in Michigan. The size of this figure surprised me, as you can believe, all the more so since I believed, just like the general opinion among us, that all the *new settlers* were Europeans.

   The land agent informed me that out of these 5,000 persons, there were not 200 emigrants from Europe. And the proportion is larger than usual. "But," I said to the agent, "what can bring this great number of Americans to leave the place of their

ourselves with joy at finally knowing a place that had not yet been reached by the torrent of European civilization.

The next day, July 23,[j] we hastened to rent two horses. Since we expected to keep them for ten days, we wanted to put a certain price in the hands of the owner; but he refused to accept it, saying that we would pay when we returned. He was not worried. Michigan is surrounded on all sides by lakes and wilderness; he let us loose in a kind of riding school, whose door he held. So after purchasing a compass as well as provisions, we got underway, rifle over the shoulder, with as much lack of concern about the future and as lightheartedly as two schoolboys who would be leaving school to go to spend their vacation at their father's house.

If in fact we had only wanted to see the forest, our hosts of Detroit would have been right to tell us that it was not necessary to go very far, for one mile from the city the road entered into the forest never to emerge again.

---

birth to come to inhabit a wilderness?" "Nothing is easier to understand," he answered me. "Since the law divides the wealth of the father equally among the children, the result is that each generation finds itself poorer than the preceding one. But as soon as the small landowner of our populated states notices that he is beginning to have difficulty making a living, he sells his field, comes with all his family to the frontier line, buys a very large farm with the small capital that he has just created, and makes a fortune in a few years.

"At his death, if this fortune is not enough for his children, they will go like him to create a new one in a new wilderness. We have, thank God, enough room to expand to the Pacific Ocean."

Do you not find, my dear friend, that an entire thick book is contained in this single response? How can we imagine a revolution in a country where such a career is open to the needs and to the passions of man, and how can we compare the political institutions of such a people to those of any other? (letter to Ernest de Chabrol, Buffalo, 17 August 1831, YTC, BIa2).

j. André Jardin and George W. Pierson noted in their edition of the letters of Beaumont (*Lettres d'Amérique,* p. 102, note) that there exist, from mid-July to August 1, 1831, differences in dates between the correspondence of Tocqueville and that of Beaumont. The two historians rely more on the dates of Tocqueville, who kept a travel notebook. Nonetheless, if you compare Tocqueville's dates to those of Beaumont's sketches (YTC, BIIb), the dates coincide for three sketches:

—watercolor of a blue bird ("Painted at Pontiac 29 July 1831"),
—sketch number 14 ("25 July 1831. Forest of Saginaw (Indian guide)"),
—sketch number 15 ("Loghouse. Saginaw. 26 July 1831").

The terrain on which the road is found is perfectly flat and often swampy. From time to time new clearings are found on the way. Since these settlements perfectly resemble each other, whether they are found deep in Michigan or at the door of New York, I am going to try to describe them here once and for all.[k]

The small bells that the pioneer carefully hangs around the necks of his animals in order to find them in the thick woods announce from afar the approach to a clearing. Soon you hear the sound of the ax that fells the trees of the forest and, as you approach, signs of destruction announce still more clearly the presence of man. Cut branches cover the road, trunks half-charred by fire or mutilated by iron, still stand upright along your passage. You continue your march and you come to a woods in which all the trees seem to have been stricken by sudden death. In the middle of summer their dry branches present nothing more than the image of winter. Examining them more closely, you notice that in their bark a deep circle has been traced that, stopping the circulation of sap, did not take long to make them die. This in fact is how the planter usually begins. Not able the first year to cut all the trees that cover his new property, he sows corn under their branches and, by killing them, he prevents them from shading his crop. After this field, an incomplete beginning, a first step of civilization in the wilderness, you suddenly see the cabin of the landowner. It is generally placed in the center of a ground more carefully cultivated than the rest, but where man still sustains an unequal battle against nature. There the trees have been cut, but not uprooted; their trunks still cover and clutter the ground that they formerly shaded. Around these dried-up remains, wheat, oak shoots, plants of all types, weeds of all kinds grow jumbled together and increase together on an intractable and still half-wild ground. At the center of this vigorous and varied vegetation arises the house of the planter, or as it is called in this country, the *log house*. Like the field around it, this rustic dwelling announces a new and

k. See p. 1287.

hurried work. Its length rarely exceeds 30 feet. It is 20 feet wide, 15 feet
high. Its walls as well as the roof are formed from tree trunks not squared
off, between which moss and earth have been placed to prevent the cold
and the rain from penetrating the interior of the house. As the traveler
approaches, the scene becomes more animated. Warned by the sound of
his footsteps, the children who were rolling around in the surrounding
debris, get up precipitously and flee toward the parental refuge, as though
frightened at the sight of a man, while two large half-wild dogs, ears upright and muzzles elongated, emerge from the cabin and come growling
to cover the retreat of their young masters.

Then the pioneer himself appears at the door of his dwelling; he casts
a searching glance at the new arrival, signals to his dogs to come back into
the house and hastens to serve as their example himself without exhibiting
either curiosity or concern.

At the entry of the *log house,* the European cannot prevent himself from
casting an astonished eye over the spectacle that it presents.

There is generally in this cabin only a single window at which a muslin
curtain sometimes hangs; for in these places, where it is not rare to see necessities missing, superfluities are frequently found. On the hearth of
beaten earth crackles a resinous fire that, better than the day, lights up the
interior of the building. Above this rustic hearth, you see trophies of war
or hunting; a long rifle with a grooved barrel, a deerskin, eagle feathers. To
the right of the chimney a map of the United States is often spread, which
the wind, coming through the chinks in the wall, flaps and agitates constantly. Near it, on a single shelf of rough hewn planks are placed a few
random volumes: a Bible whose cover and edges are already worn by the
piety of two generations, a book of prayers, and sometimes a canto of Milton or a Shakespeare tragedy [{a history of America, a few pious stories and
some newspapers}]. Along the walls are placed a few crude seats, fruit of
the owner's industry, trunks instead of armoires, agricultural implements
and some samples of the harvest. At the center of the room is a wobbly
table whose legs, still covered with foliage, seem to have grown by themselves out of the earth on the spot occupied by the table. That is where the
entire family gathers each day to take its meals. There you also see a teapot

of English porcelain, spoons usually of wood, a few chipped cups and some newspapers.

The appearance of the master of this dwelling is no less remarkable than the place that serves as his shelter.

Angular muscles, slender limbs make the inhabitant of New England recognizable at first glance. This man was not born in the wilderness where he lives. His constitution alone declares it. His first years were spent within an intellectual and reasoning society. It is his will that has thrown him into the wilderness undertakings for which he seems so little fit. But if his physical strength seems not up to his enterprise, on his features furrowed by the cares of life, there reigns an air of practical intelligence, of cold and persevering energy that is striking at first sight. His gait is slow and formal, his words measured and his appearance austere. Habit and, even more, pride have given his face this stoic rigidity that his actions belie. The pioneer scorns, it is true, what often agitates the heart of men most violently; his goods and his life will never follow the chance of a throw of the dice or the fortunes of a woman; but, to gain comfort, he has faced exile, solitude and the innumerable miseries of uncivilized life; he has slept on the bare ground; he has been exposed to forest fever and to the Indian's tomahawk. He made this effort one day, he has duplicated it for years; he will do it perhaps for another twenty years, without discouragement and without complaint. [{In the pursuit of what he regards as the goal of his entire life, every competitor, every adversary will become an enemy to whom an implacable hatred will be attached as durable as the sentiment that gave birth to it. Is that a man without passions [v: cold and unfeeling]?}] Is a man who is capable of such sacrifices a cold and unfeeling being? Shouldn't we, on the contrary, recognize in him one of those mental passions that are so ardent, so tenacious, so implacable? Concentrated on this sole goal of making a fortune, the emigrant has finished by creating an entirely individual existence; the sentiments of family have themselves merged into a vast egoism, and it is doubtful that in his wife and his children he sees anything other than a detached portion of himself. Deprived of habitual relationships with his fellows, he has learned to make solitude a pleasure. When you present yourself at the threshold of his isolated dwelling, the pioneer advances to meet you; he offers his hand as is the custom, but his physiognomy expresses neither welcome nor joy. He speaks only to interrogate you; it is a need of the head and not of the heart that he is satisfying, and scarcely has he drawn from you the news that he desired to learn than he falls back into silence. You would think you were seeing a man who withdrew in the evening into his house fatigued by troublesome individuals and the chatter of the world. Interrogate him in turn; he will intelligently give you the information you lack; he will even provide for your needs; he will look to your safety as long as you are under his roof. But so much restraint and pride reign in all his conduct, you see in it such a profound indifference about even the result of his efforts, that you feel your gratitude cool. The pioneer is hospitable in his way, but his hospitality in no way touches you because he seems, while exercising it, to be submitting to a painful necessity of the wilderness. He sees in hospitality a duty that his position imposes on him, not a pleasure. This unknown man is the representative of a restless, reasoning and adventurous race that does coldly what only the ardor of the passions explains, who traffics in everything without exception, even morality and religion.

A nation of conquerors who submit to leading savage life without ever letting themselves be carried away by its sweet pleasures, who love civilization and enlightenment only when they are useful for well-being, and who shut themselves up in the wilderness of America with an ax and some newspapers; a people who, like all great peoples, has only one thought, and who advances toward the acquisition of wealth, the only goal of its efforts, with a perseverance and a scorn for life that you could call heroic, if the word was suitable for something other than the efforts of virtue. This wandering people, not stopped by rivers and lakes, before whom forests fall and prairies are covered with shade, will, after touching the Pacific Ocean, retrace its steps and destroy the societies that it will have formed behind it.

While speaking about the pioneer, you cannot forget the companion of his miseries and of his dangers. See at the other end of the room, this young woman who, while overseeing preparations for the meal, rocks her youngest son on her knees. Like the emigrant, this woman is in the prime of life, like him she can recall the comfort of her earliest years. Her dress still announces even now a barely extinguished taste for finery. But time has weighed heavily on her. On her features faded before their time, on her weakened limbs, it is easy to see that existence has been a heavy burden for her. In fact this frail creature has already been exposed to incredible miseries. Hardly entered into life, she had to tear herself away from the tenderness of her mother and these sweet fraternal bonds that the young woman never abandons without shedding tears, even when she leaves them to go to share the opulent house of a new husband. The wife of the pioneer, removed in a moment and without hope of return from this innocent cradle of youth, has exchanged the charms of society and the joys of the domestic home for the solitude of the forests. Her nuptial bed was placed on the bare earth of the wilderness. To devote herself to her austere duties, to submit to privations that were unknown to her, to embrace an existence for which she was not made, such was the use of the best years of her life, such have been for her the sweet pleasures of the conjugal union. Deprivation, sufferings and boredom have altered her fragile structure, but not weakened her courage. Amid the profound sadness painted on her delicate features, you easily notice a religious resignation, a profound peace, and I do not know what natural and tranquil steadfastness that meets all the miseries of life without fearing or defying them.

Around this woman crowd half-dressed children, shining with health, unconcerned about tomorrow, true sons of the wilderness. Their mother from time to time gives them a look full of melancholy and joy; to see their strength and her weakness, you would say that she has exhausted herself by giving life to them, and that she does not regret what they have cost her.

The house inhabited by the emigrants has no interior walls or attic. Into the single room that it contains, the entire family comes at night to find shelter. This dwelling by itself alone forms like a small world. It is the ark of civilization lost amid an ocean of leaves, a sort of oasis in the desert. One hundred steps further the endless forest spreads its shadow and the wilderness begins again.

*   *   *   *   *

We arrived at Pontiac only after the sun went down and it was evening. Twenty very clean and exceedingly pretty buildings, forming as many well supplied stores, a limpid stream, a clearing of a quarter league square, and the endless forest around it: there is the faithful picture of the village of Pontiac that in twenty years will perhaps be a city. The sight of this place reminded me of what Mr. Gallatin had said to me a month before in New York;[m] there are no villages in America, at least in the sense that we give to the word. Here the houses of the farmers are all spread out among the fields. People do not gather in one place except to establish a kind of market for the use of the surrounding population. You see in these so-called villages only men of law, printers or merchants.

We were directed to the most beautiful inn in Pontiac[n] (for there are two) and we were brought as is customary into what is called the *bar room*. It is a room where you are given drinks and where the simplest worker as well as the richest merchant of the place come to smoke, to drink, and to talk politics together on the most perfect outwardly equal footing. The master of the place or the landlord was, I will not say a large peasant, there are no peasants in America, but at least a very large man who wore on his face that expression of candor and simplicity that distinguishes Norman horse traders. He was a man who, for fear of intimidating you, never looked you in the face while speaking, but waited to look at you when he felt comfortable, while you were occupied conversing elsewhere. Moreover, a profound politician and, following American habits, an unrelenting questioner. This respected citizen, as well as the rest of the assembly, considered us at first with astonishment. Our travel clothes and our guns hardly announced business entrepreneurs, and to travel simply to see was something absolutely unaccustomed. In order to cut explanations short, we declared

m. Conversation of 10 June 1831, non-alphabetic notebook 1, YTC, BIIa, and *Voyage, OC,* V, 1, pp. 60–61.

n. In the autumn of 1867, Charles Sumner began a series of lectures in Pontiac with the title "The Nation." He evoked the Tocqueville visit that the daughter of Judge Amasa Bagley, host of the travelers, still recalled. "He came during a severe storm, remaining several days. There was a great mystery surrounding him and his servant (the most important of the two in appearance). They got their meals alone and claimed a good share of my father's attention, seeking from him information of the then new territory of Michigan." Nancy G. Davis, "History of Amasa Bagley," in *Pioneer Collections* (Lansing, Mich.: W. S. George & Co., 1881), III, p. 600. Also see George W. Pierson, *Tocqueville and Beaumont in America,* pp. 251–52.

right at the beginning that we came to buy land. Hardly were the words said, than we noticed that by trying to avoid one evil we had thrown ourselves into another very much more formidable one.

They ceased treating us, it is true, like extraordinary beings, but each one wanted to do business with us; to get rid of them and their farms, we said to our host that before concluding anything, we would like to obtain from him useful information about the price of land and about how to cultivate it. He immediately brought us into another room, with a fitting slowness spread a map of Michigan on the oak table that was in the middle of the room and, placing the candle between the three of us, waited in an impassive silence for what we had to say to him. The reader, without having like us the intention of settling in one of the uninhabited places of America, may nonetheless be curious to know how so many thousands of Europeans and Americans who come each year to find shelter there set about to do so. So I am going to transcribe here the information provided by our host from Pontiac. Often since, we have indeed been able to verify the perfect exactness of his information.º

"Here it is not like in France," our host said to us after having calmly heard all our questions and snuffed out the candle; "in your country labor is cheap and land is expensive; here buying land costs nothing and the labor of men is beyond price. I am saying this in order to show you that, to settle in America as in Europe, capital is necessary, although it is used differently.

---

o. Tocqueville and Beaumont gathered abundant information about the expenses to provide for in order to become established as a settler in America. "I am persuaded that in France there are thousands of people who would be interested in coming to America to buy good land there at a good price, but most are unaware of the situation. Perhaps to make the situation known would be a good service to our country. Ordinarily the difficulty for those who emigrate to a new country is in the difference of language; but this obstacle would not exist in Michigan where a quarter of the population speaks French." Gustave de Beaumont, *Lettres d'Amérique,* p. 116. During their return from Saginaw, Tocqueville and Beaumont remained a day at Pontiac with the idea of obtaining new details on how to settle in the wilderness, on crops, etc. A part of the observations that Tocqueville puts in the mouth of Amasa Bagley had been made to him by Dr. Burns, a Scottish doctor who lived near Pontiac, and with whom they had spoken on July 30. See alphabetic notebook A, YTC, BIIa, and *Voyage, OC,* V, 1, pp. 233–34.

For my part, I would not advise anyone, no matter who it may be, to come to seek a fortune in our wilderness unless having at his disposition a sum of 150 to 200 dollars (800 to 1,000 francs). An acre in Michigan[1] never costs more than 10 shillings (about 6 Fr., 50 c.) when the land is still uncultivated. So a worker can earn in one day what it takes to buy an acre. But the purchase made, the difficulty begins. Here is how you generally set about to overcome it. The pioneer goes to the place that he has just bought with a few animals, salted pork, two barrels of wheat and some tea. If he finds a cabin near, he goes there and receives temporary hospitality. In the opposite case he puts up a tent in the very middle of the woods that is to become his field. His first care is to cut down the nearest trees, with which he hastily builds the crude house whose structure you have already been able to examine. Among us, the maintenance of animals scarcely costs anything. The emigrant releases them into the forest after attaching a small iron bell to them. It is very rare for these animals, left to themselves in this way, to leave the area around their home. The greatest expense is that of clearing the land. If the pioneer arrives in the wilderness with a family able to aid him in his first efforts, his task is easy enough. But it is rarely so. In general the emigrant is young and, if he already has children, they are young. Then he must provide alone for all the first needs of his family or hire the services of his neighbors. It costs him from 4 to 5 dollars (from 20 to 25 francs) to have an acre cleared. Once the land is prepared, the new owner puts one acre in potatoes, the rest in wheat and corn. Corn is the providence of these wilderness areas; it grows in the water of our swamps and sprouts beneath the foliage of the forest better than under the rays of the sun.[P] It is corn that saves the family of the emigrant from an inevitable destruction, when poverty, illness or negligence have prevented him from sufficiently clearing the land during the first year. There is nothing more difficult to get through

1. *An acre is 330 English feet long by 132 feet wide.*
p. In the margin: "≠Misery.
"Isolation.
"Illness.
"No Europeans.
"Only the Americans can bear such miseries.≠"

than the first years that follow the clearing of the land. Later comes comfort, and then wealth."

This is how our host spoke; as for us, we listened to these simple details with almost as much interest as if we had wanted to profit from them ourselves; and when he became silent, we said to him:

"The land of all these uninhabited forests is generally swampy and unhealthy; doesn't the emigrant who exposes himself to the miseries of the wilderness at least fear for his life?" "All clearing of the land is a perilous undertaking," replied the American, "and it is almost without example that the pioneer or his family escapes forest fever during the first year. Often when you travel in the autumn, you find all the inhabitants of the cabin suffering from the fever, from the emigrant to his youngest son." "And what becomes of these unfortunates when Providence strikes them like that?" "They resign themselves while waiting for a better future." "But do they hope for some help from their fellows?" "Almost none." "Can they at least obtain help from medicine?" "The closest doctor often lives 60 miles from their house. They do as the Indians; they die or are cured depending on God's pleasure." We began again: "Does the voice of religion sometimes come to them?" "Very rarely; we have not yet been able to *provide for* anything in our woods to assure the public observation of a religion. Nearly every summer, it is true, a few Methodist preachers come to travel through the new settlements. Word of their arrival spreads with an incredible rapidity from cabin to cabin; it is the great news of the day. At the time appointed, the emigrant, his wife and his children, head along the paths scarcely cleared through the forest toward the indicated meeting place. People come there from 50 miles around. The faithful do not gather in a church but in the open, under the leaves of the forest. A pulpit made from rough-hewn trunks, large trees turned over to serve as pews, these are the adornments of this rustic church. The pioneers and their families camp in the woods that surround it; there for three days and three nights the crowd practices religious exercises rarely interrupted. You have to see how ardently these men give themselves to prayer, with what reverence they listen to the solemn voice of the preacher. It is in the wilderness that they show themselves famished for religion." "A final question. It is generally believed among us that the wilderness of America is populated with the help of European emigration. So how is it that since we have been traveling through your forests, we haven't happened to meet a single European?" A smile of superiority and satisfied pride was written on the features of our host upon hearing this question:

> It is only Americans, he answered emphatically, who can have the courage to submit to such miseries and who know how to buy comfort at such a price. The European emigrant stops in the large cities that are on the coast or in the districts surrounding them. There, he becomes artisan, farm laborer, valet. He leads a more pleasant life than in Europe and appears satisfied to leave the same inheritance to his children. The American on the contrary takes possession of the land and, with it, he seeks to create a great future for himself.

After uttering these final words, our host stopped. He let an immense column of smoke escape from his mouth and seemed ready to listen to what we had to say to inform him about our plans.

We thanked him first for his valuable advice and for his wise counsel from which we assured him we would profit some day, and we added: "Before settling in your district, my dear host, we have the intention of going to Saginaw and we want to consult you on this point." At the word Saginaw a singular transformation took place in the physiognomy of the American; it seemed that we had dragged him violently out of real life to push him into the domains of the imagination; his eyes dilated, his mouth gaped and a look of the most profound astonishment was written on all his features: "You want to go to Saginaw," he cried, "to Saginaw Bay! Two reasonable men, two cultivated foreigners want to go to Saginaw Bay? It is scarcely believable." "And so why not?" we replied. "But do you know clearly," our host began again, "what you are proposing? Do you know that Saginaw is the last inhabited point until the Pacific Ocean? That from here to Saginaw you find nothing more than a wilderness and uncleared empty spaces? Have you considered that the woods are full of Indians and of mosquitoes? That you will have to bed down at least one night in the dampness of the forest shade? Have you thought about the fever? Will you know how to get out of difficulty in the wilderness and not get lost in the labyrinth of our forests?" After this tirade he paused in order to judge better the impression he had made. We resumed: "All that is perhaps true. But we will leave tomorrow morning for Saginaw Bay." Our host reflected a moment, nodded his head, and said in a slow and positive way: "Only a great interest could lead two foreigners to such an undertaking: you have almost certainly figured, very wrongly, that it was advantageous to settle in the places most remote from all competition?" We did not respond. He resumed: "Perhaps you have been charged as well by the fur trading company of Canada with establishing a relationship with the Indian tribes of the frontier?" Same silence. Our host had run out of conjectures and he was quiet, but he continued to reflect deeply about the strangeness of our plan.

"Have you never been to Saginaw?" we said. "Me," he answered, "I have been there five or six times, to my sorrow, but I had a reason to do so and no reason can be found for you." "But don't lose sight, my worthy host, of the fact that we are not asking you if we must go to Saginaw, but only what is needed to manage to do so easily." Thus led back to the question, our American regained all his composure and all the clarity of his ideas; he explained to us in a few words and with an admirable practical good sense the way in which we had to proceed in order to cross the wilderness, entered into the smallest details, and foresaw the most unlikely circumstances. At the end of his instructions he paused again in order to see if we would not finally reveal the secret of our journey, and noticing that on both sides we had nothing more to say, he took the candle, led us to a room and, very democratically shaking our hands, went away to finish the evening in the common room.

We got up with the day and prepared to leave. Our host was soon afoot himself. Night had not revealed to him what made us stick to behavior that was so extraordinary in his eyes. Since we appeared absolutely decided to act contrary to his counsel, however, he dared not return to the charge, but constantly circled around us. From time to time he repeated half-aloud: "*I can imagine with difficulty* what can lead two foreigners to go to Saginaw." He repeated this sentence several times, until finally I said to him putting my foot in the stirrup: "There are many reasons that lead us to do so, my dear host." He stopped short upon hearing these words, and looking me in the face for the first time, he seemed to prepare himself to hear the revelation of a great mystery. But, calmly mounting my horse, I gave him a sign of friendship as a concluding gesture and moved away at a fast trot. When I was fifty steps away, I turned my head; I saw him still planted like a haystack before his door. A little later he went back inside shaking his head. I imagine that he still said: "I have difficulty understanding what two foreigners are going to do in Saginaw."

*   *   *   *   *

We had been advised to address ourselves to a Mr. Williams[q] who, having traded for a long time with the Chippewa Indians and having a son settled at Saginaw, could provide us with useful information. After going several miles in the woods and afraid that we had already missed the house of our man, we encountered an old man busy working in a small garden. We approached him. It was Mr. Williams himself. He received us with great kindness and gave us a letter for his son. We asked him if we had anything to fear from the Indian bands whose territory we were going to cross. Mr. Williams rejected this idea with a kind of indignation: "No! No!," he said, "you can go without fear. For my part, I would sleep more tranquilly among Indians than among whites." I note this as the first favorable impression that I had received about the Indians since my arrival in America. In very inhabited regions they are only spoken about with a mixture of fear and scorn, and I believe that there in fact they deserve these two feelings. You could see above what I thought about them myself when I met the first of them at Buffalo. As you advance in this journal and as you follow me amid the European population of the frontier and amid the Indian tribes themselves, you will conceive a more honorable and, at the very same time, more accurate idea of the first inhabitants of America.

After leaving Mr. Williams we continued our route through the woods.

q. George W. Pierson (*Tocqueville and Beaumont in America,* p. 252) identifies him: Major Oliver Williams. The *Reports of the Pioneer Society of the State of Michigan* (Lansing: Thorp & Godfrey, 1877–1891) include numerous references that validate this identification.

From time to time a small lake (this district is full of them) appeared like a sheet of silver beneath the forest foliage. It is difficult to imagine the charm that surrounds these lovely places where man has not settled and where a profound peace and an uninterrupted silence still reign. I have traveled in the Alps through dreadful, isolated areas where nature rejects the labor of man, but displays even in its very horrors a grandeur that transports and grips the soul. Here the solitude is not less profound, but it does not produce the same impressions. The only sentiments that you feel while traveling through these flowered wilderness areas where, as in Milton's *Paradise,* everything is prepared to receive man, are a tranquil admiration, a mild melancholy, a vague disgust with civilized life; a sort of wild instinct that makes you think with pain that soon this delicious solitude will have changed face. Already in fact the white race advances across the surrounding woods and, in a few years, the European will have cut the trees that are reflected in the clear waters of the lake and forced the animals that populate its shores to withdraw toward new wilderness areas.

Always on the move, we came to a country with a new appearance. The land there was not level, but cut by hills and valleys. Several of these hills presented the most wild appearance. It was in one of these picturesque passages that, turning ourselves around suddenly to contemplate the imposing spectacle that we were leaving behind us, we noticed to our great surprise near the hindquarters of our horses an Indian who seemed to follow us step by step. He was a man about thirty years old, large and admirably proportioned as nearly all of them are. His black and shining hair fell to his shoulders except for two braids that were tied up at the top of his head. His face was daubed with black and red. He was covered with a type of very short blue blouse. He wore red *mittas;* these are a type of pants that go only to the top of the thigh, and his feet were covered with moccasins. At his side hung a knife. In his right hand he held a long carbine and in his left two birds that he had just killed. The first sight of this Indian made a not very pleasant impression on us. The place was poorly chosen for resisting an attack. To our right a pine forest rose to an immense height, to our left extended a deep ravine at the bottom of which among the rocks flowed a small stream hidden from our sight by the obscurity of the foliage and toward which we descended blindly! Putting our hands on our rifles, turning and putting ourselves in the path opposite the Indian took only a moment. He stopped as well. We remained in silence for a half-minute. His face presented all the characteristic features that distinguish the Indian race from all others. In his perfectly black eyes gleamed the savage fire that still animates the look of the half-breed and is lost only with the second or third generation of white blood. His nose was hooked in the middle, slightly flat at the end, his cheekbones very prominent, and his strikingly wide mouth showed two rows of glistening white teeth that proved well enough that the savage, cleaner than his neighbor the American, did not spend his day chewing tobacco leaves. I said that at the moment when we had turned ourselves around putting our hands on our weapons, the Indian stopped. He underwent the rapid examination that we made of his person with an absolute impassivity, a steady and unchanging look. Since he saw that we had on our side no hostile sentiment, he began to smile; probably he saw that we were alarmed. It was the first time that I was able to observe to what extent the expression of gaiety completely changes the physiognomy of these savage men. I have since had the occasion a hundred times to make the same remark. A serious Indian and a smiling Indian are two entirely different men. There reigns in the immobility of the first a savage majesty that imposes an involuntary sentiment of terror. If this same man begins to smile, his entire face takes on an expression of innocence and of kindness that gives him a real charm.

When we saw our man brighten, we addressed some words to him in English. He let us speak as much as we wanted, then gestured that he did not understand. We offered him a bit of brandy, which he accepted without hesitation and without thanks. Speaking always by signs, we asked him for the birds that he carried and he gave them to us in return for a small coin. Having thus made his acquaintance, we saluted him and left at a fast trot. At the end of a quarter hour of a rapid march, turning around again, I was surprised to see the Indian still behind the hindquarters of my horse. He ran with the agility of a wild animal, without saying a single word or appearing to lengthen his stride. We stopped; he stopped. We started again;

he started again. We raced at full speed. Our horses, raised in the wilderness, easily overcame all obstacles. The Indian doubled his pace; I saw him sometimes to the right, sometimes to the left of my horse, leaping over bushes and coming back down to earth noiselessly. You would have said one of those wolves of Northern Europe that follow riders with the hope that they will fall from their horses and can be more easily devoured. The sight of this constant figure that seemed to hover at our sides, sometimes becoming lost in the obscurity of the forest, sometimes reappearing clearly, ended up becoming disturbing to us. Not able to imagine what led this man to follow us at such a hurried pace—and perhaps he had been doing so for a very long time when we discovered him for the first time—the idea occurred to us that he was leading us into an ambush. We were occupied with these thoughts when we noticed in the woods before us the end of another carbine. Soon we were next to the man who carried it. We took him at first for an Indian; he was covered by a sort of frock coat, close-fitted around the small of his back, delineating a narrow and neat waist; his neck was naked and his feet covered by moccasins. When we came near him and he raised his head, we immediately recognized a European and we stopped.[r] He came up to us, shook our hands cordially and entered into conversation with us: "Do you live in the wilderness?" "Yes, here is my house"; amid the leaves he showed us a hut much more miserable than the usual *log houses.* "Alone?" "Alone." "And so what do you do here?" "I wander through these woods and, to the right and left, I kill the game that I meet along the way, but it is not going well now." "And this kind of life pleases you?" "More than any other." "But aren't you afraid of the Indians?" "Afraid of the Indians! I prefer to live amid them than in the society of whites. No! No! I am not afraid of the Indians. They are worth more than we are, at least as long as we have not brutalized them with our liquors, the poor creatures!" We then showed our new acquaintance the man who followed us so obstinately and who had then stopped a few steps away and remained as unmoving as a statue. "He is a Chippewa," he said, "or as the French call them

r. In the margin: "To delete, I think; has too much the appearance of being reminiscent of Cooper."

a *Sauteur.* I wager that he is returning from Canada where he received the annual presents from the English. His family must not be far from here." Having said this, the American gestured to the Indian to approach and began to speak to him in his language with an extreme facility. It was a remarkable thing to see the pleasure that these two men, so different by birth and mores, found in exchanging their ideas. The conversation turned evidently on the respective merit of their weapons. The white, after very attentively examining the rifle of the savage: "That is a beautiful carbine," he said, "the English almost certainly gave it to him to use against us and he won't fail to do so at the first war. That is how the Indians draw upon their heads all the misfortunes that burden them. But they won't know it for long, the poor fellows." "Do the Indians use these long and heavy rifles with skill?" "There are no marksmen like the Indians," our new friend resumed energetically with a tone of the greatest admiration. "Examine the small birds he sold to you, Sir, they are pierced by a single bullet, and I am very sure that he fired only two shots to take them. Oh!" he added, "there is nothing happier than an Indian in the regions where we have not yet made the game flee. But the large animals sense us at more than three hundred miles, and by withdrawing they create before us like a desert where the poor Indians can no longer live if they do not cultivate the earth."

As we retook our path: "When you pass by again," our new friend cried to us, "knock on my door. It is a pleasure to meet white faces in these places."

I have related this conversation, which in itself contains nothing remarkable, in order to show a kind of man that we met very frequently at the limits of inhabited lands. They are Europeans who, despite the habits of their youth, have ended up finding in the liberty of the wilderness an inexpressible charm. Attached to the uninhabited places of America by their taste and their passions, to Europe by their religion, their principles, and their ideas, they mix the love of savage life with the pride of civilization and prefer the Indians to their compatriots without, however, recognizing them as their equals.

So we resumed our journey and, advancing always with the same rapidity, at the end of a half-hour we reached the house of a pioneer. Before the door of this cabin an Indian family has set up a temporary dwelling. An old woman, two young girls, several children crouched around a fire to whose heat the remains of a whole deer were exposed. A few steps from there on the grass, a completely nude Indian warmed himself in the rays of the sun while a small child rolled around near him in the dust. There our silent companion stopped; he left us without taking our leave and sat down gravely amid his compatriots. What had been able to lead this man to follow the path of our horses in this way for two leagues? That is what we were never able to find out. After eating in this place, we remounted our horses and continued our march through a not very thick cluster of high trees. The thicket had been burned previously as could be seen by the charred remnants of a few trees that were lying on the grass. The ground is covered today by ferns that are spread as far as you can see beneath the forest covering.

A few leagues further my horse lost his shoe, which caused us intense concern. Near there fortunately, we met a planter who managed to reshoe it. Without this meeting I doubt that we would have been able to go further, for we were then approaching the extreme limit of cleared lands. This same man who had enabled us to continue our journey, urged us to hurry up; day was beginning to fade and two long leagues still separated us from *Flint River* where we wanted to go to sleep.

Soon, in fact, a profound darkness began to surround us. We *had to march*. The night was calm but freezing. Such a profound silence and such a complete calm reigned in the depths of these forests that you would have said that all the forces of nature were as if paralyzed there. You heard only the uncomfortable buzzing of mosquitoes and the noise of the steps of our horses. From time to time you noticed in the distance an Indian fire before which an austere and immobile profile was outlined in the smoke. At the end of an hour we arrived at a place where the road divided. Two paths opened at this spot. Which one to take? The choice was delicate; one of them led to a small stream whose depth we did not know, the other to a clearing. The rising moon then showed before us a valley full of debris. Further off we noticed two houses. It was so important not to get lost in such a place and at this hour that we resolved to get some information before going further. My companion remained to hold the horses, and throwing my rifle over my shoulder, I descended into the small valley. Soon I noticed that I was going into a very recent clearing; immense trees not yet stripped of their branches covered the ground. I managed by jumping from one to another to reach the houses rapidly enough, but the same stream that we had already encountered separated me from them. Fortunately [{the new proprietor of the place, probably wanting to establish a mill, had thrown trees into the stream to stop its flow}] its flow was hampered at this place by large oaks that the pioneer's ax had probably hurled there. I succeeded in sliding along these trees and I finally reached the other side. I approached these two houses with caution, fearing that they were Indian wigwams; they were still not finished; I found the doors open and no voice responded to mine. I returned to the banks of the stream where I could not help myself from admiring for several minutes the sublime horror of this place. The valley seemed to form an immense arena surrounded on all sides by the foliage of the woods like a black curtain, and at the center the light of the moon, breaking through, created a thousand fantastic images that played in silence amid the debris of the forest. Moreover, no noise whatsoever, no sound of life arose from this solitude. I finally thought of my companion and I cried out loudly to let him know the result of my search, to get him to cross the stream and to come to find me. My voice echoed for a long time amid the solitude that surrounded me. But I got no response. I cried out again and listened again. The same silence of death reigned in the forest. Worry seized me, and I ran along the stream to find the path that crossed its course farther down. Reaching there, I heard in the distance the step of horses and soon after I saw Beaumont himself. Astonished by my long absence, he had taken the gamble of advancing toward the stream; he was already in the shallows when I had called him. My voice had not been able to reach him. He told me that on his side he had made all efforts to make himself heard and, like me, had been frightened not to receive a response. Without the ford that served as our point of reunion, we would perhaps have searched for each other a large part of the night. We retook our route promising each other indeed not to separate again, and three quarters of an hour from there we finally noticed a clearing, two or three cabins, and what pleased us most, a light.[s] The river that extended like a purple thread to the end of the valley conclusively proved to us that we had arrived at *Flint River*. Soon in fact the barking of dogs made the woods echo, and we found ourselves before a *log house* separated from us by a single fence. As we prepared to cross it, the moon revealed to us on the other side a large black bear standing upright on its paws and pulling on its chain, indicating as clearly as it could its intention to give us a very fraternal embrace. "What the devil is this country," I said, "where you have bears as watchdogs." "We must call," my companion replied to me. "If we try to cross the fence, we will have difficulty explaining the reason to the gatekeeper." So we shouted out so loudly and so well that a man finally appeared at the window. After examining us in the moonlight: "Come in, Sirs," he said to us; "Trinc, go lie down. To your kennel, I tell you. They are not robbers." The bear waddled away and we entered. We were half-dead with fatigue. We asked our

s. I see a light; I get off my horse; I walk straight toward the light that struck my eyes. After walking for five minutes, I am near enough to distinguish a house of wood without a door and half-covered. Someone was walking around inside without appearing, and it seemed to me that someone was trying hard to hide the light that illuminated the interior. Finally, using the mildest and most humble voice in order to reassure the people of this habitation who could take me for a robber, I ask if they can point out to me the house of Mr. Todds [Todd (ed.)]. (This is the name of the person we wanted to visit at Flint River.) Then a half-dressed woman appears, carrying a torch in her hand, and says to me in the most obliging way that the house of Mr. Todds is in the neighborhood and not far away. (This unfortunate woman was alone in this abandoned house open to all the wind.) I did not have the time to sympathize more with her misfortune, and I returned to rejoin Tocqueville, not without difficulty, given that I was stuck in a swamp where I thought for an instant that I would remain. Finally we found refuge with Mr. Todds, and at 11 o'clock we were in bed, one in a bed, the other on the floor.

Letter of Beaumont to Ernest de Chabrol, 2 August 1831, *Lettres d'Amérique*, p. 113.

"Uncle John Todd" was the first settler to come to Flint. In 1830, he had constructed a small inn, "Todd's tavern," which over the years became a celebrated place in the region. George W. Pierson, *Tocqueville and Beaumont in America*, pp. 258–59.

host if we could have some oats. Surely, he said; he immediately began to reap the closest field with all American calm and doing it as he would have in full day. During this time we unsaddled our mounts and, not having a stable, tied them to the fences that we had just crossed. Having thus considered our travel companions, we began to think about our shelter. There was only one bed in the house. Since it went to Beaumont by lot, I wrapped myself in my coat and, lying on the floor, slept as profoundly as is suitable for a man who has just done fifteen leagues on horseback.

*   *   *   *   *

The next day, July 25, our first concern was to ask about a guide. A wilderness of fifteen leagues separates *Flint River* from Saginaw, and the road that leads there is a narrow path, scarcely recognizable by sight. Our host approved our plan and soon after he brought in two Indians in whom, he assured us, we could have complete confidence. One was a child, thirteen or fourteen years old. The other a young man of eighteen.[t] The body of the latter, without yet having the vigorous forms of mature age, already gave the idea of agility combined with strength. He was of average height, his stature was straight and slim, his limbs flexible and well-proportioned. Long braids fell from his bare head. In addition he had carefully painted on his face black and red lines in the most symmetrical manner. A ring passed through the septum of his nose; a necklace and earrings completed his outfit. His war gear was no less remarkable. On one side a battle ax, the famous tomahawk; on the other, a long sharp knife with which the savages remove the scalp of the defeated. Around his neck was suspended a bull's horn that served as his powder flask, and he held a carbine with a grooved barrel in his right hand. As with most Indians, his look was fierce and his smile benevolent. Next to him, as if to complete the picture, walked a dog with upright ears, elongated muzzle, much more like a fox than any other

---

t. "We were provided with an Indian guide, a young man twenty years old. *Sagan-Kuisko,* of the Chippewa nation" (pocket notebook 2, YTC, BIIa, and *Voyage, OC,* V, 1, p. 168).

type of animal, and whose fierce appearance was in perfect harmony with the countenance of the man leading it. After examining our new companion with an attention that he did not appear to notice for a single moment, we asked him what he wanted from us as the price for the service that he was going to give us. The Indian answered with a few words in his language and the American, hastening to speak, informed us that what the savage asked could be evaluated at two dollars. "Since these poor Indians," our host added charitably, "do not know the value of money, you will give me the dollars and I will gladly take charge of providing him the equivalent." I was curious to see what the worthy man called the equivalent of two dollars, and I followed him quietly into the place where the market was. I saw him deliver to our guide a pair of moccasins and a pocket handkerchief, objects whose total value certainly did not amount to half of the sum. The Indian withdrew very satisfied and I fled silently, saying like La Fontaine: Ah! if lions knew how to paint!

Moreover, it is not only Indians that the American pioneers take for fools. We ourselves were victims every day of their extreme greed for profit. It is very true that they do not steal. That have too much enlightenment to commit something so imprudent, but nonetheless I have never seen an innkeeper of a large city overcharge with more shamelessness than these inhabitants of the wilderness among whom I imagined to find primitive honesty and the simplicity of patriarchal mores.

Everything was ready. We mounted our horses and, fording the stream that forms the extreme limit between civilization and the wilderness, we entered for good into the empty forest.

Our two guides walked or rather leapt like wild cats over the obstacles in our path. If we happened to encounter a fallen tree, a stream, a swamp, they pointed with their finger to the best path, went by and did not even turn back to see us get by the difficulty; used to counting only on himself, the Indian conceives with difficulty that another man needs help. He knows how to serve you as needed, but no one has yet taught him the art of improving the service by consideration and concern. This way of acting would nonetheless have led to some comments on our part, but it was impossible to make a single word understood by our companions. And then! we felt completely in their power. There in fact the tables were turned; plunged into a perfect darkness, reduced to his own resources, civilized man walked blind, incapable, not only of finding his own way in the labyrinth that he was going through, but even of finding the means to sustain his life. It is amid these same difficulties that the savage triumphed; for him the forest had no veil, he found himself as if in his own country; he walked there with his head high, guided by an instinct surer than the compass of the navigator. At the top of the tallest trees, beneath the thickest foliage, his eye found the prey that the European would have passed and repassed in vain a hundred times.

From time to time our Indians stopped; they put their finger to their lips to indicate to us to be quiet and gestured to us to dismount. Guided by them, we came to a place where you could see game. It was a singular sight to see the disdainful smile with which they led us by the hand like children and brought us finally near the object that they had seen for a long time.[u]

But as we advanced, the last traces of man faded. Soon everything ceased even to announce the presence of the savage, and we had before us the spectacle that we had been chasing for such a long time, the interior of a virgin forest.

In the middle of a not very dense thicket, through which objects at a fairly great distance could be seen, a tall cluster of trees composed almost totally of pines and oaks arose in a single burst. Forced to grow on a very limited terrain almost entirely without the rays of the sun, each of these trees goes up rapidly in order to find air and light. As straight as the mast of a ship, each tree does not take long to rise above everything that surrounds it. Having reached an upper region, it then tranquilly spreads its branches and surrounds itself with their shade. Others soon follow it into this elevated sphere and, intertwining their branches, all form like an im-

---

u. "Seeing that I tried to kill birds, he showed them to me when I did not see them; in this way he made it possible for me to kill a very beautiful bird of prey. We hunted in this way without getting off our horses, and when we fired, our peaceful mounts did not give the least sign of emotion." Letter of Beaumont to Ernest de Chabrol (2 August 1831), *Lettres d'Amérique*, p. 114.

mense canopy above the earth that supports them. Beneath this humid and unchanging vault, the appearance changes and the scene takes on a new character. A majestic order reigns above our heads. Near the earth everything presents on the contrary the image of confusion and of chaos. Some trunks, incapable of bearing their branches any longer, have split halfway from the top and no longer present anything to view except a sharp and broken tip. Others, shaken for a long time by the wind, have been thrown whole onto the ground; torn out of the earth, their roots form like so many natural ramparts behind which several men could easily take shelter. Immense trees, held up by the branches that surround them, rest suspended in air and fall into dust without touching the earth. Among us, there is no country, no matter how unpopulated, in which a forest is left alone enough for the trees, after tranquilly following their course, to fall finally due to decrepitude.^v It is man who strikes them in their prime and who rids the

v. Also it is against the woods that all the energy of civilized man seems to be directed. With us, wood is cut for use; here, it is cut to destroy. Prodigious efforts are made to obliterate it, and often these efforts are powerless. Vegetation is so rapid that it mocks the endeavors of man. The Americans in the country spend half their life cutting trees, and their children at a young age already learn how to use the hook and the ax against the trees, their enemies. Also in America, there is a general sentiment of hatred against trees. The prettiest country houses sometimes lack shade for this reason. It is believed that the absence of trees is the sign of civilization. Nothing seems uglier than a forest; on the other hand, people find a field of wheat charming. Besides, these fields of wheat present a strange appearance. All are full of tree trunks that have been crudely cut at the height of a man and whose presence on the land still recalls, despite destruction, the memory of these forests that they would like to forget. Letter of Beaumont to his sister, Eugénie (Auburn, 17 July 1831), *Lettres d'Amérique*, pp. 92–93.

In 1851, Tocqueville writes to Madame de Circourt:

M. de Chateaubriand himself portrayed the true wilderness, at least the one that I know, with false colors. He seems to have crossed, without seeing it, this endless, humid, cold, gloomy, somber and silent forest that follows you to the top of the mountains, descends with you to the bottom of the valleys, and that more than the ocean itself gives the idea of the immensity of nature and of the ridiculous smallness of man (*Correspondance avec Madame de Circourt, OC,* XVIII, p. 52).

On the differences between Tocqueville's forest and that of Chateaubriand, see Eva

forest of their remains. [≠Our woods always present the image of youth or of strength. In the forests of the New World, on the contrary, you see trees of all ages, from the weakest shoot to the hundred-year-old oak.≠] In the uninhabited areas of America, nature in its omnipotence is the sole agent of ruin, as well as the sole power of reproduction. Just as in forests subjected to the dominion of man, death strikes here constantly; but no one takes responsibility for clearing the remains that death has caused. Every day adds to the amount. They fall, they accumulate on each other; time cannot reduce them to dust quickly enough to prepare new places. There side by side several generations of dead trees are found lying together. Some at the last stage of decay no longer offer anything to view except a long line of red dust drawn on the grass. But others, already half-consumed by time, still preserve their forms. There are some finally that, just fallen, still spread their long branches on the ground and halt the steps of the traveler with an obstacle that he had not expected. Amid these divers remains, the work of reproduction goes on without ceasing. Shoots, climbing plants, weeds of all types grow up across all the obstacles. They creep along the fallen trunks; they worm into their dust; they lift up and break the bark that still covers them. [They slip between these immobile cadavers, creep along their surface, penetrate beneath their withered bark, lift up and scatter their powdery remains.] Life and death here are as if face to face; they seem to have wanted to mix and mingle their work.[w]

We often happened to admire one of those calm and serene evenings at sea, when the sails, flapping peacefully along the masts, leave the sailors not knowing from which direction the breeze will come. All of nature at rest is no less imposing in the uninhabited areas of the New World than on the immensity of the sea. When at midday the rays of the sun beat down on the forest, you often hear echoing in its depths something like a long moan,

---

Doran, "Two Men and a Forest: Chateaubriand, Tocqueville and the American Wilderness," *Essays in French Literature*, 13, 1976, pp. 44–61.

w. Tocqueville uses the same description in *Voyage to Lake Oneida* and in the first volume, p. 39.

a plaintive cry that lingers in the distance. It is the final effort of the wind that is expiring. Then everything around you falls into a silence so profound, an immobility so complete that your soul feels penetrated by a sort of religious terror. The traveler stops, he looks around. Pressed together, intertwined in their branches, the trees of the forest seem to form only a single whole, an immense and indestructible edifice, under whose vaults reigns an eternal darkness. In no matter which direction he looks, he sees only a field of violence and destruction. Broken trees, torn trunks, everything announces that here the elements are perpetually at war. But the struggle is interrupted. You would say that at the order of a supernatural power, movement is suddenly halted. Half-broken branches still seem to hold on by a few hidden bonds to the trunk that no longer offers them support; trees already uprooted have not had the time to come to earth and remain suspended in the air. The traveler listens, he holds his breath with fear the better to grasp the slightest reverberation of existence; no sound, no murmur is heard.

More than once in Europe we happened to find ourselves lost deep in the woods, but always a few sounds of life came to our ears. It was the distant ringing from the church tower of the nearest village, the step of a traveler, the ax of the woodsman, the explosion of a firearm, the barking of a dog, or only that confused murmur that arises from a civilized country. Here, not only man is missing, but even the sound of animals is not heard. The smallest among them have left these places to move closer to human habitation; the largest, to move still further away. The animals that remain keep hidden out of the sunlight. Thus everything is immobile in the woods, everything is silent beneath its leaves. You would say that the Creator has for one moment turned His face away and that the forces of nature are paralyzed.

Not only in this case, moreover, did we notice the singular analogy that exists between the sight of the ocean and the appearance of a wild forest. In both spectacles, the idea of immensity assails you. The continuity of the same scenes, their monotony astonishes and hinders the imagination. We perhaps found the sentiment of isolation and abandonment that had seemed so heavy to us in the middle of the Atlantic stronger and more poignant in the uninhabited areas of the New World. On the sea at least the traveler contemplates a vast horizon toward which he directs his view with hope. But in this ocean of leaves, who can point out the road? Toward which objects to turn your eyes? In vain do you go up to the top of the largest trees; others still higher surround you. It is useless to climb hills; everywhere the forest seems to move with you, and this same forest extends before you from the Arctic Pole to the Pacific Ocean. You can travel thousands of leagues in its shadow, and you move always, but without appearing to change place.

*   *   *   *   *

But it is time to return to the road to Saginaw. We had already walked for five hours in the most complete ignorance of the places where we found ourselves, when our Indians stopped and the oldest who was called Sagan-Cuisco drew a line in the sand. He pointed to one end while crying: Miché-Conté-Ouinque (the Indian name for *Flint River)* and the opposite end while pronouncing the name of Saginaw, and making a dot in the middle of the line, he indicated to us that we had reached the mid-point of the road and that we had to rest for a few moments. The sun was already high above the horizon and we would have accepted with pleasure the invitation made to us, if we had noticed water within reach. But not seeing any in the vicinity, we made a sign to the Indian that we wanted to eat and drink at the same time. He immediately understood us and began to walk again with the same rapidity as before. An hour later, he stopped again and showed us a place thirty steps away in the woods where he gestured that there was water. Without awaiting our response or without helping us un-saddle our horses, he went there himself; we hastened to follow him. The wind had recently overturned a large tree in this place. In the hole where its roots had been was a bit of rainwater. It was the fountain to which our guide led us without having the appearance of thinking that someone could hesitate to use such a drink. We opened our bag; another misfortune! The heat had absolutely spoiled our provisions and we were completely reduced to dining on a very small piece of bread, the only one we had been able to find at *Flint River.* Add to that a cloud of mosquitoes attracted by the presence of the water, that had to be battled with one hand while putting the piece of bread in your mouth with the other, and you will have the idea of a rustic dinner in a virgin forest. While we ate, our Indians remained seated, arms crossed, on the fallen trunk that I spoke about. When they saw that we had finished, they gestured to us that they also were hungry. We showed them our empty bag. They shook their heads without saying a word. The Indian does not know what regular hours for meals are. He gorges himself with food when he can and then goes without until he again finds something to satisfy the appetite. Wolves act the same in similar circumstances. Soon we thought about remounting, but we noticed with great fright that our mounts had disappeared. Bitten by mosquitoes and goaded by hunger they had gone away from the path where we had left them, and it was only with difficulty that we were able to find their trail. If we had remained inattentive for a quarter-hour more, we would have awakened like Sancho with a saddle between his legs. We blessed with all our hearts the mosquitoes that had made us think so quickly about leaving, and we resumed our way. The track that we followed did not take long to become more and more difficult to recognize. At every instant, our horses had to force their way through dense thickets or jump over immense tree trunks that barred our way. At the end of two hours of an extremely difficult road, we finally reached the bank of a river that was not very deep but steeply hemmed in. We forded it and, having reached the top of the opposite bank, we saw a field of corn and two cabins quite similar to *log houses*. We realized as we drew near that we were in a small Indian settlement. The *log houses* were wigwams. Moreover, the most profound solitude reigned there as in the surrounding forest. Coming before the first of these abandoned dwellings, Sagan-Cuisco stopped, he attentively examined all the surrounding objects, then putting down his carbine and approaching us, he first drew a line in the sand, indicating to us in the same way as before that we had not yet completed two-thirds of the road; then, getting up, he showed us the sun and made a sign that it was rapidly descending toward sunset. He then looked at the wigwam and closed his eyes. This language was very understandable; he wanted us to sleep in this place. I admit that the proposition greatly surprised and scarcely pleased us. We had not eaten since morning and we didn't care very much about sleeping without eating. The somber and wild majesty of the scenes that we had witnessed since morning, the total isolation in which we found ourselves, the fierce countenance of our guides with whom it was impossible to make a connection, nothing in all of that was of a nature to give us confidence. Moreover, there was something singular in the behavior of the Indians that did not reassure us. The route that we had just followed for two hours seemed even less traveled than the one that we had followed before. No one had ever told us that we had to pass by an Indian village, and on the contrary everyone had assured us that you could go from Flint River to Saginaw in a single day. So we could not conceive why our guides wanted to keep us for the night in the wilderness. We insisted on moving. The Indians gestured that we would be surprised by darkness in the woods. To force our guides to continue on their road would have been a dangerous endeavor. We decided to tempt their greed. But the Indian is the most philosophical of all men. He has few needs and hence few desires. Civilization has no hold on him; he is unaware of or disdains its sweet pleasures. I had noticed, however, that Sagan-Cuisco had paid particular attention to a small bottle in wicker that hung at my side. A bottle that does not break is something whose utility he had grasped and that had aroused a real admiration in him. My rifle and my bottle were the only parts of my European gear that had appeared to arouse his envy. I gestured to him that I would give him my bottle if he led us immediately to Saginaw. The Indian then appeared violently torn. He looked again at the sun, then the ground. Finally making his decision, he grabbed his carbine; putting his hand to his mouth, he let out two cries of: Oh! Oh! and rushed before us into the undergrowth. We followed him at a fast trot, and forcing open a path before us, we had soon lost sight of the Indian dwellings. Our guides ran in this way for two hours more rapidly than they had done as yet; but night overtook us, and the last rays of the sun had just disappeared in the trees of the forest when Sagan-Cuisco was surprised by a violent nosebleed. However accustomed this young man as well as his brother seemed to be to bodily exercise, it was evident that fatigue and the lack of food began to exhaust his strength. We began to be afraid that they would give up the undertaking and would want to sleep at the foot of a tree. So we decided to have them alternately mount our horses. The Indians accepted our offer without astonishment or humility. It was something bizarre to see, these men half-naked seated solemnly on an English saddle and carrying our gamebags and our rifles slung over their shoulders, while we went with difficulty on foot before them. Night finally came, a freezing dampness began to spread under the foliage. Darkness then gave the forest a new and terrible appearance. The eye could no longer see anything around except masses heaped up in confusion, without order or symmetry, bizarre and disproportionate forms, incoherent scenes, fantastic images that seemed borrowed from the sick imagination of someone feverish. (The gigantesque and the ridiculous there were as close as in the literature of our time.) Never had our steps brought forth as many echoes; never had the silence of the forest seemed so fearsome to us. You would have said that the buzzing of the mosquitoes was the sole breath of this sleeping world. As we advanced, the shadows became deeper; only from time to time did a firefly crossing the woods trace a sort of luminous line in its depths. We recognized too late the correctness of the advice of the Indian, but it was no longer a matter of going back. So we continued to march as rapidly as our strength and the night allowed us to do. At the end of an hour we came out of the woods and found ourselves on a vast prairie. Our guides three times yelled out a savage cry that reverberated like discordant notes of the tom-tom. Someone answered in the distance. Five minutes later we were on the bank of a river whose opposite side the darkness prevented us from seeing. The Indians came to a halt at this place; they covered themselves with their blankets to avoid the biting of the mosquitoes; sleeping on the grass, they soon formed nothing more than a ball of wool hardly visible and in which it would have been impossible to recognize the form of a man. We ourselves stood on the ground and waited patiently for what would follow. At the end of several minutes a slight noise was heard and something approached the shore. It was an Indian canoe about ten feet long and formed out of a single tree. The man who was crouching at the bottom of this fragile small boat wore the costume and had all the appearance of an Indian. He addressed a word to our guides who at his command hastened to remove the saddles from our horses and to put them in the dugout. As I prepared to climb in, the supposed Indian advanced toward me, put two fingers on my shoulder and said to me with a Norman accent that made me start: "Don't go too fast, there are times here when people drown."[x] My horse would have spoken to me, and I would not, I believe, have been more surprised. I viewed the man who had spoken to me and whose face, struck by the first light of the moon, then shone like a copper sphere: "So who are you," I said to him; "French seems to be your language and you have the appearance of an Indian?" He answered me that he was a *bois-brulé,* that is to say the son of a Canadian man and an Indian woman. I will often have the occasion to speak about this singular race of half-breeds that covers all the frontiers of Canada and a part of those of the United States. For the moment I thought only about the pleasure of speaking my native language. Following the advice of our compatriot, the savage, I sat down at the bottom of the canoe and kept my balance as much as possible. The horse got into the river and began to swim as soon as the Canadian pushed the skiff with the paddle, all the while singing in a low voice an old French tune, of whose verse I grasped only the first two lines:

> *Between Paris and Saint-Denis*
> *There was a girl*

We thus arrived without accident on the other side. The canoe returned immediately to get my companion. I will remember all my life the moment when for the second time it approached the shore. The moon, which was full, then rose precisely above the prairie that we had just crossed. Half of the circle of the moon appeared alone on the horizon; you would have said a mysterious door through which the light of another sphere escaped toward us. The moonlight that emerged reflected on the waters of the river

---

x. "<I want to get into the boat while holding my horse by the bridle. 'The saddle must be removed,' the supposed Indian said to me, 'there are times here when people drown.' Norman accent, barely intelligible French. I remove my saddle, place it in the canoe, place myself beside it. The large Indian puts himself at the end, holding the bridle. The Canadian rows; the horse swimming>" (pocket notebook 2, YTC, BIIa, and *Voyage, OC,* V, 1, p. 170).

and glistening reached me. On the very line on which this pale light shimmered, the Indian dugout advanced; you did not notice the oars, you did not hear the noise of the paddles, it glided rapidly and without effort, long, narrow and black, similar to an alligator of the Mississippi that stretched toward the bank to seize its prey. Crouched at the front of the canoe, Sagan-Cuisco, his head leaning against his knees, showed only the shining braids of his hair. At the other end, the Canadian rowed in silence, while behind him, the horse made the water of the Saginaw splash with the effort of his powerful chest. There was in this whole spectacle a wild grandeur that then made and has since left a profound impression on our souls. Disembarked on the shore we hurried to go to a house that the moon had just revealed to us one hundred steps from the river and where the Canadian assured us that we would be able to find shelter. We managed in fact to get settled comfortably there, and we would probably have regained our strength by a deep sleep if we had been able to rid ourselves of the myriad mosquitoes that filled the house; but that we could never manage to do. The animal that is called *mosquito* in English and *maringouin* in Canadian French is a small insect similar in everything to the *cousin* of France from which it differs only in size. It is generally larger and its proboscis is so strong and so sharp that woolen fabric alone can protect against its bites. These small gnats are the plague of the American wilderness. Their presence would be enough to make a long stay unbearable. As for me, I declare that I have never experienced a torment similar to what they made me suffer throughout the entire course of this trip and particularly during our stay at Saginaw. During the day they prevented us from drawing, writing, remaining still for a single moment; at night, they circled by the thousands around us; every part of the body that you left exposed served immediately as their rendezvous. Awakened by the pain caused by the bite, we covered our heads with our sheets; their sting passed through; chased, pursued by them in this way, we got up and went to breathe the outside air until fatigue finally brought us a difficult and interrupted sleep.

* * * * *

We went out very early and the first sight that struck us as we left the house was the view of our Indians who, rolled up in their blankets near the door, slept next to their dogs.

We then saw for the first time in daylight the village of Saginaw that we had come so far to find.

A small cultivated plain, bordered on the south by a beautiful and tranquil river, on the east and on the north by the forest, makes up for the present the entire territory of the emerging city.[y]

Near us arose a house whose structure announced the prosperity of the owner. It was the one where we had just spent the night. A dwelling of the same type was noticeable from the other end of the clearing. In between and along the edge of the woods, two or three *log houses* were half lost in the foliage. On the opposite bank of the river, a prairie extended like a limitless ocean on a calm day. A column of smoke escaped then from the prairie and climbed peacefully toward the sky. By following its direction toward the earth, we discovered two or three wigwams whose conical form and pointed tips blended into the grasses of the prairie.

An overturned plow, oxen returning to plowing, some half-wild horses completed the picture.

In whatever direction you looked, your eye searched in vain for the spire of a Gothic church tower, the wooden cross that marks the road, or the moss-covered doorway of the presbytery. These venerable remnants of ancient Christian civilization have not been carried into the wilderness; nothing there yet awakens the idea of the past or of the future. You do not even find places of rest consecrated to those who are no more. Death has not had the time to reclaim its sphere or mark out its field.

Here man still seems to come furtively into life. Several generations do

---

y. Variant: "≠The village of Saginaw is made up of four or five houses scattered over a small cultivated plain surrounded on all sides by the forest {the cabins are placed a hundred steps from the river}. The river that is called the Saginaw and that has given its name to the clearing runs in {a deep bed until} Lake Huron.≠" Grateful for Tocqueville's description, the city of Saginaw has built a center for the federal administration as a reproduction of the Tocqueville château (Richard Reeves, *American Journey,* New York: Simon and Schuster, 1982), p. 188.

not gather around his cradle to express hopes that are often false, and to give themselves to premature joys that the future will belie. His name is not inscribed in the records of the city. Religion does not come to mix its touching solemnities with the solicitudes of the family. The prayers of a woman, a few drops of water poured on the head of the infant by the hand of the father, quietly open the gates of heaven to him.

The village of Saginaw is the last point inhabited by Europeans to the northwest of the vast Michigan peninsula. It can be considered like an outpost, a sort of sentry point that whites have placed amid the Indian nations.

The revolutions of Europe, the tumultuous clamor that is constantly arising from the civilized world, reach here only now and then, and are like the echo of a sound whose nature and origin the ears cannot make out.

Sometimes it will be an Indian who, while passing, will recount with the poetry of the wilderness some of these sad realities of the life of society; a forgotten newspaper in the knapsack of a hunter; or only that vague rumor that is propagated by unknown voices and almost never fails to alert men that something extraordinary is happening under the sun.

Once a year, a ship ascending the course of the Saginaw comes to reconnect this link detached from the great European chain that already envelops the world with its coils. It brings to the new settlement the diverse products of industry and in turn takes away the fruits of the land.

At the time of our passage, thirty persons alone, men, women, old people and children, composed this small society, an embryo scarcely formed, an emerging seed entrusted to the wilderness, that the wilderness is to make fruitful.

Chance, interest, or passions had gathered these thirty persons in this narrow space. Moreover, no common bond existed between them and they differed profoundly from each other. You noticed Canadians, Americans, Indians and half-breeds there.

Philosophers have believed that human nature everywhere the same only varied according to the institutions and the laws of different societies. That is one of those opinions that every page of the history of the world seems to belie. Nations, like individuals, all appear with a physiognomy that is their own. The characteristic features of their countenance are reproduced throughout all the transformations that they undergo. Laws, mores, religions change, empire and wealth are displaced; the external appearance varies, the dress differs, prejudices fade or are substituted for others. Among these diverse changes you always recognize the same people. Something inflexible appears amid human flexibility.

The men who inhabit this small, cultivated plain belong to two races that for nearly a century have existed on the American soil and obeyed the same laws. [{Before coming to America, their fathers had lived under the same European sky; an arm of the sea more narrow than the Saint Lawrence River separated their countries.}] But they have nothing in common between them. They are English and French, just as they appear on the banks of the Seine and the Thames.

Enter this cabin of foliage, you will meet a man whose cordial welcome and open countenance will announce to you from the beginning the taste for social pleasures and lack of concern about life. At the first moment you will perhaps take him for an Indian; subjected to savage life, he has willingly adopted their habits, customs and almost their mores. He wears moccasins, a hat of otter-skin, a woolen blanket. He is an indefatigable hunter, lying in wait, living on wild honey and buffalo meat. This man has nonetheless still remained no less a Frenchman, cheerful, enterprising, self-important, proud of his origins, passionate lover of military glory, more vain than self-interested, a man of instinct, obeying his first movement rather than his reason, preferring making a stir to making money. In order to come to the wilderness he seems to have broken all the bonds that attached him to life; you see him with neither wife nor children. This condition is contrary to his mores, but he submits to it easily as to everything. Left to himself, he would naturally feel the stay-at-home mood; no one more than he has the taste for the domestic hearth; no one loves more to delight his sight with the appearance of the paternal church tower; but he has been torn despite himself from his tranquil habits; his imagination has been struck by new images; he has been transplanted beneath another sky; this same man feels suddenly possessed by an insatiable need for violent emotions, vicissitudes and dangers. The most civilized European has become the worshipper of savage life. He will prefer the plains to the streets of the city, hunting to agriculture. He will make light of existence and live without concern for the future.

The whites of France, said the Indians of Canada, are as good hunters as we. Like us, they scorn the comforts of life and face the terrors of death. God had created them to inhabit the cabin of the savage and to live in the wilderness.[z]

A few steps from this man lives another European who, subject to the same difficulties, became steeled against them.

This man is cold, tenacious, mercilessly argumentative; he attaches himself to the land, and tears all that he can take from savage life. He struggles constantly against it; he despoils it daily of some of its attributes. He transports into the wilderness, piece by piece, his laws, his habits, his customs and, if he can, even the slightest refinements of his advanced civilization. The emigrant of the United States values from victory only its results; he holds that glory is a vain noise and that man comes into the world only to acquire comfort and the conveniences of life. Brave nonetheless, but brave by calculation, brave because he has discovered that there were several things more difficult to bear than death. Adventurer surrounded by his family, yet who little values intellectual pleasures and the charms of social life.

Placed on the other side of the river, amid the reeds of the Saginaw, the Indian from time to time casts a stoic glance on the habitations of his brothers from Europe. Do not think that he admires their works, or envies their lot. For the nearly three hundred years that the savage of America has struggled against the civilization that pushes and surrounds him, he has not yet learned to know and to esteem his enemy. The generations follow each other in vain among the two races. Like two parallel rivers, they flow for three hundred years toward a common abyss; a narrow space separates them, but they do not blend their waves. Not, nonetheless, that the native of the New World lacks natural aptitude, but his nature seems stubbornly to reject our ideas and our arts. Seated on his blanket amid the smoke of his hut, the Indian looks with scorn on the comfortable dwelling of the

z. Cf. "Some ideas on the reasons that go against the French having good colonies," *Écrits et discours politiques, OC,* III, 1, pp. 36–37.

European; as for him, he proudly takes pleasure in his misery, and his heart swells and rises at the images of his barbaric independence. He smiles bitterly seeing us torment our lives in order to acquire useless riches. What we call industry, he calls shameful subjection. He compares the farmer to the ox that painfully traces his furrow. What we call the conveniences of life, he calls the toys of children or the refinements of women. He only envies our weapons. When man can shelter his head for the night under a tent of leaves, when he is able to light a fire to chase away the mosquitoes in the summer and to protect himself from cold in the winter, when his dogs are good and the country full of game, what more can he ask from the eternal Being?

On the other bank of the Saginaw, near the European clearings and so to speak on the borders of the Old and the New World, arises a rustic cabin more comfortable than the wigwam of the savage, more crude than the home of the civilized man. This is the dwelling of the half-breed. When we presented ourselves for the first time at the door of this half-civilized hut, we were completely surprised to hear in the interior a soft voice that chanted hymns of penitence to an Indian tune. We stopped a moment to listen. The modulations of sound were slow and profoundly melancholy; we easily recognized the plaintive harmony that characterizes all the songs of the man of the wilderness. We entered. The master was absent. Seated in the middle of the room, her legs crossed on a mat, a young woman worked making moccasins; with her foot she rocked an infant whose coppery color and features announced its double origin. This woman was dressed like one of our peasant women, except that her feet were naked and her hair fell freely over her shoulders. Seeing us, she became quiet with a kind of respectful fear. We asked her if she was French. "No," she answered smiling. "English?" "Not that either," she said; she lowered her eyes and added: "I am only a savage." Child of two races, raised using two languages, nourished with diverse beliefs and reared with opposing prejudices, the half-breed forms a combination as inexplicable to others as to himself. The images of the world, when his crude brain happens to think about them, appear to him only as an inextricable chaos which his mind cannot escape. Proud of his European origin, he scorns the wilderness, and yet he loves the wild liberty that reigns there. He admires civilization and cannot completely submit to its dominion. His tastes are in contradiction to his ideas, his opinions to his mores. Not knowing how to be guided by the uncertain light that illumines it, his soul struggles painfully, wrapped in a universal doubt. He adopts opposing customs; he prays at two altars; he believes in the Redeemer of the world and in the amulets of the medicine man; and he reaches the end of his course not having been able to sort out the obscure problem of his existence.

So in this forgotten corner of the world the hand of God had already sown the seeds of diverse nations; several different races, several distinct peoples already find themselves face to face.

Some exiled members of the great human family have met in the immensity of the woods, their needs are common; they have to struggle together against the beasts of the forest, hunger, the harshness of the seasons. They are hardly thirty in the middle of a wilderness in which everything rejects their efforts, and they cast on each other only looks of hatred and suspicion. Skin color, poverty or comfort, ignorance or enlightenment have already established indestructible classifications among them; national prejudices, the prejudices of education and birth divide them and isolate them.

Where to find in a more narrow frame a more complete picture of the miseries of our nature? A feature is still missing however.

The deep lines that birth and opinion have drawn between the destinies of these men, do not cease with life, but extend beyond the tomb. Six diverse religions or sects share the faith of this emerging society.

Catholicism with its formidable immobility, its absolute dogmas, its terrible anathemas and immense rewards, the religious anarchy of the Reformation, the ancient paganism find their representatives here. The unique and eternal Being who created all men in His image is worshipped here in six different ways. Men fight fervently over the heaven that each man claims exclusively as his heritage. Even more, amid the miseries of the wilderness and the misfortunes of the present, the human imagination still exhausts itself giving birth to a future of inexpressible pains. The Lutheran condemns the Calvinist to eternal fire; the Calvinist, the Unitarian; and the Catholic envelops them all in a common reprobation.

More tolerant in his crude faith, the Indian limits himself to exiling his

European brother from the happy hunting grounds that he reserves for himself. As for him, faithful to the confused traditions that his fathers bequeathed to him, he easily consoles himself for the evils of life and dies peacefully dreaming of forests always green that will never be disturbed by the ax of the pioneer, and where the deer and the beaver will come to offer themselves to his shots during the days without number of eternity.

*   *   *   *   *

After breakfast we went to see the richest proprietor of the village, Mr. Williams. We found him in his shop selling to the Indians a multitude of objects of little value such as knives, glass necklaces, ear pendants. It was pitiful to see how these unfortunate men were treated by their civilized brothers from Europe. Moreover, all those that we saw there acknowledged something striking about the savages. They were good, inoffensive, a thousand times less inclined to theft than the white. It was too bad, however, that they were beginning to become informed about the value of things. And why, please? Because the profits of the trade that we conduct with them became less considerable every day. Do you see here the superiority of the civilized man? The Indian would have said in his crude simplicity, that everyday he found it more difficult to deceive his neighbor. But the white finds in the perfection of language a fortunate nuance that expresses the thing and spares the shame.

Returning from Mr. Williams we had the idea of going up the Saginaw for a distance in order to shoot the wild ducks that populate its banks. While we were busy with this hunt, a dugout came out of the reeds of the river and some Indians came to meet us in order to look at my rifle that they had seen from afar. I always noticed that this weapon, which was, however, nothing extraordinary, attracted an entirely special consideration from the savages. A rifle that can kill two men in one second and fire in the fog was, according to them, a marvel above all estimation, a masterpiece beyond price. Those who came up to us displayed as usual a great admiration. They asked where my rifle came from. Our young guide answered that it had been made on the other side of the Great Water, among the fathers of the Canadians; this did not make it, as you can believe, less precious in their eyes. They observed, however, that since the sight was not placed in the middle of each barrel, you could not be as certain about the shot, a remark to which I admit that I did not know what to answer.

When evening came we climbed back into the canoe and, relying on the experience that we had gained during the morning, we went alone to go up an arm of the Saginaw that we had only seen briefly.

[{I do not believe that I have ever in my life more strongly felt this type of pleasure, at once physical and intellectual, that beautiful nature and a serene evening make you feel.}] The sky was cloudless, the atmosphere pure and still. The river flowed through an immense forest, but so slowly that is was almost impossible to say in which direction the current went. We always felt that, to have an accurate idea of the forests of the New World, it would be necessary to follow a few of the rivers that circulate in their shadow. The rivers are like great roads with which Providence has taken care, since the beginning of the world, to pierce the wilderness to make it accessible to man. When you clear a passage through the woods, the view is most often very limited. Moreover, the very path that you walk along is a human work. Rivers on the contrary are roads that respect no trails, and their banks freely show all that a vigorous vegetation, left to itself, can offer of great and interesting spectacles.

The wilderness was there such as it probably presented itself six thousand years ago to the view of our first fathers; an uninhabited space, flowering, delicious, fragrant; a magnificent dwelling place, a living palace, built for man, but where the master had not yet entered. The canoe glided effortlessly and noiselessly; around us reigned a universal serenity and quiet. We ourselves did not take long to feel as though weakened at the sight of such a spectacle. Our words began to become more and more rare; soon we expressed our thoughts only in a low voice. Finally we became silent, and simultaneously withdrawing our paddles, we both fell into a tranquil reverie full of inexpressible charms.

Why do human languages that find so many words for all the pains meet an invincible obstacle to making the sweetest and most natural emotions of the heart understood? Who will ever portray with fidelity those moments so rare in life when physical well-being prepares you for moral tranquillity and when something like a perfect equilibrium in the universe is established before your eyes; when the soul, half asleep, balances between the present and the future, between the real and the possible; when, surrounded by beautiful nature, breathing a tranquil and mild atmosphere, at peace with himself, amid a universal peace, man lends an ear to the steady beating of his arteries, each pulse of which marks the passage of time that for him seems to flow drop by drop into eternity. Many men perhaps have seen the years of a long life accumulate without once experiencing anything similar to what we have just described. Those men cannot understand us. But there are some, we are sure, who will find in their memories and at the bottom of their hearts something to color our pictures with and, while reading us, will feel the recollection reawakened of a few fleeting hours that neither time nor the positive cares of life have been able to erase.

We were drawn out of our reverie by a rifle shot that suddenly echoed in the woods. The noise seemed at first to roll with a roar on the two banks of the river; then rumbling, it moved further away, until it was entirely lost in the depths of the surrounding forests. You would have said a long and fearsome war cry that civilization shouted out in its advance.

One evening in Sicily, we happened to get lost in a vast swamp that now occupies the place where formerly the city of Imera was built; the sight of this famous city that had become a wild abandoned place made a great and profound impression on us. Never in our path had we encountered a more magnificent witness to the instability of things human and to the miseries of our nature. Here, it was also an uninhabited place, but imagination, instead of going backward and trying to return toward the past, on the contrary rushed ahead and lost itself in an immense future. We wondered by what singular permission of destiny, we who had been able to contemplate the ruins of empires that no longer exist and to walk in the deserts of human making, we, children of an old people, were led to be present at one of the scenes of the primitive world and to see the still empty cradle of a great nation. These are not the more or less random predictions of wisdom. They are facts as certain as if they were accomplished. In a few years these impenetrable forests will have fallen. The noise of civilization and industry will break the silence of the Saginaw. Its echo will become silent. . . . Wharves will imprison its banks. Its waters that today flow ignored and tranquil amid a nameless wilderness will be forced back in their course by the prow of ships. Fifty leagues still separate this uninhabited area from the large European settlements, and we are perhaps the last travelers allowed to contemplate it in its primitive splendor, so great is the impulse that carries the white race toward the complete conquest of the New World.[a]

It is this idea of destruction, this lurking thought of a near and inevitable change that, according to us, gives to the wilderness of America so original a character and so touching a beauty. You see it with a melancholy pleasure; you hurry in a way to admire it. The idea of this natural and wild grandeur that is going to end mingles with the magnificent images given birth by the triumphant march of civilization. You feel proud to be a man, and at the same time you feel I do not know what bitter regret about the power that God granted us over nature.[b] The soul is agitated by contrasting ideas, sentiments, but all the impressions that it receives are great and leave a profound trace.

*   *   *   *   *

We wanted to leave Saginaw the next day, July 27; but because one of our horses has been hurt by its saddle, we decided to remain one more day. Lacking another way to pass the time, we went hunting in the prairies that border the Saginaw below the cleared areas. These prairies are not swampy, as you might believe. They are more or less wide plains where there are no trees although the land is excellent. The grass is hard and three to four feet high. We found only a little game and returned early. The heat was suffocating as at the approach of a storm, and the mosquitoes even more trou-

a. On a separate sheet: "In America ideas serve as the banner, not as the goal of parties./
"The head of an old man on the shoulders of a child; image of American civilization." See the note entitled "National character of Americans," in alphabetic notebook A, YTC, BIIa, and *Voyage, OC,* V, 1, pp. 208–10.

b. On the effects of a century and a half of civilization on the region crossed by Tocqueville and Beaumont, see William Serrin, "Monsieur de Tocqueville! Oh, get some water—he's fainted!" *New York Times,* 2 January 1976, p. 25, col. 2.

blesome than usual. We walked always surrounded by a dense cloud of these insects against which we had to wage a perpetual war. Woe to the man who was forced to stop. He delivered himself defenseless to a merciless enemy. I recall having been forced to load my rifle while running, so difficult was it to stand still for an instant.

As we crossed the prairie on our return, we noticed that the Canadian who served as our guide followed a small marked path and looked with the greatest care at the ground before putting down his foot. "So why are you taking so many precautions," I said to him; "are you afraid of getting wet?" "No," he answered. "But I have acquired the habit when I cross the prairies always to look where I put my foot in order not to step on a rattlesnake." "What the devil," I began again, jumping onto the path, "are there rattle-snakes here?" "Oh yes indeed," replied my American Norman with an im-perturbable sang-froid, *the prairie is full of them.*" I then reproached him for not warning us sooner. He claimed that since we wore good shoes and since the rattlesnake never bit above the ankle, he had not believed that we ran any great danger.

I asked him if the bite of the rattlesnake was fatal. He answered that you always died from it in less than twenty-four hours, if you did not appeal to the Indians. They know a remedy that, given in time, saved the patient, he said.

Whatever the case, during all the rest of the way we imitated our guide and, like him, looked at our feet.

The night that followed this scorching day was one of the most difficult that I have ever passed in my life. The mosquitoes had become so trouble-some that, although I was overcome by fatigue, it was impossible for me to close my eyes. Toward midnight the storm that had threatened for a long time finally broke. Not able to hope for sleep, I got up and opened the door of our cabin in order at least to breathe the cool night air. It was not raining yet, the air seemed calm; but the forest was already shaking and out of it came deep moanings and long clamorings. From time to time a lightning bolt happened to illuminate the sky. The tranquil flow of the Saginaw, the small cleared area that bordered the river, the roofs of five or six cabins, and the belt of foliage that surrounded us, appeared then for an instant like an evocation of the future. Afterward everything was lost in the deepest darkness, and the formidable voice of the wilderness began again to make itself heard.

I was witnessing this great spectacle with emotion, when I heard a sigh at my side, and in the flash of a lightning bolt I noticed an Indian pressed like me against the wall of our dwelling. The storm had probably interrupted his sleep, for he cast a fixed and troubled eye on the objects around him.

Was this man afraid of thunder? Or did he see in the clash of elements something other than a passing convulsion of nature? These fleeting images of civilization that loomed up as if by themselves amid the tumult of the wilderness, did they have a prophetic meaning for him? These moans from the forest that seemed to struggle in an unequal contest, did they come to his ear like a secret warning from God, a solemn revelation of the final fate reserved for the savage races? I cannot say. But his restless lips seemed to murmur a few prayers, and all his features were stamped with a superstitious terror.

* * * * *

At five o'clock in the morning, we thought about our departure. All the Indians in the neighborhood of Saginaw had disappeared; they had left to go to receive the presents that the English give to them each year, and the Europeans were engaged in the work of the harvest. So we had to accept going back through the forest without a guide. The undertaking was not as difficult as you could believe. There is generally only one path in these vast uninhabited places, and it is only a matter of not losing the trail in order to reach the end of the journey.

So at five o'clock in the morning, we recrossed the Saginaw; we received the good-byes and the final advice of our hosts, and turning the heads of our horses, we found ourselves alone in the middle of the forest. It was not, I admit, without a grave feeling that we began to penetrate its humid depths. This same forest that then surrounded us extended behind us to the Pole and to the Pacific Ocean. A single inhabited point separated us from the limitless wilderness, and we had just left it. These thoughts, moreover, only led us to hasten the pace of our horses, and at the end of three hours we reached an abandoned wigwam and the solitary banks of the Cass River.

A point of grass that went down to the river in the shade of large trees served as our table, and we began to have lunch, having before us the view of the river whose waters, as clear as crystal, meandered through the woods.

Coming from the wigwam of the Cass River we encountered several paths. Someone had indicated to us which one we should take; but it was easy to forget a few points, or to be misunderstood in such explanations. That is what we did not fail to experience that day. The person had spoken to us about two roads, there were three; it is true that among these three roads, two came together as one further on, as we learned after, but we did not know it then and our difficulty was great.

After looking carefully, discussing things well, we did as nearly all great men do and acted more or less by chance. We forded the river as well as we could and plunged rapidly toward the southwest. More than once the path seemed ready to disappear amid the undergrowth; in other places the road seemed so little used that we had trouble believing that it led any-where other than to some abandoned wigwam. Our compass, it is true, showed us that we were always going in the right direction. Nevertheless, we were completely reassured only when we found the place where we had eaten three days earlier. A gigantic pine whose trunk, broken by the wind, we had admired, led us to recognize the spot. We did not, however, con-tinue our course any less rapidly, for the sun was beginning to go down. Soon we reached a clearing that usually precedes cleared lands, and as night began to surprise us we saw the Flint River. A half-hour later, we found ourselves at the door of our host. This time the bear welcomed us as old friends and got up on its hind legs only to celebrate with joy our happy return.

During this entire day we had encountered no human face. On their side, the animals had disappeared; they had probably retreated beneath the foliage to escape the heat of the day. Only now and then did we find at the bare top of some dead tree, a hawk that, immobile on a single leg and sleeping tranquilly in the rays of the sun, seemed sculpted in the same wood that it had used for support.

It was amid this profound solitude that we thought suddenly about the Revolution of 1830 [whose clearest result until now to my knowledge is to have sent Charles X to Edinburgh, {Louis-Philippe to St. Cloud and us to Saginaw}] whose first anniversary we had just reached. I cannot say with what impetuosity the memories of July 29 took hold of our minds. The cries and the smoke of combat, the noise of the cannon, the rumble of the musketry, the still more horrible ringing of the tocsin, this entire day with its fiery atmosphere seemed to emerge suddenly from the past and to come before me like a living tableau. It was only a sudden illumination, a passing dream. When, raising my head, I looked around me, the apparition had already vanished; but never had the silence of the forest seemed more chilling, its shadows more somber, or its solitude more complete.

APPENDIX 3

Sects in America[a]

Piece that could perhaps be introduced by modifying it, by making it shorter and more striking, into the place where I will explain the type of influence that democracy exercises on the Christian religion, but [even? (ed.)] when contrary to its habits democracy accepts the principle of religion [v: some sects in America] without discussion.

* * * * *

It was Sunday. The city was as deserted as if it had been threatened by an attack that very morning and all of the people had gone to the defense of the walls. The streets were stretched with chains and the shutters of the houses were closed with so much care that you would have said that the inhabitants feared that the sun would commit some base act by coming within.

I wandered for a long time in this desert without finding anyone who could point out my route. I finally met a man whose mild and venerable appearance first attracted me. Although he was of middle age, his dress preserved a certain old-fashioned air that struck me. He wore a jacket in the French style and a hat with a wide flat brim, short trousers and flat shoes; he had neither a ruffle on his shirt nor buckles on his shoes, but his

a. This account condenses events that Tocqueville witnessed at different moments of his journey. This survey of American sects could have accompanied no matter which chapter on religion and particularly chapter 12 of the second part of the second volume. The account is on pages 9 to 15 of notebook CVa (it is a copy by Bonnel). It was published for the first time in English by James T. Schleifer in "Alexis de Tocqueville Describes the American Character: Two Previously Unpublished Portraits," *South Atlantic Quarterly* 74, no. 2 (1975): 244–58.

jacket was of very fine cloth, and you noticed over his whole person such an extreme neatness that you would have almost taken it for elegance.

"Sir," I said to him, "could you point out to me a place in this city where I can pray to God?" He considered me with kindness and answered, without even putting his hand to his hat: "Thou art right, my friend. Come with me, but let us hurry, for the congregation must already be gathered."

So we quickened our pace, and soon we were opposite a large building that I had already passed by without noticing that it was a church. My guide made me enter and entered himself, walking on his tiptoes while sliding along in silence, like a man who regrets not being a pure spirit in order to make still less noise. Having reached his pew, he finally sat down, discreetly removed his gloves and, having carefully rolled them up, seemed to fall suddenly into a profound meditation. When we were seated, I noticed that the church was full which I never would have suspected, so profound was the silence [v: the tranquillity and the immobility] that reigned there. All those around me wore the costume of my guide, even the smallest children who sat gravely in their pews, dressed in the same jacket in the French style and covered by a wide-brimmed hat.

I remained there one hour and forty minutes in the same silence and the same immobility. I finally turned toward the man who brought me and said to him: "Sir, I wanted to attend a church service and it seems to me that you have led me to a gathering of the deaf and dumb." My guide, without seeming offended by my question, looked at me with the same kindness and said: "Dost thou not see that each of us is waiting for the Holy Spirit to illumine him; learn to moderate thine impatience in a holy place." I kept quiet, and soon in fact one of those attending got up and began to speak. His accents were plaintive, and each of the words that he uttered was as if isolated between two long silences; and with a very pitiful voice he said some very consoling things, for he spoke about the inexhaustible goodness of God and about the obligation that men have to help each other, whatever their belief and the color of their skin.

When he was quiet, the gathering began to flow out peacefully. As I left, still moved by the language that I had just heard, I found myself near the man who had brought me and I said to him: "It seems to me that I have just heard spoken here the word of the Gospel. But my soul is troubled;

let me know, I beg of you, if grace can be produced in a man only if he wears a cut-away jacket and uses 'thee' and 'thou' with his neighbor." My new friend reflected at length and answered: "The majority of our brothers think that is not absolutely necessary."

Content to see that no indispensable connection existed between my soul and my jacket, I regained the street with a lighter step.

A little distance from there, I noticed another church. But far from praying to God so tranquilly there,[b] on the contrary, such a great tumult was produced and such a strange clamor arose that I could not repress a curious desire, and to satisfy it I entered. It was a Methodist church. I first saw in an elevated place, a young man whose thundering voice made the vaults of the building reverberate. His hair was standing on end, his eyes seemed to shoot flames, his lips were pale and trembling, his entire body seemed agitated by a universal trembling [v: prey to an anguish]. I wanted to break through the crowd in order to go to the aid of this unfortunate man, but stopped upon discovering that he was a preacher. He spoke of the perversity of man and of the inexhaustible treasures of divine vengeance. He probed one by one all the formidable mysteries of the other life. He portrayed the Creator as constantly busy heaping up the generations in the pits of hell and as indefatigable in creating sinners as in inventing punishments. I stopped completely troubled; the congregation was even more so than I. Terror showed itself in a thousand ways on all the faces, and repentance took on at every instant the appearance of despair and fury.[c] Women lifted their children in their arms and let out lamentable cries, others struck their forehead against the earth, men convulsed in their pews while accusing themselves of their sins in a loud voice, or rolled in the dust. As the movements of the minister became more rapid and his portraits more vivid, the passions of the assembly seemed to grow, and often it was difficult not to believe yourself in one of those infernal dwellings that the preacher depicted.

I fled full of disgust and penetrated by a profound terror. Author and preserver of all things, I said to myself, is it possible that you recognize

b. In the margin: "As in the house of the Quakers."
c. The margins contain various stylistic variants of these sentences.

yourself in the horrible portrait that your creations make of you here? Must man be degraded by fear in order to raise him up to you, and can he climb to the ranks of your saints only by delivering himself to transports that make him descend below beasts?

Full of these thoughts, I walked rapidly without looking around myself, so much so that when I came to consider the place where I was, I noticed that I had left the city and walked into the middle of the woods that surround it. Nothing prompted me to retrace my steps, and I resolved to continue my route to see if I would not arrive at an inhabited place. At the end of two hours, I in fact reached a new clearing, and soon I noticed the first houses of a beautiful village.[d] A traveler just passing informed me that these (illegible word) were the property of a small religious sect called *dansars*[e] [*sic*]. It was obvious in fact that the houses of the village had been built on a common plan and by a single association. They had cost the same amount; the same air of comfort reigned. At the center of the works arose a vast hall that served as the church. I was told that the divine service was going to be celebrated there, and curiosity led me to it.

At the end of the room already drawn up were about fifty men of different ages, but all wore the same dress. It was that of European peasants of the Middle Ages. Facing them was a more or less equal number of women enveloped in white clothes like great shrouds, from head to toe. Moreover, you saw neither pulpit, nor altar, nor anything that recalled a place consecrated by Christians to the worship of the Divinity. These men and women sang songs of a lugubrious and plaintive tone. From time to time, they accompanied themselves by clapping their hands. Other times, they began to move and made a thousand rotations without losing the beat,

d. On various occasions, Beaumont gave the account of a visit to the Quaker community of Nisquayuna, not far from Albany. See the letter to Samuel R. Wood of 24 November 1831, in the Quaker Collection of Haverford College, Pennsylvania; the letter to his sister, Eugénie, of 14 July 1831 (*Lettres d'Amérique*, pp. 86–90); and *Marie*, II, pp. 205–9. Beaumont gives a general survey of American sects in *Marie*, I, pp. 258–59, and in the appendix "Notes on Religious Movements in the United States" (II, pp. 181–225).

e. Shakers.

sometimes marching in columns, sometimes gathering in a circle. Other times, they advanced toward each other as if to fight and then withdrew without touching. I was witnessing this spectacle with astonishment, when suddenly at a given signal the whole congregation began to dance. Women and men, old people and children began to jump to the point of breathlessness. They danced so long in this way that sweat ran down their faces. They finally stopped; and one of the oldest men of the company, after wiping his brow, began with a broken voice: "My brothers, let us give thanks to the Almighty who, amid all the various superstitions that disfigure humanity, has deigned finally to show us the way of salvation, and let us pray that he opens the eyes of this crowd of unfortunates who are still plunged into the darkness of error, and saves them from the eternal torments which perhaps await them."

APPENDIX 4

Political Activity in America[a]

The first evening of my arrival in the United States,[b] I saw a large crowd assembled in one of the rooms of the inn. I learned that it was a political banquet. After the meal, I drew one of the guests aside and I said to him: "Excuse, I beg you, the curiosity of a foreigner who still only imperfectly understands your language and does not know about your customs."

"Is there something that surprises you?" he said to me wiping his mouth.

"There is a great deal. I am afraid," I answered, "that some unfortunate events have happened since I left Europe."

"What do you mean?" he replied to me, all frightened.

"Yes," I began again, "while disembarking this morning at the port I saw on all sides large posters that invited people to assemble in certain places that were indicated, and during the time that it took me to come here I heard two speeches which were concerned with public affairs, and I witnessed an election. Again, just a moment ago, while I was in a corner of the room where you held the banquet, it seemed to me that most of the guests were speaking about the dangers to the State and were seeking the means to avert them [v: I listened to the speeches of several of your orators

a. This short fragment, which is found in notebook CVa, pages 37 to 41, bears no title. We reuse that which James T. Schleifer gave it in English in "Alexis de Tocqueville Describes the American Character: Two Previously Unpublished Portraits," *South Atlantic Quarterly* 74, no. 2 (1975): 244–58. This conversation recalls ideas from chapter XVII of the third part of this volume (pp. 1089–92).

b. Tocqueville and Beaumont passed the first night on the *Havre,* which brought them from France; and the second on the steamboat *President* on the way from Newport to New York. George W. Pierson, *Tocqueville and Beaumont in America,* pp. 53–57.

proposing a great number of projects, a few of which were to save the State and all of which could not fail to prevent some great misfortunes]."

"Is that all?" the American said to me. "In truth you frightened me with your unfortunate events. What surprises you repeats itself here every day."

As he moved away while saying (illegible word), I grabbed him by his jacket and begged him to stop a moment. "Wait a bit," I said again, "I still do not see clearly (illegible word)."

"What is more clear?" he said to me. "Don't you know that we are a free people and that we take care of our affairs ourselves?"[c]

"But I imagined," I began again, "that liberty was such a great good that those who possessed it were happier and consequently more tranquil than other men. I see on the contrary that you must be prey to great difficulties to torment yourselves so much to find remedies for them."

"There is no people more enlightened, more free, more virtuous than ours," <he said to me.

He was going to add a great deal more if I had not> Interrupting him at this point, "I see," I cried. "With the aid of its enlightenment the people of the United States sees its difficulties more clearly than another, and with its liberty and its virtue it works hard to remedy them."

"<Among us," the American began again, "we have the habit of never interrupting anyone.>" The American began again: "If you had not jumped right into the middle of my comments, I was going to add that we were the happiest people in the world." "This time I don't follow," I said. "<If public affairs are in a tranquil and prosperous state, why can you not speak about something other than politics? If you have good magistrates, why work constantly to give them (words crossed out)? If your rights are guaranteed, then what leads you to occupy yourself every day with the guarantee of your rights? If you enjoy a general comfort, what good is there in seeking

c. To the side: "It would try to forget that it wants to be happy in order to try to be so."

constantly to bring about comfort? And if you have easy communications among the various parts of your territory, why are you heard to talk only about roads, ports and canals?> If you have in fact what is sufficient for the strength of the soul and the well-being of the body, what more do you ask?"

"We work constantly to improve and to increase those things," he said to me.

"<I am a foreigner," I began again, "and you must excuse my surprise.>" I answered. "As for me, I would prefer to suffer tranquilly a few disparities in my lot [v: happiness] than to tire myself constantly in this way to make it better, and I still cannot comprehend that men are happy when they make so many efforts to become happier."

"You make it very clear," the American said to me, "that you are still not very worthy to be free."

At this moment one of his friends approached us saying: "This is the time when the assembly is gathered for the Poles (illegible word) let's leave. Do you want to accompany us?" the American said to me.

"Willingly," I replied; "but what is this assembly? What is it?"

"It is," he answered, "a meeting that has the purpose of expressing the sympathy of the American people in favor of the unfortunate Poles."

"And what," I said, "would you go to war with Russia?"

"Not at all," he replied, "Russia is one of our most faithful allies. We do not want to go to war with Russia, but only to express the indignation that its current conduct causes us."

"I understand," I said, "that you are going to make speeches about Poland."

"More or less," he replied, "you have it. Consequently it is more of a diversion than a serious matter."

"Good God," I began again, "I thought you were fatigued after all the difficult efforts that you made today to increase the sum of your happiness. A European would think only of going to rest and would abandon other peoples to their fate."

APPENDIX 5

Letter of Alexis de Tocqueville to Charles Stoffels

Versailles, 21 April 1830

I have greatly delayed replying to you, my dear friend, not as much however as would be indicated by the date of your letter, which bears the date 11 April, although it arrived only on the 15th, but you know what a rush of things I am caught up in. Even today, I hardly have the time to say to you all that I would like; I cannot wait any longer, however, without risking not finding you at Metz. So pardon me if I only touch very lightly on the question that you treated in depth and remarkably well (I say it to you not as a compliment).

And first, my dear friend, I will say to you that you make me out to be much more of a *killjoy* than I am naturally; you give me a conviction where I have only expressed doubts, and an absolute opinion when I have surrounded myself with qualifications. If you have done it *for the purpose of the case,* as a lawyer would say, nothing better; but if you acted involuntarily, I must point out the error and reestablish the point of departure. In general, my dear Charles, you must not imagine that, when I am discussing something with you, I have always taken care to develop fully the ideas that I put forward. You would in truth do me an honor that I do not deserve. I do not believe that you should talk with your friends as you speak in public. To stir the mind, to give the desire to reflect, to raise in passing questions that reflection comes to elaborate, such is the goal of conversation in my opinion; and I never have another with you. So, I beg of you, never take to the letter and, above all, as definitive the opinions that I do not reexamine and that I often throw out, more as a topic than as the result of reflection.

To come back to the great question that we are debating at this moment, I can put my point of view into two sentences.

1. I doubt that the advanced state of civilization is as superior to the middling state as is proclaimed, even when the march of civilization has been well conducted;

2. I believe that almost always the intellectual education of a people is poorly done and that consequently enlightenment is often a fatal gift.

Among all half-civilized peoples, you recognize almost the same base of sentiments, ideas, passions, vices and virtues, more or less hidden it is true, but always easy to recognize. Different characters are to peoples what physiognomy is to the man: they differentiate peoples externally rather than demonstrating a profound and radical difference between them.

In the same way, you always find the mixture of the same elements among nations that have reached a very high degree of civilization; here, the bad elements are more numerous than the good ones; elsewhere, the opposite happens, but all are united solely by this social state. Thus, putting aside all special application, you can form theoretically the idea of a half-civilized people and that of a completely enlightened people; no particular circumstance, good or bad, has come to influence the development of these two principles, and I compare these two peoples with each other.

Among the first of the two, among the one still half-savage, the social state is imperfect, public force is badly organized, and the struggle between it and individual force is often unequal; there is little security for the individual, little tranquillity for the mass, mores brutal, ideas simple, religion there is almost always poorly understood. That is the bad side. Here is the good: forced back on itself in this way, the soul there finds an admirable spring of action, and individual force finds unexpected development; love of country is not rational, but instinctive, and this blind instinct brings forth miracles; sentiments are clear-cut, convictions profound; consequently devotion is not rare there, enthusiasm is common and scorn for death is deep in the heart and not on the lips.

Now let us compare to this half-civilized people the one that has attained a high degree of civilization.

Among the latter, the social body has foreseen everything; the individual gives himself the pain of being born; as for the rest, society takes hold of him in the arms of his wet-nurse, it oversees his education, opens before him the roads to fortune; it supports him in his march, deflects dangers from his head; he advances in peace under the eyes of this second providence; this tutelary power that has protected him during his life still oversees the repose of his ashes. There is the fate of civilized man. The sentiment and the spectacle of happiness soon soften the wild roughness of his nature; he becomes mild, sociable; his passions become calm; his heart seems to have expanded the ability that he had been given to feel; he finds sources of emotions and of pleasure where his fathers would never have imagined that they could exist or would have scorned looking for them. Crimes become rare, unfortunately virtues also. The soul, asleep in this long repose, no longer knows how to wake up on occasion; individual energy is almost extinguished; each man leans on the others when it is necessary to act; in all other circumstances, on the contrary, each man closes up within himself; it is the reign of egoism, convictions are shaken at the same time, for it must be clearly admitted, my dear friend, that not one single intellectual truth is established and the centuries of enlightenment are centuries of doubts and of discussion. There is no fanaticism, but there are few beliefs, consequently few of those actions, sublime in the case of another life, absurd in the opposite hypothesis. Enthusiasm there is an attack of high fever; it does not have its source in the habitual state of the soul; the taste for positive reality grows as doubts increase; the whole world ends up being an insoluble problem for the man who clings to the most tangible objects and who ends up lying down on his stomach against the earth out of fear that he, in turn, may come to miss the ground.

You cannot deny, however, that many sentiments there become purer. Thus love of country becomes more reasoned, more thoughtful, religion better understood by those who still believe in it, love of justice more enlightened, the general interest better understood, but all these sentiments lose in strength what they gain in perfection, they satisfy the mind more and act less on life.

I could undoubtedly push this portrait very much further, but I would write a volume. What I said is sufficient to make you feel that in my opinion you cannot say in an absolute manner: man improves by becoming civilized, but rather that man by becoming civilized gains at the very same time virtues and vices that he did not have; he becomes something other, that is what is most clear.

Now, I am going further and I admit that, everything balanced and weighed, I prefer the second state to the first. Security, individual happiness seem to me all in all the principal end of societies. This end is incontestably attained by civilization and if it can take place without leading to too strong an attack on human morality, it is certain that it is desirable.

But it frequently happens that the intellectual education of a people is poorly done; then, it is not precisely the enlightenment that must be blamed, but the way in which it is given. For example, one nation in the world presents a singular spectacle. For reasons easy to find but very long to enumerate, the progressive spirit or civilization, instead of marching in agreement with religious beliefs or at least not clashing with them in its march, has entered into battle with them, so that an enlightened man there has not only become the synonym of a *doubting* man, not even the equivalent of an unbelieving man, but in most cases a true enemy of religion, of country. This is not all. Political passions become mixed in with them; a man has become irreligious by pride, by opinion. This nation, I do not need to tell you, is ours. Among us, not only has enlightenment produced its usual effect; this effect is tripled by the way in which this enlightenment has been spread; if the movement was continuous, and nothing declares that it is to stop soon, we would present the example of a great social body without beliefs, a unique example in the history of men, and about which consequently it is impossible to reason.

Do not believe, however, my dear friend, that I conclude from this that enlightenment must be fought and that we must struggle against the irresistible inclination of our century. No, in truth, I believe on the contrary that the only task that remains for the government is to seek to put itself at the head of the movement in order to direct it, to lavish instruction itself in order to be sure that instruction will not become a murderous weapon in other hands. I think, above all, that its efforts must tend toward disconnecting religion from politics, for what particularly harms the first is the proximity of the second. Thus in summary, you see, we will both act more or less in the same way, you by enthusiasm and training, me by reasoning and calculations. You must notice, my dear Charles, that I have been going post-haste for a page and a half. In fact, I do not have time and must say farewell to you. I reproach myself for having philosophized in this way for an hour instead of chatting, which would have been much more valuable, but an honest man has only [interrupted text (ed.)]. (YTC, AVII)

APPENDIX 6

Foreword to the Twelfth Edition

However great and sudden the events that have just been accomplished in a moment before our eyes may be, the author of the present work has the right to say that he was not surprised by them. This book was written, fifteen years ago, with the constant preoccupation of a single thought: the impending, irresistible, universal advent of democracy in the world. May it be reread. You will find on each page a solemn warning that reminds men that society is changing form; humanity, changing condition; and that new destinies are approaching.

At the beginning these words were written:

The gradual development of equality of conditions is a providential fact; it has the principal characteristics of one: it is universal, it is lasting, it escapes every day from human power; all events, like all men, serve its development. Would it be wise to believe that a social movement that comes from so far could be suspended by the efforts of a generation? Do you think that after having destroyed feudalism and vanquished kings, democracy will retreat before the bourgeois and the rich? Will it stop now that it has become so strong and its adversaries so weak?

The man who, in the presence of a monarchy strengthened rather than weakened by the July Revolution, wrote these lines made prophetic by events, can again today call the attention of the public to his work without fear.

You must allow him as well to add that current circumstances give his book a timely interest and a practical utility that it did not have when it appeared for the first time.

Royalty existed then. Today it is destroyed. The institutions of America, which were only a subject of curiosity for monarchical France, must be a subject of study for republican France. It is not force alone that establishes a new government; it is good laws. After the combatant, the legislator. The one has destroyed, the other establishes. Each has his work. If it is no longer a matter of knowing if we will have royalty or the Republic in France, it remains for us to learn if we will have an agitated or a tranquil Republic, a regular or an irregular Republic, a liberal or an oppressive Republic, a Republic that threatens the sacred rights of property and of family or a Republic that acknowledges and consecrates them. A terrible problem, whose solution is important not only to France, but to the whole civilized world. If we save ourselves, we save at the same time all the peoples who are around us. If we are lost, all of them are lost with us, Depending on whether we will have democratic liberty or democratic tyranny, the destiny of the world will be different, and you can say that today it depends on us whether the Republic ends up being established everywhere or abolished everywhere.

Now, this problem that we have only just posed, America resolved more than sixty years ago. For sixty years, the principle of sovereignty of the people that we enthroned yesterday among us, has reigned there undivided. It is put into practice there in the most direct, the most unlimited, the most absolute manner. For sixty years the people who have made it the common source of all their laws, have grown constantly in population, in territory, in wealth, and note it well, they have found themselves to have been, during this period, not only the most prosperous, but the most stable of all the peoples of the earth. While all the nations of Europe were ravaged by war or torn apart by civil discords, the American people alone in the civilized world remained at peace. Nearly all of Europe was turned upside down by revolutions; America did not even have riots; the Republic there was not disruptive, but conservative of all rights; individual property had more guarantees there than in any country in the world; anarchy remained as unknown as despotism.

Where else could we find greater hopes and greater lessons? Let us not turn our attention toward America in order to copy slavishly the institutions that it has given itself, but in order to understand better those that are suitable for us, less to draw examples from America than instruction, to borrow the principles rather than the details of its laws. The laws of the French Republic can and must, in many cases, be different from those that govern the United States, but the principles on which the American constitutions rest, these principles of order, of balance of powers, of true liberty, of sincere and profound respect for law are indispensable to all Republics; they must be common to all, and you can say in advance that wherever they are not found, the Republic will soon cease to exist. 1848.

Works Used by Tocqueville

This appendix contains the works cited by Tocqueville in his book and those that appear in his notes and drafts (I have preceded them with *). In Tocqueville's papers are found two bibliographies (YTC, CIIa and CIIb[a]) which, in addition to certain references, allow us to identify the editions that he used. I have as well gone back when possible to the editions of the catalogue of the library of the Tocqueville château (YTC, AIe). In other cases, I cite the first edition of the works.

The inclusion of a work in the list does not necessarily indicate that it was used in the work of writing. Tocqueville was sometimes interested in texts that he was not able to obtain from the Royal Library, or he took note of a book recommended to him and never read it. Certain books greatly influenced the Democracy, such as the treatise on political economy of Villeneuve-Bargement or Rousseau's *Discours sur l'origine de l'inégalité.* If they are not mentioned in this list, it is clearly because Tocqueville does not cite them.

The library of the château also preserves a certain number of brochures, speeches, and printed materials that the author received during his journey in America. These uncut texts were never read by Tocqueville.[b] Most of these works do not appear in this list. I nonetheless cite those that interested Tocqueville enough so that their covers bear marks and annotations in his hand.

---

a. The copies of the bibliographies of Tocqueville contain numerous errors. I have omitted from the list certain nonexistent titles and authors. Thus a history of New York is attributed to Castmare when it concerns F. S. Eastman. The *Fashionable Tour* becomes the *Fashionable Tom;* the work of Judge Story is attributed to "Hury," etc.

b. Certain Americans clearly profited from the visit of Tocqueville and Beaumont in order to get rid of books that did not interest them (George W. Pierson, *Tocqueville and*

* [A. C. T., "Mouvement de la presse française en 1836," *Revue des deux mondes,*
4e série, X, 1837, pp. 453–98.]

Abridged History of the United States. [Peut-être/*Maybe:* Hosea Hildreth, *An
Abridged History of the United States of America.* Boston: Carter, Hendee and
Babcock, 1831.]

An Account of the Church of Christ in Plymouth. [Dans/*In: Collections of the
Massachusetts Historical Society for the Year 1795.* Boston: Printed by Samuel
Hall, 1795. IV, pp. 107–41.]

Adair, *History of the American Indians.* [James Adair, *The History of the American
Indians* . . . London: Printed for Edward and Charles Dilly, 1775.]

* John Quincy Adams, *President Quincy's Centennial Address.* Boston, 1830.

* *Address of the Convention to the People of the United States.*

* *Allen Biographical Dictionary.* [William Allen, *An American Biographical and
Historical Dictionary* . . . Cambridge (Massachusetts), 1809; Boston: William
Hyde, 1832.]

* *Almanach royal, 1833. [Almanach royal et national pour l'an 1833* . . . Paris:
Guyot et Scribe, 1833.]

American Almanac. [*The American Almanac and Repository of Useful Knowledge.*
Boston: Gray and Bowen, 1829–[61]. Tocqueville cite les volumes de/ *Tocqueville cites the volumes of* 1831, 1832, 1833 et/ *and* 1834.]

* *American Annual Register,* 1827–1835. [[Joseph Blunt,] *The American Annual
Register.* New York: G. and C. Carvill, 1827. New York: E. and G. W. Blunt,
1828–1830.]

American Constitution. [L'édition du *Fédéraliste* employée par Tocqueville reproduit le texte de la Constitution américaine, mais Tocqueville cite une autre
source/ *The edition of the* Federalist *used by Tocqueville reproduces the text of
the American constitution, but Tocqueville quotes another source.*]

* *American Medical and Philosophical Register.* [*American Medical and Philosophical Register, or Annals of Medicine, Natural History, Agriculture and the
Arts,* conducted by a society of Gentlemen [David Hosack and Benjamin

---

Beaumont in America, p. 537). Tocqueville received, among others, in the United States:
On the Penetrativeness of Fluids, by J. K. Mitchell (Philadelphia, 1830); *On the Storms at
the American Coasts,* by W. C. Redfield; and *An Introductory Lecture on the Advantages
and Pleasures of the Study of Chemistry in the Transylvania University,* by L. P. Yandell
(Lexington, 1831), etc. Tocqueville seems not to have read these works and their connection with the *Democracy in America* seems sufficiently vague to justify their absence
from this bibliography.

Rush entre autres/*among others*]. New York: C. S. Van Winkle, 1811–14. 4 vols.]

* *American Monthly Review.* [Peut-être celle publiée entre 1832 et 1834 par/*maybe the one published between 1832 and 1834 by* Hillard, Gray and Co., Boston. 4 vols.]

* *American Quarterly Review,* septembre 1831. [Tocqueville semble avoir été intéressé par le compte-rendu de/*Tocqueville seems to have been interested in the review of: Notices of Brazil in 1828 and 1829,* by the Rev. R. Walsh, London, 1830. 2 vols.]

* *The Anniversary Report of the Pennsylvania Society for Discouraging the Use of Ardent Spirits, 1831.* [Peut-être/*Maybe: The Anniversary Report of the Managers of the Pennsylvania Society for Discouraging the Use of Ardent Spirits, Read on the 27th May 1831.* Philadelphia: Henry H. Porter, 1831.]

* *Annual Law Register.* Voir/*See* Griffith.

* *Annual Report of the Apprentices' Library Company of Philadelphia* [Probablement/Probably: *Annual Report and the Treasurer's Account of the Apprentices' Library Company of Philadelphia.* March, 1831. "Modèle d'associations charitables," note Tocqueville/*"Model of charitable associations," notes Tocqueville.].*

* *Annuaire Militaire de 1834.*

* Marquis d'Argenson. [*Considérations sur le Gouvernement de la France.* Amsterdam [Paris]: Chez Marc-Michel Rey, 1765.]

* Francis Bacon, *Nouvel organe.*

* Edward Baines. [*History of the Cotton Manufacture in Great Britain.* London: H. Fisher, R. Fisher & P. Jackson, 1835.]

* [Odilon Barrot, "[Discours]," *Journal des débats,* 1 mars 1834.]

* Heliza Bates, *The Doctrine of Friends.* [Elisha Bates, *The Doctrines of Friends, or Principles of the Christian Religion as Held by the Society of Friends, Commonly Called Quakers.* Mountpleasant (Ohio): printed by the author, 1825.]

* Beccaria [*Traité des délits et des peines . . .* Philadelphia [Paris], 1766.].

Jeremy Belknap, *History of New Hampshire,* Boston, Philadelphia: 1784–92. 3 vols.

Jeremy Belknap, ["Queries Respecting the Slavery and Emancipation of the Negroes in Massachusetts, Proposed by the Hon. Judge Tucker of Virginia, and Answered by the Rev. Dr. Belknap," dans/*in: Massachusetts Historical Collection,* IV, p. 191–211].

Bell, *Rapport sur les affaires indiennes, 24 février 1830.* [John Bell, *Removal of*

Indians. February 24, 1830, [Documents of the House of Representatives, 21st Congress].]

Beverley, *History of Virginia from the Earliest Period.* Traduit en français en 1707/ *Translated into French in 1707.* [Robert Beverley, *Histoire de la Virginie.* Paris: Pierre Ribou, 1707.]

Blackstone. [*Commentaries on the Laws of England.* Tocqueville le juge un écrivain médiocre, incapable d'un jugement profond/ *Tocqueville considers him a mediocre writer, incapable of a profound judgment.*]

Blosseville, *Mémoires de Tanner.* [*Mémoires de John Tanner.* Traduit par Ernest de Blosseville/ *Translated by Ernest de Blosseville.* Paris: A. Bertrand, 1835. 2 vols.]

* Joseph Blunt, *A Historical Sketch of the Formation of the Confederacy.* [*A Historical Sketch of the Formation of the Confederacy, Particularly with Reference to the Provincial Limits and the Jurisdiction of the General Government over Indian Tribes and the Public Territory.* New York: Geo. & Chas. Carvill, 1825. "Curieux pour connaître les principes du gouvernement fédéral de l'Union"/ *"Interesting for knowing the principles of the federal government of the Union."*]

* Blunt, Joseph. Voir/ *See: American Annual Register.*

* Boissy d'Anglas, François Antoine comte de, *Essai sur la vie, les écrits et les opinions de M. de Malesherbes.* Paris: Treuttel et Würtz, 1819–21. 2 vols.

* Bossuet, *Discours sur l'histoire universelle, depuis le commencement du monde jusqu'à l'empire de Charlemagne, avec la suite jusqu'à l'année 1700,* 1756. [Nous n'avons pas trouvé l'édition de 1756 mentionnée dans le catalogue de la bibliothèque du château de Tocqueville. Il s'agit peut-être de l'édition de Babuty fils, Paris, 1765. 2 vols./ *I have not found the edition of 1756 mentioned in the catalogue of the library of the Tocqueville château. Perhaps it is the edition of Babuty fils, Paris, 1765. 2 vols.*]

* Bossuet, *Histoire des variations des églises protestantes.* Paris: G. Desprez et J. Dessesartz, 1730. 4 vols.

[Boston] *Nineteenth Annual Report of the Receipts and Expenses of the City of Boston and County of Suffolk. 1 May 1831.*

Brevard's Digest of the Public Statute Law of South Carolina. [Joseph Brevard, *An Alphabetical Digest of the Public Statute Law of South Carolina.* Charleston (South Carolina): John Hoff, 1814.]

* Buffon, *Histoire naturelle générale et particulière.* Paris: Imprimerie Royale, 1769–1781. 13 vols.

* Buffon, *Histoire naturelle des oiseaux.* Paris: Imprimerie Royale, 1770–83. 9 vols.

* *Burke* (mot illisible) *Register.* [*The Annual Register of World Events; A Review of the Year.* London, New York: Longmans, Green, 1758–1963. Edité par E. Burke jusqu'à 1791/*Edited by E. Burke until 1791.*]

Lord Byron, *Childe Harold.*

* Lord Byron, [*Correspondance de lord Byron avec un ami* . . . Paris: A. and W. Calignani, 1825. 2 vols].

* Candolle. [Tocqueville mentionne un ouvrage de Candolle sur l'or et l'argent. Il s'agit peut-être de/*Tocqueville mentions a work by Candolle on gold and money. Perhaps it is* Alphonse de Candolle, *Les caisses d'épargne de la Suisse considérées en elles-mêmes et comparées avec celles d'autres pays* . . . Genève: A. Cherbuliez et Cie., 1838.]

Carey, *Letters on the Colonization Society.* Philadelphia, 1833. [Mathew Carey, *Letters on the Colonization Society* . . . 7ᵉ édition. Philadelphia: Sterotyped by L. Johnson, 1833.]

Caroline du Sud. *Rapport fait à la convocation de la Caroline du Sud. Ordonnance de nullification du 24 novembre 1832.* [Il y a plusieurs éditions de ce document. Tocqueville aurait pu consulter/*There are several editions of this document. Tocqueville could have consulted: The Report, Ordinance, and Addresses of the Convention of the People of South Carolina. Adopted, November 24th, 1832.* Columbia (South Carolina): A. S. Johnston, 1832.]

Cass. Voir/*see* Clark.

Chalmer. [Probablement/*probably,* Lionel Chalmers, *An Account of the Weather and Diseases of South Carolina.* London: Edward and Charles Dilly, 1776. 2 vols.]

* "[Chambre des députés, discussion sur la loi de compétences départamentales/*Chamber of Deputies, discussion of the law on departmental jurisdiction*]," *Journal des débats,* 7 mars 1838.

* William Ellery Channing, *Discourses, Reviews and Miscellaneous.* 1 vol. [William Ellery Channing, *Discourses, Reviews and Miscellanies.* Boston: Carter, Hender and Co., 1830. 2 vols.]

Charlevoix, *Histoire de la Nouvelle France.* [Pierre-François Charlevoix, *Histoire et description générale de la Nouvelle France* . . . Paris: Chez Nyon Fils, 1744.]

Chateaubriand, *René.*

* Chateaubriand, [*Essai sur la littérature anglaise.* Paris: Charles Gosselin et Furne, 1836. 2 vols].

Clark et Cass. Rapports du 4 février 1829, 29 novembre 1823 et 19 novembre 1829/ *Reports of 4 February 1829, 29 November 1823 and 19 November 1829.*

* De Witt Clinton, *Memoirs of De Witt Clinton* [New York: J. Seymour, 1829]. Voir/ *See* David Hossak.

Code of 1650. Hartford, 1830. [*The Code of 1650* . . . Hartford (Connecticut): S. Andrus, 1830.]

* [Auguste Colin, "Lettres sur l'Egypte—Administration territoriale du Pacha," *Revue des deux mondes,* XIII, 1838, pp. 655–71.]

Companion to the Almanac for 1830. [*Companion to the Almanac; or Year-Book of General Information.* London: Stationers' Co., 1830.]

Compte général de l'Administration des Finances, [Paris, 1808– . Le titre change à l'occasion/ *The title changes on occasion*].

Connecticut. *Constitution de 1638.* [Les citations de Tocqueville appartiennent au *Code of 1650,* qui reproduit la Constitution de 1638 aux pages 11–19/ *Tocqueville's quotations are from the* Code of 1650, *which reproduces the constitution of 1638 on pages 11–19.*]

John Cook. [Voir/ *See* Look]

* [James Fenimore Cooper, *Excursion in Switzerland.* Paris: A. and W. Calignani and Co., 1836; et/ *and* Baudry, 1836.]

* [James Fenimore Cooper, *Letter of J. Fenimore Cooper to Gen. Lafayette, on the Expenditure of the United States of America.* Paris: Baudry, 1831.]

* [James Fenimore Cooper, *Notions of the Americans; Picked up by a Travelling Bachelor.* London: Henry Colburn, 1828. 2 vols. Dans ses notes, Tocqueville cite l'édition anglaise, mais il a acheté avant son départ la version française publiée sous le titre/ *In his notes, Tocqueville cites the English edition, but before his departure he bought the French version published with the title:* Lettres sur les mœurs et les institutions des États-Unis de l'Amérique du Nord. Paris: A. J. Kilian, 1828. 4 vols en 2.]

Darby's View of the United States. [William Darby, *View of the United States, Historical, Geographical, and Statistical* . . . Philadelphia: H. S. Tanner, 1828. "Cet ouvrage est estimé mais déjà ancien, il date de 1828."/ *"This work is respected but already old; it dates from 1828."*]

* *A Practical Treatise of the Peace in Criminal Jurisdiction,* by Davis. [Daniel Davis, *A Practical Treatise upon the Authority and Duty of Justices of the Peace in Criminal Prosecutions.* Boston: Cummings, Hilliard, 1824. Tocqueville jugeait curieux pour la procédure civile ce texte estimé/ *Tocqueville considered this respected text interesting for civil procedure.*]

Delolme [voir/*see* de Lolme].

Descouritz. [Michel Etienne Descourtilz, *Voyages d'un naturaliste et ses obser-vations* . . . Paris: Dufart Père, 1809. 3 vols.]

Documents législatifs. [Voir *U.S. Congress. Legislative documents.*]

* Douglas, *Histoire générale des colonies. Douglas' Summary, 1775.* [William Douglass, *A Summary, Historical and Political of the First Planting, Progressive Improvements, and Present State of the British Settlements in North America.* London: R. Baldwin, 1755. 2 vols. Nous n'avons pas pu trouver l'édition de 1775/*I have not been able to find the edition of 1775.*]

* William Alexander Duer, *Outlines of the Constitutional Jurisprudence of the United States.* [New York: Collins and Hanny, 1833.]

* Dufresne de St. Léon, *Étude du crédit public.* [Dufresne de Saint-Léon, Louis-César-Alexandre, *Étude du crédit public et des dettes publiques.* Paris: Bos-sangue Père, 1824.]

Duponceau, *Correspondance avec le Rvd. Heckewelder.* [Voir/*See* Heckewelder]

* Durand, de Dauphiné, *Voyages d'un François, exilé pour la religion, avec une description de la Virginie & Marilan dans l'Amérique.* [La Haye, [imprimé par l'auteur], 1696.]

* F. S. Eastman, *History of the State of New-York.* [New York: E. Bliss, 1828.]

* Elliot's Pocket Almanac of the Federal Government. 1832. [*Elliot's Washington Pocket Almanac.* Washington: S. A. Eliot [*sic*]. "Assez curieux comme pré-sentant le tableau des rouages administratifs du gouvernement central."/ *"Quite interesting for presenting the picture of the administrative machinery of the central government."*]

Emerson's Medical Statistics. [Gouverneur Emerson, *Medical Statistics, Consisting of Estimates Relating to the Population of Philadelphia, with its Changes as Influenced by the Deaths and Births, During Ten Years, viz. from 1821 to 1830, Inclusive.* Philadelphia: Joseph R. A. Kenett, 1831. 32 pp.]

Encyclopedia americana. [Reçue de Francis Lieber/*Received from Francis Lieber.*]

* *Encyclopédie*

Les Évangiles.

Everett. [Edward Everett, *Speech of Mr. Everett, of Massachusetts, on the Bill for Removing the Indians from the East to the West Side of the Mississippi, Delivered . . . 19th of May, 1830.* Boston, 1830.]

* *Extracts from the Ancient Roads [Records] of New Haven.* [Fait partie du *Code of 1650*/*Part of the* Code of 1650.]

* *Extrait du bulletin de la Société de géographie. Tableau de la population des États-Unis d'après les différents recensements exécutés par ordre du gouvernement.*
* *The Fashionable Tour.* [[Gideon Miner Davidson,] *The Fashionable Tour. A Guide to Travellers Visiting the Middle and Northern States and the Province of Canada.* 4ᵉ édition. Saratoga Springs and NewYork, 1830.]

Le Fédéraliste. [*The Federalist.* Washington:Thomson & Homans,1831.(Édition identifiée par James T. Schleifer/ *Edition identified by James T. Schleifer*). Au début de 1835, Tocqueville a également employée l'édition française de Buisson . . . , Paris, 1792. 2 vols./ *(Edition identified by James T. Schleifer.) At the beginning of 1835, Tocqueville also used the French edition of Buisson . . . , Paris, 1792. 2 vols.*]

* Fisher, *Pauperism and Crime.* 1831 [W. L. Fisher, *Pauperism and Crime.* Philadelphia: The Author, 1831].

Fischer, *Conjectures sur l'origine des Américains.* [Jean-Eberhard Fischer, *De l'origine des Américains.* Saint-Petersburg, 1771.]

Peter Force, *The National Calendar, and Annals of the United States, for 1833.* Washington: Printed and Published by Peter Force, [1833].

* Franklin, *An Historical Review of the Constitutions of Pennsylvania.* 1759. [Benjamin Franklin, *An Historical Review of the Constitutions of Pennsylvania . . .* London: R. Griffiths, 1759.]

* Gallatin, *Considerations of the Currency and Banking System of the United States.* [Albert Gallatin, *Considerations on the Currency and Banking System of the United States.* Philadelphia: Carey & Lea, 1831.]

* Gallatin. Voir/ *See:* *Memorial of the Committee of the Free Trade Convention Held in Philadelphia, October 1831.*

Geisberg. Voir/ *See:* Zeisberger.

Isaac Godwin, *The Town Officer.* [Isaac Goodwin, *Town Officer; or Laws of Massachusetts Relative to the Duties of Municipal Officer . . .* Worcester (Massachusetts): Dorr and Howland, 1829.]

* Daniel Gookin, *Historical Collections of the Indians in New England.* 1792. [Dans/ *In Collections of the Massachusetts Historical Society. For the Year 1792.* Boston, 1792. I, pp. 141–226.]

* Miss Grant, *The American Lady.* [[Anne Grant,] *Memoirs of an American Lady.* London: Longman, 1808, et nombreuses rééditions/ *and many reprints.*]

* William Griffith, *Annual Law Register of the United States.* [Burlington (New Jersey): David Allinson, 1822.]

* [Friedrich M. Grimm, *Nouveaux mémoires secrets et inédits historiques, politiques, anecdotiques et littéraires* . . . Paris: Lerouge-Wolf, 1834. 2 vols.]
* [François Guizot, "De la religion dans les sociétés modernes," *L'Université catholique*, 5 (27), mars 1838, pp. 231–40.]
* [François Guizot, *Histoire de la Civilisation en Europe.*]
Ebenezer Hazard, *Historical Collection of State Papers and Other Authentic Documents Intended as Materials for an History of the United States of America.* Philadelphia, 1792. [Philadelphia: Printed by T. Dobson for the author, 1792–94.]
* John Heckewelder, *Historical Account of the Indian Nature.* 1 vol. ["An Account of the History, Manners and Customs of the Indian Nations," *Transactions of the American Philosophical Society* . . . Philadelphia: A. Small, 1819–43. I, pp. 3–347.]
John Heckewelder, *Transactions of the American Philosophical Review.* [American Philosophical Society, *Transactions of the Historical and Literary Committee of the American Philosophical Society* . . . Philadelphia: A. Small, 1819–43. 3 vols. Le volume I, pages 351–448, contient/ *Volume I, pages 351–448, includes:* "Correspondence between Mr. Heckewelder and Mr. Duponceau, on the Languages of the American Indians." "Très curieux sur les langues indiennes, les mœurs et l'histoire des Indiens."/ *"Very interesting on the Indian languages, the mores and the history of the Indians."*]
* Père Hennepin, *Nouveau voyage dans la Mer du Sud et du Nord.* Utrecht, 1698. [Il semble que Tocqueville n'ait pas lu cet ouvrage/ *It seems that Tocqueville did not read this work.*]
* Hinton, *History US.* [John Howard Hinton ed., *The History and Topography of the United States.* Jennings & Chaplin & J. T. Hinton, 1830–33. 2 vols.]
* David Hosack, *Essays on various Subjects of Medical Science.* 3 vols. [New York: J. Seymour, 1824–30. 3 vols.]
* David Hosack, *Memoirs of De Witt Clinton* [New York: J. Seymour, 1829.]
* David Hosack. Voir/ *See American Medical and Philosophical Register.*
* John Howard, *Memoirs of John Howard.* [Probablement/ *probably* Thomas Taylor, *Memoirs of John Howard.* London: John Hatchard and Son, 1836.]
Hutchinson, *Histoire.* [Thomas Hutchinson, *The History of the Colony and Province of Massachusetts-Bay* . . . 2ᵉ édition/ *second edition.* London: Mr. Richardson, 1765.]
Jefferson, *Correspondance de Jefferson par Conseil.* [Louis Conseil, *Mélanges poli-*

tiques et philosophiques extraits des mémoires et de la correspondance de Thomas Jefferson . . . Paris: Paulin, 1833.]

Jefferson, *Lettres à Madison.* [Dans l'édition de Conseil/ *In Conseil's edition.*]

Jefferson, *Mémoires.* [Fragments de l'édition de Conseil/ *Fragments from Conseil's edition.*]

Jefferson, *Notes sur la Virginie.* [Thomas Jefferson, *Observations sur la Virginie.* Traduites par l'abbé Morellet/ *Translated by the Abbé Morellet.* Paris: Barrois, l'aîné, 1786.]

* Johnson, *Wonder-working Providence of Sions Saviour in New England.* London. ["Wonder-working Providence of Sions Saviour. Being a Relation of the First Planting in New England, in the Yeere, 1628," dans/ *in: Collections of the Massachusetts Historical Society,* II, pp. 51–95; III, pp. 123–61; IV, pp. 1–51; VII, pp. 1–58; VIII, pp. 1–39.]

* *Journal des débats,* 1 mars 1834. Voir/ *See* Odilon Barrot.

* *Journal des débats,* 22 janvier 1836. [Sur la Pennsylvanie et ses communication, spécialement les chemins de fer/ *On Pennsylvania and its communication networks, especially the railroads.*]

* *Journal des débats,* 27 janvier 1836. [Sur la banque américaine et sa réaction après l'incendie de New York/ *On the American bank and its reaction after the New York conflagration.*]

* *Journal des débats,* 7 mars 1838. Voir/ *See* "Chambre des députés."

* Kempis, *Imitation de Jésus-Christ.*

Kent's Commentaries. [James Kent, *Commentaries on American Law.* New York: O. Halsted, 1826. 4 vols.]

* La Bruyère. [*Les caractères de Théophraste et de La Bruyère avec des notes par Mr. Coste.* Paris: L. Prault, 1769. 2 vols.]

Lafayette, *Mémoires.* [Marquis de Lafayette, *Mémoires, correspondance et manuscrits du général Lafayette.* Paris: H. Fournier aîné, 1837–38. 6 vols. Nous avons fait remarquer que la citation des mémoires pourrait provenir de l'article de Sainte-Beuve/ *I have noted that the quotation from the memoirs could have come from the article by Sainte-Beuve,* "Mémoires de Lafayette," *Revue des deux mondes,* 4ᵉ série, 15, 1838, pp. 355–81.]

* Lafayette. [*Le général Lafayette à ses collègues de la Chambre des députés.* Paris: Paulin, 1832.]

* La Hontan. [*Voyages du Baron de La Hontan dans l'Amérique septentrionale.* Amsterdam: F. l'Honoré, 1705.]

* La Hontan. [*Nouveaux voyages de Mr. le baron de la Hontan en Amérique sep-
tentrionale*. La Haye: F. l'Honoré, 1703.]
* La Luzerne, César-Henri comte de, *Correspondence of C. A. de La Luzerne*,
dans/*in* Jared Sparks, *The Diplomatic Correspondence of the American Revolu-
tion*. Boston 1830. Vols. X et XI. Identifié par/*Identified by* George W. Pierson.
Lamartine, *Jocelyn*.
* La Rochefoucault Liancourt, *Voyage dans les États-Unis*. [*Voyage dans les États-
Unis d'Amérique, fait en 1795, 1796 et 1797*. Paris: Du Pont, Buisson, Charles
Pougens, [1799]. 8 vols.]
John Lawson, *The History of Carolina*. [John Lawson, *The History of Carolina
. . .* London: T. Warner, 1718.]
Lepage-Dupratz, *Histoire de la Louisiane*. [Antoine Simon Le Page Du Pratz,
Histoire de la Louisiane . . . Paris: De Bure, 1758. 3 vols.]
* *Letter to the Mechanics of Boston*. [[Joseph Tuckerman,] *Letter to the Mechanics
of Boston, Respecting the Formation of a City Temperance Society . . .* Boston:
Published by the Massachusetts Society for the Suppression of Intemperance,
1831. "Contenant des détails curieux sur les diverses sociétés de tempérance."
Auteur identifié par George W. Pierson. L'ouvrage est cité aussi dans le *Sys-
tème pénitentiaire./ "Containing interesting details on the various temperance
societies." Author identified by George W. Pierson. Cited also in the* Penitentiary
System.]
* *Lettres édifiantes*. [*Lettres édifiantes et curieuses écrites des missions étrangères par
quelques missionaires de la compagnie de Jésus*.]
* *Christophe Level Voyage into New England, 1623–1624*. [Christopher Levett, *A
Voyage into New England, Began in 1623 and Ended in 1624 . . .* London: Wil-
liam Jones, 1628.]
De Lolme. [Jean Louis de Lolme, *The Constitution of England*.]
Long's Expedition. [Stephen H. Long, *Narrative of an Expedition to the Source
of St. Peter's River . . .* Philadelphia: H. C. Carey & I. Lea, 1824. 2 vols.]
* Stephen H. Long, *Account of and Expedition from Pittsburgh to the Rocky Moun-
tains Performed in the Years 1819 and 1820*. [Philadelphia: H. C. Carey and I.
Lea, 1822–23.]
* *Looks' Russia*. London, 1800. [Probablement/*Probably*, John Cook. *Voyages
and Travels Through the Russian Empire, Tartary, and Part of the Kingdom of
Persia*. Edinburgh: [imprimé pour l'auteur], 1770.]
* Louisiane. *Code de procédure*. [Edward Livingston, *A System of Penal Law, for
. . . Louisiana; . . . A Code of Procedure . . .* Nouvelle Orléans, 1824.]

Digeste des lois de la Louisiane. [L. Moreau Lislet, *A General Digest of the Acts of the Legislature of Louisiana . . . from 1804 to 1827 . . .* Nouvelle Orléans, 1830.]

Mahomet, *Coran.*

[Malesherbes] *Mémoires pour servir à l'histoire du droit public de la France en matière d'impôts.* Bruxelles [Paris], 1779.

Malte-Brun. [Conrad Malte-Brun, *Annales des voyages . . .* Paris: F. Buison, 1809–14. 24 vols.]

Machiavel, *Le Prince.* [Les éditeurs des œuvres complètes de Tocqueville (*OC,* XI, p. 19) ont identifié deux éditions qui se trouvaient dans la bibliothèque de Tocqueville: *Œuvres complètes* traduites par J.-V. Périès. Paris: Michaux, 1823–26, 12 vols; et une édition en italien, publiée à La Haye, et non daté/ *The editors of the complete works of Tocqueville (OC, XI, p. 19) have identified two editions that were found in the Tocqueville library:* Œuvres complètes *traduites par J.-V. Périès. Paris: Michaux, 1823–26. 12 vols; and an edition in Italian, published in The Hague, and undated.*]

Marshall, *Vie de Washington.* [John Marshall, *Vie de George Washington. . .* Paris: Dentu, 1808. 5 vols.]

Massachusetts. *Laws of Massachusetts.* Boston, 1823. 3 vols. [*The General Laws of Massachusetts from the Adoption of the Constitution to February, 1822 . . .* Boston: Wells & Lilly & Cummings & Hilliard, 1823, 1827. 3 vols.]

Massachusetts. *Historical Collection of State Papers.*

Massachusetts Historical Collection. Boston, 1792. Réédité en 1806. [*Collections of the Massachusetts Historical Society.* Reprinted by Monroe & Francis, Boston. Voir/*See:* Gookin, Belknap, Rogers.]

* Massillon, *Sermons,* édition de 1740 en 5 vols. [Nous n'avons pas réussi à retrouver cette édition/*I have not succeeded in finding this edition.*]

Mather's Magnalia Christi Americana. Hartford, 1820. 2 vols. [Cotton Mather, *Magnalia Christi Americana: or, the Ecclesiastical History of New England. . . ,* Hartford (Connecticut): S. Andrus, 1820. 2 vols.]

* J. H. McCulloh, *Researches, Philosophical and Antiquarian Concerning the Aboriginal History of America* [Baltimore: Fielding Lucas, 1829.]

* *Memorial of the Committee of the Free Trade Convention Held in Philadelphia, October 1831.* [[Albert Gallatin,] *Memorial of the Committee Appointed by the 'Free Trade Convention,' Held at Philadelphia, in September and October, 1831, to Prepare and Present a Memorial to Congress, Remonstrating Against the Ex-*

isting Tariff of Duties; with an Appendix. New York: W. A. Mercein, Printer 1832.]

* André Michaux, *Histoire des arbres forestiers de l'Amérique septentrionale.* [Paris: L. Haussmann et d'Hautel, 1810–13. 3 vols.]

Milton, *Paradis perdu.*

* *Minutes of the Proceedings of the United States Temperance Convention.*

* *L'Utopie de Thomas Morus, chancelier d'Angleterre, . . . traduite en français par Gueudeville,* 1717. [Seule l'édition publiée à Leiden: P. Vander AA, 1715, a pu être consultée/ *I was only able to consult the edition published in Leiden.*]

Mississippi Papers.

* Mary Russel Mitford, *Stories of American Life.* London: Colburn and Bentley, 1831. 3 vols.

Montaigne [*Les essais de Michel, seigneur de Montaigne.* Paris: A. L'Angelier, 1600. 3 vols.]

* Montesquieu, *L'esprit des lois.* 1750. 3 vols. [Genève: Barrillot et fils, 1750.]

* Montesquieu, *Lettres persanes.*

* *Morrison Mental Diseases.* [Sir Alexander Morison, *Outlines of Lectures on Mental Diseases.* Edinburgh, 1825.]

Nathaniel Morton, *New England's Memorial.* Boston, 1826. [Nathaniel Morton, *New England's Memorial . . .* 5ᵉ édition. Boston: Crocker and Brewster, 1826. Bruce James Smith, dans *Politics and Remembrance* (Princeton: Princeton University Press, 1985, p. 175), note que Morton a recopié dans son livre de longs fragments de l'ouvrage de William Bradford, *Of Plymouth Plantation,* sans en faire mention. Le manuscrit de cet ouvrage a été perdu jusqu'à 1858/ *Bruce James Smith, in* Politics and Remembrance, *notes that in his book Morton recopied long fragments from the work by William Bradford,* Of Plymouth Plantation, *without mentioning it. The manuscript of this work was lost until 1858.*]

National Calendar. [Voir/ *See* Force, Peter.]

* *National Intelligencer,* 19 février 1833, 10 décembre 1833 [Voir/ *See* President], 14 janvier 1834, 6 février 1834, 5 mars 1834.

* Neal, *History of New England.* [Daniel Neal, *History of New England.* London: J. Clark, 1720; et London: A. Ward, 1747. 2 vols.]

New Haven Antiquities. ["New Haven Antiquities or Blue Laws." Fait partie du *Code of 1650,* pp. 103–19/ *Part of the* Code of 1650, *pp. 103–19.*]

New York. *Annual Report of the Comptroller with the Accounts of the Corporation of the City of New York for the Year 1830.*

New York. *Proceedings of the Indian Board in the City of New York.* [Peut-être/ *Maybe*: *Proceedings of the Indian Board in the City of New York: with Colonel M'Kenneys Address.* New York: Vanderpool and Cole, Printers, 1829.]

New York. *The Revised Statutes.* [*The Revised Statutes of New York* . . . Albany (New York): Packard & Van Benthuysen, 1829. 3 vols.]

* New York. *Rules and Orders.* 1832.

The New York Annual Register [New York: J. Leavitt, 1830–45. Compilé par Edwin Williams/ *Compiled by Edwin Williams*].

New York Spectator. 23 août 1831.

* *Reports of the Temperance Societies of the States of New-York and Pennsylvania, 1831.* Cité dans le *Système pénitentiaire/Cited in the* Penitentiary System.

* *Second Annual Report of the New York Temperance Society, 1831.*

* *Nile's Weekly Register* jusqu'à 1832/ *until 1832.* [Hezekiah Niles, *The Weekly Register.* Baltimore: H. Niles éditeur/ *editor.*]

Ohio. *Acts of a General Nature of the State of Ohio.* [*Acts of a General Nature* . . . Columbus, Ohio: P. H. Olmsted, 1820, 1831. Tocqueville a peut-être pris connaissance de cet ouvrage par le compte-rendu de l'*American Quarterly Review,* XX, 1831, pp. 29–47, le volume est cité dans ses notes/ *Perhaps Tocqueville learned about this work from the review in the* American Quarterly Review, *XX, 1831, pp. 29–47; the volume is cited in his notes.*]

* *Statutes of Ohio.* [S. P. Chase. *Statutes of Ohio . . . from 1758 to 1833.* Cincinnati, 1833–35. 3 vols.]

* Ohio. Journal of the House of Representatif [*sic*] for 1830. [*Ohio. Journal of the House of Representatives,* Chillicothe; et ensuite/ *and later,* Columbus (Ohio), 1800– . "C'est un récit de tous les actes de cette assemblée pendant 1830. Il peut être fort utile comme *spécimen.*"/ "*This is an account of all the acts of this assembly during 1830. It can be very useful as example.*"]

Pascal. [*Pensées.*]

* William Penn, *Œuvres choisies de Penn.* London, 1782. [William Penn, *The Selected Works of William Penn.* 3ᵉ édition. London: Phillips, 1782. 5 vols.]

* Pennsylvanie. *Rapport du comité des voies et moyens de (mot illisible/illegible word). Législature de Pennsylvanie. Le 19 janvier 1831.*

Pennsylvanie. *Digest of the Laws of Pensylvania.* [John Pourdon, *A Digest of the Laws of Pennsylvania, from 1700 to 1824.* Philadelphia, 1824.]

Pitkins. [Timothy Pitkins, *A Political and Civil History of the United States of America* . . . New Haven, Connecticut: H. Howe and Durrie & Peck, 1828.

2 vols. Tocqueville a pu prendre connaissance de cet ouvrage par le compte-rendu de la *North American Review,* 30 (66), 1830, pp. 1–25/ *Tocqueville was able to learn about this work from the review in the* North American Review, *30 (66), 1830, pp. 1–25.*]

* Timothy Pitkins, *Statistical View of the Commerce of the U.S.* [deuxième édi-tion, avec ajouts et corrections/ *second edition with additions and corrections,* Hartford: Hamlen & Newton, 1817.]

Platon, *La république.*

Plutarque. [*Vie de Marcellus.* Traduction d'Auguste. La bibliothèque de Tocque-ville (*OC,* XI, p. 61) contient les éditions suivantes/ *The Tocqueville library (OC, XI, p. 61) contains the following editions: Vie des hommes illustres, Grecs et Romains.* Traduction de Mayot/ *Translation by Mayot,* Paris, 1568; *Les œuvres meslées de Plutarque,* 1574. 7 vols; *La vie des hommes illustres,* Paris, 1825. 10 vols.]

* *The Presidency.* [Pamphlet contre Jackson/ *Pamphlet against Jackson.*]

Président. *Message du président du 8 décembre 1833.* [Tocqueville a pu le lire dans le *National Calendar*/ *Tocqueville was able to read it in the* National Calendar, *1833;* et le/ *and in the* National Intelligencer de 10 décembre 1833/ *of December 10, 1833.*]

Report of the Postmaster General. [Publié dans le *National Intelligencer* du 12 décembre 1833 et dans le *National Calendar, 1833.*]

* [*Project of an Anti-Tariff Convention.* "Curieux pour voir comment ces assem-blées se forment."/ *"Interesting for seeing how these assemblies form."*]

Robert Proud, *The History of Pensylvania,* Filadelfia, 1797. 2 vols. [Robert Proud, *The History of Pennsylvania . . .* Philadelphia: Zacharian Poulson, 1797–98.]

Racine, *Britannicus.* [La bibliothèque de Tocqueville contenait les *Œuvres de Jean Racine,* 1755. 3 vols./ *The Tocqueville library contains the Œuvres of Jean Racine, 1755. 3 vols.*]

* *Report Made to Congress Relative to the Bank of the United States, 1830.*

* *Report of the Commissioners of the Canal Fund.* New York, 1831.

Report of the Secretary of the Treasury. 5 dec 1833. [Peut-être dans le *National Intelligencer* du/ *Perhaps in the* National Intelligencer *of* 4 décembre 1833.]

* Reports of the Secretary of the Treasury depuis 1823 jusqu'à 1832.

* Reports of the Secretary of the Treasury Respecting the Commerce of the United States.

* Report of the Secretary of the State sur l'instruction et les pauvres pour 1832.

* *Report of the Selected Committee of the House of Representatives of Massachusetts Relating to Legalising the Study of Anatomy, 1831.*

[*Revue des deux mondes,* mai 1837, revue littéraire de l'année/ *literary review of that year.*]

[*Revue des deux mondes,* loi électorale de 19 avril 1831/*electoral law of 19 April 1831.*]

[*Revue des deux mondes,* article sur la nullification/ *article on nullification.*]

[*Revue des deux mondes.* Voir/ *See* A. C. T.]

* J. B. Say [*Cours complet d'économie politique.* Paris: Rapill, 1828–29. 7 vols.]

* Walter Scott, *The Bride of Lammermoor.*

* Arnold Scheffer, *Histoire des États-Unis de l'Amérique septentrionale.* Paris, 1825. Selon George W. Pierson, Tocqueville aurait lu ce texte/ *According to George W. Pierson, Tocqueville would have read this text.*

* Schoolcraft, *Travels in the Central Portion of the Mississippi Valley* [New York: Collins and Hannay, 1825].

Senate Documents. 18, 19 et 20 Congrès. Voir/ *See Legislative Documents.*

Thomas Sergeant, *Constitutional Law.* [Thomas Sergeant, *Constitutional Law.* Philadelphia: P. H. Nicklin and T. Johnson, 1830.]

Mme de Sevigné. [Correspondence.]

William Shakespeare, *Henri V.*

* *Siècle.* [Article sur les mines au/ *article on mines in: Siècle* du 27 juin 1837.]

* *Siècle.* [Sur Thiers au/ *on Thiers in: Siècle* de janvier 1838.]

* Claude Gabriel Simon, *Observations recueillies en Angleterre en 1835.* Paris: J. Pesrou, 1836.

John Smith, *The General History of Virginia . . .* London, 1627. [Captain John Smith, *The General History . . .* London: Michael Sparkes, 1627.]

William Smith, *History of New York.* London, 1767. [William Smith, *The History of the Province of New-York . . .* London: T. Wilcox, 1757. Tocqueville cite aussi une édition française, publiée à Londres en 1767./ *Tocqueville also cites a French edition, published in London in 1767: Histoire de la Nouvelle-York, depuis la découverte de cette province jusqu'à notre siècle.* Traduite de l'anglois par M. E***. Londres, 1767.]

Société de colonisation des noirs. 15ᵉ rapport annuel.

* *Recueil de la société de géographie.*

* *Extrait du bulletin de la société de géographie. Tableau de la population des États-Unis, d'après les différents recensements exécutés par ordre du gouvernement.*

William Stith, *History of Virginia.* [William Stith, *The History of the First Dis-covery and Settlement of Virginia* . . . Williamsburg, Virginie: W. Parks, 1747.]

Story, *Commentaires sur la Constitution des États-Unis.* [Joseph Story, *Commen-taries on the Constitution of the United States* . . . *Abridged by the Author, for the Use of Colleges and High Schools* . . . Boston: Hilliard, Gray and Company; Cambridge, Massachusetts: Shattuck and Co., Cambridge, 1833. Identifié par James T. Schleifer/ *Identified by James T. Schleifer.*]

Story, *Laws of the United States.* [*The Public and General Statutes Passed by the Congress of the United States of America. From 1789 to 1827 Inclusive. Published Under the Inspection of Joseph Story.* Boston: Wells and Lilly, 1828. 2 vols.]

* William Strachey, *The History of Travayle into Virginia Britannica* [Boston: Richardson, Lord & Holbrook, 1830.]

* *Sullivan Journal.* [George W. Pierson suggère William Sullivan, *Political Class Book* . . . Boston: Lord and Holbrook, 1830, et plusieurs rééditions/ *George W. Pierson suggests William Sullivan,* Political Class Book . . . *Boston: Lord and Holbrook, 1830, and several reissues.*]

* *Tabular Statistic Views of the Population, Revenue* . . . 1829. [Probablement/ *Probably:* George Watterston, *Tabular Statistical Views of the Population, Commerce, Navigation, Public Lands, Post Office Establishments, Revenue, Mint, Military & Naval Establishments, Expenditures, and Public Debt of the United States.* Washington: J. Elliot, 1828.]

* *Tableau général du commerce de la France pendant l'année 1832.* [Administration des douanes, *Tableau général du commerce de la France avec ses colonies et les puissances étrangères* . . . Paris: Impr. Royale, 1825–58.]

Tanner, *Mémoires de Tanner.* [Henry S. Tanner, *Memoir on the Recent Surveys, Observations, and Internal Improvements* . . . Philadelphia, [imprimé par l'auteur], 1829.] Voir/ *See* Blosseville.

* John Tappen, *County and Town Officer or a Concise View of the Duties and Offices of County and Town Offices in the State of New York.* [John Tappen, *The County and Town Officer* . . . Kingston, New York: [imprimé par l'auteur], 1816.]

The Statutes of the State of Tennessee. [Voir/ *See The Statute Law of the State of Tennessee.*]

The Statute Law of the State of Tennessee. [*The Statute Laws of the State of Ten-nessee of a Public and General Nature.* By John Haywood and Robert L. Cobbs. Knoxville, Tennessee: F. S. Heiskell, 1831. 2 vols. L'appendice du deuxième volume, qui comprend le texte de plusieurs traités avec les Indiens, semble avoir particulièrement intéressé Tocqueville/ *The appendix of the second volume, which includes the text of several treaties with the Indians, seems to have particularly interested Tocqueville.*]

Traité sur les règles des actions civiles. Nouvelle Orléans: chez Buisson, 1830. [Peut-être/ *Maybe Code of Practice in Civil Cases.* Nouvelle Orléans, 1830.]

Transactions of the American Philosophical Society. Voir/ *See* Zeisberger, Duponceau, Heckewelder.

* *Statistique du Département de l'Aude par le Baron Trouvé* [Baron Trouvé, *Description générale et statistique du département de l'Aude.* Paris: F. Didot, 1818].

Benjamin Trumbull, *A Complete History of Connecticut.* New Haven, 1818. 2 vols. [Benjamin Trumbull, *A Complete History of Connecticut . . .* New Haven, Connecticut: Maltby, Goldsmith and Co., and Samuel Wodsworth, 1818.]

Benjamin Trumbull, *La Constitution de 1639.* [Il s'agit d'un chapitre tiré de *A Complete History of Connecticut/ It concerns a chapter drawn from* A Complete History of Connecticut.]

Benjamin Trumbull, *Lois pénales du Connecticut.* [Dans son/ *In his: A Complete History of Connecticut,* chapitre VIII.]

U.S. Congress. Legislative Documents.

* Roberts Vaux, *Memoirs of the Life of Anthony Benezet* [Philadelphia: James P. Parke, 1817].

Volney, *Tableau des États-Unis.* [Constantin F. Volney, *Tableau du climat et du sol des États-Unis d'Amérique . . .* Paris: Boussangue Frères, 1822. Tocqueville l'avait acheté avant son voyage, mais il ne l'a probablement pas lu avant son retour en France/ *Tocqueville had purchased it before his journey, but he probably did not read it before his return to France.*]

* *Voyage d'un Français, avec une description de la Virginie et du Maryland publiée en 1696 à La Haye.* Voir/ *See* Durand.

* Rev. R. Walsh. Voir/ *See American Quarterly Review.*

Warden, *Description des États-Unis.* [D. B. Warden, *Description statistique, historique et politique des États-Unis . . .* Paris: Rey et Gravier, 1820. Warden a prêté ce texte à Tocqueville ainsi que d'autres publications/ *Warden loaned this text to Tocqueville, as well as other publications.*]

* Isaac Weld, *Voyage dans le Haut Canada.* [*Travel Through the States of North America, and the Provinces of Upper and Lower Canada . . .* London: John Stockdale, 1799. 2 vols. Réédité en/ *reprinted in:* 1799, 1800 et 1807.]

Roger Williams, *Key into the Language of the Indians of New England,* London,

1643. Dans la *Collection de la Société Historique du Massachusetts,* III, p. 203. [Roger Williams, *A Key into the Language of America: or an Help to the Language of the Natives in that Part of America, Called New-England*. . . London: Gregory Dexter, 1643. Dans *Collections of the Massachusetts Historical Society,* III, pp. 203–38.]

Williams Annual Register. Voir/*See New York Annual Register.*

* Samuel Williams, *Histoire de Vermont.* [*The Natural and Civil History of Vermont.* New Hampshire: Isaiah Thomas and David Carlisle, Walpole, 1794.]

David Zeisberger, "A Grammar of the Language of the Lenni Lenâpé," traduite par P. S. Duponceau dans/*translated by P. S. Duponceau in* Transactions of the American Philosophical Society, *III, 1827, pp. 65–250.*

Bibliography

I list here some works that reproduce Tocqueville documents that are interesting for the understanding of *Democracy in America* and that sometimes reproduce texts of Tocqueville not available in the *Œuvres complètes*.

Adams, Herbert Baxter, ed. *Jared Sparks and Alexis de Tocqueville*. Johns Hopkins University Studies in Historical and Political Science, 16th ser. (112). Baltimore: Johns Hopkins University Press, 1898.

Craiutu, Aurelian, and Jeremy Jennings, eds. *Tocqueville on America after 1840*. Cambridge: Cambridge University Press, 2009.

Drescher, Seymour. *Tocqueville and England*. Cambridge, Mass.: Harvard University Press, 1964.

————, ed. *Tocqueville and Beaumont on Social Reform*. New York: Harper & Row, 1968.

Engel-Janosi, Friedrich, ed. "New Tocqueville Materials from the Johns Hopkins University Collections. In *Four Studies in French Romantic Historical Writing*, 121–42. Johns Hopkins University Studies in Historical and Political Science 71, no. 2 (1955).

Grandmaison, Charles A. G. de. "Séjour d'Alexis de Tocqueville en Touraine, préparation du livre sur l'Ancien Régime, juin 1853–avril 1854." *Correspondant* 114 (1879): 926–49.

Hawkins, Richmond L., ed. "Unpublished Letters of Alexis de Tocqueville." *Romanic Review* 19 (1928): 195–217; 20 (1929): 351–56.

L'Hommedé, Edmond. *Un département français sous la Monarchie de Juillet: le conseil général de la Manche et Alexis de Tocqueville*. Preface by A. Coville. Paris: Bovin, 1933.

Jardin, André. *Alexis de Tocqueville*. Paris: Hachette, 1984.

Alexis de Tocqueville als Abgeordneter. Briefe an seinem Wahlagenten Paul Clamorgan 1837–1851 aus dem Besitz der Staats und Universitätsbibliothek Hamburg. Herausgegeben von Joachim Kühn. Hamburg: Ernest Hauswedell & Co., 1972.

Lamberti, Jean–Claude. *Tocqueville et les deux Démocraties.* Paris: PUF, 1983.

Letessier, Fernand, ed. "Cinq lettres inédites de Tocqueville à Lamartine." *Revue d'histoire littéraire* 83 (1983): 451–58.

Lingelbach, William E. "American Democracy and European Interpreters." *Pennsylvania Magazine of History and Biography* 61, no. 1 (1937): 1–25.

MacInnis, Edgar, ed. "A Letter from Alexis de Tocqueville on the Canadian Rebellion of 1837." *Canadian Historical Review* 19, no. 4 (1938): 394–97.

Marcel, Roland-Pierre. *Essai politique sur Alexis de Tocqueville.* Paris: Félix Alcan, 1910.

Mayer, J. P., ed. "Sur la Démocratie en Amérique. Fragments inédits." *Nouvelle revue française* 76 (1959): 761–68.

Nolla, Eduardo. *Autour de l'autre* Démocratie. Napoli: Instituto Suor Orsola Benincasa, 1994.

———. "La 'Démocratie' ovvero il libro chiuso." *Filosofia Politica* 6, no. 1 (1992): 132–41.

Passy, Louis. *Le marquis de Blosseville, souvenirs.* Évreux: Charles Hérissey, 1898.

Perry, Thomas Sergeant, ed. *The Life and Letters of Francis Lieber.* Boston: James R. Osgoood and Co., 1882.

Pierce, Edward L., ed. *Memoir and Letters of Charles Sumner.* 4 vols. Boston: Roberts Brothers, 1893.

Pierson, George Wilson. "Le 'seconde voyage' de Tocqueville en Amérique." In *Alexis de Tocqueville. Livre du centenaire.* Paris: Éditions du C.N.R.S., 1960.

———. *Tocqueville and Beaumont in America.* New York: Oxford University Press, 1938.

Pitman, C. B., ed. *Memoirs of the Count de Falloux.* London: Chapman and Hall Limited, 1888. 2 vols.

Pope-Hennessy, James. *Monckton Milnes, the Flight of Youth. 1851–1885.* London: Constable, 1951.

Quinet, Mme Edgar. *Edgar Quinet avant l'exil.* 2nd ed. Paris: Calman Lévy, 1888.

Rédier, Antoine. *Comme disait M. de Tocqueville.* Paris: Perrin, 1925.

Schleifer, James T. *The Making of Tocqueville's "Democracy in America."* Chapel Hill, N.C.: The University of North Carolina Press, 1980. Second edition. Indianapolis: Liberty Fund, 2000.

———. "Tocqueville and Religion: Some New Perspectives." *Tocqueville Review* 4, no. 2 (1982): 303–21.

———. "How Democracy Influences Preaching: A Previously Unpublished

Fragment from Tocqueville's *Democracy in America.*" *Yale University Library Gazette* 52, no. 2 (1977): 75–79.

———. "Tocqueville and American Literature: A Newly Acquired Letter." *Yale University Library Gazette* 54, no. 3 (1980): 129–34.

———. "Tocqueville and Centralization: Four Previously Unpublished Manuscripts." *Yale University Library Gazette* 58, nos. 1–2 (1983): 29–39.

———, ed. "Alexis de Tocqueville Describes the American Character; Two Previously Unpublished Portraits." *South Atlantic Quarterly* 74, no. 2 (1975): 244–58.

Simpson, Mary Charlotte Mair, ed. *Journals Kept in France and Italy from 1842 to 1852 . . . by Nassau William Senior.* 2 vols. London: Henry S. King and Co., 1871.

———. *Correspondence and Conversations of Alexis de Tocqueville with Nassau William Senior, from 1834 to 1859.* Ed. M. C. M. Simpson. 2nd ed. New York: A. M. Kelly, 1968.

Secondary Bibliography

L'actualité de Tocqueville. Caen: Centre de publications de l' université de Caen, 1991.

Alexis de Tocqueville. Livre du centenaire, 1859–1959. Paris: C.N.R.S., 1960.

Allen, Barbara. *Tocqueville, Covenant, and the Democratic Revolution.* Lanham, Md.: Lexington Books, 2005.

Amiel, Anne. *Le vocabulaire de Tocqueville.* Paris: Ellipses, 2002.

Ampère, Jean-Jacques. "Alexis de Tocqueville." *Correspondant* 47 (25 June 1859): 312–35.

———. "Epître à M. de Tocqueville." In *Promenade en Amérique.* vol. I, v–xi. Paris: Michel Lévy, 1855.

Analyses et réflexions sur . . . Tocqueville. De la Démocratie en Amérique. Paris: Éditions Marketing, 1985.

Angell, Robert C. "Tocqueville's Sociological Theory." *Sociology and Social Research* 26, no. 4 (1942): 323–33.

Antoine, Agnès. *L'impensé de la démocratie.* Paris: Fayard, 2003.

Aron, Raymond. "Alexis de Tocqueville et Karl Marx." *European Journal of Sociology* 5, no. 2 (1964): 159–89.

———. "The American Experience: Unique or Universal?" *Atlantic Community Quarterly* 14, no. 3 (1976): 306–13.

———. *Auguste Comte et Alexis de Tocqueville, juges de l'Angleterre.* Oxford: Clarendon Press, 1965.

———. "Idées politiques et vision historique de Tocqueville." *Revue française de science politique* 10, no. 3 (1960): 509–26.

———. "Tocqueville." In *Les étapes de la pensée sociologique.* 2 vols. Paris: Gallimard, 1967.

———. "Tocqueville." In *Les grandes doctrines de sociologie historique: Montesquieu, Auguste Comte, Karl Marx, Alexis de Tocqueville. Les sociologues et la révolution de 1848,* 162–202. Paris: Centre de Documentation Universitaire, n.d.

———. "Tocqueville et Marx." In *Dix-huit leçons sur la société industrielle.* Paris: Gallimard, 1962.

———. "Tocqueville retrouvé," *Tocqueville Review* 1, no. 1 (1979): 8–23.

Audier, Serge. *Tocqueville retrouvé.* Paris: Librairie philosophique J. Vrin et Éditions de l'EHESS, 2004.

Bagge, Dominique. "Deux écrits américains sur Tocqueville." *Politique* 16 (1961): 406–10.

———. "De Maistre à Tocqueville: la naissance de la science politique moderne." *Res publica* 6, no. 2 (1964): 169–80.

———. "Tocqueville et le renouvellement de la science politique." *Politique* 14 (1961): 5–22.

Ball, Rex Harrison. "Race in America: Three Nineteenth Century French Liberals as Critics of America." *Proceedings of the Annual Meeting of the Western Society for French History* 1 (1973): 268–79.

Barzun, Jacques. "Notes on Tocqueville's Interpreters." *Tocqueville Review* 7 (1985–1986): 149–55.

Batault, Georges. "Tocqueville et la littérature américaine." *Mercure de France* 135 (1919): 248–61.

Bathory, Peter Dennis. "The Science of Politics and the Art of Ruling: James Madison and Alexis de Tocqueville." In *Leadership in America: Consensus, Corruption and Charisma,* 11–37. New York: Longman, 1978.

———. "Tocqueville on Citizenship and Faith: A Response to Cushing Strout." *Political Theory* 8, no. 1 (1980): 27–38.

Battista, Anna Maria. "La *Democrazia in America* di Tocqueville. Problemi interpretativi." *Cultura* 9 (1971): 165–200.

———. "Il primo Tocqueville sulla 'democrazia politica.'" *Quaderni Fiorentini* 10 (1981): 9–52.

———. *Lo spirito liberale e lo spirito religioso: Tocqueville nel dibattito sulla scuola.* Milano: Jaca Book, 1976.

———. "Lo stato sociale democratico nella analisi di Tocqueville e nelle valutazioni di contemporanei." *Pensiero Politico* 4, no. 3 (1973): 336–95.

———. *Studi su Tocqueville.* Firenze: Centro editoriale toscano, 1989.

Baunard, Louis. "Alexis de Tocqueville." In *La foi et ses victoires dans le siècle présent,* vol. I, 123–249. Paris: Poussielgue Frères, 1884.

Beaumont de la Bonninière, Gustave. "Notice sur Alexis de Tocqueville." In *Œuvres et correspondance inédites d'Alexis de Tocqueville,* 3–124. Paris: Michel Lévy Frères, 1861.

———. Preface to *De la démocratie en Amérique,* i–xlvi. 14th ed. Paris: Michel Lévy, 1864.

Becker, Carl Lotus. "Why De Tocqueville Wrote *De la démocratie en Amérique.*" In *Detachment and the Writing of History. Essays and Letters of Carl L. Becker,* 167–76. Ed. Phil L. Snyder. Ithaca, N.Y.: Cornell University Press, 1958.

Bedeschi, Giuseppe. *Storia del pensiero liberale.* Roma-Bari: Laterza, 1990.

Bellah, Robert N. "Are Americans Still Citizens?" *Tocqueville Review* 7 (1985–1986): 89–96.

———, Richard Madsen, William M. Sullivan, Ann Swidler, and Steven M. Tipton. *Habits of the Heart. Individualism and Commitment in American Life.* Berkeley: University of California Press, 1985.

Beloff, Max. "Tocqueville et l'Angleterre." In *Alexis de Tocqueville. Livre du Centenaire,* 87–100.

———. "The Tocqueville Industry." *Encounter* 56, nos. 2–3 (1981): 85–87.

Benoît, Jean-Louis. *Alexis de Tocqueville. Notes sur le Coran et autres textes sur les religions.* Paris: Bayard, 2007.

———. *Tocqueville moraliste.* Paris: Honoré Champion, 2004.

Bergeron, Gérard. *Quand Tocqueville et Siegfried nous observaient . . .* Québec: Presses de l'université du Québec, 1990.

Berlin, Isaiah. "The Thought of De Tocqueville." *History* 50, no. 169 (1965): 199–206.

Berthomieu, Gérard, and Françoise Rullier-Theuret. *Styles, genres, auteurs.* Paris: Presses de l'université de Paris Sorbonne, 2005.

Bigiawi, W. "Tocqueville e il diritto romano; Tocqueville e i juristi." *Rivista di Diritto e Procedura Civile* 1 (1947): 184–88.

Biré, Edmond. "Alexis de Tocqueville." In *Mémoires et souvenirs, 1789–1830: la*

Révolution, l'Empire et la Restauration, vol. 2, 300–17. Paris: Victor Retaux, 1859–1898.

Birnbaum, Pierre. *Sociologie de Tocqueville.* Paris: PUF, 1970.

———. "Tocqueville and the Historical Sociology of State." In *Liberty, Equality, Democracy,* 91–102, Eduardo Nolla, ed. New York: New York University Press, 1992.

Blanc, Louis. "De la Démocratie en Amérique." *Revue républicaine* 5 (10 May 1835).

Bloom, Allan. "Rousseau on the Equality of the Sexes." In *Justice and Equality Here and Now,* 66–88, Frank S. Lucash, ed. Ithaca, N.Y.: Cornell University Press, 1986.

Blosseville, Bénigne, Vicomte de. "De la Démocratie en Amérique." *L'Écho français* 42 (11 February 1835).

Boesche, Roger. "Hedonism and Nihilism: The Predictions of Tocqueville and Nietzsche." *Tocqueville Review* 8 (1986–1987): 165–84.

———. "The Prison, Tocqueville's Model for Despotism." *Western Political Quarterly* 33, no. 4 (1980): 550–63.

———. "The Strange Liberalism of Alexis de Tocqueville." *History of Political Thought* 2, no. 3 (1981): 495–524.

———. *The Strange Liberalism of Alexis de Tocqueville.* Ithaca, N.Y.: Cornell University Press, 1987.

———. "Tocqueville and Le Commerce: A Newspaper Expressing His Unusual Liberalism." *Journal of the History of Ideas* 44, no. 2 (1983): 277–92.

———. *Tocqueville's Road Map: Methodology, Liberalism, Revolution, and Despotism.* Lanham, Maryland: Lexington Books, 2006.

———. "Why Did Tocqueville Think a Successful Revolution Was Impossible?" In *Liberty, Equality, Democracy,* 165–85, Eduardo Nolla, ed. New York: New York University Press, 1992.

———. "Why Could Tocqueville Predict so Well?" *Political Theory* 11, no. 1 (1983): 79–103.

Bonetto, Gerald M. "Alexis de Tocqueville's Concept of Political Parties." *American Studies* 22, no. 2 (1981): 59–79.

———. "Tocqueville and American Slavery." *Canadian Review of American Studies* 15, no. 2 (1984): 123–39.

Botana, Natalio R. "Tocqueville y la legitimidad democrática." *Revista Latinoamericana de Filosofía* 9 (1983): 117–42.

Botto, Evandro. "Libertà politica e libertà morale nel pensiero di Tocqueville."
    Rivista di Filosofia Neo-Scolastica 73, no. 3 (1981): 497–512.

Boudon, Raymond. *Tocqueville aujourd'hui*. Paris: Odile Jacob, 2005.

Bourricaud, François. "Contradiction et traditions chez Tocqueville." *Tocque-
    ville Review* 2, no. 1 (1980): 25–39.

———. "Les 'convictions' de M. de Tocqueville." *Tocqueville Review* 7 (1985–
    1986): 105–15.

Bradley, Phillips. "A Century of *De la Démocratie en Amérique." Journal of Adult
    Education* 9, no. 1 (1937): 19–24.

Bray, René. "Tocqueville et Charles Monnard: contribution à l'étude des sources
    allemandes de l'Ancien Régime et la Révolution." In *Mélanges d'histoire et de
    littérature offerts à M. Charles Gilliard*, 606–15. Lausanne: F. Rouge et Cie,
    1964.

Bressolette, Michel. "L'humanisme d'Alexis de Tocqueville." *Bulletin de la société
    toulousaine d'études classiques* 169–70 (1974): 5–18.

———. "Lamartine vu par Tocqueville." In Le comité permanent d'études la-
    martiniennes, *Centenaire de la mort d'Alphonse de Lamartine*, 241–49 Mâcon,
    1973.

———. "Tocqueville et la culture universitaire." *Études* 332, no. 1 (1970): 5–13.

Brogan, Hugh. *Alexis de Tocqueville: A Life*. New Haven, Connecticut: Yale Uni-
    versity Press, 2007.

———. "Alexis de Tocqueville and the Liberal Moment." *Historical Journal* 14,
    no. 2 (1971): 289–303.

———. "Alexis de Tocqueville: The Making of a Historian." *Journal of Con-
    temporary History* 7, nos. 3–4 (1972): 5–20.

———. "Pauperism and Democracy. Alexis de Tocqueville and Nassau Senior."
    In *Liberty, Equality, Democracy*, 129–41, Eduardo Nolla, ed. New York: New
    York University Press, 1992.

———. *Tocqueville*. London: Fontana, 1973.

———. "Tocqueville and the American Presidency." *Journal of American Stud-
    ies* 15, no. 3 (1981): 357–75.

[Brooks, Edward] "The Error of De Tocqueville." *North American Review* 102,
    no. 211 (1866): 321–34.

Brudnoy, David. " 'Liberty by Taste': Tocqueville's Search for Freedom." *Modern
    Age* 20, no. 2 (1976): 164–76.

Brunius, Teddy. *Alexis de Tocqueville, the Sociological Aesthetician*. Uppsala:
    Almqvist and Wicksell, 1960.

Bryce, James. *The Predictions of Hamilton and De Tocqueville.* Baltimore: Johns Hopkins University, 1887.

Buicks, Peter E. J. "Alexis de Tocqueville and the Ethos of Democracy." *The Netherlands Journal of Sociology* 17 (1981): 137–50.

Burrage, Michael. "On Tocqueville's Notion of the Irresistibility of Democracy." *Archives européennes de sociologie* 13, no. 1 (1972): 151–75.

Caboara, Lorenzo. *Democrazia e libertà nel pensiero di Alexis de Tocqueville.* Milano: U. Hoepli, 1946.

Callot, Emile-François. *La pensée libérale au 19 siècle.* Lyon: L'Hermès, 1987.

Canoll, John W. Henry. "The Authorship of *Democracy in America.*" *Historical Magazine* 8, no. 9 (1864): 332–33.

Caplow, Theodor. "The Current Relevance of *Democracy in America.*" *Tocqueville Review* 7 (1985–1986): 137–47.

Caprariis, Vittorio de. "Profilo di Alexis de Tocqueville." *Nord e Sud* 22, no. 83 (1961): 77–124.

———. *Tocqueville in America. Contributto alla genesi de "La Democrazia in America."* Napoli: L'Arte Tipografica, 1959.

Cavallaro, Renato. "Dall'individualismo al controllo democratico: aspetti del pensiero di Alexis de Tocqueville sull'associazionismo volontario." *Critica Sociologica* 28 (1973–1974): 99–125.

Ceaser, James. "Alexis de Tocqueville on Political Science, Political Culture, and the Role of the Intellectual." *American Political Science Review* 79, no. 3 (1985): 656–72.

Chevallier, Jean-Jacques. "De la distinction des sociétés aristocratiques et des sociétés démocratiques en tant que fondement de la pensée politique d'Alexis de Tocqueville." *Revue des travaux de l'Académie des sciences morales et politiques* 109, no. 4 (1956): 116–36.

———. "Tocqueville." In *Les grandes œuvres politiques de Machiavel à nos jours.* Paris: Armand Colin, 1949.

Chichiarelli, Ezio. *Alexis de Tocqueville, saggio critico.* Bari: G. Laterza & Figli, 1941.

———. "Note sul pensiero politico francese del secolo XIX; Alexis de Tocqueville." *Annali di Scienze Politiche* 12, nos. 3–4 (1939): 1–76.

Cioran, Émile. *Anthologie du portrait. De Saint-Simon à Tocqueville.* Paris: Gallimard, 1996.

Clark, Dympha, David Headon, and John Williams. *The Ideal of Alexis de Tocqueville. Manning Clark.* Melbourne: Melbourne University Press, 2000.

Clinton, David. *Tocqueville, Lieber, and Bagehot.* New York: Palgrave Macmillan, 2003.

Cofrancesco, Dino. *Introduzione a Tocqueville e altri saggi.* Milano: Marzorati, 1969.

———. "John Stuart Mill a Tocqueville nell'ottocento liberale." In J. S. Mill, *Sulla "De la Démocratie en Amérique" di Tocqueville,* 7–86. Napoli: Guida Editori, 1971.

———. "Rileggendo *La Democrazia in America.*" *Nord e Sud* 120, no. 181 (1969): 119–28.

———. "Tocqueville e il pensiero conservatore: riflessioni sui quaderni di viaggio e sulle lettere dell'Alexis de Tocqueville. Alle origini della sociologia." *Controcorrente* 9, no. 4 (1974): 11–40.

Cohen, David. *Chasing the Red, White, and Blue.* New York: Picador, 2001.

Cohen, Eliot A. "Tocqueville on War." *Social Philosophy and Policy* 3, no. 1 (1985): 204–22.

Colombo, A. "Attualità di due 'classici': fra Tocqueville e Stuart Mill." *Nuova Antologia* 546, no. 2139 (1981): 292–96.

Colwell, James L. "The Calamities Which They Apprehend: Tocqueville on Race in America." *MARAB* 1, no. 3 (1968): 53–8.

Commager, Henry Steele. "De la Démocratie en Amérique." In *The Search for a Usable Past, and Other Essays in Historiography,* 181–95. New York: Knopf, 1967.

———. "Democracy in America: 100 Years After." *New York Times,* 15 December 1935, sec. VII.

———. "Tocqueville's Mistake. A Defense of Strong Central Government." *Harper's* 269, no. 1611 (August 1984): 70–74.

Compagna, Luigi. "Dalle 'parti' ai 'partiti.'" *Pensiero Politico* 14, no. 2 (1981): 274–83.

———. "La modernità di Tocqueville." *Nord e Sud* 153, no. 214 (1972): 84–94.

Copans, Simon Jacob. "Tocqueville's Later Years—A Reaffirmation of Faith." *Romanic Review* 36, no. 2 (1945): 113–21.

Corcelle, Francisque de. "De la Démocratie en Amérique." *Revue des deux mondes* 2 (1835): 739–64.

———. "De l'esclavage aux États-Unis." *Revue des deux mondes* 6 (1836): 227–46.

Costner, Herbert L. "De Tocqueville on Equality: A Discourse on Intellectual Style." *Pacific Sociological Review* 19, no. 4 (1976): 411–29.

Craiutu, Aurelian. *Liberalism under Siege. The Political Thought of the French Doctrinaires.* Lanham, Md.: Lexington Books, 2003.

Crouthamel, James L. "Tocqueville's South." *Journal of the Early Republic* 2, no. 4 (1982): 381–401.

Dannhauser, Werner J. "Some Thoughts on Liberty, Equality, and Tocqueville's *Democracy in America.*" *Social Philosophy and Policy* 2 (1984): 141–60.

Darveau-Cardinal, Jacqueline. "À propos de Tocqueville et d'un voyage au Bas–Canada." *Forces* 23 (1973): 27–37.

Debu-Bridel, Jacques. "De Montesquieu à Tocqueville." *Liberté de l'esprit* 25 (1951): 267–72.

De La Fournière, Xavier. *Alexis de Tocqueville. Un monarchiste indépendant.* Paris: Librairie Académique Perrin, 1981.

Delbez, Louis. "Un défenseur lucide de la démocratie, Alexis de Tocqueville." *Revue politique des idées et des institutions* 56, no. 2 (1967): 52–60.

De Sanctis, Francesco. "The Question of Fraternity in *Democracy in America.*" In *Liberty, Equality, Democracy,* 113–28, Eduardo Nolla, ed. New York: New York University Press, 1992.

———. *Tempo di democrazia.* Napoli: Edizioni Scientifiche Italiane, 1986.

Diamond, Martin. "The Ends of Federalism." *Publius* 3, no. 2 (1937): 129–51.

Díez del Corral, Luis. "Chateaubriand und der Soziologische Aesthetizismus Tocquevilles." In *Epirrhosis. Festgabe für Carl Schmitt,* 115–52. Berlin: Duncker & Humblot, 1968.

———. *La demistificación de la antigüedad clásica por los pensadores liberales, con especial referencia a Tocqueville.* Cuadernos de la Fundación Pastor 16. Madrid: Taurus, 1969.

———. "El liberalismo de Tocqueville. (La influencia de Pascal)." *Revista de Occidente* 3, no. 26 (1965): 133–53.

———. *La mentalidad política de Tocqueville, con especial referencia a Pascal.* Madrid: Real Academia de Ciencias Morales y Políticas, 1965.

———. "Montesquieu y Tocqueville." In *Libro homenaje a Jose Antonio Maravall,* 473–82. Madrid: Centro de Investigaciones Sociológicas, 1986.

———. *El pensamiento político de Tocqueville.* Madrid: Alianza Editorial, 1989.

———. "Sobre la formación intelectual de Tocqueville. La 'noblesse de robe' y el bisabuelo Malesherbes." *Boletín de la Real Academia de la Historia* 181, no. 2, 173–205.

———. "Tocqueville y Royer-Collard." In *Historia económica y pensamiento so-*

cial. Estudios en homenaje a Diego Mateo del Peral. Madrid: Alianza Editorial, 1983: 75–86.

Dittgen, Herbert. *Politik zwischen Freiheit und Despotismus.* München: Alber, 1986.

Doran, Eva. "Two Men and a Forest. Chateaubriand, Tocqueville, and the American Wilderness." *Essays in French Literature* 13 (1976): 44–61.

Drago, Roland. "Actualité de Tocqueville (Tocqueville et l'administration)." *Revue des sciences morales et politiques* 139, no. 4 (1984): 633–49.

Draper, Theodore. "The Idea of the Cold War and Its Prophets. On Tocqueville and Others." *Encounter* 52 (1979): 34–45.

Drescher, Seymour. "America and French Romanticism During the July Monarchy." *American Quarterly* 11, no. 1 (1959): 3–20.

———. *Dilemmas of Democracy: Tocqueville and Modernization.* Pittsburgh: University of Pittsburgh Press, 1968.

———. *Tocqueville and Beaumont on Social Reform.* New York: Harper & Row, 1968.

———. *Tocqueville and England.* Cambridge, Mass.: Harvard University Press, 1964.

———. "Tocqueville's Two Democracies." *Journal of the History of Ideas* 25, no. 2 (1964): 201–34.

———, and Lynn Marshall. "American Historians and Tocqueville's Democracy." *Journal of American History* 55, no. 3 (1968): 512–32.

Drolet, Michael. *Tocqueville, Democracy, and Social Reform.* New York: Palgrave Macmillan, 2003.

Dubois, Christian. *Alexis de Tocqueville.* Paris: Ellipses, 2004.

Dumas, Jean-Louis. "Alexis de Tocqueville ou la compréhension efficace." *Revue de métaphysique et de morale* 78, no. 4 (1973): 525–43.

———. "Tocqueville philosophe de la liberté." *Cahiers de philosophie politique et juridique* 1 (1982): 71–92.

Eden, Robert. "Tocqueville on Political Realignment and Constitutional Forms." *Review of Politics* 48, no. 3 (1986) 349–73.

d'Eichtal, Eugène. "Alexis de Tocqueville à propos d'un livre récent." *Séances et travaux de l'Académie des sciences morales et politiques* 173 (1910): 569–79.

———. *Alexis de Tocqueville et la démocratie libérale: étude suivie de fragments des entretiens de Tocqueville avec Nassau William Senior (1808–1858).* Paris: Calmann Lévy, 1897.

————. "Tocqueville et *De la Démocratie en Amérique.*" *Revue politique et parlementaire,* April–May 1896, 47–66, 350–76.

Einaudi, Mario. "L'avenir de la démocratie américaine." *Cahiers de la république* 6, no. 33 (1961): 27–39.

————. "Riflessione sopra Tocqueville." In *La rivoluzione di Roosevelt, 1932–1952.* Torino: G. Einaudi, 1959.

Eisenstadt, Abraham S., ed. *Reconsidering Tocqueville's "Democracy in America."* New Brunswick, N.J.: Rutgers University Press, 1988.

Elster, Jon. *Alexis de Tocqueville. The First Social Scientist.* Cambridge: Cambridge University Press, 2009.

Engel-Janosi, Friedrich. "New Tocqueville Material from the Johns Hopkins University Collections." In *Four Studies in French Romantic Historical Writing.* Johns Hopkins University Studies in Historical and Political Science 71, no. 2 (1955): 121–42.

Epstein, Joseph. *Alexis de Tocqueville. Democracy's Guide.* New York: Harper-Collins, 2006.

Fabian, Bernhard. *Alexis de Tocquevilles Amerikabild; Genetische Untersuchungen über Zussamenhänge mit der zeitgenössischen, insbesondere der englischen Amerika-Interpretation.* Heidelberg: Carl Winter, 1957.

————. "Die sogenannte definitive Ausgabe von Alexis de Tocquevilles *De la Démocratie en Amérique.*" *Archiv für Kulturgeschichte* 38, no. 3 (1955): 358–63.

Facon, Nina. "La 'Questione Meridionale' in Alexis de Tocqueville." In *Saggi di letteratura italiana. In onore de Gaetano Trombatore,* 187–99. Milano: Instituto Edit. Cisalpino–La Goliardiaca, 1973.

Faguet, Emile. "Alexis de Tocqueville." *Revue des deux mondes* 121 (1894): 641–73.

Faucher, Léon. "De la démocratie aux États-Unis par M. Alexis de Tocqueville (inédit)." *Courier français* 358 (24 December 1834).

————. "De la Démocratie en Amérique." *Courier français,* 20 January 1841.

Faught, Jim. "Tocqueville's Utilitarianism." *International Social Science Review* 61, no. 1 (1981): 21–34.

Feuer, Kathryn B. "Alexis de Tocqueville and the Genesis of *War and Peace.*" *California Slavic Studies* 4 (1967): 92–118.

Filipiuk, Marion. "Tocqueville in Translation in Mill's Reviews of *De la Démocratie en Amérique.*" *Mill News Letter* 13, no. 1 (1978): 10–17.

Fogelman, Edwin. "Alexis de Tocqueville and the Commitment to Freedom." *Western Humanities Review* 14, no. 3 (1960): 271–82.

Freund, Dorrit. *Alexis de Tocqueville und die Politische Kultur der Demokratie.* Berne: Paul Haupt, 1974.

Furet, François. "The Intellectual Origins of Tocqueville's Thought." *Tocqueville Review* 7 (1985–1986): 117–29.

———. "Naissance d'un paradigme. Tocqueville et le voyage en Amérique (1825–1831)." *Annales, économies, sociétés, civilisation* 39, no. 2 (1984): 225–39.

———. "Le système conceptuel de *De la Démocratie en Amérique*." *Commentaire* 12 (1980–1981): 605–13.

Galasso, G. "De Socrate a Tocqueville." *Nord e Sud* 12, nos. 66–67 (1965): 14–41.

Gannett, Robert T., Jr. *Tocqueville Unveiled.* Chicago: The University of Chicago Press, 2003.

Gargan, Edward T. *Alexis de Tocqueville: The Critical Years, 1848–1851.* Washington: Catholic University of America Press, 1955.

———. "The Formation of Tocqueville's Historical Thought." *Review of Politics* 24, no. 1 (1962): 48–61.

———. "The Purpose of Tocqueville's Democracy." *Tocqueville Review* 7 (1985–1986): 67–75.

———. "The Silence of Tocqueville on Education." *Historical Reflections* 7, nos. 2–3 (1980): 565–75.

———. "Some Problems in Tocqueville Scholarship." *Mid-America* 41, no. 1 (1959): 3–26.

———. "Tocqueville and the Postmodern Refusal of History." In *Liberty, Equality, Democracy,* 187–92, Eduardo Nolla, ed. New York: New York University Press, 1992.

———. *De Tocqueville.* New York: Hillary House Publishers, 1965.

———. "Tocqueville and the Problem of Historical Prognosis." *American Historical Review* 68, no. 2 (1963): 332–45.

Garret, Stephen A. "Foreign Policy and the Democracies: De Tocqueville Revisited." *Virginia Quarterly Review* 48, no. 4 (1972): 481–500.

[Gaudio, Angelo.] "Ortega e Tocqueville." *Nuova Antologia* 2149 (January–March 1984): 458–69.

Geiss, Imanuel. *Tocqueville und das Zeitalter der Revolution.* München: Nymphenburger Verlagshandlung, 1972.

———. "Tocqueville und Karl Marx, eine Vergleichende Analyse Anlässlich des

100 Todestages von Alexis de Tocqueville." *Neue Gesellschaft* 6 (1959): 237–40.

Genco, Maria Francesca. *Alexis de Tocqueville. Un liberale deluso.* Milano: Gastaldi, 1969.

George, William Henry. "Montesquieu and De Tocqueville and Corporative Individualism." *American Political Science Review* 16, no. 1 (1922): 10–21.

Georgin, René. "Tocqueville et le langage de la démocratie." *Vie et Langage* 17, no. 201 (1968): 740–44.

Gershman, Sally. "Alexis de Tocqueville and Slavery." *French Historical Studies* 9, no. 3 (1976): 467–83.

Gibert, Pierre. "L'éducation de la liberté selon Tocqueville." *Projet* 69 (1972): 1087–99.

———. "Fragile et nécessaire démocratie selon Tocqueville." *Projet* 51 (1971): 5–16.

———. "Incroyance nouvelle et religion à venir selon Alexis de Tocqueville." *Études,* 1966, 611–27.

Gideonse, Harry. "De Tocqueville, Liberal of a New Type." *American Journal of Economics and Sociology* 19, no. 4 (1960): 411–12.

Gilman, Daniel C. "Alexis de Tocqueville and His Book on America—Sixty Years After." *Century* 56, no. 1 (1898): 703–15.

Gojat, Georges. "Les corps intermédiaires et la décentralisation dans l'œuvre de Tocqueville." In *Libéralisme, traditionalisme, décentralisation,* 1–43. Paris: Armand Colin, 1952.

Goldstein, Doris Silk. "Alexis de Tocqueville's Concept of Citizenship." *Proceedings of the American Philosophical Society* 108, no. 1 (1964): 39–53.

———. "The Religious Beliefs of Alexis de Tocqueville." *French Historical Studies* 1, no. 4 (1960): 379–93.

———. *Trial of Faith, Religion, and Politics in Tocqueville's Thought.* New York: Elsevier, 1975.

González Pedrero, Enrique. "Alexis de Tocqueville y la teoría del Estado democrático." *Cuadernos americanos* 15, no. 6 (1956): 159–84; also in Alexis de Tocqueville, *De la democracia en América,* 8–27. Méjico: Fondo de Cultura Económica, 1963.

Goring, Helmut. *Tocqueville und die Demokratie.* Berlin: R. Oldenburg, 1928.

Gorla, Gino. *Commento a Tocqueville. L'idea dei diritti.* Milano: A. Giuffrè, 1948.

Graebner, Norman A. "Christianity and Democracy: Tocqueville's Views of Religion in America." *Journal of Religion* 53, no. 3 (1976): 263–73.

Grandmaison, Charles Alexandre Geoffroy de. "Séjour d'Alexis de Tocqueville en Touraine, préparation du livre sur l'Ancien Régime, juin 1853–avril 1854." *Correspondant* 114 (1879): 926–49.

Greilsamer, I. "The Ideological Basis of French Regionalism." *Publius* 5, no. 3 (1975): 83–100.

Guellec, Laurence. *Tocqueville. L'apprentissage de la liberté.* Paris: Éditions Michalon, 1996.

———. *Tocqueville et les langages de la démocratie.* Paris: Honoré Champion, 2004.

———, ed. *Tocqueville et l'esprit de la démocratie.* [Paris:] Presses de la Fondation des Sciences Politiques, 2005.

Guicciardi, Jean-Pierre. "Tocqueville et les Lumières." *Studies on Voltaire and the Eighteenth Century* 163 (1976): 203–19.

Guillemain, Bernard. "Tocqueville et le féodalisme." *Francia* 4–5 (1973): 42–51.

Guizot, François. "Discours de M. Guizot, Directeur de l'Académie française." In *Réponse au discours prononcé par M. Lacordaire pour sa réception à l'Académie française (séance de l'Académie française, du 24 janvier 1861).* Paris: Didier et Cie., 1861.

Hadari, Saguiv A. *Theory in Practice. Tocqueville's New Science of Politics.* Stanford: Stanford University Press, 1989.

Hamburger, Joseph. "Mill and Tocqueville on Liberty." In John M. Robson and M. Laine, eds. *James and John Stuart Mill. Papers of the Centenary Conference,* 111–25. Toronto: University of Toronto Press, 1976.

Harrison, Katherine. "A French Forecast of American Literature." *South Atlantic Quarterly* 25, no. 4 (1926): 350–60.

Heimonet, Jean-Michel. *Tocqueville et le devenir de la démocratie: la perversion de l'idéal.* Paris: L'Harmattan, 1999.

Henderson, Christine Dunn. "Beaumont y Tocqueville." In *Alexis de Tocqueville. Libertad, igualdad, despotismo,* 73–99, Eduardo Nolla, ed. Madrid: Gota a gota, 2007.

Hennis, Wilhelm. "La 'nueva ciencia política' de Tocqueville." *Revista de Estudios Políticos* 22 (1981): 7–38.

Hereth, Michael. *Alexis de Tocqueville. Die Gefährdung der Freiheit in der Demokratie.* Stuttgart: W. Kohlhammer, 1979. English edition, Durham, N.C.: Duke University Press, 1986.

————, and Jutta Höffken, eds. *Alexis de Tocqueville—Zur Politik des Demok-ratie.* Baden-Baden: Nomos Verlagsgesellschaft, 1981.

Heroux, Maurice. "De Tocqueville, Prophet of Democracy." *Culture* 16 (1955): 363–75; 17 (1956): 10–24.

Hirsh, Jeffrey L. "Tocqueville and the Frontier Press." *Journalism Quarterly* 51 (1974): 116–19.

Hoeges, Dirk. "Alexis de Tocqueville: Freiheit und Gleichheit." *Historische Zeit-schrift* 219 (1974): 412–14.

————. "Der vergessene Rest: Tocqueville, Chateaubriand und der Subjekt-wechsel in der französischen Geschichtsschreibung." *Historische Zeitschrift* 238, no. 2 (1984): 287–310.

————. "Guizot und Tocqueville," *Historische Zeitschrift* 218 (1974): 338–53.

————. "Tocqueville Literatur im Zeitalter der Gleichheit." *Siegener Hoch-schulblätter* 5, no. 2 (1982): 44–55.

L'Hommedé, Edmond. *Un département français sous la Monarchie de Juillet: le conseil général de la Manche et Alexis de Tocqueville.* Preface by A. Coville. Paris: Bovin, 1933.

Hoog, M. J. "Tocqueville et les 'bois-brûlés.'" *Actes du 3ᵉ congrés de la FIPF* 1976–1977, 327–36.

Hornung, Klaus. "Die Dialektik von Emanzipation und Despotismus. Alexis de Tocqueville und Karl Marx." *Staat* 15, no. 3 (1976): 305–33.

Horwitz, Morton J. "Tocqueville and the Tyranny of the Majority." *Review of Politics* 28, no. 3 (1966): 293–307.

Isay, Raymond. "Les oracles de Tocqueville." *Revue des deux mondes* 130 (1959): 48–65.

Jacoby, Henry. "Hobbes und Tocqueville." *Zeitschrift für die Gesamte Staats-wissenschaft* 109, no. 4 (1953): 718–25.

Jacovella, Guido. "Religión y política en el pensamiento de Tocqueville." *Revista de estudios políticos* 110 (1960): 143–54.

Jacques, Daniel. *Tocqueville et la modernité.* Québec: Boréal, 1995.

Jacques, Heinrich. *Alexis de Tocqueville, ein Lebens und Geistesbild.* Wien: C. Gerald's Sohn, 1976.

Janara, Laura. *Democracy Growing Up. Authority, Autonomy, and Passion in Tocqueville's "Democracy in America."* Albany: State University of New York Press, 2002.

Janet, Paul. "Alexis de Tocqueville et la science politique au XIXᵉ siècle." *Revue*

des deux mondes 34 (1861): 101–33; reprinted in *Les problèmes du XIXe siècle,*
37–130. Paris: M. Lévy, 1873.

Jardin, André. *Alexis de Tocqueville.* Paris: Hachette, 1984; also Hachette-Pluriel,
1986.

———. "Alexis de Tocqueville." *Histoire* 55 (1983): 26–33.

———. "Alexis de Tocqueville, Beaumont et le problème de l'inégalité des
races." In *L'idée de race en la pensée politique française contemporaine,* 200–19.
Paris: CNRS, 1977.

———. "Tocqueville, député sous la Monarchie de Juillet." *Contrepoint* 22–23
(1976): 167–85.

———. "Tocqueville en Amérique." *H. Histoire* 4 (1980): 227–40.

———. "Tocqueville et l'Algérie." *Revue des travaux de l'Académie des sciences
morales et politiques* 115 (1962): 61–74.

———. "Tocqueville et la décentralisation." In *La décentralisation, VIe colloque
d'histoire,* 89–117. Aix-en-Provence: Publication des Annales de la Faculté des
Lettres, 1961.

Jennings, Jeremy. "Democracy Before Tocqueville: Michel Chevalier's America," *Review of Politics,* 68 (2006): 398–427.

———. "Tocqueville, América y la libertad." In *Alexis de Tocqueville. Libertad,
igualdad, despotismo,* 57–62, Eduardo Nolla, ed. Madrid: Gota a gota, 2007.

Johnson, Ellwood. "Individualism and the Puritan Imagination." *American
Quarterly Review* 22, no. 2 (1970): 230–37.

Kahan, Alan Sidney. *Aristocratic Liberalism.* New Brunswick, N.J.: Transaction
Publishers, 2001.

———. "Tocqueville's Two Revolutions." *Journal of the History of Ideas* 44, no.
4 (1985): 585–96.

Kaledin, Arthur. "Tocqueville's Apocalypse: Culture, Politics, and Freedom."
Tocqueville Review 7 (1985–1986): 3–38.

Keeney, James. "Tocqueville and the New Politics." *New Politics* 1, no. 3 (1962):
58–65.

Kellenberger, Paulfritz. "Il y a des cantons, il n'y a pas de Suisse." *Rorschacher
Neujahrsblatt* 49 (1959): 46–48.

Kelly, George Armstrong. "Faith, Freedom, and Disenchantment: Politics
and the American Religious Consciousness." *Daedalus* III, no. 1 (1982): 127–
48.

Kergorlay, Louis de. "Étude littéraire sur Alexis de Tocqueville." *Correspondant*
52 (1861): 750–66.

Keslassy, Eric. *Le libéralisme de Tocqueville à l'épreuve du paupérisme.* Paris: L'Harmattan, 2000.

Kessler, Sanford. "Tocqueville on Civil Religion and Liberal Democracy." *Journal of Politics* 39, no. 1 (1977): 119–47.

King, Preston. "Liberalism: Alexis de Tocqueville." In *Fear of Power: An Analysis of Antistatism in Three French Writers,* 17–42. London: Frank Cass, 1967.

Kinzer, Bruce L. "Tocqueville and His English Interpreters, J. S. Mill and Henry Reeve." *Mill News Letter* 13, no. 1 (1978): 2–10.

Kirk, Russell. "Liberal Conservatives: Macaulay, Cooper, Tocqueville." In *The Conservative Mind,* 161–95. Chicago: Henry Regnery, 1953.

———. "The Prescience of Tocqueville." *University of Toronto Quarterly* 22, no. 4 (1953): 342–53.

Koritansky, John C. *Alexis de Tocqueville and the New Science of Politics: An Interpretation of Democracy in America.* Durham, N.C.: Carolina Academic Press, 1986.

———. "Decentralization and Civic Virtue in Tocqueville's 'New Science of Politics.'" *Publius* 5, no. 3 (1975): 63–81.

———. "Democracy and Nobility: A Comment on Tocqueville's *De la Démocratie en Amérique.*" *Intercollegiate Review* 12 (1976): 13–27.

———. "Two Forms of the Love of Equality in Tocqueville's Political Teaching for Democracy." *Polity* 6, no. 4 (1974): 488–99.

Kotsovolou, Y. "La décentralisation chez Tocqueville: un aspect historique du droit public français." *Revue hellénique de droit international* 24, nos. 1–4 (1971): 330–42.

Kraynak, Robert P. "Tocqueville's Constitutionalism." *American Political Science Review* 81, no. 4 (1987): 1175–95.

Kummings, Donald D. "The Poetry of Democracies: Tocqueville's Aristocratic Views." *Comparative Literature Studies* 11, no. 4 (1974): 306–19.

Laborie, Léon d'Estresse Lanzac de. "L'amitié de Tocqueville et de Royer-Collard d'après une correspondance inédite." *Revue des deux mondes* 58 (1930): 876–911.

———. "Barante, Tocqueville, Turgot." *Correspondant* 171 (1893): 152–68.

Laboulaye, Édouard. "Alexis de Tocqueville." *Journal des débats,* 30 September, 1, 2, and 4 October 1859; also in *L'État et ses limites,* 138–201. Paris: Charpentier, 1863.

Lacordaire, Abbé. "Discours de M. l'Abbé Lacordaire élu en remplacement de Monsieur de Tocqueville." In *Anthologie de l'Académie française. Un siècle de discours académiques 1820–1920,* vol. I, 290–313. Paris: Librarie Delagrave, 1921.

Lacour-Gayet, Robert. "Tocqueville et l'énigme américaine." *Revue de Paris* 66, no. 10 (1959): 96–106.

La Fournière, Xavier de. *Alexis de Tocqueville, un monarchiste indépendant.* Paris: Perrin, 1981.

Lamberti, Jean-Claude. "De Benjamin Constant à Tocqueville." *France Forum* April–May 1983, 19–26.

———. "La liberté et les illusions individualistes selon Tocqueville." *Tocqueville Review* 8 (1986–1987): 153–64.

———. *La notion d'individualisme chez Tocqueville.* Paris: PUF, 1970.

———. *Tocqueville et les deux Démocraties.* Preface by François Bourricaud. Paris: PUF, 1983.

Landy, Remy. "Tocqueville moraliste, une lecture de *De la Démocratie en Amérique.*" *Information littéraire* 20, no. 3 (1968): 114–18.

Lange, Victor. "Visitors to Lake Oneida. An Account of the Background of Sophie von La Roche's Novel *Erscheinungen am See Oneida.*" *Symposium* 2 (1948): 48–74.

Lawler, Peter Augustine. "The Human Condition: Tocqueville's Debt to Rousseau and Pascal." In *Liberty, Equality, Democracy,* 1–20, Eduardo Nolla, ed. New York: New York University Press, 1992.

———. *The Restless Mind: Alexis de Tocqueville on the Origin of Perpetuation of Human Liberty.* Lanham, Maryland: Rowman and Littlefield Publishers, 1993.

———. "Tocqueville on Metaphysics and Human Liberty." *Teaching Political Science* 14, no. 2 (1987): 81–88.

———. "Tocqueville on Religion and Human Excellence. A Neglected Aspect of Political Education in Democracy." *Southeastern Political Review* 11, no. 2 (1983): 139–60.

———. "Tocqueville on Slavery, Ancient and Modern." *South Atlantic Quarterly* 80, no. 4 (1981): 466–77.

———. "Tocqueville on the Place of Liberal Education in a Democracy." *Liberal Education* 69, no. 4 (1983): 301–6.

———, ed. *Democracy and Its Friendly Critics: Tocqueville and Political Life Today.* Lanham, Maryland: Lexington Books, 2004.

———, and Joseph Alulis, eds. *Tocqueville's Defense of Human Liberty: Current Essays.* New York: Garland, 1993.

Lawlor, Sister Mary. *Alexis de Tocqueville in the Chamber of Deputies: His Views on Foreign Policy.* Washington, D.C.: Catholic University of America Press, 1959.

Leclerq, Jean-Michel. "Alexis de Tocqueville au Canada (du 24 août au 2 septembre 1831)." *Revue d'histoire de l'Amérique française* 22, no. 3 (1968): 356–64.

Ledeen, Michael A. *Tocqueville on American Character.* New York: Truman Talley Books, 2001.

Lefort, Claude. "De l'égalité à la liberté." *Libre* 340 (1978): 211–46.

———. "Réversibilité." *Passé présent* 1 (1982): 18–35.

———. "Tocqueville, a Phenomenology of the Social." In *Liberty, Equality, Democracy,* 103–12, Eduardo Nolla, ed. New York: New York University Press, 1992.

Legaz y Lacambra, Luis. *La actualidad de Tocqueville.* Santiago de Compostela, 1951.

Legros, Robert, dir. *Tocqueville. La Démocratie en questions.* Cahiers de philosophie de l'université de Caen. Caen: Presses universitaires de Caen, 2008.

Leon, D. H. "The Dogma of the Sovereignty of the People: Alexis de Tocqueville's Religion in America." *Journal of Church and State* 14, no. 2 (1972): 279–95.

Lerner, Max, "Culture and Personality in Tocqueville's America." *Southern Review* 1, no. 3 (1965): 590–605.

———. "Tocqueville's *De la Démocratie en Amérique:* Politics, Law, and the Elites." *Antioch Review* 25, no. 4 (1966): 543–63.

———. *Tocqueville and American Civilization.* New York: Harper & Row, 1966.

Leroy, Maxime. "Alexis de Tocqueville." *Politica* 1, no. 4 (August 1935): 393–424.

———. "Tocqueville.," In *Histoire des idées sociales en France,* vol. III, 49–53, 511–22. Paris: Gallimard, 1962.

———. "Tocqueville." In *Les précurseurs français du socialisme, de Condorcet à Proudhon,* 256–67. Paris: Éditions du Temps Présent, 1948.

Liebersohn, Harry. *Aristocratic Encounters.* Cambridge: Cambridge University Press, 1998.

Lively, Jack. *The Social and Political Thought of Alexis de Tocqueville.* Oxford: Clarendon Press, 1962.

Locke, Jill, and Eileen Hunt Botting, eds. *Feminist Interpretations of Alexis de Tocqueville.* University Park, Pennsylvania: Pennsylvania State University Press, 2009.

Lombardo, Paul A. "Historic Echoes: Romantic Emphasis in Tocqueville's *Democracy in America.*" *Journal of Thought* 16 (1981): 67–80.

Loménie, Louis Léonard de. "Publicistes modernes de la France, Alexis de Tocqueville." *Revue des deux mondes* 21 (1859): 402–28.

Lucchini, Laurent. *De la Démocratie en Amérique, ce que ce texte a d'essentiel pour la politique aujourd'hui.* Paris: Seghers, 1972.

Lukacs, John A. "Alexis de Tocqueville: A Historical Appreciation." *Literature of Liberty* 5, no. 1 (1982): 7–42.

———. "The Last Days of Alexis de Tocqueville." *Catholic Historical Review* 50, no. 2 (1964): 155–70.

McCarthy, Eugene Joseph. *America Revisited: 150 Years After Tocqueville.* New York: Doubleday, 1978.

McDonagh, Eileen. "De Tocqueville's *De la Démocratie en Amérique:* A Sociology of Knowledge Perspective." *Journal of Political Science* 12, nos. 1–2 (1985): 39–52.

Mahieu, Robert G. *Les enquêteurs français aux États-Unis de 1830 à 1837.* Paris: Librairie Ancienne Honoré Champion, 1934.

Mancini, Matthew J. *Alexis de Tocqueville and American Intellectuals: From His Times to Ours.* Lanham, Maryland: Rowman and Littlefield, 2006.

———. "Too Many Tocquevilles: The Fable of Tocqueville's American Reception." *Journal of the History of Ideas,* 69, 2 (2008): 245–68.

Manent, Pierre. "Commentaire." *Tocqueville Review* 4, no. 1 (1982): 22–30.

———. *Tocqueville and the Ambiguities of Modern Liberty.* London: University of London, 2000.

———. "Tocqueville, filósofo político." In *Alexis de Tocqueville. Libertad, igualdad, despotismo,* 269–88, Eduardo Nolla, ed. Madrid: Gota a gota, 2007.

———. *Tocqueville et la nature de la démocratie.* Paris: Julliard, 1982.

———. "Un commentaire." In Michael Hereth and Jutta Höffken, eds., *Alexis de Tocqueville—Zur Politik des demokratie,* 53–60.

Mansfield, Harvey C., Jr., Delba Winthrop, and Philippe Raynaud. *Tyranny and Liberty.* London: University of London, 1999.

Mantica, Giuseppe. "Liberalismo e democrazia in Tocqueville." *Studi Storici* 11 no. 2 (1970): 373–84.

Marcel, Roland-Pierre. *Essai politique sur Alexis de Tocqueville (avec un grand nombre de documents inédits).* Paris: Félix Alcan, 1910.

Marshall, Margaret. "Notes by the Way: Alexis de Tocqueville's Discussion of Cultural Matters." *Nation* 162, 2 February 1946, 170–72.

Martelli, Paolo. "Alexis de Tocqueville e il liberalismo della Restaurazione." *Humanitas* 13, no. 3 (1958): 219–22.

Martonyi, Eva. "Une contribution à l'étude du vocabulaire politique du XIXe siècle. L'usage du terme 'égalité des conditions' par Tocqueville." *Acta Romanica* 5 (1978): 235–49.

Matsumoto, Reiji. "Tocqueville on the Family." *Tocqueville Review* 8 (1986–1987): 127–52.

Matteucci, Nicola. *Alexis de Tocqueville.* Bologna: Il Mulino, 1990.

———. *Alla ricerca dell'ordine politico: da Machiavelli a Tocqueville.* Bologna: Il Mulino, 1984.

———. "Il problema del partito politico nelle riflessioni d'Alexis de Tocqueville." *Pensiero Politico* 1, no. 1 (1968): 39–92.

Matthiessen, F. O. "A Classic Study of America: Tocqueville." In *Responsibilities of the Critic; Essays and Reviews Selected by John Rackliffe,* 141–45. New York: Oxford University Press, 1952.

Mayer, Jacob Peter. *Prophet of the Mass Age: A Study of Alexis de Tocqueville.* Trans. M. M. Boxman and C. Hahn. London: J. M. Dent and Sons, 1939; New York: Viking Press, 1940; Paris: Gallimard, 1948; Stuttgart: Deutsche Verlagsanstalt, 1954; Madrid: Tecnos, 1965.

———. "Alexis de Tocqueville. A Commentated Bibliography." *Revue internationale de philosophie* 49, no. 3 (1959): 350–53.

———. "Alexis de Tocqueville: sur *De la Démocratie en Amérique,* fragments inédits." *Nouvelle revue française* 76 (April 1959): 761–68; also under the title "De Tocqueville: Unpublished Fragments." *Encounter* 12 (April 1959): 17–22; also under the title "Sur la Démocratie en Amérique. Fragments inédits." *Revue internationale de philosophie* 49, no. 3 (1959): 300–12.

———. "Alexis de Tocqueville und Karl Marx." *Geist und Tat,* January 1957; also under the title "Alexis de Tocqueville und Karl Marx. Affinitaten und Gegensatze." *Zeitschrift für Politik* 13, no. 1 (1966): 1–13.

———. "Tocqueville as a Political Sociologist." *Political Studies* 1 (1953): 132–42.

———. "Tocqueville Today." *Revue internationale de philosophie* 49, no. 34 (1959): 313–19.

———. "Tocqueville on India." *Encounter* 18, no. 5 (1962): 55–57.

———. "Tocqueville, prophète de l'État moderne." *Critique* 12, nos. 100–101 (1955): 883–92.

————. "Tocqueville's Influence." *History* 3 (1960): 87–103.

————. "Les voyages de Tocqueville et la genèse de sa sociologie politique." *Nouvelle revue française* 9 (June 1957): 372–84.

————, ed. "Alexis de Tocqueville. The Art and Science of Politics. An Unpublished Speech." *Encounter* 36, no. 1 (1971): 27–35.

Meaglia, Piero. "Tocqueville e il problema della democrazia." *Teoria Politica* 1, no. 3 (1985): 41–70.

Mélonio, Françoise. "La religion selon Tocqueville. Ordre moral ou esprit de liberté?" *Études* 360 (1984): 73–88.

————. "Tocqueville et la restauration du pouvoir temporel du pape (juin–octobre 1849)." *Revue historique* 271 (1984): 109–23.

————. *Tocqueville et les Français.* Paris: Aubier, 1993.

————. "Tocqueville et les malheurs de la démocratie américaine." *Commentaire* 10, no. 38 (1987): 381–89.

————, and José-Luis Díaz, eds. *Tocqueville et la littérature.* Paris: Presses de l'Université Paris–Sorbonne, 2005.

Mendras, Henri, and Jean Étienne. *Les grands auteurs de la sociologie.* Paris: Hatier, 1996.

Mennell, Stephen, and John Stone, eds. *Alexis de Tocqueville on Democracy, Revolution, and Society.* Chicago and London: University of Chicago Press, 1980.

Meuwly, Olivier. *Liberté et société.* Geneva: Droz, 2002.

Meyers, Marvin. "The Basic Democrat: A Version of Tocqueville." *Political Science Quarterly* 72, no. 1 (1957): 50–70.

Michel, Henry. "L'école démocratique." In *L'idée de l'état,* 317–26. Paris: Librairie Hachette et Cie., 1896.

Michel, Pierre. "Démocratie et barbarie: Alexis de Tocqueville." In *Un mythe romantique. Les barbares, 1789–1848,* 267–91. Paris: Presses universitaires de Lyon, 1981.

Mignet, François. "Notice historique sur la vie et les travaux de M. Alexis de Tocqueville." *Mémoires de l'Académie des sciences morales et politiques* 13 (1872): 41–71.

Mignoli, A. "Tocqueville." *Rivista Trimestrale di Diritto e Procedura Civile,* 1949: 128.

[Mill, John Stuart.] "De la Démocratie en Amérique." *Edinburgh Review* 72, no. 145 (1840): 1–25.

————. "State of Society in America." *London and Westminster Review* 30 (1836): 365–89.

————. "De Tocqueville on Democracy in America." *London and Westminster Review* 30, no. 2 (1835): 85–129.

Miller, Perry (Pseud. of M. Cabot Powell). "The Responsibility of Mind in a Civilization of Machines." *American Scholar* 31, no. 1 (1961): 51–69.

Mitchell, Harvey. *America after Tocqueville*. Cambridge: Cambridge University Press, 2002.

Mitchell, Joshua. *The Fragility of Freedom*. Chicago: Chicago University Press, 1995.

Molé, Louis-Mathieu, Count. "Réponse de M. le comte Molé au discours de réception de M de Tocqueville à l'Académie française." In Alexis de Tocqueville, *Études économiques, politiques et littéraires*, 607–16. Paris: Michel Lévy, 1866.

Molnar, Thomas Steven. *Le modèle défiguré: l'Amérique de Tocqueville à Carter*. Paris: PUF, 1978.

"Le moment tocquevillien." *Raisons politiques* 1 (2001).

Monconduit, François. "Introduction." In Michael Hereth and Jutta Höffken, eds., *Alexis de Tocqueville—Zur Politik des demokratie*, 91–92.

————. "Liberté et égalité dans la pensée d'Alexis de Tocqueville." In *Mélanges offerts à Georges Burdeau*, 315–32. Paris: Librairie générale de droit et de jurisprudence, 1977.

————. "Tocqueville: la décentralisation, impératif démocratique." In *L'objet local, colloque dirigé par Lucien Sfez*. Paris, 1975.

Monnier, Luc. "Tocqueville et la Suisse." In *Alexis de Tocqueville. Livre du centenaire*, 101–13.

————. "Alexis de Tocqueville et Auguste de la Rive à travers leur correspondance." In *Mélanges offerts à M. Paul Martin*. Genève, 1961.

————. "Tocqueville et le colonialisme." *Journal de Genève*, 19–20 September 1964; also in *Cahiers Vilfredo Pareto* 15, no. 41 (1977): 44–46.

Montesquiou, Léon de. "M. de Tocqueville est un criminel." *Action française* 9, no. 92 (1903): 169–78.

Moreau, Pierre. "Tocqueville pour et contre le traditionalisme." In *Alexis de Tocqueville. Livre du centenaire*, 133–43.

Morton, F. L. "Sexual Equality and the Family in Tocqueville's *De la Démocratie en Amérique*." *Canadian Journal of Political Science* 17, no. 2 (1984): 309–24.

Mueller, Iris W. *John Stuart Mill and French Thought*. Urbana: University of Illinois Press, 1956.

Muller, H. J. *"De la Démocratie en Amérique:* Some Reconsiderations. Alexis de Tocqueville." In *In Pursuit of Relevance,* 181–97. Bloomington: Indiana University Press, 1971.

Murphy, William J., Jr. "Alexis de Tocqueville in New York: The Formulation of the Egalitarian Thesis." *New York Historical Society Quarterly* 60, nos. 1–2, 69–79.

Muzzey, David S. "Alexis de Tocqueville: Pioneer Student of American Democracy." *Columbia University Quarterly* 30 (1938): 85–90.

Nantet, Jacques. "L'attitude de Tocqueville à l'égard d'une éventuelle séparation des églises et de l'état et, entre autres, d'un enseignement laïc." *Revue des travaux de l'académie des sciences morales et politiques* 12 (1967): 23–33.

———. "Correspondance d'Alexis de Tocqueville avec Louis de Kergorlay." *France-Forum,* Novembre–December 1978, 45–46.

———. "L'esprit de liberté et l'esprit d'égalité chez Alexis de Tocqueville," 120–26. In *Analyses et réflexions sur . . . Tocqueville. De la Démocratie en Amérique.*

———. "Alexis de Tocqueville. Homme d'hier ou d'aujourd'hui?" *Critique* 20, no. 203 (1964): 364–77.

———. "Royer-Collard, Guizot, Tocqueville et le parti du mouvement." *Revue des deux mondes* 3 (March 1972): 570–81.

———. *Tocqueville.* Paris: Seghers, 1971.

———. "Trois cents lettres de Tocqueville." *Quinzaine littéraire* 27 (1 May 1967): 19–20.

Nef, John. "Truth, Belief, and Civilization: Tocqueville and Gobineau." *Review of Politics* 25, no. 4 (1963): 460–82.

Negro Pavón, Dalmacio. "Individualismo y colectivismo en la ciencia social. Ensayo sobre Tocqueville y Stuart Mill." *Revista internacional de sociología* 28, nos. 113–14 (1970): 5–32; 29, no. 115 (1970): 47–76.

———. "El liberalismo de Alexis de Tocqueville y de John Stuart Mill." *Revista de estudios políticos* 167 (1969): 117–54.

———. *Liberalismo y socialismo. La encrucijada intelectual de Stuart Mill.* Madrid: Instituto de Estudios Políticos, 1975.

———. "Tocqueville y Stuart Mill." *Revista de Occidente* 5, no. 55 (1967): 104–14.

———. "Tocqueville sobre Hispanoamérica." *Revista internacional de sociología* 28, nos. 109–110 (1970): 5–19.

Newman, Edgar Leon. "The French Background of Tocqueville's *De la Démocratie en Amérique." Tocqueville Review* 7 (1985–1986): 39–45.

Nicholas, H. G. "Tocqueville and the Dissolution of the Union." *Revue internationale de philosophie* 49, no. 3 (1959): 320–29.

Nimitz, August H., Jr. *Marx, Tocqueville, and Race in America.* Lanham, Md.: Lexington Books, 2003.

Nisbet, Robert. "Tocqueville." In *The Sociological Tradition.* New York: Basic Books, 1967.

———. "Many Tocquevilles." *American Scholar* 46, no. 1 (1977): 59–75.

Nolla, Eduardo. *Autour de l'autre Démocratie.* Napoli: Istituto Suor Orsola Benincasa, 1994.

———. "La 'Démocratie' ovvero il libro chiuso." *Filosofia Politica* 6, no. 1 (1992): 132–41.

———, ed. *Liberty, Equality, Democracy.* New York: New York University Press, 1992.

———, ed. *Libertad, igualdad, despotismo.* Madrid: Gota a gota, 2007.

Olgiatti, Giancarlo. "Attualità di Tocqueville: la compatibilità fra liberalismo e democrazia." *Cenobio* 32, no. 4 (1982): 327–38.

Ortega y Gasset, José. "Tocqueville y su tiempo." In *Meditación de Europa,* 135–41. Madrid: Revista de Occidente, 1966.

Ossewaarde, M. R. R. *Tocqueville's Moral and Political Thought.* London: Routledge, 2004.

Palmer, R. R. *The Two Tocquevilles. Father and Son.* New Jersey: Princeton University Press, 1987.

Pappe, H. O. "Mill and Tocqueville." *Journal of the History of Ideas* 25, no. 2 (1964): 217–44.

Parieu, E. de. "La philosophie politique de M. Alexis de Tocqueville." *Revue contemporaine et athenaeum français* 53, no. 18 (1860): 561–85.

Passy, Louis. *Le marquis de Blosseville, souvenirs.* Évreux: Charles Hérissey, 1898.

Pergolesi, F. "Alexis de Tocqueville e l'attualità della sua storiografia politica." *Rivista di Studi Politici Internazionale* 19, nos. 1–2 (1952): 107–48.

———. "Appunti sulla storiografia politica di Alexis de Tocqueville." *Sociologia* 4, no. 4 (October–December 1959): 547–609.

Pessen, Edward. "The Egalitarian Myth and the American Social Reality, Wealth, Mobility, and Equality in the 'Era of Common Man.'" *American Historical Review* 76, no. 4 (1971): 989–1034.

———. "Tocqueville's Misreading of America, America's Misreading of Tocqueville." *Tocqueville Review* 4, no. 1 (1982): 5–22.

Peyrefitte, Alain. "Les paradoxes de Tocqueville." *Commentaire* 10 (1980): 280–81.

──────. "Tocqueville, cet inconnu." *Actes académiques. Bordeaux* 5, no. 9 (1984): 189–202.

──────. "Tocqueville, professeur de liberté," *Figaro* 17 (December 1979): 32.

Philo, Gordon. "Tocqueville, the Prophetic Historian." *History Today* 11, no. 2 (1952): 770–77.

Pierson, George Wilson. "Alexis de Tocqueville in New Orleans." *Franco-American Review* 1 (1936): 25–42.

──────. "On the Centenary of Tocqueville's *Democracy in America.*" *Yale University Library Gazette* 10 (1936): 33–38.

──────. "The Manuscript of Tocqueville's *Democracy in America.*" *Yale University Library Gazette* 29 (1955): 115–25.

──────. "Le 'seconde voyage' de Tocqueville en Amérique," 71–85. In *Alexis de Tocqueville. Livre du centenaire.*

──────. *Tocqueville and Beaumont in America.* New York: Oxford University Press, 1938. Abridged edition by Dudley C. Lunt. *Tocqueville in America.* New York: Doubleday, 1959.

──────. "Tocqueville's Visions of Democracy." *Yale University Library Gazette* 51 (July 1976): 4–17.

Pisa, Karl. *Tocqueville Prophet des Massenzeiltalters. Eine Biographie.* Stuttgart: Deutsche Verlags-Anstalt, 1984.

Plongeron, B. "Égalité sociale et liberté politique." *Études* 348 (February 1978): 275.

Pochon, Jacques. "Quinet lecteur et utilisateur de Tocqueville." In *Edgar Quinet, ce juif errant. Actes du colloque international de Clermont-Ferrand,* 133–44. Clermont-Ferrand: Publications de la Faculté des Lettres et Sciences Humaines de Clermont–Ferrand, 1978.

Poggi, Gianfranco. "Tocqueville e lo staendestaat. Lettura sociologica della seconda parte della Démocratie." *Rassegna Italiana di Sociologia* 12, no. 3 (1971): 395–427.

Pope, Whitney. *Alexis de Tocqueville: His Social and Political Theory.* Beverly Hills, Calif.: Sage Publications, 1986.

Pouthas, Charles H. "Le corps électoral de l'arrondissement de Valognes au temps de Tocqueville." *Mémoires de la société nationale académique de Cherbourg,* 1961.

──────. "Un observateur de Tocqueville à Rome pendant les premiers mois de l'occupation française (juillet–octobre 1849)." *Rassegna Storica del Risorgimento* 37 (1950): 417–30.

———. "Plan et programme des œuvres, papiers et correspondances d'Alexis de Tocqueville," 35–43. In *Alexis de Tocqueville. Livre du centenaire.*

Pranger, Robert J. "Tocqueville and Political Ambivalence." *Studies in Romanticism* 2, no. 3 (1963): 129–54.

Qualter, Terence H. "John Stuart Mill, Disciple of Tocqueville." *Western Political Quarterly* 13, no. 4 (1960): 880–89.

Rahe, Paul A. *Soft Despotism, Democracy's Drift.* New Haven, Connecticut: Yale University Press, 2009.

Rau, Hans-Arnold. *Demokratie und Republik. Tocquevilles Theorie der politische Handelns.* Würzburg: Königshausen und Neumann, 1981.

———. *Tocquevilles Theorie des Politischen Handelns (Demokratie Zwischen Verwaltungsdespotismus und Republik).* Cologne: F. Hansen, 1975.

Rausch, Heinz. "Erziehung zur Demokratie. Zur Deutschen Gesamtausgabe der Werke Alexis de Tocqueville." *Neue Politische Literatur* 11, no. 2 (1966): 151–71.

Read, Herbert E. "De Tocqueville on Art in America." *Adelphi,* October–December 1946, 9–13; reprinted in *The Tenth Muse. Essays in Criticism,* 138–46. New York: Horizon Press, 1958.

Rédier, Antoine. *Comme disait M. de Tocqueville.* Paris: Perrin, 1925.

———. "Tocqueville." *Correspondant* 220 (1905): 239–45.

———. "Tocqueville et la Révolution." *Revue universelle* 19, no. 17 (1924): 536–52.

Reeve, Henry. "Posthumous Writings of Alexis de Tocqueville." *Edinburgh Review* 250 (1865): 456–81; also in *Royal and Republican France,* 79–144. London: Longmans Green, 1872.

———. "Remains of Alexis de Tocqueville." *Edinburgh Review* 113, no. 230 (1861): 427–60; also in *Royal and Republican France,* 145–90. London: Longmans Green, 1872.

Reeves, Richard. *American Journey.* New York: Simon and Schuster, 1982.

———. "*De la Démocratie en Amérique,* Reconsidered." *Washington Monthly* 14, nos. 5–6 (1982): 44–52.

Rémond, René. *Les États-Unis devant l'opinion française, 1815–1882.* 2 vols. Paris: Armand Colin, 1962.

———. "Tocqueville et la Démocratie en Amérique." *Bulletin de la société d'histoire moderne* 58, no. 1 (1960): 2–4; also in *Alexis de Tocqueville. Livre du centenaire,* 181–90.

Rémusat, Charles de. "L'Ancien Régime et la Révolution." *Revue des deux mondes* 4 (1856): 652–70.

———. "De l'esprit de réaction: Royer-Collard et Tocqueville." *Revue des deux mondes* 35 (1861): 777–813.

Resh, Richard. "Alexis de Tocqueville and the Negro. De la Démocratie en Amérique Reconsidered." *Journal of Negro History* 48, no. 4 (1963): 251–59.

Revel, Jean-François. "L'erreur de Tocqueville ou la menace extérieure." *Commentaire* 6, no. 22 (1983): 422–24.

Riccobono, Francesco. "Osservazioni su eguaglianza e democrazia in Alexis de Tocqueville." *Rivista Internazionale di Filosofia del Diritto* 54, no. 4 (1977): 887–903.

Richter, Melvin. "Comparative Political Analysis in Montesquieu and Tocqueville." *Comparative Politics* 1, no. 2 (1969): 129–60.

———. "A Debate on Race: Tocqueville-Gobineau Correspondence." *Commentary* 25 (1958) 151–60.

———. "Modernity and Its Distinctive Threats to Liberty: Montesquieu and Tocqueville on New Forms of Illegitimate Domination," 61–80. In Michael Hereth and Jutta Höffken, eds., *Alexis de Tocqueville—Zur Politik des demokratie.*

———. "Tocqueville on Algeria." *Review of Politics* 25, no. 3 (1963): 362–98.

———. "Tocqueville's Contribution to the Theory of Revolution." In C. Friedrich, ed. *Revolution,* 75–121. New York: Atherton, 1966.

———. "Toward a Concept of Political Illegitimacy: Bonapartist Dictatorship and Democratic Legitimacy." *Political Theory* 10, no. 2 (1982): 185–214.

———"The Uses of Theory: Tocqueville's Adaptation of Montesquieu." In *Essays in Theory and History. An Approach to the Social Sciences,* 74–102. Cambridge, Mass.: Harvard University Press, 1970.

Rickey, H. Wynn. "A French Judgment of Early American Ideas and Manners." In *Homage to Charles Blaise Qualia,* 47–54. Lubbock: Texas Technological Press, 1962.

Riesman, David. "Commentary." *Tocqueville Review* 7 (1985–1986): 97–101.

———. "Tocqueville as Ethnographer." *American Scholar* 30 (1961): 174–87.

Riviale, Philippe. *Tocqueville ou l'intranquilité.* Paris: L'Harmattan, 1997.

Roldán, Darío, ed. *Lecturas de Tocqueville.* Madrid: Siglo XXI, 2007.

Rollet, Jacques. "De l'individualisme selon Tocqueville." *Projet* 196 (1985): 75–90.

———. *Tocqueville.* Paris: Éditions Montchrestien, 1998.

Roquette, A. de Forcade de la. "Le gouvernement impérial et l'opposition nouvelle." *Revue contemporaine et athéneum français* 29 (1856): 5–29.

Rosenberg, Bernard, and Dennis H. Wong. "De la Démocratie en Amérique: An Appreciation on the Occasion of the Centennial of Tocqueville's Death." *Diogenes* 33 (1961): 127–37.

Rostow, Walt Whitman. "The American National Style." *Daedalus* 87, no. 2 (1958): 110–44.

———. "The Domestic Determination of Foreign Policy: Or Tocqueville Oscillation." *Naval War College Review* 23, no. 1 (1970): 4–16.

Roz, Firmin. "Cent ans après: Alexis de Tocqueville et la Démocratie en Amérique." *Revue des deux mondes* 28 (1935): 152–67.

———. "Tocqueville en Amérique et son actualité." *Revue des deux mondes* 110, no. 1 (1940): 720–25.

Sainte-Beuve, Charles-Agustin. "Alexis de Tocqueville. De la Démocratie en Amérique." *Temps,* 7 April 1835; reprinted in *Premiers lundis,* vol. II, 277–90. Paris: Michel Lévy, 1974.

———. "Oeuvres et correspondances inédites de M. de Tocqueville." In *Causeries du lundi,* vol. XV, 93–121. Paris: Garnier, 1876; also in *Nouveaux lundis,* vol. X, 280–334. Paris: Michel Lévy, 1865.

Salomon, Albert. "Alexis de Tocqueville: Moralist and Sociologist." *Social Research* 2 (1935): 405–38.

———. "Einleitung." In *Alexis de Tocqueville. Autoritat und Freiheit: Schriften, Reden und Briefe,* 1–28. Zurich-Leipzig-Stuttgart: Rascher, 1935.

———. "Tocqueville 1959." *Social Research* 26, no. 4 (1959): 449–70.

———. "Tocqueville's Philosophy of Freedom: A Trend Towards Concrete Sociology." *Review of Politics* 1, no. 4 (1939): 400–31.

Santis, Vittorio de. *La libertà e l'uguaglianza nel pensiero di Alexis de Tocqueville.* Louvain: Frankie, 1972.

Sapper, Neil. "'I Been There Before': Huck Finn as Tocquevillian Individual." *Mississippi Quarterly* 24, no. 1 (1971): 35–45.

Sauca Cano, José María. *La ciencia de la asociación de Tocqueville.* Madrid: Centro de Estudios Constitucionales, 1995.

Schapiro, J. Salwyn. "Alexis de Tocqueville: Pioneer of Democratic Liberalism in France." *Political Science Quarterly* 57, no. 4 (1942): 545–63.

Schleifer, James T. "How Many *Democracies?*" In *Liberty, Equality, Democracy,* 193–205, Eduardo Nolla, ed. New York: New York University Press, 1992.

———. *The Making of Tocqueville's "Democracy in America."* Chapel Hill: University of North Carolina Press, 1980; second ed., Indianapolis, Ind.: Liberty Fund, 2000.

———. "Tocqueville and Religion: Some New Perspectives." *Tocqueville Review* 4, no. 2 (1982): 303–21.

———. "How Democracy Influences Preaching: A Previously Unpublished Fragment from Tocqueville's *De la Démocratie en Amérique.*" *Yale University Library Gazette* 52, no. 2 (1977): 75–79.

———. "Images of America After the Revolution: Alexis de Tocqueville and Gustave de Beaumont Visit the Early Republic." *Yale University Library Gazette* 51, no. 3 (1977): 125–44.

———. "Tocqueville and American Literature: A Newly Acquired Letter." *Yale University Library Gazette* 54, no. 3 (1980): 129–34.

———. "Tocqueville and Centralization. Four Previously Unpublished Manuscripts." *Yale University Library Gazette* 58, nos. 1–2 (1983): 29–39.

———, ed. "Alexis de Tocqueville Describes the American Character: Two Previously Unpublished Portraits." *South Atlantic Quarterly* 74, no. 2 (1975): 244–58.

Schlesinger, Arthur. "Tocqueville and American Democracy." *Michigan Quarterly Review* 25 (1986): 493–505.

Schlüter, Gisela. "Democratic Literature: Tocqueville's Poetological Reflections and Dreams." In *Liberty, Equality, Democracy,* 153–64, Eduardo Nolla, ed. New York, New York University Press, 1992.

———. *Demokratische Literatur.* Frankfurt am Main: Verlag Peter Lang, 1986.

Schmitt, Carl. "Alexis de Tocqueville." In *Ex Captivitate Salus,* 25–33. Cologne: Greven-Verlag, 1950.

———. "Historiographia in nuce Alexis de Tocqueville." *Revista de estudios políticos* 23, no. 43 (1949): 109–14.

Schuettinger, Robert. "Tocqueville and the Bland Leviathan." *New Individualist Review* 1, no. 2 (1961): 12–17.

Schwartz, Joel. "The Penitentiary and Perfectibility in Tocqueville." *Western Political Quarterly* 38, no. 1 (1985): 7–26.

Schwartz, Robert M., and Robert A. Schneider. *Tocqueville and Beyond.* Newark: University of Delaware Press, 2003.

Secretan, Philibert. "Alexis de Tocqueville: pronostic et prophétie." *Esprit* 346 (1966): 246–58.

Segal, Howard P. "Tocqueville and the Problem of Social Change: A Reconsideration." *South Atlantic Quarterly* 77 (1977): 492–503.

Sennett, Richard. "What Tocqueville Feared." *Partisan Review* 46, no. 3 (1979): 406–18.

Sidoti, Francesco. "Honesty et Virtus in America: Tocqueville et Weber." *Sociologia e Ricerca Sociale* 7, no. 21 (1986): 49–73.

Simon, G. A. Abbé. *Les Clarel à l'époque de la conquête d'Angleterre et leur descendance dans la famille Clerel de Tocqueville.* Caen: Société d'Impression de Basse Normandie, 1936.

Simon, Walter, ed. "Alexis de Tocqueville: French Liberalism in the Light of American Democracy." In *French Liberalism 1789–1848,* 117–36. New York: John Wiley and Sons, 1972.

Smelser, Neil J. "Alexis de Tocqueville as Comparative Analyst," 6–37. In *Comparative Methods in the Social Sciences.* New Jersey: Prentice-Hall, 1976.

Smith, Bruce James. "Alexis de Tocqueville: The Politics of Affection." In *Politics and Remembrance,* 155–250. Princeton: Princeton University Press, 1985.

Smith, Louis. "Alexis de Tocqueville and Public Administration." *Public Administration Review* 2 (1942): 221–39.

Smith, T. V. "Hindsight on de Tocqueville's Foresight." *University Review* 9, no. 1 (1942): 17–26.

Sorgy, Giuseppe. *Per uno Studio della Partecipazione politica. Hobbes, Locke, Tocqueville.* Lecce: Milella, 1981.

Spender, Harold. "America Now and in the Thirties: In the Steps of De Tocqueville." *Fortnightly Review* 110 (1921): 1–13.

Spitz, David. "On Tocqueville and the Tyranny of Public Sentiment." *Political Science* 9, no. 2 (1957): 3–13.

Spring, David. "An Outsider's View: Alexis de Tocqueville on Aristocratic Sociey and Politics in Nineteenth Century England." *Albion* 12, no. 2 (1980): 122–31.

Stanley, John Langley. "Majority Tyranny in Tocqueville's America: The Failure of Negro Suffrage in 1846." *Political Science Quarterly* 84, no. 3 (1969): 412–35.

Stein, Gary C. "Indian Removal As Seen by European Travelers in America." *Chronicles of Oklahoma* 51, no. 4 (1974): 399–410.

Stoke, Harold W. "De Tocqueville's Appraisal of Democracy—Then and Now." *South Atlantic Quarterly* 36, no. 1 (1937): 14–22.

Strout, Cushing. "Tocqueville and American Literary Critics." In *Liberty, Equality, Democracy,* 143–52, Eduardo Nolla, ed. New York: New York University Press, 1992.

————. "Tocqueville and Republican Religion: Revisiting the Visitor." *Political Theory* 8, no. 1 (1980): 9–26.

————. "Tocqueville and the Idea of an American Literature (1914–1971)." *New Literary History* 18, no. 1 (1986): 115–27.

————. "Tocqueville's Duality: Describing America and Thinking of Europe." *American Quarterly* 21, no. 1 (1969): 87–99.

Strowski, Fortunat. "La Démocratie en Amérique d'Alexis de Tocqueville, et l'Amérique actuelle." *Revue des cours et conférences* 26, no. 4 (1925): 366–74.

Sutter, Jean François. "Tocqueville et le problème de la démocratie." *Revue internationale de philosophie* 49, no. 3 (1959): 330–40.

Swedberg, Richard. *Tocqueville's Political Economy.* Princeton, New Jersey: Princeton University Press, 2009.

Tagliacozzo, Enzo. *"Democrazia e libertà in Tocqueville." Nuova Antologia* 540, no. 2133 (1980): 292–311.

————. "Tocqueville profeta dell'età delle masse." *Nuova Antologia* 536, no. 2129 (1979): 264–82.

Tanner, Tony. "Pigment and Ether: A Comment on the American Mind." *Bulletin of the British Association for American Studies* 7 (1963): 40–45.

Taylor, Alan J. Percival. "Books in General. (Aesthetic Pleasure from the Play of Ideas: Tocqueville)." *New Statesman and Nation* 42 (8 September 1951): 257–58.

Thimonier, Christian. "La foi et la liberté. Un dialogue entre Tocqueville et Madame Swetchine." *Communio,* July–August 1984, 102–15.

Tilton, Timothy A. "Alexis de Tocqueville and the Political Sociology of Liberalism." *Comparative Social Research* 2 (1979): 263–87.

Tolles, Frederick B. "Tocqueville on American Destiny." *Christian Century* 64, no. 49 (1947): 1480–81.

Trías Vejarano, Juan. "La autonomía local y las asociaciones en el pensamiento de Tocqueville." *Revista de estudios políticos* 123 (1962): 133–94.

Uhde, Ute. *Politik und Religion: zum Verhältnis von Demokratie und Christentum bei Alexis de Tocqueville.* Berlin: Duncker & Humblot, 1978.

Utzinger, Ernst. "Der Prophet des Massenzeitalters und die Gemeindefreiheit: Alexis de Tocqueville." *Schweizer Monatschefte* 86 (1957): 376–79.

Villemain, A. "De la Démocratie en Amérique." *Journal des savants* 25 (1 May 1840): 257–63.

————. "Rapport sur les concours de l'académie française en 1836." In *Discours et mélanges littéraires,* 275–85. Paris: Didier, 1856.

Virtanen, Reino. "Tocqueville and the Romantics." *Symposium* 13, no. 2 (1959): 167–85.

———. "Tocqueville and William Ellery Channing." *American Literature* 22 (1951): 21–28.

———. "Tocqueville on a Democratic Literature." *French Review* 23, no. 3 (1950): 214–22.

Volkmann-Schluck, Karl-Heinz. *Politische Philosophie: Thukydides, Kant, Tocqueville.* Frankfurt: Klostermann, 1974.

Von Barloewen, Constantin. *Portraits croisés.* Paris: Éditions des Syrtes, 2004.

Vossler, Otto. *Alexis de Tocqueville: Freiheit und Gleichheit.* Frankfurt: Klosterman, 1973.

Wach, Joachim. "The Role of Religion in the Social Philosophy of Alexis de Tocqueville." *Journal of the History of Ideas* 7 (1946): 74–90.

Wade, L. C. "Tocqueville and Public Choice." *Public Choice* 47, no. 3 (1985): 491–508.

Ward, John W. "The Ideal of Individualism and the Reality of Organization." In *Red, White, and Blue. Men, Books and Ideas in American Culture,* 227–66. New York: Oxford University Press, 1969.

Wasser, H. "Alexis de Tocqueville and America." *South Atlantic Quarterly* 47, no. 1 (1948): 352–60.

Watkins, Sharon B. *Alexis de Tocqueville and the Second Republic, 1848–1852.* Lanham, Md.: University Press of America, 2003.

Watson, George. "Tocqueville and the Burden of Liberty." *The Hudson Review* 38, no. 3 (1985): 365–75.

Welch, Cheryl. *De Tocqueville.* New York: Oxford University Press, 2001.

West, Paul. "Literature and Politics. Tocqueville on the Literature of Democracies." *Essays in Criticism* 12, no. 3 (1962): 254–72.

Westfall, William. "Tocqueville, Emerson, and the Abolitionists." *Journal of Thought* 19 (1984): 56–64.

White, Hayden. "The Structure of Historical Narrative." *Clio* 1, no. 3 (1972): 5–20.

———. "Tocqueville: Historical Realism as Tragedy." In *Meta-History. The Historical Imagination in Nineteenth Century Europe,* 191–229. Baltimore: Johns Hopkins University Press, 1974.

White, Paul Lambert. "American Manners in 1830: Tocqueville's Letters and Diary." *Yale Review* 12, no. 1 (1922): 118–31.

Whitridge, Arnold. "Chateaubriand and Tocqueville: Impressions of the American Scene." *History Today* 12, no. 8 (1963): 530–38.

Wilson, Francis G. "Tocqueville's Conception of the Elite." *Review of Politics* 4, no. 3 (1942): 271–86.

Winthrop, Delba. "Tocqueville on Federalism." *Publius* 6, no. 3 (1976): 93–115.

———. "Tocqueville's American Woman and 'the True Conception of Democratic Progress.'" *Political Theory* 14, no. 2 (1986): 239–61.

———. "The Voluntary Spirit of Tocqueville." *American Spectator* 15 (1982): 18–20.

Wolfe, Don Marion. "The Plastic Mind: Tocqueville and Horace Mann." *Western Humanities Review* 11, no. 3 (1957): 233–49.

Wolin, Sheldon S. "Archaism and Modernity." *Tocqueville Review* 7 (1985–1986): 77–88.

———. *Tocqueville Between Two Worlds.* Princeton: Princeton University Press, 2001.

Zafra Victor, Manuel. *Tocqueville.* Madrid: Ediciones del Orto, 2000.

Zanfarino, A. "Alexis de Tocqueville politico e moralista." *Studii Politici* 5, no. 1, 33–44.

Zeitlin, Irving M. *Liberty, Equality, and Revolution in Alexis de Tocqueville.* Boston: Little, Brown, 1971.

Zemach, Ada. "Alexis de Tocqueville on England." *Review of Politics* 13, no. 3 (1951): 329–43.

Zetterbaum, Marvin. "Alexis de Tocqueville." In Leo Strauss and Joseph Cropsey, eds. *History of Political Philosophy,* 715–36. Chicago: Rand McNally College Pub., 1963.

———. "Tocqueville: Neutrality and the Use of History." *American Political Science Review* 58, no. 3 (1964): 611–21.

———. *Tocqueville and the Problem of Democracy.* Stanford: Stanford University Press, 1967.

Zuckert, Catherine H. "Not by Preaching: Tocqueville on the Role of Religion in American Democracy." *Review of Politics* 43, no. 2 (1981): 259–80.

———. "The Role of Religion in Preserving American Liberty—Tocqueville's Analysis 150 Years Later." In *Liberty, Equality, Democracy,* 21–36, Eduardo Nolla, ed. New York: New York University Press, 1992.

Zunz, Olivier, and Alan S. Kahan, *The Tocqueville Reader.* Oxford: Blackwell, 2002.

Index

This project would not have been possible without the outstanding efforts of the following Editorial Committee, which assisted in the preparation of the English text:

Paul Seaton (Primary Reader)

Christine Dunn Henderson
Peter A. Lawler
Pierre Manent
Eduardo Nolla
Emilio Pacheco
Melvin Richter
Alison Schleifer
James T. Schleifer
Catherine H. Zuckert

This book is set in Adobe Garamond, a modern adaptation
by Robert Slimbach of the typeface originally cut around 1540
by the French typographer and printer Claude Garamond.
The Garamond face, with its small lowercase height and
restrained contrast between thick and thin strokes, is a classic
"old-style" face and has long been one of the most influential
and widely used typefaces.

This book is printed on paper that is acid-free and meets
the requirements of the American National Standard for
Permanence of Paper for Printed Library Materials,
Z39.48-1992. ∞

Book design by Louise OFarrell
Gainesville, Florida

Typography by Grapevine Publishing Services, LLC
Madison, Wisconsin

Printed and bound by Worzalla Publishing Co.,
Stevens Point, Wisconsin